Vietnam: The Second Front:

Winning the War, Losing the Homeland.

The Peace Movement, 1968-1972

Dr. Roger B. Canfield

Published by Amazon.com

Photo: 9th division soldier in cambodia
reading about protests back home.

Cover designed by Cathy Joyce
Cover Photo: U.S. Army.

Peace movement, Vietnam War, military history,
strategy, political science, propaganda, media,
Tom Hayden, Jane Fonda, Bill Ayers,
Cora Weiss, Howard Zinn

In memory of

Nguyễn Ngọc Bích
Hon. Mickey Conroy
Ngo Dinh Diem
Hon. Gil Ferguson
Madame Nhu
Armond Noble
Douglas Pike
Pfc. Dr. Harold W. "Bill" Rood

Photos

Photo: Maoist revolutionary poster.

Photo: Victory for the Viet Cong, peace protestors.

Photo: *Dien-Tin*, Saigon's Leading Opposition Newspaper.

Photo: Genie Plamondon, Nancy Kurshan and Judy Gumbo Albert in Hanoi.

Photo: Iconic Kent State photo, Mary Ann Vecchio, War Remnants Museum.

Photo: Eric Holder, Columbia 1973.

Photo: 9th Division soldier in Cambodia reading about protests back home.

Photo: General Giap with Cleaver Anti-Imperialist Delegation.

Photo: Peace Conference, Versailles, France February 1972.

Photo: Hanoi Propaganda Poster Showing American Protesters.

Photo: Roads and buildings at flood risk on both sides of levees.

Photo: DOD, Bach Mai Airport.

Photo: Hitler with Nixon Mask Propaganda Poster ca. 1970

Photo: Dr. Roger Canfield, Mekong Delta, Vietnam March 2008.

Reviews.

The ULTIMATE source on Vietnam and the Left. LT. COL. ROBERT "BUZZ" PATTERSON, US Air Force (Ret) Author *Dereliction of Duty, Reckless Disregard, War Crimes.*

Very impressed. NGUYEN NGOC TAN, Ph.D. Reeducation camp survivor, refugee 1978, Australia, Author *The Vietnam War Revisited: A Revolutionary View of U.S. Foreign Policy, Vietnamese Nationalists in Diaspora,* 2012.

Wow! ...an invaluable reference...monumental achievement. FEDORA, Free Republic.

Dissects...US fronts for Hanoi, BRUCE KESLER, Sgt., USMC, Intelligence, Vietnam 1969-70, founder of Vietnam Veterans for a Just Peace, 1971, familysecuritymatters.org, blogs on Maggie's Farm.

Great...facts we will never see in the liberal media DAN NGUYEN, Boat People

Intriguing...raises never-before asked questions. MELODY CONROY, W.W. Norton.

GREAT...impressive. ... VOA Comments from *Viet Kieu* are positive. NGHIA VO, Saigon Arts, Culture & Education Institute, author *Bamboo Gulag, The Viet Kieu in America* and *The Vietnamese Boat People.* SACEI07.org.

Utterly amazed...Astounding research. Outstanding...Should drive a stake in the heart of the grand myths. BILL LAURIE, Co-author *Whitewash Blackwash: Myths of the Vietnam War,* 1st Lt. US Army (Ret) and defense attaché (1971-1975).

A damn good piece of work. MIKE BENGE, contributor to History Channel, POW (1968-73), Vietnam: US Marines, 1956-1959, International Voluntary Services (IVS), 1963-65; Foreign Service Officer, USAID, 1963-68.

Wow. Impressive...tour de force. ...LT. COL. JAMES K. BRUTON, Army SFT, Counterinsurgency Vietnam 1972.

A tremendous project. SCOTT SWETT, co-author *To Set the Record Straight* Webmaster, Swift Boats Veterans and POWs for Truth, wintersoldier.com, tosettherecordstraight.com

Massive study of the Hanoi Lobby. MAX FRIEDMAN, National Mobilization Committee to End the War in Vietnam, New Mobilization, Student Mobe, Washington Mobe. Co-author *The Human Cost of Communism in Vietnam, 1972.*

A monumental work of original historical research, a gold mine for future generations of historians. JAMES McLEROY, 1st Lt., Army Special Forces, I Corps, 1967-68.

I have been waiting for this book for 40 years. JACK J. GOERHRING III, Psychological War, Capt. USA, Vietnam 1968-69.

Truly a fantastic masterpiece. Takes the whole antiwar-activists-as-sincere-liberators myth and trashes it… sets fire to the pile of pieces. Wow. … truly monumental achievement. R. J. DEL VECCHIO Co-author *Whitewash Blackwash: Myths of the Vietnam War,* Cpl. Marine combat photographer, 1st Marine Div. Vietnam (1967-8),

Amazing…dig so deep and see so far ahead. THU-MINH HUYNH, daughter of Gen. Huynh Cao.

Recorded as the author has written. GEN. HUYNH VAN CAO, Cdr. ARVN, 7th Division, 1961-63.

Unfolds the ugly, shameful and mischievous acts of the anti-war liberals and leftists in the USA. JOACHIM THONG LE, *The Vietnamese-American Nationalists in Diaspora,* Ngo Dinh Diem Foundation.

Your Masterpiece has been making the Vietnamese diaspora boil. HUNG LE, translator into Vietnamese of *Comrades in Arms.*

A library of the mind clear and clean. Thank You. Thank You. VIET TRAN, Refugee August 1975.

Great work. Harsh. Painfully honest. Looking forward to your next installment in *Military* magazine. JIM BREEN, machine gunner, Cav. First Air Cavalry Div. ...RVN, 1966-67.

Commentary on author's works on Chinese Operations in USA Today

Congratulations on your book---you are a patriot and a great American. JUDGE WILLIAM P. CLARK, former Chief of Staff, National Security Advisor to Governor and President Ronald Reagan.

It's really scary. God bless JANE RUSSELL, film star

A wake up call… a must read for every American…. The People's Republic of China [has] launched an all-out underground war with the U.S. to invade our technology and [increase their] influence around the world…. CLIVE CUSSLER, novelist and sea hunter.

The so-called 'Stealth Invasion' by 'Red' China [is] false and groundless...absurd...farce... WANG YUNXIANG, Consul General, People's Republic of China.

***

ACKNOWLEDGEMENTS, 1964-2019.

In thirty years there are many to thank, especially my editor at Radix Press, Steve Sherman, and friends at Vietnam Veterans for a Factual History (VVFH.org). In the California Legislature Pete Conaty, Mickey Conroy and Gil Ferguson. Richard Delgaudio of the United States Intelligence Council. From the *Sacramento Union,* Patrick Joyce, Thanks to everyone who has written reviews of project published above. Others in alphabetical order: Michael Benge, Prof. Larry Berman, Nguyễn Ngọc Bích, Prof. George Blair, Richard Botkin, Hon. John Briggs, Lt. Col. Robert Brown, B. G. Burkett, Mary Noel Morse Canfield, Gen. Huynh Van Cao, Bill Cavala, Peter Collier, Victor Comerchero, Col. Pete Conaty, Hon. Mickey Conroy, Ellen Cousins, Richard Delgaudio, R.J. Del Vecchio, John Del Vecchio, David Demshki, Stephen Denney, Cathy Pirie Evans, Mike Faber, Joe Farah, Fedora, John Feliz, Col. Col. Andy Finlayson, Hon. Gil Ferguson, Max Friedman, Pat Henning, David Horowitz, Kyle Horst, Thu-Minh Huynh, William F. Jasper, Christopher Jenks, Pat Joyce, Anita Kando, Peter Laurence, Bill Laurie, Hung Le, Mark Leddy, Edward Humberger Marshall, Phil Nails, Hon. Bob Naylor, Armond Noble, Carl Oglesby, Doug Pike, Major and Prof. Harold W. "Bill" Rood, Mike Rocco, Paul Schmehl, Hon. John Schmidt, Stephen Sherman, Jonathan Slevin, Sol Stern, Hon. Larry Sterling, Scott Swett, Ted Thomas, Robert Turner, George "Jay" Veith, Nghia "Paul" Vo, John Vieg, Nghia "Paul" M. Vo, Dirk Werkman, Col. Earl Von Kaenel.

Thousands of small contributors to Hon. Gil Ferguson's Oust Tom Hayden PAC and Richard Delgaudio's U.S. Intelligence Council provided early funding. None relied on graduate student labor, tenure, sabbatical, foundation or any NGO.

New Left Collection of Hoover Institute at Stanford University, Palo Alto; Indochinese Studies, Institute of East Asian Studies of University of California, Berkeley; California State Library, Sacramento; FBI, Freedom of Information.

Principal electronic sources: FBI, Freedom of Information; FRUS; CIA SNIE, Texas Tech; National Archives and Presidential libraries; Swarthmore; Syracuse Peace Council, Vanderbilt Television archives, www.paperlessarchices.com, and, of course Google and Bing.

TABLE OF CONTENTS.

---

[1] Does not include Radio Hanoi broadcasts, correspondence, telephone contacts in FBIS broadcasts and NSA intercepts. Many are in text below.
[2] With minor edits from: Clinton, James, *The Loyal Opposition: Americans in North Vietnam, 1965-1972,* University of Colorado, 1995. Posted by redvet Facilitator, Vietnam Veterans against the War/Anti-Imperialist
http://www.oz.net/~vvawai/ Hawaii Chapter
http://groups.google.com.vc/group/alt.gossip.celebrities/msg/ 428da4d0fc9af29b Does not include meetings in Paris and across the globe.

Part I 1968 Summary
A Year of War, Revolution, and Infamy

What conventional histories tell us about the peace movement in 1968 is mostly wrong, a figment of visions from an alternative universe, a compendium of myths, narratives and assumptions now largely accepted as gospel. The legendary year of 1968 in the Vietnam War did not happen as it is almost universally reported.

Critical points were Hanoi's invasion of South Vietnam during Tet; riots at Democrat convention in Chicago; foreign assistance to American deserters; A clueless CIA; and Cubans and Vietnamese Communists inspiring American antiwar activists.

Peace Movement. The National Mobilization to End the War in Vietnam, a coalition of "peace" groups, planned riots at the Democrat convention in Chicago. Some draft deferred, trust-funded students and "red diaper baby" activists blasted GIs and POWs with Hanoi propaganda. Scores f movement leaders traveled[3] across the planet to attend multiple meetings[4] with top peace group leaders, Hanoi and the "peace" movement coordinated scheduling of antiwar demonstrations, propaganda themes and psychological war.

Tet: Hanoi and Peace Movement Solidarity. Media. The media, Walter Cronkite et al, falsely declared the allied victory at Tet against a communist invasion/uprising was an American "defeat." A village, Ben Tre, was allegedly "destroyed" to save it. The media reported false claims of American war crimes, using outlawed chemical weapons and targeting women, children, schools and hospitals. At the same time the media ignored systematic communist terror and assassinations everywhere[5] and horrific atrocities of murdered innocent civilians in Hue.

Many American peace activists visited Hanoi in late 1967[6] and in early 1968.[7] Except for Mary McCarthy, they did not

---

[3] See: Appendix II-U.S. Citizens Who Traveled to North Vietnam: 1965-1972, By Name/Affiliation/Year.

[4] See: Appendix I--American "Peace Activist" Meetings[4] with Enemy During War, 1968-1972 by Date and Place.

[5] Appendix III: Viet Cong War Crimes Against Civilians, Compiled by Vietnamese American Youth, Petition to the U N.

[6] Dagmar Wilson, Ruth Krause and Mary Clarke of WSP. Tom Hayden, Rennie Davis, Carol McEldowney, Vivian Rothstein, and Norm Fruchter of SDS.

[7] Howard Zinn, Daniel Berrigan, Harry Ashmore, William Baggs, Franz Schurmann,

2

report ship, train and truck-loads of arms and armor supplying the invasion.

Hanoi Reemphasizes *Dich Van* Campaign in USA

Despite Hanoi's horrific battlefield losses, Tet did prove the effectiveness of political influence operations on the media and the antiwar movement. Gen. Leonard F. Chapman said Hanoi's politburo fully recognized *dich van,* political struggle among the people of the U. S. "could be employed effectively" to "win the war "in the United States.

***

Mary McCarthy and CBS's Charles Collingwood.

Chapter 1. Sleeping with the Enemy:
Vietnamese, Cubans, Riotors, Deserters.

U.S. at Fault in Tet -- National Council of Churches, Dove Senators. Early in Tet when the massive scale of Hanoi's attack on 100 cities in South Vietnam was on the evening news every night, the tax exempt National Council of Churches, allied with the Soviet dominated World Council of Churches, met in solemn general assembly in San Diego to prayerfully demand the U.S "stop the bombing of North Vietnam" so that peace talks could begin. Dove Senators Mansfield, John Sherman Cooper, Robert Kennedy, and Eugene McCarthy, also called for a U.S. bombing halt during Hanoi's massive Tet invasion. Radio Hanoi thanked the Senators for choosing the "right way."[8]

At the North Vietnamese Embassy in Vientiane, Laos during Tet on February 9 secret American communist Howard Zinn said, "There was a lot of feeling of victory in Hanoi ..."[9]

Left pacifist priest Daniel Berrigan said the Hanoi Vietnamese "are too humane to rake over our losses [in Tet]..." They are so courteous and gentle "during a week of humiliation of the Allies."[10]

In fact, on suicide missions the Viet Cong were dying by the tens of thousands. The people of South Vietnam rose up, not to the welcome their "liberators," but to help kill them.

Comrades: New York, Moscow, London, Sweden

With communist military forces mostly defeated in Tet in South Vietnam, political comrades set forth in a flurry of activities in the USA, the second front. On March 2 and March 24, the *New York Times* reported 16 and then 24 Vietnamese students in the U.S., led by Harvard's Ngo Vinh Long, appealing for peace.[11] On March 17 in London and on March 19 in Moscow, the faithful expressed solidarity. In London a sign read, "Young Communists Accuse Johnson of Murder." Meanwhile communist assassination squads with clip-board lists were

---

[8] Peter Braestrup, *Big Story*, 473, 591-2n10 cites "Hanoi Lauds Four Senators for Asking Halt in Bombing," *Washington Post,* Mar. 2, 1968, A10.
[9] FBI, FOIA, Howard Zinn, BS 100-35505
[10] Berrigan, *Night*, 31.
[11] "16 South Vietnamese in U.S. and Canada Support a Halt," *New York Times*, March 2, 1968; Ngo, V.L., T.M.V. Lr, and H.Q. Nguyen, "Vietnamese Students' Appeal, *New York Times*, March 24, 1968; Chris Norlund, "The First Vietnamese to Attend Harvard," *Migration Letters*, Volume 2, No. 1. 78-9.

methodically going from door to door in Hue, South Vietnam seeking thousands for summary executions.[12] In April 1968, Steve Halliwell revisited Hanoi[13] and Ken Cloke met a Hanoi delegation in Sweden.[14]

NVA Troops Instructed: Declare Tet a Success

By April 4, a Directive of Unit 491, the political staff of the 3rd Division of the NVA was telling the troops that the general offensive and uprising were a "big and all-sided success." The directive reminded troops to "closely coordinate our military and political struggles [*dau tranh*] with diplomatic offensives."[15] In the event, save Arnaud de Borchgrave, nearly every American reporter called the game over.

President Johnson Quits

Tet shocked and depressed President Johnson.[16]

On March 31, 1968, LBJ announced he would not run for re-election. Mary McCarthy, swilling Bulgarian alcohol in KGB agent Wilfred Burchett's hotel room in Hanoi, toasted the good news of LBJ quitting and bombing halt[17] At the Metropole hotel, Mary McCarthy hugged Ashmore and Baggs with the good news.

Hue Massacre Deniers-Burchett, Porter

After the Communist occupation, KGB agent Wilfred Burchett, ever the master of invention, attributed the 2,800 bodies found in Hue to American actions. D. Gareth Porter wrote a total denial of Hue.[18] After the Hue massacres young South Vietnamese teenagers voluntarily took up arms. One said, "We used to hate foreigners, first the French, then the Americans. But after Tet we just hate the Communists—all of us: from schoolboys all the way up to the Dowager Empress."[19]

---

[12]Memorialized in captions and photos at War Remnants Museum in Saigon, Author's photo numbers Viet II DSC_349, 351, 361-2.

[13]House, Committee on Internal Security, Investigation of Students Exhibit no. 3, 2321.

[14] "Declassified U.S. 13 at www.americasurvival.org.

[15] Directive dated April 4, 1968, issued by Unit 491, (Political Staff), Third NVA Div., HQ), "Unit 491 to all units, #487, attached to Press Release #75-68, U.S. Mission Press Center, Saigon, April 28, 1968, Pike Collection, Unit 4-Political Settlement, TTU, Virtual Archive, Item Number 2300602031.

[16] Later Cronkite would condemn minor American victories in Grenada and Tripoli. See: *Newsweek*, December 1988, "Cronkite: An Anchor Unchained."

[17] Mary McCarthy, *The Seventeenth*, 31-32.

[18] D. Gareth Porter, "The 1968 'Hue Massacre," *Indochina Chronicle*, No. 33, June 24, 1974, 2-13.

[19] Uwe Siemon-Netto *Duc*...241.

Meanwhile on the home front, the radical left sought to bring the war home.

On June 29, 1968, *Ramparts* published a Hayden article, "Talk, Talk; Fight, Fight." Hayden claimed military successes, military victories, for the North Vietnamese in Tet. Moreover, he publicly adopted the Vietnamese strategy of "fighting and talking, talking and fighting" -- *Danh Va Dam, Dam Va Danh.* The ink still drying on his letter of June 4 to Col. Ha Van Lau, Hayden wrote for *Ramparts:*

> ... The Tet offensive was ... one of the great achievements in the history of warfare; ...As *victory* [for NLF] comes closer ... [the politics] ... favors a central role for the *victorious* NLF.

Hayden was thrilled with Vietnamese military victories. Though Tet was a horrific defeat for Viet Cong cadre, "once in a lifetime" suicide mission on orders from Hanoi,[20] it was a political victory for Hanoi in the American media and in the "peace" movement.

The Viet Cong's COSVN Resolution # 6 said Tet intended to "create conditions for pacifist movements in the USA to radically change [US] VN policy."[21] Hayden told his *Rampart's* readers that a Viet Cong victory would bring a peace that most Americans could support: Reconciliation, universal suffrage, a national union government, protection of private property, and trade and cultural relations. Hayden praised the NLF "concessions" of postponing reunification and promising a non-socialist South Vietnam. Of course, Hayden favored only a peace followed by a successful Socialist revolution. He shared the Soviet concept of "a just peace" -- there could be no just peace in Vietnam until the victory of Socialism.[22] Hayden's salutation, "Victory," meant what the questioning Congressman Conley thought it meant -- victory politically and militarily for the Viet Cong.

Peace Groups Meet Communists in Paris in September

September 5-6, 1968 four American scholars, including Howard Zinn, met the North Vietnamese delegates in Paris for

---

[20] Dung, "Strategic," *Nhan Dan*, January 30-31, 1988; FBIS-EA, 88-028. Also: Peter Collier & David Horowitz, *Destructive Generation Second Thoughts about the '60s,* New York: Summit Books, 1989, 232.

[21] Gen.William Westmoreland in Gettleman, (ed.), 1985, 354.

[22] Mikhail Heller and Aleksandr M. Nekrich, (trans. Phyllis B. Carlos), *Utopia in Power: The History of the Soviet Union from 1917 to the Present*, New York: Simon and Schuster, 1985, 504, 631.

an "exchange of views."[23] Later in September, the North Vietnamese invited a larger American delegation to their residence at Choisy-le-Roi in Paris for thirteen hours of talks. Attendees were Jonathan Mirsky, George Kahin of Cornell, Howard Zinn, Marilyn Young of University of Michigan, and Douglas Dowd.

The communists said, "Vietnamese have a sacred right to defend their country anywhere they choose," still denying they had troops in the south. Despite their Tet defeat, Vietnamese and the peace group agreed U.S. "attempt to defeat the NLF and to maintain a puppet government has not succeeded."[24] Tet was declared a victory. Zinn's *Vietnam: the Logic of Withdrawal* was required reading[25] for American POWs in Hanoi.

October 24-30, 1968 members of Clergy and Laymen Concerned About Vietnam, CALC, traveled to Paris and Stockholm to meet the North Vietnamese, NLF and American deserters. CALC found no fault with the Viet Cong despite a report from Catholic scholar Michael Novak that Tet had proved the South Vietnamese hated and feared the VC. In Stockholm, for two days CALC attended speeches by deserters.[26]

***

Hanoi Approves Riots at Democrat Convention in Chicago. The National Mobilization to End the War in Vietnam, a coalition of "peace" groups, planned riots at the Democrat convention in Chicago. The 1968 Presidential election, particularly the Democrat Convention in Chicago, presented a unique opportunity to provoke "police state" violence while the whole world was watching.

Out of Vietnam: Tom Hayden, Rennie Davis Plan a Riot at the Chicago Democrat Convention. What is to be Done?

The idea of staging militant protests against the Vietnam War during the upcoming Democratic Convention in Chicago in

---

[23] FBI, FOIA, Howard Zinn cites *The First Issue*, Ithaca New York, September 27, 1968.

[24] Jonathan Mirsky, "The North Vietnamese in Paris II. What They Don't Say," *New York Review of Books*, October 24, 1968, https://www.coveredca.com/; Timothy Patrick McCarthy (ed) *The Indispensable Zinn, Howard Zinn: A Life on the Left,* The New Press, 149. books.google.com/books?isbn=159558840X; Martin Duberman.

[25] Mary Hershberger, *Jane Fonda's War: A Political Biography of an Antiwar Icon*, New York: New Press, 2005, 96 cited in Paul Kengor, Dupes:

[26] FBI, memo, "Clergy and Laymen Concerned About Vietnam, Information Concerning—Internal Security, November 4, 1968, 123418-123420 in FBI, FOIA, C, CALC.

August 1968 took months of planning and discussions.[27] In late October 1967, two weeks out of Hanoi and days after a mass "peace" assault upon the Pentagon, Rennie Davis had "returned to Chicago..." There he and "others, including Tom Hayden, began to think seriously about the Democratic convention..."[28]

Tom Hayden remembered, "Rennie and I had been in Vietnam [in October, November] ... just before the idea of Chicago seized us and we began talking about it."[29] Rennie Davis said, "Chicago was really conceived coming out of Vietnam." Then Jerry Rubin, an organizer of the October 1967 assault on the Pentagon, told the *Village Voice,* "...see you ... [in] Chicago ... Bring pot ... smoke bombs ... also football helmets."[30]

Communists Help Fund Office to Disrupt Democrat Convention. On February 11, 1968, in an antiwar planning meeting of the National Mobilization for the Democrat Convention, Tom Hayden and Rennie Davis presented a detailed riot plan.[31] Davis and Hayden intended to disrupt the convention and to provoke the police in Chicago.[32]

---

[27] It began brewing about Labor Day 1967. In early September Paul Booth, President of Students for a Democratic Society, SDS, proposed "massive demonstrations at the National Party conventions." On October 17, 1967 known Communist John J. Abt chaired a meeting of the New York chapter of the National Conference of New Politics at Schermerhorn Hall at Columbia University to plan massive demonstrations at the Democrat convention in August 1968 in Chicago. In late October, after thousands assaulted the Pentagon, Dave Dellinger of National Mobilization to End the War in Vietnam, back from months consulting with Hanoi, suggested using "the Pentagon siege ... as one possible model for future physical confrontation." He urged planning for the Democratic convention. Dellinger wrote to Mobe members: "One of [National Mobe's] continuing aims must be to disrupt and block the war machine ... We might discuss ... trying to disrupt the nominating conventions." See: Francis X. Gannon, *A Biographical Dictionary of the Left,* [1969-1973], Belmont (Mass.): Western Islands, Vol. III, 37; House Committee on Un-American Activities, House of Representatives, *Subversives Involvement in Disruption of 1968 Democratic Party National Convention,* 90th Congress, Second Session, Hearings December 2 and 3, 1968, Washington: U.S. Government Printing Office, Part I, 2269-72, cited at Paul Kengor, *Dupes: How America's Adversaries Have Manipulated Progressives for a Century,* Wilmington: ISI Books, 2010, 295N34; Dave Dellinger, *Liberation,* Nov. 1967, cited in Jeffrey St. John, *Countdown to Chaos; Chicago, August, 1968, Turning Point in American politics,* Nash Publishing, 1969, 21. See: David Farber, *Chicago 1968,* University of Chicago Press, 1988, 70N38 who cites *Mobilization Report,* N.D.

[28] Zaroulis, Nancy, and Gerald Sullivan. *Who Spoke Up?: American Protest against the War in Vietnam 1963-1975.* Garden City, NY: Doubleday, 1984, 133.

[29] Tim Findley, "Tom Hayden: The Rolling Stone Interview (Part One)" *Rolling Stone,* OCTOBER 26, 1972.

[30] "Lighting the Fuse," *Village Voice,* November 16, 1967, cited in St. John, *Countdown* 25.

[31] Memo To: National Mobilization Staff: Chicago Organizers, Not for Circulation Publication., From: Rennie Davis, Tom Hayden, "Discussion of Democratic Convention Challenge," February 11, 1968, text can be found at House Committee on Un-American

"In March 1968, an FBI report said a member of the CPUSA coordinated the CP Party with the New Left, "He is to assist in setting up a coordinating office to be financed in part by the party and to recruit full-time personnel to man it."[33] Dr. Quentin Young, a member of the Bethune Doctors Club of the Communist Party of the North Side of Chicago[34] as well as an activist in Communist fronts paid $1,000 to a realtor named Sudler for a partial rental payment for an office for National Mobe at 407 South Dearborn in Chicago.[35]

"We were keeping secrets for Tom Hayden," said *Ramparts* writer Sol Stern.[36]

Bring the War Home. Attending a National Lawyers Guild meeting on January 28, 1968, planning disruptions in Chicago, Tom Hayden sought to "bring the war home" for America's Viet Cong -- the SDS. Tom Hayden, Rennie Davis and others, the Chicago Seven, were making plans for the upcoming Democratic Convention in August and coordinating their activities with the "Spring Offensive" of the SDS. For a Lake Villa conference on March 23, they wrote,:

> The *imperialistic* role of the United States in the world. Actions should concentrate on ... war targets, ... draft boards, ...induction centers, ... and major war corporations like Dow Chemical. [They wanted] draft cards turned in to the convention and ... teach-ins for soldiers.

US Army Intelligence Monitors Antiwar Protesters. The U.S. Army expanded its existing intelligence collection capability. Besides reading newspapers and FBI and local

---

Activities, House of Representatives, Subversives Involvement in Disruption of 1968 Democratic Party National Convention, 90th Congress, Second Session, Hearings December 2 and 3, 1968. Washington: U.S. Government Printing Office, 2556-2559.
[32]Memo To: National Mobilization Staff: Chicago Organizers, Not for Circulation Publication., From: Rennie Davis, Tom Hayden, "Discussion of Democratic Convention Challenge," February 11, 1968, text can be found at HCUA, December 1968, 2556-2559
[33] Herbert Romerstein and Stanislav Levchenko, The KGB *Against the "Main Enemy": How the Soviet Intelligence Service Operates Against the United States,* Lexington (Mass): Lexington Books, 1989, 274.
[34] Paul Kengor, *Dupes*: 301.
[35] Transcripts of Quinton Young testimony before House Committee on Un-American Activities, October 3-4, published in *Health Rights News*, provided by Max Friedman to author in email April 2, 2008; Romerstein and Levchenko, *The KGB*, 274.
[36] *Ramparts* did not publish its one scoop of the Chicago convention, the plan to disrupt the convention by provoking the police. Sol Stern, "The Ramparts I watched," *City Journal*, Winter 2010.

police files, the U.S. Army actively infiltrated groups and monitored public speeches. Of near immediate concern was the National Mobilization Committee to End the War in Vietnam, Dellinger, Hayden and Rennie Davis, actively planning to disrupt the Democratic Convention in Chicago in August.

1968 Intensifying Antiwar Sentiment. The FBI observed, "The purpose…was to intensify the anti-war sentiment in the United States. … [Since Bratislava September 1967 and Havana July of 1968]…the influence of Vietnamese representatives on the…SDS leadership became sharply pronounced."[37] The Vietnamese were particularly interested in Hayden, Dellinger, Davis and Greenblatt leading the Chicago convention protests. Besides the discussions about the POWs, the North Vietnamese were "very interested in demonstrations or activities in the United States against the war."

Progress Reports—Hayden, Greenblatt. The protests in Chicago were only a month away. Hayden "returned [from Paris] in a revolutionary mood" what Andrew Kopkind called "an NLF high."[38] Long planned protests in Chicago unfolded.

After meetings with Vietnamese communists in Hanoi, Prague and Paris, Tom Hayden returned, planned and led actions to provoke riots at the Democrat Convention in Chicago in August 1968. It was only after Tom Hayden and Rennie Davis had returned from Hanoi with a plan in mind in late 1967 that others, David Dellinger and National Mobe, began early planning including legal, medical services[39] and martial arts.

"Blood Might Have to Be Shed." On July 25th, 1968 Tom Hayden, Cora Weiss, and Beulah Sanders spoke before the Fifth Avenue Parade Committee at the Hotel Diplomat in New York.[40] At 8:00 p.m. Hayden spoke to the "peace" parade group. The *Guardian*, the Long Island *Newsday* and the FBI recorded Hayden's speech. Hayden said, "... come to Chicago prepared to shed their blood."[41]

According to Cora Weiss, Hayden said, "it would not be the first time that blood might have to be shed, our blood, as demonstrators for a cause."[42] According to Linda Morse, he said,

---

[37] FBI, FOIA, Weather, 1.
[38] Newfield, *Village Voice*, July 18,1968 cited in St. John, 28-29; See Also: "Capital Briefs," *Human Events*, 1968; Hayden, "The Impasse in Paris," *Ramparts*, August 24, 1968, 18.
[39] Romerstein and Levchenko, *The KGB…*, 275.
[40] Clavir, (ed.), *Transcript*, 320.
[41] Tom Hayden, *Reunion, A Memoir*, New York: Random House, 1988, 297.

10

"It was the duty of every American to protest ... by any means possible because it was going to be (nuclear weapons and) genocide in Vietnam in a short time otherwise."[43] Linda Morse "was training with a squad [Hayden's International Liberation School][44] in California for armed rebellion, which Tom Hayden was a part of," David Dellinger remembers.[45] In Paris during August Bernardine Dohrn briefed the Viet Cong on last minute plans for Democratic Convention.[46]

Bill Ayers remembers,

Tom Hayden was our Captain Ahab…[a] group gathered at our house…[Tom said] This demonstration…has the potential…to expose the face of the enemy, to strip him naked, to force him to reveal himself as violent, brutal, totalitarian, evil. It will be difficult…taunting the monster, stabbing him…but it's got to be done."[47]

Provoked as planned, there was bloodshed in Chicago. With the "whole world watching," there were riots in the parks and streets of Chicago and around its convention hotels. The Army's covert "Midwest Video Associates," taped hundreds of hours of protest speeches in Grant Park and conducted interviews of leaders

At Democrat Convention; "New Escalation of the War"

At the convention in late August, Hayden wrote his views on Vietnam in the *RAT* Convention special flyer:

The U.S. is trying to end the anti-war movement rather than its policy in Vietnam....The U.S. is … turning the South into a wasteland. Nearly one-fourth of the South Vietnamese people are uprooted and homeless refugees in "camps." Bubonic Plague and other epidemics are

---

[42] Cora Weiss testimony in Clavir, (ed.), *Transcript*, 431.

[43] Linda Morse testimony in Clavir, (ed.), *Transcripts...*, 321; See also: Testimony of Frank D. Sweeney in Clavir, (ed.), *Transcripts...*, 132; See: David Farber, 161N99 who cites the complete Chicago trial transcripts, 3969. The Seventh Court of Appeals later wrote on *July 25, 1968...*" at a meeting in New York of the Fifth Avenue Peace Parade Committee... He [Hayden] said that the U.S. was an outlaw nation... It had broken all the rules, and therefore the peace demonstrators could break all rules too... The North Vietnamese were shedding blood and the peace demonstrators... [in] Chicago should be prepared to shed blood too..." [*U.S. vs. Dellinger*, 300]. The Appeals court felt this indicated an intent to incite a riot by Hayden and not the police.

[44] Materials on International Liberation School, ILS, is in the New Left Collection at Hoover Institute at Stanford. Copies in possession of author.

[45] James W. Clinton interview of David Dellinger, Mary Clarke, January 23, 1991 in Clinton, *Opposition*, 41.

[46] Declassified U.S. 28 at www.americasurvival.org

[47] Bill Ayers, *Fugitive Days: A Memoir, Penguin Books, 2001*, 121-122.

spreading ... chemicals ... napalm and phosphorous bombs ... the U.S. is using genocidal methods.[48]

In fact, masses of refugees were fleeing the Communists, not Americans, like they would in 1972 and 1975.

Press Roughed Up in Streets of Chicago. Chicago Police hit newsmen as well as rioters. When CBS reporter Dan Rather was manhandled on the convention floor, CBS anchor of "CBS Evening News," Walter Cronkite, said, "I think we've got a bunch of thugs here, Dan."

In September 1968, a majority of the American people in a Gallup Poll did not believe the police were violent in Chicago.[49] While the whole world had been watching police force and demonstrator violence, what most saw was "... a mob of long-haired kids ... hurling curses and chanting slogans and waving Communist flags."[50]

Joan Baez would tell *Esquire* that come the revolution, she expected Tom Hayden, who had planned the disorders, "would be the one to shoot her."[51] Meanwhile inside the Democratic Convention Democrat delegates rejected an antiwar plank 1,500 to 1,000.

Hanoi Happy With Chicago Riots. On September 14, 1968 the South Vietnam People's Committee in Solidarity with the American People *(Viet My)* sent a letter to National Mobe thanking it for the "seething, resolute and courageous struggle …at the convention of the Democratic Party." *Viet My* extended, "our heartfelt thanks for…recent actions in Chicago. We also voice the high indignation [over]… masked policemen…using tear gas and truncheons and firing at them." The protests helped the struggle in Vietnam. "You have shed your blood…in defense of the Vietnamese people's right to self-determination….[52]

Chicago Seven. Tom Hayden and six others would stand trial as the Chicago Seven. A Jury would convict five of the seven.[53] The Chicago Seven symbolically represented dissent in

---

[48] Tom Hayden, "Democracy Is In The Streets," *R.A.T. Convention Special*, Vol. 1, #14, August 1968 at New Left collection at Stanford University.

[49] Gallup, Sept 1968.

[50] James Miller, *Democracy is in the Streets: From Port Huron to the Siege of Chicago*, Cambridge: Harvard University Press, 1987, 305.

[51] Steven V. Roberts, "Will Tom Hayden Overcome," *Esquire*, December 1968.

[52] Subversive Involvement in Disruption of 1968 Democratic Party Convention, Part 2, December 3, 1968, 2683.

[53] Some of the others co conspirators on the streets of Chicago, cited in United *States of*

America, some of it in collaboration with the enemy in war. In the midst of the enemy's interference in the body politic during war what was the nation to do?

Facts about Police State Are Not Compelling. The Left condemned the FBI and the military for gathering intelligence on those antiwar activists closely tied to enemy foreign powers during war. Under authority of either court orders and/or the Omnibus Crime Control Act of 1968, over the 15 years between 1960 through October 1975, the FBI entered homes and businesses 454 times targeting 290 separate targets- averaging 30 entries and 10 targets a year out of a population of 200 million people.

Claims of an American police state notwithstanding by the Chicago Seven and Cora Weiss, Americans meetings with agents of Hanoi continued apace without interference of the U.S. Government.

National Mobe: September 14, 1968. In Washington on September 14, 1968, the National Mobe met to discuss the aftermath of the Chicago riots. The Mobe group was old left apologists and new left revolutionaries.[54] Sidney Lens briefed Chicago, over 700 arrests, 100 needing travel money, $8,900 in debt, 100 sympathetic newsmen, favorable press coverage,

---

America vs. David T. Dellinger et al were: Sidney M. Peck, former CPUSA; Stewart E. Albert, a Berkeley Free Speech Movement activist, VDC leader, and street fighter in Chicago; Kathie Boudin, red diaper baby, Weatherman, and daughter of leftist attorney and identified CPUSA member, Chair of NLG committee, Leonard Boudin; Newark (NCUP), Columbia activist and roommate of Hayden, Connie (Sara C.) Brown; and Newark (NCUP) activist, Corina F. Fales. Others cited were Wolfe B. Lowenthal, Benjamin Radford, Bradford Fox, Thomas W. Neuman, Craig Shimabukuro, Bo Taylor, and David A. Baker. To be an unindicted conspirator a presiding judge concluded the person's statements or acts were in furtherance of the conspiracy.
[54] Among the Chicago Seven attendees were Hayden, Dellinger, Rennie Davis. Some of the others were: Arnold Johnson, Public Relations Director of the CPUSA; Helen Gurewitz, identified member of CPUSA; Sid Lens, Communist-dominated Chicago Peace Council; Walter Schneir, an author who defended not only the Chicago conspirators, but also Soviet spies, the Rosenbergs, years after their convictions; Barbara Bick, Women's Strike for Peace and identified member of CPUSA; Weathermen to be (Bill Ayers, Terry Robbins); Soviet (non-Trotskyite) Radical Organizing Committee (Alan Gross, Irwin Gladstone, Josh Brown (Hanoi 1967); Lee Webb, NACLA expert on intelligence; Trotskyites Harry Ring and Lew Jones, Susan Lamont, Mike Maggi, Larry Siegel, Pat Grogan, Richie Lesnick; assorted SDS (Karl Baker, Tim McCarthy). Also Gerald Schwinn, Comm. Of Returned [Peace Corps] Volunteers; Irving Beinin, Guardian,; Abe Bloom, Washington Mobe; Thomas L. Hayes, Episcopal Peace Fellowship; Eric Weinberger, Fifth Avenue Vietnam Peace Parade Committee; Barbara Deming, Liberation; Ron Young, Fellowship of Reconciliation; Arthur Waskow, a founder of the Soviet-friendly Institute for Policy Studies. Dan Dellinger, "Summary of Administrative Committee Held in Washington on September 14, (1968) chaired by David Dellinger; see: also HCUA, 1968, 2614.

13

support of National Council of Churches, and collections of statements of police brutality.[55]

Hanoi Confident on Second Front. The South Vietnam People's Committee in Solidarity with the American People (*Viet My)* wrote on October 20, 1968 to its "America friends" expressing

"warm…appreciation (for) strong developments of the antiwar movement…from the 21 October 1967 confrontation at the Pentagon…to the seething and bloody demonstrations at the Democratic convention in Chicago [August 1968] …"

***

KGB, Japanese, Swedes, Canadians, Help America Deserters.
KGB Aids Deserters

In February 1968, the Soviet secret police, the KGB, instructed "the Soviet Committee of Solidarity with the Nations of Asia and Africa…to receive the American deserters arriving from Japan, to work with them in a plan that is beneficial to the Soviet Union, and to provide for their departure to countries offering them political asylum."[56] Japanese *Beheiren* peace activists and professor Taketomo Takahashi formed Japan Technical Committee for Assistance to U.S. Antiwar Deserters, JATEC, to help deserters get to asylum in Europe, e.g. Sweden and France. That fall JATEC sent 16 Americans to Sweden.[57] The KGB provided financial and material support to JATEC, and to KGB agents inside *Beheiren.* [58]

Swedes Harbor Deserters

The Swedish government claimed to welcome deserters for purely humanitarian reasons. Yet Soviet bloc secret services financed leftist factions inside the Swedish ruling Social Democratic Party, SDP, and directed or influenced forty percent of the SDP in the mid-sixties.[59] Prime Minister Olaf Palme was a public supporter of Viet Cong, NLF.[60] Within three months, thirty American deserters resided in Stockholm, from bases in

---

[55] David Dellinger, "Summary of Administrative Committee Held in Washington on September 14, (1968) chaired by David Dellinger."

[56] Document 315 KGB, 699.

[57] Holloran; Shigeru Sekiya and Yoshie Sakamoto, (eds.), *A Period When Deserters Were Your Neighbors*, (Tonari ni Dasso-hei gai ta Jidai), Shiso no Kagakusha, 1988.

[58] Mikio Haruna, *Secret Files: CIA Operations in Japan*, (Himitsu No File; CIA No Tainichi Kosaku), Shincho-sha, 2003.

[59] Jan Sejna, *We Will Bury You,* London: Sidgwick & Jackson, 1982, 122.

[60] *Svenska Dagbladet*, Stockholm, January 8, 1968 cited Robert K. Brigham, *Guerrilla*, 81-82.

West Germany as well as from the *Beheiren*-KGB pipeline. In Sweden on February 28, 1968, 22 deserters formed the American Deserters Committee, ADC, to encourage further desertion. ADC soon became the English language wing of Kfml, a Maoist party, condemning alleged American atrocities in Vietnam.[61] The ADC attended the Soviet sponsored Stockholm Conference on Vietnam in November 1968. Maoists and Stalinists communist factions among deserters like such splits among American communists, had one common enemy—US imperialism. American deserters eventually troubled the Swedes. Of 335 deserters, over 50% were unemployed and nearly 10% in jail for selling drugs.[62]

Deserters Network-Canada, Sweden

In May 1968 Alan McEachan, the Canadian Minister of Immigration, had announced desertion from American military services would not prevent a deserter from establishing legal immigration, "landed status," in Canada.

Vietnamese Hug and Kiss American Youth Delegates, Sofia, Bulgaria — July 28-August 6, 1968

July 28-August 6, 1968 the Ninth World Youth Festival was held in Sofia, Bulgaria to express "solidarity with the Vietnamese people in their struggle against the American imperialist aggressors." The festival boasted 17,898 delegates from 143 nations.[63] Some fifty[64] to seventy-one[65] American attendees—11 SDSers, e.g. Howard Jeffrey Melish, Leslie Cagan[66] met Vietnamese Communists, U. S. deserters and Soviet representatives and visited the Chinese Embassy.[67] William Cathcart, Chairman of the American Deserters Committee in Stockholm, said the communist Bulgarians financed the American deserters.[68]
. "...Vietnamese girls hug & give flowers to American guy…and US army deserters speak on camera."[69]

---

[61] Thomas Ekman Jorgensen, "Scandinavia," in Martin Klimke and Joachim Scharloth, 1968 *in Europe*, 246-7.
[62] Calculated from Frank J. Rafalko, *MH/CHAOS:* 144.
[63] Frankfurter Rundschau, 3 August 1968 cited in "The Ninth World Youth Festival: A Review," Radio Free Europe Research, East Europe, Bulgaria/15, 23 August 1968 at http://files.osa.ceu.hu/holdings/300/8/3/text/7-1-101.shtml
[64]Barbara Bright letter to Richard H. Nolte, Institute of Current World Affairs, 9 September 1968 at ICWA Website http://www.icwa.org/articles/BWB-2.pdf?
[65] Frank J. Rafalko, MH/CHAOS:, 151.
[66] *Leslie Cagan,* "Being Left: It Should Be Possible, It Has To Be Possible," http://www.zmag.org/cagan.htm
[67] FBI, FOIA, *Weather*, 332.
[68] Tom Charles Huston, Special Report, 44.

Kyoto Conference

In Kyoto, Japan August 11-14, 1968, *Beheiren,* sponsored a conference of 250 anti-war activists including 23 Americans. *Beheiren* claimed solidarity with the North Vietnamese Communist Party.[70]

The conference focused on helping deserters and draft dodgers as well as coordinating peace movements worldwide.[71]

After Budapest at the behest of National Mobe, John Davis also visited Prague and deserters in Stockholm and SDS, Danny "The Red" Cohn-Bendit, in Germany.[72]

On September 10, 1968, the FBI Legate in Paris forwarded a Department of the Army memo, "Assistance Provided U.S. Servicemen by Anti-Vietnam War Elements in Europe," listing, in part, the American Deserter Committee in Sweden, and the Second Front and French Union for American Resistors and Deserters (FUARD) in France.[73]

German SDS Works on U.S. GIs. Frankfurt, September 12-16, 1968

Bernardine Dohrn and Bill Ayers attended the German SDS national conference in Frankfurt, West Germany. The German New Left sought to "organize American soldiers and establish a

---

[69] Description in text is from Footage Farm, "Civil Rights and Anti-Vietnam War Protests," x 22112 21:09:55-21:18:54 1968 Bulgaria; Vietnam; COL SD Time to Live R2 of 6 at footagefarm.co.uk; quote "Film is "A Time To Live (Bulgaria Youth Festival)(Vietnam War). This colorful documentary of the Ninth Annual Communist Youth Festival, held in Sofia, Bulgaria in 1968, is an anti-American film. Attacking the Vietnam War and stressing solidarity, world peace and, of all things, freedom, this film is an excellent example of how the Soviets manipulate the minds of youth. Opening with a rousing parade, with groups from Europe, China, Japan, Vietnam, Africa and South America, the film features spirited songs, ethnic dances, native costumes, and a New Orleans-style carnival, including a jazz band. A popular song of the time, "Hands Off Vietnam," is sung by the famous singer Gilda Maziukaite. Also present are sad-faced deserters from the US armed forces, who mumble statements on how awful America is. Beautifully filmed in color by real technicians, the film reflects intense excitement, often on the edge of hyteria. USSR, 1968, Color, 55 minutes, English narration." End quote http://www.ihffilm.com/278.html

[70] Fumiko Holloran, NBR Book Review of Taketomo Takahishi, *We Helped American Deserters Cross National Borders*, ("Watashi-tachi wa Dasso America-hei wo Ekko Saseta"), NBR'S Japan Forum (POL), April 15, 2008.

[71] Tom Charles Huston, Special Report, 44.

[72] *The Marcolian*, May 16, 1969. Until an attempted assassination, Rudi Dutschke was the charismatic leader of the German SDS who had shouted, "Ho, Ho, Ho Chi Minh" at the Free University in Berlin. Like Dohrn's SDS, the German variety was descending into the terrorist Red Army Faction, RAF, and the Baader-Meinhofe gang. Jeffrey Herf, "Unpleasant Truths," *New Republic*, 2008.

[73] FBI, memo, Legat, Paris to Director, FBI September 10, 1968 at FBI, FOIA, A, American Deserters Committee.

Europe-wide 'underground railroad' to help them desert from their German bases to France and Scandinavia."[74]

CALC Meets Vietnamese Communists and US Deserters—
Paris and Stockholm, October 24-30, 1968

October 24-30, 1968 members of Clergy and Laymen Concerned About Vietnam, CALC, traveled to Paris and Stockholm to meet the North Vietnamese, NLF and American deserters In Paris, an NLF spokesman claimed Communists in the NLF. CALC had supper with the Union of Draft Resisters and Deserters. In Paris, an NLF spokesman claimed Communists in the NLF. CALC had supper with the Union of Draft Resisters and Deserters. In Stockholm, for two days CALC attended speeches by deserters.[75]

What was the American Deserters Committee and what impact did it have upon American troops?

***

American Deserters Committee: Worldwide Support Network
The Communist and Moscow Aids U.S. Deserters

A top Secret KGB report of KGB director Andropov to the Central Committee of the CPUSSR describes the transport of the four sailors[76] from the *Intrepid* to Moscow and the KGB's financial support of and friendly contacts with BEHEIREN.[77] Levchenko says a Marine, probably working for the Office of Naval Intelligence, later broke the news of the *Beheiren*-KGB pipeline and testified before Congress.[78] Open Soviet assistance stopped after it was revealed.

---

[74] Mari Hohn, workshop, Vassar College, April 12, 2008 cited in Frank J. Rafalko, *MH/CHAOS:*, 143.

[75] FBI, memo, "Clergy and Laymen Concerned About Vietnam, Information Concerning—Internal Security, November 4, 1968, 123418-123420 in FBI, FOIA, C, CALC.

[76] At first deserters boarded Russian ships at Kushiro Port in Hokkaido, Japan sailed to Russian Sakhalin and then traveled across the USSR to Moscow and eventually to Sweden

[77] Document 315 KGB report to the Central Committee on cooperation with Japanese peace groups during the Vietnam War in 1968, SPECIAL FOLDER/ Top Secret, Politburo Minutes No. 73, Point 47, USSR, KBG, Council of Ministers of the USSR, February 24, 1968, No. 438. A Central Committee [TSK] of the Communist Party of the Soviet Union KPSS] published in Diane P. Koenker and Ronald D. Bachman, (eds.), *Revelations from the Russian Archives,* Library of Congress, Washington, 1997, 699; Fumiko Holloran, NBR Book Review of Taketomo Takahishi, *We Helped American Deserters Cross National Borders,* ("Watashi-tachi wa Dasso America-hei wo Ekko Saseta"), NBR'S Japan Forum (POL), April 15, 2008.

[78] Stanislav Levchenko, *On the Wrong Side*, Pergamon-Brassey's, 1988, 50-53; Lora Soroka, *Fond 89: Communist Party of Soviet Union on Trial*, Stanford: Hoover

Deserter Influence on Morale of GIs.

Terry Whitmore told Mark Lane about a Marine massacre in 1967 of 300 innocent civilians in Quang Tri. In fact, the U.S. prosecuted two marines for killing not 300, but a single woman. U.S. troops killed some civilians in the midst of a firefight.[79] That was not a war crime.

Apart from the political impact on American policy, the impact of the GI movement on the battlefield was disputable.

Less than 300 U.S. troops would desert inside South Vietnam out of 2.6 million who served there and only 5,000 deserted worldwide. These few, plus thousands of draft dodgers did have high political value as false, but effective, indicators of low morale in the U.S. armed forces.

Military Justice

Punishment of GIs started tough and faded away fast: In 1967, two black Marines at Camp Pendleton got six and ten years allegedly just for discussing the war. In 1968, two privates got four years each for handing out antiwar leaflets. GIs claiming to be in trouble for protesting the war had lots of legal assistance. For example, the New York Military Law Panel[80] at 5 Beekman St., provided legal aid to the Fort Dix 38 who in June 1968 had rioted protesting poor conditions and treatment in the stockade.

Despite the extensive efforts of Hanoi and its agents and dupes to erode the morale of the American servicemen, most served honorably. Veterans of the war were bands of brothers performing tough duties in mean places trying to survive without the full support of their commanders in chief and Congress. The U.S. Government honorably discharged 97% of Vietnam era vets.

The South Vietnam People's Committee in Solidarity with the American People (*Viet My*) wrote on October 20, 1968 to its "America friends" The solidarity committee favored, "antiwar acts...among...GI's" It expressed "admiration" for

---

Institute, 2001, 302.

[79] Gary Kulick, "Apocryphal Now: The Psychology and Mythology of the Vietnam War," *Weekly Standard,* April 22, Apr 22, 2013, Vol. 18, No. 30;

[80] Lawyers on the New York Military Law Panel providing their services were Lynn Adleman, Frank Askin, Carl Broge, Fred Cohn, William Crain, Henry DiSuvero, Stephen Fine, Steve Hyman, Mark Kadish, Sanford M. Katz, Michael and William Kunstler, Gerald Lefcourt, John Lubbell, Victor Rabinowitz, David Rein, and Eric Schmidt. Also Leonard Boudin, Stanley Faulkner and Arthur Kinoy.

American youth [who]…deserted, refused induction, or refused to go to Vietnam…"

Montreal Conference for Solidarity on Vietnam
November 28-December 1, 1968. Canadian Hospitality
Montreal, Quebec, Canada was always a friendly venue. The Canadian Voice of Women for Peace traveled to Vietnam, provided aid to North Vietnam, disseminated the atrocity stories of GI deserters in Canada, [81]

***

President Seeks Intelligence
on Foreign Connections of Antiwar Activists

At the request of President Lyndon Baines Johnson, CIA Director Richard Helms ordered CHAOS's Richard Ober to prepare a report on foreign connections of the antiwar movement. Ober had only two weeks to collect information from uncooperative CIA field offices and domestic U.S. agencies and to read, analyze and write a report.[82] The superficial CIA report said, "contacts and communications on the international peace network appear to have dropped off," but noted, "Continuing coordination between U.S. peace activists and the North Vietnamese. Hanoi kept in touch with peace activists….[83]

There was underreported evidence of Soviet/CPUSA and Cuban funding. And the deaf, dumb and blind CIA found no contacts with foreign embassies[84] missing many American visitors to Chinese, Cuban, Laotian, NLF, Soviet, and North Vietnamese outposts across the globe.

American POWs and GIs remained targets for political war

CIA. The CIA, unlike military intelligence, missed entirely the Tet invasion. The CIA did not see or report either Hanoi's political war on the Second Front—America nor significant foreign or communist influence in the antiwar movement. The CIA's congenital blindness occurred in the presence of multiple meetings during 1968 of representatives of Hanoi/Viet Cong and Communist bloc nations with American activists in Bucharest,

---

[81] Kay Macpherson, Viewpoint, Canadian Broadcasting Corporation, National Television Network, January 11, 1971.
[82] Rockefeller Report, formally a *Report to the President [Ford], Commission on CIA Activities within the United States*, U.S. Government Printing Office, Washington, D.C. June 1975, 692.
[83] CIA, FOIA, case number EO11978-00207, "International Connections of US Peace Groups—III," 2-3.
[84] Helms to President Johnson, November 15, 1967 cited in Rockefeller report 693.

19

Budapest, Frankfurt, Hanoi, Havana, Kyoto, Ljubljana, Montreal, Moscow, Paris, Phnom Penn, Sofia, and Stockholm.

Hence, CIA and American history became what it was not.

CIA Sees No Evil, No Treason
No Fault Treason

Today only a few "second thought" former leftists believe anti-war protesters were guilty of treason. Peter Collier, a *Ramparts* editor and an advocate of Robert Scheer for Congress, says that many of the most prominent antiwar leaders during the Vietnam War engaged in "no fault" treason. Yet in November and December of 1967 two CIA reports[85] minimized the meaning of contacts between the antiwar movement and Hanoi:

CIA Criterion: Control

The CIA insisted that the Communists did not "control" the peace movement. Short of generous travel vouchers, KGB and friends did not provided peace activists with paychecks, health insurance or pensions. Hayden, Davis, David Dellinger and many other giddy enthusiastic were volunteers, not employees. Close in in Canada and in Cuba American cadre trained for the political struggle, *dich van,* against the war in Vietnam. In WWI this would have been treason, but Vietnam was an undeclared war.

1968 would prove extensive political cooperation, coordination, and influence, but not mechanical control.[86]

Politicians Disaffected from CIA Analysts and Bureaucrats

Political leaders were the real experts on politics and their careers depended upon knowledge and experience with political recruitment, organization, influence, power, authority, loyalty and betrayal. Similarly, military leaders understood the concepts of psychological warfare, influence operations in war.

The Vietnamese with the help of KGB dominated Cuban intelligence, the DGI, recruited hundreds of Americans into their revolutionary cadre. The CIA did a much better job of covering Cuban operations among the New Left[87] than it did Vietnamese and Soviet operations.

---

[85] "The Peace Movement: a Review of Developments Since November 15," of December 21, 1967 and "Student Dissent and its Techniques in the U.S." of January 5, 1968.

[86] Romerstein and Levchenko, The KGB ..., 274-5.

[87] Frank J. Rafalko, MH/CHAOS: The CIA's Campaign Against the Radical Left and the Black Panthers, Annapolis: Naval Institute Press, 2011, 158-171.

CIA: Hanoi believes…peace sentiment…politically potent." An essential element of Hanoi's strategy was the antiwar movement. The CIA opined, for once correctly, "Hanoi's leaders…believe the widespread desire for peace and opposition to the Vietnam War …places political pressure on Washington…" Indeed, "North Vietnam's leaders probably believe the US was 'compelled' to restrict the bombing and enter into talks by mounting domestic political pressures." And "Hanoi believes that peace sentiment in the U. S. is widespread and politically potent." It looked like "At a minimum the talks offer opportunities for political warfare."[88]

"What is spontaneous and what is organized?" Kissinger to Hoover. Within ten days of Nixon's swearing in, Dr. Henry A. Kissinger called J. Edgar Hoover. The CIA was writing a report on students protests overseas, could Hoover contribute his "reflections on…the relationship of what goes on abroad and to what goes on in this country. …[and] What is the connection between what is spontaneous and what is organized?"[89] Professor of political science, ought to have known that there is no such thing as a spontaneous demonstration.[90]

Presidents kept asking and getting nothing from the CIA about flurry of antiwar activist ties to the enemy in war. Exception Cuba.

***

Communist Cuban Ties to Peace Movement.

Fanciful preoccupation with… ruthless dictators like… Castro and search for manifestations of [international] civility …[in] the arts and sciences…obscure the sinister meaning of such dictatorships. Harold W. Rood[91]

---

[88] CIA, "Hanoi's Negotiating position and Concept of Negotiations," Secret, Intelligence Memorandum, No. 0587/68, Case Number: DS-2004-00003, 6 May 1968.
[89] Hoover to Tolson, memo, January 30, 1969.
[90] All demonstrations are organized—dates, times, places, speakers, entertainers, and themes chosen, permits acquires, publicity produced and distributed, funds raised, participants invited, transportation and accommodations arranged, signs made, equipment acquired, lawyers and emergency medical personnel recruited, monies expended. A useful list is found in Charles DeBenedetti; Charles Chatfield, *An American Ordeal: The Antiwar Movement of the Vietnam Era.* Syracuse: Syracuse University Press, 1990, 174. On a modest scale short of several thousand the author has helped on a score of demonstrations.
[91] Harold W. Rood, *Kingdoms of the Blind: How the Great Democracies Have Resumed the Follies That Nearly Cost Them their Life,* St.Petersburg: Hailer publishing, 2005, 133. Originally published in 1980 by the University of North Carolina.

Cuban Communications During Chicago Riot. During the midst of rioting, Hayden and "red diaper baby" Michael Klonsky called Cuba for a report from an SDS contingent there. Jackie Goldberg, a future member of the California Assembly was there. She was a sister of Art Goldberg, a firearms instructor for Hayden's International Liberation School.

As an Assemblyman, Goldberg, advocated homosexual rights and recycling of toilet water. Remembering Havana, she said she was free to say anything in Havana, but the US was a "police state."[92] On August 29, Radio Havana interviewed Mike Klonsky. Klonsky said the SDS would continue to battle at the convention and called for the creation of "Many Chicagos."[93]

Acculterating Cadre-Cuba, January 1968. A day after attending a National Lawyers Guild meeting (January 28, 1968) planning disruptions in Chicago, Tom Hayden and about 50 other Americans attended a Fidel Castro sponsored International Cultural Conference in Havana, Cuba.[94] Other SDS groups would follow in March, July and September 1968[95] and thereafter many contingents of the Venceremos Brigade through #46 in 2015.[96]

---

[92] Jackie Goldberg, "interview' in Episode 13 Make Love Not War (*The Sixties*), George Washington University.

[93] Bernardine Dohrn Letter (n.d.), to "Cuba Trippers-Brothers and Sisters," August 5, 1968; Radio Havana interview of Mike Klonsky in Chicago, August 29, 1968; "NIC Discusses Chicago, Elections, Elitism," *New Left Notes*, Sept 9, 1968; FBI, FOIA, *Weather*, 87-8.

[94] Other SDS leaders included Carl Davidson, Todd Gitlin,[94] Gerry Long, Susan Sutheim, Ed Jennings, Joe Horton, Paul Hugh Shinoff, and Les Coleman. Todd Gitlin later wrote it was to be the "first of many junkets to that island in the next few years." *National Guardian*, February 3, 1968: 1, 6; *Florida Alligator*, February 20, 1968; Testimony of Sergeant Grubsic, Senate Permanent Subcommittee on Investigations, June 30, 1969, 4485; Tom Charles Huston, Special Report for the President, TOP SECRET, EYES ONLY- Very Sensitive, *Foreign Communist Support of the Revolutionary Protest Movement in the United States*, July 1969, 43, declassified 11/10/2008 at request of Max Friedman. "Declassified U.S. Government intelligence information regarding the communist and foreign connections of the Weather Underground. Presented as evidence, on the agreement of the prosecution and defense counsel, in the trial of W. Mark Felt and Edward S, Miller," 12 at www.americasurvival.org; Kirkpatrick Sale, *SDS: The Rise and Development of Students for a Democratic Society, 1973,* 405.

[95] House, Committee on Internal Security, Investigation of Students for a Democratic Society, Part 7-A, December 9-11, 16, 1969, Appendix A, Committee Exhibit No. 2, 2318-20.

[96] http://venceremosbrigade.net/

Castro's Cultural Conference, Havana January 1968.
They met Vietnamese communists in Cuba. Before the HCUA in
the fall of 1968, Congressman Conley said the conference was "a
gathering of Communists and other revolutionaries whose aim is
to destroy non-Communist governments of the world." Tom
Hayden said, "I don't remember those aims being enunciated in
quite that way. ... It was essentially a meeting of intellectuals ...
film makers, painters." Those who "initiated" the Congress,
described its mission, "armed revolutionary struggle for
Socialism is the key to [cultural] developments;"[97]

Within a year, Castro closed Cuba's Museum of Modern Art,
cut the cultural budget and arrested the longhaired.[98]
Homosexuals, evidence of bourgeois decadence, were detained
in street sweeps and sent to forced labor camps.[99]

Yet the self-described painters and poets met with the North
Vietnamese, Viet Cong (NLF), North Koreans and the Red
Chinese.[100] Not surprisingly, they pledged to support the
Vietnamese struggle. The Vietnamese praised Susan Sherman
and three SDS members "We have to fight… You support us by
choice."[101]

Among the Vietnamese there was the Cuban, Soviet and
Laotian medal recipient Nguyen Quang Phong. Phong conducted
"American proselyting work…to persuade progressive
Americans to support the Vietnamese revolution and to oppose
the unjust [American] war." Phong, remembers, "I went to Cuba
to persuade Americans who were harvesting sugar cane…to
oppose the war."[102] At lunch and dinner,[103] "We formed
American proselyting groups to … create anti-war movements."

---

[97] Tom Charles Huston, Special Report, 43. House Committee on Un-American
Activities, House of Representatives, Subversives Involvement in Disruption of 1968
Democratic Party National Convention, 90th Congress, Second Session, Hearings
December 2 and 3, 1968. Washington: U.S. Government Printing Office, 2554-2555.
[98] Paul Hollander, *Political Pilgrims: Travels of Western intellectuals to the Soviet
Union, China, and Cuba*, New York: Harper Colophon, 1981, 226-27, N 13-14.
[99] Reinaldo Arenas, *Before Night Falls*, 1992.
[100] "Declassified U.S. Government intelligence information regarding the communist
and foreign connections of the Weather Underground. Presented as evidence, on the
agreement of the prosecution and defense counsel, in the trial of W. Mark Felt and
Edward S, Miller," 20-21 at www.usasurvival.org.
[101] Carol Brightman, "Carol Brightman on the 1960s," Truthdig.com, Jan 3, 2008 cites
Susan Sherman's *America's Child*, Curbstone Press, 2007.
[102] "Major General Quang Phong Discloses Security Secrets," *Vietnamese Historical
Artifacts*, Web page, 1 November, 2013 at
http://www.kyvatlichsucand.vn/vn/news/2121/355/thieu-tuong-quang-phong-tiet-lo-
nhung-bi-mat-an-ninh.html
[103] *Ibid*

Phong also propagandized the many Americans traveling to France to meet Vietnamese communists.[104]

Some Received Intelligence Training. From Cuba, two SNCC leaders flew via Moscow to North Korea where the North Koreans instructed them in military intelligence to act as "eyes and ears" on "latest plans, newest weapons, blueprints and actual weapons."[105] When American attendees of the Cultural Congress crossed the Canadian border, U.S. Customs and Immigration officials found large quantities of North Korean, Soviet, and Cuban propaganda, a Soviet-manufactured five-band radio and informative notebooks and diaries.

SDS Trained in Cuba in February. From August 1967 through February 20, other SDS groups[106] visited Cuba. Jesus Jimenez Escobar, a DGI officer serving as the first Secretary of the Cuban mission at the UN arranged the tour.[107] Apparently, Alberto Boza Hildago Gato gave final approval to those Americans seeking to visit Cuba.[108] On February 6, 1968, Cuba paid all expenses[109] for twenty-two SDS members leaving Mexico City accompanied by two Cuban UN officials on a Cubana Airlines flight to Havana. Their mission was to "to talk with representatives of North Korea and the NLF of North (sic) Vietnam" and "to spend some time…working in Cuban Fields."

North Vietnamese met the SDS group at the airport in Havana. Over Cuban radio, Joe Horton said, "I will not go to Vietnam to defend the interests of the Rusks and the Rockefellers and the Imperialists of my country." Hanoi used Cuban radio "to send our military proselyting propaganda into the 'bedrooms' of the American people."[110] Rather than cutting sugar cane the SDS group spent nearly three weeks meeting a large Communist delegation of soldiers, party members and diplomats.[111]

---

[104] *Ibid.*

[105] Tom Charles Huston, Special Report, 25-6.

[106] Sale, *SDS* 405.

[107] "Declassified U.S." 21 at www.americasurvival.org ; Tom Charles Huston, Special Report, 23; Mark Rudd, *Underground: My Life With the SDS and the Weathermen*, New York: Harper Collins, 2009, 38.

[108] Frank J. Rafalko, *MH/CHAOS:*, 159.

[109] "Declassified U.S." 12 at www.americasurvival.org.; Mark Rudd remembers paying his way by selling "opiated hashish" brought back from Vietnam. Mark Rudd, *Underground:*, 38-9.

[110] Quang Huy, "The 'psychological attack' Aimed at American Servicemen," *Events and Witnesses* [*Sur kien va nhan chung*]People's Army [*Quan Doi Nhan Dan*] monthly supplement) April 2013.

[111] Mark Rudd, *Underground:*, 39.

Training in Revolutionary and Guerrilla Tactics. The select SDS group of 22 attended the Cuban Institute for Friendship between Peoples, ICAP, a cultural front for "training foreign radicals in revolutionary and guerrilla tactics," according to FBI sources.[112] The Vietnamese Ambassador said, "This will be a long war…Eventually the American people will tire of the war. …Then the war will end." Rudd says, "I passionately wanted to be a revolutionary like Che, no matter what the costs. …Our goal was…ending the capitalist system that caused the war."

Kissing the Rings. Mark Rudd says the SDS group received "souvenir rings made of extremely lightweight titanium. The number 2017 was stamped inside to indicate that each ring had been made from debris from the 2017th American plane shot down in Vietnam. I wore mine proudly for years afterwards."[113] While publicly claiming over 2,000 shoot downs in rings and commemorative stamps[114] in fact Hanoi had downed "well under 1,000."[115]

Reports on a Cuban Paradise. Ted Gold later wrote, "The biggest organizer of the Vietnam antiwar movement has been the Viet Cong. The Viet Cong organized the [upcoming 1969] Moratorium and they organized us." The Viet Cong "are struggling and winning."[116] Also in June 1968 Sam Brown, major peace organizer of the upcoming "moderate" Moratorium, told Dr. Martin Abend privately that the Viet Cong was the best future for South Vietnam[117] and later publicly celebrated the VC victory.

---

[112] Those taught revolutionary tactics were Karen Lynn Ashley, Dena Marie Clanage, Les Coleman[112], Mary Elson, Alice Embree, Mike Herman Goldfield, Thomas Mark Hardesty, Holly Maureen Hart, Joe Richard Horton, Ed John Jennings, Alan Thomas Levin, Joseph Sharon Michael, Mary Jane Nelson, Dick Johnson Reavis, Joan Marie Rockwell, James Rockwell, Mark Rudd[112], Phil Low Russell, Sheila Patricia Ryan, Mike Sharon. Also Paul Hugh Shinoff[112], Mark Ben Steiner, Bob Samuel Tumposky, Jean Barbara Weisman. "Declassified U.S." 13 at www.americasurvival.org. Mark Rudd, *Underground:*, 40. By December 1966 Hanoi had claimed 1,600 shot down while the U.S. tally was less than 400. Harrison E. Salisbury, *Behind the Lines-Hanoi*, New York: Harper & Row, 1967, 139-140. Rochester and Frederick Kiley, *Honor Bound, American Prisoners of War in Southeast Asia 1961-1973*, Annapolis: Naval Institute Press, 1999, 403n.

[113] Mark Rudd, *Underground:*, 40.

[114] By December 1966 Hanoi had claimed 1,600 shot down while the U.S. tally was less than 400. Harrison E. Salisbury, *Behind...*, 139-140.

[115] Rochester and Frederick Kiley, 13.

[116] FBI, FOIA, Weather Underground. The primary source is Acting SAC Chicago to Director, memo, "Foreign Influence-Weather Underground Organization," August 20, 1976, 204.

Back from Cuba SDS leaders implemented Plan A-5.[118] On April 22, the SDS published a newspaper *Up Against the Wall!* Up Against the Wall was English for Al Paredon! the cry of Cuban execution firing squads.

The FBI believed the Columbia protest was planned in Cuba.

Cuban guerrilla Che Guevara had said, create "One, Two, Three, Many Vietnams" at a Tricontinental Conference in Havana.[119] Mark Rudd now said, "Thus we have our slogan: create one, two, three, many Columbias."[120]

One poll found in December 1968 more college students (20 percent) identified with Che Guevara than with either of the candidates for President, Nixon or Humphrey.[121]

SDS in Havana, July 1968. On July 26, 1968, the tenth anniversary of the Cuban Revolution, Fidel Castro accepted an "official the group of five hardcore American SDS radicals for an eight-day celebration of his "holy day for Cuban Communists."[122] Most importantly, the SDSers met fourteen representatives of the North Vietnamese—Huynh Van Ba--and the Viet Cong, NLF. Ruben Salazar of the *Los Angeles Times* reported five Americans selected out of 300 studied revolution at the Fifth of May Camp in Pinar del Rio Province.[123]

Symposium on Yankee Genocide and Cuban Torture. In Havana October 18-21, 1968 the Communist international and the Cuban Solidarity with Vietnam Committee brought Cubans and Vietnamese together for the Second Symposium Against Yankee Genocide in Vietnam. Professor Miguel A. D'Estafano told *El Mundo*, he had completed a Cuban program in Vietnam to "to collect extensive information" on "genocide in Vietnam." Three Cubans, Major Fernando Vecino Alegret, Luis Perez Jaen, Dr. Miguel Angel Bustamente-O'Leary, presented films and tapes to the symposium. The symposium received five committee

---

[117] Alice Widner, "Moratorium's Coordinator Favors Viet Cong Victory," *Houston Tribune*, October 23, 1979.

[118] Tom Charles Huston, Special Report, 23.

[119] "The Weather Underground Organization," *Information Digest*, Vol. XIV, #22, November 13, 1981, 337.

[120] Francisco Tortela interview of Mark Rudd on *Prensa Latina*, (Cuban News Agency) New York, June 11, 1968.

[121] Todd Gitlin, *The Sixties: Years of Hope, Days of Rage* , New York: Bantam, 1987, 344.

[122] *New Left Notes*, June 24, 1968:8; Anthony Bryant, *Hijack*, Freedom Press International, June 1984, 184.

[123] Ruben Salazar, "Aliens Get Training in Cuba," *Los Angeles Times*, August 13, 1968.

reports.[124] The Cubans were very likely the Cuban interrogators of POWS.

Meanwhile, indoctrination in Cuba and meetings with Vietnamese communists in Hanoi Europe inspired the SDS. The hard-core SDS leadership formed the Weathermen faction to bring the war home to start an American revolution resulting in street fighting for peace in Days of Rage in Chicago and the formation of the Venceremos Brigades in Cuba to recruit and train revolutionaries, and finally the major SDS leadership split off into the terrorist Weather Underground and their above ground protectors.

***

---

[124] "Five Committees Report from Second Genocide Symposium," *Granma*, (Spanish), October 21, 1968, 3, Sum. No. 46, 845, FBIS, November 12, 1968.

Chapter 2. Fellow Travelers And the Hard Core.

January Quakers Seduced

Repeating a mission in 1967, on January 23, 1968 the yacht *Phoenix* sailed into Haiphong, North Vietnam where A Quaker Action Group, AQUAG, delivered $5,000 in surgical supplies and $2,500 in medicines for the Red Cross of the NLF.[125] South Vietnam had turned away a landing at Da Nang intending to provide Quaker medicine to the NLF and the United Buddhists. So too Cambodia "did not want to offer the U.S. another pretext for charging [actually noticing] that... Sihanoukville (is a) supply route for NLF."[126]

Upon arrived in Haiphong,[127] "dozens of beautiful girls carrying flowers" welcomed them.[128] Vietnamese officials, "Red Cross" and the Vietnam Peace Committee greeted them. The Americans briefed the Vietnamese on " the United States peace movement" who "were counting on the U.S. peace movement to force America to withdraw from Vietnam." On tour, the Quakers were shown bombed out residential area where no military targets were revealed visited war victims in a hospital. At an Historical Museum they saw the personal effects of America's pilots, dead and imprisoned.[129]

The Quakers thought "this war must be stopped before it destroys Vietnam and plunges all mankind into an atomic holocaust."[130] Back home AQAG refused to pay taxes, rejected the draft and protested Dow Chemical making napalm.[131]

Senator Ted Kennedy—One Man VC Propaganda Show.

During January 1968, Senator Ted Kennedy (D-MA) made a fact-finding tour of refugee camps in South Vietnam. He

---

[125] "Phoenix Docks in Haiphong With $7,000 in Medicine," *The Evening Bulletin*, Philadelphia, February 1, 1968, 6.

[126] George Lakey, "South Vietnam Rebuffs Aid Haiphong in the Picture Again," A Quaker Action Group, *Newsletter* No. 9, January 1968, 2.

[127] William Mimms, National Fair Housing Association; Maryann McNaughton, Committee for Nonviolent action; John Braxton, Swarthmore College; Robert Eaton, captain, Annapolis; Beryl Nelson, Kokomo, Ind; and Christopher Crowley, London; "Phoenix Crew Reports Delivery to N. Vietnam," *Daily News*, Philadelphia, February 14, 1968, 6; "The Phoenix Windup," newsletter #11, April 1968-zaFS.

[128] "Phoenix *Daily News*, 6.

[129] "The Phoenix Windup," *newsletter* #11, April 1968-zaFS

[130] Lawrence Scott, "Dear Friend" letter, A Quaker Action Group, March 10, 1968 in FBI, FOIA, "A", AFSC.

[131] A Quaker Action Group, "Human Rights Are For Everyone," pamphlet, N.D. 1968.

described a corrupt and brutal regime. The junior Senator from Massachusetts believed "half of the 30 million dollars a year the United States has given South Vietnam for refugee relief...[went into]...the pockets of government officials..." Kennedy did not mention corruption and brutality in Hanoi, let alone in his home state of Boston, Massachusetts.[132] Senator Kennedy falsely declared, "the vast majority [of the South Vietnamese refugees] -- ...over 80 percent -- ...either deposited in camps by the Americans or fled to camps in fear of American airplanes and artillery. Only a handful claimed they were driven from their homes by the Viet Cong."[133]

Hanoi POW Releases—Berrigan and Zinn

After the Vietnamese Peace Committee told Dellinger that several POWs had "a repentant attitude," on February 17, 1968, Tom Hayden and Dellinger coordinated[134] a POW release to Father Daniel Berrigan[135] and professor and secret Communist, Professor Howard Zinn. Upon arrival in "the destroyed city" of Hanoi, Catholic priest and poet, Daniel Berrigan thought, "the loveliest fact of all ... we had been received with flowers"[136] and the poems of Ho Chi Minh.[137]

Col. Ha Van Lau, a frequent mentor of peace activists, gave a six-hour lecture to Zinn and Berrigan.[138] They guided to bomb debris, a damaged hospital, war museums and shown a film on the life of Ho. Hanoi showcased the damaged body parts (e.g. "brain and skull and heart and viscera") of victims of bombings in jars. Berrigan thought America was waging "a monstrous and intentionally genocidal war."[139]

---

[132] Corruption was "so pervasive in the 1960's and 1970's that it became 'a way of life,' ...It was not a matter of a few crooks... [it was] broad and pervasive... where money and power came together, the system has been rotten,." Michael Knight, "Massachusetts Told of Wide Corruption," *New York Times*, January 1, 1981.

[133] Adam Clymer, *Edward M. Kennedy: a Biography,* New York: Harper Perennial, 2000, 80-82, 99-103; Spock and Zimmerman, Spock on Vietnam, 15, 45-46, 4849 cited in Paul Kengor, *Dupes*, 318-319; See also Paul Kengor, "Ted Kennedy's Vietnam Plot," *American Thinker*, March 11, 2011.

[134] FBI, FOIA, Howard Zinn.

[135] In 1967, Berrigan had had considerable conflict with superiors in his Jesuit order over his desire to go to Hanoi with the Fellowship of Reconciliation to bring medical supplies. Thomas Merton, a Communist while at Columbia University and then a dupe of communist front groups, advised Berrigan to follow his individual conscience, [not Catholic teaching about Communism.]

[136] Daniel Berrigan, *Night Flight to Hanoi*, New York: Macmillan, 1968, 38, 134 cited in Paul Hollander, *Political Pilgrims, 356.*

[137] Berrigan, *Night*, XIV, cited in Paul Hollander, *Political Pilgrims, 371.*

[138] Berrigan, *Night*, 50-6.

[139] Berrigan, *Night*, 65.

Premier Pham Van Dong:
"great intelligence...great reserves of compassion."

On February 16, 1968, Berrigan and Zinn met Premier Pham Van Dong at his French villa and garden behind armored doors. Berrigan saw in the "face of this man... great intelligence, and yet also great reserves of compassion."

"We are in combat here, and you there."

In Berrigan's notes, Dong said, "we have a common front. We are in combat here and you there."[140] Comrades in arms. "We must continue to coordinate our efforts. ...We will be in touch with representatives of your movement... (in) future meetings...here or in another place, such as Bratislava."[141] Bratislava was where Tom Hayden and Dan Dellinger had already led over thirty of Hanoi's American fans to meet a like number of Vietnamese communists in September 1967.

POWs: "Correct Attitude."

The Vietnamese asked, "Is it possible, that (the pilots will)... do something for the antiwar movement in the United States?"[142] Hanoi declared, "Three of the captured pilots were released in view of their correct attitude...."[143] Maj. Norris Overly and Lt. Col. Jon David Black "taped statements of contrition...as a condition of their release."[144]

After his arrival in New York, Berrigan told POW families the Vietnamese acted "humanely toward prisoners."[145] "[W]ithout prompting," the POWs readily told Berrigan how good their food and medical care was.[146]

Media Covers Protests

During the height of Tet, the *Times* gave 70% of its domestic news coverage to antiwar activists and 30% to hawks or the administration.[147] Berrigan got his share of free publicity.

POW Escort Berrigan: Jesuit Napalms Draft Cards

---

[140] Berrigan, *Night*, 128.
[141] Berrigan, *Night*, 129.
[142] Berrigan, *Night*, 42-3.
[143] Harry S. Ashmore and William C. Baggs, *Mission to Hanoi: A 1968 Chronicle of Double Dealing in High Places*, New York: Putnam, September 1968, 145.
[144] Stuart I. Rochester and Frederick Kiley, 367.
[145] (Rev) Daniel Berrigan to Dear Friends, Cornell University, Ithaca, New York, March 3, 1968.
[146] Daniel Berrigan, *Nighti*, 78-9, 86, 111 cited in Paul Hollander, *Political Pilgrims*,353.
[147] Peter Braestrup, *Big Story*, 494-95.

On May 17, 1968, Maj. Norris Overly's escort Daniel Berrigan and eight others[148] earned considerable media notoriety as the Cantonsville Nine. They staged the napalming of the draft files of 378 persons in wire trashcans before an assembled crowd of reporters at the Catonsville, Maryland draft board. "Their major accomplishment was scaring the hell out of the little old ladies at the office of the Catonsville draft board," remembers Pat Joyce, an editor of several Catholic newspapers and the Baltimore *Evening Sun.* [149]

Mary McCarthy in Hanoi

In March 1968, Mary McCarthy, self-described utopian socialist arrived in Hanoi in the midst of the Tet Offensive. Also visiting was Franz Schurmann, a Berkeley professor, a Marxist active in the Vietnam Day Committee, an angry drunk,[150] and a fellow at the Pro-Hanoi Institute for Policy Studies. Also self-described peace negotiators Harry Ashmore and William Baggs and CBS's Charles Collingwood. Mary McCarthy had long believed it was the special moral obligation of intellectuals to get the U.S. out of the Vietnam War. It was a separate responsibility of politicians and the military, not her, to predict the fate of the South Vietnamese people after a Hanoi victory. Diana Trilling told Mary McCarthy, "No choice which is careless of its consequences is a moral choice." Mary McCarthy felt badly about the 50,000 or so killed in earlier northern land reforms, but Hanoi had "rectified" that mishap. McCarthy believed the alternative to Communism, capitalist materialism, was far uglier than socialist ideals.

Hanoi: Revelry, Rebirth, Resistance

Arriving in Hanoi at night the lights were on, no blackout curtains and the Peace Committee met McCarthy and Prof. Schurmann with bouquets of flowers. Air raid alerts led to scrambles to shelters. "All that nocturnal movement and chatter gave an impression of revelry." McCarthy, unlike many visitors, saw and wrote about the massive movement of military supplies wherever she went.

Fine Food and Nicely Arranged Toilet Paper

The French colonial Metropole Hotel had hot water and toilet paper laid out in a fan pattern. She contrasted her

---

[148] Philip Berrigan, David Darst, John Hogan, Tom Lewis, Marjorie Melville, Thomas Melville, George Mische and Mary Moylan.
[149] Joyce to author.
[150] *Time* March 29, 1968.

delicious meals with "99% of the Vietnamese" eating "rice and bean curd for dinner tonight." Moreover, "a guest of a Vietnamese organization was not allowed to pay for anything—I never had to change so much as a dollar or a Dong." Over loud speakers came voices "feminine and soothing, sugared in tone." In Hanoi McCarthy saw no beggars, "no ragged children with sores," no prostitutes. The streets of Hanoi were cleaner than New York City, no trash.[151]

Bombing Alerts, But No Bombing

Despite the Tet offensive, there was no bombing of downtown Hanoi during McCarthy's stay. Practiced host of antiwar Americans, Col. Ha Van Lau served beer at the War Crimes Museum while displaying particularly "fiendish" cluster bombs and pellets imbedded in human skulls. Col. Lau doubtless knew the military value of such weapons for disabling Hanoi's fire control radar and defending against Vietnamese human wave attacks, (Ia Drang, Khe Sanh).

Rings, "A Medal pinned"

At the War Crimes Museum, Mary McCarthy and party received "rings made from downed U.S. aircraft"… (2,818 and counting every day). "Like a wedding ring mine is engraved August 1, 1966." And a woman's comb too. It was "a medal pinned." She was uncomfortable wearing the ring and writes she never passed the comb through her hair.

Down to business Mr. Phan of the Peace Committee said the leper colony of Quynh Lap had been bombed 39 times. Quynh Lap was a coal-mining region perhaps of some interest as a bombing target in war. They were shown a headless statute of John the Baptist at the Church of the Little Flower.[152]

Meeting POW Risner: "Low Mental Attainments."

At the Show Room of the Plantation, "a Hanoi Villa," Mary McCarthy met POW Robbie Risner with questions "submitted in advance." She "was taken …by a stiffness of phraseology and naïve rote-thinking, childish, like handwriting…(of Risner)" He "speaks English very slowly, like a Vietnamese practicing the language." Risner "fawns on Vietnamese officers. Servile. … Grateful: 'Oh, gee, bananas

---

[151] New York was a pigsty at that time. Garbage collectors, entertainers and artists alike were on strike.

[152] Mary McCarthy, *Seventeenth Degree: How It Went, Vietnam, Hanoi, Medina, Sons of the Morning*, New York: Harcourt Brace, 1967, 1968, 1972, 1973, 1974, 73-4, 182, 184-5, 191-3, 197-98, 201-5, 208-9, 211-2, 215-6, 222-4, 232.

too?' McCarthy decided the college-educated American pilots had "low mental attainments."[153]

Alas, Mary McCarthy of the Inteligencia could not discern POW Risner's signaling he was under duress, poorly fed, and had been tortured. In *Passing of the Night*, POW Risner says he was tortured before meeting visitors. Of the Vietnamese McCarthy said, "I don't think they understand me." Risner raised his eyebrows and said, "I think they do." McCarthy "knocked on wood," hoping for an early end of the war. For three hours, guards interrogated Risner about the meaning of knocking on wood and the raising of eyebrows.[154]

CBS's Collingwood Sees No Bombing, No Genocide.

On March 20, 1968, the North Vietnamese cleared Walter Cronkite to go to Hanoi,[155] but CBS sent Charles Collingwood instead. For eight days, Collingwood describes his companions and "three bureaucrats" traveling to bombsites. The Vietnamese "trotted out survivors to stare" at them. Collingwood was no fool. "Their little faces fell..." when Collingwood refused to go to bomb shelters believing the U.S. would not bomb "population centers." For an hour, Collingwood met Pham Van Dong, the Foreign Minister and a Colonel (likely Ha Van Lau) who made "ritual charges of genocide" in "propaganda phraseology" and expressed optimism about prevailing.[156]

Committee for Concerned Asian Scholars Sees U.S. Imperialism, March 22-24, 1968.

Meanwhile some members of the faculties and graduate students of Harvard, Stanford, University of Michigan, University of California at Berkeley, and Columbia came together at a conference of the Association of Asian Studies, AAS, at the Benjamin Franklin Hotel in Philadelphia on March 22-24, 1968. AAS had not taken a position on the war. So the dissenters formed the Committee of Concerned Asian Scholars, CCAS, for the expressed purpose to oppose the "brutal

---

[153] Mary McCarthy, *Seventeenth... 299.*
[154] Robinson Risner, *The Passing of the Night*, New York: Random House, 1973 cited in James Banerian, 252.
[155] Ashmore and Baggs, *Mission*, 160.
[156] "Television: Mission to Hanoi," *Time* Apr. 19, 1968; "The War: Hopeful Half Steps, *Time* Apr. 12, 1968.

aggression of the United States in Vietnam" and to encourage "anti-imperialist research."[157]

Photo: Maoist revolutionary poster.

The CCAS promoted Mao's cultural revolution. CCAS has supported several generations of pro-Hanoi historians up to the present.[158] An early CCAS member and later a prominent historian of the Vietnam War, Marilyn Blatt Young has said,

---

[157] The formal founding convention of Concerned Asian Scholars occurred a year later in Boston, March 28-30, 1969. Its mission "to develop a humane and knowledgeable understanding of Asian societies and their efforts… to confront…poverty, oppression and imperialism" and to create "alternatives to prevailing trends…which…serve selfish interests and expansionism." Today its direct successor Critical Asian Studies retains this mission and further states "the historical tradition of socialist thought remains a source of inspiration for some of us…" Richard Baum, *China and The American Dream: a Moral Inquiry*, Seattle: University of Washington, 2010, 236-9.

[158] Almost universally pro-Hanoi Vietnamese contributors to the CCAS *Bulletin* were: Ngo Vinh Long, To Hu, Ho Chi Minh, Mao Tse-Tung, Nguyễn Kim Nghan, Truong Quoc Khanh, Ly Phong Lien, Nguyen Khac Vien, Nguyen Cong Binh, Mai Ho, Le Van Hao, Liu Van Nong, Ly Chanh Trung. Early founders, staff, contributors, and advisors of *Bulletin of Committee of Concerned Asian Scholars* were Kathleen Gough Aberle, Nina Adams, Frank Akerman, R. David Arkush, Marianne Bastid, Dennis Bathroy, Sidney Beech, Michael Bierman, Herbert Bix, Fred Branfman, Noam Chomsky, John Collins, Bruce Cumings, John Dower, Tom Engelhardt, Joseph Esherick, Thomas Ferguson, Cynthia Frederick, Ed Friedman, William Haseltine, Jon Halliday, Charles Hayford, David Horowitz, Carl Jacobson, Leigh Kagan, Richard Kagan, Madeleine Levine, Perry Link, Jon Livingston, Ngo Vinh Long, Jonathan Mirsky, Edwin Moise, Ray Moore, Jim Morrell, Victor Nee, Cheryl Payer, Jim Peck, Elizabeth J. Perry, Daniel Pool, Jim Sanford, Earl C. Ravenal, Larry Rottman, Orville Schell, Franz Schurmann, Mark Selden, Jon Sherwood, Douglas Spelman, Susan Shirk, James C. Thomson, John Wheeler, James A. Whitson, Ernest Young, Marilyn B. Young, Yamashita Tatsuo. The most noteworthy and published American and western contributors to the *Bulletin of Committee of Concerned Asian Scholars* during the Vietnam War and its immediate aftermath, 1968-1977, were: Iqbal Ahmad, Doug Allen, Frank Baldwin, Dan Berrigan, Marc Blecher, James K. Boyce, O Edmund Clubb, Jacque Decornoy, Doug Dowd, John Fairbanks, Edward Freedman, Cynthia Fredrick, Nigel Gray, Chalmers Johnson, Michael Klare, Gabriel Kolko, David Marr, Andre Menras, Richard Minear, Michael Morrow, Liane Ellison Norman, Bruce Gareth Porter, Moss Roberts, Stanley Sheinbaum, Stanley Spector, Ezra Vogel, Arthur Waskow, Christine and Gordon White, William Appleman Williams, William Wray. Some collectively contributed as unnamed authors the CCAS book *The Indochina*

The Sixties – to use the general noun currently in use – were centrally about the recognition, on the part of an ever growing number of Americans, that the country in which they thought they lived – peaceful, generous, honourable, just – did not exist and never had."[159]

CCAS and Marilyn Young loved communists Mao, Ho and Castro. They hated capitalist imperialist America.

Ashmore Sees Humanity, Integrity and Romanticism in Hanoi's Leaders. Both Harry Ashmore and William Baggs[160] had met Ho Chi Minh in January 1967. Meeting Hoang Tung, editor of *Nhan Dan,* Ashmore said socialism was "tolerable so long as it was run by humane men of demonstrated integrity like Ho Chi Minh." Touring with Vu Qhoc Thanh, Nguyen Hap and Thinh Hai, Ashmore and Baggs saw spires of churches amidst rubble.[161] Also increased rail and truck traffic.

***

SDS "Bring the War Home...Ten Days to Shake an Empire."

On February 10-11, 1968, a SDS Eastern Regional Conference planned "Ten Days to Shake an Empire," ...a major step ... in a struggle... to expose and attack the imperialist nature of our society."[162] A leaflet, said, "In the last year or so, ...[w]e have organized ...militant demonstrations ... to direct confrontations with the war machine and the cops."[163]

On April 21-30, in a steam heated and sweaty sub cellar game room at Weinberg Residence Hall, New York University Stalinist ...literature was plentiful,[164] including the *Spark,* an

---

Story in 1970 including Frank Ackerman, R. David Arkush, Dennis Bathoy, Sidney Beech, Richard Bernstein, Michael Bierman, Herbert Bix, Karen Burke, Noam Chomsky, John Collins, John Dower, Thomas Engelhardt, Thomas Ferguson, Cynthia Fredrick, William Hazeltine, Charles Hayford, Carl Jacobson, Leigh Kagan, Richard C. Kagan, Madeleine Levine, Perry Link, Ngo Vinh Long, Edwin Moise, Victor Nee, James Sanford, Cheryl Payer, James Peck, Daniel Pool, Earl C. Ravenal, Larry Rottman, Jon Sherwood, Douglas Spelman, James C. Thomson, Jr., John Wheeler, James A. Whitson, and Ernest Young.

[159] Marilyn B. Young, "Reflections on the Anti-war Movement, Then and Now," http://www. nnet.gr/historein/historeinfiles/ histvolumes/hist09/historein9-young.pdf

[160] Oberdorger, *Tet!* Cited in Peter Braestrup, Big Story, 596n88; Ashmore Baggs, *Mission.*

[161] Ashmore and Baggs, *Mission,* 132-6, 150-1.

[162] *Firebomb* [SDS newsletter], March 11, 1968 cited in "Ten Days in April," *Barron's,* March 11, 1968.

[163] "Ten Days in April," *Barrons,* March 11, 1968.

[164] Some literature included the Russian word and Cyrillic alphabetical spelling for SPARK -- the Leninist/Bolshevik publication in Lenin's years of exile.

artifice of V.I. Lenin. Participants considered spreading garbage at Lincoln Center and setting fires in subways. The New York Police prevented any such acts.[165]

West Berlin Conference Countered by Anticommunists

February 17-18, 1968 the German SDS organized an International Vietnam Congress at the Technical University in West Berlin gathering 5,000-6,000 antiwar activists who showed solidarity with the Vietnamese shouting "Ho, Ho, Ho Chi Minh."

In response, some 60,000 experienced anticommunist West Berliners mobilized against Communist conquests.[166]

Hanoi Organizes American Women

On February 11, 1968, Vietnam News Agency reported letters from Vietnamese women and youth to Americans, "on occasion of current concerted struggle." Bill Ayers' companion and ring bearer in Toronto, Nguyen Thi Thanh wrote, "more and more American women have risen up valiantly against the U.S. war in Vietnam." Thanh wrote urgently,

[W]e earnestly call on you to raise your voice strongly, … to demand an early end to this dirty war and …the repatriation of your husbands and sons…"[167]

Paris Propaganda: Women Defiled

From April 3-6, 1968, a WSP contingent met Vietnamese women at the Paris Conference of Women to End the war in Vietnam. The Vietnamese women told the WSP women tales of snakes put in female trousers, which "wiggled into the internal organs of girls" and of American troops bayoneting pregnant women.[168]

---

[165] Among the 200 SDSers in attendance were Trudy Bennett, Bernardine Dohrn, Steve Halliwell, Naomi Jaffe, Tom Neuman, Sue Shargell, Gerry Tenney, and Bob Tomashevsky. See: Alice Widener, "Subcellar Student Subversion," *U.S.A. Magazine*, March 1, 1968, also in *Barron's* March 1, 1968.

[166] Jessica C.E. Gienow-Hecht and Frank Schumacher, *Cultural and International History*, New York: Berghahn books, 2003, 145; Martin Klimke and Joachim Scharloth,*1968 in Europe*, New York: Palgrave Macmillan, 2008, 103-4.

[167] "Women, Youth Send Letter to Groups in U.S.," VNA International News Service, Hanoi, 1608 GMT, Feb. 11, 1968, FBIS Feb. 15, 1968. TTU Archive. Cited in Rothrock, p.147-148N22.

[168] Amy Swerdlow, *Women Strike For Peace: Traditional Motherhood and Radical Politics in the 1960s*, 220-21. http://books.google.com/books?id=y5BQXBB520IC&pg=PA220&lpg=PA220&dq =anne+bennett+vietnam&source=web&ots=uwNz5rcHj4&sig=FV-9YP4qoVNQ9Oe9 Qo1utk6jmY#P PP1,M1o; The graphic portrayal of intermingling snakes and women can be seen in stone carvings at ancient Hindu inspired ruins in Cambodia at Ankhor Wat.

***
King, Kennedy, Columbia: Assassinations and Disorder. On April 4, 1968, James Earl Ray assassinated Martin Luther King in Memphis, Tennessee and riots broke out in over twenty cities.[169]

In an atmosphere of civil disorder, the U.S. Army prepared for the worst.[170]

US Army Intelligence Monitors Antiwar Protesters. The U.S. Army expanded its existing intelligence collection capability. Besides reading newspapers and FBI and local police files, the U.S. Army actively infiltrated groups and monitored public speeches. Its operation grew to 1,000 undercover officers operating from 300 offices following 18,000 individuals.[171] Army intelligence covered every major demonstration, including antiwar groups such as CALC, WRL, National Mobe and WSP. Information was fed into four computers and mug books at Fort Holabird, Maryland.[172]

SDS Occupies Columbia University, April 23-30, 1968. Flying the Viet Cong flag from atop a math building April 23-30, 1968 the SDS[173] and hundreds of others occupied five buildings at Columbia University[174] in protest of the Institute for Defense Analysis there. Protesters held a Dean hostage, looted the files of the university president, occupied buildings

---

[169] Atlanta, Ga.; Baltimore, Md.; Boston, Mass.; Buffalo, N.Y.; Chicago, Ill.; Denver, Colo.; Des Moines, Iowa; Detroit, Mich.; Gainesville, Fla.; Greensboro, N.C.; Los Angeles, Calif.; Memphis, Tenn.; Nashville, Tenn.; New Orleans, La.; Oakland, Calif.; Pittsburgh, Pa.; Richmond, Va.; St. Louis, Mo.; Tampa, Fla.; Trenton, N.J.; Washington, D.C.; Youngstown, Ohio; Clay Risen, "Spies Among Us," *American Scholar*, WINTER 2009, theamericanscholar.org/spies-among-us/#.UhjYNxuTh9A 1/11

[170] And the author began his writing and research on black ghetto riots and campus disorders.

[171] "Army Spied on 18,000 civilians in two-year operation" *New York Times*, January 18, 1971.

[172] Christopher H. Pyle, "CONUS Intelligence: The Army Watches Civilian Politics," *Washington Monthly*, January 1970; Robert O'Harrow interview of Chris Pyle, "No Place to Hide," PBS, http://americanradioworks.publicradio.org/features/noplaceto hide/pyle.html; Ralph Michael Stein, *Laird v. Tatum: The Supreme Court and a First Amendment Challenge to Military Surveillance of Lawful Civilian Political Activity*, School of law, Faculty Publications, Pace University 1973 at http://digitalcommons.pace.edu/lawfaculty/285.

[173] Mark Rudd, Ted Gold, John Jacobs, Nick Freudenberg, Tom Hurwitz, Ted Kaptchuk, Bob Feldman, Tony Papert, David Gilbert, Juan Gonzalez, Lew Cole, Robert Roth, Martin Kenner, Eleanor Stein Raskin, Joseph Raskin, Abbie Hoffman, and Tom Hayden.

[174] Mark Rudd, *Underground: ,* 55-77; "Declassified U.S., 2 at www.americasurvival.org; Senate, Committee on the Judiciary, Subcommittee to Investigate the Administration of the Internal Security Act and Other Internal Security Laws, *The Weather Underground*, Committee Print, January 1975.

occupied for a week until the President of called the New York City Police for help. Seventeen police were injured in arresting 700 persons, some not students. Tom Hayden escaped into the early morning fog before the police raid. The FBI believed the Columbia protest was planned in Cuba. Indeed, *Prensa Latina* interviewed Mark Rudd about the Columbia insurrection. Carl Davidson and others spent three hours with Castro who told them a socialist revolution was possible in the U.S.[175] Gus Hall, CPUSA General Secretary, said Communists had played an active role in campus protests including Columbia.[176]

"One, Two Three More Columbia's" and Vietnams. "One, Two Three More Columbia's" and "One Two Three More Vietnams" soon became siren calls for revolution. Riots in France in June led to hopes for worldwide assaults upon capitalist imperialism. The SDS in East Lansing, Michigan June 8-15, discussed a paper by Bernardine Dohrn, Tom Bell and Steve Halliwell calling for the creation of urban centers of revolution.. "Confrontation politics puts the enemy up against the wall."

Hayden and Scheer's "Red Family.' Tom Hayden saw revolutionary opportunities. Hayden would work to build cadre, his own "AmeriCong" and his own "foci," cell, in his Red Family in "liberated" Berkeley. Also in Madison and Ann Arbor.[177] Anne Weills Scheer remembers, "The Cubans and Vietnamese were trying to build new Socialist men and women, and that's what we were trying to be. …We went so far as to collectivize our underwear." Also women.[178] Hayden later provided weapons and combat medical training in his and Stew Albert's International Liberation School. Hayden had visions of the AmeriCong turning Berkeley, Isla Vista, Ann Arbor, East Village into liberated territory. The blacks got the Republic of New Africa, the southern states and the Chicanos got the Atzlan, the southwestern United States.[179] Creating

[175] "Declassified U.S. 2 at www.americasurvival.org.
[176] "U.S. Reds Claim Role in Campus Uprisings," *Los Angeles Times*, July 5, 1968.
[177] Peter Collier, "Life Along the 'Ramparts," *New Criterion*, January 2010.
[178] Unger, "Special Issue: Private Lives (Robin Williams cover). Michael J Fox, Tom Hayden, Muhammad Ali, Groucho Marx, James Woods," *Esquire*, June 1989, 190.
[179] Tom Hayden, "The Trial," *Ramparts* July 1970; Tom Hayden, *Trial,* New York: Holt, Rinehart and Winston, 1970, 157-8; Tom Hayden, "The New American Revolution," *Ramparts*, July 1970, reprinted in *Trial*, 155-165; Peter Collier, "I Remember Fonda," *New West*, September 24, 1979.

revolution now seemed an option in the United States and the world with Cuba and Vietnam the models.

SDS Weather Cadre at Columbia. Among the future SDS revolutionaries-to-be, some Weathermen were at Columbia. Some would go underground and take new names. [180]

Robert Kennedy Assassinated. On June 5, 1968, 12:15 am, a Palestinian Arab, Sirhan Sirhan assassinated Senator Robert F. Kennedy with a .22 revolver. Kennedy, a former staffer to anti-communist Senator Joseph McCarthy, was running an antiwar campaign for President. Robert Kennedy had visited North Vietnamese Ambassador Mai Van Bo in Paris[181] just as George McGovern would meet Hanoi negotiators in 1972. The Weather Underground, e.g. Bill Ayers, Bernardine Dohrn *et al*, would later dedicate a book to the Kennedy's assassin Sirhan Sirhan. Hayden attended the Kennedy funeral at St. Patrick's Cathedral wearing a Castro field military cap.

COSVN Resolution #6 – "pacifist movements in the USA." In May 1968 the Viet Cong inside South Vietnam was showing greater interest in antiwar movement. The precise Vietnamese interest in American politics was to "create conditions for pacifist movements in the USA to radically change its VN policy," according to COSVN Resolution #6 of May 1968.[182] Nguyen Tuong Lai, a Viet Cong guerrilla leader, said, "We knew there was a large antiwar movement in America who would not allow the American army to cross the border."[183]

Hanoi's Spies Recruiting Americans

In 1968 Ho Nam (real name Hoang Gia Huy), a secret agent of Department A13 of Foreign Intelligence Directorate of the Ministry of Public Security was assigned to the North Vietnamese mission in Paris. Ho Nam was tasked to recruit Americans as agents or friendly contacts. Tran Quoc Hoan, Minister of Public Security (equivalent to KGB) instructed Ho

---

[180] Nick Freudenberg, Dave Gilbert, Ted Gold, Norris Grossner, John Jacobs (a.k.a. JJ, Anthony Frank Rocco, Jr., Robert Carnie Morgan), Robb Roth, Mark Rudd, Nancy Cantelmo, Andrea Boroff Gedal, Martin Herman Kenner, Shinya Ono, Jonah Raskin, Stephen Joseph Tappis; .FBI, FOIA, Weather, 83.

[181] Ashmore and Baggs, *Mission*, 118.

[182] Gen. William Westmoreland, in Marvin E. Gettleman, Jane Franklin, Marilyn B. Young, and H. Bruce Franklin (eds.), *Vietnam and America; A Documented History*, New York: Grove Press, 1985, 354.

[183] Nguyen Tuong Lai, "Soldier of the Revolution," Al Santoli, *To Bear Any Burden*, 146.

Nam, "You must do everything you can to recruit people from among the ranks of Americans whose revolutionary consciousness has been awakened, from among those Americans who oppose the American war." Nam directed covert propaganda operations with his American contacts Ho Nam says, "I was able to select and recruit a network that worked actively and...helped to reduce our casualties and to gain victory."[184] Jane Fonda was one of his contacts.

Also operating in Paris as part of Hanoi's intelligence operations among Americans antiwar activists were overseas Vietnamese Huynh Trung Dong, Nguyen Ngoc Giao and NLF representative Phan Thanh Nam. Other persons of interest later signed Nguyen Ngoc Giao's several declarations of innocence— A Letter From the Heart in 1989-90 and the "Organizational relationship between the Viet Kieu and the Communist Party of Vietnam (1945-1990)" and early Vietnamese witnesses for Bertrand Russell in 1966-67. Giao lists are comprised mostly of students and intellectuals[185] claiming falsely that Hanoi did not organize or recruit *Viet Kieu* (expatriates) in France and USA. Chung Nguyen,[186] besides Giao, lists as pro-Hanoi *Viet Kieu* "actively involved in the antiwar movement" ...mostly members of "Hoi Viet Kieu Yeu Nuoc Tai Phap" (Association of Vietnamese Patriots in France). [187]

---

[184] Interview of Ho Nam in *Thanh Nien*, official newspaper of Vietnamese Communist Party's Ho Chi Minh Youth Group, 2005; Ho Nam, "The Late Minister Tran Quoc Hoan and His Relationship with an Intelligence Warrior;" 2004; Both cited by Merle L. Pribbenow, "Jane Fonda and Her Friendly Vietnamese Intelligence Officer," *Washington Decoded*, 10 August 2011.

[185] They were Soviet trained mathematician Phan Dinh Dieu, economist Tran Huu Dung, Marxist economist Tran Hai Hac, historian Le Thanh Khoi, Philosophy professor Thai Thi Kim Lan, Alexandre Le, historian Ngo Vinh Long, Vinh Sinh, classical philosopher and translator Bui Van Nam Son, chemist Nguyen Minh Tho, Japan based economic advisor to Vietnam Tran Van Tho, Vietnam-published political scientist Cao Huy Thuan, Dao Van Thuy, Nguyen Tung, and UN economist and advisor to Vietnam Vu Quang Viet.

[186] Chung Nguyen at umb.edu

[187] Chung Nguyen at umb.edu Fri May 4 05:43:56 PDT 2007 economist Tran Hai Huc, mathematician Ha Duong Tuong, writer and literature instructor Dang Tien as well as Council president of Overseas Vietnamese in France Huynh Trung Dong. Top leaders were economist Tran Hai Huc, mathematician Ha Duong Tuong, writer and literature instructor Dang Tien as well as Council President of Overseas Vietnamese in France Huynh Trung Dong. Berkeley sociologist and writer Tran Tuong Nhu Miller names "Vietnamese exiles in Paris" Mathematician and historian Hoang Xuan Han, Hoang Xuan Man, teacher and writer Nguyen Tien Lang, Catholic South Vietnamese politician Nguyen Ton Hoan, professor of music Tran Van Khe, painter Vo Lang, Pham Bich, Pham Ngoan, Pham Hoan, third force nationalist and journalist Ton That Thien, painter Nguyen Cam, and the NLF honored airline high jacker Nguyen Thai

Hanoi Ops in USA.

Hanoi's American operation included Nguyen Thi Ngoc Thoa in Washington, D.C., former sailor and OSS recruit Nguyen Van Luy in San Francisco and later Dinh Ba Thi in New York at the United Nations.[188] Both Luy and Thoa were active in the American antiwar movement, in Berkeley and in Hayden-Fonda's IPC respectively. In April 1968 under a Viet Cong flag at a University of California rally, Nguyen Van Luy, Hanoi intelligence agent, is pictured conferring with students of sponsoring group, the pro-Viet Cong Tri-Continental [Communist] Progressive Students Association.[189] The ACLU provided Luy with legal assistance on an immigration matter. In the USA a very small number few South Vietnamese students openly protested the war. They were the pro-Hanoi hard core.[190]

On May 10, 1968, Hanoi came to the peace table in Paris and sat there for five years until, as John Negroponte says, the U.S. had bombed North Vietnam into accepting American concessions.

Hanoi Journeys: Greenblatt, Sontag, Kopkind—April-May 1968

May 3-17, 1968, Robert Greenblatt joined Susan Sontag and Bratislava veteran Andrew Kopkind[191] in Hanoi. Sontag wrote her impressions in *Esquire*, "Trip to Hanoi and Styles of Radical Will." Sontag recognized "being plied with gifts and flowers and rhetoric and tea and seemingly exaggerated kindness."[192] It was flattery with a purpose. She said, "We are in the hands of skilled bureaucrats (Oanh, Hieu, Phan, Toan) specializing in relations with foreigners."[193] She and the others were "reduced to the status of a child: scheduled, led about, explained to, fussed over, pampered, kept under benign

---

Binh.

[188] Yung Krall, *A Thousand Tears Falling*, Atlanta: Longstreet Press, 1995.

[189] Photo in *Washington Daily Freedom,* April 2, 1968
http://fultonhistory.com/newspaper%2010/Kingston%20NY%20 Daily%20
Freeman/Kingston%20NY%20Daily%20 Free
man%201968%20Grayscale/Kingston%20NY%20Daily%20 Freeman%201968%20
Grayscale%20-%202176.pdf

[190] They included "patriotic Vietnamese" were: Le Anh Tu, Nguyen Huu An, Nguyen Thai Binh, Tran Khanh Tuyet, David Truong, Doan Hong Hai, Tran Vu Dung, Ngo Vinh Long, Vu Ngoc Con, Vu Quang Viet, Do Hoang Khanh, and Nguyen Trieu Phu.

[191] Susan Sontag, "Trip to Hanoi," *Esquire* magazine, December 1968, 131-141 in Susan Sontag, *Styles*, 205-274.

[192] Sontag, *Styles*, 207, 237.

[193] Sontag, *Styles*, 226.

surveillance..." Still "I'm not a child, though the theatre of this visit requires that I play the role of one."[194] She, "a veteran signer of petitions and an anti-war demonstrator,"[195] said, "the trip to Hanoi is a kind of reward or patronage ... a treat being granted for our unsolicited efforts."[196] Herbert Mitgang wrote, Sontag had "spent a couple of weeks in Hanoi in the spring as a reward for what the North Vietnamese regarded as a proper anti-American war attitude."

Meeting Premier Pham Van Dong for an hour late in the afternoon of May 16, 1968, Sontag found him "praising the moral character of his country's people with tears in his eyes..."[197] Among the Vietnamese waging war against her countrymen Susan Sontag found much love. Sontag, remarked, "... Radical Americans have profited from having a clear-cut moral issue [like Vietnam] on which to mobilize discontent and expose the camouflaged contradictions in the system." She said, "Vietnam offered the key to a systematic criticism of America."[198] Though she recognized the theatre, the staging, of most tours and sites she was seduced. Observing the absence of hospital and school supplies, Sontag wondered just what had happened to the "vaunted aid from Russia and China."[199] Though critical of flattery and propaganda, Susan Sontag took the whole Hanoi hook, line and sinker on the Vietnam War, e.g. virtual destruction of "all the schools and hospitals... pagodas, and Catholic churches..." and the building of 21 million bomb shelters.[200]

Unlike most visitors, Sontag recognized that North Vietnam was not "a model of a just state. One only had to recall the most notorious crimes committed by the present government. ... persecution ....execution, ...forcible collectivization of agriculture."[201] Still, Sontag concluded that "Victory for Vietnam' is the only credible slogan...."[202]

---

[194] Sontag, *Trip to Hanoi*, New York: Farrar, Straus and Giroux, 1968, 212 6, 12, 33 cited in Hollander, *Political Pilgrims*, 368, 371, 375-6.
[195] Sontag, *Styles*, 203.
[196] Sontag, *Styles*, 214. Susan Sontag, "Trip to Hanoi," *Esquire*, December 1968.
[197] Sontag, *Styles*, 238, 262.
[198] Sontag, *Styles*, 271.
[199] Sontag, *Styles*, 253.
[200] Sontag, *Styles*, 208.
[201] Sontag, *Styles*, 259.
[202] Sontag, *Styles*, 269-70.

Sontag wrote, "Toward the close of my stay" she advised government officials that Hanoi's "bombastic, shrill" propaganda betrayed their revolution.[203] Their propaganda needed improvement. That was a sentiment many Americans were anxious to communicate to their hosts.

Greenblatt—"Red and Gold Badges"

Robert Greenblatt distributed antiwar buttons to the Vietnamese and the Americans received "red and gold badges,"[204] perhaps Ho Chi Minh medals.

Other Literati Seek
Immediate Ceasefire, Surrender After Victory in Tet

With the NVA defeated and VC decimated in Tet, in August 1968 some 534 writers signed a petition to the White House, Congress and the UN urging an immediate ceasefire and a US bombing halt. In effect coming to the defense of the enemy in war, the literati called for a unilateral surrender after a battlefield victory. "This is an immoral, senseless war, the most un-American in our history.[205]

Naomi Jaffe--SDS

Half way through the Sontag tour, North Vietnam had received four SDS sponsored students as visitors.[206] Hanoi International Service and the *Washington Star* reported on May 15, 1968, that Naomi Jaffe, a women's anti-draft leader, was one of the four unidentified SDS members visiting Hanoi in the second week of May 1968.[207] They met Do Van Hien, visited war crimes museums and talked to students about the American antiwar movement.[208] During June 1968, Naomi Jaffe (Aka. Naomi Esther Safier, Mrs. William Irving Safier, Leona) said she had just returned from Hanoi when speaking at Michigan State University. Jaffe claimed she had "shot down an American fighter plane with an antiaircraft gun…observed the capture of an America pilot. …Jaffe wore a small piece of fuselage on a chain around her neck…from the plane."[209] Shortly before going

---

[203] Sontag, *Styles*, 262.

[204] Sontag, *Styles*, 215.

[205] UPI, "Cease-Fire Urged by Writers Group," August 12, 1968. Some of those who signed were Bishop James A. Pike, Dr. Benjamin Spock, Nat Hentoff, Dwight MacDonald, Mark Van Dorn, Joseph Heller, John Hersey, Muriel Rukeyser, Terry Southern and William L. Shirer.

[206] Susan Sontag, *Styles*, 207.

[207] *Esquire* magazine, December 1968, 131 cited in House, Committee on Internal Security, Investigation of Students Exhibit No. 2, 2319.

[208] Senate, Committee on the Judiciary, *The Weather Underground*, 75.

[209] FBI, FOIA, Acting Senior Agent in Charge (SAC), Chicago, Memo to Director FBI

underground in February 1970 Jaffe would accompany Bill Ayers to Canada and come back with $2,000 after visiting the Quebec Liberation Front.[210]

POW Kasler Refusing to Meet Antiwar Group is Tortured

Sometime in late June 1968, POW Jim Kasler refused to meet an antiwar delegation. An outraged "Fidel" beat Kasler, put him in ropes and gave him 300 lashes. In a semi coma, Kasler did not meet with the delegation and made no usable written statement.[211] One time Kasler saw a photo of antiwar demonstrators. "I saw in the background two elderly gentlemen with smiles and American Legion hats cocked.... They were holding a sign...' Drop the Bomb.' It gave Kasler a new burst of courage.[212] Lt. Col. Earl Cobeil was not so lucky. Fidel sadistically tortured Cobeil to death...slowly. In August 1968, "Fidel" returned to Cuba a failure. POW Mike Benge later identified "Fidel" as Maj. Fernando Vecino Alegret.[213]

"Good Fortune, Victory"

In a letter dated June 4, 1968, Tom Hayden wrote to North Vietnamese Col. Ha Van Lau:

June 4, 1968

Dear Col. Lao [sic];

This note is to introduce to you Mr. Robert Greenblatt, the Coordinator of the National Mobilization to End the War in Vietnam. He works closely with myself and Dave Dellinger, and has just returned from Hanoi.

If there are any pressing questions you wish to discuss, Mr. Greenblatt will be in Paris for a few days.

Subject: Foreign Travel and Contacts with Representatives of Foreign Governments which Influenced the WHO, in Weather Underground Summary, August 20, 1976, 208; Rothrock, *Divided,* 178.

[210] FBI, FOIA, Weather, 190; Larry Grathwohl testimony before Subcommittee to Investigate the Administration of the Internal Security Act and Other Internal Security Laws of the Committee on the Judiciary, U.S. Senate, *Terrorist Activity Inside the Weatherman Movement*, 93rd Cong., 2nd Sess., Part 2, October 18, 1974, 106.

[211] John G. Hubbell, *P.O.W.: A Definitive History of the American Prisoner-of War Experience in Vietnam, 1964-1973*, New York: Readers Digest Press, 1976, 440, 444 cited in Craig Howes, *Voices of the Vietnam POWs*, New York: Oxford University Press, 1993, 103n106.

[212] House, Hearings on *Restraints on Travel to Hostile Areas*: Hearings before the Committee on Internal Security, 93rd Cong., 1st sess., 1973, 32-33 cited in Rothrock *Divided...* 195-6n14.

[213] Mike Benge to R.J. Del Vecchio, October 28, 2008; Humberto Fontova, "The Left Tries to Find John McCain's Bill Ayers," *American Thinker*, October 27, 2008,

We hope that the current Paris discussions go well for you. The news from South Vietnam seems very good indeed.

We hope to see you this summer in Paris or at a later time.

Good Fortune!
Victory!
[signed]
Tom Hayden[214]

The Mysterious Col. Ha Van Lau

Ha Van Lau (correct spelling) was Secretary General of the North Vietnamese Commission to Investigate U.S. War Crimes. True, but Col. Lau was more than a mere propagandist. Col. Lau was a key North Vietnamese functionary in negotiations in 1954, 1962 and 1968. Less than a month before Hayden wrote him, Lau met with Cyrus Vance to work out details of the upcoming Paris negotiations.[215] Hayden had previously met Col. Lau three times in Hanoi (December 1965, January 1966, October 1967), once in Bratislava, and briefly (after his letter) in Paris in July 1968.[216] Hayden's five documented contacts with Lau were as politically intimate as any could be between people living halfway around the world from each other.

Two questions reveal the significance of Hayden's letter to Col. Lau.

1. What did Hayden mean by "Good fortune! Victory!"?

2. Why did Robert Greenblatt, back from Hanoi, need a letter of introduction to Hanoi?

The HCUA record shows:

Mr. Conley: Mr. Hayden ... [Your] ... letter concludes "Victory!" Am I to imply ... you are wishing victory to Colonel Lau and his people?

Mr. Hayden: No. When I say "Victory" I mean that the end of the war in Vietnam and the withdrawal of the American troops would be the greatest victory possible for the people of this country and for the people of Vietnam.[217]

---

[214] Hayden's letter to Col. Ha Van Lau is in House Committee on Un-American Activities, House of Representatives, *Subversives Involvement*.... 2586.

[215] Lyndon Baines Johnson, *Vantage Point*, New York: Popular Library, 1971, 502, 507.

[216] *Human Events*, August 3, 1968.

[217] House Committee on Un-American Activities, House of Representatives, Subversives Involvement in Disruption of 1968 Democratic Party National Convention, 90th Congress, Second Session, Hearings December 2 and 3, 1968.

"A Word...Means What I Choose It to Mean

Years later called a traitor, Hayden objected: "This is a little like 'Alice in Wonderland' ... that words can be used to mean anything you want."[218] Humpty Dumpty said, "When I use a word, it means just what I choose it to mean; neither more nor less." To HCUA, like Humpty Dumpty, Hayden said, "... when I mean victory, I mean... the end of the war in Vietnam and the withdrawal of American troops..." Hayden said, his "Good Fortune, Victory" did not mean a military victory for the North Vietnamese. And no, "the news ... seems very good indeed" did not mean a Viet Cong victory in Tet.

Tom Hayden was North Vietnam's Humpty Dumpty. It was simple for Hayden. "Victory" meant whatever he said it meant.[219]

Introducing Mr. Robert Greenblatt

Clearly, with Hayden's worldwide broadcast "I am Viet Cong," in September in Bratislava before a room filled with Vietnamese Communists, he did not need to send a letter. How could Hayden's introduction have helped Robert Greenblatt?

What were Robert Greenblatt's credentials?

By June of 1968, Robert Greenblatt was already a very well established leader in the American anti-war movement.[220] On November 12, 1967, Greenblatt had become the coordinator of National Mobe (Dellinger was chairman).[221] In 1967-8 he was an active participant in planning meetings for the Democratic Convention.

Washington: U.S. Government Printing Office, 2547-8.

[218] Mike Otten, "Demos Beat Back Move to Expel Former Activist," *Sacramento Union*, June 24, 1986, 1; See also: Hayden Letter to members of his Campaign California, July 28, 1986 in possession of the author.

[219] HCUA, December 1968, *op cit* 2550.

[220] Greenblatt had participated in the founding conference of the November 8 Mobe held in Cleveland September 10-11, 1966. Greenblatt's name appeared on the letterhead of the November 8 Mobe along with 15 others (including Aptheker and Lynd) all known to the North Vietnamese. Greenblatt was one of four vice chairmen of the November Mobe's successor, the Spring Mobe, founded at a November 26-27, 1966 conference in Cleveland. Greenblatt drafted a working paper on the Spring Mobilization and his name appeared on its letterhead and in its promotional literature. By May of 1967, Greenblatt was Vice Chairman of the successor to the Spring Mobe, the National Mobe. In August 1967, Dellinger appointed Greenblatt (also Rubin and Halstead) to the Administration Committee for the October 1967 demonstrations of National Mobe at the Pentagon. The Pentagon actions had received rave reviews in Hanoi. See: Greenblatt, working paper of SMC conference, Catholic Peace Fellowship Records, University of Notre Dame Archives, CCPF 7/10 Folder.

[221] A flyer of the Philadelphia Mobilization Committee, announcing National Mobilization sponsored rally on October 21, 1967 lists Dellinger and Greenblatt. Also James Bevel as national director and co-chairmen Ralph Abernathy, Donald Kalish, Edward Keating, Sidney Lens, Sidney Peck, Dagmar Wilson and others.

In Paris Mr. Greenblatt Gets a New Job?

Greenblatt had many more meetings with the North Vietnamese and Viet Cong after Hayden's letter. Greenblatt and Dellinger met Col. Ha Van Lau on June 16, 1968 and in July in Paris. Tom Hayden, who also met NLF leaders in Paris in July,[222] may have accompanied Greenblatt.[223] The North Vietnamese Ambassador to Paris, Mai Van Bo, regularly met American war dissenters, including candidate Robert Kennedy.[224] Upon Greenblatt's return from Paris, via Canada, Greenblatt's letter of introduction from Tom Hayden was seized.[225] After his Paris meeting with the North Vietnamese, Greenblatt would later travel to Prague and to Budapest to perform international communist services Hanoi would value highly.

POW Release, Hayden, Paris -July 1968
Hayden Chooses Delegation: Meacham, Grizzard, Weills

In the meantime, the North Vietnamese, on July 1, 1968, sent a cablegram to Mobe "requesting that either Hayden or Dellinger fly to Paris immediately."[226] Arriving in Paris on July 3, Hayden "spent ten sleepless days talking to the North Vietnamese and American negotiators." On July 3 or 4, 1968 Rennie Davis told AFSC's Stuart Meacham, an advocate of physically obstructing the "warfare" state,[227] that the North Vietnamese wanted three people to travel to Paris and Hanoi to pick up three prisoners of war, POWs. On July 6, a serial supporter of Communist fronts[228], Stuart Meacham, flew to Paris. There, Hayden and his handpicked trio, Vernon Grizzard, Stewart Meacham and Anne Weills Scheer,[229]met North Vietnamese, Col. Ha Van Lau, Nguyen Minh Vy, and Xuan Oanh, and Ambassador Averill Harriman. They arranged the third POW release of the war from

---

[222] *Human Events*, August 3, 1968.

[223] John Feliz, Louis Barnet, Daniel Orr, *Network of Networks,* Los Angeles: National Foundation to Fight Political Corruption, Inc., 1983, 12.

[224] David Kraslow and Stuart H. Loory, *The Secret Search For Peace in Vietnam*, New York: Random House, 1968, 177; See also: Mai Van Bo, *Diplomacy: Attack and Secret Contacts,* Hanoi: Ho Chi Minh Publishing House, 1985; *The Vietnamese People's Struggle in the International Context*, Hanoi: Foreign Language Publishing House, 1986.

[225] Stephen Denney, *Religion and Communism in Vietnam, 1975-1992*, (manuscript), August 1992, 7-8; HCUA *op cit.*

[226] Jack Newfield, "Saigon Will Fall in the Dry Season," *Village Voice*, July 18, 1968.

[227] Richard Greenleaf, "Quakers' storehouse of brotherly love," *Daily World,* July 18, 1969.

[228] ECLC, *New York Times* October 10, 1960; CCL, *National Guardian*, March 7, 1964; and VALB, letterhead and invitation, January 31, 1967.

[229] *Guardian*, July 13, 1968, 6.

North Vietnam. Weills later observed, "If we had loyalties, they definitely were for the Vietnamese." About an hour and a half with Premier Pham Van Dong, Weills later said, "He talked a lot...about the peace talks...what their strategy was, tactically...We were sort of ...their fifth column...clearly helping them...We could be considered, I guess, traitors or whatever....[W]e were not brain washed and we were not agents. But the way we thought...we, in some ways, probably were."[230]

Hanoi Picks POWs to Release

Maj. Joe Victor Carpenter, Maj. James Frederick Low, and Maj. Fred Neale Thompson[231] freshly captured--4 months to 7 months—were relatively healthy. At the Plantation show camp the communist Vietnamese groomed the POWs for possible release, prevented them from communicating with other POWS, and thoroughly indoctrinated them. They made the obligatory taped messages over camp radio. Maj. Low had disobeyed orders not to accept release.[232] Major Thompson said, "We were safe bets to release. People would see us and say, 'Maybe they do take good care of their prisoners." Still in captivity in Hanoi, Stuart Meacham told the press that all three men "agreed...the basic conditions of their life in the detention camps... were adequate." Meacham later told Congress, "Where threatening or harsh treatment has occurred ...it has typically come not at the hands of military or prison authorities but...at the hands of angry villagers."[233]

Under AFSC letterhead, Vernon Grizzard, Anne Weills Scheer, and Stewart Meacham wrote to American families of other POWs that the release was "a humanitarian gesture ...to the growing sentiment...for an end to military intervention in Vietnam." The prisoners had excellent health care, "food is well balanced" and the Vietnamese were "humane and considerate." The AFSC coauthors wrote, "...US military intervention...has neither rational purpose nor moral justification. We do not believe that the Vietnamese can be defeated."[234]

POW Release Delayed: Hanoi or U.S.?

---

[230] Clinton interview of Anne Weills, November 14, 1990 in Clinton, *Opposition:* 122-123, 125.
[231] American Prisoners, Hearings 1971.
[232] Stuart I. Rochester and Frederick Kiley, 369-70.
[233] American Prisoners, Hearings 1971.
[234] Vernon Grizzard, Anne Weills Scheer, and Stewart Meacham, Dear Friend [POW families], AFSC, August 6, 1968.

From July 17-August 1, the released POWs stayed in a Hanoi hotel and were paraded out for two weeks of ceremonies, tapings, press conferences[235] The POWs had closely controlled meetings with the "peace group."[236] Tom Hayden was "insult[ed]" when Ambassador Harriman said the POWs had a right to return by American military aircraft once they arrived in Vientiane, Laos.[237] A compromise was struck, a commercial flight with joint escort, both antiwar and U.S. military.

Released POWs Deny Treatment was "humane and considerate"

Freed the POWs described what "humane and considerate" meant to the communists. Carpenter was held in a bamboo cage, feet in stocks and his hands in rusty handcuffs, until he graduated to sleeping on concrete. For ten days, he was moved from village to village for public ridicule, humiliation and degradation...and physical abuse. People hit him with rocks, sticks and clods. He survived a mile-long gauntlet of people hitting and kicking him. Meacham had said the Vietnamese fed the POWs a "thick kind of soup or stew" which "was probably prepared with its nutrient properties rather carefully considered." Major Thompson said, "You could hold the bowl up to the light, and if you saw grease on top you knew that meat had been in it at some time. The only meat I ever saw was pork fat and very little of that."

Back from Paris only two weeks, on July 25 at 8:00 p.m., before the Fifth Avenue Parade Committee, Hayden gave his insiders report.[238]

Linda Morse remembered Hayden reporting:

> the Vietnamese were feeling...(July 1968) ...that ... they had won the war militarily and politically and ... that there was nothing to negotiate ... (Hayden) said that the United States had only two alternatives ... withdrawing

---

[235] Stuart I. Rochester and Frederick Kiley, 370.

[236] FBI, Interview of Fred Neale Thompson on October 12, 1970 at Randolph Air Force Base, Texas, FD-302, October 16, 1970.

[237] James W. Clinton telephone interview of Harold Supriano, November 14, 1990 in James W. Clinton, *The Loyal Opposition: Americans in North Vietnam, 1965-1972*, Niwot: University Press of Colorado, 1995; *The Conspiracy Trial: The Extended Edited Transcript of the Trial of the Chicago 8* Bobbs-Merrill, 1970, 378; "Capital Briefs," *Human Events*, 1968; Hayden, "The Impasse in Paris," *Ramparts*, August 24, 1968, 18.

[238] The Vietnamese agreed to negotiate - the shape of conference table.

or genocide. ... the U.S. was seriously considering nuclear weapons ... therefore … protest ...by any means possible.[239]

The Greenblatt Reports

Meanwhile, Robert Greenblatt, now anointed by Tom Hayden, Dave Dellinger and Col. Ha Van Lau, joined Dellinger in a conference in Prague on June 16, 1968. Greenblatt met two Viet Cong officials and five Czechs.[240] He agreed to supply reports on "work of the anti-draft movement…since the Tet Offensive and…anti-war agitation…among members of the armed forces." Greenblatt also agreed to make tape recordings for use against U.S. troops.[241]

Lawyers for Vietnam—Grenoble July 1968

During an International Conference of Lawyers for Vietnam[242] sponsored by an international Communist front, the International Association of Democratic Lawyer, the Vietnamese and Americans wrote the conference's final resolution.[243]

Vietnamese Hug and Kiss American Youth Delegates, Sofia, Bulgaria — July 28-August 6, 1968

July 28-August 6, 1968 the Ninth World Youth Festival was held in Sofia, Bulgaria to express "solidarity with the Vietnamese people in their struggle against the American imperialist aggressors." The festival boasted 17,898 delegates from 143 nations.[244] Some fifty[245] to seventy-one[246] American attendees—11 SDSers, e.g. Howard Jeffrey Melish, Leslie Cagan[247] met Vietnamese Communists, and Soviet representatives and visited the Chinese Embassy.[248]

---

[239] Clavir, (ed.) *Transcripts...*

[240] Frank J. Rafalko, MH/CHAOS, 155.

[241] Denney, 7-8; See also: John Ashbrook, "Washington Report" undated (October 1979?); Ashbrook, "The Hayden-Fonda Road Show," *Congressional Record,* September 28, 1979, H8784.

[242] Five Americans represented the Lawyers Committee on American Policy toward Vietnam, LCAPC. Prominent members of LCAPC were William Standard, Carey McWilliams, Richard Falk, Hans Morganthal, and Quincy Wright.

[243] Tom Charles Huston, Special Report, 44.

[244] Frankfurter Rundschau, 3 August 1968 cited in "The Ninth World Youth Festival: A Review," Radio Free Europe Research, East Europe, Bulgaria/15, 23 August 1968 at http://files.osa.ceu.hu/holdings/300/8/3/text/7-1-101.shtml

[245] Barbara Bright letter to Richard H. Nolte, Institute of Current World Affairs, 9 September 1968 at ICWA Website http://www.icwa .org/articles/BWB-2.pdf?

[246] Frank J. Rafalko, MH/CHAOS:, 151.

[247] *Leslie Cagan,* "Being Left: It Should Be Possible, It Has To Be Possible," http://www.zmag.org/cagan.htm

[248] FBI, FOIA, *Weather,* 332.

Soviets Finance and Select American Delegates to Sofia Conference

One invitee, Gerald Wayne Kirk, only had to pay $20.[249] The Soviet controlled sponsors, the World Federation of Democratic Youth, WFDY, the International Union of Students, IUS, and the Club members[250] carefully picked delegates. The CPUSA, SDS and Mobe: "the organizers appear to have relied on local Communist youth organizations for the selection of delegates," according to Radio Free Europe.[251] After the Sofia conference, the Soviets sponsored a delegation of eight for a tour of the USSR.[252]

As many as 40,000 Bulgarians were herded out to "the support of the entire festival for the fighting [people of] Vietnam." An official Declaration on Vietnam was adopted with no discussion..[253] SDSers led shouts, "Ho, Ho, Ho Chi Minh."[254]

Soviets Film Festival

The Soviets made a film showing peace demonstrators hugging, kissing and exchanging gifts with Vietnamese delegates, protests of the American Embassy, and a U.S. flagged bus pulling up. An "Anti-Vietnam War American delegation" exited the bus shaking the hands of Vietnamese. The Americans "enter meeting w/ big sign—'Vietnam will win." An American woman sits with her arm around a Vietnamese woman. Vietnamese present flowers.[255] Barbara Bright, a *Newsweek*

---

[249]Testimony of Gerald Wayne Kirk, Hearings Before the Subcommittee to Investigate the Administration of Justice and other Security Laws of the Committee on the Judiciary, March 1970 cited in Frank J. Rafalko, *MH/CHAOS:* , 151.

[250] Tom Charles Huston, Special Report, 44.

[251] "The Ninth World…" 11-16 July 1968

[252] Tom Charles Huston, Special, 44.

[253] *Narodna Mladezh*, 30 July 1968 cited in "The Ninth World…", 23 August 1968, 1-2.

[254] Bright to Nolte,

[255] Description in text is from Footage Farm, "Civil Rights and Anti-Vietnam War Protests," x 22112 21:09:55-21:18:54 1968 Bulgaria; Vietnam; COL SD Time to Live R2 of 6 at footagefarm.co.uk; quote "Film is "A Time To Live (Bulgaria Youth Festival)(Vietnam War). This colorful documentary of the Ninth Annual Communist Youth Festival, held in Sofia, Bulgaria in 1968, is an anti-American film. Attacking the Vietnam War and stressing solidarity, world peace and, of all things, freedom, this film is an excellent example of how the Soviets manipulate the minds of youth. Opening with a rousing parade, with groups from Europe, China, Japan, Vietnam, Africa and South America, the film features spirited songs, ethnic dances, native costumes, and a New Orleans-style carnival, including a jazz band. A popular song of the time, "Hands Off Vietnam," is sung by the famous singer Gilda Maziukaite. Also present are sad-faced deserters from the US armed forces, who mumble statements on how awful America is. Beautifully filmed in color by real technicians, the film reflects intense

freelancer reported the Vietnamese wore battle fatigues and figure flattering *ao dai*. The fifty or so Americans "looked the scruffiest."[256]

Leslie Cagan Loves It All

Antiwar activist and Venceremos Brigade traveler to Cuba Leslie Cagan's memories were indistinguishable from the Soviet film.

Most important for me was our interaction with the Vietnamese delegation. ... It was a matter of moments before everyone was crying. ... We spontaneously gave one another rings, pins, handkerchiefs...a connection came to life. The emotion in the room escalated when one of the men in the U.S. group took out his draft card and burned it. ...most of us...donate[d] blood for the Vietnamese to take home.[257]

Czechs Force Way on Agenda

"While the Vietnam question was officially brought up at every possible opportunity, interest in Czechoslovakia gained momentum spontaneously." A Soviet insisted, "Only enemies of socialism and...revisionists ...would turn the correction of past mistakes into a campaign against socialist democracy...."[258] Bulgarian police units easily dispersed SDS protests, beat up Czechs and western journalists, including NBC staff.[259]

---

excitement, often on the edge of hysteria. USSR, 1968, Color, 55 minutes, English narration." End quote http://www.ihffilm.com/278.html

[256] Bright to. Nolte,

[257] Cagan stayed active in the U.S. Peace Council, an affiliate of the Soviet controlled World Peace Conference and was engaged in the soviet influenced "nuclear freeze" movement. In April 2000, Leslie Cagan organized and collected checks for the Vietnam Peace 25th Anniversary Committee. Since 2002 his has led protests against U.S. involvement in Iraq. In 2011, Cagan recruited 30 Americans for a flotilla aiming to forcefully break Israel's arms embargo of Gaza. Cagan *Z Magazine*, June 1998. http://zena.secureforum.com/ Znet/ZMag/articles/caganjune98.htm; Also Rep. John Conyers, Jack O'Dell, Bernie Sanders. "End the Cold War, Fund Human Needs," U.S. Peace Council's Tenth Anniversary, November 10-12, 1989, *Guardian*, November 8, 1989; Leslie Cagan email requesting funds from Walter Teague on 11 May 2000 15:33:09-0400

[258] The Bulgarians refused to admit 50 Czechs into the country,[258] confiscated Czech material,[258] and uniformed Bulgarians "accompanied" Czech ...journalists in the streets, restaurants, and hotels of Sofia."[258] In an opening ceremony Czechs, shouted "Dubcek, Dubcek, Svoboda ....Our Democracy is our own Business"...[258]" The crowd was silence with scattered timid clapping. *Komsomolskaya Pravda*, 1 August 1968 cited in "The Ninth World..." 23 August 1968; Czechoslovak Television, 27 July 1968, cited in "The Ninth World..." 23 August 1968 l; Radio Bratislava, 28 July 1968, cited in "The Ninth World..."23 August 1968; Radio Bratislava, 28 July 1968, cited in "The Ninth World..." 23 August 1968; *Zemedelske Noviny*, 30 July 1968 cited in "The Ninth World..." 23 August 1968, Bright letter to Nolte.

[259] Bright to Nolte,

Brutality the westerners had never experienced. It was a hint of Soviet tanks coming to Czechoslovakia only weeks later. In 2008 Hanoi still memorialized the Sofia choreographed show of solidarity[260] *sans* Czechs.

Meanwhile, fearing the impact of violence at the upcoming Democratic Convention upon negotiations in Paris, the State Department belatedly warned the Vietnamese to stay out of American politics.[261] This according to columnist Drew Pearson whose legman David Karr was a soviet asset.[262]

USSR Invades Czeckoslovakia

Finally, Soviet Warsaw Pact forces, advised by the "liberal Westernized" KGB chief, Yuri Andropov, invaded Czechoslovakia. Sen. George McGovern blamed the U.S. for its negative attitudes. There were no campus protests or rallies against Soviet oppression of Czech freedom.[263]

Kyoto Conference

In Kyoto, Japan August 11-14, 1968, *Beheiren,* sponsored a conference of 250 anti-war activists including 23 Americans. *Beheiren* claimed solidarity with the North Vietnamese Communist Party.[264] The Americans attending represented SNCC, SDS, WSP, Socialist Workers Party, AFSC, and AQUG. Ken Cloke said, "In the U.S. workers are aiding North Vietnam. I...joined SDS to engage in this activity."[265] The conference

---

[260] Caption and photo of friendly French press coverage is displayed at Hanoi Hilton Museum in Hanoi, author's photo number Viet I DSC 190.

[261] Drew Pearson, *Chicago Daily News* in *Congressional Record* H8260, (September 4, 1968), and St. John, 29.

[262] M. Stanton Evans and Herbert Romerstein, *Stalin's Secret Agents; The Subversion of Roosevelt's Government*, New York: Simon and Schuster, 2012, 139.

[263] A handful of members of the conservative Young Americans for Freedom, YAF, such as Dana Rohrabacher, David Keene, Paul A. Mapes, Lawrence Reed, Donald Harte and James Farley visited Czechoslovakia, formed Student Committee for Freedom in Czechoslovakia, burned Soviet flags and held protests in Detroit, Atlanta, Honolulu, and Pittsburgh Wayne Thorburn, *A Generation Awakes: Young Americans for Freedom and the Creation of the Conservative Movement*, Ottawa (Illinois): Jameson Books, Inc., 2010, 202-205 cites Dana Rohrabacher, "Young Czechoslovakians for Freedom," *New Guard*, October 1968, 9-10; Paul A. Mapes, "Youth Under Soviet Communism," *New Guard*, October 1968, 12-15; David A. Keene, "What Happened to the Bridges We Built," *New Guard*, October1968, 6-7;2008 YAF Alumni Survey Responses of Lawrence W. Reed and Donald E. Harte; John Hebers, "McGovern Charges US Is Partly to Blame for Crisis in Czechoslovakia, *New York Times*, August 24, 1968.

[264] Fumiko Holloran, NBR Book Review of Taketomo Takahishi, *We Helped American Deserters Cross National Borders*, ("Watashi-tachi wa Dasso America-hei wo Ekko Saseta"), NBR'S Japan Forum (POL), April 15, 2008.

[265] FBI, FOIA, *Weather Underground*, 261.

focused on helping deserters and draft dodgers as well as coordinating peace movements worldwide.[266].

"Anti-Imperialists and Anti-Capitalist Struggle"
Ljubljana, Yugoslavia, August 25-28, 1968.

August 25-28, 1968 the German SDS[267] and the International Confederation for Disarmament and Peace called a conference on the "Anti-Imperialists and Anti-Capitalist Struggle."[268] SDS's Bernadine Dohrn and other Americans were invited.[269] Representatives of the NLF and Hanoi attended. Dr. No Vasiljev, a member of the Czechoslovak peace committee who had met over 30 peace activists at Bratislava in September 1967 spoke to the Yugoslav conference. According to Daniel Dean Swinney eleven Americans burned their draft cards at a reception at the NLF embassy.[270] Bernardine Dohrn felt she now had Vietnamese friends since they had given her a ring of comradeship doubtless made from the debris of a shot down American aircraft.[271]

Bernadine Dohrn spent August and September 1968 in Europe in Yugoslavia, Hungary, Germany and Sweden.[272]

Budapest Planning: Actions against the U.S. Military—
September 5-9, 1968

On September 3, 1968, twenty-eight Americans organized by David Dellinger[273] flew off to Budapest, Hungary. September 5-9, 1968, they met North Vietnamese and five NLF. The plan was to coordinate strategy on US campuses, an apparent repeat of the Bratislava meeting of September 1967. Elinor Langer thought:

> It was like being caught up in some splendid fairy tale of revolution peopled with live heroes and

---

[266] Tom Charles Huston, Special Report, 44.

[267] German SDS members were Frank Wolff, Hans-Werner Koblitz, Holger Klotzbach, Michaela Wundzte and Klaas Behnken.

[268] Martin Klimke, *The Other Alliance: Student Protest in West Germany & the United States in the Global Sixties*, Princeton: Princeton University Press, 2010, 100-1.

[269] Americans were Judi Bernsten, Larry Bloom, Jeff Blum, Ruth Chamberlain, Bernardine Dohrn, Bryan Flack, Ruth Glick, Martin Kinner, Ellen and Fred Lessinger, Miles Mogulescu, Paul Schollmen, Mollje Struerer, and Daniel Swinney; ICDP-SDS Student Conference/List of Participants, Ljubljana, American SDS Records, 3, 19, Box 55, SHSW, cited in Klimke, *The Other*....

[270] Sale, *SDS*, 316; Swinney talk at University of Wisconsin, Madison, October 29, 1968; cited in FBI, FOIA, *Weather*, 93.

[271] Martin Klimke, *The Other*, 104.

[272] Senate, Committee on the Judiciary, *The Weather Underground*, 56.

[273] "U.S. War Foes Met with Hanoi Group," *Washington Post*, September 21, 1968, A-3.

heroines…Each of them was wonderful: physically beautiful, warm sensitive, smart.[274]

David Dellinger, National Mobe, and eight other veterans of the Chicago riots were joined by Vernon Grizzard returning from his pick-up of three POWs and by Robert Greenblatt back from talks with Col. Han Van Lau in Paris in June and July. Bernardine Dohrn was back from Yugoslavia, Hungary, Germany and Sweden.

The Vietnamese wanted information on antiwar activities including further student and draft unrest.[275] Grizzard said the Vietnamese "talked about methods of organizing and mobilizing students in universities" as well as among GIs.[276] Robert Greenblatt, National Mobe, gave a report to the North Vietnamese and the Viet Cong about anti-draft, GI organizing and GI broadcasts in North Vietnam. Dohrn meet with two Viet Cong, undercover intelligence officers, who specialized in getting information from GIs in Saigon,[277] military intelligence.

After Budapest Bernardine Dohrn, and many from Budapest contacted the German SDS in Frankfurt and traveled to Sweden. Another contingent of the Budapest group, including John Davis, brother of Rennie Davis, spent thirteen days in Paris from September 10- September 23[278] talking with NLF, Viet Cong.[279] They discussed an international conference of peace organizations, the upcoming Stockholm Conference in 1969.

After Budapest at the behest of National Mobe, John Davis also visited Prague and deserters in Stockholm and SDS, Danny "The Red" Cohn-Bendit, in Germany.[280]

---

[274] This party included Gerald Borenstein, Thompson Bradley, Perry Cannon, Bruce Dancis, John Willard Davis, Ray Dellinger, Frank Dimon, Mrs. Sharie Fate Dickey, Frank Debunks, Howard Emmer, Paul Golden, Vernon Grizzard, Harold Hector, Daniel Jaffe, David Komatsu, David Landau, Elinor Langer, Vicki Ann Mittlefendt, William Spires, Finley Schaef. See Elinor Langer, "Notes for Next Time," *Working Papers*, Fall 1973, 65, cited in Todd Gitlen, *Sixties*, 262; *Washington Post*, September 21, 1968 cited in Frank J. Rafalko, *MH/CHAOS*, 152; Tom Charles Huston, Special Report, 45; FBI, FOIA, Weather, 269.
[275] John G. Schmitz, et al *The Viet Cong Front in the United States*, Congressional Record, April 21, 1971, Belmont: Western Islands, 1971, 58; *Washington Post*, September 21, 1968 cited in Frank J. Rafalko, *MH/CHAOS*, 152.
[276] *Washington Post*, September 21, 1968, A-3.
[277] Frank J. Rafalko, MH/CHAOS, 152; *Washington Post*, September 21, 1968 and *USA*, September 27-October 11, 1968 cited in Senate, Committee on the Judiciary, *The Weather Underground*, 56-57.
[278] FBI, FOIA, *Weather*, 269.
[279] *The Marcolian*, May 16, 1969.
[280] *The Marcolian*, May 16, 1969. Until an attempted assassination, Rudi Dutschke was the charismatic leader of the German SDS who had shouted, "Ho, Ho, Ho Chi Minh" at

On September 10, 1968, the FBI Legate in Paris forwarded a Department of the Army memo, "Assistance Provided U.S. Servicemen by Anti-Vietnam War Elements in Europe," listing, in part, the American Deserter Committee in Sweden, and the Second Front and French Union for American Resistors and Deserters (FUARD) in France.[281]

National Mobe: September 14, 1968
Organizing GIs and Heightened Militancy

Donald Kalish endorsed the GI Week and urged pressure on draft boards and Dow Chemical. And less than a week after the Budapest confab with Vietnamese Communists discussing activities among GIs, the National Mobilization decided to localize GI's against the war during a national GI Week of leafleting USO Centers, and visiting military bases.

German SDS Works on U.S. GIs. Frankfurt, September 12-16, 1968

Bernardine Dohrn and Bill Ayers attended the German SDS national conference in Frankfurt, West Germany. After the massive 'revolutionary" May 1968 protests in France BBC had interviewed radical European students,[282] who sang the "Communist Internationale." Dohrn and comrades were developing coordinating networks of international solidarity on Vietnam, anti-imperialism and anti-capitalism.[283] The German New Left sought to "organize American soldiers and establish a Europe-wide 'underground railroad' to help them desert from their German bases to France and Scandinavia."[284]

American Violence Worse than Communist Violence

At UCLA, Hayden claimed violence was American history. Any criticism of New Left violence was a fiasco.

Our (antiwar) violence is not yet equivalent to ... a B52 raid on South Vietnam.... Mark Hopkins [builder of railroads] could have taught Joseph Stalin a thing or two about forced industrialization.

---

the Free University in Berlin. Like Dohrn's SDS, the German variety was descending into the terrorist Red Army Faction, RAF, and the Baader-Meinhofe gang. Jeffrey Herf, "Unpleasant Truths," *New Republic*, 2008.

[281] FBI, memo, Legat, Paris to Director, FBI September 10, 1968 at FBI, FOIA, A, American Deserters Committee.

[282] Daniel Cohn-Bendit, Alan Geismar, Tariq Ali, Karl-Dietrich Wolff, Jan Kavan and Dragana Starijel,

[283] Martin Klimke, *The Other*, 3-5, 8.

[284] Mari Hohn, workshop, Vassar College, April 12, 2008 cited in Frank J. Rafalko, *MH/CHAOS:*, 143.

Leftist violence, including Stalinist massacre and starvation of millions, was a lesser evil than the violence of America's military-industrial complex.[285] Indeed, in Hanoi on September 18, 1968 Politburo member Truong Chinh on Radio Hanoi threatens violence to its own dissenters:

> It is absolutely necessary for people's democratic dictatorship to use violence against counterrevolutionaries and exploiters who refuse to submit to reforms. …We must pay continuous attention to consolidating the repressive apparatus of the people's (state, army, police, control institute, tribunal) and so forth.[286]

Montreal Conference for Solidarity on Vietnam
November 28-December 1, 1968.

In Budapest during February 1968, some 67 Western Hemispheric Communists parties met to declare its sympathy and support for the valiant stand of North Vietnam against "American aggression."[287] The parties planned a later conference on Vietnam to be organized by the Communist Party-USA and the Canadian Communist Party and largely paid for by the Communist Party of the Soviet Union.[288]

The follow up Soviet sponsored[289] conference in Montreal provided free lodging and food. Irving Sarnoff's Peace Action Council provided subsidized round trip tickets to Montreal for $150.[290]

In Montreal, Canada in the basement of the St. James United Church from November 28-December 1, 1968 the Conference for Solidarity on Vietnam, also the Hemispheric Conference to End the U.S. War in Vietnam War, was held. The communist parties there invited U.S. antiwar activists and seven Vietnamese Communists headed by Hoang Minh Giam,

---

[285] Tom Hayden, "The Battle for Survival" (adapted from a speech at UCLA in May 1969), in Peter and Deborah Babcock and Bob Abel (Eds.), *The Conspiracy*, N.Y. 1969, 171-172.

[286] P.J. Honey, "Vietnam:, 23-4 cites Radio Hanoi broadcast.

[287] J. Edgar Hoover cited at Senate, *Extent of Subversion in Campus Disorders*: Hearing before the Subcommittee to Investigate Security Act and Other Internal Security Laws, Committee on Judiciary, 91st Cong., 1st sess., 1969, 148.

[288] Tom Charles Huston, Special Report, 46; Frank J. Rafalko, *MH/CHAOS:* 142.

[289] Frank J. Rafalko, MH/CHAOS:, 99.

[290] "Dear Peace Worker" letter from Los Angeles Organizing Committee, Hemispheric Conference to End the U.S. War in Vietnam, Peace Action Council, October 15, 1968 Exhibit III, in Senate, State of California, *Fifteenth Report of the Senate Fact-Finding Subcommittee on Un-American Activities*, Sacramento, CA, 1970, 41.

Minister of Culture.[291] Some of the key American sponsors were Douglas Dowd [292] and Howard Zinn.[293]

Many identified Communist Party members attended the Montreal conference.[294]

Though Moscow friendlies largely ran the show others also participated, Trotskyites, Maoist, Black Panthers. Some 1,700 attended; among the over 500 Americans were 90 from Los Angeles alone; 25 Black Panthers[295] and other Americans came from Havana. Among members of the American antiwar left who met seven representatives of the North Vietnamese and NLF were twelve members of the National Mobe and its successor, the New Mobe, 1969.[296]

---

[291] Tom Charles Huston, Special Report, 45.

[292] "The Seattle Liberation Front," *Information Digest*, May 2, 1970, 4 speccoll.library.kent.edu/4may70/box107/107f9p8.html.

[293] FBI, FOIA, Howard Zinn

[294] Linda Appelhaus, Canadian Prof. Raymond Boyer, Carl and Anne Braden, Ben Dobbs, Robert Duggan, Mike Eisencher, Jim Fite, Carlton Goodlett, James Jackson, Arnold Johnson, Sam Kushner, Mike Myerson, Harvey O'Connor, Irving Sarnoff, Eugene Tournour, Jarvis Tyner, Frank Wilkinson, and Prof. Leon Wolfsy; see: Tom Charles Huston, Special Report, 46.; FBI, *Information Digest Special Report on VVAW*, Aug. 25, 1972 cited in Fedora post to FreeRepublic.comhttp://http://www.winter-soldier.com/staticpages/index.php?page=InfoDigestonVVAW ; Also: Rothrock p 110N55 cites House, Subversive...New Mobilization..., 1970 VII-VIII.

[295] Tom Charles Huston, Special Report, 46.

[296] FBI *Information Digest* cited in Fedora post to FreeRepublic.comhttp://http://www.wintersoldier.com/staticpages/index.php?page=Info DigestonVVAW; Also: Rothrock p 110N55 cites House, *Subversive...New Mobilization...*, 1970 VII-VIII; New Mobe leadership participating were: Norma Becker of Fifth Avenue Peace Parade Committee, War Resisters League and later CPUSA spin-off Committee of Correspondence for Democracy and Socialism; Richard Fernandez, Robert Greenblatt; Prof. Donald Kalish from "left of the Communist Party"; Lincoln Lynch, Stewart Meacham, Sidney Peck and John Wilson. See: Hemispheric Conference to End the War in Vietnam, Montreal 1968, Records of the Fellowship of Reconciliation, USA, (FOR-USA), DG 013, Section 2, Series G, Swarthmore College Library: Fair Play for Cuba, at ronridenoue.com; later Chair of Harry Bridges Memorial Committee in San Francisco; . http://depts.washington.edu/pcls/chronology-jacoby.html.; Dorothy Healy and Maurice Isserman, *California Red*, 147; Correspondence of Communist Mary Inman, Inman Papers, Harvard Library; person of interest to J.B. Matthews of the Senate Internal Security Committee, Matthews Collection, Duke University Library; FBI, FOIA, *Weather*, 276; California, Senate, *Fifteenth Report*, 32-33.; *Washington Post*, November 29, 1968, A-26; Max Friedman to Canfield, June 5, 2008; Also Alfred Hassler of the Fellowship for Reconciliation, representative(s) of Women's International League for Peace and Freedom, Bobby Seale of Black Panthers, Front du Liberation de Quebec, QLF, Robert Eugene Duggan, SDS; Rev. Stephen Fritchman of Los Angeles Unitarian Church and an "unfriendly" witness before HCUA, Fr. James Groppi, Benjamin Spock, Mario Savio of Free Speech Movement and Maryknoll and Marxist "liberation theology" Priest and guerrilla supporter Blase Bonpane.

Some delegates wanted to denounce Soviet imperialism in its invasion of Czechoslovakia in August 1968, but were shouted down. In the closing ceremony in Montreal, Hoang Minh Giam, North Vietnamese Minister of Culture, joined by Mexican Communist Galdino Guzman Cadena burned 25 American draft cards. "The audience went wild when ... (the) cards were burned in a tinfoil dish," reported police undercover agent David E. Gumaer in *American Opinion* in February 1969. The crowd waved red flags and Viet Cong banners and sang the Communist International. New York's AFSC and the War Resisters League gave the Viet Cong a $2,000 check.[297]

Canadian Hospitality

Montreal, Quebec, Canada was always a friendly venue. The Canadian Voice of Women for Peace traveled to Vietnam, provided aid to North Vietnam, disseminated the atrocity stories of GI deserters in Canada, [298] and brought Vietnamese women to hold mass rallies and to meet American women, WSP and SDS/Venceremos, at border points.[299]

Greetings and Salutations Ending 1968

In early December 1968, Tom Hayden testified before the HCUA about his letter to Colonel Lau on behalf of Robert Greenblatt. Hayden told the Committee that in using the word "victory," he merely meant U.S. withdrawal, and a bombing halt, but not a Communist victory against America, even though he supported the "revolutionaries" (the Viet Cong) in Vietnam.

In a sympathetic article about Tom Hayden published in the December 1968 issue of *Esquire,* Steven V. Roberts, talented reporter (the lesser half of Senator Hale Bogg's daughter, Cokie Boggs Roberts) wrote,

Few Americans have spent more time in North Vietnam in recent years, and are more trusted by its leaders than Tom Hayden.

He has a large say in which Americans get visas to travel there; he serves as an informal conduit for messages to and from prisoners; during July (1968) he helped arrange another prisoner

---

[297] "Hanoi Official Burns 25 U.S. Draft Cards," *Chicago Tribune*, Dec. 2, 1968, 8; Senate, State of California, *Fifteenth Report*, 33-35.
[298] Kay Macpherson, Viewpoint, Canadian Broadcasting Corporation, National Television Network, January 11, 1971.
[299] http://home.ca.inter.net/~vow/history.htm also http://aabc.bc.ca/WWW.aabc.archbc/display.UBCSP-969

release and spent several weeks talking to North Vietnamese negotiators in Paris.[300]

One journalist told Roberts said, "When Hanoi is ready to discuss peace, it will say to us, 'we will only talk to Hayden.'"

On December 20, 1968, "Twenty-seven members of WSP, (e.g. Cora Weiss, Barbara Bick (CPUSA) and a dog named Prince walked two miles to the White House to present President Johnson a wreath and telegrams urging an end to the war."[301]

POW Christmas: Well-staged and Sabotaged

The POWs' Christmas at the Movie House at the Plantation in Hanoi was a well-staged propaganda operation subtly sabotaged. Sitting at tables laden with good food the POWs had not been served in their cells, the POWs took the opportunity to openly exchange information separate prison camps and solitary confinement had made difficult. With Japanese cameras recording, Stratton and Stafford dipped their middle fingers in paste while decorating the room with posters.[302]

Ho Christmas Message

On December 31, 1968, Ho Chi Minh sent a New Year's message to his "American friends." Ho thanked them for opposing the war and called Johnson's October Surprise, an election eve bombing halt a "Great Victory."[303]

***

[300] Steven V. Roberts, *Esquire*, Dec. 1968.
[301] Zaroulis, *Who Spoke Up*, 207.
[302] Stuart I. Rochester and Frederick Kiley, 371.
[303] Zaroulis, *Who Spoke Up*, 208.

Part II. 1969 Summary

During 1969 antiwar protesters, played a larger role in the pursuit of peace than diplomats diplomats and their peace prize chasing surrogates,. Radical leaders of the peace movement favored, not peace but outright communist victory. Others seeking to distinguish themselves from extremists merely advocated a unilateral US withdrawal. In short, the self-defined pacifists were efectively working toward US surrender and communist victory by other means and names. Hanoi saw protesters, one and all, as friends. With the Viet Cong militarily decimated in South Vietnam during 1968 and Tet still a political/psychological defeat for the USA, Hanoi refocused on political struggle, *dau tran*, allied with antiwar movements, in America. Through individual and conference meetings with Americans, Hanoi actively "proselytized," communicated, its strategies, tactics and guidance to its friends in the USA.

As a candid revelation, SDS noted "...the (NLF) is now opening a major political offensive to isolate the US imperialists...from the masses of people in South Vietnam...Because war is political, political tasks—the international communist revolution—must guide it," said the SDS Weatherman Statement of June 1969 and its November 9 Movement.[304] In 1969, the antiwar movement cooperatively ramped up the scale and militancy of its operations in the USA with the active and increasingly open assistance and guidance from Fidel Castro's Cuba, Hanoi, Moscow and the East Bloc in unifying and coordinating antiwar events and propaganda themes. The National Mobe intentionally provoked police and rioting at the 1968 Democratic convention[305] and at the Pentagon. The now infamous National Mobe and its indicted leaders forced the major antiwar groups to transform themselves into new organizations and coalitions with new names and brands. With the leaders of National Mobe indicted in March for inciting riots, the National Action Group, New Mobe and the Moratorium formed. At large conferences in Stockholm and East Berlin, the North Vietnamese/Viet Cong, and the Soviet Bloc, advised Americans, New Mobe,

---

[304] The Weatherman Statement paper was signed by Karen Ashley, Bill Ayers, Bernardine Dohrn, John "J.J." Jacobs, Jeff Jones, Gerry Long, "Howie" Machtinger, Jim Mellen, Terry Robbins, Mark Rudd and Steve Tappis; November 8th Movement Planned by SDS cited at speccoll.library.kent.edu/4may70/box107/107f9p8.html.
[305] Hayden and Davis Memo.

Moratorium and allied coalition members to unite and coordinate common strategies, demonstration schedules and propaganda themes with Vietnamese communists. New Mobe (and other organizations[306] and members[307]) openly favored a Viet Cong victory and others, like Moratorium, favored immediate or rapid unilateral U.S. withdrawal.[308] What Nixon called "precipitous" withdrawal, (usually offered without elections in South Vietnam) was ultimately American surrender and a communist victory by other names.

New Mobe scheduled a militant mass rally, a March Against Death, in November. At the insistence of Hanoi, East bloc and American Communists, New Mobe worked cooperatively with Moratorium, a broader coalition of peace groups opposing the war for any and all reasons. Moratorium helped organize local actions nationwide including a Washington D.C. event in October. The far left, "communist dominated" National Mobe/New Mobe, at the prompting of Hanoi and with overlapping leaderships and members, influenced Moratorium. Moratorium and New Mobe shared leaders and office space, spoke together, promoted the others' events, and coordinated events.[309]

Though the Moratorium and the New Mobes March against Death successfully mobilized as many as two million Americans, Nixon's "Silent Majority" speech mobilized the

---

[306] Counter- Inaugural, SDS, CRV, IPS, FOR, Stockholm Conference any many, many affiliated organizations in these coalitions. See: *CRV Newsletter*, October 1969, 1; FBI, FOIA, *Weather Underground*. The primary source is Acting SAC Chicago to Director, memo, "Foreign Influence-Weather Underground Organization," August 20, 1976, 284-285; Senate, Committee on the Judiciary, Subcommittee to Investigate the Administration of the Internal Security Act and Other Internal Security Laws, *The Weather Underground*, Committee Print, January 1975, 136-7;House, Subversive...New Mobilization, 1970; Church committee final report.

[307] Most prominent leaders below find--Bernardine Dohrn, Sidney Peck, Doug Dowd, John McAuliff, Allan Brick, Richard Barnet, Ron Young, Irving Sarnoff, Fred Halsted, Cora Weiss.

[308] Moratorium's most prominent leader, Sam Brown, said so as did the group leaders in the coalition, American Friends Service Committee, Americans for Democratic Action, Business Executives Move for Peace, SANE, Women's International League for Peace and Freedom, WILPf, Women Strike for Peace. Charles DeBenedetti; Charles Chatfield, *An American Ordeal: The Antiwar Movement of the Vietnam Era*. Syracuse: Syracuse University Press, 1990, 248, 256.

[309] U.S. House, Committee on Internal Security *Subversive Involvement in the Origin, Leadership and Activities of the New Mobilization Committee to End the War in Vietnam, and its Predecessor Organizations,* Washington, US Government Printing Office, 1970; Fedora, "Road to Moscow: Bill Clinton's Early Activism from Fulbright to Moscow," Original FReeper research, *Free Republic*, 08/22/2007, unpaginated page 4;

majority of citizens not protesting. Some 52,000 letters supporting the President, massive majorities in opinion surveys, and a nationwide "National Honor Week" mobilizing hundreds of thousands demonstrating their support of the President.

It all proved only a small, though very passionate, minority supported the peace movement. Popular support was a thin illusion.

Meanwhile, Tom Hayden, David Dellinger and Cora Weiss collaborated closely with Hanoi in exploiting POWs and their families with selective POW releases and POW interviews. At the request of Hanoi, they formed the Committee of Liaison with Families of Servicemen Detained in North Vietnam, COLIFAM, to correspond with and try to recruit POW family members into the antiwar movement.

Chapter 3. Vietnam 1969: Hanoi and Antiwar Movement Unite.[310]

Photo: Victory for the Viet Cong, peace protestors, January 19, 1969, *Washington Star.*

Viet Cong Directive. On January 31, 1969, the Viet Cong issued a directive to political cadre to increase "our determination to annihilate tyrants and eliminate traitors."[311] **Oglesby Purged.** Like the Viet Cong, Bernardine Dohrn, now SDS's charismatic leader of Weatherman wanted the Brigades not to cut sugar cane, but to make and win Communist revolutions and to "Bring the War home." Bernardine Dohrn said Oglesby's cutting sugar cane was too "Peace Corp," lacked a solid political theory, and would not "bring back more committed revolutionaries" to the U.S. In March 1969, in Austin, Texas, Dohrn and Bergman "star-chambered" Oglesby accusing him of rejecting Marxist-Leninism and cavorting with the imperialists. Oglesby had written critical comments about the Cuban revolution in *Life* magazine. A sneering Arlene Bergman recited Oglesby's errors in political correctness in his article in *Life* magazine: "The Cubans can't vote. The economy is stagnant. Everything depends on Soviet aid." Dohrn and Bergman purged Carl Oglesby.[312]

---

[310] Adapted from Roger Canfield "Winning the War: Losing on the Second Front in the USA,--1969" Volume II, Part IV of *Comrades in Arms: How the Americong Won the War in Vietnam Against the Common Enemy-America.* All three volumes are available as one e-book at http://americong.com

[311] Security Section of the Que Son District cited in Robert F. Turner, "The Viet Cong Tactic of Assassination," U.S. Mission in Vietnam, 1970, 35-36; also testimony of Daniel E. Teodoru, U.S. Congress, Senate, Committee on Judiciary, *The Human Cost of Communism in Vietnam-II*, Washington; U.S. Government Printing Office, January 5, 1973, 37.

[312] Carl Oglesby, *Ravens in the Storm: A Personal History of the 1970s Antiwar*

Arlene Eisen Bergman was a Marxist-Leninist believer.[313] Always towing the party line, Bergman's later book on *Women in Vietnam* was indistinguishable from the official history of the Indochina Communist Party.[314]

Dohrn and Bergman had treated Carl Oglesby just as if the Viet Cong Directive had given them instructions. **SDS Materials Favor Viet Cong Victory.** On January 15, the Illinois Crime Investigating Commission acquired SDS materials from 4943 North Winthrop Street in Chicago which Gerald Long, soon a weatherman, had vacated in October after the landlord objected to its use by persons not on Long's lease.[315] "We found mail from the Communist Viet Cong government, including official news releases; mail from Communist regime in Cuba; from militant persons in West Germany." Materials advocated "outright support for victory of the Communist regimes in North and South Vietnam."[316]

Viet Cong Favors a Counter-Inaugural as Nixon takes Office. Meanwhile on January 20, 1969 a new President was to take office. Several antiwar factions worked on the event. Those trying to avoid the notoriety of the radical, extremist violence of the National Mobe, brought together a new, short lasting coalition, the National Action Group, NAG, to peacefully protest the Inaugural.[317] A Washington Mobilization Committee[318]

Movement, New York: Scribner, 2008, 245-257; Zaroulis, Who Spoke Up..., 213.

[313] Her husband, Lincoln Bergman, program director radio KPLA, Berkeley, and Maoist Leibel Bergman her father-in-law and founder of the Revolutionary Union (later Revolutionary Communist Party); *Combat*, Vol. 1, No. 28, October 15, 1969; Declassified U.S. Government intelligence information regarding the communist and foreign connections of the Weather Underground. Presented as evidence, on the agreement of the prosecution and defense counsel, in the trial of W. Mark Felt and Edward S, Miller," 11 at www.usasurvival.org

[314] Arlene Eisen Bergman, *Women of Vietnam*, San Francisco: People's Press, 1974.

[315] Robert C. Tomashevsky, Bernardine Dohrn, Jeffrey Blum, John G. Jacobs, and Peter Clapp.

[316] Members of the Washington Mobe were Bob Auerbach, Abe Bloom, Norm Borlin, Bill Caraway, Kathy Coram, James Dill, P.K. Downey, Thelma Duvinage, Bob Falk, Max Phillip Friedman, Tom Fulcher, Don Gurewitz, Helen Gurewitz, , Charlie Kimball, Keith Lappe, (Lampe), Carol Lipman, Anne Newton, Tom Palmer, Bill Peters, Charlie Rather, and Jane Silverman. See: Senate, Committee on the Judiciary, Subcommittee to Investigate the Administration of the Internal Security Act and Other Internal Security Laws, *The Weather Underground*, Committee Print, January 1975, 136-7.

[317] Stewart Meacham of AFSC, Dave Reynolds of WRL, Richard Fernandez of CALC, James Bevel of SCLC and the Spring Mobe, Tudja Crowder, Catherine Camp of WILPF, Paul Lauter of RESIST, Brad Lytte of CNVA, William Davidon of Hartford College, Otto Nathan of of NY Peace Committee, Allan Brick, Ron and Trudi Young, and Jim Forest of FOR.

previously meeting at the Dumbarton Methodist Church relocated to 1029 Vermont Avenue to work on Counter-Inaugural protests. Formed in 1967 after Hayden and Dellinger led meetings in September-October in Bratislava, Hanoi and Phnom Penh between Americans and Vietnamese communists, on January 17, the South Vietnam People's Committee in Solidarity with the American People (*Viet My*), sent a message to National Mobe in connection with a campaign intended for January 19 and 20... We warmly welcome ...large-scale demonstrations...on Nixon's assumption of the presidency, to ...bring U.S...troop[s] home...[Further] Your antiwar acts will stimulate us more strongly....[319]

On Jan 20, 1969, the Counter-Inaugural for Nixon was a bust – only 6,000 protestors. Some 300-400, openly supporting a Viet Cong victory, hurled rocks and bottles at Nixon's limousine. The National Mobe was still kicking and the nominal pacifists silenced. **Communists Speak Clearly to its American Friends.** At the request of Hanoi's peace delegation in Paris, on January 30, 1969 David Dellinger and Rennie Davis of National Mobe, Cora Weiss of WSP, and Richard Barnet of IPS flew to Paris.[320] The focus was upon the formation of a group to help the Vietnamese communists handle American POW interviews, mail, families and releases. The organization would become COLIFORM.

Oriana Fallaci Interviews and Penetrates Gen. Giap's Lies. In Hanoi in February 1969, Oriana Fallaci, a critic of both the South Vietnamese regime and the war, interviewed General Giap at his large villa and garden of flowering trees.[321] They sat "around a table loaded with delicacies: fried cheese balls,...meat coquettes, comfits and little glasses of red liquor."[322]

---

[318] *Extent of Subversion in Campus Disorders*, Testimony of Max Phillip Friedman, Hearings before the Subcommittee to Investigate the Administration of the Internal Security Act and other Internal Security Laws of the Committee of the Judiciary, United States Senate, 91st Cong., 1st Sess., Part 2, August 12, 1969, 90, 100

[319] "U.S. Demonstrations for End War Praised," *Liberation Press Agency* 1514 GMT 17 January 1969, TTU archive. Cited in Rothrock, p. 137N11.

[320] FBI, SAC WFO to Director, Memo Bufile 105-185148, May 4, 1970, 2,3.

[321] Robert Templer, "Imagining Vietnam," *Richmond Review*, United Kingdom, at richmondreview.co.uk/features/temple01 cites her interview published in *L'Europeo*, February 1969 and *Washington Post*, April 6, 1969, B1, B4; Oriana Fallaci, (Trans. John Shepley), *Interview With History*, New York: Liveright 1976, 74-87; Oriana Fallaci, *Nothing, And So Be It*, New York: Doubleday, 1969.

[322] Oriana Fallaci, "General Giap," *Interview with History*, (Trans. John Shepley), Boston: Houghton Mifflin, 1977, 78.

The charming Giap told stories of the glories of the Revolution. During his 45-minute filibuster, Fallaci interrupted Gen. Giap with questions. What was the role of North Vietnamese Army in the military defeat of Tet? Giap, "The (Tet offensive) didn't depend on us: it was conducted by the Front," "I don't know if the Front foresaw or desired the population to rise up."[323] **How long will the war last?** "So, then, general, how long will the war go on? How long will this poor people be asked to sacrifice itself, to suffer, and to die?" The General replied, "As long as is necessary.... "Ten, fifteen, fifty years. ...We're not in a hurry..."[324]" A half million already dead, Giap was indifferent to the losses of North Vietnamese lives, nearly a million were to come, the equivalent of 28 million Americans. Vietnamese flesh, blood and lives were expendable. The refrain was "born in the north to die in the south," by hunger, malaria, anemia, open sores as well as war.[325] Such suffering was just more useful propaganda.

COSVN Instructions to American Cadre: Mass Actions of Peace Supporters. On February 27, 1969 in Circular No. 75, the communist Central Office on Viet Nam, COVN, reminded its political cadre, ...We must exploit our diplomatic victories... ...[V]ictories are due to...the struggle capabilities of our people and that of the peace-loving people...including the Americans.[326]

First National Convocation on the Challenge of Building Peace. On March 5, 1969, the First National Convocation on the Challenge of Building Peace was at the Hilton Hotel in New York. Attendees claimed a broad range of perspectives.[327] Viet Cong flags unfurled, but no American flag flew. There were no prayers for peace, wisdom or anything else. Among the speakers were Senators Fulbright, Javits and McGovern. A few shouted, "Ho, Ho, Ho Chi Minh, NLF is going to win." Saigon reporter Neil Sheehan, told the bellicose pacifists, "In some countries a

---

[323] Fallaci, "General Giap," *Interview with History*, (Trans. John Shepley), Boston: Houghton Mifflin, 1977, 82-83.

[324] Fallaci, "General Giap," 82, 87.

[325] Bao Ninh, *The Sorrow of War*, 58-59 cited in Nghia M. Vo, "The War Viewed From All Sides," in Nghia M. Vo, Chat V. Dang, Hien V. Ho (eds.), *War and Remembrance*, SACEI Forum #6, Denver: Outskirts Press, Inc, 2009, 14.

[326] Circular No. 75/CTNT, "Intensification of...Diplomatic Struggles...to Gain Greater Victories," Feb. 27, 1969 in U.S Mission to South Vietnam, Viet-Nam Documents and Research Notes, Document No. 101, Part IV, Saigon, January 1972, 2,10-11.

[327] The invited included Corliss Lamont, Stewart Rawlings Mott, Jerome B. Wisner, former Senator Joseph Clark, Col. Donald H. Humphries, Rev. William Sloan Coffin, Howard Zinn and New York Timesman Neil Sheehan.

Communist government may be the best government." He described "anticommunism as destructive as Stalinism."[328] He was now an open cheerleader for the Viet Cong.

Circular 79 Gives Instructions on Propaganda Themes. In Vietnamese circular 79 informed political cadre, "U.S. imperialists and their henchmen...have been confronted... by those American people who demand the rapid withdrawal of U.S. troops and the end of the war."[329] Soon the Moratorium's chief spokesman, Sam Brown, called Hanoi's theme of rapid withdrawal the peace movement's common denominator.

Committee of Concerned Asian Scholars. In late March 1969 in Boston, the Committee of Concerned Asian Scholars, CCAS, passed its statement of purpose, in part, "in opposition to the brutal aggression of the United States in Vietnam ...[and] to create alternatives ...for the development of anti-imperialist research."[330] Its *Bulletin of Concerned Asian Scholars* soon became an academic front for pro-Hanoi propaganda from a Maoist Chinese perspective. CCAS member Marilyn Young's "anti-imperialist research" is now the ruling orthodoxy of the Vietnam War ably assisted by Edwin Moise, Noam Chomsky Ngo Vinh Long, Orville Schell.

Peace Mobilization, New York April 4-6, 1969. In New York, the National Mobe and the Fifth Avenue Peace Parade Committee, FAVPPC,[331] cosponsored a march of 30,000 to 100,000 from Bryant Park to Central Park to protest the war, condemn American capitalism, racism and imperialism, and advocate a socialist revolution. "Bring the Troops Home," became code words for unilateral U.S. withdrawal. Indeed, the *New York Times* declared, "Thousands March Here to Demand Vietnam Pullout."[332] **Madame Binh Speaks.** Dellinger

---

[328] Alice Widener, "The Coo of the Doves: From Waldorf to Hilton, 1949-1969," *U.S.A.* Vol. XV, No. 26, March 14, 1969.

[329] Circular No. 79/CTNT, March 29, 1969, "U.S. and Puppet schemes used in making a public proposal for private talks," in U.S Mission to South Vietnam, Viet-Nam Documents and Research Notes, Document No. 101, Part IV, Saigon, January 1972, 3, 15-18.

[330] Doug Allen, "Universities and the Vietnam War: A Case Study of Successful Struggle," *Bulletin on Concerned Asian Scholars*, Vol. 8, No. 4: October–December 1976.

[331] Key participants were Richard Cartwright, Ossie Davis, David Dellinger, Al Evanoff, Fred Halstead, Abbie Hoffman, Frederick Douglass Kirkpatrick, Paul O'Dwyer, Jerry Rubin, Buelah Sanders, Ron Wolin, Howard Zinn, representing groups such as Catholic Peace Fellowship, Mobilization for Peace Action, Veterans for Peace in Vietnam, Workers World Party, Student Mobilization, SDS, Veterans of the Abraham Lincoln Brigade, Women Strike for Peace.

introduced an eight-minute tape of Mrs. Nguyen Thi Binh speaking English with a heavy Vietnamese accent. Binh condemns Nixon for "indicting Dave Dellinger, Tom Hayden, Rennie Davis [National Mobe members] and five other friends, in an attempt to stamp out the anti-war movement." Regularly consulting with Dellinger, Hayden, Bernardine Dohrn, Steve Halliwell, and others, Binh revealed details of the peace mobilization program in New York. Binh said B-52 bombing is "resulting in massacre of civilians," and "daily raining napalm to incinerate South-Vietnamese children." No mass massacre ever occurred and B-52s did not drop napalm. All that needs to be done is to unconditionally withdraw troops.

National Action Group, NAG--Easter protests, April 6-9

Stewart Meacham of AFSC put together a new coalition of pacifist groups[333], the National Action Group, NAG, to conduct local protests. NAG tried to avoid the notoriety of National Mobe radicalism and violence at the Pentagon in 1967 and in Chicago in 1968. NAG's participation in the Counter Inaugural in 1969 had gone badly with violence.

In the event at Easter 1969, some 150,000 people gathered in 40 cities.

Most of the NAG's member groups, AFSC, CALC, CNVA, FOR, soon turned to hard core collaboration with Hanoi.

FBI Reports communist and foreign connections of the Weather Underground. In April 1969, the FBI said the new left was participating in guerrilla training in Cuba, making repeated contacts with the KGB in East Berlin and continuing cooperation" with the Viet Cong and Hanoi. In April 1969, the Viet Cong NLF cabled the Chicago office of the SDS asking Bratislava veterans, Bernardine Dohrn and Steve Halliwell, to come to Prague for discussions.[334]

---

[332] FBI, FOIA, Abbie Hoffman, Hoffsum3, Madame Binh transcript at 123-126.
Original FBI, New York, memo, "Peace Mobilization April 4-6, 1969," April 22, 1969; "Thousands March Here to Demand Vietnam Pullout," *New York Times*, April 6, 1969, A-1.
[333] Stewart Meacham of AFSC, Dave Reynolds of WRL, Richard Fernandez of CALC, James Bevel of SCLC and the Spring Mobe, Tudja Crowder, Catherine Camp of WILPF, Paul Lauter of RESIST, Brad Lytte of CNVA, William Davidon of Hartford College, Otto Nathan of NY Peace Committee, Allan Brick, Ron and Trudi Young, and Jim Forest of FOR.
[334] "Declassified U.S. Government intelligence information regarding the communist and foreign connections of the Weather Underground. Presented as evidence, on the agreement of the prosecution and defense counsel, in the trial of W. Mark Felt and Edward S, Miller," 28 at www.usasurvival.org.

VC's New 10 Point Peace Plan

On May 4, 1969, Circular 89 instructed cadre to promote the new Vietnamese, unannounced, 10-point peace plan inside the United States:

> [T]he (Peace Plan) statement... encompasses tactics designed to win the support of...all political forces. ... [T]he U.S. people are initiating an intense movement to end U.S. aggression in Vietnam. This (10-point) solution...will motivate the U.S. people...This is the most favorable time to proselyte the enemy..."[335]

The Ten Point plan was one of other plans, numbers 7, 8, 9 and 10, all giving propaganda value to peace forces.[336]

AFSC: "American-led holocaust" Genocide in South Vietnam. On May 5, AFSC's leaders Gilbert White and Bronson Clark, pacifist Quakers, wrote an inflammatory and false[337] letter to mobilize its members. The letter said that America was "decimating the population... borders... on Vietnamese genocide. ...The American-led holocaust must come to an end."[338] There was no U. S. genocide campaign. After the war, Communists conducted genocide upon Khmer, Montagnards and Hmong.

Stockholm Conference on Vietnam—May 16-18, 1969. May 16-18, 1969, the 14-member Paris delegations of Hanoi and the NLF conducted an Emergency Action Conference in Stockholm hosted by two Communist members of the World Peace Council-funded Swedish International Liaison Committee, Carl H. Hermansson and Dr. John Takman. Of 350 to 400 attending the Communist dominated event were 33 Americans representing eleven organizations,[339] many were advertised

---

[335] Circular No. 89/CTNT, May 4, 1969,"Concerning... Significance of the solution presented...at the Paris Conference," in U.S Mission to South Vietnam, Viet-Nam Documents and Research Notes, Document No. 101, Part IV, Saigon, January 1972, 4, 19-21; See also Doan Van Tien, T.20, Standing Committee, 5 Truong directive, [possibly COSVN] PRP C.C. Directive on NLF May 8 1969 Paris Talks Statement, May 19, 1969, Pike Collection, TTU, Virtual Archive, Item Number 2121313022.
[336] "67. Memorandum ...(Kissinger) to President Nixon," May 10, 1969. FRUS, 1969-1976, Vol. VI, Vietnam, January 1969-July 1970.
[337] Unlike Cambodia, where a real genocide was to occur, the populations of North and South Vietnam increased throughout the war despite heavy casualties among its military forces.
[338] Gilbert White and Bronson Clark, "A Call from the Board of Directors..." May 5, 1969 in FBI, FOIA, AFSC.
[339] National Mobe (soon renamed New Mobe) committee, American Friends Service Committee, AFSC, Clergy and Laity Concerned About Vietnam, CLC, Lawyers Committee on American Policy Toward Vietnam, National Lawyers Guild, NLG, Women Strike for Peace, WSP, RESIST, SNCC, SANE, War Resistor's League and American Deserter's Committee, HISC, Staff Study, *Subversive Involvement in the*

pacifists.[340] The Vietnamese purpose was to unify antiwar organizations and to coordinate mass demonstrations on Vietnam worldwide[341] and to sell the Ten Point Peace Plan. The Stockholm Emergency Action Conference sought "to listen to what our Vietnamese friends will have to tell us" and to "discuss, in common, what has to be done. ...It is the wish of our Vietnamese friends that these contacts will develop into permanent ones."[342]

The Vietnamese, Nguyen Minh Vy and Nguyen Thi Binh, expressed concern about a "deteriorating anti-war movement" in the U.S. "Without public opinion in the U.S. calling for American troops withdrawal, their efforts to achieve victory would be handicapped."

To "revitalize...anti-war sentiment" the conference had prepared a TO DO list from A to F for the U.S. antiwar movement including newspaper ads, demonstrations July 4, boycotts, draft and GI resistance, and the 10-Point Peace Plan.[343] Like Hanoi, the conference appeal for "the complete withdrawal of all U.S...troops without any conditions whatsoever... ,"[344]

By November a directive to VC cadre still reporting on a conference in Sweden passing a resolution supporting the people's struggle in the USA and "calling for all youth and student movements ...to demand the U.S. end the war in Viet-Nam and withdraw all U.S. and satellite troops..." VC Cadre on the ground in South Vietnam were being taught that political, military and diplomatic victories "activated the struggle

---

Origin, Leadership and Activities of the New Mobilization Committee to End the War in Vietnam And Its Predecessor Organizations, 1970,XII-XIII, 28. HISC, Staff Study, 1970, 28.

[340] Leadership of "pacifists" attending were William Davidon, CPUSA Carlton Goodlett, Rev. Episcopalian Thomas Lee Hayes and Bratislava veteran John Wilson. American Deserter delegates were George Carrano and Donald McDonough. Other notables attending were Anatol Rapaport, Noam Chomsky and Gabriel Kolko. HISC, Staff Study, *Subversive Involvement in the Origin, Leadership and Activities of the New Mobilization Committee to End the War in Vietnam and Its Predecessor Organizations,* 1970, II-XIII, 28.

[341] International Liaison Committee, Stockholm Conference on Vietnam, Information Letter No. 2, April 26, 1969; *Militant* July 18, 1969. Both cited in HISC, Staff Study, 1970, 26-27.

[342] International Liaison Committee, Stockholm Conference on Vietnam, Information Letter No. 2, April 26, 1969, 2.

[343] Tom Charles Huston, Special Report for the President, TOP SECRET, EYES ONLY- Very Sensitive, *Foreign Communist Support of the Revolutionary Protest Movement in the United States,* July 1969, 46-7, Declassified 11/10/2008 at request of Max Friedman.

[344] Mailing on May 23, 1969; Both cited I HISC, Staff Study, 1970.

movement in the U. S. people…"[345] New Mobe would urge, as had the Stockholm conference, that withdrawal be "immediate and total."[346]

Sec. Defense Laird Accuses Hanoi of Torturing POWs. May 19, 1969 Sec. of Defense, Melvin Laird accused Hanoi of torturing POWs. Laird traveled to Paris to give the Vietnamese photos of beaten and starved POWs, Lt. Robert Frishman, Cdr. Dick Stratton and Seaman Doug Hegdahl. "The Geneva Conventions says you shall release all sick and wounded prisoners… Why aren't they released?"[347] Responding to Laird on June 2, 1969 Hanoi recorded admiral of the 7th fleet's son, John McCain. McCain's voice, "I received very good medical treatment. …I was given an operation on my leg …and a cast upon my right arm…. The doctors…knew a great deal about the practice of medicine…."[348] McCain's words, though unnatural, reflected Hanoi's themes. The Weathermen would later give another more successful pro-Hanoi answer, Vietnam: "Laird cries—for the POWs while [South] Vietnamese are tortured in Saigon's tiger cages."[349]

Disinformation, Political Oppression: Study Team on Freedom in South Vietnam-- From May 25-June 10, 1969 Allan R. Brick, Gene Stolzfus, Tom Fox of Fellowship of Reconciliation, FOR, led a nine-person group[350] on an 11-day tour of South Vietnam called the U.S. Study Team on Religious and Political Freedom in Vietnam.[351] From Phnom

---

[345]Le Minh Nguyen, "To Various K's and H's (Regions and Districts)," October 27, 1969, Australians captured Nov 4, 1969 attached to "Viet Cong Units Directed to Intensify Struggle to Take Advantage of U.S. Peace Movement," Press Release, No. 98-69, November 30, 1969 United States Mission in Vietnam.

[346]New Mobe, Fact Sheet in press kit prior to November 1969 demonstrations.

[347] Lieut. Commander John S. McCain III, U.S. Navy, "How the POW's Fought Back," *US News & World Report*, May 14, 1973.

[348] [redacted] Hanoi in English to American Servicemen in South Vietnam at 1300 GMT 2 Jun 69 B, B000S BVA 0002, (Eugene C.) Cannon 2 Jun 69; (U.S. wire service, AP or UPI?) "PW Songbird Is Pilot Son of Admiral, June 4, 1969.

[349] Weather Underground communication #8, copy in FBI, FOIA, Weather Underground. The primary source is Acting SAC Chicago to Director, memo, "Foreign Influence-Weather Underground Organization," August 20, 1976, 168.

[350] The rest of the group included Bishop James Armstrong, President of United Methodists, member of World Council of Churches, largest contributor to the tax exempt National Council of Churches; Mrs. John C. Bennett, "Protestant churchwoman" and wife of the president of the National Council of Churches; Rep. John Conyers, D-Michigan; Robert F. Drinan, S.J. of Boston College; John J. Pemberton of ACLU; Rabbi Simore Siegel of Jewish Theological Seminary; Admiral Arnold E. True, USN, Ret.

[351] Inspector Quang to DOC, Nguyen Phu Sanh, "Congressional /Religious Delegation Visit Con Son", June 3, 1969; U.S. Study Team on Religious and Political Freedom in

Penh, Don Luce, who had previously written about South Vietnamese political prisoners in the *National Catholic Reporter*[352], provided key contacts and materials. The team traveled freely throughout South Vietnam without minders. Jesuit Father and future Congressman Robert F. Drinan claimed he "saw dreadful things.... the bombing, ... poisonous defoliants and thousands of political prisoners." Drinan wanted war crime trials for Americans.[353]

On July 11, 1969, Thomas Fox published an article in *Commonweal*, "Devil's Island of Vietnam; The Price of Political Dissent." The *Commonweal* piece names prisoners not there. One prisoner at Con Son, Ho Duc Thanh, claimed to have been falsely convicted for assassinating Assemblyman Tran Van Van, but the actual convicted murderer was Nguyen Xuan An, not Thanh. The group were shown segregation cells—14 feet high, 24 wide and 30 feet long, but claimed falsely they only 4 feet by 5 feet.[354] The Tom Fox report was phony from start to finish, but that did not prevent wide distribution of its allegations.[355] Thereafter FOR published "America's Political Prisoners in South Vietnam" alleging widespread brutality and torture, incarcerations without trials, and "reputed small barred cells in which prisoners...were chained to the floor in a prone position." FOR launched a five-year program to free South Vietnam's political prisoners culminating in the very successful "Tiger Cage" vigil before Congress in July 14-20, 1974.

"Climate of political and religious suppression." In a letter to President Nixon, the FOR study group wrote, in part,

---

Vietnam, "Findings on Trip to Vietnam, May 5, 1969-June 10, 1969, for the *Congressional Record*; "Transcription of taped Interview of Don Luce," Shirley Bordenkircher, December 11, 1992 (accompanied by Jerry Snider); cited in D.E, Bordenkircher, S.A. Bordenkircher, *Tiger Cage: Untold Story,* Abby Publishing, *1998, 103.*

[352] Don Luce, "Vietnam's overflowing Prisons: Where 'one day is 1,000 years," *National Catholic Reporter*, January 16, 1969.

[353] Robert F. Drinan, "When will the American conscience demand justice for Vietnam?" *National Catholic Reporter*, March 17, 2000.

[354] Bordenkircher to Colby, "Study Team on Religious and Political Freedom, January 17, 1970;cited in D.E, Bordenkircher, S.A. Bordenkircher, *Tiger Cage: Untold Story,* Abby Publishing, *1998*

[355] June 17, 1969 Sen. Abraham Ribicoff, Rep. Ogden Reid, D-New York, distributed a report. Hanoi used the study group as powerful propaganda. Records of FOR-USA, DG 013, Section 2, Series G, G-3, box 8,G-4, Box 10-11, Swarthmore College Library at Swarthmore.edu/library/peace; Tiger Cage Vigil and Fast, Catholic Peace Fellowship Records, University of Notre Dame Archives, CCPF 7/12 Folder

"Religious and political suppression is widespread. The facts do not match FOR feelings.[356] Saigon had many free critical newspapers,[357] bookstalls and music.[358] Antiwar activists Nguyen Cong Hoan, Ngo Ba Thanh, Huynh Tan Mam, and other critics freely roamed and met anti-war Americans largely unmolested by the government.

Photo: *Dien-Tin*, Saigon's Leading Opposition Newspaper.[359]

In stark contrast, Hanoi had no free press during the war; after victory it closed down newspapers and burned books in South Vietnam.[360] **Viet Cong Massacres.** Yet AFSC, and like

---

[356] U. S. Study Team on Religious and Political freedom in Vietnam," June 1969, 10-9. See also "Study Team on Religious and Political Freedom, January 17, 1970."

[357] By 1970-71 there were 24 daily **newspapers.** The largest, *Tin Sang*, was "incredibly anti-government" according to Robert Turner. Robert Turner to Max Friedman and others, May 25, 2009. Turner and Friedman both took photos of books and newspapers. By September of 1970, Daniel Sutherland wrote in the *Christian Science Monitor*, "…South Vietnam has one of the freest presses in Southeast Asia, and the daily paper with the largest circulation here happens to be sharply critical of President Thieu….The government has not been able to close down *Tin Sang* or any other newspaper among the 30 now being published in Saigon." Other independent papers were *Chinh Luan*, *Saigon Times*, and *Le Journal D'Extreme Orient*. Bill Laurie remembers the Saigon newspapers, "They slammed corruption, criticized Thieu, and exhibited all the caustic pugnacity a free press, can muster." Though "sometimes… censored…by blackouts, so readers knew censorship had been applied." A paper might be closed, but it would reopen in a week so. Indeed, on the advice of Malay counterinsurgency expert Sir Robert Thompson, the Saigon government subsidized newsprint.

[358] Saigon had hundreds of **bookstalls** selling anything and everything in English, French and Vietnamese including General Giap's *Peoples War, People's Army,* Ho Chi Minh's *On Revolution* and Che Guevara too. While **music** of all kinds was banned in North Vietnam, in South Vietnam the recordings of antigovernment popular artists, like Khanh Ly, were readily available. Bill Laurie to Roger Canfield, May 25, 2009.

[359] John Spragens, Jr., "Corruption in South Viet Nam: Pervasive, Profound and Permanent," CALC, *American Report, July 22, 1974.*
http://www.enigmaterial.com/dateline/dateline_main.html

[360] In 1991, on Little Saigon Radio, Duong Thu Huong, author of *Novel without a Name and Paradise of the Blind*, said, "Only after I got to South Vietnam [in 1975] did I realize that the Northern regime was a barbarian regime because it punches blind people's eyes, it plugs up people's ears. While in the South people could listen to any international radio they wanted whether it's French, British or American. Such is a civilized society. …I cried…. I was flabbergasted …all the works of South Vietnamese authors were freely published. Tons of authors that I have never heard of have works displayed in the bookstores and even on street curbs; and the people had all sorts of access to information such as the television, radio and cassettes galore. Such

groups, never mentioned VC atrocities. A secret directive of the Can Duoc District Unit, Subregion 3, of May 18, 1969 instructed, "We must motivate the...people to join the 'deep hatred for the enemy' movement... We must seek all means to destroy people who surrender, traitors and pacification personnel."[361]

CIA-CHAOS and NSA Progress Reports. On June 20, 1969 Tom Huston, staff Assistant to the President requested a CIA review on its CHAOS project on foreign governments support of the antiwar movement? "Support" meant "...Foreign communists [seeking] to encourage or assist revolutionary protest movements in the United States." Huston said, "...[O]ur present intelligence collection capabilities...may be inadequate."[362] It took the CIA's Deputy Director Cushman a scant ten days to write a report that was conclusive and dismissive:

> The information collected...provides only a very limited amount of foreign Communist assistance to revolutionary protest movements...There is very little reporting on...funding or training and no evidence of communist direction or control of any United States revolutionary protest movement...

The CIA's report of June 30 was "conspicuous for absence of hard facts....CIA coverage of contacts...is totally inadequate. ...I am convinced that CIA has failed to assign an adequate priority ...."[363] The CIA had only noticed "encouragement of these movements through propaganda methods."[364]

---

apparatuses to the North Vietnamese could only be in dream. In the North, all the media and publications are under government control. In 2008 liberated Vietnam still ranked very low in freedom of the press--168 out of 173 nations surveyed. By 2014 it was worse still. Vietnam is ranked 174th out of 180 countries in the Reporters Without Borders press freedom index. It is hard to conclude that the FOR delegation that toured Con Son, saw the "tiger cages," and yet saw no oppression of political freedom anywhere else in South Vietnam. Was FOR entirely populated by fools and dupes? Indeed, they had become transparent partisans for America's enemy in the war in South Vietnam.

[361] Doc. Log No. 06-1939-69 cited in Thanh Nam Le, "Viet-Cong Repression: Control and Polarization of the Populace" at http://25thaviation.org/history/id926.htm

[362] Memo Tom Huston to Deputy Director of the CIA, June 20, 1969.

[363] Tom Charles Huston, Special Report for the President, TOP SECRET, EYES ONLY- Very Sensitive, *Foreign Communist Support of the Revolutionary Protest Movement in the United States*, July 1969, 1,3, 29-30,33 Declassified 11/10/2008 at request of Max Friedman.

[364] Gen. Robert Cushman to Tom Charles Huston, June 30, 1969 in Church Committee 700.

Huston Report, July 1969. A July 1969 special report for the President by Tom Charles Huston[365] responds to the poor performance of U.S. intelligence, in particular the CIA. There was no *"iron-clad* proof that foreign powers were helping to finance campus disorders in this country." This was likely out of a "political sensitivity of surveillance of domestic political organizations,"

Finances. The NSA, DIA and CIA, had not done much to find communist financing. Huston found Cuban and Chinese financial support for the Progressive Labor Party,[366] known to local officials and HCUA since 1966. Huston concluded "individual (CPUSA) party members play a role in the demonstrations, activities and workings of these groups." **Close Cooperation.** "There is overwhelming evidence pointing to close cooperation and coordination between the U.S. 'peace movement' and the North Vietnamese and the National Liberation Front for South Vietnam." Huston cited the Stockholm Conference in May 1969 and communications with David Dellinger about the Bratislava meeting of September 1967.

The CIA had separate files on 9,944 out of 250,000 protesters[367]—4 tenths of one percent of antiwar activists.[368] CHAOS had an active interest in very few organizations such as PCPJ, NPAC, SDS, Student Mobe, Black Panther Party, Dispatch News Service, Newsreel, Liberation News Service, *Ramparts*.[369] All actively collaborated with the enemy in war. **NSA.** According to Lt. Gen. Lew Allen to the Church Committee the NSA monitored the foreign communications of only about 300 activists and terror suspects.[370] "All messages had at least one foreign terminal" and "over 90 percent had at least one foreign communicant." **Monitoring communications to and from Hanoi.** "The (NSA) communications were obtained, for example by monitoring communications to and

---

[365] Tom Charles Huston, Special Report for the President, TOP SECRET, EYES ONLY- Very Sensitive, *Foreign Communist Support of the Revolutionary Protest Movement in the United States*, July 1969, pp. 52, Declassified 11/10/2008 at request of Max Friedman.

[366] Old news from the testimony of Phillip Abbott Luce before Congress.

[367] Frank J. Rafalko, MH/CHAOS: The CIA's Campaign Against the Radical Left and the Black Panthers, Annapolis: Naval Institute Press, 2011, 24.

[368] Frank J. Rafalko, MH/CHAOS: 24.

[369] Frank J. Rafalko, MH/CHAOS: 38-39.

[370] Testimony of Lt. Gen. Lew Allen, Jr., director, NSA on October 29, 1975 to Church Committee at cryptime.org/nsa-4th.htm.

from Hanoi." By the end in 1973, NSA had intercepted the messages of 168 American citizens and groups.[371]

In 1969, leaders of the antiwar movement had engaged in extensive coordination of political activities with the enemy in Stockholm, Hanoi, Berlin and elsewhere.

COORDINATING PEACE ACTIONS: STOCKHOLM, HANOI, EAST BERLIN

Stockholm Conference on Vietnam. May 16-18, 1969 the Soviet-Czech-Vietnamese run Stockholm Conference on Vietnam held an "Emergency Action Conference on Vietnam" in Stockholm seeking closer consultation with between Americans and North Vietnamese.[372] The World Peace Council Conference noted, "The Vietnamese and U.S. delegations[373] were numerous and took a leading part in the deliberations of the conference." At 33, the Americans[374] were the largest delegation out of 340 persons from 60 countries. Among the dozen US organizations officially represented were American Friends Service Committee, SNCC, SANE, WSP, Clergy and Laity Concerned, CALC, and Lawyers Committee on American Policy Towards Vietnam.[375]

The Agenda. Americans met Hanoi's Nguyen Minh Vy and the Viet Cong's Nguyen Thi Binh[376], and accepted congratulations on their "spring offensive" and planned the October antiwar demonstrations.[377] The Lawyers Committee presented a Five-Point program to end the war.[378] *Daily World*,

---

[371] Christian W. Erickson, UC Davis, "Securing Cyberspace: Part 2-US Cryptography in the 20th Century."

[372] Frank J. Rafalko, MH/CHAOS: 138.

[373] See: Gannon, *A Biographical Dictionary of the Left*, [1969-1973] Belmont (Mass.): Western Islands, Vol. III, 571.

[374] Americans attending were: John Wilson and Sherman Adams of SNCC; Amy Swerdlow, Serita Crown, Althea Alexander of WSP; Noam Chomsky; Joseph Elder, Bob Eaton and Bronson Clark of AFSC; Joseph Crown, Richard Falk, Stanley Swerdlow of the Lawyers' Committee on American Policy Towards Vietnam; Doris Roberson of NLG; Carlton Goodlett of National Mobe; George Carranog and Donald McDonough of American Deserters Committee and John McAuliff of the Committee of Returned [Peace Corps] Volunteers.

[375] House members Rep. John Conyers, Rep. Bella Azbug and "avowed socialist" Rep. Ron Dellums were among the Lawyers Committee's most prominent supporters. .Frank J. Rafalko, MH/CHAOS: 139.

[376] Frank J. Rafalko, MH/CHAOS: 139.

[377] FBI *Information Digest Special Report on VVAW*, Aug. 25, 1972 at www.wntersoldier.com/staticpages/index. php?page= InfoDigestGuide; also cited in Fedora post to FreeRepublic.com www.wintersoldier.com/staticpages/index.php? page=Info Digeston VVAW

[378] Tom Charles Huston, Special Report for the President, 44,

an official CPUSA newspaper covered the conference positively. The Stockholm Conference declared it "stands with the people of Indo-China" and

> their legitimate representatives: the Government of the Democratic Republic of Vietnam, the Provisional Revolutionary Government of the Republic of South Vietnam, the Lao Patriotic Front and the Royal Cambodian Government of National Unity." The American pacifists of the WPC were seeking not peace in Vietnam, but a communist victory, like Ho Chi Minh, in the whole of Indochina. The tactical purposes of the Stockholm conference was unity among peace groups, "..action coordinated and supported ... (worldwide that) … lead to results than separate action, different methods and different dates....

Conditions for "Peace." A call to action was adopted to help the NLF and the antiwar movement,

> "[T]he unconditional withdrawal of US troops and the ten-point program of the NLF should be raised as widely as possible… Increase international support for resistance in America and by Americans abroad in refusing the draft, in defecting from the US armed forces, for carrying on propaganda within the army and for militant actions against the Selective service system."[379]

The Soviets and the East Bloc quashed a resolution to end the military draft in the communist world.

Circular No. 4, Directive No. 96—Unify and Coordinate

Circular No. 4 of the Central Office of South Vietnam on May 28, 1969, like the Stockholm conference, explicitly called for a "Front for United Action." Directive No. 96 described the antiwar movement as an integral part of Vietnamese diplomacy:

> in coordination with our diplomatic offensive, we should promote the struggle movement of the people in the U.S. and throughout the world and incite them to intensify their pressure on Nixon..." Directive 96 repeated: "We must also develop the Front for United Action…. We must make best use of all forms of propaganda such as leaflets, letters, overt press…to create public opinion.

---

[379] House, Subversive…New Mobilization. 1970, 28 cited in Rothrock, 110N56.

The Directive described an antiwar movement in non-pacifist terms, Vietnamese military victory. "We must ...support antiwar actions, military revolts, and desertion..."[380]

Adopting United Front Strategy—Moscow.

In May and June 1969, the Soviet Union provided advice to key activists in the antiwar movement. June 5-17, 1969 representatives of some 70 communist parties met in Moscow. American communists[381] and New Mobe activists[382] went to Moscow to work on the details of the propaganda messages for an upcoming World Peace Assembly in East Berlin, June 21-24, 1969.[383] Frank J. Rafalko, a CIA/CHAOS analyst, concluded the New Mobe was "a tool of Soviet propagandists. ...They had the same ideology, using the same patterns of organization and virtually the same propaganda tactics."[384] In Moscow, Soviet boss, Leonid Brezhnev, recognized the value of student and black movements in opposing the Vietnam War, the draft and racism. He said they "will do great things" once they master Marxism-Leninism.[385]

New Mobe's Irving Sarnoff –United Front. Briefed in May in Moscow, Irving Sarnoff, said in late June (21-24), in East Berlin,

"Our task is to broaden the base ... to include groups in motion around specific issues, -- wages, welfare, prices, taxes, racism,

---

[380] Circular No. 4 and Directive No. 96/CTNT, May 31,1969, "Development of...diplomatic Struggles in conjunction with military and Political Struggles..." in U.S Mission to South Vietnam, *Viet-Nam Documents and Research Notes*, Document No. 101, Part IV, Saigon, January 1972, 22-27.

[381] Irving Sarnoff, CPUSA member and a leader in both the National Mobe (and successor New Mobe) and the Peace Action Council of Los Angeles, Barbara Bick of New Mobe, a Robert Kennedy identified CPUSA Legislative Director, Arnold Samuel Johnson, and Charles Fitzpatrick, CPUSA member and an FBI informant. Sarnoff had flown from the Montreal conference on a Soviet plane booked by identified Communist Martin Hall and in November to the Sudan on a ticket paid by the Soviet front, the WPC.

[382] New Mobe visitors to Moscow included Barbara Ruth Bick, Rennie Davis, David Tyre Dellinger, William Douthard, Douglas Fitzgerald Dowd, Carlton Benjamin Goodlett, Terrence Tyrone Hallinan, Gersho Phineas Horowitz, Arnold Johnson, Sylvia Kushner, Stewart Meacham, Sidney Peck and Irving Sarnoff. Frank J. Rafalko, MH/CHAOS: 141.

[383] Subversive Involvement in Disruption of 1968 Democratic Party Convention, Part 1, October 1, 1968, 2369; HISC, Staff Study, Subversive Involvement in the Origin, Leadership and Activities of the New Mobilization Committee to End the War in Vietnam And Its Predecessor Organizations, 1970, 38; *Combat*, Vol. 1, No. 30, November 30, 1969; Senate Internal Security Subcommittee, Hearings, *The Nationwide Drive Against Law Enforcement Intelligence Operations*, part 2, July 14, 1975, 149.

[384] Frank J. Rafalko, MH/CHAOS: 141.

[385] Tom Charles Huston, Special Report for the President, 3, 13.

repression, housing -- and to make them understand that there can be no improvement until the war in Vietnam is ended.

AFSC Begs to Go to Hanoi. June 10-17.

At Stockholm AFSC's Bronson Clark arranged AFSC meetings with Xuan Oanh in Paris. Clark offered $25,000 in medical supplies, but expected to learn from Vietnamese medical expertise.[386] Bob Eaton showed 1967 photos of the Phoenix sailing trip to Haiphong. AFSC got a week in Hanoi. On June 10, Elder meet Houng Bac asking to visit POWs and acquire a POW list. Bac said maybe later. Bob Elder saw evidence of "air attacks" on hospitals. The Vietnamese wanted antibiotics and antimalarial medicines. Dr. Ton That Tung, director of Viet-Duc hospital, wanted equipment for open-heart surgery. Elder left with a list.[387] The Nixon administration approved. In October, deliveries were made and continued thereafter.[388]

There are no reports that kind and gentle Dr. Tung had performed open-heart surgery on an American POW, but he had administered lethal doses of drugs to political dissidents.[389]

THE SDS's CUBAN CONNECTION

SDS /Venceremos Aid Cuban Intelligence Operations. In early 1969, the SDS continued its contacts with Cubans inside the U.S. In March 1969, the SDS, likely Bernardine Dohrn and Arlene Eisen Bergman, made "several phone calls a day …to the (Cuban) Mission at the UN in New York"[390] On June 4, 1969 Bernardine Dohrn told Mike Klonsky she was meeting Cubans the next day.[391] A former DGI officer and defector, Gerardo Peraza, later reported (on February 26, 1982) that Julian Torres-Rizo, First Secretary of the Cuban Mission to the UN[392] was [one

---

[386] Bronson Clark 1967 and Joseph Elder, Letter to Charles Read and Martin Teitel, 20 May 1969, AFSC, Philadelphia cited in Hershberger, 134

[387] "Notes of Dr. Elder's Meeting on November 12, 1969 at Hamline University, November 12, 1969."

[388] Joseph Elder, Letter to Charles Read and Martin Teitel, 20 May 1969, AFSC, Philadelphia cited in Hershberger, 134-137.

[389] James Banerian and the Vietnamese Community Action Committee, *Losers Are Pirates: A Close Look at the PBS Series "Vietnam: A Television History,"* Phoenix: Tieng Me Publications, 1984, 22.

[390] Georgie Anne Geyer and Keyes Beech, "Cuba: School for US Radicals," *Chicago Sun Times*, October 1970 cited in FBI, FOIA, Weather Underground. The primary source is Acting SAC Chicago to Director, memo, "Foreign Influence-Weather Underground Organization," August 20, 1976, 42.

[391] Georgie Anne Geyer and Keyes Beech, "Cuba: School ….," 141.

[392] James L. Tyson, Target America: The Influence of Communist Propaganda on U.S. Media, 46-47.

of a succession of] DGI control officer(s) for the Venceremos Brigadiers, the Weathermen, and the Puerto Rican F.A.L.N.[393] "Under control of Cuban Intelligence Operatives," a Cuban defector said, "the Venceremos Brigade brought the first great quantity of information [intelligence] through American citizens that was obtained in the U.S."[394]

SDS WEATHERMEN STATEMENT.

Action Faction—You Don't Need a Weatherman--June 18-22, 1969. On June 18, 1969, the "Action faction" of SDS issued an ideological treatise in SDS's *New Left Notes* concluding: "You don't need a weatherman to know which way the wind blows,"[395] a line from *Bob Dylan*'s "Subterranean Homesick Blues." The Weathermen were born. **SDS Joins Viet Cong**. The statement was the seminal position paper for the Weathermen faction at the SDS convention of June 18-22, 1969 in Chicago. The Weatherman paper said "the Vietnamese are winning…[and] Vietnam heightens the possibilities for struggle here" (in USA.) To do so required a "united anti-imperialism movement. Because war is political, political tasks—the international communist revolution—must guide it." An SDS resolution planning a November 8th movement, "The current struggle of the Vietnamese people for self-determination is the vanguard struggle against US imperialist." Following the lead of the NLF, "Clearly, we must …launch our own Political Offensive in the United States…to isolate the imperialist war makers from the mass of the people…"[396]

Hanoi Seeks Help-U.S. Shelling Across DMZ. On June 24, 1969, Hanoi telegraphed the SDS office in Chicago objecting to artillery shelling on the DMZ and bombing of Quang Binh province and Minh Linh on June 14, 16, and 19. Hanoi asked, "Appeal you take immediate measures prevent US war AVTS demand US government stop encroachments …sovereignty. Sincere Thanks. Vietmy"[397] Quang Binh was the heavily

---

[393] *New York Times*, Oct. 10, 1977; *Rev. Lobby*, 150.
[394] Collier and Horowitz, *Destructive Generation...*, 152-3.
[395] "You Don't Need A Weatherman To Know Which Way The Wind Blows," *New Left Notes*. June 18, 1969.
http://www.antiauthoritarian.net:80/sds_wuo/weather/weatherman_document.txt The paper was signed by Karen Ashley, Bill Ayers, Bernardine Dohrn, John "J.J." Jacobs, Jeff Jones, Gerry Long, "Howie" Machtinger, Jim Mellen, Terry Robbins, Mark Rudd and Steve Tappis.
[396] November 8th Movement Planned by SDS cited at
www.speccoll.library.kent.edu/4may 70/box107/ 107f9p8.html
[397] Copy of telegram is in *New Left Notes,* Vol. 4, No. 23, June 25, 1969 and in FBI,

defended province across the DMZ in North Vietnam. Of course, units of the NVA had been violating the sovereign territories of Laos, Cambodia and South Vietnam for decades.

Many Vietnams. The Weathermen were "one division of the International Liberation Army…[and] "its battlefields are added to the many Vietnams which will dismember and dispose of US imperialism."[398] Though later denying it, in 1969 Tom Hayden was an advocate of Weathermen. In his Red Family and International Liberation School in Berkeley Tom Hayden promoted reading the Weatherman paper.[399] The Weathermen used Hayden and Stew Albert's *Firearms and Self Defense—A Handbook for Radicals, Revolutionaries, and Easy Riders*, December 1969.[400]

Hanoi Thanks SDS. On June 29 Hanoi telegraphed the SDS national office, rejoicing "at the big success at Chicago' in passing a resolution condemning Nixon. The telegram gave SDS leader Nick Egelson's "warmest greetings" for his congratulating the formation on the Provisional Revolutionary Government, PRG,[401] NFL's political front.

WORLD PEACE ASSEMBLY EAST BERLIN-- JUNE 21-23, 1969

"Find a road to a common coordinated action…without exception." June 21-23, after the May Stockholm Conference, the World Peace Assembly met in East Berlin, The World Peace Council, (WPC), invited 900 "supporters of peace." Eighteen, mostly communist Americans attended.[402]The Soviet

---

FOIA, Weather Underground. The primary source is Acting SAC Chicago to Director, memo, "Foreign Influence-Weather Underground Organization," August 20, 1976, 118. Expressing similar sentiments, but focusing upon purging the Progressive Labor Party, PLP is *New Left Notes*, Vol. 4, No. 23, June 25, 1969.

[398] FBI, FOIA, Weather Underground. The primary source is Acting SAC Chicago to Director, memo, "Foreign Influence-Weather Underground Organization," August 20, 1976, 10, 13-14, 15; H.C.I.S., *Terrorism*, p.

[399] Art Goldberg, *Bay Guardian*, 1979; *Firearms and Self Defense—A Handbook for Radicals, Revolutionaries, and Easy Riders*, December 1969, Berkeley in New Left collection Hoover Institute and copy in possession of author; See also The Red Family, [Tom Hayden and Carol Kurtz], "To Stop a Police State: The Case for Community Control of Police," Pamphlet, Berkeley, early 1971.

[400] Senate, Committee on the Judiciary, Subcommittee to Investigate the Administration of the Internal Security Act and Other Internal Security Laws, *The Weather Underground*, Committee Print, January 1975, 11.

[401] FBI, FOIA, Weather Underground. The primary source is Acting SAC Chicago to Director, memo, "Foreign Influence-Weather Underground Organization," August 20, 1976, 119.

[402] Dick Gregory; Stanley Faulkner (NLG); Valeri Mitchell (Peace Action, Los Angeles); Sonia Karose (American-Russian Institute); Estelle Cypher (WSP); Susan

82

controlled WPC paid for the tickets.[403] The Americans stated, "Forces for peace must mobilize...to end the war in Vietnam." It praised, "The courage of our [North] Vietnamese friends (who)... are manning humanities front line in the defense...of the cause of human freedom." The Americans delegates demanded "unconditional and total withdrawal."[404]

Soviet Instructions, Unite, Coordinate. The foreign communists encouraged coordination of fall activities of Vietnamese and National Mobe/New Mobe. Soviet leaders Leonid Brezhnev and Alexei Kosygin sent messages. Alexia Kosygin stressed, "Mass actions of peace supporters and...various anti-war movements have achieved...results in the struggle to thwart the aggressive plans of the imperialist circles."[405] The Soviet delegate, E.K. Federov urged, "find a road to a common coordinated action of all movements...without exception."[406]

Irving Sarnoff. Irving Sarnoff, spearheading New Mobe, condemned America in great detail, but declared Vietnam was the key issue, "Our task...is to broaden and unify the anti-war movement" (to) ...to include...many organized groups...We struggle against a common enemy..."[407] Still later in July, Irving Sarnoff, privately met North Vietnam's Nguyen Minh Vy and Vietcong's Nguyen Thi Binh to plan the fall demonstrations.

CLEVELAND AREA PEACE ACTION, JULY 5-9, 1969. With a long, A-F to-do list from the May 1969 meeting at the Stockholm Conference and the June World Peace Council meeting in East Berlin, antiwar planning moved in July to Cleveland, Ohio. In May, Jerry Gordon of Cleveland Area Peace

---

Borenstein (DuBois and Venceremos); Karen B. Ackerman (DuBois and Venceremos); Herbert Aptheker (CPUSA); Barbara Bick (CPUSA); Mary Clarke (WSP); Martin Hall (CPUSA), Jarvis Tyner (CPUSA/YWLL); Irving Sarnoff (National Mobe, CPUSA); Mary Angie Dickerson, (CPUSA); Eleanor Ohman (Peace Action, San Francisco); Pauline Rosen (WSP, CPUSA); and Carlton Goodlett, (CPUSA and National Mobe). "Provisional List of Participants," World Peace Assembly, June 21-24, 1969, 78 cited in HISC, Staff Study, 1970, 30.
[403] 20 [Soviet] Aeroflot tickets from New York to East Berlin for Angie Dickerson, three for Carlton Goodlett, one for Herbert Aptheker and two KLM-LOT tickets for comedian-activist Dick Gregory. HISC, Staff Report, 1970, 30-31; House, *Subversive...New Mobilization...* 1970, 31, cited in Rothrock, 112N59.
[404] HISC, Staff Study, 1970, 31.
[405] House, *Subversive...New Mobilization...* 1970, pp.30-31, cited in Rothrock, 111N58.
[406] House, *Subversive...New Mobilization...* 1970, 30, cited in Rothrock, 111N57.
[407] HISC, Staff Study, 1970, 33-4.

Action Council, a Socialist Workers Party spokesman, cast a wide net of invitations for an who's who in peace movement to come to Case Western Reserve University in Cleveland, July 4-5, 1969 intending to disrupt competing Cleveland events of National Mobe. The invited were many communists of contending stripes—all favoring a Viet Cong victory. Initiating sponsors of the Cleveland meeting were many top antiwar activists.[408] Many others attended came from groups all over the nation.[409]

NEW MOBE REPLACES NATIONAL MOBE

New Mobe Actions Planning Viet Cong Victory: Cleveland. In Cleveland Sidney Peck led[410] the Cleveland Peace Conference also known as the National Anti-War Conference.[411] There were well over a hundred identified[412]

---

[408] Norma Becker, Barbara Bick, Thompson Bradley, Charles Cairnes, Stephanie Coontz, Rennie Davis, David Dellinger, Douglas Dowd, Al Evanoff, Richard Fernandez, Jerry Gordon, Robert Greenblatt, Fred Halstead, Arnold Johnson, Donald Kalish, Arthur Kinoy, Sidney Lens, Carol Lipman, John McAuliff, Stewart Meacham, Dean Pappas, Sidney Peck, Max Primack, Andrew Pulley, and Rt. Rev. Monsgr. Charles Rice, Carl Rogers, Irving Sarnoff, Ken Shilman, Dr. Benjamin Spock, Cora Weiss, Dagmar Wilson and Prof. Howard Zinn.

[409] Of the 600-900 who attended the Cleveland meeting July 4-5, 1969 Max Friedman and another unnamed observer both compiled their own list of those attending and/or invited, both lists combined here. Others invited were Joe Aber, Rev. Ralph Abernathy, Larry Austin, Bill Ayers, Prof. Rev. Henry Bass, Prof. James Beck, Norman Becker, Kathy Beird, Fr. Phillip Berrigan, Barbara Bick, Al Bilik, Dave Bliss, Abe Bloom, Francis Boardman, Eleanor Bockman, Syn Bockman, Julian Bond, Paul Booth, Kathy Boudin, Al Brick, David Brown, Brenda Brdr, David Brown, Prof. McAfee Browne, John Browne, Prof. Robert S. Browne, Gloria Browning, Al Budka, Julian Bulley Andy Bustin, Debbie Bustin, William Caraway Ceaser [sic] Chavez, Barbara Chis, Prof. Noam Chomsky, Wm. Sloan Coffin, Ruth Gage-Colby, Nancy Collison (AFSC), William Davidon, Barbara Deming, Steven Deutch, Jim Dill, Donald Duncan, Robert Eaton, Ralph Featherstone Abe Feinglass, Leo Fenster, W.H. Ferry, James Forman, Michael Galizan, Harold Gibbons, Allen Ginsburg, Corky Gonzales, Patrick Gorman, Jerry Grossman, Mrs. Gurewitz, James Hansen, Charles Hayes, Prof. David Herreshoff, Russell Johnson, Prof. Arnold Kaufman, *Rampart*'s Edward Keating, Charlie Kimball, Evelyn Knapp, Clark Lowenstein, Bradford Lyttle, Eric Mann, Naomi Marcus, Sharon Naimon, Otto Nathan, Rev. Richard Neuhaus, John Oster, Oleg Penn, Britt or Nan Prendergast, Mark Raskin, Cleveland Robinson, Frank Rosenblum, Dr. Robert Rutman, Robert Scheer, Mulford Q. Sibley, Jane Silverman Michael Smith, Jack Spiegel, Morris Starsky, Amy Swedlow, Ethyl Taylor, Prof. Arthur Tuden, Anne Utterman, Rev. Richard Venus, Mary Walter, Robert Zelner.

[410] Cleveland Area Peace Action Council, "Call to a National Anti-War Conference, Cleveland, Ohio, July 4 & 5, 1969; Biographical Data on New Mobilization Co-Chairmen, 4.

[411] *Extent of Subversion in Campus Disorders*, Testimony of Max Phillip Friedman, Hearings before the Subcommittee to Investigate the Administration of the Internal Security Act and other Internal Security Laws of the Committee of the Judiciary, United States Senate, 91st Cong., 1st Sess., Part 2, August 12, 1969, 90.

[412] Peter Camejo, Bill Caraway, Margie Culver, Tony Cummins, Betsy Davis, Rennie Davis, Dave Dellinger, Ted Dostal, Douglas Dowd, Dave Edwards, Pam Edwards,

attendees. There National Mobe leaders reformed into the New Mobilization to End the War in Vietnam. The New Mobe included old leftists, Communists of all stripes,[413] new left friends and associates Rennie Davis, Dave Dellinger, Cora Weiss, and many others.[414] The cochairmen of New Mobe were David Dellinger, Douglas Dowd, Terrance Hallinan, Donald

---

Howie Emmers, Jim Estes, Al Evanoff, Linda Evans, Abe Feinglass, Leo Fenster, Richard Fernandez, Clive Fetzer, Richard Finkel, Ishmael Flory, Irv Fox, Phil Friedman, Bob Galayda, Dave Gass, Stephanie Gass, Gene Gladstone, Gene Glasgo, Lynn Glixon, Jerry Gordon, Eric Greenberg, Robert Greenblatt, Don Gurewitz, Helen Gurewitz, Fred Halstead, Bill Harraway, Sue Hathaway, David Hawk, James Harris, Sari Herzig, Bill Hillenbrand, Terry Hillman, Paul Hoffman, Gus Horowitz, Don Ingerson, Ron Jamison, Lew Jones, Arnold Johnson, Donald Kalish, Chuck Kanavan, Charlie Kimball, Herman Kirsch, Max Kirsch, Molly Kirsch, Sandy Knoll, Bob Kos, Sylvia Kushner, Roberta Lee, Kathy Levine, Nick Lindan, Carol Lipman, Sidney Lens, Ilene Lock, Dave Maristock, John McAuliff, Bernie McLaughlin, Stewart Meacham, Bob Meers, Ralph Meister, Al Meyers, Joe Miles, Tom Moore, Norman Oliver, Louise Peck, Sandy Peck, Sidney Peck, Robert Pinkerton, Claudette Piper, Earl Price, Roger Priest, Maxwell Primack, Andrew Pulley, Harry Reems, Dr. Richard Recknagle, Betsy Reeves, Brother Rice, Jacqueline Rice, Harry Ring, Mike Robbins, Terry Robins, Mr/Mrs Stuart Robinson, Carl Rogers, Nancy Rozman, Marty Rudenstein, Roger Rudenstein, Mark Rudd, Arnie Schwartz, Bob Schwartz, Irving Sarnoff, Doug Seaton, Jane Silverman, James Smid, Bobbie Smith, Ed Smith, Mike Smith, James Smith, Jack Spiegel, Syn Stapleton, Martha Stillman, Dan Stryon, Jim Susyanski, Andrew St. Laurent, Peggy Swingle, Tony Thomas, Jeannette Tracy, Carol Travis, Sue Tryon, Anne Utterman, Ron Walden, Ted Walker, Charlotte Weeks, Marty Weinstein, Cora Weiss, Abe Weisburd, Prof. Robert H. Whealey, Paul White, Steve Wilcox, John Wilson, Mike Wolpert, Dan Wood, LeRoy Wolins, Dave Wulp, Ted Yanow, Ron Young, Elvie Zell, and Paul Zinsel; Extent of Subversion in Campus Disorders, Testimony of Max Phillip Friedman, Hearings before the Subcommittee to Investigate the Administration of the Internal Security Act and other Internal Security Laws of the Committee of the Judiciary, United States Senate, 91st Cong., 1st Sess., Part 2, August 12, 1969, 126-128 (Friedman) 153-154 (observer).

[413] House, Subversive Involvement in the Origin, Leadership, and Activities of the New Mobilization Committee to End the War in Vietnam and its Predecessor Organizations, staff study by Committee on Internal Security, 91st Cong., 2nd sess., VII, Texas Tech cited in Rothrock, 108N52; "Student in Peace Groups Repeats Red Charges," Sunday (Washington) Star, October 26, 1969, a news clip from Max Friedman to author.

[414] Norman Becker, Irving Beinin, Barbara Bick, Abe Bloom, Irwin Bock, Allan Brick, Balfour Brickner, Katherine Camp, Marjorie Colvin, Bill Davidon, Tom Cornell, Rennie Davis, Gerhard Elston, Al Evanoff, Myrtle Feigenburg, Richard Fernandez, Gene Gladstone, Jerry Gordon, Bob Green, Robert Greenblatt, Robert Haskell, Dave Hawk, Dave Herrseshoff, Betty Johns, James A. Johnson, Gloria Karp, Sylvia Kushner, Brad Lyttle, John McAuliff, Joe Miles, Joseph Miller, Allan Myers, Otto Nathan, Ann Peery, Max Primack, Carl Rogers, Irving Sarnoff, Lawrence Scott, Arthur Waskow, John Wilson, Peter Yarrow and Ron Young. Letter sent with August 21, 1969 edition of Student Mobilizer, and July 4-5 National Antiwar Conference Steering Committee, both at Extent of Subversion in Campus Disorders, Testimony of Max Phillip Friedman, Hearings before the Subcommittee to Investigate the Administration of the Internal Security Act and other Internal Security Laws of the Committee of the Judiciary, United States Senate, 91st Cong., 1st Sess., Part 2, August 12, 1969, 101-2; New Mobe letterhead, Steering Committee (in Formation) at Combat, Vol. 1, No. 30, November 15, 1969; New Mobilization, letterhead, "1969: No Christmas As Usual."

Kalish, Sidney Lens, Stewart Meacham, Sidney Peck and Cora Weiss.[415] New Mobe's steering committee were communist[416] or SDS revolutionaries[417] Many Mobe leaders and other active members had past and future contacts with the Vietnamese Communists, e.g. Ayers, Cornell, Davis, Dellinger, Evans, Fernandez, Greenblatt, McAuliff, Meacham, Rudd, Sarnoff, Weiss. Other members were in various peace movement organizations most supporting unilateral withdrawal.

United Peace Front. A Student Mobilization flyer conformed to Soviet advice saying, "The National Antiwar Conference on July 4-5 achieved an important unity in the antiwar movement... (A mass march)...can involve sections of the population not previously organized"[418] Fred Halstead, Sidney Lens and Sidney Peck[419] kept the Cleveland conference from splitting between various leftist factions, including an attempted Socialist Workers Party take-over of the convention. Perhaps following advice from comrades in Stockholm and East Berlin conferences,

The antiwar movement has every possibility of transforming itself from a movement of dissenting activists to a mass social force...We must plan...on action which the mass of people can identify with...This action is the way for every citizen opposed to the war to make his voice heard."[420]

The Conference endorsed the Moratorium in October and a Death March in Washington in November. New Mobe planned for fall 1969 activities to show support for communist negotiators in Paris, not President Nixon. [421]

---

[415] New Mobilization, letterhead, "1969: No Christmas As Usual."

[416] Arnold Johnson, CPUSA, and SWP/YSA members, Fred Halstead, Gus Horowitz, Carol Lipman and Larry Siegel. Senate, Committee on the Judiciary, Subcommittee to Investigate the Administration of the Internal Security Act and Other Internal Security Laws, *The Weather Underground*, Committee Print, January 1975, 17.

[417] SDS delegates were Bill Ayers, Linda Evans, Terry Robbins, and Mark Rudd. House, Subversive Involvement in the Origin, Leadership, and Activities of the New Mobilization Committee to End the War in Vietnam and its Predecessor Organizations, staff study by Committee on Internal Security, 91st Cong., 2nd sess., VII, Texas Tech cited in Rothrock, 108N52; "Student in Peace Groups Repeats Red Charges," Sunday (Washington) Star, October 26, 1969, a news clip from Max Friedman to author.

[418] Student Mobilization, printed flyer, "Join the Fall Antiwar Offensive," n.d. fall 1969.

[419] *Cleveland Plain Dealer*, July 5, 1969, A-4.

[420] Senate, *Extent of Subversion in Campus Disorders*: Hearing before the Subcommittee to Investigate Security Act and Other Internal Security Laws, Committee on Judiciary, 91st Cong., 1st sess., 1969, 134-6.

[421] *Combat*, Vol. 1, No. 30, November 15, 1969

Representing New Mobe, National Action Group, the Moratorium and the Weathermen respectively, Irving Sarnoff, Stewart Meacham, David Hawk, and Mark Rudd each spoke in turn on various plans for protests.[422]

The New Mobe concentrated on two key events--a cooperative event with Sam Brown and Hawk's national "Moratorium" on October 15, 1969 and a New Mobilization "March on Washington" on November 15, 1969. Both events reflected the coordination of overt "mass actions of peace supporters" which the Soviets had advised in Moscow, Stockholm and in East Berlin in May and June.

New Mobe immediately got work on its November event.[423]

Communist Front? Was New Mobe following advice given it in Stockholm and East Berlin and instructions given in captured Viet Cong Circular 4 and Directive 96? It seemed so. A House committee discovered that New Mobe members had actively participated in the Soviet-controlled and financed World Peace Council, the Stockholm Conference on Vietnam and the World Peace Assembly. Max Friedman who had infiltrated the Washington Mobe and attended the Cleveland meeting told a Senate Subcommittee on internal security, "The overall peace movement in the United States has become a Communist front organization." Senator Paul J. Fannin (R-Az) said, some 900 "Communists, well-known Communist sympathizers" met.[424]

New Mobe dismissively mocked such claims, "We met together, planned together, worked together. We have crossed many state lines and we have talked with many people. …We conspired—literally breathed together—to engage in peaceful protest against U.S. aggression in Vietnam. …If this be

---

[422] August in California, Labor Day demonstrations in Washington, October and SDS protests in Chicago and in September school and business "moratoriums" respectively.
[423] Directing the planned November 15 demonstration were Abe Bloom, Sidney Peck, Stewart Meacham, Bunny Knopp and Ron Young. Hired staff for the Washington Action Committee was Steve Wilcox, Don Gurewitz, and Trudy Young. Sidney Peck and Steve Wilcox soon flew off to San Francisco to appoint cadre for San Francisco protests on November 15: Berkeley City Councilman and future Congressman Ronald Dellums, DuBois member Terence Hallinan, SWP member Marjorie Colvin, CPUSA member Irving Sarnoff, peace activist Louise Lovett and Rev. Bryan Drolet. Senate, Extent of Subversion in Campus Disorders: Hearing before the Subcommittee to Investigate Security Act and Other Internal Security Laws, Committee on Judiciary, 91st Cong., 1st sess., 1969, 137; New Mobilization, letter and petition to Attorney General John Mitchell, November 19, 1969.
[424] "Behind the Coming 'March on Washington," *U.S. News & World Report*, Nov. 3, 1969.

87

conspiracy, let the Justice Department make the most of it."[425] Perhaps taking up the public challenge the government wiretapped some members of the peace movement cheering for a Hanoi military victory.[426]

Open Support of Viet Cong. Sidney Peck, former CPUSA member and New Mobe co-chairman said, "We want the complete and total withdrawal of American forces from Vietnam. If that results in a victory for the National Liberation Front we are pleased...." Professor Doug Dowd said, "If there had to be a side...we would be on the other side."[427] A workshop on Washington actions supported U.S. troop withdrawal and the Viet Cong.[428]

Max Phillip Friedman, an undercover volunteer for the Washington Mobilization Committee, told a Senate Committee in mid-October "that the Communists have completely and utterly taken over the peace movements in the United States." Friedman said the role of seven Communists and others was covert, but coincided with the interests of communism.[429]

Communists Sign the Checks and Leases. Besides being the prime organizers, additional domestic Communists were also taking care of office space. Irving Sarnoff's Peace Action Council provided New Mobe office space in Los Angeles and a $1,000 loan.[430] August- December 1969, Carol Lipman, Trotskyite SWP, joined the New Mobe in signing leases for office space at 1029 Vermont Ave NW, Washington, D.C. for the Student Mobilization Committee to End the War in Vietnam.[431] CPUSA members or their associates, Abe Bloom (CP), Sid Peck (CP), and Brad Lyttle (WRL, and a pro-Marxist activist supporting CP fronts[432]) signed checks of both the New

---

[425] New Mobilization, letter and petition to Attorney General John Mitchell, November 19, 1969.

[426] Church committee final report.

[427] House, Subversive...New Mobilization, 1970 VII cited in Rothrock, 109N54.

[428] *Extent of Subversion in Campus Disorders,* Testimony of Max Phillip Friedman, Hearings before the Subcommittee to Investigate the Administration of the Internal Security Act and other Internal Security Laws of the Committee of the Judiciary, United States Senate, 91st Cong., 1st Sess., Part 2, August 12, 1969, 121-2.

[429] "Student in Peace Groups Repeats Red Charges," *Sunday (Washington) Star,* October 26, 1969, a news clip from Max Friedman to author.

[430] Senate, State of California, Fifteenth Report of the Senate Fact-Finding Subcommittee on Un-American Activities, Sacramento, CA, 1970, 31.

[431] *National Peace Action Coalition, NPAC and People's Coalition for Peace and Justice, PCPJ,* Part I, Hearing, Committee on Internal Security, House of Representatives, 92nd Cong, 1 Sess., May 18-21, 1971. Washington, D.C., 1782-84. US Government Printing Office $1.75.

Mobe and later the People's Coalition for Peace and Justice, PCPJ.[433] July 1969-late February 1970, Abe Bloom, CPUSA, signed leases for the New Mobe at 1029 Vermont Ave NW.[434]

Americans Meet Viet Cong in Canada.

On July 7, 1969 the Canadian Voice for Women invited American women, members of WSP, Cora Weiss, Mia Adjali, Carol Andreas, Willis Hardy, and Dorothy Hayes, to meet delegates of Hanoi and the NLF.[435] The Canadians arranged a Vietnamese speaking tour during June and July and arranged other meetings with American women at the border.[436]

---

[432] A Brad, different spelling, Lytell was a fundraiser for the CPUSA's official newspaper, the *Daily World* in December 1974.

[433] http://www.wintersoldier.com/staticpages/index.php?page=KGBKerry

[434] *National Peace Action Coalition, NPAC and People's Coalition for Peace and Justice, PCPJ*, Part I, Hearing, Committee on Internal Security, House of Representatives, 92nd Cong., 1st sess., May 18-21, 1971. Washington, D.C., 1782-84. US Government Printing Office $1.75.

[435] HISC, Staff Study, Subversive Involvement in the Origin, Leadership and Activities of the New Mobilization Committee to End the War in Vietnam And Its Predecessor Organizations, 1970, XII-XIII.

[436] "Vietnamese Women Visit Canada," (July 1969) Voice of Women Records, SCPC; CVW Website, "Our History," http://home.ca. inter.net/ ~vow/history.htm; Papers of Cora Weiss, http://www.swarthmore.edu/library/peace/DG201-225/dg222cweiss.htm .

Chapter 4. Action Factions: SDS, Cubans and Moritorium.

SDS WEATHERMEN MEETS VIETNAMESE IN CUBA, JULY 9-15.

One month after the SDS convention of June 18-22, 1969 the Vietnamese invited select SDS members to meet them in Cuba. Assisted in part by a $1,500 grant from Wennergren Foundation, a reliably revolutionary SDS delegation (and a Latino delegation) of 34 persons traveled to Havana via plane from Mexico[437] Beginning in early July, they spent "five weeks in Cuba, two of them meeting and traveling around with the Vietnamese," according to the *New Left Notes*.[438]A printed program for July 9-15 sparsely outlined "reports by North American and Vietnamese delegations," reception by Hoang Bich Son of PRG, reading of papers, small group discussions, "showing of North American...South Viet Nam NLF ...Democratic Republic of Viet Nam films."[439]

Committed cadre had multiple educational opportunities. They traveled to *Cuba* to meet representatives of the enemy in war to discuss strategy for winning the war.

Little Sugar Cane. No cutters of sugar cane, no Peace Corp volunteers. They were *machetismos* of a special sort. Corky Benedict told FBI informer Larry Grathwohl that he received training in propaganda, firearms and explosives in Cuba. Naomi Jaffe told Grathwohl that she received such training in North Korea as well as Cuba.[440] Peter Clapp, an SDS organizer at Western Michigan claimed that summer he was taught "revolutionary tactics, a la Fidel Castro style. We got instructions from Cuba."[441] They met with Cuban and Soviet officials, but they were most impressed by the North Vietnamese

---

[437] Senate, Committee on the Judiciary, Subcommittee to Investigate the Administration of the Internal Security Act and Other Internal Security Laws, *The Weather Underground*, Committee Print, January 1975, 59.

[438] *New Left Notes*, August 29, 1969 cited in "The Weather Underground Organization," *Information Digest,* Vol. XIV, #22, November 13, 1981, 339, 341.

[439] Senate, Committee on the Judiciary, Subcommittee to Investigate the Administration of the Internal Security Act and Other Internal Security Laws, *The Weather Underground*, Committee Print, January 1975, 139-140.

[440] Larry Grathwohl testimony before Subcommittee to Investigate the Administration of the Internal Security Act and Other Internal Security Laws of the Committee on the Judiciary, U.S. Senate, *Terrorist Activity Inside the Weatherman Movement*, 93rd Cong., 2nd Sess., Part 2, October 18, 1974, 108-9.

[441] *Western Herald*, September 19, 1969, 1.

and the new PRG of South Vietnam. The Vietnamese communists had a delegation of over fifteen.[442] Americans were nearly fifty.[443] Hanoi's clearest message was "[T]hey had the job of building the American Movement to the point where it could put invincible pressure upon the U. S. government to withdraw.[444] The meetings mapped an "antiwar campaign during an eight-day seminar with representatives of Hanoi and the Viet Cong"[445] They also discussed building a revolutionary movement in the USA to "kick ass."

Dohrn Notes: July 9-15, 1969,
Reveal Full Hanoi Indoctrination. Viets Winning, US Losing.

Bernardine Dohrn's notes show that on July 9, Nguyen Thai said the war strained U.S. military morale. U.S. troops were "not trained for close-in fighting." Van Trong, said the people of South Vietnam support the "anger of public opinion in U.S."[446] Fidel Castro said the U.S.A could not win in Vietnam. **Importance of Antiwar Movement to Hanoi.** The Vietnamese said their strategy had three fronts—Vietnam, Paris and the United States.[447] The decisive role was to be the antiwar

---

[442] From Viet Cong south came Le Thi Tranh Tra, Doan Chau Tranh, Nguyen Thi Quy, Hoang Van Dinh, Dinh Thi Tru, Nguyen Phuc, and Pham Van Chuong. From North Vietnam came Nguyen Van Trong, Vu Quang Chuyen, Nguyen Thai Tran Duc Tien, Ngo Qui Du, Le Tuan, Dao Cong Doan, Nguyen Thi Van, Le Thanh, Van Trong, and Le Thi Thanh Mai. See: Ron Koziol, Chicago *Tribune*, April 27, 1970 in Senate, Committee on the Judiciary, Subcommittee to Investigate the Administration of the Internal Security Act and Other Internal Security Laws, *The Weather Underground*, Committee Print, January 1975, 27, 138, 141.

[443] The SDS group included Carlos Antonio Aponte, Robert Jay Barano, Christopher Kit Bakke, Thomas Wilson Bell, Edward "Corky" Benedict, Kathie Boudin, Cristina Bristol, Aubrey Brown, Robert Burlingham, George Cavalletto, Peter Clapp, Luis John Cuza, Lucas Daumont, Carl Alfred Davidson, Dianne Donghi, Bernardine Dohrn, Diane Westbrook Faber, Richard Rees Fagen, Ted Gold, Kenneth Alan Hechter, Frank Petras James, Nino Jeronimo, Gregory, Nina, Saul Irwin and Valerie Landau, Sandra Hale Levinson, Gerald "Jerry" William Long, Robert Schenk Love, Beth Susan Lyons, John "Shorty" Marquez, Albert Martinez, Howard Jeff Melish, David Millstone, Robert Edward Norton, Orlando Ortiz, Diana Oughton, Rose Paul, Verna Elinor Richey Pedrin, Jesus Maria Ramirez, Jose Ramirez, Eleanor Raskin, Patricia Ellen Shea, Jane Spielman, Jeronomi Ulpiano, Joanne Washington, Robert Wetzler, Myra Ann Wood, and Mary Woznich-- less Oglesby.

[444] Kirkpatrick Sale, *SDS*, 414, 593

[445] Georgie Anne Geyer and Keyes Beech, "Cuba: School for US Radicals," Chicago Sun Times, October 1970; Ron Jacobs, *The Way The Wind Blew: A History Of The Weather Underground* Verso, 1997, 28.

[446] Senate, Committee on the Judiciary, Subcommittee to Investigate the Administration of the Internal Security Act and Other Internal Security Laws, *The Weather Underground*, Committee Print, January 1975, 143-146

[447] Carl Davidson, *Guardian*, August 30, 1969 cited in FBI, FOIA, Weather Underground. The primary source is Acting SAC Chicago to Director, memo, "Foreign Influence-Weather Underground Organization," August 20, 1976, 99.

movement in the United States.[448] Van Trong recommended the lessons of French resistance. Use progressive journals, "go deep" into all forms of mass organizations and keep slogans understandable to promote unity. On July 13, Dohrn's notes again show Vietnamese concern for coordination of antiwar groups among themselves. On July 14-15, her notes outline Viet Cong concerns about GI's, their motivation, morale and involvement in antiwar movement and the objective of "work w/GIs" to "weaken the enemy."[449]

Status of Propaganda War in USA? Van Trong, DRV wanted to know the current status of American popular opinion. Did the American people think that withdrawal was surrender?

SDS Weatherman Assignment: "kick ass." Huynh Van Ba of the PRG delegation, said, "When you go into a city, look for the person who fights the hardest against the cops."[450] He said, "You must begin to wage armed struggle as soon as possible to become the vanguard and take leadership of the revolution"

Rings and Accolades. The "Americans" were given "rings forged from salvaged metal stripped off American fighter aircraft."[451] Nguyen Thai who impressed Eleanor Stein Raskin so much she named her and Jeff Jones' son Thai Jones.[452] Fonda and Hayden would follow with a son named Troi. Homebound on the Cuba freighter, Manuel Ascunce, there was much talk of "kicking ass." Ted Gold soon wrote, "defeat in Vietnam will be a vital blow" and do "decisive damage to the U.S. ruling class's plans to…expand its world rule."[453]

WHAT IS TO BE DONE?

Debriefing SDS Cadre: Caution or Revolution? Bill Ayers debriefed the returning July 1969 hardcore group, Dohrn, Gold, Oughton, Donghi and Raskin, upon their arrival

---

[448] Carl Davidson, *Guardian*, August 30, 1969 cited in FBI, FOIA, Weather Underground. p. 99.

[449] Senate, Committee on the Judiciary, Subcommittee to Investigate the Administration of the Internal Security Act and Other Internal Security Laws, *The Weather Underground*, Committee Print, January 1975, 145-146.

[450] *New Left Notes*, August 29, 1969 cited in "The Weather Underground Organization," *Information Digest*, Vol. XIV, #22, November 13, 1981, 339.

[451] Peter Collier and David Horowitz, *Destructive Generation, Second Thoughts about the '60s,* 82-83.

[452] Juliet Wittman, "Memoirs: Radical parents, Red shoes and a poet up close and personal," *Washington Post*, November 21, 2004, BW13.

[453] Carl Davidson, *Guardian*, August 30, 1969 cited in FBI, FOIA, Weather Underground. The primary source is Acting SAC Chicago to Director, memo, "Foreign Influence-Weather Underground Organization," August 20, 1976, 100-1.

at St. John, New Brunswick, Canada on August 16th.[454] They "exchanged views on strategies and tactics for ending the war...."[455] Mark Rudd remembers Bernardine Dohrn saying the Vietnamese "To convince the Americans to withdraw, the antiwar movement... had to become even broader...The Vietnamese need unity of the American antiwar forces to end the war."[456]

Press conference: U.S. Losing. On August 19, 1969 at Diplomat Hotel in New York, the SDS-- Kathy Boudin, Bernardine Dohrn, Ted Gold, Dionne Donghi, Jeff Melish and Eleanor Raskin released a statement, *"Quyet Chien Quyet Thang* (Dare to Struggle, Dare to Win).... They said, "...United States imperialism is being completely defeated in Vietnam. ...[457]

SDS Cadre Following Instructions from Cuba. Reporters Georgie Anne Geyer and Keyes Beech say Castro provided "Hanoi with a base where their agents could link up with sympathetic Americans." The Americans "were instructed to organize more antiwar demonstrations, emphasize...American casualties,...planes shot down and the high cost of the war." Huynh Van Ba gave the "orders" to disrupt the U.S. military with draft resistance and agitation inside the active duty armed forces. Ba also counseled not to use the word communism, it was always avoided in the early stages of a revolution. Mention instead free health care. Clearly Hanoi had found "ready-made collaborators in the young American radicals" in their efforts to "exploit (antiwar) dissent" in the "battlefield for the 'hearts and minds' of the American people." And "more and more Americans returned from Cuba proudly wearing rings made from the metal of U.S, planes shot down over Vietnam."[458]

---

[454] FBI, FOIA, Weather Underground. The primary source is Acting SAC Chicago to Director, memo, "Foreign Influence-Weather Underground Organization," August 20, 1976, 188.

[455] Bill Ayers, *Fugitive Days*, 158, 160-61; FBI, FOIA, Weather Underground. The primary source is Acting SAC Chicago to Director, memo, "Foreign Influence-Weather Underground Organization," August 20, 1976, 188.

[456] Mark Rudd, *Underground: My Life With the SDS and the Weathermen*, New York: Harper Collins, 2009, 167-8.

[457] FBI, FOIA, Weather Underground. The primary source is Acting SAC Chicago to Director, memo, "Foreign Influence-Weather Underground Organization," August 20, 1976, 108.

[458] Georgie Anne Geyer and Keyes Beech, "Cuba: School for US Radicals," *Chicago Sun Times*, October 1970 cited in FBI, FOIA, Weather Underground. The primary

BUILDING THE VENCEREMOS BRIGADES

Revolutionary Cadre: Accepting Applications for Venceremos brigade. After July, Julie Nichamin was the organizational genius of the new Venceremos brigade. Dave Dellinger, an old Cuban hand in the Fair Play for Cuba Committee, later became "a principal spokesman and a prime organizer"[459] of the brigades.

Nationwide Organization and Recruitment. After training in Cuba from January through April 1969 in training in Cuba,[460] Julie Nichamin divided the U.S. into eight and later fifteen regions[461] for serious and systematic nationwide recruitment for late November 1969 - February 1970. Recruitment took most of 1969. On July 29 at the University of Oregon Bill Ayers told applicants to contact either the SDS national office or Bill Thomas of Portland.[462] Radio Havana named Arlene Bergman, Mike Klonsky, Gerald Long and Dianna Oughton to whom applicants could apply.[463]

Only Revolutionaries May Apply:
Street fighters, Marxist-Leninists

Not everyone was worthy of recruitment to Venceremos groups. A public recruitment poster, headlined – "Venceremos Brigade Cuba...," said, "The youth made the revolution and the youth will keep it and youth will go on making the revolution throughout Latin America and the world."[464] Contemporary internal Venceremos documents specify the Brigades were for

---

source is Acting SAC Chicago to Director, memo, "Foreign Influence-Weather Underground Organization," August 20, 1976, 101-104.

[459] Eastland, 7463.

[460] FBI, FOIA, Weather Underground. The primary source is Acting SAC Chicago to Director, memo, "Foreign Influence-Weather Underground Organization," August 20, 1976, 120.

[461] The first regional leaders were Nichamin, Diana Oughton, John Butney (phonetic) Bruce Goldberg, Brian Murphy, Bill Thomas, Bill Drew, Phoebe Hirsch, Jerry Long. From Havana, the Cuban Communist Party organ, *Granma*, also credited Arlene Bergman of The Movement; Allen Young of Liberation News Service; Jerry Long of Chicago Newsreel; John McAuliff of Committee of Returned [Peace Corps] Volunteers; Al Martinent of La Raza; Dave Dellinger of Liberation magazine; the Black Panther Party and the Revolutionary Union Movement. "Vietnam Supplement," SDS, *New Left Notes*, 1969, cited in Gannon, *A Biographical Dictionary of the Left*, [1969-1973] Belmont (Mass.): Western Islands, Vol. II, 245.

[462] FOIA, FBI, Weather Underground, Vol. II, Section IV, Individuals, Present WUO Members, William Charles Ayers.

[463] Senate, Committee on the Judiciary, Subcommittee to Investigate the Administration of the Internal Security Act and Other Internal Security Laws, *The Weather Underground*, Committee Print, January 1975, 48.

[464] Copy of Venceremos recruitment brochure is in the New Left archives at Hoover Institute at Stanford University.

serious revolutionaries only. The Venceremos visits to Cuba were for " Marxist-Leninists …for …revolutionary action within the United States."[465] The Venceremos Brigade was "prepar[ing] for revolution in America."[466] The application materials for the Venceremos Brigade refers to Cuba as " …building...the new man." Pamphlets sought "people who are involved in … the progressive movement ... [or] social change."[467] **Closely Vetted Applicants.** Applicants were warned the work would be hard, drugs forbidden, and married couples separated. Persons with poor health need not apply. All applicants apparently received background checks."[468] Venceremos brigade conducted interviews in Oakland where "numerous individuals [were] turned down…"[469] Like Carl Oglesby, SDS leader Todd Gitlin, privately expressing reservations about parts of the Cuban Revolution, was rejected.[470]

FBI Concerned, CIA Not Much. In September 1969, J. Edgar Hoover testified, "The protest activity of the new left and the SDS, under the guise of legitimate dissent, has created an insurrectionary climate…"[471] The US Attorney General approved an FBI microphone, on September 15, 1969, in a Chicago residence of the SDS.[472]

POW RELEASE-AUGUST 4, 1969

Paris and Hanoi Meetings. On July 1, 1969 Xuan Oanh cabled David Dellinger from Paris saying Hanoi would release some POW to honor July 4. Dellinger spent three days with Xuan Oanh, Col. Ha Van Lau and Madame Nguyen Thi Binh and returned to New York to round up an American team of seven[473] led by Bratislava, Hanoi, and Democratic Convention

---

[465] H.C.I.S., *Annual Report*, 1972, H. Rpt. 93-301, June 21, 1973, 136-7; H.C.I.S. *Terrorism*, August 1974, 58, 216.

[466] Venceremos (mimeographed) *Newsletter*, No. 1, January 1974, 2.

[467] February 1976 pamphlet cited by Hollander, *Political Pilgrims*, 228 N 19.

[468] Denver, Memo, "VVAW National Steering Committee Meeting, Denver, Colorado, February 18-21, 1972 Internal Security-new Left," March 17, 1972, 9.

[469] *State Secrets*, 150, cites an FBI memo on its investigation of one person. A full FBI report on Venceremos is: FBI, *The Report on Foreign Influence in the Weather Underground Organization*, 20 August, 1976, 90, 120, 126, cited in both Romerstein, 23 and in Fontain, 137N28.

[470] Hollander, 231, 245, 247, 250; Ronald Radosh in Collier and Horowitz (eds.), *Second Thoughts...* 132.

[471] Rothrock, *Divided...* p. 90-91N18 cites *House Investigation of Students for a Democratic Society*, Part I-A, (Georgetown University), Hearings before the Committee on Internals Security, 91st cong., 2nd sess., 1969, 6.

[472] FBI, top Secret, Re: Surreptitious Entries, FBIHQ file 100-439045, Chicago 100-47094, 56 at FBI, FOIA, Weather Underground.

[473] Weatherman Linda Sue Evans, Newsreelers Norm Fruchter, Robert Kramer, and

veteran Rennie Davis representing the New Mobe, Fort Hood Three and SDS aligned Newsreel.[474]

Tall Tales of Destruction, Extermination and Massacres. Arriving in Hanoi on July 8, the group took a six-day jeep ride to the DMZ where they saw bombed roads and bridges (along Hanoi's supply and invasion routes). Rennie Davis claims, "Some 80% of thatched and straw houses had been demolished." Robert Kramer, Norm Fruchter, and John D. Douglas of the Newsreel collective kept three cameras rolling later producing the "People's War," a moody montage of citizen soldiers using small arms to deter invasion from the seashore, beautiful girls, and singing children. Punctuated by the sounds of gunfire, air raid sirens and voice-overs of Ho Chi Minh, the "People's War," declared Vietnamese commitment to democracy and peace while fluent English speakers claimed America was waging a war of extermination. Robert Kramer was an SDS community organizer in Newark with Tom Hayden, known to speak fondly of "heroic periods in the (Communist) party's past."[475] Rennie Davis reported a meeting with Pham Van Dong who said, Hanoi's two goals were total victory and high U.S. casualties—killing many Americans.[476] There is no record that Davis or anyone objected to killing more Americans.

POW Releases: Hegdahl, Fishman and Rumble. After a "lavish farewell party" with plenty of rice liquor,[477] August 4 1969, Hanoi made their fourth POWs release. Mme. Bui Thi Cam said while U.S. imperialists had "Massacred...women, children and old folks,"[478] the POWs had been treated humanely.[479] There were three prisoners, Doug B. Hegdahl, Navy Lt. Robert F. Fishman and Air Force Capt. Wesley L.

John D. Douglas. Also Grace Paley (activist writer) and James A. Johnson, Jr. (Fort Hood Three). Fruchter, a Newark cadre, had been part of Hayden's Bratislava-Hanoi entourage in September and October 1967. "How the Prisoners Were Released," *Time*, Aug. 15, 1969.

[474] House, Committee on Internal Security, *Investigation of Students for a Democratic Society*, Part 7-A, December 9, 1969, 2185-6.

[475] G. Roy Levin, "Robert Kramer and John Douglas interviewed, Reclaiming our past, reclaiming our beginning," *Jump Cut*, no. 10-11, 1976, 6-8.

[476] Bob Phillips and Arthur Berg, "New Mobe's November action: The Reds, the Doves and the Gulls," *Combat*, vol. 1, No. 30, November 15, 1969.

[477] "How the Prisoners Were Released," *Time*, Aug. 15, 1969.

[478] Vietnamese News Agency cited in Louis R. Stockstill, "The Forgotten Americans of the Vietnam War," *Air Force Magazine*, October 1969, Vol. 52, No. 10.

[479] CIA, FOIA, Case number EO-1995-00063, "FBIS Trends-Vietnam-Introduction: Paris talks," August 6, 1969

Rumble. Hegdahl was 75 pounds lighter, Fishman had a useless elbow and 65 pounds and Rumble was in a body cast for his broken back.[480] A month earlier on July 4, 1969 Italian journalist Oriana Fallaci had interviewed Frishman, Rumble and Hegdahl eating food and drinking beer and tea. Cat, the Plantation camp commander, had told the three they would be released if they cooperated.

Staged Good Bye. In the interim, the POWs were fattened, tanned and indoctrinated. Hegdahl "butchered his scripted speech" and stole Cat's cigarette holder. Hegdahl, thought a fool, had memorized the names of more than 300 fellow POWs, their Social Security numbers and personal traits, e.g. pet's names.[481]

At a farewell press conference, the Vietnamese brought out three other POWs Robbie Risner, Roger Ingvalson and Edwin Miller. Asked about the food Risner said he hoped to get recipes.[482] Weatherman Linda Evans said the POWs had "extremely humane treatment..."[483] Back home Hegdahl and Frishman renounced their farewell remarks as "coerced and contrived" and described torture far from "humane and lenient."[484]

Later Risner said antiwar visitors "only encouraged the Vietnamese, prolonged the war, worsened our condition and cost the lives of more Americans on the battlefield."[485]

Bring the War Home. Weatherman Linda Evans was thrilled to see the Vietnamese "winning total victory."[486] Evans had cradled an antiaircraft gun, "Wishing this: an American

---

[480] Lieut. Commander John S. McCain III, U.S. Navy, "How the POW's Fought Back," *US News & World Report*, May 14, 1973.

[481] Bethanne Kelly Patrick, "Seaman Apprentice Douglas Hegdahl: Young Seaman's Remarkable Memory Brought Home News of Fellow POWs," Military.com http://www.military.com/Content/MoreContent?file=ML_hegdahl_bkp

[482] Stuart I. Rochester and Frederick Kiley, *Honor Bound, American Prisoners of War in Southeast Asia 1961-1973,* Annapolis: Naval Institute Press, 1999, 373; Oriana Fallaci, "Two American POWs," *Look* Magazine, July 15, 1969.

[483] FBI, FOIA, Weather Underground. The primary source is Acting SAC Chicago to Director, memo, "Foreign Influence-Weather Underground Organization," August 20, 1976, 284.

[484] Stuart I. Rochester and Frederick Kiley, *Honor Bound, American Prisoners of War in Southeast Asia 1961-1973,* Annapolis: Naval Institute Press, 1999, 374-5.

[485] James Banerian and the Vietnamese Community Action Committee, *Losers Are Pirates: A Close Look at the PBS Series "Vietnam: A Television History,"* Phoenix: Tieng Me Publications, 1984, 227.

[486] Sale, SDS 414; also cited in FBI, FOIA, Weather Underground. The primary source is Acting SAC Chicago to Director, memo, "Foreign Influence-Weather Underground Organization," August 20, 1976, 2-3.

plane would come over."[487] Evans said, "Immediate withdrawal is what the Vietnamese define as total victory...."[488] Evans had joined the other side. "...[I]t is our responsibility...to help (the Vietnamese) in their fight by *opening another battle front* here. We should *bring the war home*."[489]

Rennie Davis and POW Letters. On August 9, 1969, Rennie Davis telegrammed POW families messages from POWs' unsealed letters. Rennie Davis and *Time* magazine contacted a POW's wife asking *Time* magazine to publish her husband's message. She refused.[490]

POW Releases: An Evaluation.

POW Sam Johnson said Ho Chi Minh, "danced us across the stage of world opinion and presented the world with the best orchestrated propaganda show this century has beheld." Rochester and Kiley say, "until Frishman and Hegdahl gave compelling testimony..., the peace travelers' whitewashes and ...lavishly courted journalists, were the only versions of captivity available in firsthand accounts." The contrast between the Vietnamese staged "humane" treatment of POWs and the death and destruction of U.S. bombing [of military targets] gave the Vietnamese the appearance of moral superiority.[491]

POW Families Told to Contact Rennie Davis, Cora Weiss or COLIFAM. POW families tried to discover whether their loved ones were alive, dead or healthy. On September 14, a group of POW family members traveled to Paris to meet Vietnamese seeking mail and information. "Tom"—Tam-- told them to contact Rennie Davis. Tam said the U. S. government was confiscating POW mail and offered a film showing how well the POWs were doing.[492] Two weeks later on September

---

[487] FBI, FOIA, Weather Underground. The primary source is Acting SAC Chicago to Director, memo, "Foreign Influence-Weather Underground Organization," August 20, 1976, 109, 286.

[488] FBI, FOIA, Weather Underground. The primary source is Acting SAC Chicago to Director, memo, "Foreign Influence-Weather Underground Organization," August 20, 1976, 284-285.

[489] FBI, electronic FOIA, W, Weather Underground, contains: FBI, FOIA, Weather Underground. The primary source is Acting SAC, Chicago, Memo to Director, *Weather Underground Organization WUO Formerly Weathermen, 1976* p. 208, 283-4; Also cited in Rothrock pp. 181-182N48.

[490] FBI, Oklahoma City, interview of [REDACTED] December 12, 15 and 16, 1970, FD-302 December 28, 1970.

[491] Stuart I. Rochester and Frederick Kiley, *Honor Bound,* 376-7.

[492] FBI, Dallas, interview of [REDACTED], August 31, 1970, FD-302, September 2, 1970.

28, another group[493] traveled Paris to ask the Vietnamese to release sick and wounded POWs and to deliver letters to their loved ones. They met for three hours with three Vietnamese. A furious Xuan Oanh angrily told them to contact Rennie Davis, Cora Weiss or COLIFAM. Go home and demonstrate against the war. A Texas POW family member was to "remain quiet or gather the masses to protest American intervention in South Vietnam."[494] Mrs. Shuman said, "They absolutely told us to go out and demonstrate." Meanwhile back in Hanoi, POWs Shuman and Doss, were threatened and Shuman tortured for refusing to meet antiwar delegations.[495]

Peace Group. "A Little Band of Traitors." Hearing this testimony in June 1970, Rep. William J. Scherle called Hanoi's POW family minders, "a little band of traitors" exploiting POW families in the interest of Communist propaganda.[496]

October 10-17 Quakers and POWs. Returning to Hanoi, October 10-17, 1969 with AFSC promised medical equipment, AFSC's Joseph Elder again brought up POW conditions, a POW list and mail services. Joseph Elder said the pacifist Quakers could act as a go between with the POWs. Moreover, the AFSC had already condemned the US, but not the Vietnamese.

Mr. Toan accepted 200 family letters. On October 16 the Vietnamese told Elder "Your government is using the families of the missing men and POWs for propaganda purposes." Elder replied, "Release of a prisoner list would end the propaganda." Thanking Americans active in the upcoming October moratorium, the Vietnamese sent Elder on his way. Later, Elder told a Hamline University crowd Vietnamese bureaucrats surely had accurate POW lists.[497] Among anti-war advocates, Joseph Elder's skepticism of the Vietnamese was unique.

---

[493] Mrs. Edwin A. Shuman III, Mrs. Dale Doss and others from Maryland, Texas, California and Minnesota.

[494] FBI, Dallas, interview with [REDACTED], FD-302, September 1, 1970; FBI, Dallas, fragment, DL 100-12009, memo, n.d. [post December 1969], 2 (copied as 17 in a packet).

[495] House, Hearings on Restraints on Travel to Hostile Areas: Hearings before the Committee on Internal Security, 93rd Cong., 1st sess., 1973, 4-5 cited in Rothrock *Divided...* 188-96n11.

[496] "Band of Traitors; Rep. Scherle Assails POW Liaison Group," Washington Evening Star, June 11, 1970; FBI, Norfolk, Interview of [REDACTED], June 26, 1970, FD-302, June 30, 1970; FBI, Norfolk (NF-100-6833), fragment, LHM, n.d. [post October 1969]; FBI, Dallas, Interview of [REDACTED], September 31, 1970, FD-302, October 1, 1970.

POW Family Vigil Continues. Other POW families returned to Paris and Stockholm in November and December. In November, the September POW family group returned to Paris. My Van Bo had replaced Xuan Oanh. My Van Bo said the POWs were "air pirates and war criminals and did not deserve human treatment" and called the wives of POWs "agents of the U.S. government." The family members flew to Stockholm. They filmed Le Ky Giai saying return home, contact Rennie Davis and protest the war.[498]

Having treated the POW families with contempt, the Communists turned to its American collaborators to handle POW matters.

Hanoi Asks Davis, Dellinger, Kunstler to Help with Another POW Release

Paris Meeting. Having rebuffed AFSC's Joseph Elder and the POW families, the Vietnamese again summoned Rennie Davis and David Dellinger to Paris. As members of the Chicago Seven, Davis and Dellinger were prohibited from travel to Paris. Their attorney William Moses Kunstler went to Paris instead.[499] Kunstler said the North Vietnamese would release POW information only through National Mobilization. The release of POW information was intended to give credibility to peace groups.[500]

Viet Cong Releases "Progressive" POWs November 1969, Tinsley, Strickland, Watkins. On November 5, 1969, the Viet Cong released Coy Tinsley, Army Pfc. James Henry Strickland and Willie A. Watkins in Cambodia. Watkins, a strong black man "always had a Bible and a machete." Strickland, a tough small man, was a hard worker. The Vietnamese saw both as "progressive" prisoners.[501] The Viet Cong said Watkins was released in support of New Mobe's upcoming November protests. A recorded Watkins, thanked the Liberation Front for releasing him and condemned racism.[502]

---

[497] "Notes of Dr. Elder's Meeting on November 12, 1969 at Hamline University, November 12, 1969."

[498] FBI, Dallas, Dallas 100-12009, Interview with [Redacted male]. August 19, 1970, FD-302, August 28, 1970; FBI, Dallas, fragment, DL 100-12009, memo, n.d. [post December 1969], 2 (copied as 17 in a packet).

[499] FBI, Norfolk, Interview of [REDACTED], June 26, 1970, FD-302, June 30, 1970.

[500] Vanderbilt Television News Archive http://openweb.tvnews.vanderbilt.edu/1969-10/1969-10-27-ABC-3.html

[501] http://www.pownetwork.org/bios/s/s132.htm

[502] Craig Howes, Voices of the Vietnam POWs: Witnesses to Their Fight, New York: Oxford University Press, 1993, 131.

Strickland hinted soldiers had fragged their hated commanding officer. Both made statements, but they had survived Viet Cong camps where most lost more than half their weight and where half of the captives died of malnutrition, malaria, dysentery, boils.[503] While their survival was welcomed, their antiwar statements served the enemy.

"BRING THE WAR HOME" STREET FIGHTING FOR PEACE

Weathermen "National Action"-Cleveland. August 28-September 2, 1969 the SDS held a "National Action" conference in Cleveland. Georgie Anne Guyer and Keyes Beech write, "In August 1969 (Cuban UN) mission intelligence personnel... counseled Mark Rudd and Jeff Jones concerning acceptable slogans to be used..."[504] Bill Ayers said, "Bring the War Home...that's going to help the NLF..."[505] The August 23, 1969 issue of *New Left Notes*, said National Action is "a movement ...allies with and proposed material aid to the people of Vietnam....Its primary task.. not only to defeat the imperialists in Vietnam but to BRING THE WAR HOME! Our tactics...we move in tight groups...affinity groups. Spending the summer learning karate...and first aid."

Weather Women Go Wild for Ho Chi Minh. On Wednesday night, September 3, in Pittsburgh, a weatherman contingent "commemorated the death of Ho Chi Minh..., by taking small guerrilla actions." Carrying an NLF flag, they chanted "Ho Lives" and "Free Huey,"[506] On September 4, 1969, police arrested 26 Weathermen women running through South Hills High School screaming antiwar slogans. The Weather account reads,

The pigs attacked and the women fought back, protecting their sisters and the Viet Cong flag. ...and left... chanting "Ho Ho Ho Chi Minh, the Viet Cong is Going to Win.[507]

---

[503] Craig Howes, *Voices of the Vietnam POWs: Witnesses to Their Fight*, New York: Oxford University Press, 1993, 211-15.

[504] Georgie Anne Geyer and Keyes Beech, "Cuba: School for US Radicals," *Chicago Sun Times*, October 1970 cited in FBI, FOIA, Weather Underground. The primary source is Acting SAC Chicago to Director, memo, "Foreign Influence-Weather Underground Organization," August 20, 1976, 42.

[505] Bill Ayers at the conference and in "A Strategy to Win," *New Left Notes*, September 12, 1969 cited in FBI, FOIA, Weather Underground. The primary source is Acting SAC Chicago to Director, memo, "Foreign Influence-Weather Underground Organization," August 20, 1976, 36, 110.

[506] Harold Jacobs (ed.) *Weatherman*, Ramparts Press 1970, 97, http://www.sds-1960s.org/books/weatherman.pdf

Save your tears for Ho for victory. "Save your tears for victory," wrote Bernardine Dohrn and 100 SDS women co-signers in a telegram on September 9, 1969,[508] to Huynh Van Ba, DRV Ambassador to Cuba and to Pham Van Dong. In North Vietnam, a 15-day political drive commemorated on the legacy of Ho, an "eminent combatant of the international Communist and worker movement." He was "a great Communist combatant."[509] Some Ho-inspired Americans, like the Weathermen, saw themselves as Communist combatants.

Liberation News Services Hanoi: "the Vietnamese need our help." After meeting with Vietnamese Communists in Havana, George Cavalletto of the Liberation News Service wrote "for Internal Consumption Only—Not for Publication, Please" saying, "the Vietnamese need our help." In an LNS editorial, "...Their fight and our fight are one."[510] **Some Peace Corps Support for Viet Cong Victory.** On September 15, 1969 John McAuliff's Committee of Returned [Peace Corps] Volunteers, CRV, declared, "We support the heroic struggle of the Vietnamese people... Only...victory [is] true national liberation."[511]

On October 5, the International Liaison Committee of the World Peace Council's Stockholm Conference on Vietnam endorsed New Mobe's November 15 protest for uniting active groups. The ILC called it "the widest spectrum of forces yet to unite in opposition and resistance to the war."[512]

SDS National Action—September and October 1969
Planning Days of Rage: Fort Dix, Chicago, Washington.
The Weathermen, back from spring and summer visits to Cuba, were prepared for an invasion of Fort Dix carrying Viet Cong flags to kick (GI) ass," destruction orgies in October "Days of Rage" in Chicago, and a November rampage in Washington.

---

[507] Harold Jacobs (ed.) *Weatherman,* Ramparts Press 1970, 98, http://www.sds-1960s.org/books/weatherman.pdf

[508] FBI, FOIA, Weather Underground. The primary source is Acting SAC Chicago to Director, memo, "Foreign Influence-Weather Underground Organization," August 20, 1976, 119.

[509] Directive of the Political Bureau of the Party Committee on the Political Activity Drive to Study and Comply with President Ho's Will, *Hoc Tap*, Vietnamese, No 10, October 1969, 9-13 Pike Collection, TTU, Virtual Archive, Item Number 2360511013.

[510] "Liberation News Service Rallies U.S. Left for Cong," *Combat*, Vol. 1, No. 28, October 15, 1969.

[511] CRV Newsletter, October 1969, 1.

[512] International Liaison Committee, World Peace Council, Information Letter No. 5," October 5, 1969.

DAYS OF RAGE, CHICAGO, OCTOBER 8-11, 1969.-

SDS Street Fighters. On October 8, 1969, the SDS Weathermen converged upon Chicago for "Days of Rage" smashing property and fighting police in the streets of Chicago, but only several hundred street fighters showed up, not the expected 20,000. Carrying large Viet Cong flags Kathy Boudin and Linda Sue Evans led the charge[513] with Bill Ayers, Jim Mellen, Peter Clapp and John Jacobs armed with chains and pipes.[514] Organizer and street fighter Bill Ayers remembers,

....The crowd roared...HO, HO, HO CHI MINH, the VIET CONG ARE GONNA WIN. ...Bernardine (Dohrn)...shouted, 'BRING THE WAR HOME.[515]

At an October 9, 1969 press conference Weatherman Jonathan David Lerner bragged, "The ring I am wearing on my hand was made in North Vietnam from the wreckage of an American Fighter...".[516] Journalists Geyer and Beech write, "They were opening a second front in Chicago to help their embattled comrades in Vietnam."[517]

Government Refuses to Reveal "Foreign Intelligence Sources." Judges in the federal and one Detroit case dismissed charges after the government refused to reveal "foreign intelligence sources." Those foreign intelligence sources of most interest to the FBI, CIA and NSA were likely contacts

---

[513] FBI, FOIA, Weather Underground. The primary source is Acting SAC Chicago to Director, memo, "Foreign Influence-Weather Underground Organization," August 20, 1976, 388.

[514] FBI, FOIA, Weather Underground. The primary source is Acting SAC Chicago to Director, memo, "Foreign Influence-Weather Underground Organization," August 20, 1976, 389.

[515] Bill Ayers, *Fugitive Days*, 266-269. *New Left Notes* of October 21, 1969 reveled in such accomplishments as: 500 of us moved through the richest sections of Chicago, with VC flags in front, smashing luxury apartment windows and storefronts, ripping apart the loop and injuring scores of pigs....SDS women with clubs battled armed pigs...8 of our people were shot, and over 100 were busted....It was war—we knew it and the pigs knew it. We came to Chicago to join the other side...start fighting with the VC. ..."

[516] FBI, FOIA, Weather Underground. The primary source is Acting SAC Chicago to Director, memo, "Foreign Influence-Weather Underground Organization," August 20, 1976, 318; Herbert Romerstein, "What Was the Weather Underground," America's Survival, 39 contains a copy of his testimony before House Committee on Internal Security, Investigation of Students For A Democratic Society, Part 7-B, December 17-8, 1969, 2470.

[517] Georgie Anne Geyer and Keyes Beech, "Cuba: School for US Radicals," Chicago Sun Times, October 1970 cited in FBI, FOIA, Weather Underground. The primary source is Acting SAC Chicago to Director, memo, "Foreign Influence-Weather Underground Organization," August 20, 1976, 113.

with Cuban, Chinese, Soviet, East Berlin and Vietnamese communists.

The Fort Dix 38

Meanwhile by October 12, 1969, a large antiwar coalition of 12 organizations formed to support the Fort Dix 38.[518] Besides supporting the Fort Dix 38, the coalition also demanded the withdrawal of all U. S. (not Hanoi) occupation forces in Vietnam.

Deserters Terry Klug and Donald Williams. Among the few known antiwar activists at Fort Dix was Terry Klug. After volunteering for Officer's Candidate School, learning he was going to Vietnam, Klug claimed to be a conscientious objector and deserted the Army on June 26, 1967 and a year and a half on the lam. Klug described RITA, "a Resister Inside the Armed Forces, ...His reasons may be political, pacifistic or whatever." Klug became active in the Andy Stapp's American Servicemen's Union, ASU, founded to organize "soviets inside the U.S. imperialist army,"[519] **The Principal Protesters: Coffee House, SDS Action Faction.** Among the individual leaders[520] of the October protest worked at the Fort Dix Coffee House, most being active members of SDS, [521] Black Panthers,[522] Committee for Returned Volunteers [of Peace Corps][523] and the Fifth Avenue Parade Committee.[524] Action faction SDSers, Bob Tomaschevsky and Sam Karp, wrote *The GI Movement: Its Importance in Defeating Imperialism,* worked at the Fort Dix Coffee House and published *Shakedown* at Fort Dix, both SDS projects.

The Ft. Dix Committee Organizes. Tactical leaders of the October 12 protest were "Larry," Barbara Reilly, Maryann Weissman, Jim Eagan, Richard Rosman. Showing up to

---

[518] The organizations included The Resistance, Fifth Avenue Peace Parade Committee, Student Mobe, Black Panther Party, the Young Lords, Clergy and Laity Concerned About Vietnam, Women Strike for Peace, the W.E.B. Dubois Clubs, Movement for a Democratic Society, all SDS factions, Catholic Peace Fellowship, Greenwich Village Peace Center, War Resisters League.

[519] *Terrorism*, a Staff Study, August 1, 1974,102.

[520] "Josephine Drexel Duke Is Engaged To John Marshall Geste Brown Jr." New York *Times*, August 31, 1969, 49 Ronald Carver, Saul Shapiro, Gary Harris, James Wallen, Herb Dreyer, Corina Fales, Steve Ornstein, Bob Tomaschevsky, tobacco heir and SDS financier Josephine Drexel Duke Brown, John Marshall Brown and Haven Logan.

[521] Ronald Glick, Fred Bogardus, Carl Broege, Fred Halper and Dick Fried.

[522] Carl Nichols, Frank Kaiser, Mac Feggin, and Frank Hall.

[523] John McAuliff.

[524] Abe and Debbie Weisbud.

participate were anarchists belonging to the Black Panthers, U.S. Committee to Aid the National Liberation Front, Workers Youth World Party, Youth Against War and Fascism.[525] **Media Coverage of Dix Protest.** Leftists, like Newsreel (Melvin Margulis, Roz Payne), Liberation News Service (Howie Epstein, Barbara Rothkrug, and David Fenton) and photographer Louis Salzberg, an FBI informant, covered the event.[526]

The Rally Assembles Outside Fort Dix, October 12. On October 12, 1969, a rally assembled at the coffeehouse outside Fort Dix where Barbara Dane sang anti-war songs followed by speakers.[527] A Woman's Brigade led a march eight abreast and half a mile long carrying banners, "Free the Fort Dix 38" and "Bring the GIs home now." Peking Radio reported,

8,000 American people bravely stormed the Fort Dix Army base in New Jersey...protesting against the U.S. imperialist aggression in Vietnam and against the reactionary base authorities persecution of the American servicemen who opposed the U.S. war of aggression...[528]

It was the event the Weather had always wanted. Chuck Sollish, a Fort Dix GI, had warned, "Attacking the GIs...we would be looked upon as their enemies."[529] Weather Underground, considered Fort Dix servicemen their enemies as an explosion of bombs intended for a dance at Fort Dix proved accidentally exploded killing three weathermen in March 1970.

HOLLYWOOD AND HANOI
ENDORSE OCTOBER AND NOVEMBER PROTESTS
Hollywood. In Hollywood Jane Fonda's 's brother Peter Fonda, Bert Schneider, Dennis Hopper, Paul Newman, and Jon

---

[525] Black Panthers (Zahed Shakur, Suzanne Bellamy, "Sabu") U.S. Committee to Aid the National Liberation Front (Karen Atkin) pacifists (Peter Kiger), Veterans for Peace and Reservists for Peace (Mike Spector, John Seeley, Robert Levine, Frank Hoffman, Jack Godoy, Jerry Chodick, Bob Marinaro) the Workers Youth World Party group, Youth Against War and Fascism (Sam Marcy (Balan), Dave Axel, Andy Stapp, Dierdre Griswold Stapp, Arthur Rosen, Rita Freed, Shirley Joels, Sharon Martin, Joel Meyers).

[526] *Combat* (*National Review*), Vol. 1, No. 29, November 1, 1969.

[527] Herb Dreyer of the coffee house; Kathy Russell, wife of Fort Dix soldier, Jeff Russell; Zayed Malik Shakur and "Sabu" of the Black Panthers; "preacherman" William Fensterman;

[528] Peking Radio New China News Agency, International Service in English, 1526 Greenwich Mean Time 14 October 1969 in *Combat* (*National Review*), Vol. 1, No. 29, November 1, 1969.

[529] *Combat* (*National Review*), Vol. 1, No. 29, November 1, 1969.

Voight co-sponsored a one-day movie strike in Hollywood in support of the Moratorium. **Hanoi.** Hanoi publicly endorsed both the upcoming Moratorium and New Mobe demonstrations in October and November. On October 4, 1969, the Moratorium and the New Mobe announced that they had joined forces in a "Fall Offensive" against the war.[530] **NLF** On October 5, 1969 the Liberation Press Agency in South Vietnam the South Vietnam People's Committee for Solidarity with the American People, *Viet My,* messaged, "We are very elated...you will launch a big fall campaign against the Nixon administration's war policies, urging it to ...bring all troops home immediately." The message concluded that withdrawal was to end immediately "without posing any conditions."

World Peace Council. On the same day the International Liaison Committee, LIC, of the Soviet controlled World Peace Council, WPC called November New Mobe actions, "the widest spectrum of forces yet to unite in opposition and resistance to the war."[531]

Vietnamese Students. On October 6, Tran Buu Kiem, South Vietnam Liberation Students Union, broadcast a letter to American students praising "the heroic struggle of the friends in New York, Washington, Oakland and Berkeley, has been appreciated by South Vietnamese youth and students." The message also praised the July 4th Cleveland Peace Conference, the SDS (Terry Robbins, Bill Ayers, Mark Rudd and Linda Sue Evans)[532] and the Spring Mobe.

Tran Buu Kiem had an underground relationship with New Mobe and SDS.[533] On October 13, 1969, a rally in Hanoi sent another telegram supporting New Mobe's "struggle" of 13-15 November. Dr. Nguy Nhu Kon Tum, president of Hanoi University, "expressed unity" with American intellectuals, students, and people" and with their demands that the "Nixon administration withdraw all...troops..."[534]

---

[530] New York *Times*, Oct 5, 1969.

[531] The International Liaison Committee, "Nov 15 Day of International Mobilization to End the War in Vietnam," *Information Letter,* No. 5, October 5, 1969, Stockholm Conference on Vietnam, Stockholm, Sweden.

[532] Senate, Committee on the Judiciary, Subcommittee to Investigate the Administration of the Internal Security Act and Other Internal Security Laws, *The Weather Underground*, Committee Print, January 1975, 17 cites Illinois Crime Investigating Commission report, in Part 4 of "Extent of Subversion in the New Left, 377.

[533] Frank J. Rafalko, *MH/CHAOS: The CIA's Campaign Against the Radical Left and the Black Panthers*, Annapolis: Naval Institute Press, 2011, 140 cites Jack Anderson, "U.S. Revolutionaries Linked to Hanoi," *Washington Post*, October 15, 1969, E11.

Stockholm Conference. On October 11-12, 1969 Irving Sarnoff and Ron Young, representing New Mobe[535] attended the International Liaison Committee, ILC, meeting of the Soviet funded Stockholm conference,[536] supporting an International Mobilization on November 15. The ILC was the "principal body" of WPC "coordinating and planning international support for the domestic antiwar movement in the United States."[537] The Stockholm Conference hailed New Mobe for doing "the crucial work of mobilizing the American people against the war of aggression and counterrevolution in Vietnam." An ILC letter, noting the "full cooperation with our American friends" in the New Mobe, named Ronald Young and Irving Sarnoff. "The Stockholm Conference on Vietnam welcomes the formation of the broadest coalition of US antiwar forces yet known...in the New Mobilization. ..." All demonstrations supported "the demand of the Vietnamese appeal ...the immediate, total and unconditional withdrawal ...from South Vietnam."[538]

Pham Van Dong Endorses both the 'Moderate" Moratorium and New Mobe. The self-proclaimed moderates were allegedly running the Moratorium events in October. Sam Brown privately wanted a VC victory. On October 14, North Vietnamese Prime Minister Pham Van Dong sent a telegram to New Mobe, not the Moratorium;
STRUGGLE OF ...PROGRESSIVE PEOPLE IN THE UNITED STATES AGAINST U.S. AGGRESSION WILL END IN TOTAL VICTORY. I WISH YOUR 'FALL OFFENSIVE' A BRILLANT SUCCESS.[539]

On Radio Hanoi on October 15 Pham Van Dong praised, "peace-and justice loving Americans...launching a broad and

---

[534] "Hanoi Students Send Telegram Supporting Antiwar Activities," *Nhan Dan,* Hanoi, Nov. 14, 1969 from Joint Publications Research Service in TTU archives cited in Rothrock, 146N20.

[535] Frank J. Rafalko, MH/CHAOS: The CIA's Campaign Against the Radical Left and the Black Panthers, Annapolis: Naval Institute Press, 2011, 136.

[536] HISC, Staff Study, Subversive Involvement in the Origin, Leadership and Activities of the New Mobilization Committee to End the War in Vietnam And Its Predecessor Organizations, 1970, XII-XIII.

[537] Frank J. Rafalko, MH/CHAOS: 142.

[538] International Liaison Committee, Stockholm Conference on Vietnam, letter, October 18, 1969, Staff Study, 1970, 42-3.

[539] *Combat*, Vol. 1, No. 30, November 15, 1969; Frank J. Rafalko, *MH/CHAOS: The CIA's Campaign Against the Radical Left and the Black Panthers*, Annapolis: Naval Institute Press, 2011,139.

powerful offensive." Dong felt confident, "the struggle of Vietnamese people and of progressive people in the United States against U.S. aggressions will end in total victory."[540] Fred Halstead drafted a New Mobe reply, "We know the American people and the Vietnamese people share…a common desire for the immediate withdrawal of all U.S. forces in Vietnam." Fearing embarrassment, New Mobe tried to keep both the Dong telegram and Halstead's reply a secret. Yet on October 14, the President learned about a letter using "very flowery red rhetoric" from Pham Van Dong to the American people supporting the Moratorium. By its silence, "Radical" New Mobe was now covering for the "moderate" reputation of Moratorium.[541]

Innocents Being Used. Presidential advisor Haldeman arranged for the letter's release to "try to make the innocents see they are being used."[542] On October 13th and 18th, 1969 *Washington Post* articles described Vietnamese plans in articles headlined, "VC Woman Encourages U.S. Protests" and "VC to Cultivate U.S. Antiwar Groups."[543]

OCTOBER 15, MORATORIUM

On October 15, 1969, the long planned Fall Offensive was a nationwide one-day student strike, a "Moratorium," against the war in Vietnam all across the country. **Moderate Supporters.** Many liberal, former supporters of Robert Kennedy and Eugene McCarthy, including Jerome Grossman, Sam Brown, David Hawk, and David Mixner were the original organizers, endorsed by the Cleveland conference, joined by prominent others e.g. Senators Cranston, Goodell, Javits, Kennedy, Tydings and NYC Mayor John Lindsay in the October Moratorium.[544] Notable speakers were Senators George McGovern and Frank Church, SDS/IPS's Art Waskow, Dr. Benjamin Spock.[545] Tom Hayden recalls, "We (the Chicago Conspiracy) had to fight their bureaucracy even to appear on

---

[540] Herschensohn, 94.

[541] *Combat*, Vol. 1, No. 30, November 15, 1969.

[542] H.R. Haldeman, *The Haldeman Diaries: Inside the Nixon White House*, New York: Berkley Books, 1994, 120.

[543] "Answer This Question, Mr. Kerry," *Pittsburgh Tribune*-Review, internet service, October 17, 2004 cites "VC Woman Encourages U.S. Protests," UPI, *Washington Post,* Oct. 13, 1969 and "VC to Cultivate U.S. Antiwar Groups," Stanley Karnow, *Washington Post,* Oct. 18, 1969.

[544] *Combat*, Vol. 1. No. 28, October 5, 1969.

[545] New Mobilization, "A schedule of events, October 15, 1969,"

stage in Chicago Moratorium..."[546] Hayden also appeared on a Moratorium stage in An Arbor, Michigan,[547] where he scorned liberals. "They want to end the war but also save the system....They remain a loyal opposition. ..[548] Near Schenectady FOR's Allan Brink called for ousting (Saigon's) government and withdrawing U.S. troops, the complete recipe for communist victory[549] and U.S. defeat and surrender.

ASTONISHING SUCCESS AND SURPRIZING FAILURE.

Success: One Million Protesters. Across the nation, no less than one million participated in Moratorium rallies, large and small, town and city, campus to campus, from coast to coast.[550] The Fifth Avenue Parade Committee rented "six hundred busses and three or four trains."[551] **Popular Support Misinterpreted.** *Time* **magazine** joined many in mistakenly calculating popular support for the antiwar movement. *Time* said the **Harvard faculty** had voted 255-81 to condemn the war, only 6.6% of Harvard's faculty of 7,330 had bothered to vote. While 79 **college presidents**, 4% wanted to accelerate US withdrawal, about 1,900 college presidents, 96% took no such position. Though 17 Senators and 47 representatives, 14% supported the Moratorium, 86% of **Congress**, did not support the Moratorium. Seven percent of Harvard faculty, 4% of college presidents and 14% of Congress did not a majority make. Then, of course, there was the public opinion that was supposed to change. It didn't.

Public Opinion: Protesters "giving aid and comfort to the Communists." On November 3, 1969, a Harris Poll showed that by a margin of 65%-25 percentage the American people thought that anti-war protesters were "giving aid and comfort to the Communists."[552] And in late 1969, 60% of the

---

[546] Hayden, *The Trial*, 1970, 137.

[547] Photo of Hayden, captioned "Tom Hayden speaking at the National Moratorium against the Vietnam War rally in Michigan Stadium, October 15, 1969, Jay Cassidy photograph, Bentley Historical Library, University of Michigan, p. 64 in Richard Gull, "The New Left of the 1960s Turns 50: and An Interview with Howard Brick," *The Crazy Wisdom Community Journal*, September-December 2012.

[548] Tom Hayden, "All for Vietnam," *Ramparts*, July 1970, 27.

[549] "Local Protests in the Vietnam War," History of Mohonasen Central School District.

[550] Wells, 371.

[551] According to FBI checks of its bank account and surveillance at 57 locations. *Combat*, Vol. 1. No. 28, October 5, 1969.

[552] Herbert S. Parmet, *Richard Nixon and His America*, New York: Konecky & Konecky, 1990, 580.

public thought antiwar demonstrators were harming prospects for peace,[553] not the President.

Viet Cong Targets GIs. On the battlefield in South Vietnam, the Viet Cong distributed leaflets to GIs quoting Moratorium speakers[554] A VC pamphlet declared that "Millions of Americans... [were in]...a just struggle for peace and justice..." and called for the "immediate and total repatriation of U.S. troops." It urged GIs in Vietnam to "Leave your firearms aside, refuse to move out..."[555] Handfuls of GIs in Vietnam wore black armbands supporting Moratorium. A news photographer reported that in a platoon on patrol near Da Nang, about half of the men were wearing black armbands.[556] In Hanoi today a museum at the site of the prison for U.S. POWs, the "Hanoi Hilton" honors the Moratorium protests of 1969.[557]

On Oct 27, 1969, the Viet Cong sent an encouraging message to regional and district comrades informing them that Americans were working "in conjunction" or "in coordination" with Hanoi, Moscow and its front organizations in event scheduling and propaganda themes.[558]

Nixon called off Duck Hook. Despite public opinion polls favorable to the President in late October and early November of 1969, Nixon thought the completed October Moratorium and the upcoming November Mobe had eliminated Duck Hook, massive mining and bombing of North Vietnam. Nixon said, "After all the protests and the Moratorium, American public opinion would be seriously divided by any military escalation of the war."

---

[553] David L. Anderson, John Ernst (eds.) *The War Never Ends: New Perspectives on Vietnam War*, Lexington: University of Kentucky, 2007, 259.

[554] U.S. Senators Charles Goodall, Frank Church, Mike Mansfield, George McGovern, Edmund Brooke, as well as Benjamin Spock, Roger Hilsman, and Coretta King.

[555] VC leaflets, "Opinion of US Senators on the 'fall offensive' against the US aggressive war in south VN," and "End the War in Vietnam Now!, Dan Teoduro to Max Friedman in November 1970 from a JUSPAO II collection of pamphlets, "Not So Loud...The Enemy is Listening." Max Friedman to author and others October 11, 2011.

[556] Howard Zinn, "GI opposition the Vietnam War," http://libcom.org/library/soldiers-opposition-to-vietnam-war-zinn 1965-1973

[557] Author's 2008 photo Viet I DSC_202.

[558] Le Minh Nguyen, "To Various K's and H's (Regions and Districts), October 27, 1969, Australians captured Nov 4, 1969 attached to "Viet Cong Units Directed to Intensify Struggle to Take Advantage of U.S. Peace Movement," Press Release, No. 98-69, November 30, 1969 United States Mission in Vietnam.

Silent Majority Speech- November 3, 1969. After the Moratorium, the President hoped to take the steam out the second, New Mobe, event of the "fall offensive." On November 3, President Nixon gave a speech arousing a "silent majority." to support of his Vietnam policies.

The precipitate withdrawal...from Vietnam would be a disaster.... This first defeat in our nation's history would result in a collapse of confidence in American leadership...throughout the world. ...If a vocal minority, however fervent its cause, prevails over reason and the will of the majority, this nation has no future as a free society. ...To you the great silent majority of my fellow Americans – I ask for your support...North Vietnam cannot defeat or humiliate the United States. Only Americans can do that.[559]

Also on November 3, preempting the President by two and a half hours, CBS and NBC showed a "news" film of South Vietnamese troops abusing Viet Cong troops at some date unspecified. Only days later, CBS stories of the Viet Cong shelling and mortaring 116 hamlets received a few sentences and no pictures.[560]

***

An American student participating in protests in London, dodging the draft, volunteering for Moratorium, and exploring the East Bloc, just kept running into leftists and communists.

BILL CLINTON's WORK FOR PEACE: WINTER in LONDON, OSLO, PRAGUE, MOSCOW[561]

As an Arkansas graduate of Georgetown University in Washington, D.C. and a Rhodes Scholar at Oxford University, in 1968-1969, Bill Clinton found the "atmosphere ...decidedly anti-American," but still joined the leftist U.K. antiwar movement. Bill Clinton joined a British antiwar demonstration at Trafalgar Square.[562] **Summer Moratorium.** That summer of

---

[559] *Public Papers: Nixon*, 1969, 901-909; Richard Nixon's Address to the Nation on the War in Vietnam, "The Silent Majority Speech," November 3, 1969 at Pacifica Radio/UC Berkeley Social Activism Sound Recording Project, Media Research Center, Moffitt Library, UC Berkeley, at www.lib.berkeley.edu/MRC/Pacificaviet.

[560] *Combat*, Vol. 1, No. 30, November 15, 1969.

[561] Fedora, "Road to Moscow: Bill Clinton's Early Activism from Fulbright to Moscow," *Original FReeper research* , Free Republic, 08/22/2007.

[562] Nick Ruford and David Leppard, with James Adams in Washington, Geordie Greig in New York, Susan Ellicott in Los Angeles, Jonathan Bastable in Moscow, Peter Green in Prague, Christine Toomey in Berlin and Ian Burrell, Miranda Devine, Charles Hymas and Simon Reeve in London, "A Yank at Oxford," *The Times*. October 25,

1969 Clinton planned to work on the Vietnam Moratorium Committee, VMC, in its office CPUSA member Abe Bloom leased at 1029 Vermont Avenue NW in Washington, DC. In September in Martha's Vineyard, Clinton joined members for the Vietnam Moratorium Committee—Sam Brown, David Mixner, Mike Driver, Eli Segal, Richard Stearns, Branch Taylor, Strobe Talbott.[563] **Clinton's Fall Protests.** Back in Oxford in the fall of 1969, Clinton and Richard Stearns attended meetings of Group 68, formed out of the Stop It Committee of the radical Viet Nam Solidarity Committee. Bertrand Russell's leaders of his [U.S.] War Crimes Tribunal, Ralph Schoenman, Trotskyite Tariq Ali and the pro-Soviet British Peace Committee funded the Vietnam Solidarity Committee[564] of which Clinton's Group 68 was a spin-off. Along with Richard Stearns and others, Bill Clinton helped organize the Moratorium's London rally on October 15, 1969 outside the U.S. embassy on Grosvenor Square. Actors Paul Newman and Joanne Woodward participated. Also sponsoring the London Moratorium were members of the British Peace Council, an affiliate of the Soviet controlled WPC, the Stockholm Conference, and the International Confederation for Disarmament and Peace.[565] The British press reported demonstrators crying, "Ho Chi Minh, the Viet Cong is gonna

1992 cited in Fedora, "Road to Moscow: Bill Clinton's Early Activism from Fulbright to Moscow," http://www.freerepublic.com/focus/f-news/1884984/posts
[563] Cullen, Tom. "War, Unrest Haunt American Scholars at Oxford". *The Post* (Frederick, Maryland). June 9, 1969, A8; Maraniss, David. "Bill Clinton and Realpolitik U.: In '68, 5 Georgetown Students Shared A House With a View of the World". *The Washington Post.* October 25, 1992, F1. Roberts, Steven V. and Matthew Cooper. "Clinton, Oxford and the Draft: Clinton still shows his ambivalence about those painful years". *U.S. News & World Report.* October 11, 1992; Clinton, Bill. *My Life.* New York: Alfred A. Knopf, 2004, Chapters 9-16; all http://www.freerepublic.com/focus/f-news/1884984/posts
[564] Wilkie, Curtis. "Red-baiting reflects strain of desperation". *Boston Globe.* October 7, 1992, 12; Maraniss, David. "Bill Clinton and Realpolitik U.: In '68, 5 Georgetown Students Shared A House With a View of the World". *The Washington Post.* October 25, 1992, F1; Nick Ruford and David Leppard, With James Adams in Washington, Geordie Greig in New York, Susan Ellicott in Los Angeles, Jonathan Bastable in Moscow, Peter Green in Prague, Christine Toomey in Berlin and Ian Burrell, Miranda Devine, Charles Hymas and Simon Reeve in London, "A Yank at Oxford", *The Times.* October 25, 1992; all http://www.freerepublic. com/focus/f-news/1884984/posts
[565] Dr. Rhiannon Vickers, "Harold Wilson, the Labour Party, and the War in Vietnam," British International Studies Association Annual Conference, 18-20 December, 2006, Cork, 20-21; Tariq Ali, *1968 and After: Inside the Revolution,* London: Blond and Briggs, 1978; Walter Cronkite, CBS Evening News, October 15, 1969 at Vanderbilt Television News Archive: Record display, University; BBC, October 15, 1969;

win."[566] Clinton also "helped to put together a teach-in at the University of London,"[567] details still unknown.

A month later on November 16, 1969, Clinton helped organize a protest of 200 or so in front of the U.S. Embassy on Grosvenor Square in London.[568] Actress leftist Vanessa Redgrave and singers Peggy Seeger and Judy Collins participated. On November 17, Clinton helped organize a church protest at St. Mark's allowing some protesters to be distinguished Marxist radicals.[569] Jesuit Father Richard McSorley, Georgetown Professor says, "As I was waiting for the ceremony to begin Bill Clinton ...came up and welcomed me. He was one of the organizers." Other organizers of the November event included Tariq Ali's Trotskyite Vietnam Solidarity Campaign and Bertrand Russell's Peace Council and War Crimes Tribunal. Seeking reelection in 1992, President George H. W. would say, "I can't understand someone mobilizing demonstrations in a foreign country when poor kids, drafted out of the ghettos, are dying in a faraway land."[570]

Oslo, Stockholm, Helsinki.

Clinton spent the rest of December 1969 in Oslo, Prague and Moscow into early 1970. On December 12, Clinton joined Fra. McSorley in Norway visiting the **Oslo Institute for Peace Research** at Oslo University. Russell's International Committee for Inquiry into United States War Crimes was also headquartered in Oslo. From Oslo Clinton spent several days in Stockholm[571] and Helsinki and then took trains to Leningrad (St. Petersburg) and Moscow.

---

[566] Joel A. Roth, "Clinton's Czech-communist connection," WorldNetDaily, April 30, 1999.

[567] John Greenwald, "Anatomy of a smear," *Time* Magazine, October 19, 1992.

[568] Terence Hunt, "Clinton softens views on LBJ's role in Vietnam War," *AP*, November 15, 2000. Richard McSorley, *Peace Eyes*, 1977; *Washington Times*, September 18, 1992;

[569] Roberts, Steven V. and Matthew Cooper. "Clinton, Oxford and the Draft: Clinton still shows his ambivalence about those painful years". *U.S. News & World Report.* October 11, 1992; McSorley, Richard, S.J. *Peace Eyes.* Washington, DC: Center for Peace Studies, 1978; Nick Ruford and David Leppard, with James Adams in Washington, Geordie Greig in New York, Susan Ellicott in Los Angeles, Jonathan Bastable in Moscow, Peter Green in Prague, Christine Toomey in Berlin and Ian Burrell, Miranda Devine, Charles Hymas and Simon Reeve in London, "A Yank at Oxford," *The Times.* October 25, 1992 all http://www.freerepublic.com/focus/f-news/1884984/posts.

[570] Andrew Rosenthal, "Bush questions Clinton's Account of Vietnam-Era Protests and Trip," *New York Times*, October 8, 1992, A-1.

[571] Bill Clinton must have had rather generous financial backers—Rhoades Scholar, Georgetown, KGB, or CIA funding—to explain his extensive travels. Three years

Moscow: KGB Contacts? In winter, December 31-January 6, 1970, Bill Clinton stayed at the expensive Hotel National in Moscow, "mostly just a tourist"[572] [Why not south of France, Spain, Italy] during "a very friendly time." Bill Clinton met the girlfriend of Tom Williamson, Anik "Nikki" Alexis, a daughter of a French diplomat. Nikki attended **Patrice Lumumba People's Friendship University** called "KGB U,"[573] because of its Marxist curriculum and KGB recruiting ground.[574] At Lumumba University the young Bill Clinton had dinner with Niki, Helene from Haiti and Oleg Rakito "assigned to keep an eye on me."[575] In the Russian translation of Clinton's autobiography, *My Life*, Vyacheslav Nikonov said, "a good old man from the KGB…held salutary talks with the young American,"[576] perhaps Rakito or anyone of the university's 90% KGB faculty. Coincidentally, Clinton's roommate Strobe Talbott was also in Moscow at this time. Strobe Talbott was translating former Soviet Premier Nikita Khrushchev's memoirs[577] through Victor Louis (Vitali Yevgenyevich Lui) a KGB disinformation agent.[578]

---

earlier in the summer and winter of 1966 the author as a student at Claremont Men's College, later renamed Claremont McKenna, also visited Stockholm *sans* any government grant, hitchhiking across the United States, Sweden and Europe, living in youth hostels and with a gracious Swedish family, and working as a common laborer in a plastics factory. Clinton had substantial financial backing.

[572] John Greenwald, "Anatomy of a smear," *Time* Magazine, October 19, 1992.

[573] According to KGB defectors, 90 percent of its faculty and staff were on the KGB's payroll. Like the Venceremos Brigade in Cuba, Lumumba's students were receptive to "working for peace" serving the Soviet Union or conducting revolution in their homelands.

[574] The KGB recruited some of Lumumba's students for further training in revolution, terrorism, and guerrilla warfare such as, Illich Ramirez Sanchez AKA Carlos the Jackal, future Iranian dictator Ayatollah Ali Khamenei and Palestinian Authority Chairman, PLO chief and KGB agent Mahmoud Abbas.

[575] Clinton, Bill. *My Life*. New York: Alfred A. Knopf, 2004, Chapters 9-16; Maraniss, David. "Bill Clinton and Realpolitik U.: In '68, 5 Georgetown Students Shared A House With a View of the World," *The Washington Post,* October 25, 1992, F1.; all cited in http://www.freerepublic.com/focus/f-news/1884984/posts

[576] "Bubba's Book Sales Stalled," NewsMax.com July 23, 2004 http://archive.newsmax.com/archives/ic/2004/ 7/23/101 123.shtml

[577] Clinton, Bill. *My Life*. New York: Alfred A. Knopf, 2004, Chapters 9-16; Jerrold and Leona Schecter, *Sacred Secrets: How Soviet Intelligence Operations Changed American History*, (forward, Strobe Talbott) Washington, DC: Brassey's, 2002 all http:// www.freer epublic.com/focus/f-news/1884984/posts .

[578] In *Comrade J*, Sergei Tretyakov, a Soviet spy later described Strobe Talbot as a very useful dupe of Russian intelligence, SPECIAL, UNOFFICIAL CONTACT, an "11-2" source, trusted contact (spy) who was greatly distrusted by the FBI and CIA during the administration of President Bill Clinton.

114

Clinton's "friendly times" Soviets, were subsidizing the anti-war movement, openly in Europe, and supplying North Vietnam with intelligence and arms killing Americans. The Moscow friendlies were also recruiting terrorists like the namesake of Nikki's university. Patrice Lumumba ordered the use of "terrorism, essential to subdue the population" in the Congo.

Prague: Warm in Winter. Arriving in Prague January 6, 1970 Bill Clinton stayed with the family of Oxford classmate Jan Kopold, son of a top Czech Communist party leader[579] who had by some happy coincidences survived both the Soviet Warsaw Pact invasion of Czechoslovakia and post-Dubcek purges of freedom advocates only months earlier. Clinton's friend Jan Kopold was married to the granddaughter of Czech communist party founder, Jan Sverma. She gave Bill Clinton a guided tour of still Communist Prague. During the 1992 election—Bush v Clinton-- the now free Czech news media, including a newspaper *Mlada Fronta Dnes,* reported that the Czech secret police, the Federal Security and Information Service (FSIS), provided information about Clinton's travel to Prague and Moscow and his connections inside Czechoslovakia. Nothing substantive was provided.[580]

Clinton: CIA, KGB? Some believed Bill Clinton was cavorting with the KGB, others the CIA. Both are plausible, but unproven. The KGB connections were available in the British peace movement as well as Clinton's friendly visits with Communists in Moscow and Prague. A former Czech political prisoner and publisher of Czech secret police files, Petr Cibulka, later said, "I'm personally convinced that Clinton is a communist agent as well as his vice-president, Al Gore."[581]

Clinton: CIA Agent/Informer? In 1996, Roger Morris, former White House aide to LBJ and Nixon, wrote an astonishing book, *Partners in Power.* Morris claimed unnamed CIA sources said the agency recruited Bill Clinton at Oxford or Georgetown[582] to make reports on his fellow anti-war

---

[579] Bob Momenteller, www.etherzone.com/1998/reich1.html

[580] http://www.consortiumnews.com/2004/101804.html

[581] August Interview with Petr Cibulka, Questions posed by Jan Malina, Translation by Jan Malina. Cibulka, a five-time political prisoner, in 1991 began publishing his paper, *Uncensored News,* and secret police files, including the names of over 200,000 communist spies and collaborators. Gore, Sr., was a business partner with Armand Hammer, longtime friend of top Soviet leaders granting him monopoly business franchises inside the USSR.

115

protestors in UK and GI deserters in Scandinavia.[583] That might explain how Clinton could pay for "luxury" and long-term travels.[584] Certainly, CIA's CHAOS, did recruit Americans, many from Georgetown, for service overseas targeting some peace movement Americans working with foreign powers.

NEW MOBE: "HAWKS ON THE OTHER SIDE"

From Hong Kong on October 17, 1969, in *Christian Science Monitor*, John Hughes wrote the Vietnamese communist view of the battlefield includes capturing public opinion in the USA." The Vietnamese gave "extensive daily coverage to the 'Fall Offensive against the Nixon administration..." A letter to U.S. students called "them a 'shock force' in the ...hard revolutionary struggle."[585]

Yet the Young People's Socialist League, YPSL, in *Washington Post* of October 18, 1969, said the New Mobe was acting contrary to peace. "Many in the leadership [of New Mobe] are more committed to an NLF victory than to peace." YPSL leader Josh Muravchik said, "many people involved" in New Mobe "are active, proclaimed supporters in every public speech they make of the -- what they call the 'liberation movement' in Vietnam -- the Viet Cong." Muravchik said, "I think those people do not properly belong in the peace movement. They are not for peace. They are hawks on the other side." [586]

Confirmation came from the Vietcong. On Oct 27, 1969, the Viet Cong sent an encouraging message to regional and

---

[582] Roger Morris to Suzan Mazur, "Scoop: Deeper into the Clinton's Drug Nexus scoop.co.nz/stories/HL070/S00058.htmssis

[583] Roger Morris, *Partners in power: The Clintons and Their America*, New York: Henry Holt, 1996; George Archibald, "Partners in power: The Clintons and Their America," *Insight on the News*, July 22, 1996; "Student Bill Clinton 'spied' on Americans abroad for CIA," Sunday Telegraph, 9 June, 1996.

[584] At the time, many young people hitch hiked and slept in youth hostels in Europe, including the author, but there is no record that either Clinton or other players in our tale ever did Europe on $5 a day. Reports on FBI raids on Weather targets found abandoned apartments with evidence of half dozens of residents. Cathy Wilkerson later claimed to live on peanut butter while Ayers and Dohrn lived a higher style.

[585] "Hanoi Keys Appeal to US Mood," *Christian Science Monitor*, Hong Kong, October 17, 1969. TTU archives. Cited in Rothrock, 131-132N5.

[586] William S. White, "Moratorium Demonstration Against the War Boomeranged," *Washington Post*, October 18, 1969, A15 quotes Josh Muravchik "Behind the Coming 'March on Washington," *U.S. News & World Report*, Nov. 3, 1969, 24; Staff Study by the Committee on Internal Security, House of Representatives, 91st Congress, 2nd Session, quoted in *Exclusive,* March 6, 1970 cited in Frank J. Rafalko, MH/CHAOS: The CIA's Campaign Against the Radical Left and the Black Panthers, Annapolis: Naval Institute Press, 2011, 141-2..

district comrades informing them that Americans were working "in conjunction" or "in coordination" with Hanoi, Moscow and its front organizations in event scheduling and propaganda themes.[587]

IPS Advocates Viet Cong Victory. One of the hawks on the other side was identified Communist Richard Barnet on Hanoi Radio in November 1969 saying, "The Vietnamese will continue to fight against the aggressors, the same aggressors that we continue to fight in our own country." [588] Barnet and Marcus Raskin founded the $1 million a year[589] Institute for Policy Studies, IPS, most of whose trustees and officers,[590] and paid fellows,[591] took an active role on the Hanoi side of the Vietnam War.

***

Hanoi's Friends in America:
Cronkite, New Mobe, Weathermen, New York Times

Cronkite. On November 10, 1969, CBS's Walter Cronkite opined that U.S. captured Viet Cong documents claiming the VC planned military actions to coincide with November antiwar protests could be propaganda plants,[592] despite a yearlong flurry of Hanoi and VC messages coordinating and advising leaders of the October and November protests. From North Vietnam Pham Van Dong sent messages to New Mobe: "The Vietnamese people thank their friends in America and wish them great success in their mounting movement."

New York Times Reveals Mai Lai, November 12, 1969.

On November 12, 1969, the Seymour Hersh of the *New York Times* reported a rogue Army unit murdering hundreds of women and children in My Lai, South Vietnam during March 1968. Long covered up and publication delayed, My Lai provided grist for the Hanoi propaganda mill. Years of false claims of intentional napalming of children and bombing civilians, hospitals, pagodas, schools and dikes now seemed true for those already predisposed

[587] Le Minh Nguyen, "To Various K's and H's (Regions and Districts), October 27, 1969, Australians captured Nov 4, 1969 attached to "Viet Cong Units Directed to Intensify Struggle to Take Advantage of U.S, Peace Movement," Press Release, No. 98-69, November 30, 1969 United States Mission in Vietnam.

[588] FBI, SAC WFO to Director, Memo Bufile 105-185148, May 4, 1970, 1-2.

[589] IRS 990s for IPS for 1970 and 1971.

[590] Barnet, Raskin, Charlotte Bunch, Christopher Jencks, Robert Levin and Peter Weiss.

[591] Barbara Bick, Fred Branfman, Saul Landau, Staughton Lynd, Paul Jacobs, and Sol Stern.

[592] Walter Cronkite, CBS Evening News, November 10, 1969, Vanderbilt Television Archives.

to hate America. Finding believers the American government routinely practiced genocide suddenly became easier to sell. The timing was perfect, three days before New Mobe's March Against Death. What a coincidence?

House Committee on Internal Security Chairman Richard H. Ichord (D-Mo.) called the November March against Death, "a propaganda maneuver designed and organized by Communists and other revolutionaries." Members of Mobe were certainly the communist Vietnamese's "friends in America." A Lou Harris Poll showed that 65 percent of Americans agreed with Internal Security Chairman Richard H. Ichord (D-Mo.), "Protesters against the war are giving aid and comfort to the Communists." Only 25 percent did not.

SDS Turns Peaceful Protest Violent. On Saturday November 13, 1969 in a 40-hour vigil, some 45,000 peacefully filed past the White House carrying the names of American war dead. Intimidated and fearing a mob attack, a solid ring of closely parked buses blocked access to the White House.

Some 100 broke out of the peaceful, if intimidating, White House procession shouting "Ho, Ho, Ho Chi Minh, the NLF is Gonna Win." The SDS Weathermen, "Mad Dogs and Crazies," carried Viet Cong flags. Later that night, led by Bill Ayers and his Weathermen, some 1,000 to 2,000, rampaged and laid siege to the South Vietnamese Embassy.[593] Bill Ayers remembers that a "counter demonstrating frat boy" had seized and set fire to a Viet Cong flag. "I ...burned my left hand and broke my ring finger rescuing" the Viet Cong flag.[594]

Protesting the trial of the Chicago 8, on Monday, November 15, the Weathermen attacked everything on route to the Department of Justice. Bruce Herschensohn, a Nixon staffer, writes that at the Department of Justice, the SDS ripped down and burned the American flag and raised the Viet Cong.[595]

Meanwhile, the New Mobe sponsored other protests.

***

New Mobe's "March against Death"—November 13-15, 1969

With Sid Peck, Stewart Meacham and Cora Weiss taking leadership, the New Mobe "March against Death" in Washington

---

[593] Bui Diem, The Jaws of History,
[594] Ayers, *Fugitive Days*, 120.
[595] Herschensohn, *An American Amnesia*, 95.

on November 15 was, like the Moratorium, a success. Nationwide, the March attracted 250,000 to 500,000 people by various counts (100,000 in San Francisco). This was a broad-based mass action in which moderates, liberals, pacifists, and Trotskyites participated. Hanoi's call for unity and coordination among contending peace groups in 1969 in Moscow, Stockholm, East Berlin, like its political directives to the Viet Cong cadre, had successfully mobilized in the face of the president and his silent majority.[596]

On December 2, 1969 Madame Ma Thi Chu of the South Vietnam People's Committee in Solidarity with the American People (*Viet My*) sent a message to the New Mobe and the Moratorium saying, "We highly *value* your achievements in forming the anti-Vietnam front...[Y]ou have succeeded with the strength of your *unity...*"[597]

***

COMMITTEE OF LIAISON WITH FAMILIES OF SERVICEMEN DETAINED IN NORTH VIETNAM (COLIFAM)

"Only Communications...Between POWs and Their Families."

In late October 1969, the North Vietnamese asked for Tom Hayden's help. Later Hayden would say, "I helped construct the only communications system there was between POWs and their families."[598] At the request of the North Vietnamese, Tom Hayden (and then Cora Weiss, William Kunstler, Dave Dellinger, Richard Fernandez, Stewart Meacham, and the New Mobilization) developed, staffed, formed, announced, and ran the Committee of Liaison with Families of Servicemen Detained in North Vietnam (COLIFAM) from October 28, 1969 through January 15, 1973. **COLIFAM Hanoi Controlled.** COLIFAM became the sole conduit, an absolute Communist monopoly, on all POW/family mail until the Vietnam War ended for America. All POW mail was addressed "Via Moscow, Soviet Union" according to COLIFAM's instructions to POW families. A COLIFAM information sheet said: "The committee will function

---

[596] Sindlinger poll cited by Howard K. Smith, ABC Evening News on November 14, 1969.
[597] Mass Organizations Back Antiwar Efforts, Liberation Press Agency (Clandestine) 1533 GMT 2 Dec. 69, TTU archives cited in Rothrock, 139N13.
[598] A.P. "Hayden Reveals His CIA Role During the Vietnam War," *San Francisco Examiner*, June 21, 1986.

entirely apart from the U.S. government." Moreover, COLIFAM accused the U.S. government of "using the [POWs'] families' genuine desires as a propaganda ploy." COLIFAM said the U.S. government was jeopardizing "existing communications and the possibility of future releases for the sake of propaganda."

The facts are directly contrary to the COLIFAM information sheet. **Hanoi's COLIFAM Exploited POWs.** All propaganda levers were in the hands of COLIFAM and the Communists, hardly the Pentagon as the COLIFAM claimed. Clearly, the North Vietnamese held all the hostages and controlled the means to generate favorable propaganda. COLIFAM handled all POW mail prior to its transmittal through Moscow to Hanoi. The Defense Department told the Washington *Daily News*, that the Liaison Committee was "in a position…to blackmail and punish (wives) by withholding mail from their husbands."

Some Families "we have to play their game." One wife said, "…any information about our husbands is so precious that if dealing with these so called peace groups will open up communications with Hanoi—even if the North Vietnamese are using us for propaganda, and they are--we have to play their game."[599] Mrs. Peyton McCleary thanked Cora Weiss for the letters and said she was never asked for contributions. Contributors to COLIFAM were told to look "forward to sending more letters" to POWs and receiving strong antiwar messages from them. One sad case was Delia Alvarez, sister of POW Everett Alvarez. Her brother, a victim of torture sent coded, wildly exaggerated, confessions. Jane Fonda persuaded Delia Alvarez to join her in a protest at the Republican Convention in 1972.[600]

Hanoi/COLIFAM Pressured Families to Join Antiwar Movement. COLIFAM repeatedly used its leverage over POWs and their families to spread communist propaganda and to urge prisoner's families to aid the peace movement. Joy Jeffrey noticed that all of Bob Jeffrey's letters came with enclosures, "(propaganda like) Bob was getting in prison every day." Letters from antiwar groups were "a torture treatment …on the families…"[601] POW wives said Cora Weiss offered mail from

---

[599] Jim G. Lucas, "POW wives Show Ire," *Washington Daily News*, Feb. 5, 1970, p.1. Texas Tech.
[600] *San Francisco Chronicle*, Aug. 19, 1972; Hubbell, *POW*, 224.
[601] "Room Prepared for Son's Return," New York Times, 2:1:18 1973; J.M. Heslop and Dell R. Van Orden, *From the Shadows of Death: Stories of POWs*," Salt Lake City:

their husbands if the wives publicly opposed the war. Robert Turner says,

Most ... showed incredible courage.., refusing to cooperate even when they were told that if they denounced the war their husbands or sons would get better treatment in Hanoi.

I was--and I remain--tremendously proud of them.[602]

Cora Weiss's loyalties to the North Vietnamese were never in doubt.

Some Families Resisted. A horrific case is that of Janis Dodge, wife of POW Lt. Ronald Dodge. According to Janis Dodge, Cora Weiss

was absolutely horrible. She told me-- and many other wives and mothers-- that if I wanted to correspond with my husband, I would have to go through her. And she wanted the families to make antiwar statements.[603]

They killed Ron...kept it a secret for fourteen years.

Then in July 1981, Hanoi decided to return Ron's body.[604]

Carol McCain, wife of POW John McCain, refused to send letters through COLIFAM insisting on using the channels of the Geneva Convention. John McCain got approximately one letter a year.[605]

Hanoi Selected What POWs to Reveal to Families. The Vietnamese cadre categorized American POWs in their detention as ... "progressive" or "stubborn." A CIA report: "prisoners were listed as, "A," for special information, "B," high intelligence value, but uncooperative, and "C," little value to DRV.[606]

No attempt was made to contact relatives in the U.S. of ...categories "A" and "B"... because it might [lead to]...their identities [as live POWs].

Deseret, 1973, 21-22; cited in Craig Howes, Voices of the Vietnam POWs, New York: Oxford University Press, 1993, 155N163.

[602] Dr. Robert Turner, "On the Edge of Treason?: John Kerry's exploitation of POWs and their Families," http://www.winter soldier.com/staticpages/index.php?page=EdgeofTreason

[603] Janis Dodge, in Santoli, *To Bear*... 243.

[604] Janis Dodge, in Santoli, *To Bear*... *243-4;* Garnett "Bill" Bell with George J. Veith, *Leave No Man Behind: Bill Bell and the Search for American POW/MIAs from the Vietnam War*, Madison: Goblin Fern Press, 2004,177, 443.

[605] Lieut. Commander John S. McCain III, U.S. Navy, "How the POW's Fought Back," *US News & World Report*, May 14, 1973.

[606] Bell and Veith

The identity of category "A" (information possessed) prisoners were carefully guarded to [prevent corrective] …countermeasures…

Similarly, the identity of the category "B" (uncooperative) prisoners was kept secret because they may not have survived the interrogations…"[607]

The wife of POW Allen Shuman said before the House Committee on Internal Security, that

One of the cruelest activities of … COLIFAM … was … releasing a handful of names of POWs they claimed … were still alive.

They never put out full lists, just a trickle…to increase the anguish.[608]

Sybil Stockdale said the WSP women "seemed not to care whether we ever got the mail as long as they got credit for the North Vietnamese in the newspapers. …They were giving aid and comfort to the enemy, but there was just the usual silence from our side."[609] The North Vietnamese made it chillingly clear that "cooperating" with COLIFAM was the perquisite for gaining the freedom of American POWs: "The success of … COLIFAM … would be the first step toward the release of the pilots."[610] For three years, the North Vietnamese used COLIFAM to release an occasional POW and to dribble out very small quantities of mail (2 letters per year per POW) and incomplete lists of POWs (e.g. 336) held. COL was a front for North Vietnamese propaganda to end the war on Vietnamese terms. For example, COLIFAM practiced techniques right out of the Viet Cong manual:

Mobilize the soldier's dependents as the key spear … to attack the enemy … Each relative should be encouraged to write a letter to their soldier relative telling …how they are miserable and sick … Letters may be anonymous.[611]

Thus, COLIFAM was merely another Viet Cong front, like the Soldier's Mother's Association, Families of Patriotic Soldier's Association etc.

COLIFAM Carried Hanoi War Propaganda

[607] Bell and Veith

[608] Stephen Powell, *Covert Cadre*, p. 39, N 57 cites: U.S., Congress, House Committee on Internal Security, *Annual Report,* 1973, 93rd Cong., 1st Sess. January 24, 1974, 25.

[609] James and Sybil Stockdale, In Love and War: The Story of a Family's Ordeal and Sacrifice during the Vietnam Years," Maryland: Naval Institute Press, 1990, 204 cited in Craig Howes, Voices of the Vietnam POWs, New York: Oxford University Press, 1993, 71N77.

[610] *Covert Cadre*, 39N56 cites Liberation News Service press release, March 14, 1970. Gannon, *A Biographical Dictionary of the Left*, [1969-1973] Belmont (Mass.): Western Islands, Vol. III, 54 cites both Robert Horner of HISC and COLIFAM publications.

[611] Douglas Pike, *Viet Cong*, 260-61.

- COLIFAM press conferences and newsletters covered such topics as:
  - South Vietnamese torture of its POWs;
  - Grand living conditions and the humane treatment of American POWs in the "Hanoi Hilton" (coined by POW Edwin Shuman as a joke, but appropriated by Cora Weiss);
  - American atrocities and massacres in Vietnam; and
  - The need for immediate American withdrawal from Vietnam.

After investigating COLIFAM, the House Committee on Internal Security concluded:

> The (COLIFAM) is a propaganda tool of the North Vietnamese government, playing upon the hopes and anxieties of the wives of American prisoners of war for Communist propaganda purposes. The activities of the Committee of Liaison aid and abet a nation with which the United State is engaged in armed conflict. The Committee of Liaison appears to be acting as an agent for a foreign power-- the Government of North Vietnam.[612]

From 1970-1973 the FBI investigated (COLIFAM) for being a North Vietnamese propaganda organ, but the FBI concluded, "No information was developed warranting prosecution of COLIFAM for solicitation under the Foreign Agents Registration Act." Obviously the FBI, actually the Justice Department, passed on prosecuting any other crimes that may have occurred besides solicitation. As the war continued, there would be mounting evidence that COLIFAM was a vehicle of North Vietnamese propaganda. The Justice Department simply decided not to prosecute COLIFAM under the Foreign Agents Registration Act, FARA.[613]

***

While COLIFAM was a vehicle for psywar, the Venceremos Brigade would perform a wider range of chores for Hanoi and the international communist movement, for a few espionage, terror, spying.

---

[612] House Committee on Internal Security, Annual Report, 1970, 149.
[613] Dale Van Atta, *With Honor: Melvin Laird in War, Peace and Politics*, Madison: University of Wisconsin, 2008, 209.

THE FIRST CONTINGENT OF VENCEREMOS
BRIGADE, December 1-5.

The first contingent of the Venceremos brigade, a group of 216, left in late November and early December 1 and 5. 1969.[614] Among the first contingent were many weathermen.[615]

Upon arriving at their destination their camp director greeting them said, "The sugar harvest was dedicated to the heroic Vietnamese people (and was) to fight American aggression in Vietnam." The first brigade met Vietnamese who gave them "rings made of metal from U.S. airplanes downed in Vietnam."[616] The blood of dead and wounded American aircrews paid for the rings.

Psychological Conditioning. The Cubans and Vietnamese immersed the Brigadiers in an ideological boot camp, basic military training, breaking down their individuality and developing their collectivist consciousness. There were continuous meetings of self-criticism - Blacks of whites, women of men, etc. Individuals criticized others for their racism, selfishness, cleanliness, drug use or bourgeois attitudes.[617]

Revolutionary Indoctrination. Cuban Communists, Viet Cong, North Vietnamese and a delegation from the Soviet Union[618] indoctrinated the Venceremos brigade in revolutionary propaganda and tactics and praised the anti-war movement as the vanguard of a revolution in the U.S. The Cuban Committee of Solidarity with South Vietnam declared, "Cuba, Vietnam and you shall conquer." Over "five weeks...long discussions...Weatherman was told to raise the level of

---

[614] Adair *Cong Record*, February 24, 1970, H1195; Chicago *Tribune*, Nov. 28, 1969.
[615] Nichamin, Pierre Joseph Barthel, Neal Birnbaum, Marianne Camp, Sonia Helen Dettman, Linda Sue Evans, Laura Ann Obert, Nicholas Britt Riddle, Sheila Marie Ryan, Jeffrey David Sokolow, Mallorie N. Tolles, Robert Greg Wilfong, and Donna Jean Willmott. Also Bert Garskof, Sandy Pollack, Leslie Cagan. CPUSA, WPC and SDS member Sandy Pollack would serve on Venceremos's national committee (1971-1985), help found the U.S. Peace Council (1979) and travel widely as its international solidarity coordinator, lead mass protests favoring a nuclear freeze and Communists in Central America before she was killed in a Cuban airlines flight to Nicaragua. Leslie Cagan would head Mobilization for Survival and successor organizations including United for Peace and Justice protesting America's "permanent warfare and empire-building" in Iraq and elsewhere. FBI, FOIA, Weather Underground. The primary source is Acting SAC Chicago to Director, memo, "Foreign Influence-Weather Underground Organization," August 20, 1976, 96; Hollander, 357N26; Hollander, 244N66;. Adair, *Cong Record*, February 24, 1970, H1195.
[616] Adair, *Cong Record*, February 24, 1970, H1195.
[617] Hollander, 229-230N126.
[618] Eastland, 7465.

confrontation in the U.S. in order to help the NLF and North Vietnamese win in Vietnam."[619]

Skillful Statecraft: Terrorists. Propagandists. Spies. The Cuban program turned out sweet products of nonagricultural value, skillful statecraft including thousands of propagandists, an unknown number of intelligence operatives, and a score or so of Weatherman terrorists. Some traveled covertly to the Soviet Union, China, North Korea, North Vietnam and Eastern Europe, perhaps to receive espionage training.[620]

Terrorists. Propagandists. Spies. Some of the Brigade members received extensive training in the tools of revolutionary terrorism -- bombs, propaganda, finance, etc.[621] Upon their return some veterans of the Venceremos brigade turned to revolutionary terrorism.

Intelligence Agents. Besides propaganda and outright terrorism, another mission of the Venceremos Brigade was to gather military, political, and economic intelligence on the U.S. for the Cuban equivalent of the Soviet KGB, the DGI.[622] Nichamin's most important task was establishing contact with the Cuba Mission,[623] and perhaps the Vietnamese Mission.[624] After meetings in July, Huynh Van Ba, had also kept telephone contact with the Weatherman controlled SDS national office[625] making requests of Bernardine Dohrn and talking to Mark Rudd. Rudd told Huynh Van Ba about an eight-page issue of *New Left Notes*, "Vietnam has Won" of August 29, 1969.[626]

---

[619] Ron Jacobs, The Way The Wind Blew: A History Of The Weather Underground, Verso, 1997, 28.

[620] "Declassified U.S. Government intelligence information regarding the communist and foreign connections of the Weather Underground. Presented as evidence, on the agreement of the prosecution and defense counsel, in the trial of W. Mark Felt and Edward S, Miller," 64 at www.usasurvival.org.

[621] See: Testimony of Geraldo Peraza, Senate, Subcommittee on Security and Terrorism, Hearing, February 26, 1982, 21-24, cited in S. Steven Powell, *Covert Cadre,* 31N18; Eastland, p. 7465; James L. Tyson, *Target America: The Influence of Communist Propaganda on U.S. Media,* 27; Fontain, 138N34 cites Passony and Bouchey, 82.

[622] Bittman, 28.

[623] Fontain, p. 138 N 34 cites Passony and Bouchey, 82. Also: Eastland, 7464.

[624] James L. Tyson, Target America: The Influence of Communist Propaganda on U.S. Media, 27.

[625] FBI, FOIA, Weather Underground. The primary source is Acting SAC Chicago to Director, memo, "Foreign Influence-Weather Underground Organization," August 20, 1976, 96.

[626] FBI, FOIA, Weather Underground. The primary source is FBI, FOIA, Weather Underground. The primary source is Chicago to Director, memo, "Foreign Influence-Weather Underground Organization," August 20, 1976, 105.

The Venceremos Brigade were clearly agents of the Soviet-Cubans. They were propagandists, and some were terrorists and intelligence operatives.

Venceremos in Cuba. On December 10, 1969 in an interview on *Granma,* the official Cuban communist newspaper, Venceremos leader Julie Nichamin said, in part, "The battle of the Vietnamese is the battle…against American imperialism. …The way for us to fight American imperialism is by fighting on many fronts."[627] And from Cuba in the December 21, 1969 issue of *Verde Olive*, the official publication of the Cuban armed forces, came a letter from Julia Nichamin after a meeting with Cuban and Vietnamese Communists:

> The meeting we had today with the Cubans and the Vietnamese people has shown us the true meaning of internationalism: 'all of us are involved in the same struggle against Yanqui imperialism. … "[628]

***

National Council of Churches.

"No Christmas as Usual," On December 5, 1969 the Communist *Daily World* reported that the tax exempt National Council of Churches, NCC, in a convention of 790 delegates had unanimously "condemned the massacre of Vietnamese civilians by U.S. troops." President Dr. Cynthia Wedel announced plans to collect funds in churches during the Christmas season to provide "emergency medical relief to civilian Vietnamese casualties."[629] The NCC, formally endorsed both the October Vietnam Moratorium and the November March against Death. For years the National Council proved itself loyal to Hanoi and Moscow.[630]

---

[627] Julie Nichamin interview, *Granma*, December 10, 1969 cited in FBI, FOIA, Weather Underground. The primary source is Acting SAC Chicago to Director, memo, "Foreign Influence-Weather Underground Organization," August 20, 1976, 121-2.
[628] Georgie Anne Geyer and Keyes Beech, "Cuba: School for US Radicals," *Chicago Sun Times*, October 1970.
[629] William Allen, *Daily World*, December 5, 1969 quoted in David Emerson Gumaer, "The National Council of Churches," *Apostasy, at* www.thephora.net/forum/showthread.php?t=4623
[630] Within months in April 1970, James Armstrong would tell General Conference of United Methodists in St. Louis the military dominated the USA, South Vietnam was a "corrupt police state," and Americans killed had died in vain for "an immoral and unjust war." For decades thereafter the tax exempt NCC, a founder of the National Emergency Committee of Clergy Concerned (the predecessor to Clergy and Laity Concerned) supported Communist Vietnam under virtually all circumstances. The NCC claimed that postwar Vietnam was "building a new society" despite its millions imprisoned in reeducation camps and millions of fleeing boat people; said the U.S. shared blame for the Cambodian holocaust with Pol Pot; and universally condemned all anticommunist governments across the globe. The NCC paid for "instructional

The New Mobilization, allies of the NCC declared "1969: No Christmas As Usual," to disrupt the religious observance of Christianity, by public vigils and reading lists of the war dead.[631]

***

HEGDAHL, FRISHMAN AND FAMILIES CONFRONT CORA WEISS

December 9-11, the alleged POW benefactors of communist lodgings, recreation, Christmas parties, cuisine, recreation, and leniency, Doug Hegdahl and Robert Frishman told their story to Congress. Robert Frishman said:

> I don't think solitary confinement, forced statements, [being] in a cage for three years ... removed fingernails, being hung from the ceiling [with] an infected arm without medical treatment ... [being] dragged with a broken leg and not allowing exchange of mail for prisoners are humane.[632]

As a "war criminal," Cora Weiss said, Frishman was lucky to have any arm at all. Only Americans brutalized prisoners.

WSP and POW Families, Laos in December. In early December 1969 Cora Weiss, Ethel Taylor and Madeleine Duckles of WSP traveled to Hanoi to talk to North Vietnamese officials. **Cora Weiss in Charge.** Duckles remembers Cora Weiss hustling off the other WSP women to "go to nursery schools or something." Cora said, "the Vietnamese wanted to talk to *her* about the issue of political prisoners" and POW mail.[633] Weiss described POWs quarters as immaculately clean concrete wardrooms, dormitory bedrooms, with showers, and shade trees. They had cards, chess sets and barbells.[634] Duckles

---

materials for the PBS, WGBH Boston, production the pro-Hanoi "Vietnam: A Television History," gave a half million dollars to help, in part, the funding of labor camps in New Economic Zones. NCC's James Armstrong said, Hanoi "should be hailed for its moderation and its extraordinary efforts to achieve reconciliation among all its people." Robert Wilson, Biases and Blind Spots: Methodism and Foreign Policy Since World War II, Chapter 4, The Reemergence of Radicalism, 5; Rael Jean Isaac, "Do You Know Where your Church Offerings Go?," *Reader's Digest*, January 1983, 12-0-125; David Emerson Gumaer, "APOSTASY: The National Council of Churches," at nccwatch/articles/apostasy.htm200815; James Banerian and the Vietnamese Community Action Committee, *Losers Are Pirates: A close Look at the PBS Series "Vietnam: A Television History,"* Phoenix: Tieng Me Publications, 1984, 15-16.

[631] Stewart Meacham, Dave Dellinger, and Cora Weiss, New Mobilization, Dear Friend letter, postmarked 12/8/69, Friedman to Canfield e-mail, December 3, 2008.

[632] House, Committee on Internal Security, Investigation of Students for a Democratic Society, Part 7-A, Frishman testimony, December 9-10, 1969, 2187-2258. Also in Richard Nixon, *No More Vietnams*, 129-30.

[633] Wells interview of Duckles, Wells, *The War Within*, 339.

[634] "A Chosen Few Tread a Productive Path," *Virginian-Pilot*, June 26, 1970; FBI,

was charmed. Music, patriotic songs, a music conservatory, a concert and sailing among the majestic islands in the emerald waters of Ha Long Bay somehow persuaded her of the innate peacefulness of the Vietnamese communists and the barbarity of Americans. Duckles, says, if asked, would deny she was either a Communist or a traitor. "The Vietnamese are not my enemy." **POW Wives Turned Away.** Meanwhile in Vientiane, Laos two wives tried to deliver letters to the North Vietnamese embassy. The wives were told to keep the letters, take them back home and contact the peace movement.

Weiss claimed she had no POW letters to return. She said the State Department was holding up POW mail.[635] In the event Taylor and Duckles did return with 138 letters from POWs. At a press conference on December 23 they showed photos of a POW whose mother WSP had telephoned.[636] WSP forwarded the POW letters to their families with a note under the masthead of WSP.[637] By early January, AFSC's Louis Schneider would bring back another 69 letters[638]—traded for medical equipment. Unstated, the US government did not confiscate POW mail as Weiss had claimed.

***

VC Losing War in Shadows?

In North Vietnam, the 85,000 casualties of VC cannon fodder in Tet 1968 led to a shift in 1969 from armed struggle to midnight terror and political struggle. The official history of the People's Army of Vietnam reports:

> By the end of 1969, the enemy had retaken almost all of our liberated zones.... Units were forced to begin alternately eating rice for one meal and manioc for the next..."[639]

In South Vietnam under directive 04/CT70 VC cadre and troops were re-indoctrinated upon their political tasks, the three prong attack to defeat the enemy and reminded "the war will

---

Norfolk, NF-100-6833, LHM, n.d. 115-116

[635] FBI, Albuquerque, fragment AQ 100-3655, n.d. 4-5.

[636] FBI, Boston, interview of [Redacted]on August 4, 1970, FD-302, August 14, 1970; FBI, fragment COLIFAM, n.d. 2-3 of 6.

[637] Ethel Taylor to Dear, Women Strike for Peace, Philadelphia, December 17, 1969.

[638] Louis W. Schneider and Roger G. Fredrickson to Dear Friend, AFSC, Philadelphia, January 20, 1970.

[639] *Victory in Vietnam: The Official History of the People's Army of Vietnam*, William J. Duiker (Foreword), Merle l. Pribbenow (Translator) 249.

turn in our favor on all three fronts: military, political and diplomatic...[640]

The antiwar movement in America had become a growing part of the Vietnamese political strategy for victory since communist military force had failed on the battlefield in 1968 and modest pacification was also succeeding against the Viet Cong cadre in many villages and hamlets. The CIA thought that Hanoi did not consider antiwar activity as "decisive" and that victory was "not dependent on the U.S. antiwar movement."[641]

The events of 1969 suggested otherwise.

US government's pacification of its own AmeriCong was not going as well as Saigon's counterinsurgency in South Vietnam.

***

---

[640] Directive 04/CT70, COSVN (U), ABSOLUTE SECRET, TV.C.69 to (all) units; Instructions for the implementation of Directive No. 4/CT70 and accomplishment of the political mission in Campaign X," 20 February 1970, COMUSMAC, CDEC Doc Log No. 05-3134-70.

[641] Frank J. Rafalko, *MH/CHAOS: The CIA's Campaign Against the Radical Left and the Black Panthers*, Annapolis: Naval Institute Press, 2011, 158.

Part III. 1970 Summary

Ending 1969, positive responses to Nixon's "Silent Majority" speech and surveys ultimately would show the Anerican public held contempt for the peace movement. Undeterred, during 1969 Hanoi and friends stayed on task, meet frequently and events moved in their favor.

Jane Fonda. In 1970 stories of an active political war in America filled the news. Police arrested Jane Fonda returning from Canada. Jane Fonda twice gave public speeches saying she thought everyone ought to be on their knees praying for communism. Fonda's F--- The Army, FTA, toured military bases and campuses. With a French communist tour guide of America, Elizabeth Vialland, Fonda soon became a revolutionary. "The Russians had started it all, Vailland convinced Jane."

After homemade bombs exploded in a Greenwich Village townhouse killing and scattering the body parts of three Weathermen, two naked women terrorists escaped. There after the Weather Underground fulfilled a bombing pledge from Santa Barbara to Boston.

Havana, Hanoi and the SDS created Venceremos Brigades indoctrinating and training American revolutionaries for decades.

Hanoi and the Americong formed COLIFAM to showcase POWS and to intimidate families into joining the pro-Hanoi antiwar movement. POW wives desperately toured the planet in search of news and letters from their husbands.

Antiwar activists met Vietnamese Communists in Stockholm, Hanoi, Vientiane, Moscow, Paris, Helsinki, Stockholm, Vancouver and Canada. The Soviet controlled Stockholm Conference on Vietnam pressured the peace movement to coordinate mass actions and propaganda. At Hanoi's urging, the movement organized GIs and deserters. At the Paris peace talks, Le Duc Tho mocked Henry Kissinger about the peace movement.

Lt. John Kerry joined the executive committee of VVAW and led VVAW Operation RAW (Rapid American Withdrawal), an 86-mile march to Valley Forge where John Kerry and Fonda both gave speeches though in 2004 Kerry denied any significant association with Fonda.

A Congressional delegation "finds" "Tiger Cages" at Con Son Island allegedly abusing political prisoners. The Tiger Cages propaganda launches Tom Harkin's long political career and ultimately persuades Congress to abandon Indochina.

Communists hail the "comrades in arms" in Eldridge Cleaver's large cavalcade to Hanoi and other communist capitols.

Nixon's invasion "violates' North Vietnam's Cambodian sanctuary. Students killed at Kent State and Jackson State mobilize thousands of protesters snuffing out news of victory in Cambodia.

Ending 1970, Hanoi and friends wrote and promoted a People's Peace Treaty outlining Hanoi's conditions for a settlement and promising the good life in Vietnam after peace. Ignored, anti-communist Saigon quietly takes back villages and wins many hearts and minds. The media, falsely, reports otherwise.

Chapter 5. Coordination, Conspiracy, and Boom

"Christian" Clergy Hate Capitalist Imperialism. In January 1970, Clergy and Laity Concerned, CALC, sought "not simply an end to the war in Vietnam, but a struggle against American imperialism...Our task is to join those who ...hate...corporate power...."[642]

Caught U.S. Army Drops Domestic Intelligence. In the January 1970 issue of *Washington Monthly,* a former Army intelligence officer, Christopher Pyle, blew the whistle on the Army gathering intelligence on the antiwar movement: "The U.S. Army has been closely watching ...protests of all kinds..."[643] Unmolested in rallies of hundreds of thousands, the ACLU, WSP, National Mobe, CALC etc claimed the Army cast a chill upon First Amendment rights.[644]

Pyle and others[645] concluded the Army had collected data useless to its legitimate mission of restoring public order. Among those monitored without reason, were conservative *National Review*, John Birch Society, and Young Americans for Freedom. After bad press, on 19 February 1970, the Army ordered all civil disturbance and civilian biographic data destroyed.[646] Two years later, a communist front, Alliance to End Repression said the Army had files on 28 million.[647]

Army intelligence did not chill collaboration with Hanoi, but the Ohio National Guard heated up the confrontations at Kent State

---

[642] *Information Digest*, Vol. XIII, #6, March 21, 1980, 86.

[643] Christopher H. Pyle, "CONUS Intelligence: The army Watches Civilian Politics," *Washington Monthly*, January 1970; C. H. Pyle "CONUS Revisited: The Army Covers Up" *Washington Monthly*, July 1970; Robert O'Harrow interview of Chris Pyle, "No Place to Hide," PBS, http://americanradioworks.publicradio.org/features/noplaceto hide/pyle.html

[644] Ralph Michael Stein, *Laird v. Tatum: The Supreme Court and a First Amendment Challenge to Military Surveillance of Lawful Civilian Political Activity*, School of law, Faculty Publications, Pace University 1973 at http://digitalcommons.pace.edu/lawfaculty/285.

[645] Paul Cowan, Nick Egelson, and Nat Hentoff, *State Secrets: Police Surveillance in America* (New York: Holt, Rinehart, and Winston, 1974), 13.

[646] John P. Finnegan, *Military Intelligence,* compiled by Romana Danysh, Army lineage series, Center of Military History, United States Army, Washington, D. C., 1998 Chap.9: Vietnam and Beyond, 163. http://www.history.army.mil/books/Lineage/mi/ch9.htm

[647] Senate Internal Security Subcommittee, Hearings, *The Nationwide Drive Against Law Enforcement Intelligence Operations*, part 2, July 14, 1975, 115.

French Reds Join Peace Movement. In Saigon Jean Debris and Andre Menras, members of French Red Youth International Cooperation Mission,[648] climbed a statute, unfurled a Viet Cong flag and tossed 6,000 leaflets urging U. S. withdrawal. [649] Saigon imprisoned Debris and Menras on Con Son Island. They later join Hayden/Fonda's IPC.

Among defenders of Debris and Menras was the *Secours Populaire Francais,* a humanitarian aid organization for decades reserving its outrage for communists causes (Sacco and Vanzetti, Dimitrov, Spanish Republicans, Henri Martin).[650]

At a Soviet dominated World Peace Council, WPC, meeting in Africa in January, CPUSA leaders Carlton Goodlett, Irving Sarnoff and Ron Young plan a meeting in Vancouver February 7-8, 1970.

***

COLIFAM Launched:
Committee of Liaison with Families of Servicemen Detained in North Vietnam

Hanoi Created COLIFAM. On January 15, 1970 Cora Weiss and David Dellinger, co-chairmen, debuted the Committee of Liaison with Families of Servicemen Detained in North Vietnam, COLIFAM.[651] WSP and AFSC promptly told POW families their official contact with their loved one was now COLIFAM, not the U.S.Post Office. The *New York Times* and *AP* dutifully wrote Hanoi "agreed" or "approved" the COLIFAM's control of POW mail.[652] The CPUSA newspaper *Daily World* said Hanoi formed COLIFAM. The COLIFAM Information Sheet said, "The Committee of Liaison was …an initiative created by the North Vietnamese." (Legal disclaimer) "It is not in any sense representing the government of North Vietnam." To clarify, "the committee will be dealing solely with (Hanoi)…entirely apart from the United States Government." In

---

[648] "First foreigner granted Vietnamese citizenship," at http://vietnamese language.wordpress.com/2011/06/first-foreign…

[649] "Frenchman interned in Nam speaks on 'Thieu prisoners', *Jambar*, Youngstown State University, November 2, 1973, 5.

[650] Observatoire de l'action humanitaire, "Secours populaire francais (French People's Aid)," www. Observatoire-humanitaire.org/fusion.php?1=GB&id=2

[651] Additional committee members representing various organizations were Rennie Davis, Rev. Richard Fernandez, Maggie Geddes, Stewart Meacham, Prof. Bea Seitzman, Ethel Taylor, Barbara Webster, and Trudi Young.

[652] "Foes of War Form Group to Forward Letters to P.O.Ws," New York Times, January 16, 1970; "Antiwar Group Seen as Liaison to U.S. POWS," AP, San Diego Union, January 19, 1970.

a COLIFAM letter to POW families, Hanoi "...has decided to use our committee as a channel for communications..."[653]

COLIFAM Propaganda. COLIFAM said, the return of the POWs "can only come with ... withdraw(al) from Vietnam."[654] In effect, the POWs were hostages of COLIFAM and Hanoi. The Navy noted , "The action of (Hanoi) ...is an obvious propaganda ploy designed to promote the credibility of those who oppose the United States position in Vietnam." Yet, unlike Hanoi, the U.S. Navy would not impede communications,[655]whatever the conduit to servicemen.

Cora Weiss Introduced COLIFAM to Congress. Cora Weiss invited POW families to her speech on January 27, 1970 in the Cannon Office Building. Only two POW wives and a daughter showed up. Weiss concentrated upon US war crimes, only briefly touching conditions of POW. The camps were nice and POWs treated very well.

Weiss attacked former POWs Frishman and Hegdahl "kept under wraps" until "fabrications" of torture could be prepared.[656] The former POW's were "making inflammatory remarks... intended to influence the American people to hate the North Vietnamese.[657]

***

Coordination in Quebec and Vancouver. Quebec. On January 31, 1970, peace activists representing the Chicago Peace Council (Sylvia Kushner, identified CPUSA) and the New Mobe (Katherine Camp, Arnold Johnson, and Stewart Meacham) met with the North Vietnamese and representatives of the Soviet-controlled WPC in Quebec. Other Americans in Quebec were Stanley Faulkner, Joseph Crown, Pauline Rosen, Rev. Richard Norford of New Mobe.[658] They discussed plans for New Mobe's spring 1970 offensive.[659]

---

[653] Richard Fernandez (CALC), Stewart Meacham (AFSC), and Ethel Taylor to POW families, COLIFAM, no letterhead, n.d.; Quote also cited in "'Peace Leader' Says No Hope of Prisoner Return Short of Red Victory," *Combat*, Vol. 2, No. 8, April 15, 1979, 1.

[654] "Ready to Assist POW Families," *Daily World*, January 19, 1970; News Release, COLIFAM, n.d. January 15, 1970; Information Sheet, COLIFAM n. d.; Functions of the Committee.

[655] D.H. Chinn to Navy Wives and Parents, January 21, 1970.

[656] FBI, Norfolk, interview of [Redacted] June 11, 1970, FD-302, June 22, 1970; FBI, Baltimore, interview of [redacted], on December 16, 1970, FD-302, December 19, 1970.

[657] "A Chosen Few Tread a Productive Path," Virginian-Pilot, June 26, 1970.

[658] HISC, Staff Study, Subversive Involvement in the Origin, Leadership and Activities

Vancouver: World Peace Council.[660] New Mobe invited 125 Americans including nine SDS/Weathermen[661] to the WPC in Vancouver.[662] Vietnamese were Paris negotiators Tran Cong Tuong and Ha Huy Oanh. WPC representatives were Krishna Menon, Pastor Martin Niemoller and Romesh Chandra. The conference endorsed upcoming protests on April 15, immediate withdrawal of U.S., and a war crimes confab. New Mobe West falsely declared, "The conference was ...the *first time* ... the DRV ...have met with US citizens."[663]

***

Marines in Son Thang: War, Crime and Punishment. "Literally millions of military patrols encountered Vietnamese civilians without incident," according to Gary D. Solis, author of *Son Thang: An American War Crime.* **Hot, Tired, Dirty and Angry.** Yet the war crimes of a few troops, however infrequent, alienated the Vietnamese and defamed the reputation of the USA. The hamlet of Son Thang was in "Arizona Territory," Viet Cong country, where the 7th Marines ran patrols day and night and spent up to ninety sleep-deprived and dirty days on patrol in sweltering and enervating 100-degree tropical heat.

    Civilian Combatants Kill Marines. Many civilians acted as enemy combatants. Old women planted bobby-traps. Children lured troops into ambushes. Lt. Col. Jim King said, "In this shadowy war where friends, enemy and neutral are virtually indistinguishable, and where women and children have often set booby-traps...'minimizing noncombatants

---

of the New Mobilization Committee to End the War in Vietnam And Its Predecessor Organizations, 1970, 34, 35, 47-48.

[659] Max Friedman Lawyers Committee file to Author.

[660] FBI *Information Digest Special Report on VVAW*, Aug. 25, 1972 cited in Fedora post to FreeRepublic.comhttp:/http://www.wintersoldier.com/staticpages/index.php?page=Info DigestonVVAW; British Columbia Peace Council, Library of University of British Columbia, Box 8-11a, contains World Peace Council: Conference Vancouver 1970; Frank J. Rafalko, *MH/CHAOS: The CIA's Campaign Against the Radical Left and the Black Panthers*, Annapolis: Naval Institute Press, 2011, 137.

[661] Frank J. Rafalko, *MH/CHAOS: The CIA's Campaign Against the Radical Left and the Black Panthers*, Annapolis: Naval Institute Press, 2011, 137.

[662] HISC, Staff Study, Subversive Involvement in the Origin, Leadership and Activities of the New Mobilization Committee to End the War in Vietnam And Its Predecessor Organizations, 1970, XII-XIII.

[663] *Emphasis* added. "Vancouver Peace Conference," New Mobilization Committee West, Newsletter Number 4, February 13, 1970 cited in HISC, Staff Study, Subversive Involvement in the Origin, Leadership and Activities of the New Mobilization Committee to End the War in Vietnam And Its Predecessor Organizations, 1970, 48.

casualties' is translated in the field, rightly or wrongly...to shoot anything that moves at night..."[664]

Son Thang-4 Kills Marines. Nearly continuous Viet Cong mortar and M-79 fire on February 12, 1970 killed nine men of Company B, 1st Battalion, 7th Marines patrolling the thatch-roofed hamlet of Son Thang-4 south of Danang. A woman and a child ran luring troops into an ambush.[665] Two days later on February 14, Marines captured an 11-year Viet Cong. The next day on February 15, Marines killed an armed Viet Cong woman. Two days later on the 17th a child lured a patrol into another ambush killing two Marines.[666] And on the morning of February 19, 1970, a booby trap killed the well-liked Pfc. Richard Whitmore in Company B. After a week of encounters with "civilian" enemy combatants, American troops were in a very foul mood.

Revenge Patrol. Just after dark on February 19, a five-man patrol, Lance corporal Randall Dean Herrod, Private Michael A. Schwarz, Pfc. Thomas R. Byrd, Pfc. Michael S. Krichten, and Pfc. Samuel A. Green, Jr., conducted a night ambush patrol.

The Marines entered Son Thang-4 and methodically murdered 16 women and children. The victims were six women and ten children: a fifty-year-old, a blind twenty-year-old, a sixteen-year-old, a five-year-old, a forty-three year old woman, a twelve year old boy, two ten-year old girls and two little boys - one five and the other three years old.

Immediate Investigation. Immediate investigations found no evidence of enemy fire. The patrol killed unarmed civilians. Some may have been Viet Cong-- local officials said so,[667]but they were unarmed. Whether civilians or POWS, the unarmed were due protection.

Maj. Dick Theer said, Son Thang after dark was "extremely hostile. The people...are the VC cadre... and they support actively the enemy forces."[668] Le Thi Thuong testified

---

[664] Lt. Col. Jim King, Article 32 interim Report to CO, Marines, 18 Apr. 1970 cited in Gary D. Solis, *Son Thang: An American War Crime*, New York: Bantam, 1998,114n17
[665] Gary D. Solis, *Son Thang: An American War Crime*, New York: Bantam, 1998,165
[666] Operations Journals of 1/7, Command Chronology, Feb. 1970 entry 171315H, 20; 151115H, 19; 141620H, 18; cited in Gary D. Solis, *Son Thang: An American War Crime*, New York: Bantam, 1998, 163.
[667] cited in Gary D. Solis, *Son Thang: An American War Crime*, New York: Bantam, 1998, 87n27
[668] Gary D. Solis, *Son Thang: An American War Crime*, New York: Bantam, 1998,107.

her dead son was VC, another a member of a VC front, and one an active VC. [669]

VC or not, Theer's investigation brought the atrocity to higher authority. By September four courts martial had plea-bargained immunity for Pfc. Krichten for his testimony. Two, Schwarz and Green were guilty. Private Herrod and Byrd were acquitted.

Oliver North and James Webb: Character Witnesses.

Aiding Herrod's acquittal, Oliver North testified Randall Dean Herrod had saved his life. Future Navy Secretary, U.S. Senator and candidate for President, James H. Webb worked to change Samuel A. Green's dishonorable discharge. Pfc. Green had been in Vietnam only 11 days, was of low intellect and his company B had had "three direct [violent] encounters involving women and children."[670] Webb's testimony was too late to stop Green's suicide.

Battle Fatigue. Oliver North argued, "Only men who had served in combat could appreciate the pressures that Herrod must have been under." [671] Dr. Hayden Donahue, a psychiatrist, believed Herrod suffered from "battle fatigue." Herrod and the others—faced extensive combat and death day after day. Dr. Donahue said instinct had supplanted reason.[672] Fatigue came from marching for hours in hot, humid and insect infested conditions with fitful sleep on hard or wet ground. "You were not the same person you were …at hotel bar in Saigon."[673]

Codes of Morality and War. Nonetheless, men who committed atrocities violated every moral code of man including the rules of war. The Marines were properly prosecuted as war criminals. Of the twenty-seven Marines convicted of crimes during the Vietnam War most received light sentences equivalent to sentences back home.[674]

---

[669] Gary D. Solis, *Son Thang: An American War Crime*, New York: Bantam, 1998, 163-164.

[670] James H. Webb, "The Sad Conviction of Sam Green: The Case for the Reasonable and Honest War Criminal," *Res Ipsa Loquitar*, Georgetown University Law School, 26, Winter 1974, 11 cited in Gary D. Solis, *Son Thang: An American War Crime*, New York: Bantam, 1998, 320.

[671] Doubtful says Gary D. Solis, *Son Thang...* 1997, 247.

[672] Gary D. Solis, *Son Thang*, 247.

[673] From Armond Noble, Army Signal Corps, and on assignment to Vietnam for *Time magazine* and Westinghouse Broadcasting.

[674] CG of 1st Marine Division to II MAF Da Nang, Fleet marine Forces, Commandant,

***

Public Opinion: Hanoi, Peace Groups, POWs. In February 1970, Ross Perot's United We Stand commissioned a Gallup Poll.

Some 51% felt that peace groups did not have a true reflection of the situation in Vietnam. Six in ten believed that South Vietnamese would be killed or imprisoned if the US withdrew.[675]

Of the 68 per cent who had heard or read about the treatment of POWs only seven per cent, one in twelve, believed the POWs were "treated well." Of this specific types of mistreatment believed were: 77 percent felt POWs were not allowed to write letters; 61 percent PWs suffered solitary confinement; 60 per cent POWs tortured; 46 percent POWs starved; 33 per cent POWs killed. Only two percent said the POWs had not experienced any of these things.

Vietnamese Bring US Opinion to Talks. February 21, Kissinger asked Le Duc Tho to take U.S. public opinion out of the talks.

> Tho: "We must take it into account."

> Kissinger: "We will take care of U.S. public opinion. You can take care of opinion in North Vietnam."

> Tho: "Okay, but we must make an assessment... too."

Kissinger felt "caught between the hammer of antiwar pressure and the anvil of Hanoi."[676]

South Vietnam's President Thieu told Ambassador Ellsworth Bunker, "Hanoi's major objectives were ...psychological...attempting to influence U.S. and free world opinion."[677]

Marine Corps, Specat Marine Corps eyes only, Daily Report #2, 27 February 1970 cited in Gary D. Solis, *Son Thang: an American War Crime*, Annapolis: Naval Institute Press,1997; Robinson O. Everett, review of Solis book, Did Military Justice Fail or Prevail? *Michigan Law Review, Vol. 96, No. 6, May 1998*
http://www.law.duke.edu/lens/publications/050698.html
[675] American Prisoners of War in Southeast Asia, Subcommittee on National Security Policy and Scientific Developments of the Committee on Foreign Affairs, House of Representatives, 91st, 2nd, April 29, May 1,6, 1970, 128-30.
[676] Henry Kissinger, Whitehouse Years, Boston: Little Brown, 1979, 444, 260-261 cited in Rothrock *Divided...* 282-283.
[677] Larry Berman, *No Peace, No Honor*, 71-72.

A good reflection of American opinion was a Chicago jury.

Jury Convicts Chicago Conspirators.

February 18, 1970 a Chicago jury convicted five of the Chicago Seven (eight less one-Bobby Seale), Tom Hayden, David Dellinger, Rennie Davis, Abbie Hoffman, and Jerry Rubin, of violating Federal Antiriot laws by crossing state lines with the intent to incite a riot during the Democratic Convention in August 1968. The jury acquitted Lee Joel Weiner and John Radford Froines.

Guilty On Facts: Free on Errors of Judge.

On February 20, 1970, Judge Hoffman sentenced the conspirators to five years in prison and a $5,000 fine, but free them during appeals. Appeals would uphold in copious details the jury's judgment of the facts. They were guilty. Yet on November 21, 1972, the 7th Court of Appeals throw out the jury's decision based on the errors of the trail and the Judge, Julius Hoffman. The Judge failed to resist responding angrily to the Chicago Seven's disruptions of the trial—trial tactics of the National Lawyers Guild and the Communist Party.[678]

One judge declared the defendants lacked a jury of their peers, hippies and revolutionaries. The DOJ did not pursue the case further.

Public opinion had played no part. In March 1970 a rally to support "The Conspiracy" in New York's Central Park expected 100,000 people but only 30 showed up[679] in support of the Chicago Seven.

"Guilty as hell....We wanted disruption. We planned it."

Jerry Rubin later said we were "Guilty as hell. Guilty as charged...Let us face it. We wanted disruption. We planned it." Rubin insisted, " 'guilty' does not mean 'wrong.'[680]

While several Chicago Seven defendants travel was limited, their women ably manned the assaults on capitalist imperialism.

***

Yippie Wives of Chicago Conspirators Meet

---

[678] HCUA, Report on the National Lawyers Guild, *Legal Bulwark of the Communist Party,* Union Calendar No. 1078, 81st Congress, 2d Session, House Report 3123, September 17, 1950, 5.
[679] *Combat*, Vol. 2, No. 7, April 1, 1970, 4.
[680] Rubin column in the *Chicago Sun-Times* cited in " How Long Ago It Seems," *Time*, Mar. 22, 1976 http://www.time.com/time/printout/0,8816,911745,00.html.

North Vietnamese
in Hanoi, Stockholm, Moscow, Cuba

In Stockholm. On March 24, 1970 red diaper baby and Weatherman Nancy Kurshan Rubin and Anita Susan Kushner Hoffman, wives of two of the convicted Chicago Five, Jerry Rubin and Abbie Hoffman, announced they were going to Stockholm to meet Vietnamese leaders. Anita Hoffman, identified herself as "Hanoi Rose. Also accompanying Kursan Rubin and Anita "Hanoi Rose" Hoffman was Judith Gumbo Albert (aka Judy Clavir, Judith Lee Hemblem), wife of Stew Albert and also a red diaper baby.[681] Genie Plamondon, White Panther and Communications Secretary of the World People's Party, WPP, was wife of Lawrence Robert "Pun" Plamandon, WPP's Minister of Defense and convicted bomber at CIA office, Ann Arbor, Michigan.

In Hanoi. Planning demonstrations for the fall, the experienced North Vietnamese greeter of Americans, Do Xuan Oanh,

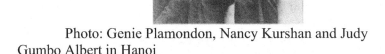

Photo: Genie Plamondon, Nancy Kurshan and Judy Gumbo Albert in Hanoi

invited the women to Hanoi. Do Xuan Oanh charmed the women. Forty-three years later Judy Gumbo Albert Gumbo wrote, he was

a composer, a poet in the romantic Vietnamese/French style, a water color artist and a translator of Mark Twain's *Huckleberry Finn*. Everyone from the inner core of the U.S. anti-war movement knew (Oanh).[682]

Nancy Kurshan wanted to "be a more effective antiwar organizer" …and to "…to address …GIs …on Vietnamese radio and to encourage them to lay down their arms."[683]

---

[681] Judy Gumbo Albert, "Back to Vietnam," *Counterpunch,* January 13, 2014.
[682] Judy Gumbo Albert, "Back to Vietnam," *Counterpunch,* January 13, 2014.

In Stockholm. In late March Kurshan Rubin, Anita Hoffman, and Judith Hemblem attended the Fifth Stockholm Conference.

In Moscow. "We are the Ameri-Cong." On June 10, 1970 the women in Moscow at the American Embassy carried posters, "Ho Chi Minh, The NLF is gonna Win," and "We are the Ameri-Cong."

In Cuba. On August 27, 1970 Robert Greenblatt joined the women meeting a group of North Vietnamese in Cuba.[684]

Forty years later, on Thursday, January 23, 2013, Nancy Kurshan and Judy Gumbo Albert, invited to Hanoi, celebrated the 40th anniversary of the Paris Peace Accords.[685] A ceremony honored Mme. Binh standing behind red velvet curtains on which hung a giant gold star, hammer and sickle. A gold bust of Ho Chi Minh, three times their size gazed down. As a 'red diaper baby,' I understood the symbolism…equivalent to a Lifetime Achievement Award.[686]

***

Venceremos, Weathermen, and Mad Bombers

The second contingent of the Venceremos brigade, 687 strong, was "riddled with agents." Karen Nussbaum says, she "didn't need money because transportation, food, clothing and shelter were free,"[687] Many Weathermen[688] were on the trip. Others of interest were "Daren" [Karen] B. Ackerman,[689] Carol Brightman, CPUSA leader Angela Davis, Karen Beth Nussbaum, Shari Whitehead.

We are Viet Cong. With "NLF banners…hats, headbands, …machetes," Americans met ten smiling

[683] Nancy Kurshan, "From Tiger Cages to Control Units," *Counterpunch*, November 1-3, 2013.

[684] FBI, FOIA, Weather Underground. The primary source is Acting SAC Chicago to Director, memo, "Foreign Influence-Weather Underground Organization," August 20, 1976, 307.

[685] Nancy Kurshan, "From Tiger Cages to Control Units," *Counterpunch*, November 1-3, 2013; Judy Gumbo Albert, "Back to Vietnam," *Counterpunch,* January 13, 2014.

[686] Judy Gumbo Albert, "Back to Vietnam," *Counterpunch,* January 13, 2014.

[687] "How I Cut Cane and Met Fidel," *New York Post,* August 10, 1970.

[688] Include Edith Crichton, David Ira Camp, John De Wind, Nancy Frappier, Vicki Gabriner, Joyce Greenways, Ann Hathaway, Robert Hackman, Marguarita Hope, Lenore Ruth Kalom, Jonathan Lerner, Jeffrey Melish, Jed Proujansky, Daniel Ross Slick, Marguerite "Mini" Smith, Carlie Tanner (Aka. Dr. Caroline Margaret Tanner, M.D., Shirley Jackson, Meg Johnson, Shirley Jameson, Margaret Ann Harmony, Beth Stewart.

[689] "How I Cut Cane and Met Fidel," *New York Post,* August 10, 1970.

Vietnamese. "[W]e are the same fighters on the same front," Martha Trolin said, "To be considered comrades in struggle by the Vietnamese...was the thing."[690]

Focus on GIs. Huynh Van Ba, said, "G.I. organizing is one of the most important things the movement in the U.S. is doing." He was particularly interested in deserters and GI newspapers.[691]

***

Did Bernardine Dohrn Murder Sgt. Brian V. McDonnell?

At 10:44 pm, February 16, 1970 a pipe bomb killed San Francisco Police Sgt. Brian V. McDonnell, permanently disabled Officer Robert Fogerty and injured Sgt. Paul Kotta and officers Ron Martin, Al Arnaud, Gerry Doherty, Edward Buckner, Robert O'Sullivan and Frank Rath at the Golden Gate Park Station.[692]

No one took public credit, but many San Francisco police believe Bernardine Dohrn was responsible.[693] In March 2009, elected leaders of the police union in San Francisco accused Ayers and Dohrn of the murder of Sgt. Brian V. McDonnell in February 1970.

Bill Ayers Attributes SF Bombing To Dohrn. FBI informer Larry Grathwohl says Bill Ayers ordered slacking weathermen to "raise the level of the struggle." Bernadine Dohrn had to "plan, develop and carryout the bombing of the police station ... (all by herself) and he [Ayers] specifically named her... committing the act." Ayers said, "The bomb was placed on the window ledge." Ayers described the bomb and the shrapnel used [heavy metal staples and lead bullets]. [694]

---

[690] Sandra Levinson and Carol Brightman, (eds.), *Venceremos Brigade: Young American Sharing Life and Work of Revolutionary Cuba*, New York: Simon and Schuster, 1971, 332, 327.

[691] Sandra Levinson and Carol Brightman, (eds.), *Venceremos Brigade: Young American Sharing Life and Work of Revolutionary Cuba*, New York: Simon and Schuster, 1971, 336-7.

[692] Irene Michaud, "Victim of Park Station Bombing: Memorial Scheduled for Sergeant Brian V. McDonnell," *POA Journal*: San Francisco Police Officers Association, Volume 39, Number 2, February 2007, 1.

[693] Demian Bulwa, "S.F. Police Union Accuses Ayers in 1970 Bombing," *San Francisco Chronicle*, March 12, 2009; Tamara Barak Aparton, Police Union Targets '60 Radical, *San Francisco Examiner*, March 12, 2009. See Cliff Kinkaid's www.usasurvival.org.

[694] Larry Grathwohl, testimony, *Terrorist Activity: Inside the Weatherman Movement*, Hearings before the Subcommittee to Investigate the Administration of the Internal Security Act and other Internal Security Laws of the Committee on the Judiciary United States Senate, 93rd Congress, 2nd, Part 2, October 18, 1974, 106-7; Also Larry Grathwohl, *Bringing Down America: An FBI Informer with the Weathermen*, New

Dohrn Was in Town. The Berkeley Police placed Bernardine Dohrn in Berkeley February 8-21 at the time of the bombing, February 16, 1970.[695] Persons of interest would be leaders of Bay Area Weather who were Lincoln Bergman, Arlene Eisen Bergman, Clayton van Lydegraf, Jeff Jones, Julie Nichamin, Karen Latimer and Scott Braley.[696]

Dynamite and Detonators Traced to Weathermen Bomb Factory. Inspector Earl Bergfeld of the Berkeley Police Department said local police agencies traced the dynamite in both the Weather bomb factory in Chicago and the San Francisco bombing to a lawful Boulder Colorado supplier. Forged signatures might identifiable by handwriting experts. The detonators used matched the bombing in San Francisco and unexploded bombs near an Oakland paint factory.[697]

Matthew Landy Steen, Karen Latimer Witnessed Planning the Bombing. In September 2009, Peter Jamison of the *SF Weekly* interviewed former FBI agents Willie Reagan and Max Noel. They described the testimony of two independent witnesses, a writer for the *Berkeley Tribe*, Matthew Landy Steen and a Weatherman, Karen Latimer. FBI agent Reagan infiltrated the Revolutionary Committee included Clayton Van Lydegraf, Communist and Weatherman in town at the time of the bombing took Sgt. McDonnell's life. While Steen was a hippy writer, Karen Latimer was a Weatherman vet in Chicago and Flint. She wanted to talk. Steen and Latimer attended two planning meetings for the bombing of the Park Station. They said Bernardine Dohrn was the ringleader and Howard Machtinger[698]

Rochelle: Arlington House, 169.

[695] Ronald Koziol, "Police Link National Bomb Plot to Weatherman Revolutionaries," Chicago *Tribune*, May 27, 1970 copy in Senate, Committee on the Judiciary, Subcommittee to Investigate the Administration of the Internal Security Act and Other Internal Security Laws, *The Weather Underground*, Committee Print, January 1975, 30.

[696] "The Weather Underground Organization," *Information Digest*, Vol. XIV, #22, November 13, 1981, 341.

[697] Ronald Koziol, "Police Link National Bomb Plot to Weatherman Revolutionaries," Chicago *Tribune*, May 27, 1970 copy in Senate, Committee on the Judiciary, Subcommittee to Investigate the Administration of the Internal Security Act and Other Internal Security Laws, *The Weather Underground*, Committee Print, January 1975, 29-30.

[698] Howard Machtinger in 2009 in wrote the Weathermen were 'we were wrong and destructive" but by grace escaped being terrorist by not killing anyone. Howard Machtinger, "You Say You Want a Revolution," [IPS] *In These Times, February 18, 2009.* Yet in 2015 he is reported to have said, "The myth, and this is always Bill Ayers' line, is that Weather never set out to kill people, and it's not true — we did," Howie Machtinger said. "You know, policemen were fair game." Greg Richter, "Radical

was the bomb builder. Latimer cased the police station and handled the bomb,[699] like a Weather bomb plot Larry Grathwohl broke up in targeting a Detroit police station. Machtinger was a coconspirator in the Detroit case[700] also a windowsill.

Weather's Supporters. In Cleveland the Weathermen decided to go underground.[701] They had an extensive network of family, friends, true believers and groups protecting them for years. E.g., the Communist parents of Howard Emmers[702] provided a phone checkpoint and housing to fugitives Rudd, Handelsman, Smith and Fuerst. Bernardine Dohrn's sister, Jennifer Dohrn, was part of this extensive[703] support network.

Weather Buys Dynamite. On February 28, 1970, several phone calls were made from a Greenwich Village Townhouse to Goddard College. On March 2, 1970, Ella Fulwood of New England Explosives in Keene, New Hampshire sold 100 sticks of dynamite, 100 blasting caps and 100-foot rolls of safety fuse for $56.40. The buyer was "David Beller," claiming to buy the dynamite for his father, John Beller, a construction contractor in Shelburne Vermont (Shelburne Limestone, Inc was a long standing customer of New England Explosives).

Weather Underground Bombmaker Taught in NYC Schools for 25 Years," newsmax, 29 Mar 2015 09:43 AM.

[699] Peter Jamison, "Time Bomb: Weather Underground leaders claimed their bombings were devised to avoid bloodshed. But FBI agents suspect the radical '70s group killed a S.F. cop in the name of revolution," *SF Weekly*, September 16, 2009.

[700] Senate, Committee on the Judiciary, Subcommittee to Investigate the Administration of the Internal Security Act and Other Internal Security Laws, *The Weather Underground*, Committee Print, January 1975, 87.

[701] Larry Grathwohl, testimony, *Terrorist Activity: Inside the Weatherman Movement*, Hearings before the Subcommittee to Investigate the Administration of the Internal Security Act and other Internal Security Laws of the Committee on the Judiciary United States Senate, 93rd Congress, 2nd, Part 2, October 18, 1974, 107.

[702] "Declassified U.S. Government intelligence information regarding the communist and foreign connections of the Weather Underground. Presented as evidence, on the agreement of the prosecution and defense counsel, in the trial of W. Mark Felt and Edward S, Miller," 20-21 at www.usasurvival.org.

[703] Among the others identified as above ground supporters of the Weather Underground revealed at National Hard Times Conference in Chicago, January 30- February 1, 1976 were: Nancy Barrett, Arlene Eisen Bergman, Alan Berkman, Diane Block, Bob Cantor, Mike Deutsch, Melody Ermachild, Brian Flannigan, Marc Fliegelman, Penny Grillos, Jeff Haas, Sarah Kaplan, Connie Keresy, Kitty Kimatsu, Lisa Lawrence, Sarah Loft, Shelly Miller, Judith Mirkinson, Russ Neufeld, Julie Nichamin, Jed Proujanski, Miles Pustin, Melina Rorick, Eve Rosahn, Nancy Ryan, David Saxner, Mara Seigel, Annie Stein (mother of Eleanor Stein Raskin), Flint Taylor, Susan Tipograph, Sylvia Warren, Susan Waysdorf, Barry Weinberg, Laura Whitehorn.

The FBI suspected SDS member Ronald Fliegelman of Goddard College may have been "David Beller" and "Henry Skirball" who had earlier tried to make other explosive and arms purchases, but all Goddard College leads, Joan Zimmerman, Steve Rappaport, Andrew Higgins, Russ Neufeld, were uncooperative.[704] Indeed, Ronald Fliegelman later admitted to being a bomb maker for Weatherman.[705]

Also at Goddard College were Marc Lee Fliegelman, Venceremos and brother of weatherman Ronald David Fliegelman, and friend of weatherman Thomas Brainerd Cook. In June New England Explosives in Keene turn away Cook's attempt to buy still more dynamite.

Ample dynamite supplies, notwithstanding Weather was poorly prepared, so some things went wrong on the way to the revolution. Cathy Wilkerson allowed her weather friends to use her father's house while he was away on vacation.

***

Revolution Goes Boom in Greenwich Village: Weather Underground Townhouse Bombs.-- March 6, 1970

A little after noon on Friday March 6, 1970 a homemade bomb, dynamite and steel nails, exploded destroying a four-story townhouse, a Weather Underground safe house, at 18 West 11th Street near Fifth Avenue in Greenwich Village, New York. The antipersonnel bomb loaded with sixteen-penny, 3 ½ inch, and roofing nails killed Ted Gold, Terry Robbins and Diana Oughton. The bomb was intended for a U.S. Army dance at Fort Dix in New Jersey endangering hundreds.[706]

In the event, Bill Ayer's lover, Diana Oughton, 28, was decapitated in the explosion and identified by a surviving fingertip.[707]

---

[704] Senate, Committee on the Judiciary, Subcommittee to Investigate the Administration of the Internal Security Act and Other Internal Security Laws, *The Weather Underground*, Committee Print, January 1975, 133-5.

[705] Greg Richter, "Radical Weather Underground Bombmaker Taught in NYC Schools for 25 Years," Newsmax, 29 Mar 2015, cites Fliegelman in Bryan Burrough, Days of Rage: America's radical Underground, the FBI, and the forgotten age of Revolutionary Violence.

[706] Howard Machtinger, "You Say You Want a Revolution," [IPS] *In These Times, February 18, 2009.*

[707] "Body discovered in Rubble Identified," *Chicago Daily News*, March 18, 1970; Lucinda Franks and Thomas Powers, "A Final Family Christmas, a Lull and then the

Hollywood Enablers: Fonda, Hoffman. Cathy Wilkerson and Kathy Boudin, survivors of the townhouse explosion, climbed, Wilkerson topless, Boudin naked, bloodied and bruised through a hole in the townhouse rubble to the sidewalk into the arms of two good Samaritans. Susan Wager Fonda, actor Henry Fonda's former wife and Ann Hoffman, wife of actor Dustin Hoffman,[708] provided a shower and borrowed clothes.[709] Wilkerson and Boudin slipped back underground.

Gerald William Long suggested the surviving Weathermen take six months of technical training in explosives.[710] Cathy Wilkerson later studied and designed a safer circuit.[711] Ron Fleigelman took 100 pounds of dynamite and boxes of .38 shells, to Philadelphia.[712]

Political Assassinations Planned. On March 18, 1970 the New York office of the FBI learned three weathermen told a reporter Weather planned to kill President Nixon, Vice President Agnew, Attorney General John Mitchell and Governor Nelson Rockefeller.[713]

Cuban and Family Money, Oatmeal and Peanut Butter. Eleanor Raskin gave Cathy Wilkerson a disguise.[714] The families of Bernardine Dohrn and Kathy Boudin routed money through the Kuwaiti Ambassador's diplomatic mail pouch to Canada.

Blast," *Chicago Daily News, September 19, 1970, 16.*

[708] Senate, Committee on the Judiciary, Subcommittee to Investigate the Administration of the Internal Security Act and Other Internal Security Laws, *The Weather Underground*, Committee Print, January 1975, 25.

[709] Cathy Wilkerson, *Flying Close to the Sun*, New York: Seven Stories Press, 2007, 346-7, 349.

[710] FBI, FOIA, Weather Underground. The primary source is Acting SAC Chicago to Director, memo, "Foreign Influence-Weather Underground Organization," August 20, 1976, 327.

[711] Cathy Wilkerson, *Flying Close to the Sun*, New York: Seven Stories Press, 2007, 361.

[712] "Declassified U.S. Government intelligence information regarding the communist and foreign connections of the Weather Underground. Presented as evidence, on the agreement of the prosecution and defense counsel, in the trial of W. Mark Felt and Edward S, Miller," 59 at www.usasurvival.org.

[713] "Declassified U.S. Government intelligence information regarding the communist and foreign connections of the Weather Underground. Presented as evidence, on the agreement of the prosecution and defense counsel, in the trial of W. Mark Felt and Edward S, Miller," 61 at www.usasurvival.org.

[714] Juliet Wittman, "Memoirs: Radical parents, Red shoes and a poet up close and personal," *Washington Post*, November 21, 2004, BW13; hair dye according to Cathy Wilkerson, *Flying Close to the Sun*, New York: Seven Stories Press, 2007, 349.

After the townhouse explosion four members of Venceremos, Ann Hathaway, Eleanor Ruth Kalom, Jonathan David Lerner and Carlie Tanner were in Cuba in the 2nd Venceremos Brigade.[715] Fearing arrest, the Cuban government paid their way to Prague, Czechoslovakia. Returned U.S. they created an underground NY foco group.[716] On the west coast, Wilkerson lived on oatmeal and peanut butter.[717]

Cuban Intelligence. Both prosecution and defense testimony in the trial of the FBI's W. Mark Felt and Edward S. Miller showed KGB controlled Cuban intelligence/secret police meeting regularly with SDS/Weather Underground leadership, Bernardine Dohrn, Martin Kenner, Mark Rudd, Julie Nichamin, Karen Koonan, Kathy Boudin, Gerry Long, Karen Ashley, Jeff Jones and Jennifer Dohrn.

Cuban intelligence gave advice, money and some instructions to the Weathermen.[718] During March 1970, someone firebombed a research center at Case Western University. FBI had evidence Weatherman John Fuerst and others followed Bill Ayers' plan.[719]

During 1970 there were 3,000 bombings and 50,000 bomb threats.[720] Bill Ayers says the Weathermen "claimed half a dozen bombings…5,000 bombings (since spring of 1969), about six a day, and the Weather Underground had claimed six, total."[721] From Weather sources, the FBI counted no less than forty

---

[715] House, Committee on Internal *Security, The Theory and Practice of Communism in 1972* (Venceremos Brigades) October 16,18 and 19 1972, Appendix B, 8135-40, contains the Venceremos manifesto of the 2nd Brigade, originally published in Sen. James O. Eastland, "Americans Train in Cuba for Revolution," Congressional record, November 8, 192, E 9089-E 9098.

[716] "Declassified U.S. Government intelligence information regarding the communist and foreign connections of the Weather Underground. Presented as evidence, on the agreement of the prosecution and defense counsel, in the trial of W. Mark Felt and Edward S, Miller," 59 at www.usasurvival.org; FBI, FOIA, Weather Underground. The primary source is Acting SAC Chicago to Director, memo, "Foreign Influence-Weather Underground Organization," August 20, 1976.

[717] Cathy Wilkerson, *Flying Close to the Sun*, New York: Seven Stories Press 2007, 379.

[718] "Declassified U.S. Government intelligence information regarding the communist and foreign connections of the Weather Underground. Presented as evidence, on the agreement of the prosecution and defense counsel, in the trial of W. Mark Felt and Edward S, Miller," 40, 90 at www.usasurvival.org.

[719] "Declassified U.S. Government intelligence information regarding the communist and foreign connections of the Weather Underground. Presented as evidence, on the agreement of the prosecution and defense counsel, in the trial of W. Mark Felt and Edward S, Miller," 61 at www.usasurvival.org.

[720] History of the FBI, Vietnam War Era, www.fbi.gov/libref/history/vietnam.htm

[721] Bill Ayers, *Fugitive Days*, 228.

bombings through September 1976, nearly seven times Ayers's deflated half dozen. By May 1974, the Weathermen claimed credit for 19 bombings in their publication *Prairie Fire*. Ayers, Bernardine Dohrn, Jeff Jones and Celil Sojourner signed this admission of 19 bombings "carried out by the Weather Underground."[722] Ayers once proudly claimed 19, not six.

Under the Freedom of Information Act, Jennifer Dohrn received her FBI file. Top FBI officials Mark Felt and Edward Miller were convicted despite WUO ties to foreign agents justifying FBI's investigations. President Reagan pardoned Felt and Miller. They helped to "end the terrorism that was threatening our nation."[723]

Reagan unhappy with militants. Ronald Reagan took a hard line. Elected "to clean up the mess at Berkeley," on April 7, 1970, asked about campus militants, California Governor Reagan said: "If it takes a bloodbath, let's get it over with. No more appeasement." In the interest of student safety, the tough talking Governor gave California's state institutions of higher learning a long weekend off.[724]

Meanwhile the families of POWs and MIAs in Vietnam continued their quest for information about their loved ones.

***

POW Families Appeal to Vietnamese, COLIFAM, Attorney General

Day after day, March 9-23, 1970, POW wives Susan Hanley and Carolyn Dennison picketed Hanoi's Embassy in Paris. On the 18th the Embassy gave them a letter, "The policy of the DRV" was to contact the "New York Committee of Liaison…[and] give that committee the necessary time to have information to give you." A sheet, "Policy of the Government of the Democratic Republic of Viet-Nam on US Pilots Captured in North Viet-Nam" claimed the pilots were

---

[722] Bernardino Dohrn, Bill Ayers, Jeff Jones, and Celia Sojourn, *Prairie Fire: The Politics of Revolutionary Anti-imperialism; Political Statement of the Weather Underground*, Communications Co. 1974, 4-5.

[723] Amy Goodman interview of Jennifer Dohrn, "Exclusive …Jennifer Dohrn: I Was the Target of Illegal FBI Break-ins Ordered by Mark Felt asks "Deep Throat", *Democracy Now.org*, June 2, 2005.

[724] Disclosure: As a speaker for Republican Associates of Los Angeles County the author supported Governor Reagan's policies at the University of California; See Republican Associates, "Education is your responsibility. Be Informed." Pamphlet of speaker's bureau, undated circa 1969-70.

"captured in the act of committing a crime…[namely] …massacred a great number of Vietnamese civilians, including women and children." Rep. Bob Wilson (R. CA) demanded the State Department assist the women and condemned Hanoi for its use of "an element of the peace movement as a propaganda instrument…"[725]

No one named either Hanley or Dennison appeared on a list of live POWs. Major Larry J. Hanley died in captivity. Lt. Terry Dennison, shot down in Laos, listed as MIA, declared dead.

POW Wives Meet the Reverend Fernandez. On March 24, 1970, five wives of POWs, some affiliated with the National League of Families of American Prisoners in Southeast Asia, met the Rev. Richard Fernandez of CALC, in Virginia Beach. Fernandez promised to try to exchange letters and gain information on MIAs.[726]

On April 8, 1970, Mrs. James Plowman said though she resented pressure to join peace groups, but "I don't care if the Devil brings it to me, I'll take a letter from my husband…"[727]

The Devil moved in mysterious ways. No Plowman was released after the Paris Peace Accords. LTJG Jim Plowman disappeared near Chinese border on March 24, 1967. Hanoi denied he was a POW. The US listed him as MIA until declared dead. Family doubts this.[728]

COLIFAM Registration as a Foreign Agent? On March 25, 1970 Rep. Bob Wilson (R-San Diego) asked Attorney General John N. Mitchell to require COLIFAM to register as a foreign agent of Hanoi under the Foreign Agents Registration Act, FARA. Registration would have required COLIFAM to reveal who financed its operations and extensive

---

[725] FBI, San Diego, Interview of [redacted, likely Susan Hanley] on June 5, 1970 FD 302, June 9, 1970; Rep. Bob Wilson, News Release, March 18, 1970.

[726] FBI, Norfolk COLIFAM IS- Misc: Registration, AIRTEL June 26, 1970; FBI, Norfolk LHM fragment n.d. 34-35, 39, 43.

[727] Donnie Radcliffe, "POW Wives Pressed to join 'Peaceniks'" *Washington Evening Star*, April 9, 1970.

[728] POW Network reports, "There is no indication that they died when their plane disappeared, and unofficial reports that they have been unable to verify suggest that one or both may have been captured. A photo of a POW in the front of a march conducted in China was identified by Navy officer and returned POW Robert Flynn who was released by the Chinese in 1973 as being James E. Plowman. Flynn also saw a photo of Ellison while held in China. Plowman's wife identified him from a North Vietnamese photo just prior to December 1970, and his parents identified him from a 1967 North Vietnamese photo." http://www.pownetwork.org/bios/p/p043.htm

travel. Rep. Wilson said, COLIFAM had engaged in "callous exploitation" and "a cruel traffic in human misery." Joining COLIFAM was a *quid pro quo* for release of POWS. The families might ask about the life or death of their loved ones only through COLIFAM.[729]

POW Wives Refuse Letters. On April 3, 1970, Mrs. Arthur Doss and Mrs. Sue Shuman announced they would no longer accept letters from WSP/COLIFAM. Mrs. Doss: "I can no longer allow my husband's precious letters to be used as a devise for torture and torment of U.S. prisoners of war."[730] Hanoi did release Dale Walter Doss and Edwin Arthur Shuman after the war.

FBI Investigation of COLIFAM as Hanoi Agent. On April 6, 1970, J. Walter Teagley, Assistant Attorney General asked the FBI Director to conduct investigations of COLIFAM. Was there admissible evidence COLIFAM was an agent of North Vietnam? That is, was COLIFAM acting within the United States at the request of Hanoi? Was it engaged in either political activity or as a publicity agent as defined in FARA? Over several years, the FBI would answer yes, and yes, but the Justice Department never prosecuted.

COLIFAM Releases Hanoi's Incomplete List of POWs. On April 7, 1970 COLIFAM's Cora Weiss and David Dellinger announced Hanoi's release of a list of 335 POWs. They wrote POW families, saying the "North Vietnamese had confirmed through (COLIFAM)" 335 POWs of which 81 were new names. "We continue to work toward the immediate and complete withdrawal of U.S. troops…so that all families, American and Vietnamese, can be united again."[731] WSP's Ethel Brown said Fernandez and two others (Sidney Peck and an unknown person) received the list in Stockholm.[732]

MIA Family Appeals Denied. In early April 1970 mothers and wives[733] of servicemen missing in action, MIAs,

---

[729] Rep. Bob Wilson, News Release, March 25, 1970.

[730] "POW Wives Decline Husbands' Letters," Ledger-Star (Norfolk), April 4, 1970.

[731] Cora Weiss and David Dellinger, Dear Mrs. [redacted], COLIFAM, April 7, 1970; FBI, New York to Director, COLIFAM-Information concerning IS, TELETYPE xx55 PM Urgent, April 7, 1970.

[732] FBI, Norfolk, Interview of [redacted] on July 20, 1970, FD-302, July 31, 1970.

[733] The women were Mrs. Dorothy Bodden (Sgt. Timothy Roy Bodden), Mrs. Irene Davis (Capt. Robert Charles Davis), Mrs. Sharon Walsh (Lt. Col. Richard Walsh III), Mrs. Elizabeth Brashear (Maj. William James Brashear), and Mrs. Gordon Perisho (Lt. Cdr. G. S. Perisho).

flew to Vientiane, Laos to visit Hanoi's embassy to ask for information. Phan Tam told one wife to contact COLIFAM and told Mrs. Gordon Perisho he would relay her request to Hanoi. When there was no response, Phan told Mrs. Perisho to contact "peace groups." At the Red Chinese Embassy, guards laughed at the women and they received cold shoulders at East Bloc embassies.[734]

Fernandez Meets Families in Vientiane. Several relatives of POWs ran into CALC's Richard Fernandez in Vientiane. He "spent most of the time being critical" of U.S. policy in Southeast Asia.[735] Fernandez said prominent people were contributing heavily to CALC.[736] Actually the tax exempted National Council of Churches, NCC, and the Washington Square United Methodist Church were the major sources of funds for CALC.[737] DJB Foundation used NCC to launder money to CALC.[738]

Hanoi. POW Letters Rejected. In early June three members of AFSC, Seattle—Kenneth Kirkpatrick, Mark S. Patshne, and Egbert W. Feiffer—traveled to Hanoi with 700 letters. Tran Trong Quat refused letters to any person not on the official list of 335. Quat also rejected any letters directed to Laos, Cambodia, or South Vietnam where Hanoi refused to admit it had troops or influence there.[739]

Help to MIA Families. While aiding Hanoi, COLIFAM, CALC and AFSC did little for the MIA families. No MIAs returned alive from Laos. Still waiting in 2004, Sharon Walsh wrote. [740]

---

[734] Committee on Foreign Affairs, hearings May and June 1972, Appendix A-Statement of Mrs. Gordon Perisho, Mother of Lt. Cdr. G. S. Perisho, 655540/1329, USN, Missing in Action Over North Vietnam Since 31 December 1967; Max Vanzi, "Women Weep While Guards Laugh," UPI, n.d.

[735] FBI, Minneapolis, MP 100-15134, interview with [redacted]on June 22, 1970, FD-302, June 26, 1970, 3; FBI, Springfield, LHM, COLIFAM, October 6, 1970.

[736] FBI, Newark, interview with [redacted]on October 20, 1970, FD-302, October 27, 1970.

[737] "Methodist Church Funding examined," *Information Digest*, May 16, 1980, 160; Max Friedman, Council for Inter-American Security, study in lieu of testimony to Chairman of House Ways and Means Committee, *Lobbying and Political Activities of Tax-Exempt Organizations*, Hearings, Committee on Oversight, March 12-13, 1987, 404.

[738] *New York Times* May 1, 1975.

[739] FBI, Milwaukee, Interview of [redacted] on July 13, 1970, FD-302, July 20, 1970; Kenneth Kirkpatrick, Dear Mrs. [redacted]AFSC, July 27, 1970; Barbara Webster, Dear Mrs. [redacted], COLIFAM, New York, July 27, 1970.

[740] www.virtualwall.org/dw/WalshRAO1a.htm

We the survivors, are always with them now…to live our long goodbye, not to see their beloved faces again here, as they walk on. In Flanders Field where poppies grow, or near the Mekong River in the foothills of Laos they rest.

Except for their propaganda value, indifferent to the flight of POW/MIA families, Hanoi's envoys enthusiastically traveled the world spending weeks meeting hundreds of American antiwar activists.

**

Antiwar Activists Meet Vietnamese communists: Vancouver, Stockholm, Hanoi, Vientiane, Paris, Helsinki, Toronto.

International Liaison Committee, ILC, of the Soviet controlled Stockholm Conference, coordinating Hanoi, VC[741] and international support for the US antiwar movement,[742] urged "world support for … the initiatives taken by the U.S. [antiwar] movement."[743] Key ILC members were Alexander Berkov of Soviet Peace Committee, Romesh Chandra of WCP, Irving Sarnoff, CPUSA member and a New Mobe leader,[744] and John McAuliff of New Mobe.

KGB Funds New Mobe. Michael Dobbs, a Moscow correspondent, *Washington Post,* reported a KGB financial subsidy [through Agent SOLO?] of the CPUSA to support agents of influence in front groups,[745] i.e., the New Mobe. Similar subsidies of Mao,[746] Ho[747] and the CPUSA[748] ran for decades.

Vancouver. In January-February in Vancouver 125 members of New Mobe, CPUSA and West Coast antiwar groups gathered [749] to plan the Fifth Stockholm conference.

---

[741] John McAuliff, "Report from Stockholm," *New Mobilizer*, February, 1970, 3 cited in Frank J. Rafalko, *MH/CHAOS: The CIA's Campaign Against the Radical Left and the Black Panthers*, Annapolis: Naval Institute Press, 2011, 140.

[742] Frank J. Rafalko, *MH/CHAOS: The CIA's Campaign Against the Radical Left and the Black Panthers*, Annapolis: Naval Institute Press, 2011, 135-6.

[743] William T. Poole, The Anti-Defense Lobby Part 2: "The Peace Movement, Continued," *Institutional Analysis #11,* September 19, 1979.
http://www.heritage.org/Research/GovernmentReform/IA11.cfm,

[744] Frank J. Rafalko, *MH/CHAOS: The CIA's Campaign Against the Radical Left and the Black Panthers*, Annapolis: Naval Institute Press, 2011, 136.

[745] Reed Irvine and Joseph C. Goulden, "U.S. Communists and U.S.S.R. Gold," *Sacramento Union*, March 26, 1992.

[746] Jung Chang *Mao*

[747] Robert Tucker.

[748] Harvey Klehr.

[749] Hearings before the Committee on Internal Security House of Representatives, Part

152

Fifth Stockholm Conference. March 28-30, 1970 in Stockholm 44 Americans out of 350 attendees met officials of Hanoi and the NLF.[750] The New Mobe delegation was Irving Sarnoff, Noam Chomsky, William Davidon, Doug Dowd, Carlton Goodlett, Robert Greenblatt, Sylvia Kushner, and Richard Fernandez.

The Stockholm delegates declared international "cooperation with the antiwar movement" in the USA and adopted Hanoi's ten-point plan.[751] New Mobe planned an "immediate withdrawal," OUT-NOW project for April. Xuan Thuy said the antiwar movement "constitutes …a great source of encouragement for our people."

Hanoi. At a Hanoi rally, "welcoming the America People's spring offensive" against the war in Washington and across the nation, April 13-14 1970 Noam Chomsky, Douglas Dowd and Rev. Richard Fernandez (CALC and COLIFAM) made speeches on Radio Hanoi.[752]

Hating America: Chomsky and Dowd. Radio Hanoi, April 14, Chomsky alleged, "villages mutilated by savage bombardments…" Hating America, he saw, "the savagery of a technological monster …the rulers of the American empire…." Doug Dowd said, "One of the incurable hatreds I will have for the rest of my life is …for what they did to these people…just absolutely incredible savagery…"[753]

The Vietnamese and Americans generated hate for America, a lasting legacy of the Vietnam War.

Meeting POWs: Schweitzer, Wilber, and Miller. Chomsky, Dowd and Fernandez talked to three POWs—Cdr.

2, 91st Congress, , Parts 1-3, 1971 cited in Frank J. Rafalko, *MH/CHAOS: The CIA's Campaign Against the Radical Left and the Black Panthers*, Annapolis: Naval Institute Press, 2011, 140n22.

[750] "Declassified U.S. Government intelligence information regarding the communist and foreign connections of the Weather Underground. Presented as evidence, on the agreement of the prosecution and defense counsel, in the trial of W. Mark Felt and Edward S, Miller," 61 at www.usasurvival.org. Frank J. Rafalko, *MH/CHAOS: The CIA's Campaign Against the Radical Left and the Black Panthers*, Annapolis: Naval Institute Press, 2011, 140.

[751] Hon. John Schmidt, Hon. Fletcher Thompson, Hon. Roger H. Zion, *The Viet Cong Front in the United States*, Western Islands 1973, 154. Originally, a report prepared by minority staff and printed in the *Congressional Record* on April 21, 1971.

[752] Hanoi in English to Southeast Asia 1000 GMT, 14 April 1970,Speeches by Professor Noam Chomsky, Prof. Douglas Dowd, and clergyman Richard Fernandez at Hanoi meeting welcoming the 1970 American people's spring offensive.

[753] Tom Wells, *The War Within: America's Battle over Vietnam*, NY: Henry Holt, 1994,162.

Robert Schweitzer, Cdr. Walter Wilber, and Lt. Col. Edison Miller. Dowd said the POWs were "lively and friendly and wanted the war ended so they could get home." The POWs "were being educated with anti-war literature." Fernandez commended their health, exercise and reading material.[754]

The Vietnamese said the three prisoners were cooperative. Fernandez told a POW wife the prisoners were "obviously prompted by their captors." Actually, Walter Wilber and Edison Miller were enthusiastic members of the POW Peace Committee. Schweitzer, made radio broadcasts and signed confessions.[755] The POWs hated all three. Repentant and forgiven, Schweitzer became a MIA advocate at home.

MIAs. No Help. Fernandez provided a list of 87 MIA servicemen to the Vietnamese, but they had no information. Fernandez told POW wives Hanoi short listed the number of POWs.[756]

In Hanoi. Institute for Policy Studies. On April 12, 1970 an IPS delegation of Charlotte Bunch-Weeks, Gerald Shin, Frank Joyce and Elisabeth Sutherland-Martinez, left Washington for 10 days in Hanoi.[757] The IPS group met Lao, Cambodian, and Vietnamese communists including future winner of Lenin Peace Prize, Nguyen Huu Tho and Premier Pham Van Dong.

"Everything ...written... understated the... destruction." It was genocidal and ecocidal.[758] To the Chicago Women's Liberation Union, Charlotte Bunch Weeks described massive destruction of Vinh City, Hanoi was winning and the U. S. ought to withdraw completely.[759]

Toronto--World Jurist Conference on Vietnam. May 22-24, 1970 the Lawyers Committee on American Policy Towards Vietnam (Joseph H. Crown, William Standard, Richard Falk) sponsored a World Jurist Conference on

---

[754] Richard Fernandez, To: Families of the 335 presently confirmed prisoners in North Vietnam, May 4, 1970.

[755] Craig Howes, *Voices of the Vietnam POWs: Witnesses to Their Fight*, New York: Oxford University Press, 1993,110-111, 198.

[756] Steve Halliwell to Dear Mrs. [redacted]COLIFAM letter, April 20, 1970; FBI, Norfolk LHM fragment n.d. 40-41.

[757] FBI, Washington Field to Director, COLIFAM, Information concerning (internal security), NITEL 645, April 17, 1970.

[758] FBI, New York, LHM, COLIFAM, June 9, 1970, 15-18.

[759] "Back from Hanoi," *CWLU News*, Newsletter of the Chicago Women's Liberation Union, 2875 W. Cermak, Rm. 9, 1-2.

Vietnam, renamed The Lawyers Conference on Vietnam, Laos and Cambodia, of 100 U.S. lawyers and 50 foreign lawyers, including Ho protégé Tran Cong Tuong. Room and board was only $11. Attendees were members of the National Lawyers Guild, CALC, the Law Center for Civil Rights (Peter Weiss and Morton Stavis), National Committee for a Citizens' Commission on Inquiry on United States War Crimes in Vietnam (Dr. Howard Levy, Noam Chomsky, Ralph Schoenman, Eric Seitz), and Education/Action Conference on U.S. Crimes of War in Vietnam (CALC, AFSC).[760]

In Toronto jurists condemned U.S. war crimes. "By a strange coincidence" the same claims as Communists, wrote John H. Vincent. The agenda was: Illegality and Immorality of Vietnamization and Pacification; Application of Nuremberg Principles to the Vietnam War; Biological and Chemical Warfare; Deceptions…: Reparations…..

Helsinki. May 29-31, the World Peace Conference Control Committee in Helsinki instructed Romesh Chandra, Secretary of WPC, to expand anti-war activities among pacifist organizations.[761]

***

Paris. John Kerry Meets Vietnamese in Paris.
According to John Kerry and Gerald Nicosia, in late May 1970 during their honeymoon Kerry and his new wife Julia Thorne met[762] with Vietnamese communists. Max Friedman says "It's

---

[760] John Ashbrook, *Congressional Record—Extension of Remarks*, May 12, 1970, E 4182-3; John H. Vincent, "US Leftist to Hold Parley on U.S. 'War crimes," *Twin Circle*, (Catholic), May 17, 1970; Lawyers Committee on American Policy Toward Vietnam, "Mark Your Calendar", Rec'd April 29, 1970.

[761] Frank J. Rafalko, *MH/CHAOS: The CIA's Campaign Against the Radical Left and the Black Panthers*, Annapolis: Naval Institute Press, 2011, 136, 146.

[762] Scott Swett and Tim Ziegler, *To Set the Record Straight: How the Swift Boat Veterans, POWs and the New Media Defeated John Kerry*, New American Media Publishing, 2008 5n19 cites Michael Kornish, *Boston Globe*, Mar 25, 2004 citing Michael Meehan, Kerry spokesman; "I have been to Paris. I have talked with…" Gerald Nicosia author of *Home to War: A History of the Vietnam Veterans' Movement*, citing redacted FBI files in an article in the *Los Angeles Times* on May 23, 2004. The author has many of the same files on an FBI FOIA VVAW DVD. In addition, see: Fedora, "John Kerry's Fellow Travelers, Part 3: Hanoi John: Kerry and the Antiwar Movement's Connections, www.freerepublic.com/focus/f-news/1241847/posts note 11 cites Brinkley, *Tour of Duty*, 340-341; Michael Kranish and Patricia Healy, "Kerry spoke of meeting negotiators on Vietnam, the *Boston Globe*, www.bostonglobe. com/news/nation/articles/2004/03/25kerry spoke of meet March 2004 (Sept 4, 2004); Marc Morano, "FBI Files Show Kerry Met with Communists More than Once," CNSNews.com www.cnsnews.com//viewspecialreports.asp?page=\special reports\ archive\200406\SPE20040604a.html, June 4, 2004 (June 18,2004); John E. O'Neill and Jerome Corsi, *Unfit for Command: Swift Boat Veterans Speak Out Against John*

not something you just walk into on your honeymoon."[763] The War Resisters League, WRL, identified David Dellinger as Kerry's contact with the Vietnamese. French intelligence said Kerry met Le Duc Tho, chief negotiator.[764] Gerald Nicosia says John Kerry met Madam Nguyen Thi Binh to discuss the VC peace plan he endorsed.

Kerry says, "I have been to Paris. I have talked with both [communist] delegations at the peace talks, that is to say the Democratic Republic of Vietnam and the Provisional Revolutionary Government (PRG)." Kerry spoke only to the enemy, not the U.S. side in Paris. In 1971, Kerry met the enemy again[765] and sought a third meeting.

Paris. Minnesotans Meet Indochina Comrades.

In Paris, June 25-July 2, 1970 "hard core Communist" Adam Schesch led a group of 31 Minnesotans, "a jury" conducting a "commission of inquiry" assisted by Madame Binh. French participants were Maoist Jean Chesneaux, Anneck Levy, and anti-Diem historian Philippe Devillers. The jury talked over many days with officials of Hanoi, the NLF, the PRG and the National United Front of Cambodia, NUFK, and the Patriotic Laotian Front, Pathet Lao in Paris.

Adam Schesch wrote a report James Dennis of Wisconsin Committee to Stop the War delivered to Robert Kastenmeir (D-Wisc) for the *Congressional Record* of September 28.

The report supported the PRG's Ten Point Plan for peace and every major Communist propaganda claim:

- NLF and PRG were independent military and political forces not "playing second fiddle" to the North Vietnamese Communists; [COSVN controlled]
- PRG was a very broad coalition including only 2% Communists; [Communist Hanoi controlled]

Kerry, Wash DC: Regnery Publishing, Inc., 2004, 127-129.

[763] Scott Swett interview of Max Friedman in July 2005 cited in Scott Swett and Tim Ziegler, *To Set the Record Straight: How Swift Boat Veterans, POWs and the New Media Defeated John Kerry*, New American Media 2008,5n21.

[764] "Answer This Question, Mr. Kerry," *Pittsburgh Tribune-Review*, Internet service, October 17, 2004.

[765] Gerald Nicosia, *Home to War: A History of the Vietnam Veterans' Movement*, Crown, 2001 citing redacted FBI files in *Los Angeles Times* on May 23, 2004.

- PRG favored free elections, protection of women, minorities and religious freedom for Catholics, Buddhists etc.
- Hanoi was "quite clearly excluded from every step of the (reconciliation) process"; [false on every count]
- PRG favored reconciliation with all parties including Saigon officials and military and opposed retribution and retaliation with collaborators; [executions, reeducation camps say otherwise]
- the PRG sought land reforms, land for the tiller; [executions, confiscations, forced relocations]
- the PRG wanted coalition government, gradual peaceful reunification of North and South; [conquest]
- The allies lost [won] the ground war, pacification failed [succeeded] and US "terror' air war targeted civilians[false]
- The PRG said only a few would flee after the war "with suitcases full of dollar bills;" [penniless millions fled]
- There would be no "bloodbath"[65-85,000 executed].
- Hanoi's delegation said Saigon had 500,000 political prisoners.[766] [7,000 April 1975]

***

Progressive Reporters Captured in Cambodia
Dudman, Pond and Morrow

Covering the U.S. incursion into Cambodia, [767] on May 7, 1970 NVA troops in Cambodia captured American reporters, Michael Morrow of pro-Hanoi *Dispatch News Service* and of pro-VC *Liberation News Service*, Elizabeth Pond of the *Christian Science Monitor* and Richard Dudman of the *St. Louis Post Dispatch*

Credentialed "International" and "Progressive" Journalists. The *curriculum vitae* of Morrow, Dudman and Pond were good. "We had all been personally opposed to the Vietnam War for a long time," said Dudman.[768]

---

[766] 116 *Cong. Rec.* 34001-005, September 28, 1970.
[767] Richard Dudman, *Forty Days With The Enemy*, New York: Liveright, 1971.
[768] Richard Dudman, *Forty Days With The Enemy*, New York: Liveright, 1971, 5.

Vietnamese-speaking **Michael Morrow** was a founder[769] of the Dispatch News Service (DNS), publishing the stories of KGB agent Wilfred Burchett, communist atrocity denier Gareth Porter and "tiger cage" propagandist Thomas Fox.

Richard Dudman wrote America was "very close to imperialism,"[770] acquired Pentagon Papers from KGB agent I.F. "Izzy" Stone and accompanied Allen Brick and Rep. John Conyers to view "tiger cages" on Con Son island. Dudman accepted Peter Arnett's fabricated canard America policy was to destroy villages to save them.[771] Dudman said the communists had massacred thousands in Hue but it was only in "the heat of battle" [lists on clipboards], an "exception" to VC practice.[772]

Elizabeth Pond believed Saigon was flushing "endless dollars into an unwinnable war." Yet Pond tried "diligently to leave no ideological fingerprints in ..[her].. stories."[773] Pond later wrote about the killing fields of Cambodia, Soviet disinformation and the fall of the Berlin Wall.

NVA Propaganda. Pond noticed the "narrative of the American invader and the longsuffering patriotic defenders of Vietnam."[774] Vietnamese-speaking Michael Morrow whining said they were "international journalists" now in "liberated territory" interested in "truth and peace."[775] Dudman said the people of Cambodia supported the communists. Cambodians turn out in crowds to scream and wave their fists at the foreign journalists.[776] After a few days their Vietnamese captors, Anh Ba (Bay Cao[777]), Anh Tu, Wang, Ban Tun and Anh Hai, treated and fed them well and protected them[778] from angry Cambodians and American bombs and artillery.

---

[769] Richard Dudman, *Forty Days With The Enemy*, New York: Liveright, 1971,96.

[770] Richard Dudman, *Forty Days With The Enemy*, New York: Liveright, 1971, 96.

[771] Richard Dudman, *Forty Days With The Enemy*, New York: Liveright, 1971,5; Bill Laurie to author, August 1, 2019 says) Peter Arnett asked the military briefer if the U.S. had to "destroy Ben Tre in order to save it." The briefer brushed the question aside responding "if that's what you want to call it."

[772] Richard Dudman, *Forty Days With The Enemy*, New York: Liveright, 1971, 13, 51-52.

[773] Joyce Hoffmann, *On Their Own: Women Journalists and the American Experience in Vietnam*, 7.

[774] Elizabeth Pond, "What Would My Viet Cong Captors Think?" *Christian Science Monitor*, January 21, 2011.

[775] Richard Dudman, *Forty Days With The Enemy*, New York: Liveright, 1971, 7, 8, 15,27.

[776] Richard Dudman, *Forty Days With The Enemy*, New York: Liveright, 1971, 11-13

[777] Identified by Richard Dudman, *Bangor Daily News*, March 8, 1994.

[778] Richard Dudman, *Forty Days With The Enemy*, New York: Liveright, 1971, 68.

Captive Reeducation. Leading informal sessions of reeducation, Anh Hai (Bay Cao) said the war was a "unified" struggle in Vietnam, Cambodia and Laos for the "independence"[779] of each. (No Vietnamese occupation of Cambodia and Laos mentioned.) Hai thought the American invasion had "strengthened the opposition in Congress and among the students."[780] Anh Ba said he shot down a helicopter and four planes with his AK-47.[781] He said Cambodians fled liberated zones, not to escape communists, but to escape American bombing.[782] Unmentioned was the communist "liberation" of Cambodia defended Hanoi's supply lines, the Ho Chi Minh Trails and the port of Sihanoukville.

Collaborating and Cooperative Journalist. Michael Morrow voluntarily wrote news of the "cooperation and growing friendship" between the Cambodians and the Vietnamese. He contrasted the good behavior of Vietnamese with the looting and raping of Saigon's troops.[783] Dudman thought the Cambodians hated America and Nixon had widened the war in Cambodia [Hanoi troops there since 1959], and waged "… an unprovoked war against the Cambodian people."[784]

Execution or Release. Dudman learned the Vietnamese initially decided to execute them. Their detailed dossiers, mentioning Wilfred Burchett, Harrison Salisbury, and Senators Fulbright, Mansfield, McGovern and McCarthy, confirmed they were journalists, sympathetic to Hanoi. Elizabeth Pond said, they were finally judged to be "especially progressive" journalists.[785] Super spy Pham Xuan An claimed he intervened for Elizabeth Pond's release.[786]

The Communists executed many journalists considered combatants. In June 1971, the Khmer Rouge executed AP combat photo journalists Sean Leslie Flynn, son of actor Errol Flynn, and Dana Stone of *Time* and CBS. [787] The Khmer

---

[779] Richard Dudman, *Forty Days With The Enemy*, New York: Liveright, 1971,76.

[780] Richard Dudman, *Forty Days With The Enemy*, New York: Liveright, 1971, 56, 60.

[781] Richard Dudman, *Forty Days With The Enemy*, New York: Liveright, 1971, 125-6

[782] Richard Dudman, *Forty Days With The Enemy*, New York: Liveright, 1971,61.

[783] Richard Dudman, *Forty Days With The Enemy*, New York: Liveright, 1971,65.

[784] Richard Dudman, *Forty Days With The Enemy*, New York: Liveright, 1971, ." 67, 69-70.

[785] Elizabeth Pond, "Out from Cambodian Captivity," *Christian Science Monitor*, 22 June, 1970.

[786] Joyce Hoffman, *On Their own: Women Journalists and the American Experience in Vietnam*, Philadelphia: Da Capo Press, 2008, 233-4.

787 Richard Linnett "THE UNREDACTED SEARCH FOR THE SON OF CAPTAIN

Rouge murdered some 25 unarmed journalists in Cambodia in 1970-71. The Khmer Rouge murdered as many as 2 million fellow, noncombatant Cambodians.

Comradeship. "[F]riendship and comradeship… developed between …us…"[788] said Dudman. "..[W]e now consider you our friends."[789] Captors had many virtues, except reverence.[790]

Propaganda Statement Upon Release. They enthusiastically wrote an acceptable statement:

> Cambodians…have been led to hate all Americans by the invasion of Cambodia. …
>
> [W]e have…a very positive impression of the [Vietnamese] Liberation Army. … (They) were always polite and cordial…[and] differ sharply from our impressions of …of the Saigon troops. …[who had] …broken into houses and stores and stolen the contents. …We believe…the invasion of Cambodia …cannot be successful. …[791]

Cambodian Commander of Region 203 of the Khmer Rouge in a final faux press conference gave a two hour speech.[792] No public admission North Vietnamese troops, their captors, were in Cambodia.

***

BLOOD," October 18,2002 http://richardlinnett. files.wordpress.com/2010/06/unredacted-captain-blood3.pdf; Bass, Thomas A., *The Spy Who Loved Us: The Vietnam War and Pham Xuan An's Dangerous Game,* PublicAffairs, 2009, 187; Tim Page, *Derailed in Uncle Ho's Victory Garden: Return to Vietnam and Cambodia,* Scribner: 1999, 171.

[788] Richard Dudman, *Forty Days With The Enemy*, New York: Liveright, 1971,102, 126, 141.

[789] Richard Dudman, *Forty Days With The Enemy*, New York: Liveright, 1971,145.

[790] Richard Dudman, *Forty Days With The Enemy*, New York: Liveright, 1971, 156-7.

[791] Richard Dudman, *Forty Days With The Enemy*, New York: Liveright, 1971, 137-138.

[792] Richard Dudman, *Forty Days With The Enemy*, New York: Liveright, 1971, 166.

Chapter 6. Resurgence: Chaos, Cambodia, Kent State

Peace Movement Split.

Despite Hanoi's demand for unity various American communist factions in the American peace movement were continually at each other's throats. In mid-1970, New Mobe split into the People's Coalition for Peace and Justice, PCPJ, and National Peace Action Coalition, NPAC. NPAC was Trotskyite and a single issue organization--Vietnam. Members of the Trotskyite Communist SWP, Patricia Grogan and Syd Stapleton, signed the checks of National Peace Action Coalition, NPAC.[793] Sydney R. Stapleton, SWP signed leases for office space at 1029 Vermont Ave, NW for both the National Peace Coalition and the National Peace Action Coalition. In March 1971, Brad Lyttle, WRL, and a Marxist active in CP fronts, signed office leases for National Action Group also at 1029 Vermont Ave. NW. [794]

PCPJ opened shop at 917 15th Street, NW in Washington.[795] Heavily larded with CPUSA members[796] and joiners of fronts,[797] it claimed a broad sweep "of peace, anti-poverty, labor groups."[798]

Richard H. Ichord, Chairman of the House Committee on Internal Security said, NPAC was "not interested in obtaining peace in Vietnam except on the terms of the enemy"[799]

---

[793] http://www.wintersoldier.com/staticpages/index.php?page=KGBKerry

[794] *National Peace Action Coalition, NPAC and People's Coalition for Peace and Justice, PCPJ*, Part I, Hearing, Committee on Internal Security, House of Representatives, 92nd Cong, 1st Sess., May 18-21, 1971. Washington, D.C., 1782-84, US Government Printing Office $1.75.

[795] PCPJ letterhead, September 1, 1971.

[796] Max Friedman identified "CP" members on [796] PCPJ letterhead, September 1, 1971 and at http://keywiki.org/index.php/Peoples_Coalition_for_Peace_and_Justice are: Althea Alexander, Abe Bloom, Lucile Berrien, Carl Braden, Al Evanoff, John Gilman, Carlton Goodlet, Dave Gordon, Gil Green, Terrance Hallinan, Dorothy Hayes, Sylvia Kushner, Sid Peck, Pauline Rosen, Irving Sarnoff, Jack Spiegel, Jarvis Tyner, Abe Weisburd.

[797] Kay Camp, Mary Clarke, Dave Dellinger, William Kunstler, Cora Weiss, on PCPJ letterhead, September 1, 1971.

[798] The American Friends Service Committee, National Welfare Rights Organization, Fellowship of Reconciliation, Southern Christian Leadership Conference, Clergy and Laymen Concerned, Women's International League for Peace and Freedom, Women Strike for Peace, National Student Association, and War Resisters League [798] PCPJ letterhead, "Dear Friend," in a "Call to Action to End the War in Indochina," September 1, 1971.

[799] House, National Peace Action Coalition NPAC) and People's coalition for Peace

and so did PCPJ. Both were united in opposing the U.S. in Vietnam and dedicated to a Communist victory.[800]

The Committee of Returned [Peace Corps] Volunteers, CRV, complained in August 22, 1970 Liberation News Service, an "International Committee" of 10-15 New Mobe leaders had "perpetuated itself by selecting people for trips or meetings with the Vietnamese…"[801] Indeed, Hanoi chose PCPJ for vetting applicants. Hanoi's reliable agents in PCPJ, assisted Hanoi's control of mail and visitors.

***

Nixon Violates North Vietnam's Cambodian Sanctuary.

Hanoi's Agents Provide Early Warnings. On April 29, 1970 someone phoned Cora and Peter Weiss's elegant home at 4022 Waldo Avenue, Bronx, New York during a New Mobe meeting. David Dellinger relayed the news. President Nixon was sending South Vietnamese and American troops into Cambodia.[802]

Ten thousand miles away, super spy and *Time* magazine reporter, Pham Xuan An gave his own advanced warning to Hanoi's headquarters in South Vietnam, COSVN. allowing top North Vietnam officials in their Cambodian base camps to escape death or capture.[803] Spy An received one of his sixteen exploitation medals for providing details of the operation in Cambodia.[804]

Nixon only told one member of Congress, the likely leaker to New Mobe and Hanoi was in Saigon, the White House or the Pentagon.

New Mobe Mobilized. Forewarned, on the evening of the 29th, New Mobe set the date, May 9, for a mass Washington

---

and Justice (PCPJ), 91st Cong.,1st sess., 1971 1446 cited in Rothrock, 115N64.

[800] "Dear Friend," in a "Call to Action to End the War in Indochina," September 1, 1971.

[801] Cited in "Answer This Question, Mr. Kerry," *Pittsburgh Tribune-Review*, internet service, October 17, 2004; See also James Sherod, "A Case Study of Elitism: A Critique of the Planning and Organization for the Conference with the Indochinese in Cuba, August 1970," New York Chapter of the Committee of Returned Volunteers, July 30, 1970. www.jamesherod.info/index.php?sec=paper&id=43&print=y.

[802] Tom Wells, *The War Within: America's Battle over Vietnam*, NY: Henry Holt, 1994, 420-21

[803] Thomas A. Bass, *The Spy Who Loved Us: the Vietnam War and Pham Xuan An's Dangerous Game*, New York: Public Affairs, 2009, 6, 260, 278n.

[804] Kyle Horst to author, March 2008.

protest of the Cambodian incursion still unknown to the American people.[805] In one day Norma Becker's cadre stuffed, stamped and mailed 10,000 anti-war activists and organizations.

***

COSVN Does Not Exist. The antiwar movement and the media had another theory. Hanoi's Central Office of South Viet Nam, (COSVN) did not exist[806] despite captured documents self-identified as COSVN.[807] The official history of the People's Army of Vietnam from 1961-1975 makes frequent, over thirty, references to COSVN,[808] ordering, directing, instructing or guiding its forces in South Vietnam.

Journalists and peace protesters thought COSVN in Cambodia was mostly a figment of American imagination.[809]

If COSVN did not exist or was a minor operation, then perhaps Hanoi's troops in Cambodia were imaginary just as Hanoi said. Better, if Hanoi had no troops in Cambodia, then the US was violating Cambodian neutrality.

Cambodia: Enemy Sanctuary and War Materials. Nixon's full-force move into Cambodia, recommended by the Joint Chiefs of Staff since 1964, was not a senseless slaughter of innocent peasants and a violation of Cambodian neutrality. Nearly a quarter of Cambodia had long provided an unchallenged sanctuary for the North's military forces. It provided safe haven for base camps and munitions bunkers for the communists off limits to the U.S. military for most of the war.

War Materials. As early as 1966, military intelligence, Joe Christian, said Chinese merchant vessels delivered war material to Cambodian ports. The CIA thought MACV was "overstating the significance of Cambodia to the Communists fighting in South Vietnam." Maps of infiltration

[805] Zaroulis, *Who Spoke Up...,* 316; General Bruce Palmer, Jr., *The 25-Year War; America's Military Role in Vietnam,* New York: Simon Schuster, 1985, 100-101.
[806] Asprey, Robert B. *War in the Shadows: The Guerilla in History* New York: William Morrow and Company, 1994, 996-997; Mark Rudd, *Underground: My Life With the SDS and the Weathermen,* New York: Harper Collins, 2009, 208-9.
[807] Hanoi's Central Office for South Vietnam (COSVN): A Background Paper, US Mission in Vietnam, Saigon, July 1969.
[808] The Military History Institute of Vietnam, Merle L. Pribbenow (Trans.) *Victory in Vietnam: The Official History of the People's Army of Vietnam, 1954-1975,* Lawrence: University Press of Kansas, 2002, 58, 84,100, 113, 116, 117, 129, 134,138,144, 145, 176, 177, 183, 191, 192, 194, 196, 197, 209, 214, 246, 248, 255, and many more.
[809]Joyce Hoffman, *On Their own: Women Journalists and the American Experience in Vietnam,* Philadelphia: Da Capo Press, 2008, 195-196, 197, 199, 215-6, 222, 227.

routes, showed no Cambodian ports. Sec. Robert McNamara said, "Evidence was insufficient to support that thesis [of Cambodian ports]." Johnson's "policy of secrecy and lack of candor" about Cambodia silenced Gen. Westmoreland and public discussion of the matter.

By end of 1969, some 21,600 metric tons of arms, ammunition, rockets, clothing and medicines had been delivered through Cambodian ports.[810] Moreover, by 1970, canvas-covered trucks carried 70-80% of the bulk of battlefield supplies, not down the Ho Chi Minh Trail from the north, but from the port of Sihanoukville in Cambodia.[811]

The US Attack. The field commander of the first American brigade to attack Cambodia, General Arthur Collins, had the same 48 hour warning as Cora Weiss's intelligence agent in Washington, D.C. The president would not tell the American people until the next day. The main attack came on May 1, 1970.

Cambodian Invasion. Finally announced on April 30, 1970, Nixon's Cambodian invasion was intended to disrupt its sacred status as a decade-long untouchable sanctuary for North Vietnamese infiltration of party cadre, troops, and supplies into South Vietnam. In the spring of 1970, the North Vietnamese had 35,000- 40,000 troops in eastern Cambodia. A year of well-known "secret" B-52 strikes had had little military effect. The invasion was a significant escalation of previously limited bombing inside Cambodia.

"Neutrality" Violated. Under the laws of war, both the Sihanouk and the successor Lon Nol governments were obligated to approve the American attack upon Vietnam's years-long violations of Cambodia's territorial sovereignty. Soon Lon Nol cut enemy access to the Cambodian port of Sihanoukville forcing

---

[810] Gen. William C. Westmoreland, *A Soldier Reports*, New York: Dell, 1976, 237-38.
[811] Thomas L. Ahern, *Good Questions, Wrong Answers: CIA's Estimates of Arms Traffic Through Sihanoukville, Cambodia During the Vietnam War* CIA Center for the Study of Intelligence, February 2004; 70% John Prados, *The Blood Road: The Ho Chi Minh Trail and the Vietnam War*, New York: John Wiley, 1998, 296; 80 % "Danger and Opportunity in Indochina," *Time*, March 30, 1970; McAlister Brown, Gordon Hardy, and Arnold Isaacs, *Pawns of War*, Boston: Boston Publishing, 1987, 73; Clinton's CIA Director, John Deutch told the 911 Commission, "Group think...did then happen.... [I]n Vietnam it became the house view in CIA that all the supplies for operations in the south came down the trail.... They defended it and got more entrenched as the war went on - when in fact, it turned out some 80 percent came in through Sihanoukville. We only found that out afterwards."[811]

total reliance on the Ho Minh Trail stockpiles of military supplies in Laos.[812]

Left Outraged. The American left, internationalists who did not give a whit about any nation's borders, territorial integrity, national aspirations, or sovereignty, was absolutely outraged by U.S.'s violation of Cambodian "neutrality," a neutrality Hanoi North Vietnamese gang raped for five years and twenty miles inside Cambodia.

Hanoi's America friends never protested Hanoi's violations of Laotian and Cambodian neutrality. The Saigon corps press gave scant coverage to Cambodia's Prince Norodom Sihanouk's complaints, nor of his successor Lon Nol, of Hanoi violations of their territorial integrity. They cared less about Cambodia's secret approval of secret U.S. bombing of Hanoi occupying Cambodia.[813]

Battlefield Successes in Cambodia. The Cambodia incursion succeeded on the battlefield. Allied forces lost 1,200 KIA, but killed ten times that number of enemy troops. "Perhaps of greater importance…thousands of tons of rice, millions of rounds of …ammunition, and…vital supplies were captured or destroyed."[814] The Communists said so. "The destruction of their Cambodian sanctuary has been disastrous for the Viet Cong. Overnight Chua (VC village secretary) and his comrades have been denied …medical facilities, schools, ammunition dumps and food storage."[815]

The year-end report from the Soviet Embassy in Hanoi said, "the intensification of hostilities in Laos and Cambodia...truly created an extremely difficult position in Vietnam. … …"[816]

---

[812] William Westmoreland, *A Soldier Reports*, 474 cited James Banerian and the Vietnamese Community Action Committee, *Losers Are Pirates: A Close Look at the PBS Series "Vietnam: A Television History,"* Phoenix: Tieng Me Publications, 1984, 191.

[813] Robert Elegant, "How to Lose a War: The Press and Vietnam," *Encounter*, (London), Vol. LVII, August 1981, 73-9- at Wellesley.edu/Polisci/wj/Vietnam/readings/elegant.htm

[814] Richard Botkin, *Ride the Thunder: A Vietnam War Story of Honor and Triumph*, New York: WND Books, 2009, 205.

[815] Mark Moyar, *Phoenix and the Birds of Prey; The CIA's Secret Campaign to Destroy the Viet Cong*, Annapolis: Naval Institute Press, 1997, 245n20 cites Herrington, 34.

[816] CIA, FOIA, "Political Report of the Embassy of the USSR in the Democratic Republic of Vietnam For the Year 1970," [TFR 136-22A, [handwritten "22"] Top Secret, Copy No. 3 "12" Mar 71, Issue No. 114 [Stamp "TsK KPSS, 10987, 16 Mar 71 180-A/ Subject to Return to the General Section TsK KPSS"] DRV, city of Hanoi,

PRG Justice Minister General Truong Nhu Tang wrote the operation in Cambodia

Largely accomplished its immediate goals (I barely survived it myself)...Nixon and Kissinger [said it]...gained an essential year of time. ...Yet this "victory" ...undermine[d] American unity. ...[and] incurred a propaganda defeat whose effects... have entered the American national psyche....[817]

Public Supports Cambodian Invasion. American elites may have been psychologically compromised, but were the American people? Harris surveys in May showed 60% of the American people supported Nixon's Cambodian invasion and a majority favored a resumption of the bombing of North Vietnam.[818] Nixon's approval 59% in early June.[819]

The war in the streets of American would trump battlefield successes and the views of the American people yet again.

***

Students Killed at Kent State and Jackson State

"Tin soldiers and Nixon coming,
We're finally on our own.
This summer I hear the drumming
Four dead in Ohio."
"Ohio" lyrics by Neil Young of
Crosby, Stills, Nash and Young[820]

Poorly understood and historically distorted events at Kent State in April 1970 turned millions against the war.

National Guardsmen killed four students and wounded nine without readily apparent reason. Kent State became another exemplar of how the U.S. government was waging a uniquely illegal and immoral war in Vietnam and on the very streets of America.

It was not entirely as it seemed.

March 1971, [TFR 136-40][handwritten "128", "161"].

[817] Tang, *A Viet Cong Memoir* 211-12.

[818] James Webb, "Peace? Defeat? What Did the Vietnam Protesters Want?" speech at American Enterprise Institute, jameswebb.com/articles/variouspubs/aeiprotesterswant.htm http://www.discoverthenetworks.org/ individual Profile.asp?indid=1624

[819] H.R. Haldeman, *The Haldeman Diaries: Inside the Nixon White House*, New York: Berkley Books, 1994, 204.

[820] Thanks to Richard Botkin, *Ride the Thunder: A Vietnam War Story of Honor and Triumph*, New York: WND Books, 2009,208, for reminding us of the emotional propaganda power of music describing events of the era.

SDS Agitation at Kent State. Two years before the student deaths at Kent State University in Ohio[821] Weatherman Terry Robbins, SDS regional traveler, helped Rick and Candy Erickson, SDS Weatherman and red diaper baby Howie Emmer organize[822] a radical and militant chapter of the SDS ranging from six to 30 members.[823] Other SDS members at Kent State were Tim Butz, Joyce Cecora, and Mark Real. They operated out of the "Haunted House" on Ash Street up the hill from the "Bates Motel" in Alfred Hitchcock's classic "Psycho."[824]

Those SDS leaders visiting the House and Kent State campus, were Ayers, Dohrn, Rubin, Corky Benedict, Katie Boudin, Lisa Meisel, Jim Mellen, Carl Oglesby, Diana Oughton, and Mark Rudd.

In 1969 a year before the student deaths, Robbins and Meisel declared *The War At Kent State*, demanded the end of ROTC and of police training programs "protect[ing] imperialism."[825] Debbie Shryock of the *Kent Daily Stater*, wrote, "They were…bent on destroying the university. They were determined to start revolution here."[826]

On April 8, 1969, the SDS had organized a rally of 400 people. About 200 marched on buildings forcing their way past police.[827] Dan Berger in his *Outlaws of America* says, Robbins and other SDS members "moved past an army of athletes and policemen to successfully disrupt a university hearing on disciplinary and student-power issues."[828] Six SDS members (No first name) Dimarco, Colin S. Neiberger, George Gibeaut, Howard Emmer, Edward Erickson and Jeff David Powell, were arrested for assaulting campus cops.[829]

---

[821] Ron Jacobs, *The Way The Wind Blew: A History Of The Weather Underground*, Verso, 1997, 49-50.

[822] Mark Rudd, *Underground: My Life With the SDS and the Weathermen*, New York: Harper Collins, 2009, 210; James A. Michener, *Kent State: What Happened and Why*, New York: Random House, 1971, 92; Cathy Wilkerson, *Flying Close to the Sun*, New York: Seven Stories Press, 2007, 228, 356.

[823] "Active Members in SDS," T.F. Kelly to D.L. Schwartzmiller, Kent State University [n.d.1969] in a special collection, "4 May 1970," Box 107, at the Kent State University Library at speccoll.library.kent.edu/4may70/box 107/107f9p12.gif.

[824] James A. Michener, *Kent State: What Happened and Why*, New York: random House, 1971, 80.

[825] Robbins and Meisel (1968) *The War At Kent State* cited in Wikiipedia.

[826] James A. Michener, *Kent State: What Happened and Why*, New York: random House, 1971, 88-89, 98.

[827] Ibid.

[828] Berger *Outlaws…*, 112.

[829] Neil Wetterman report attached to T.F. Kelly to D.L. Schwartzmiller, Kent State University, May 1, 1969 in a special collection, "4 May 1970," Box 107, at the Kent

One, Colin Nieberger, faced a trial on April 16, 1969 opposed by a rally of 2,000 and a march of 700. Robbins was arrested, sentenced to three-months, served six weeks, in December 1969.

On April 28, 1969, Bernardine Dohrn told Kent State students to arm for revolution. VDC's Jerry Rubin said, "Until you are ready to kill your parents, you're not ready to change this country."[830]

Other groups at Kent State were the Young Socialist Alliance (YSL), Student Mobilization and Moratorium Committee—all vigorous opponents of ROTC on campus. Senior Professor Sidney L. Jackson, a lifelong CPUSA activist was the faculty advisor to Kent State Committee to End the War,[831] among whose members were red diaper baby Howie Emmer, Bob Erlich, Joe Walsh, Rick Erickson and Robin Marks. YSLer Mike Alewitz led Kent State Mobilization.

Early May 1970. Weathermen Arrive on Scene: "Join the AmeriCong..." In early May 1970, cars arrived from Illinois and New York, home turfs of the Weather SDS. Requesting aid from the Governor of Ohio, Kent Mayor Leroy told a grand jury two out of town cars of Weathermen had arrived[832] and emerged with walkie-talkies and armbands. The SDS Weather controlled Revolutionary Printing Cooperative Committee distributed a leaflet showing white radicals carrying rifles captioned, "Join the AmeriCong...Be an Outlaw. The Time is right for fighting in the streets."[833]

In two years before, the SDS Weather had surely prepared the ground for battle at Kent State—by others. Some of the most prominently identified leaders of the 1970 riots, Jerry Rupe, Rick Felber, Doug Cormak, Peter Bleik, Thomas Foglesong and Thomas Miller, were not students of Kent State University.[834] Witnesses later reported overhearing talk of meetings planning riots and the burning of the ROTC building on campus[835] including gathering rocks[836], railroad flares, and

---

State University Library at speccoll.library.kent.edu/4may70/box 107/107f9p12.gif.
[830] Alan Stang, "Kent State," *American Opinion*, June 1974, 2,4,10.
[831] "Ohio notables at rites for Prof. Jackson," *Daily World*, May 16, 1979, 11.
[832] "Entire text of special grand jury report," *The Record* (Kent-Ravenna), October 16, 1970.
[833] Senate, Committee on the Judiciary, Subcommittee to Investigate the Administration of the Internal Security Act and Other Internal Security Laws, *The Weather Underground*, Committee Print, January 1975, 27-29.
[834] C.D. Brennan to W.C. Sullivan, FBI Memo, June 10, 1970.

machetes. Threatening students demanded merchants post signs protesting the war or face damages to their stores.[837]

Kent City and Campus, Days of Rage. Replicating the Weathermen "Days of Rage" in the streets of Chicago in October 1969, for three days May 1-3, 1970 mobs hit and ran through the streets of Kent, Ohio and the university campus breaking windows, setting fires, burning the ROTC building, attacking photographers, firemen and policemen and cutting fire hoses.[838]

Ohio Governor James Rhodes compared the mobs to Nazi brown shirts, communists, nightriders and vigilantes. They were "well-trained, militant" revolutionaries."[839] SDS Weather had trained some.

Twenty-three of Kent State's faculty distributed hundreds of leaflets deploring the National Guard and defending the burning of the ROTC building in the "larger context of the daily burning …by our government in Vietnam, Laos and now Cambodia."[840]

Only after the trashing of the city and the burning of the ROTC building, on May 4, 1970 the Governor called the Ohio National Guard.

Mobs Attack National Guard. Hundreds of students and nonstudents advanced upon the Guardsmen shouting obscenities and yelling KILL, KILL, KILL."[841] According to witnesses and photographs the mob bombarded the Guardsmen with bricks, concrete, golf clubs, baseball bats, spiked golf balls, slingshots, ball bearings, razor-embedded blocks of wood and bags of excrement.

---

[835] FBI, FOIA, Kent State, CV 98-2140, 302 interview of [redacted] on 5/19/70 at Canton Ohio; FBI, FOIA, Kent State, CV 98-2140, 302 interview of [redacted] at Ravenna, Ohio 5/16/70.

[836] FBI, FOIA, Kent State, CV 98-2140, 302 interview of [redacted] at Kent Ohio, May 26, 1970.

[837] "Entire text of special grand jury report," *The Record* (Kent-Ravenna), October 16, 1970.

[838] Francis L. Brininger, State Arson Bureau, to Eugene Jewell, Chief August 6, 1970, in "ROTC building arson May 2, 1970: Witness statements taken August 6, 1970, Kent State University in a special collection, "4 May 1970," Box 107, at the Kent State University Library at speccoll.library.kent.edu/4may70/box 107/107f9p12.gif.

[839] Cathy Wilkerson, *Flying Close to the Sun*, New York: Seven Stories Press, 2007, 356.

[840] "Entire text of special grand jury report," *The Record* (Kent-Ravenna), October 16, 1970.

[841] "Entire text of special grand jury report," *The Record* (Kent-Ravenna), October 16, 1970.

Sniper Fire Reported. Radios of both the National Guard and State Police reported sniper fire. While retreating up a hill there were one or more shots, not from the Guard's M-1 rifles according to contemporary witnesses, rang out.[842] A TV reporter, Fred DeBrine of WKYC, claimed to have witnessed Kent State student, FBI informant and photographer, Terry Norman, handing a revolver to a police officer and saying "I was afraid they were going to kill me, so I took out my revolver, and I fired it the air and into the ground."[843]

Kent State Gunfire Confirmed in 2010. Such gunfire prior to the Ohio National Guard shootings was widely denied at the time. In October 2010 a digitally mastered copy of an audiotape of that day revealed new evidence. Kent State student and law enforcement photographer, Terry Norman, was surrounded by an angry mob. A voice shouted, "They got someone" followed by other voices "Kill Him, Kill Him." Thereafter, the sound of a digitally identical .38 caliber revolver is heard followed by "Whack that [expletive]"and three more .38 caliber shots. Again, the Guardsmen were using M-1 rifles with a distinctly different sound than a .38 pistol.

After the .38 shots, a Guard commanded, "prepare to fire."[844] A contemporary photo shows Terry Norman in the protection of Ohio National Guardsmen.[845] Perhaps guilt-ridden, Terry Norman has since told many stories, denied firing his .38 and avoided interviews, but the forensic evidence now seems to place him in self-defense precipitating a human tragedy killing innocent students and outraging a nation.

13 Seconds of Hell. Seventy seconds after the .38 gunfire, frightened and undisciplined members of the National

---

[842] FBI, FOIA, Kent State, CV 98-2140, 302 interview of [redacted], by [redacted] JJD/jky, Cleveland, 5/15/70.

[843] Norman repeated his story off camera to DeBrine the next day; John Mangels, "Kent State tape indicates altercation and pistol fire preceded National Guard shootings (audio), Cleveland Plain Dealer, October 8, 2010.

[844] Terry Strubbe, tape recording from the ledge of his dorm room at Kent State, April 4, 1970: AP, "Report: Pistol shots preceded Kent St. shootings," *Cleveland Plain Dealer*, October 8, 2010; Robert F. Turner, "Turner: Not a massacre but a mistake: New evidence indicates source of gunfire of shots that triggered shootings," *Washington Times*, October 12, 2010; "Kent Tribunal Hears New Evidence of Clear Order to Fire at Kent State, Backs Rep. Kucinich in Call to Open Inquiry: Audio Tape Shows Evidence of Pistol Firing Seconds Before Verified Order to Shoot," Common Dreams.Org, Press Release, October 12, 2010; Testimony of Stuart Allen bit.ly/dakhWw;

[845] John Mangels, "Kent State tape indicates altercation and pistol fire preceded National Guard shootings (audio)," *Cleveland Plain Dealer*, October 8, 2010.

Guard, 29 out of 77 guardsmen, returned rifle fire 67 times for 13 seconds killing four students, Allison Krause, Jeffrey Miller,[846] Sandra Scheuer, William Schroeder, and wounding nine others.

Fateful Photo Forever Condemns U.S. Government. In a Pulitzer Prize winning John Filo photo, a tall 14-year-old runaway girl from a Florida junior high school, Mary Ann Vecchio, was forever remembered kneeling, screaming with arms outstretched over the dead prostate body of innocent student bystander Jeffrey Miller.[847] (There is a similar photo of a woman holding the head of Benno Ohnessorg shot by a West German policeman in a 1967 protest.) The Filo photo and news coverage radicalized thousands.

"Radicalized, revolutionized and yippized." About the bloodshed, Rubin said, "In 48 hours more young people were radicalized, revolutionized and yippized than in any single time in American history."[848] According to Bob Haldeman's diary, President Nixon was "very disturbed. Afraid his (Cambodian) decision set it off, and that is the ostensible cause of the demonstrations there."[849]

Kent Makes Effective Soviet Propaganda. Kent State provided the stuff for Soviet agit-prop[850] such as Soviet poet Yevgeny Yevtushenko's *Bullets don't like people / who love flowers,* published in *Pravda,* the official newspaper of the Communist Party of the Union of Soviet Socialist Republics. The poem was a eulogy for 19-year-old protester and victim Allison Krause. The day before she was quoted as saying, "Flowers are better than bullets." Yevtushenko's poem was both a condemnation of the war and a call to arms to overthrow capitalism to "become a legion of flowers... armed with bullets."[851]

To this day, a duplicate photo of Mary Ann Vecchio hangs in Hanoi's war museums.

---

[846] A search of Miller's clothing turned up a scrap paper with the number 673-1759 and words "communications center." FBI, FOIA, Kent State, Teletype, FBI Cleveland to Director FBI Washington, Unsubs: Firebombing of Army ROTC Bldg., Kent State Univ. (KSU), Kent Ohio, 5-6-70.

[847] The Filo photo of Vecchio is honored in the War Remnants Museum in Saigon, author's photos Viet II DSC_327-8.

[848] Alan Stang, "Kent State," *American Opinion*, June 1974, 2,4,10.

[849] H.R. Haldeman, *The Haldeman Diaries: Inside the Nixon White House*, New York: Berkley Books, 1994,191.

[850] Bill Rood to author, April 1, 2011.

[851] Solomon Todd, "Ten Years After: Kent State in the Rearview," *The Nation*, May 1980.

Bốn sinh viên Đại học Kent, Bang Ohio, Mỹ – bị lính cảnh vệ quốc gia bắn chết trong một cuộc biểu tình chống chiến tranh của Mỹ ở Việt Nam (năm 1970).

Four students of Kent University, Ohio State, the US were shot dead by national guards in a demonstration against the US war in Vietnam (in 1970).

Photo: Iconic Kent State photo, Mary Ann Vecchio, War Remnants Museum wall, Roger Canfield, March 2008.[852]

***

The Investigations of Kent State:
FBI, Justice, Commission, Grand Jury, District Court.

FBI Director Hoover privately reported FBI investigations showed rioters, students and nonstudents, were at fault, as would ultimately a Special Ohio Grand Jury and the families of the student victims.

Yet Jerris Leonard of the **Justice Department**, who had prosecutorial responsibility (and political vulnerability) publicly claimed the FBI had concluded the Guard was at fault[853] and on June 15, 1970 J. Walter Yeagley, Assistant Attorney General for Internal Security wrote Hoover, "the evidence was insufficient to warrant presentation ...to a grand jury." Hoover scrawled on the memo, "The usual run around by the do nothing Div."[854]

Scranton Commission on Kent State. Nixon appointed Pennsylvania Governor William Scranton to lead a Commission on Kent State that called the actions of the National Guard "unnecessary, unwarranted, and inexcusable."

---

[852] Author's photos, Viet II, 237, 238.

[853] H.R. Haldeman, *The Haldeman Diaries: Inside the Nixon White House*, New York: Berkley Books, 1994,220.

[854] FBI, FOIA, Kent State, Memo, C.D. Brennan to W. C. Sullivan, 6/10/70; FBI, FOIA, Kent State, J. Walter Yeagley, Assistant Attorney General, Internal Security Division to Director, FBI. June 15, 1970.

Ohio Grand Jury on Kent State. Thinking otherwise, Ohio Governor James Rhoades called a Special Ohio Grand Jury, which indicted 25 students[855] and no Guardsmen.[856]

U.S. District Court on Kent State. On October 16, 1970. Eight Guardsmen (James Daniel McGee, Mathew Junior McManus, Barry William Morris, William Earl Perkins, James Edward Pierce, Lawrence Anthony Shafer, Leon Herbert Smith, Ralph William Zoller) were prosecuted for violating the civil rights of students, but U.S. District Court Judge Frank J. Battisti acquitted the guardsmen. They lacked willful intent to deprive victims of their civil rights.[857]

FBI assessments. On May 11, 1970, J. Edgar Hoover told White House aide Egil Krogh, "The national guardsmen (at Kent State) would have been killed if they had not fired because students were throwing lead pipes, rocks, and bricks at Guardsmen. …We have…photos of bruises of the Guardsmen in color, some of which are shocking." Hoover reminded Krogh the burning of an ROTC building two nights before had precipitated the calling out of the National Guard.[858]

Firearms. On May 18th, Hoover told Vice President Agnew, "We found a considerable amount of firearms in the

---

[855] The following were indicted: David O. Adams, William G. Arthrell, Peter C. Bliek, Alan M. Canfora, Roseann Canfora, Douglas Charles Cormack, Joseph B. Cullum, Michael Erwin, Richard G. Felber, Thomas Graydon Foglesong, John Gerbetz, Ruth Gibson, Kenneth J. Hammond, Jeffrey D. Hartzler, Joseph J. Lewis, Dr. Thomas S. Lough, Thomas D. Miller, Carol Lynn Mirman, Craig A. Morgan, Mary Helen Nicholas, James M. Riggs, Jerry H. Rupe, Larry A. Shub, Allen Tate, Ronald Weissenberger; FBI, FOIA, AIRTEL, SAC, Cleveland to Director [redacted] et al Sabotage; Sedition; Destruction Government Property, civil Rights Act of 1968—interference with Federally Protected Facility, 10/20/70, 1-3; "Kent 25," *The Burr,* May 2000 at http://www.burr.kent.edu/ archives/may4/twentyfive/twentyfive1.html. Only three of the indicted were SDS-Ruth Gibson, Ken Hammond and Ron Weissenberger. Eyewitnesses identified the following either throwing rocks, starting fires, beating up witnesses and firemen or cutting fire hoses: Mike Brock, Peter Bliek, Tony Compton, Debbie Durham, Richard Felber, Tom Grace, James Harrington, Jimmy Riggs, Jerry Rupe, Larry A. Shub, Allen Tate, Donald Weisenberger. For eye witnesses see: Francis L. Brininger, State Arson Bureau, to Eugene Jewell, Chief August 6, 1970, in "ROTC building arson May 2, 1970: Witness statements taken August 6, 1970, Kent State University in a special collection, "4 May 1970," Box 107, at the Kent State University Library at speccoll.library.kent.edu/4may70/box 107/107f9p12.gif

[856] H.R. Haldeman, *The Haldeman Diaries: Inside the Nixon White House,* New York: Berkley Books, 1994,242.

[857] FBIB, FOIA, Kent State, FBI note, JJB, 11/8/74; FBI, FOIA, Kent State, SA Martin V. Hale, Killing of Four Students at Kent State University, Kent, Ohio, --May 4, 1970; Allison Krause, ET AL – Victims.

[858] Hoover to Tolson etc, memo, May 11, 1970 found at FBI FOIA website under Tolson.

173

...rooms of students (at Kent State)...Some say there was sniping and some say there was not. ...The same is true at Jackson ...allegations of sniping at the troops before they fired and denials." Media reports said the FBI had found no justification for the Kent State shootings. An angry Hoover told Nixon that was the view of Assistant Attorney General Jerris Leonard, not the FBI. The FBI did not draw conclusions. "...[T]he press [was]...attributing (absolutely untrue) things to the FBI.[859]

Kent State Prosecutions and Culprits Fade Away. Thomas S. Lough, a sociology professor and faculty advisor to SDS,[860] was indicted for inciting a riot. Only two of the wounded students were among the 25 indicted, Joe Lewis and Alan Canfora. Canfora was an identified Maoist member of the Revolutionary Communist Party[861] and a member of the National Lawyers Guild.[862] Despite two years of SDS agitation only three of the indicted were SDS members in the action, Ruth Gibson, Ken Hammond and Ron Weissenberger.

Thomas Graydon Fogleson, witnessed pulling fire hoses,[863] and Larry A. Shub both pled guilty to first-degree riot. Jerry Rupe who was witnessed setting fire to the ROTC building with a gasoline soaked rag, burning an American flag, and assaulting firemen[864] was found guilty by a hung jury only for interfering with a fireman by cutting fire hoses.[865] During trial charges were dismissed against Peter Bleik, witnessed leading the action at the ROTC fire scene,[866] but not identified at trial.[867] Charges against Mary Helen Nicholas were also dismissed at trial. On December 23, 1971, all charges against the remaining 20 were also dismissed.

Two of the indicted fled, Carol Mirman to California and Allen "Alfie" Tate, a Black Panther, to New York and

---

[859] Hoover to Tolson, memo, July 24, 1970 at FBI FOIA website under Tolson; Hoover to Tolson, memo, 8:47 AM July 24, 1970 at FBI FOIA website under Tolson.
[860] Ken Hammond, Thomas Lough, Papers May 4 Collection, Box 21 http://speccoll.library.kent.edu/4may70/21.html
[861] Max Friedman to Roger Canfield, May 6, 2010.
[862] The NLG National Convention, February15-19, 1979, *Information Digest*, 9.
[863] FBI, FOIA, Kent State, Cleveland FD 204 June 23, 1970.
[864] FBI, FOIA, Kent State, Cleveland FD 204 June 23, 1970; FBI, FOIA, Kent State, CV 98-2140, 302 interview of [redacted]at Kent Ohio, May 26, 1970; FBI, FOIA, Kent State, CV 98-2140, 302 interview of [redacted] at [redacted] Ohio on June 18, 1970.
[865] FBI, FOIA, Kent State, Teletype, Cleveland to Director, 11-30-71.
[866] FBI, FOIA, Kent State, Cleveland FD 204 June 23, 1970.
[867] FBI, FOIA, Kent State, Teletype, Cleveland to Director, 11-30-71.

were never arrested or prosecuted. Tate helped set fire the ROTC building. [868]

Payday for Kent State Rioters. Two wounded indicted students, Joe Lewis and Alan Canfora, and one witnessed riot participant, Thomas Grace, received money settlements in civil suits equal to or larger than the $675,000 settlements given to parents of the four dead students.

Every subsequent year since 1970 commemorative ceremonies are held at Kent State as perpetual symbols of the evil empire and its war in Vietnam.

Mark Rudd, weatherman and an SDS visitor to Kent State, in retrospect wrote, "In some measure, the militancy of the university's Cambodia demonstrations resulted from the confrontational politics that Weatherman had helped to create at Kent." The Kent State chapter of SDS "had produced dozens of Weather cadre."[869]

Buying Dynamite. On the same day as the student deaths, on May 4, 1970, taking no time to mourn, Weatherman John Allen Fuerst (Aka Jeremy Pikser, Phil) and Roberta Brent Smith, illegally bought 30 pounds of dynamite, under the alias William Allen Friedman and took the explosives to California.[870]

Public Blames Kent State Protesters

In mid-1970, a Gallup poll asked Americans to rate groups. 42% rated the SDS highly unfavorable and the Black Panthers 75% highly unfavorable.[871] A Gallup poll revealed that 58% of Americans blamed the protesters and only 11% the National Guard.[872]

***

Hardhats: "Kill the Commie Bastards."

On May 8, 1970, in New York some two hundred, hard-hatted construction workers, following the example of their AFL-CIO leader, George Meany who supported the war, opposed the leftists. Apparently not having read Karl Marx's

---

[868] FBI, FOIA, Kent State, LHM Cleveland [redacted] et al, February 8, 1972.

[869] Mark Rudd, *Underground: My Life With the SDS and the Weathermen*, New York: Harper Collins, 2009, 210.

[870] FBI, FOIA, Weather Underground. The primary source is Acting SAC Chicago to Director, memo, "Foreign Influence-Weather Underground Organization," August 20, 1976, 199.

[871] Adam Garfinkle, *Telltale Hearts: The Origins and the Impact of the Vietnam Antiwar Movement*, NY: St. Martin's Griffin, 1997, 8n44, 306.

[872] Robert F. Turner, "Turner: Not a massacre but a mistake: New evidence indicates source of gunfire of shots that triggered shootings," *Washington Times*, October 12, 2010.

Das Kapital, these workers of the world united chanting, "Kill the Commie Bastards," while defending capitalist Wall Street from a leftist assault. The hardhats roughed up seventy students. In the weeks that followed pro-war hardhats in the thousands took to the streets in response to antiwar protests. J. Edgar Hoover told Egil Krogh, "I'm glad (the construction guys) did what they did…[T]hey really chased them down Broadway."[873]

***

Washington Protest of Kent Killings.

Assisted by Cora Rubin Weiss's intelligence network, organizational apparatus and public outrage over the killing of innocents at Kent State in a few days, on May 9th up to 50,000-100,000 peaceful demonstrators converged on Washington, D.C.

Major speakers and organizers were Barbara Bick, Rennie Davis, Dave Dellinger, Richard Fernandez, Fred Halstead, Phil Hirschkop, Abbie Hoffman, Brad Lyttle, John McAuliff, Stuart Meacham, Sidney Peck, Jerry Rubin, Arthur Waskow, and Ron Young. The protest concluded with demonstrators picking up caskets and marching them down 15th Street toward the White House ringed by tightly packed buses and an invisible thousand National Guardsmen.

Police and National Guard Ignore Provocations. The mass of demonstrators on the 9th were calm, angering Norma Becker, Arthur Waskow and Sidney Peck seeking massive civil disobedience to provoke the police to excessive force.[874] Marshals directed the caskets away from the White House, but an angry thousand rushed down H Street breaking windows of buses until police tear gas turned them back.

---

[873] Hoover to Tolson, memo, 10:27 AM, May 11, 1970 at FBI FOIA website under Tolson. DISCLOSURE-The author was a leader, chairman of Campus Mobilization for the Committee for Academic Freedom, which successfully fought to keep the Claremont Graduate School open during debates about US Cambodian operations. Other activists of the committee were Gary Gammon, Sue Leeson, Jo Ellen Schroeder, Richard Reeb, Steve Schlesinger. See: Leeson, Canfield and Schroeder, "A Plea for Academic Freedom," spring 1970. The author subsequently gave speeches supporting Governor Ronald Reagan's policies at the University of California. Some members of Claremont doctoral examination committee were unhappy—delaying completion of the author's PhD for several years. Perpetrators of bombings in February 1969 at Scripps College, Claremont Men's College, CMC, and at Pomona college, one injuring a Pomona professor's secretary and burning down a CMC campus landmark, Story House, were never prosecuted in Claremont.

[874] Stewart Meacham, "May Ninth," *Win Magazine*, July 1970; Wells, *The War Within…*, 437-445.

On May 10, trespassers, fleeing the occupied office of the Peace Corps said, "Like the Viet Cong, we escape back into the people." That day, the Weather Underground bombed the National Guard's Washington Headquarters in retaliation, they said, for the killings of anti-war protesters at Jackson and Kent State Universities.

Fonda-Nixon: "Bunch of Bums." Jane Fonda called President Nixon a "warmonger" for sending U.S. troops against the Vietnamese in their sanctuary of Cambodia. Nixon replied that Fonda and kind were "a bunch of bums." At a Washington rally Fonda welcomed her "fellow bums," clenched her fist and declared "Power to the People."

Anti-ROTC Protesters on Campuses. Harassment and disruption of ROTC and military recruiting on campus, e.g. Wisconsin, Northwestern, Dartmouth, Berkeley, Princeton, reduced ROTC enrollments by two-thirds from the mid-1960s to the 1970s,[875] diminishing the quality of both recruits and junior officers in combat, e.g. William Calley at My Lai.

Eric Holder at Columbia ROTC Protest. In the spring of 1970, before Kent State, April 11-16, an armed group of the Black Students Organization at Columbia University occupied the abandoned Naval ROTC office demanding it be renamed the Malcolm X Lounge. Renamed it was. Among the armed group occupying the ROTC Office for five days was allegedly Eric Holder, future Attorney General of the United States for Barack Obama.[876] A "peaceful sit-in" he says A sit-in is a forceful occupation of a property, a trespass. ML King accepted an arrest as acceptable in civil disobedience, a breaking of the law.

---

[875] Rothrock *Divided*... 242-3.
[876] "As college student, Eric Holder participated in 'armed' takeover of former Columbia University ROTC office," *Daily Caller*, September 30, 2012.

Eric Holder, Jr.

Photo: Eric Holder, Columbia 1973.

Jackson State Killings. On May 15, two more students protesting the war were shot and killed at Jackson State College in Mississippi. Hoover said Guardsmen were "severely provoked" at Jackson and Kent State.[877]

Shutting Down Universities, Nationwide. The organized left, joined by the outraged, shut down universities nationwide for teach-ins on the Vietnam War. The objective was not debates. The organizers sought to win the Vietnam "debate" by superior force. And they did. More than 400 universities were shut down. There were protests on 57% of college campuses and even junior high schools experienced protests.[878] An FBI report, "Campus violence hits new high during period of May 1-15" said, "Campus violence hits new high during period of May 1-15." May's two-week total was equal to the previous eight months—844 campus demonstrations, 3,000 arrests, 166 injuries, six deaths. Property losses were $4.5 million ranging from vandalism, 115 arsonist attacks, 3 bombings--often targeting ROTC facilities. Of 458 injuries, two-thirds, 295 were of police officers. &&&&&

Public and Youth Opposed Campus Shutdowns. "Less than 3% of student enrollment ...(had)...taken part"[879] in a near 100 percent shutdown of the nation's colleges and universities. Indeed, when answering Gallup's question, "Do you think the U.S. made a mistake sending troops to fight in

---

[877] Hoover to Tolson, memo, 9:49 AM, May 18, 1970 at FBI FOIA website under Tolson.

[878] Roger B. Canfield, *Democratic Legitimacy and American Political Violence, 1964-1970,* doctoral dissertation, Claremont Graduate School, Claremont, California 1972, 3.

[879] FBI, FOIA, "Campus violence hits new high during period of May 1-15,"file number 65-73268-127, May 21, 1970,at seanet.com/...

Vietnam? throughout the war young people under thirty were far less likely to think the war was a mistake than those over thirty"[880] By June Gallup found 82% disapproved of "College students going on strike…to protest the way things are run in this country."[881]

***

Antiwar Activists Pro-Viet Cong.

At UCLA Tom Hayden spoke of "revolutionizing youth" going through "a series of sharp and dangerous conflicts, life and death conflicts."[882] From the Weather Underground, on May 21, 1970 Bernardine Dohrn issued the WUO's "Declaration of a State of War." Like Hayden in 1967 in Bratislava, the WUO describes itself, in pertinent part, as "adapting the classic Viet Cong…to our situation here…." They were "Fighting Amerikan imperialism" using "our strategic position behind enemy lines to join forces in the destruction of the empire." Inspired by "Eldridge Cleaver… and all black revolutionaries…[for] their fight behind enemy lines."[883] Hayden had said in Bratislava, "We are all Viet Cong—NOW."

American troops in Cambodia read about Viet Cong friendly militant actions against the U.S. military at home.

Photo: 9th Division soldier in Cambodia reading about student protest back home, US Army. [884]

---

[880] "Support for the Vietnam War," 21 November 2002.
[881] Joseph A. Fry, "Unpopular Messenger; Student Opposition to the Vietnam War," cited in David L. Anderson, John Ernst (eds.) *The War Never Ends: New Perspectives on Vietnam War*, Lexington: University of Kentucky, 2007, 237.
[882] Miller, *Democracy is in the Streets,* 310N124 cites: Tom Hayden, "The Battle for Survival" (adapted from a speech at UCLA in May 1969), in Peter and Deborah Babcock and Bob Abel (Eds.), *The Conspiracy*, N.Y. 1969, 171-172.
[883] Bernardine Dohrn, "A Declaration of War," May 21, 1970, Pacifica Radio/UC Berkeley Social Activism Sound Recording Project, Media Research Center, Moffitt Library UC Berkeley, at www.lib.berkeley.edu/MRC/Pacificaviet; a copy also appears in FBI, FOIA, Weather Underground, Acting SAC Chicago to Director, memo, "Foreign Influence-Weather Underground Organization," August 20, 1976, 158-60.

***

[884] THE U.S. ARMY IN VIETNAM: FROM TET TO THE FINAL WITHDRAWAL, 1968-1975 at
http://images.google.com/imgres?imgurl=http://www.history.army.mil/books/amh-v2/amh%2520v2/p354.jpg&imgrefurl=http://www.history.army.mil/books/amh-v2/amh%2520v2/chapter11.htm&usg=__tvQEmh-t6bv__7oa1TzC2leeeew=&h=300&w=445&sz=23&hl=en&start=16&itbs=1&tbnid=Pj wYZ4XzCkWo7M:&tbnh=86&tbnw=127&prev=/images%3Fq%3DArmy%2Bassassi nation%2BOR%2Batrocity%2BOR%2Bmassacre%2B%2522viet%2Bcong%2522%26 hl%3Den%26sa%3DG%26as_st%3Dy%26tbs%3Disch:1

180

Chapter 7. GIs, Inquiries, Cages, Fonda.
Left Organizing GIs and Deserters.

During 1970, Jane Fonda toured military bases and USA, leftists created antiwar films, GI newspapers, coffee houses, old left foundations pay United States Servicemen Fund, USSF, to finance activities among GIs, deserters met Tom Hayden in Canada, and many deserters gathered in Canada, France and Sweden.

Fonda Forms F--- The Army. In April 1970, Jane Fonda and Donald Sutherland formed the FTA, F--- The Army, organized antiwar road shows before American troops. After April 16, 1970, FTA traveled the U. S during 1970 and for a month in 1971 toured Pacific bases.[885] Jane's tax-exempt leftist U.S. Servicemen Fund helped pay.

John Wayne Supports Troops and War against Communism. During 1970 actor John Wayne and singer Martha Ray narrated a film, "No Substitute for Victory,[886]" featuring Generals Mark Clark, A.C. Wedemeyer, William Westmoreland, Paul Harkin, Admiral U.S. Grant Sharp, broadcaster Lowell Thomas and Los Angeles Mayor Sam Yorty.

Howard Levy, a doctor refusing to teach medical skills to Green Berets, spent 2 1/2 years in prison. An admirer of Che Guevara and an advocate of a revolution to overthrow the government of the United States,[887] Levy advised Jane Fonda and Donald Sutherland. "...Bob Hope, Martha Ray and other companies of their political ilk have cornered the market..."[888] So "the time has come for entertainers who have a different view ...to reach the soldiers."[889]

Underground Media: Newsreel—Europe. According to Army intelligence, on May 24, the staff of Newsreel, socialist producer of antiwar films, pitching American Servicemen in Germany, met at Club Voltaire in Frankfurt, Germany to discuss how to expand its reach. Newsreel had contacts with Second Front International in France and the

---

[885] *Ramparts,* May 1972, 32.
[886] Amazon reviews, all liberal, trash Wayne, and any idea the war had any good purpose.
[887] Stuart Auerbach, "Dr. Levy Says Che Is His Hero," *Washington Post,* Nov. 11, 1969.
[888] *New Republic,* March 13, 1971, 9; Dennis Lim, "Jane Fonda's antiwar years with the FTA," *Los Angeles Times,* February 22, 2009.
[889] Christopher Andersen, 238.

American Deserters Committee in Sweden. Newsreel conducted 45-minute film discussions attracting 700 GIs during 1969.The report of Army intelligence of Newsreel's play in European politics understated its significance.

Melvin Margolis and others incorporated Newsreel in late 1967 in New York. Santiago Alvarez, a producer of pro-Castro films, heavily influenced Newsreel. Newsreel recruited talent from the SDS, SNCC and groups committed to revolution. Newsreel produced 40 films by 1973, many focusing on Vietnam. Robert Kramer, Douglas and Norm Fruchter's "People's War" covered their Hanoi sponsored trip in July 1969. Newsreel made films on draft resistance, 1967 Pentagon protest.

Roz Payne remembers, "Our cameras were used as weapons as well as recording the events." Literally, "Melvin [Margolis] had a cast iron steel...camera that could ...(break) plate glass windows."[890]

On May 24, 1970, Newsreel decided to produce a newsletter in Europe. At a follow up meeting May 30-31, 1970, the American Deserters Committee participated in "GI Summit Conference in Copenhagen" where it was use leftist publications.[891] By 1970, more than fifty underground newspapers circulated e.g. *About Face* in Los Angeles, *Fed Up!* in Tacoma, Washington; *Short Times* at Fort Jackson; *Vietnam GI* in Chicago; *Graffiti* in Heidelberg, Germany; *Bragg Briefs* in North Carolina; *Last Harass* at Fort Gordon, Georgia; *Helping Hand* at Mountain Home Air Base, Idaho.[892]

In 1976, Robert Kramer observed, "We've had a very privileged existence as filmmakers...we haven't had to raise money that much ourselves."[893] distributors David and Barbara Stone booked Newsreel films in theatres and universities in Europe and America.

Funding Newspapers and Coffeehouses: United States Servicemen's Fund, USSF. In 1969 Cora Weiss, Rev.

---

[890] "Film Love: Protesting the Vietnam War, 1966-1971," October 2, 2004. andel.home.mindspring.com/antwar_notes.htm.

[891] FBI, Washington Memo, "Newsreel" May 11, 1970; FBI, Washington Memo, "The following information has been received from the Office of the Deputy Chief of Staff, Intelligence, Headquarters, United States Army, Europe," June 18, 1970.

[892] Howard Zinn, "GI opposition the Vietnam War," http://libcom.org/library/soldiers-opposition-to-vietnam-war-zinn 1965-1973

[893] G. Roy Levin, "Robert Kramer and John Douglas interviewed, Reclaiming our past, reclaiming our beginning," *Jump Cut*, no. 10-11, 1976, 6-8.

Richard Fernandez, Jack Newfield, Dwight McDonald, Robert Zenin, Fred Gardner, and Donna Mickelson incorporated the tax-exempt United States Servicemen's Fund, USSF.[894] In 1970 Jane Fonda, joined wealthy leftist foundations in helping finance the tax exempt USSF. USSF was the primary financier of a network of antiwar GI Coffee House around military bases distributing antiwar newspapers.

Coffee Houses. Investor and Fair Play for Cuba activist, Robert Zevin, former *Scientific American* and *Ramparts* editor, and free-lance writer Fred Gardner, and organizer of UFO coffee house, Donna Mickleson, founded coffee houses in the spring of 1969. [895] USSF granted monthly stipends to GI newspapers, coffeehouses, counseling centers, bookstores, and other projects. [896] USSF supported *Binh Van,* political actions among active servicemen and provided financial and legal support to antiwar soldiers, deserters and protesters. According to the FBI, from May 1969 to November 1970 the USSF spent $125,667 on its projects from an income of $166,714.[897]

Senate Investigation of USSF. On May 28, 1970, the Senate Subcommittee on Internal Security acting under its authority to discover "infiltration by persons who are or may be under the domination of the foreign government," began an investigation of the activities and finances of (USSF). USSF asserted[898] it did not know the sources of its funds and filed legal actions to prevent subpoenas of its bank accounts. It would take five years to resolve the case in favor of the Senate records search.

Along the way a dissenting judge observed, "There is … [a] valid legislative interest of the federal Congress" in discovering money for USSF activities "came from foreign sources or subversive organizations."[899] It was a valid inquiry

---

[894] "Hanoi Visitor, Liberal Gurus Among Founders of Anti-GI Oufit," *Combat*, Vol. 2. No. 2, January 15, 1970, 4.
[895] "Combat Exclusive – Tax Exempt Group aims at Servicemen's Morale," *Combat [National Review]*, Vol. 1. No. 29, November 1, 1969.
[896] Introduction To USSF, *About Face! The U.S. Servicemen's Fund Newsletter*, vol. 2, no. 4
http://www.sirnosir.com/archives_and_resources/library/articles/aboutface_05.html
[897] FBI *Information Digest Special Report on VVAW*, Aug. 25, 1972, 8 (PDF 39); House Internal Security Committee *Investigation of Attempts to Subvert the U.S. Armed Services,* October 1971.
[898] 421 U.S. 491, 507, Eastland V. United States Servicemen's Fund (1975).
[899] id., at 377, 378, 488 F.2d, at 1277, 1278 at Find Law,

whether USSF had interfered with the loyalty, discipline, or morale of the Armed Services. It was legitimate to ask whether the anonymity of USSF donors disguised persons subject to the Foreign Agents Registration Act.

On Jan. 14, 1975, the Senate committee was abolished before it won its case against USSF. The Supreme Court ruled, too late, "it is clear that the subpoena to discover the bank records of the United States Servicemen's Fund "may fairly be deemed within [the Subcommittee's] province."[900]

Cora Rubin Weiss: Financier of USSF. As it turned out the [Samuel] Rubin foundation's Fund for Tomorrow, a financier of some CPUSA activity, administered by Cora Rubin Weiss and Peter Weiss, financed, in part, the USSF. Faberge millionaire Samuel Rubin was a CP member and friend of Armand Hammer, who laundered Soviet money[901] and whose father, Julius, was Lenin's first bagman from the United States. Rubin's daughter was, of course, the one and only Cora Rubin Weiss of Women Strike for Peace and Hanoi's COLIFAM, exploiter of POW families.

Extensive Communist Provenance. Stern Fund, created by heirs of Sears, Roebuck & Company chairman Julius Rosenwald, also financed USSF. Being indicted for spying for the Soviet Union, the second director of the Julius Rosenwald Fund, Alfred K. Stern and his wife Martha Dodd Stern, fled to Czechoslovakia in 1958. Martha Dodd Stern recruited Jane Foster, a friend of Julia and Paul Child, as a Soviet spy.[902] From 1960 to 1963, the Sterns contributed $16,000 to the CPUSA through FBI Agent SOLO, a long time CPUSA apparatchik Morris Childs[903] (no relation to Julia and Paul), in Prague.[904] Communist and Soviet spy Alfred Stern,

http://caselaw.lp.findlaw.com/scripts/getcase.pl?court=us&vol=421&invol=491
[900] Tenney v. Brandhove, supra, at 378. See also Find Law,
http://caselaw.lp.findlaw.com/scripts/getcase.pl?court =us&vol=421 &invol=491
[901] John Earl Haynes, Harvey Klehr, *In Denial: Historians, Communism and Espionage*, Encounter Books, 2005, 63.
[902]http:/http://www.wintersoldier.com/staticpages/index.php?page=InfoDigestGuide; Jennet Conant, *A Covert Affair: Julia Child and Paul Child* in the OSS, Simon & Schuster.
[903] Max Friedman retrieved from National Archives in October 16, 2013 of a report of a meeting of State Bureau of the Communist Party of Illinois on July 5, 1940 in Chicago, distributed August 18, 1940 by Counterintelligence Branch, G-2, Office of Assistant Secretary of War, CONFIDENTIAL report 10-266, RG 107, A1, Entry 88, Secretary of War, classified file, 1932-42, box 2.
[904] R.W. Smith to W.C. Sullivan, "Communist Party, USA, Solo Funds, September 16, 1965 at FBI, FOIA, SOLO, 94, 25.

like Communist Frank Marshall Davis[905], was known to the maternal grandfather, Communist Robert Rochon Taylor, and father, Dr. James Edward Bowman of Valerie Jarrett, President Obama's personal confident[906] living in the White House and vacationing with the Obama's family.

Whether any of the $1 billion KGB budgeted for the antiwar movement ever reached USSF through the Stern and Rubin funds is unknown. It is an hypothesis of interest. Notable public supporters of USSF besides Jane Fonda were Congresswomen Bella Abzug and Shirley Chisholm, Noam Chomsky, Betty Freidan and Nat Hentoff.[907]

***

Montreal. Deserters Greet Hayden. May 29-June 1, 1970 the American Deserters Committee invited Tom Hayden to Montreal, Canada for a Pan-Canadian Conference of "Deserters and Anti-war Organizations." Canadians opposing the Vietnam War welcomed and assisted American draft dodgers. Canadian immigration accepted as many as 125,000 Americans. Perhaps half stayed permanently.[908]

FBI investigations show Students for a Democratic Society, The Black Panthers, The Revolutionary Union, The Resistance, American Friends Service Committee, War Resisters League and The Committee for Peace and Freedom assisted American deserters who had fled to Canada and formed the American Deserters Committee of Montreal, Canada.[909]

Hayden Urges Deserters to Join the Revolution. Speaking at the deserters conference, Hayden said, Nixon was seeking a nuclear confrontation with China. Only "overthrowing the U. S. government" could stop Nixon. He said the 20 to 25 per cent opposing the war would have to ignore the same number (sic) favoring an American victory as well as the silent majority. "You have to make a go for it with ... the numbers you have." The deserters were thinking of reassembling "as a larger force back in the United States."[910]

---

[905] Paul Kengor, *The Communist: Frank Marshall Davis; The Untold Story of Barack Obama's Mentor*, New York: Simon and Schuster, 2012, 293

[906] Judicial Watch, "FBI Files Document Communism in Valerie Jarrett's Family, June 22, 2015 cites FBI, FOIA Airtel New York 3/18/55 Chicago; Director to FBI Chicago, Airtel March 22, 1955; FBI, Chicago, James Edward Bowman, 4/22/55.

[907] http:/http://www.wintersoldier.com/staticpages/index.php?page=InfoDigestGuide

[908] *Wikipedia.*

[909] http://foia.fbi.gov/foiaindex/adc.htm

The American Deserters Committee- Sweden chapter also decided to move beyond desertion to resistance.[911]

Malingering in Montreal. None marched south to join Hayden's revolution. Few deserters protested the Vietnam War. Most simply avoided military service. Few desertions ever occurred from battle forces inside Vietnam. Those temporarily Absent Without Leave, AWOLs, arriving hours to days late for duty were not deserters. When AWOLs were counted they inflated numbers of "deserters."

***

Foreign Connections to Peace Movement?

V.P. Agnew Wants to Know Worldwide Connections. On May 14th, Kent Crane, an aide to Vice President Spiro Agnew called J. Edgar Hoover want information on violence prone groups. Agnew thought, said Crane, with "student demonstrations all over the world...it is time somebody looked at the possibility of connections."[912]

As we have seen the connections of the antiwar movement, New Mobe, CALC, IPS, AFSC, with the Vietnamese in April and May 1970 in Stockholm, Vancouver, Toronto, Helsinki, Hanoi and Paris were multiple.

Huston Plan: "Potential...Foreign-Directed Intelligence." After the May 1970 bloodshed at Kent State, weatherman bombings, mass rallies and campus takeovers, the Nixon administration considered stronger covert actions than previously. On June 5, 1970, Nixon ordered the heads of all of the intelligence agencies to the White House. He excoriated them for ineffectiveness in providing intelligence on the antiwar movement.

NSA Monitoring Overseas Communication of U.S. Citizens. The President signed an "Eyes Only" memo authorizing the National Security Agency, NSA, monitoring "the communications of U.S. citizens using international facilities."[913] Nixon was reaffirming ongoing NSA operations

---

[910] "Nixon Seeking War With China, Hayden Tells Meeting in Montreal," *Globe and Mail*, Toronto, Ontario, June 1, 1970.

[911] "American Exiles in Sweden-a short political history," N.D. [early 1973] at FBI, FOIA, A, American Deserters Committee, File: 105-185434.

[912] Hoover to Tolson, memo, 10:27 AM, May 11, 1970 at FBI FOIA website under Tolson.

[913] James Bamford, "Statement, NSA Lawsuit Client (of ACLU)," at aclu.orgsafefree/nsaspying/2347res20060116.html

against foreign terminals, MINARET, picking up Americans contacts with foreign governments and agents.

NSA targeted only a few Americans contacting foreign entities. NSA intercepted 168 persons. NSA created a "Watch List" of about some 300 individuals worthy of continued monitoring, hardly, a drift net endangering civil rights of speech, assembly and association. Except for a few leaders, protesters were of no interest whatsoever.

Interagency Intelligence Report: Foreign Opportunities among Dissidents. An interagency intelligence report in June 1970 said, "Leaders of student (antiwar) protest groups" who traveled abroad were "considered to have potential for recruitment and participation in foreign-directed intelligence activity." CIA said, "...Soviet and bloc intelligence services are committed at the political level to exploit all domestic dissidents wherever possible."

The interagency report said,
The dissidence and violence in the United States today present adversary intelligence services with opportunities unparalleled for forty years.'[914]

FBI director Hoover headed a committee to develop a plan for expanded surveillance on anti-war groups.

President, FBI, Army: Reject Expanded Intelligence Ops.

Hoover[915], the Army,[916] and Nixon all rejected[917] the infamous Huston Plan for expanded intelligence activities, directed entirely against the Black Panthers, White Hate Groups, and the Weather Underground. All three targets publicly advocated assassinations and bombings. On September 22, 1970

---

[914] Special Report, Interagency Committee on Intelligence (Ad Hoc), June 1970; substantial portions of this report appear in Hearings, Vol. 2, 141-188.cited in "Church Committee Report."

[915] Hoover file 0825 Folder 90. March 25-April 12, 1971, "Intelligence Coverage, Domestic and Foreign" containing memo on FBI technical (wiretap)and microphone coverage of black extremist and New Left individuals and groups as background information for meeting with CIA's Richard Helms, NSA's Admiral Noel A. Gaylor and AG John N. Mitchell. Also Hoover memo reporting Helm's desire to broaden operations and Hoover's objections due to hazards of public disclosure.

[916] Robert O'Harrow interview of Chris Pyle, "No Place to Hide," PBS, http://americanradioworks.publicradio. org/features/ noplaceto hide/pyle.html; John P. Finnegan, *Military Intelligence*, compiled by Romana Danysh, Army lineage series, Center of Military History, United States Army, Washington, D. C., 1998 Chap.9: Vietnam and Beyond, 163.
http://www.history.army.mil/books/Lineage/mi/ch9.htm

[917] Court TV, Crime Library, "J Edgar Hoover," "Nixon."

Secretary of State William Rogers sent a "talking paper" to H.R. Haldeman indicating his approval of a Hoover plan to quietly station FBI agents as legal attaches to U.S. embassies. Rogers did not tell the CIA about these FBI assignment. The President did "not have confidence" in the CIA[918]

Though formally rejected, the Huston Plan was extended far beyond even its original intent. According to General Bruce Palmer, military intelligence covered many radicals[919] Christopher Pyle, the original whistle blower and expert claims the Army [at least] stopped all surveillance in the summer of 1970.[920] The Army collected mounds of materials of questionable value without competent analysis.

Leaks Source of Intelligence. The continuing publication and broadcast of military and diplomatic secrets was also an open source of intelligence for foreign adversaries, leaks to the press. Multiple leaks had motivated Congressman Richard Ichord, Chairman of the House Internal Security Committee, to ask the CIA what was being done about secrets published about Cambodian's dealings with the Communists.

Some desperate anti-leak measures were being taken.

In late November 1970, H. R. Haldeman called J. Edgar Hoover on behalf of President Nixon. Haldeman wanted a "rundown on the homosexuals known and suspected in the Washington press corps." Hoover writes, "I told Mr. Haldeman I would get after that right away...not later than Friday."[921] Hoover's response was destroyed. Haldeman and Erlichman deny ever having received such materials.[922] Hoover kept such information on homosexuals in his private files[923] including reporters spreading false rumors about each other.[924]

---

[918] Secretary Rogers Talking Paper to HR Haldeman, September 22, 1970.
[919] General Bruce Palmer, Jr., *The 25-Year War; America's Military Role in Vietnam*, New York: Simon Schuster, 1985.
[920] Robert O'Harrow interview of Chris Pyle, "No Place to Hide," PBS, http://americanradioworks.publicradio.org/ features/noplaceto hide/pyle.html
[921] Hoover to Tolson, memo, 4:34 PM November 25, 1970. Hoover had also gathered information on Martin Luther King's sex life as a consequence of national security concerns involving of some of King's communist advisors.
[922] LOU CHIBBARO JR., "White House disavows 'smear' of gay reporter: Gay Drudge Report says Bush staff leak called attention to ABC journalist, *Washington Blade, Friday, July 25, 2003.
[923] Hoover files on Joseph Alsop containing "copies of memoranda between Hoover and the CIA recording Hoover's conversations with ...Attorneys General Herbert Brownell, Jr....and William Rogers regarding Alsop's admission to the CIA that he was a homosexual and had been compromised in Moscow by Soviet police. 0028 Folder 26. http://www.lexisnexis.com/documents/academic/upa_cis/10756_FBIFileHooverOffCo

Soviet Influence Operations in the U.S. Congress, 1964-1970. By the end of 1969, the FBI reported Soviet Embassy contacts with 53 Senators, 10 Representatives, and 239 staff employees.[925] "The (FBI) review...disclosed more frequent contacts with staff employees of ...Senate Foreign Relations Committee, House Foreign Affairs Committee and Senate and House Armed Services committees."[926]

Further, by July 1970 the FBI had moved from believing most of the Soviet contacts were mostly for legitimate diplomatic purposes to now believing the Soviets wanted to influence elected officials upon Vietnam and other issues. "...Soviets apparently making more contacts with...[those]...who have depicted themselves as 'doves'...such as Senators Fulbright, McCarthy, McGovern and Muskie, than with other U. S. Legislators. Majority of Soviet personnel maintaining contacts on Capitol Hill are either known or suspected intelligence personnel...".

"[M]ost...contacts appear to conform with overt diplomatic duties... .[Yet]..communication points out we cannot completely disregard possibility of Soviet intelligence recruitment efforts (on) Capitol Hill. The FBI cites "Soviet recruitment of former employee of Representative Alvin E. O'Konski (R-Wisc.), whose activities we directed with Congressman's concurrence... . [Also]...effort by female Cultural Attaché to establish social relations with Congressman Kenneth J. Gray are included without identifying any individual involved by name.[927]

---

nfFile.pdf

[924] Hoover file on Richard Nixon 0622 Folder 119. June 13-July 3, 1969 contained allegations received from Jack Anderson that unidentified persons were homosexuals and their denials.

[925] W. A. Branigan to C.D. Brennan, Subject: Contacts...Russia, July 28, 1970 in Federal Bureau of Investigation (FBI) File, 105-HQ-229897, *Contacts between representatives of the Soviet Union and members or staff personnel of the United States Congress, 1964 – 1972*, Released 16-February-2011, Posted 10-June-2013, Section IV, 967.

[926]W. A. Branigan to C.D. Brennan, "Subject: Contacts...Russia," July 28, 1970 in Federal Bureau of Investigation (FBI) File, 105-HQ-229897, *Contacts between representatives of the Soviet Union and members or staff personnel of the United States Congress, 1964 – 1972*, Released 16-February-2011, Posted 10-June-2013, 967, 970.

[927] W. A. Branigan to C.D. Brennan, "Subject: Contacts...Russia," July 28, 1970 in in Federal Bureau of Investigation (FBI) File, 105-HQ-229897, *Contacts between representatives of the Soviet Union and members or staff personnel of the United States Congress, 1964 – 1972*, Released 16-February-2011, Posted 10-June-2013, Section IV 967.

The FBI was running eight Capitol staffers as its own counterintelligence operation against the Soviets.

Meanwhile, hundreds of American citizens were meeting the Vietnamese across the globe.

Hanoi had its own agent in the bowels of the Congress- Tom Harkin.

***

Congress "Finds" the "Tiger Cages" July 2, 1970

In early 1970, a former CPUSA member, Rep. Augustus Hawkins (D-CA) sought to "find a factual basis for an emotional response to end the war in Vietnam."[928]

Tom Harkin. Meanwhile a Congressional aide, Tom Harkin, thought he had such a story, shopped it around, and finally made a $10,000 deal to sell photos about his unproven theory,[929] a still fact-less story.[930] Facts never got in the way of a good story. Harkin had one.

Don Luce. On July 2, 1970 moments before getting on the plane to Con Son at 7:00 am, Tom Harkin announced a person was joining the Congressional party at the last minute.[931] The mystery man was Don Luce, a freelance writer, formerly of International Voluntary Services, IVS, having press credentials as an employee of the Soviet-influenced World Council of Churches, WCC. Staff aides Harkin and Ken Lester met Don Luce and student Cao Nguyen Loi, 26, days before. Loi described horrendous prison mistreatment at Con Son.[932]

Luce's bad reputation explained his stealth arrival. Col. Nguyen Phu Sanh, Director of the South Vietnamese prison

---

[928] D.E, Bordenkircher, S.A. Bordenkircher, *Tiger Cage: Untold Story,* Abby Publishing, *1998, 9.*

[929] David Marsh of *Newsweek* to Frank Walton at lunch on June 20, 1972 in Walton memo, June 20, 1972, "Dave Marsh of Newsweek said to me he knew of Harkin's plan to set up Con Son..." cited in D.E, Bordenkircher, S.A. Bordenkircher, *Tiger Cage: Untold Story,* Abby Publishing, *1998,189*

[930] Transcript tape-recorded visit 7/2/70 on CONDEL to Con Son, U.S. House of Representatives, July 7, 1970; *Congressional Record*—volume 116, Part 19, July 21- July 29, 1970 pages 2551355-26488, "Congressman Crane Reports on Con Son," *Congressional Record*-house, July 22, 1970, "Question of Personal Privilege," Hawkins v. Crane regarding Con Son island; cited in D.E, Bordenkircher, S.A. Bordenkircher, *Tiger Cage: Untold Story,* Abby Publishing, *1998, 9, 132.*

[931] Berkeley Fact Sheet, July 4, 1970, 'Chronological Sequence of Events-CONDEL visit to Con Son on 7/2/70. Sent to Colby; Berkeley Fact Sheet to W. Colby, "Con Son National... Center, July 7, 1970; "Transcript of Taped Interview of Don Luce," Shirley Bordenkircher, December 11, 1992 (accompanied by Jerry Snider); cited in D.E, Bordenkircher, S.A. Bordenkircher, *Tiger Cage: Untold Story,* Abby Publishing, *1998*

[932] Thomas R. Harkin, "Vietnam Whitewash: The Congressional Jury the Convicted Itself," *The Progressive,* Vol. 34, No. 10, October 1970, 17-18.

system had considered Don Luce "Persona-Non-Grata…a Communist sympathizer… probably a Communist himself."[933]

The rest of the party included former Communist, Rep. Augustus Hawkins, Rep. William R. Anderson of Tennessee and Tom Harkin, a Congressional aide to Rep. Neal Smith.

The Prisoners of Con Son Island. Harkin-Luce inspired group was an official fact-finding mission for the House Select Committee on United States Involvement in Southeast Asia. The delegation was determined to see the bad prison conditions at Con Son Island where Saigon housed 9,500 prisoners, an island 50 miles off South Vietnam.

In fact, most of the well-behaved 9,500 prisoners no supervision—one guard per 100 prisoners. Some 1,500 worked vegetable gardens, 1,100 vocational training and crafts. As trustees 2,000 had small houses.[934] Many sun bathed in this island paradise of beaches.

Months before in January, the International Red Cross, IRC, gave Con Son a generally favorable report with identified deficiencies needing corrections. Between 1965 and 1973, the Red Cross made 475 inspections of Saigon POW camps and zero inspections of Hanoi's.[935]

"Tiger Cages" at Con Son 4. Using the maps of student Nguyen Cao Nguyen Loi,[936] the delegation focused like a laser on Con Son 4, which prisoners had been calling the "Tiger Cages" since French colonial days. Other's were "Cow Cages" and "Pig Barn" etc. Though he had never been there, Don Luce told a FOR delegation in May-June 1969 there was brutality and torture at the "Tiger Cages."

The "Tiger Cage" facility, Con Son 4, was a disciplinary camp reserved for a hard-core few, some four percent, 400 prisoners out of the nearly 10,000 on the island. The facility was what would be "the hole" in an American prison. "Tigers," tough prisoners, had been housed there for decades.

Under the Saigon government, most of the other 9,000 prisoners housed in Con Son's cells had been charged or

---

[933] D.E, Bordenkircher, S.A. Bordenkircher, *Tiger Cage: Untold Story,* Abby Publishing, *1998, 82.*

[934] D.E, Bordenkircher, S.A. Bordenkircher, *Tiger Cage: Untold Story,* Abby Publishing, *1998, 199.*

[935] Herschensohn, An American Amnesia, 103.

[936] Tom Harkin, *Congressional Record*, May 23, 2007, S6560; "Senator returns to South Vietnam's 'tiger cages," Knight-Ridder, July 5, 1995.

convicted of sedition, espionage or treason. Communists who committed criminal acts, were not housed in the "Tiger Cages."

Most of the 400 in Con Son 4 were not political prisoners as alleged, but simply those troublemakers requiring special attention in all prisons everywhere. The prisoners of Con Son 4 were segregated, separated from the general prison population at Con Son. They were not separated because of either their politics, Communism, or their crimes. They were disruptive. Con Son 4, the "tiger cages" were for the incorrigibles setting fires, attempting murder, organizing riots, and violating rules, e.g. raucously refusing to salute the flag of South Vietnam.

Women Rioters: Naked and Beaten? Some 312 of those imprisoned were from a 400 block of women of recent participants in Viet Cong organized riots at prisons in Thu Duc and Chi Hoa. A night police raid at the Chi Hoa prison found the women armed with homemade gas masks, shanks and shivs. It took an hour to subdue the women with tear gas and fly them to Con Son.

Don Luce wrote, "The women were stripped naked, transported naked, and loaded on the planes naked." Don Bordenkircher said, "I was witness to every move [of the women]..." It hadn't happened, but Don Luce believed the Viet Cong women and no one else.[937] Col. Nguyen Phu Sanh claimed Don Luce's version of the truth always favored the Communists. Similarly, Arlene Eisen Bergman wrote, "The women (at Chi Hoa) had to be beaten unconscious before the guards were able to transfer them to Con Son."[938] Naked, beaten great story.

Sizes of the Cages. The so called "tiger cages," were ground floor level, concrete cells, roughly 10 feet long, 5 feet wide and 10 feet high. (Other larger holding cells housing three to five prisoners each were 24 feet by 30 feet with 14-foot ceilings). The concrete cells were not the cramped spaces, underground concrete "airless" pits later described.[939] These

[937] Luce to Shirley Bordenkircher; McPhee to Berkeley, "Transfer of Female Prisoners to Con Son, December 28, 1969; Berkeley to Colby, "Transfer of Female Prisoners to Con Son," November 28, 1969 cited in D.E, Bordenkircher, S.A. Bordenkircher, *Tiger Cage: Untold Story,* Abby Publishing, *1998, 107-113.*
[938] Arlene Eisen Bergman, *Women...* 110 cites Jean Pierre Debris and Andre Menras [Ho Cuong Quiet and Ho Tat Thang], *We Accuse: Back from Saigon's prisons, Santa Minicab/Washington,* Indochina Mobile Education Project/IPC, 1973; IPC, "Women Under Torture, 7-8.

ground floor cells had bars and catwalks on the roofs of the cells. The windowless cells were open to sunlight and ventilation through the iron bars above. There was a second story above the cell bars with large windows and a steep roof.

Tom Harkin's Phony Photos of "Tiger Cages." Congressional aide Tom Harkin snapped photos in a 30-minute walk through the two-story facility.

Two dishonest methods made the cells look like crowded airless pits. One, using a 135-millimeter camera with a telephoto lens,[940] looking down through the bars at the top from the second story. The telephoto lens compressed the actual distance, while a wide-angle lens would have expanded the actual distance. Two, cropping the occupants of two cells into one photo.[941] *Life* published the phony compressed photography.

Phonier still were the mock 5 x 9 bamboo cages Don Luce used in a "tiger cage" road show, the Indochina Peace Campaign's anti-war demonstrations, and in testimony before Congress.

Phony Claims. In their walk-through Don Luce interviewed and translated the stories of Viet Cong prisoners making claims of being doused with lime and urine, beaten and shackled, denied food and water; fed rice with sand, live lizards and beetles, and suffered paralysis from cramped quarters.[942]

Tom Harkin said, "They were never let out, the food was minimal and they are given little water." Worse "Many are forced to drink their own urine. Most…could not stand up, their legs having been paralyzed by beatings and by being shackled to a bar. …" Moreover, "there were buckets of lime dust …above the cages… [to] throw down on the prisoners when they beg for food and water."[943]

Harkin: "Looks Like We Put It Over." On the way back to the airport in a jeep Harkin was overheard saying to

[939] Patsy Truxaw, "House Committee Staffer Sees 'Tiger Cages' at Con Son, Quits When Committee Produces Whitewash Report," *Liberation News Service*, July 22, 1970, 5.

[940] Viet-myth.net/Session08.htm

[941] Madsen Pirie, "The Tiger Cages Revisited," *National Review*, September 27, 1974; D.E., Bordenkircher, S.A. Bordenkircher, *Tiger Cage: Untold Story,* Abby Publishing, *1998, 12*

[942] "The Cages of Con Son island," *Time,* Jul. 20, 1970;

[943] Patsy Truxaw, "House Committee Staffer Sees 'Tiger Cages' at Con Son, Quits When Committee Produces Whitewash Report," *Liberation News Service*, July 22, 1970, 5.

Luce, "Looks like we put it over. ...Now we can write the book. ...I'm a paid investigator."[944]

No Press tour. Afterwards, American and Vietnamese officials wanted to conduct a press tour to reveal the truth Harkin, Luce and Hawkins had distorted. William Colby said he thought the story would go away. Some thought Colby a coward, either a wimp or protecting Don Luce, perhaps a CIA asset with access to the Communists.

Rep. Crane Tours Con Son. On July 20, Rep. Phil Crane (R-Indiana), accompanied by two military photographers, reported:

> 1...I saw no evidence of open sores, eye disease, or malnutrition...
>
> 2. ...Out of hundreds of prisoners only one experienced difficulty in standing.
>
> 3. All prisoners appeared healthy, well fed.
>
> 4. ...The cells...were well ventilated, well lighted, and relatively cool.
>
> 5. I found the cells cleaner than the average Vietnamese home.
>
> 6. Not one prisoner showed any evidence of paralysis or any adverse effect from being shackled (at night).
>
> 7.... Not one prisoner showed any evidence of ...nor did they complain of beating.
>
> 8... Not one prisoner complained of lack of medical care.

Cells An Improvement Over Native Abodes. Indeed, for many Vietnamese, including the unarmed prison guards who lived in thatched huts with dirt floors or on stilts above pigs and chickens, the cells were cleaner quarters than most hamlet Vietnamese and the prison staff lived in. Before the recent shipment of Viet Cong women, requiring segregated space, the prison staff had actually occupied the Tiger cages, a housing upgrade they lost to incorrigible female Viet Cong.

As if validating a threat Madame Binh had once made, Rep. Crane said Rep. Augustus Hawkins had "inadvertently

---

[944] Berkeley Fact Sheet to W. Colby, "Con Son National... Center, July 7, 1970 cited in D.E, Bordenkircher, S.A. Bordenkircher, *Tiger Cage: Untold Story,* Abby Publishing, *1998, 125.*

jeopardized the safety of the American soldiers being held prisoners of war…"

At a Crane news conference the press was hostile. "Either Hawkins was lying or you got a snow job." Rep. Crane's conference got minimal coverage. The media was already committed to the stories and the photos, they had rushed to publish and broadcast. On July 29, 1970, Rep. Phil Crane spoke for 45 minutes on the floor of the House refuting all of his critics. The media gave nary a mention, but the complete text of Crane's refutation is in Appendix D of Don and Shirley Bordenkircher's book, *Tiger Cage: Untold Story*.

Harkin Profits. Rep. Neal Smith of Iowa, Harkin's boss, did not want to publish the photos,[945] but Harkin (who had already made a $10,000 deal), stole away with the photos and took them, the paid property of the U.S. government, to *Life Magazine* for publication July 17. 1970.

Media Spreads Story. Luce's UPI story ran nationwide. Luce described the tiger cages as "small stone compartments." Tom Harkin gave detailed interviews to the *Progressive* and the *Daily World*[946] based on his 30-minute tour of Con Son. A *Washington Post* story described prisoners as "chained and beaten," and alternatively kept "locked up in windowless cages and disciplined with a dusting of choking lime" and residing in concrete cages… 6-7 feet tall, and floor space …5x9." Not one of the male prisoners was able to stand. AFSC, FOR, Oriana Fallaci and others wrote their own descriptions of cramped physical conditions.

Other Investigations. Robert F. Turner was himself photographed proving the true measurements of the cells were 10 feet high, 10 feet long and 5 feet wide.[947] Later medical studies proved the prisoners were in good health and none had neurological evidence of paralysis.[948] January 5-6, 1971 U.S. Army doctors examined 116 prisoners and found "no objective evidence of organic neurological disease." They attributed claims of paralysis to "malingering or hysteria" In a series of

[945] Harkin in *Progressive* magazine in October 1970 cited in James M. Perry, "Candidate Harkin Stretches the Truth," *Wall Street Journal*, Dec. 26, 1991.

[946] Thomas R. Harkin, "Vietnam Whitewash: The Congressional Jury the Convicted Itself," *The Progressive*, Vol. 34, No. 10, October 1970; Lowell Ponte, "The Bark of Tom Harkin" FrontPageMagazine.com, Sept. 16, 2004.

[947] Viet-myths.net/Session08t.htm.

[948] D.E, Bordenkircher, S.A. Bordenkircher, *Tiger Cage: Untold Story*, Abby Publishing, 1998, 176-179.

weekly and monthly follow-up reports through January 1973, found the same.[949]

Astronaut Frank Borman toured the "tiger cages" as they were being torn down. They appeared adequate. The Communists countered saying the prisoners had now been moved to caves, pits, dungeons and tunnels. A search was made and no hidden caves or prisoners were found.[950]

Myth of Tiger Cages Lives On Forever. The false stories had been told. The myth was fixed in time.

Tom Wells, *The War Within*, a magnum opus history of the antiwar movement describes a "tiger cage" as a "steamy, dark, filthy stone compartment measuring 5' by 9'" and "stone pits." Weatherman Cathy Wilkerson described, "thousands dead ...or rotted in three-foot-high below ground cages with grating on top..."[951]

Mothers of Political Prisoners. On August 30, 1970 an official English-language publication of the National Front for Liberation, the Viet Cong, published a Don Luce letter supporting a group claiming to be mothers of political prisoners, the Committee of Women Action for the Right to Live. The notorious Mrs. Ngo Ba Thanh, a "third Force" Viet Cong agent and serial greeter of antiwar Americans led the mothers.

In a letter to Vice President Spiro Agnew, who was visiting Saigon, the twenty-one unnamed women described beatings, torture, no food, no medicine as punishment of their children because they were "struggling for the cause of peace."[952] Military tribunals suggested the mothers' children just may have been combatants in war rather than peacemakers. In May 1971, after Don Luce reported the U.S. was building more "tiger cages," the Saigon government finally expelled Don Luce. In July, Hanoi's own *Vietnam Youth* published an article featuring Don Luce, "The US-PUPPETS' BARBAROUS PENITENTIARY Regime." Luce said, the US was building

[949] Michael G. McCann, CORDS, to DV Brown, M.D./aos 927-4602,"Paralyzed' Prisoners—Con Son National Correctional Center," DEPCORUSMACV FOR CORDS, 26 January, 1973.
[950] News clips cited in D.E, Bordenkircher, S.A. Bordenkircher, *Tiger Cage: Untold Story,* Abby Publishing, *1998, 177-178.*
[951] Cathy Wilkerson, *Flying Close to the Sun*, New York: Seven Stories Press, 2007, 309.
[952] Don Luce, "A Letter From Don Luce, Saigon, August 30, 1970," *South Viet Nam In Struggle*, No 77, October 20, 1970, 1.

new, smaller cell. For up to 400,000 political prisoners,[953] at least ten times any measure.

Tiger Cage Propaganda Tour, 1972-75. During 1972-3, Don Luce's Mobile Education Project[954] toured the U.S. with mock, cramped bamboo "tiger cages" and NLF flags. Yet in March 1973, Hanoi's own *Vietnam* magazine published a story about torture in Tiger Cages. The article did not describe the cells in any of the invidious detail found in Hanoi's political campaign in the USA.[955] The Luce tour went on covering high visibility locations in smaller cities for one to three days seeking local news coverage and speaking engagements.[956]

Tiger Cages at Capitol. In June 1974, at the entrance of the U.S. Capitol protesters began a seven-week "Tiger Cage Vigil and Fast." It displayed mock prisoners shackled in cramped bamboo, tiger cages, [VC cells for American POWs]. The Indochina Peace Campaign published "Reports and Comments from participants" and requested contributions be made to the tax exempt American Friends Service Committee of Providence, Rhode Island.[957]

September 29-October 6, 1974 "tiger cages" took stage in an "International Week of Concern"[958] providing the communists moral support for their impending invasion of prisoner abusing Saigon.

Communist Cages Worse. After April 1975, the Communists conquerors would house their prisoners not in well-ventilated and roomy concrete cells with open, well-ventilated roofs, like those at Con Son, but often in large Connex[959] metal boxes, leftover American cargo containers, far worse than the real "tiger cages." Doan Van Toai, former Viet Cong agent, described cells five by eight meters holding between sixty and one hundred prisoners.[960]

---

[953] In possession of author.

[954] Indochina Mobile Education Project, 1973, Catholic Peace Fellowship Records, University of Notre Dame Archives, CCPF 3/24 Folder.

[955] Ho Thanh Dam, "I've just Escaped from a 'Tiger Cage," *Vietnam*, March 8, 1973, 1, 15-16.

[956]Indochina Education Council, brochure, N.D.

[957] Testimonials were signed by, Carol Bragg, Sharon Breakstone, Mary Davis, Mike DeGregory, Doug Plante, Merlin Rainwater, , H. Marie Slaton, Lynda Smith-Starks, Diane Spaugh, Lesley Turner, Ron Young.

[958] Tom Wells, *War Within*, 456-7, 568, 574.

[959] Joan Baez, "Open Letter to the Socialist Republic of Vietnam," *Washington Post*, May 30, 1979, A17.

Senator Tom Harkin, visiting Vietnam in July 1995, claimed the communist regime was "not allowing freedoms it should, but it [is] better than the ousted South Vietnamese regime."[961] Don Luce later compared the humiliation of prisoners in Abu Ghraib, Iraq to the Tiger Cages story of 1970. A good story has eternal life.

Bordenkircher: "most successful operations...by Hanoi's Department of Psychological Warfare." Don Bordenkircher, helping reform South Vietnamese prisons and having intimate knowledge of Con Son, wrote *Tiger Cage: An Untold Story.* "The Tiger Cage story put out in 1970 stands as one of the most successful operations ever undertaken by Hanoi's Department of Psychological Warfare."[962]

After the Tiger Cage affair: South Vietnam expelled Don Luce; Tom Harkin, claiming falsely, to having been a combat fighter pilot in Vietnam, was elected to Congress (1974) and the US Senate (1984). Tom Harkin was a combat fighter, a combatant, only in the Communist sense, a comrade-in-arms for Hanoi's propaganda mill. Harkin had other comrades back home.

Building Opposition in Congress. The "Tiger Cages" served to delegitimize the war and build opposition in Congress.

***

Set the Date for U.S. Withdrawal

Happy About Vietnam On July 9, the Nixon White House hoisted cocktails to celebrate the defeat of the Senate passed Cooper-Church by 84 votes in the House. The Nixon's approval rating was down to 53-55% according to two polls.[963] The truth is the President ranked lower on all major public concerns, except for the issue of South East Asia.

Set the Date. On July 15, 1970, Viet Cong radio praised 100 Senators and House Members—and Sen. McGovern by name, for their three-week antiwar conference calling for a "definite withdrawal schedule," on a "set date."[964]

---

[960] Doan Van Toai, "No war, No Peace," in Santoli, *To Bear...,*272.

[961]"Senator returns to South Vietnam's 'tiger cages," Knight-Ridder, July 5, 1995.

[962] Bordenkircher is quoting Philip C. Clarke, American Legion Magazine, February 1979, D.E. Bordenkircher, S.A. Bordenkircher, *Tiger Cage: Untold Story,* Abby Publishing, *1998, 11, 197.*

[963] H.R. Haldeman, *The Haldeman Diaries: Inside the Nixon White House,* New York: Berkley Books, 1994, 216.

[964] "Liberation Press Agency Cites Varied Antiwar Sentiment in America," Liberation

About one in five members of Congress, had taken up what was to become Hanoi's political mantra, "set the date."

A policy Baraka Obama used in Iraq, a strategic disadvantage giving rise to ISSIL terrorist state.

In 1970, the antiwar movement still had a lot of work to do and turned to a movie star and pinup girl for help.

***

Jane Fonda's tour of Military Bases

Hanoi promoted *Binh Van,* political actions in the U.S. military, in meetings with antiwar leaders, such as Robert Greenblatt in 1969. The left in 1970 used GI Coffee Houses as outposts for political agitation near U.S. military bases. Jane Fonda lent her celebrity to these efforts decided in foreign capitals in 1969. Fonda made a whirlwind two-month tour of military bases and colleges, flitting from place to place, feeding the media "good copy."

Fort Carson. At Fort Carson in Colorado Springs, Fonda said blacks in the post's stockade, jail, were there for "giving the peace sign and saying that they are sick of the war." At the Home Front coffee house outside Fort Carson, Jane said the Vietnamese were fighting "for the same reason the French Underground fought the Nazis." The Viet Cong filled mass graves, not Saigon. Fonda said, "The majority of the rural population of Vietnam are in concentration camps and we put them there." Huh! (millions) "They are tortured and killed."

The Military Police who hauled her off for release outside the gates of the base.[965]

Fort Hood. Back on the road, she appeared at Oleo Strut Coffee House Group at Fort Hood, Killeen, Texas. Fonda declared unlike Bob Hope, she did not "glamorize war or urge young men to fight." Actually, she urged U.S. troops to malinger, desert and mutiny.

Universities, Texas, Maryland. Adding several college stops, at the University of Texas, "No order goes unchallenged ... We should be proud of our new breed of soldier. It's not organized, but its mutiny and they have every right,"[966] said Fonda.

Press Agency (Clandestine) in English to East Europe and Far East 1545 GMT 15 July 70,1 cited in Rothrock *Divided...* 291n73.

[965] Andersen, 217-218.

[966] Poole, Institutional Report, No. 13, "Campaign for Economic Democracy ..., " Heritage Foundation, 1980, 12.

At the University of Maryland, Jane proclaimed, like John Kerry, "It's normal to throw prisoners out of helicopters ... [to] ... make them talk." A claim repeatedly made, much investigated and never found, except as a staged media stunt reported as news.[967] Christopher Boyce, an employee of TRW, believing these claims and induced by money, stole spy satellite secrets for the Soviet Union.[968]

Fort Meade. Expelled from Fort Meade, Maryland, Fonda screamed out to her press groupies below "We are being searched ... We're going to get them on a charge of brutality...."

Jane Fonda: Revolutionary

In Jane's two-month tour, she had visited about 10 bases. In New York, she said, "When I left the West Coast I was a liberal. When I landed in New York I was a revolutionary." One politically naive journalist quipped, "She may well be the only revolutionary with her own PR man."[969] Steve Jaffe was her publicist.

A Fonda interview with the French Communist newspaper, *L'Humanite',* revealed her as the very image of the spoiled rich. A darkly sun glassed Jane Fonda spoke "of "people ... dying of hunger in a country ... so rich." She told the Cuban Communist Party's newspaper *Granma,* "Revolution is a natural ...part of life; ...an act of love."[970] She told the Cuban Communist newspaper *Juventude Rebelde*, (also in July 18, 1970, *People's World*), "To make revolution in the United States... requires patience and discipline..." Admitting she benefited "from a capitalist society, I find that system which exploits other people...should not exist. ... The system is corrupt...and is the problem ... while nothing is done against the imperialist system; all the rest will be artificial."[971]

"She thinks like a calliope programmed at the Lenin Institute,"[972] said Bill Buckley. In aiding a prison gang, the Soledad brothers whose leader George Jackson was an admitted

---

[967] Guenther Lewy, "Vietnam: New Light Upon the Question of American Guilt," *Commentary*, February 1978. See also, Paul Johnson, *Modern Times: From the Twenties to the Nineties,* New York: Harper Collins, 1991, 636, 878.

[968] Denise Noe, "Dirty Twickses," Tru Crime Library, http://www.trutv.com/library/crime/terrorists_spies/spies/boyce_lee/2.html

3937 Kiernan, 2, 224; Andersen 219-221; Frock, 53.

[970] Cited in Poole, Heritage Foundation report, report # 13, 13.

[972] William F. Buckley, "And Now Jane Fonda, Miss Secretary of State," August 1, 1972.

drug dealer and accused murderer, Jane said, "the system ... is ... racist, oppressive, totalitarian, and monstrous. ... This is not Los Angeles in 1970, it is Berlin in 1936, and we are all Jews ... I think, that we are niggers to the system."[973] Jane had had a good rehearsal for many things to come.

Fonda's Critics. Roger Vadim, her spouse of record, said, "I feel as if I were baby-sitting Lenin."[974] Riding in her limousine with Richard Grenier, a movie critic, Jane kept talking "peace" and... "Pick up a gun".[975] She oozed with enthusiasm over China's Cultural Revolution—[Red Guards, anarchy, death]. In New York, Jane asked her vet groupies and Angela Davis to educate her father, Henry Fonda. Father Fonda "thought, 'what foreign agent is manipulating my daughter?" [Editor: Answer. Ho Nam]. After FBI agents talked to Henry Fonda, he told his wayward daughter, "Jane, if I ever discover...that you're a Communist...I, your father, will be the first to turn you in."[976]

Filming *Klute,* the story of a New York call girl, Fonda said the story was "a significant social statement. ... These women are a product of a society in which the emphasis is on money. ..."[977] Jane was making $400,000 a film in 1970. *Klute* movie crews festooned their trailers with American flags.

***

July 1970--Sam Anson, Hanoi Prisoner in Cambodia. Secret Hanoi spy Pham Xuan An tutored and befriended[978] 24-year-old Robert Sam Anson, a *Time Magazine* reporter who arrived on scene in early 1970 as an experienced war protester who already believed the war was colonial, immoral, illegal and unwinnable.[979] For his outspoken opposition to the war, *Time* magazine exiled Anson from Saigon to Cambodia. In Cambodia Anson had friendly relations with East German Communists Eric Dieters and Otto Bernke interested in Anson's antiwar views.[980]

Out in the countryside the road-running Anson discovered and wrote stories of the inept and corrupt Lon Nol

---

[973] Andersen, 221-222.
[974] Andersen, 224 recites a news clip without attribution.
[975] See: Richard Grenier, "Jane Fonda & Other Political Thinkers," *Commentary*, June, 1979, 67. Also: Joseph Sobran, "Fonda Weeps", *Washington Post* (August 7, 1979).
[976] Andersen, 223.
[977] Andersen, 225.
[978] Robert Sam Anson, *War News*, New York: Simon and Schuster, 1989, 63-4.
[979] Robert Sam Anson, *War News*, New York: Simon and Schuster, 1989, 26, 40, 69
[980] Robert Sam Anson, *War News*, New York: Simon and Schuster, 1989, 111-113.

forces and Cambodian massacres of Vietnamese civilians at Prasaut and Takeo.[981] Anson rescued two-dozen Vietnamese from Cambodian military brutality. Front page stories of these atrocities of an American ally made "Takeo...the last time Vietnamese civilians were slaughtered in Cambodia."[982]

Who Saved Sam Anson? "One of us. A soldier of the revolution." The now adventurous Anson wandered into NVA regulars and was held as a prisoner where terrified he "whimpered" *Hoa-binh*, peace to his captors. A North Vietnamese officer, Hoa, gave Anson a sweater and cigarettes and talked with Anson about Jane Fonda, the Moratorium, Kent State and Norman Morrison. In time, Anson convinced the Communists he was one of them. Finally, they decided to release Anson, they owed him a blood debt for saving children at Takeo. Number One said, "You are one of us. A soldier of the revolution." Anson negotiated a spoken statement expressing gratitude for his treatment and his antiwar sentiments. Anson also edited his journal removing offending passages on NVA troops occupying Cambodia and the Vietnamese eating dog meat.[983]

At a press conference Anson said, "They weren't...my enemy. I believed in peace...and so they treated me like a friend. ...We really got to be brothers." Comments trumped Anson's script on Radio Hanoi.[984]

Once released Anson refused to debrief either the Cambodian government or the CIA about the number and disposition of NVA troops.

In August 1986, revisiting Vietnam, Anson met Pham Xuan An who informed Anson he had been a spy for Hanoi and told the NVA about Anson's rescue of Vietnamese children in Takeo.[985] Mnay believed, Pham Xuan An, "the spy who loved us," had saved Anson's life. Perhaps Anson had saved his own life as a "soldier of the revolution" reliably reporting the war was illegal, immoral and unwinnable.

Anson dedicated his book *War News* to Pham Xuan An, Hanoi's top secret agent in South Vietnam.

---

[981] Robert Sam Anson, *War News*, New York: Simon and Schuster, 1989, 120-1; story covered in *CBS Evening News* with Walter Cronkite and in *Time magazine*..
[982] Robert Sam Anson, *War News*, New York: Simon and Schuster, 1989, 135-143.
[983] Robert Sam Anson, *War News*, New York: Simon and Schuster, 1989, 257, 271-2; East of Hanoi in March 2008 the author saw bicycles whose cargo was young caged dogs.
[984] Robert Sam Anson, *War News*, New York: Simon and Schuster, 1989, 280-1, 283-5.
[985] Robert Sam Anson, *War News*, New York: Simon and Schuster, 1989. 312.

***

Mobilizing GIs

GI Office. July 1970. After concluding her road show, Jane Fonda joined KGB assisted JFK conspiracy theorist Mark Lane in opening a GI Office to protect GI rights, protest the war, and to provide lawyers for malingering, AWOL and deserting GI's. The GI Office urged antiwar businesses to hire deserters. Fonda said "a growing number of guys ... don't want to fight the war..."[986] Fonda was helping deserters, malingerers and the enemy just as the Vietnamese had instructed the SDS/Weather delegation to Cuba in July.

Cooperative GI. Cooperative G.I. might count on easier releases than uncooperative POWs.

After his capture on February 19, 1969 Jon Sweeney made broadcasts from Hanoi. He requested return to the US. Accompanied by North Vietnamese chaperones, the Red Cross flew Sweeney from Hanoi to Moscow where he gave a press conference. On August 17, 1970, SGT and former POW Jon Sweeney surrendered to the custody of the American Ambassador in Sweden.

In court-martial, the USMC was unable to prove Sweeney had aided the VC and NVA of his own free will. Sweeney testified, "Some [had] held a gun to his head." The court martial acquitted Sweeny.[987]

By September 9, 1971 (if not before) with no gun at his head John M. Sweeney, former cooperative POW, was a featured speaker of the pro-Viet Cong Pennsylvania VVAW at the Hanoi-friendly Friends Meeting House in Reading, Pennsylvania.[988]

The Hanoi comings and goings of anti-Americans continued.

***

Helsinki. Dave Dellinger, Bernardine Dohrn and others met some 50 Vietnamese communists in Helsinki, August 25-27 at a Soviet fronted event of the International Union of Students and World Federation of Democratic Youth,

---

[986] Lerman, 330;

[987] "The Case of Robert Garwood, PFC, USMC," Section II: In North Vietnam, 1970 – 1979 http://www.miafacts.org/grwd_2.htm

[988] FBI, fragment, "Anti-war March and Demonstration, Harrisburg, PA., September 9-14, 1971, Sponsored by Pennsylvania VVAW," n.d. [after] September 11, 1977, 5.

"World Meeting of Youth and Students for the Final Victory of the Vietnamese People." Bernardine Dohrn spoke:

> The movement in the U.S. must make clear which side we are on: the side of the Vietnamese people, for self-determination...Long Live The Victory of People's War. Vietnam Will Win.[989]

***

[989] Senate, Committee on the Judiciary, Subcommittee to Investigate the Administration of the Internal Security Act and Other Internal Security Laws, *The Weather Underground*, Committee Print, January 1975, 146-7.

Chapter 8. Comrades On Tour: Cleaver, Leary, Dohrn and Kerry
Eldridge Cleaver's Long Journey to Communist Capitols and His comrades.

Eldridge Cleaver praised the North Koreans for being the first to fight U.S. imperialism. Cleaver met a North Korean Ambassador at a Pan-African Festival who invited him to North Korea for a National Conference of Revolutionary Journalists. On September 11, 1969, he arrived in Pyongyang along with Byron Booth for the conference scheduled for September 18-23. Cleaver spoke to the conference and wrote two articles for *Pyongyang Times* and *The Black Panthers*. The North Koreans asked him to lead a larger group of progressives back to North Korea.[990]

Algeria. Kathleen Cleaver arrived in Soviet aligned Algeria in May 22, 1970. In Helsinki, Finland May 29-31, 1970 the Soviets had instructed the secretary of WPC to recruit black militants to the antiwar movement.[991] The Cubans, anxious to get rid an agitator among Cuban blacks, ticketed Eldridge Cleaver to Algeria to rejoin his wife.[992]

In Algeria Cleaver visited the diplomatic missions of North Vietnam, NLF, Cuba, China, and North Vietnam.[993]

Cleaver: Tour Guide to the Communist World. In late August and early September 1970, Black Panther Eldridge Cleaver led his 11-man U.S. Peoples Anti-imperialist entourage on a grand tour showing solidarity with the major Communist paradises on earth: USSR, North Korea, North Vietnam, Algeria, and China.[994]

Cleaver's group included Robert Scheer, Regina Blumenfeld, Randy Rappaport (Women's Liberation), Alexander Hing (Chinatown Red Guards), Janet Austin (*Ramparts*), Hideko Pat Sumi (Movement for a Democratic Military, Venceremos Brigade) Anne Froines (Panther Defense

[990] Frank J. Rafalko, *MH/CHAOS: The CIA's Campaign Against the Radical Left and the Black Panthers*, Annapolis: Naval Institute Press, 2011, 114-115.

[991] Frank J. Rafalko, *MH/CHAOS: The CIA's Campaign Against the Radical Left and the Black Panthers*, Annapolis: Naval Institute Press, 2011, 99.

[992] Frank J. Rafalko, *MH/CHAOS: The CIA's Campaign Against the Radical Left and the Black Panthers*, Annapolis: Naval Institute Press, 2011, 101.

[993] Frank J. Rafalko, *MH/CHAOS: The CIA's Campaign Against the Radical Left and the Black Panthers*, Annapolis: Naval Institute Press, 2011, 113.

[994] FBI, New York, LHM, Travel of US Delegation to North Korea and North Vietnam July-August, 1970, Led by Eldridge Cleaver, September 23, 1970

Committee), Janet Kranzberg (*Newsreel*), Elaine Brown (Black Panther), Judith Clavir (alias of %% nee Stew Albert, Berkley Red Family, International Liberation School.), and Andrew Truskier.

Cleaver on Radio Hanoi. On August 30, 1970, Radio Hanoi broadcast a Cleaver speech at a solidarity rally in Hanoi on August 22, 1970, "The struggle of black people...is a sure sign...the days of U.S. imperialism are numbered... [E]xternal (and internal) revolutionary forces...are going to crush U.S. imperialism."[995]

A Communist leaflet praised black riots in the USA "A million ...black men...armed with weapons, have risen up against...terrorism and cruel suppression.... The U.S. racial capitalist authorities sent tens of thousands policemen and soldier...tanks and helicopters...to suppress it...."[996]

Rev. Phil Lawson on Radio Hanoi. Methodist Rev. Phil Lawson of Kansas City (accompanied by Martha Westover and Anthony Avirgan[997]) representing the Fellowship for Reconciliation, FOR, stood at Cleaver's side at the Hanoi rally. The Rev. Lawson's said, "you must...say no [to]...criminal orders" and "you can disobey all racist officers.... The real war is being fought in the United States."[998] Rev. Lawson was asking U.S. servicemen to desert their posts in the midst of battle—a capital offense.

Robert Scheer on Radio Hanoi. Robert Scheer made his broadcast on Radio Hanoi on September 5, 1970.[999] Scheer, according to the August 8, 1970 issue of *The Black Panther,* signed a statement:

---

[995] Hanoi in English to American Servicemen in s. Vietnam 1300 GMT speeches by Eldridge Cleaver and Phil Lawson at 22 August Hanoi rally in solidarity with the struggle of black people in the U.S; Rothrock, *Divided...*, 221.

[996] SGM Herbert A. Friedman, "Race as a Military Propaganda Theme," 6 at psywar.org/race.php.

[997] FBI, Director to SACs of Kansas City, New York and Philadelphia, "Possible Travel to North Vietnam by Anthony Avirgan, Phil Lawson and Martha Westover— August Nineteen Seventy, Internal Security—Miscellaneous," Top Secret, NITEL August 18, 1970; FBI, Philadelphia 100-49298 fragment n.d. circa August 20, 1970; FBI, Kansas City, LHM, [redacted] August 11, 1970; "Phil Lawson Will Take Letters From Home to Prisoners of War on Forthcoming Trip to Hanoi," Kansas City CAL (illegible), Kansas City, August 8, 1970.

[998] Hanoi in English to American Servicemen in S. Vietnam 1300 GMT 20 Sep 1970. Talk by Phil Lawson to black GI's in S. Vietnam; Rothrock, *Divided...*, 222.

[999] Hanoi in English to American Servicemen in S. Vietnam 0830 GMT 5 Sep 70. Robert Scheer talks about his visit to both zones of Vietnam.

Since the peoples of the world have a common enemy, we must begin to think of revolution as an international struggle against U.S. imperialism. … Understanding the Korean people's struggle and communicating this to the American movement is a crucial step in developing this internationalist perspective."[1000]

Ellen Brown and Pat Sumi on Radio Hanoi. An interview of Ellen Brown, a Black Panther, was on Radio Hanoi on September 6th.[1001] Pat Sumi broadcasted over Radio Hanoi on September 9th.[1002]

Pat Sumi. On March 22, 1969, in Portsmouth Square, in San Francisco's Chinatown, Pat Sumi joined Chinese Americans, the Red Guard Party, wearing black berets revealing a "10-Point Program." Their 10 Point Program mimicked the Black Panthers program (breakfast and revolution), free breakfasts and the "removal of colonialist police from Chinatown."[1003] Bowing to the Black Panther icon, Eldridge Cleaver, Sumi had surely earned her airline tickets for Cleaver's Black Panther delegation to North Korea, North Vietnam, and China. Sumi helped form the Movement for a Democratic Military, MDM.

On Radio Hanoi, September 9, Pat Sumi spoke to U.S. troops in South Vietnam. "I am in Hanoi, …as part of the U.S. People's Anti-Imperialists Delegation…" Sumi described antiwar activities among GIs; the assault on Fort Dix in October 1969, the massive nationwide protests in October/November 1969, sentencing the Army to death at Fort Lewis, and closing 22 base celebrations[1004] on People's Armed Forces Day on May 17, 1970.

"So when you guys get back to the world, it will be a lot different." Sumi said, "Bring our GI brothers home right

---

[1000] August 8, 1970, The Black Panther cited in David Horowitz, FrontpageMagazine.com on May 6, 2003.
[1001] Hanoi in English to American Servicemen in S. Vietnam 1300 GMT 6 Sept 70. Interview with Ellen Brown.
[1002] Hanoi in English to American Servicemen in S. Vietnam 1300 GMT 9 Sept 70. Statement by Pat Sumi to black GIs in S. Vietnam.
[1003] Daryl J. Maeda, "Black Panthers, Red Guards, and Chinamen: Constructing Asian American Identity through Performing Blackness, 1969-1972," *American Quarterly*, Volume 57, Number 4, December 2005, pp. 1079-1103, at http://muse.jhu.edu/ login? uri=/ journals/american_quarterly/v057/57.4maeda.pdf
[1004] http://www.sirnosir.com/archives_and_resources/library/articles/gigline_08.html

now. We need all young people together to fight the pigs, not the Vietnamese people."[1005]

Ann Froines on Radio Hanoi. On September 10, 1970, Ann Froines, wife of John Froines, an acquitted member of the Chicago Seven, broadcast over Radio Hanoi.[1006] According to the October 21, 1970 issue of the communist party, *Lao Dong*, publication, Ann Froines said, "we learned of the widespread and formidable destruction [of] 100 million pounds of chemical poisons…" and "we also learned [about] victims of torture… the building…tiger cages." Yet "these crimes cannot weaken the determination of the Vietnamese people to fight bravely until final victory…"[1007]

Citing Douglas Pike in a contemporary report, Lt. Col. James Rothrock, USAF (ret.), says Froines had not "learned" anything about VC atrocities. Hanoi and NLF committed 158,000 terrorist attacks, 30,000 assassinations and 42,000 kidnappings from 1961 to mid-1970.[1008] Froines had been taught only the latest propaganda theme, "Tiger Cages."

Great Thoughts of Kim IL Sung. Returning September 16, 1970 at JFK in New York, Customs checked six packages of literature by by Kim IL Sung and V.I. Lenin and North Korean films. Robert Scheer praised the thoughts of Kim IL Sung in Tom Hayden's Red Family and in *Ramparts* magazine.[1009] Urging the withdrawal of (U.S.)forces from South Korea, in November 1974, Hayden/Fonda's IPC cosponsored a North Korean film, "The Flower Child" at Washington Square Methodist Church.[1010]

Press Conference: Who "Stole" POW Mail

Alex Hing, American Red Guard, led off, "The pigs have just stolen the letters…"

[1005] Hanoi in English to American Servicemen in South Vietnam, 1300 GMT 9 SEP 70 B, R 110448Z SEP 70 ZNZI, FBIS Okinawa.

[1006] Hanoi in English to American Servicemen in S. Vietnam 1300 GMT 10 Sep 1970. Talk by Ann Froines to black GI's in S. Vietnam; Suzanne Kelly McCormack, *Good Politics is Doing Something: Independent diplomats and anti-war activists in the Vietnam-era peace movement. A collective biography* (Carol McEldowney, Rona Shoul and Ann Froines), Dissertation, Boston College, 2002.

[1007] Rothrock, *Divided…*, 174-5 cites Joint Publications Research Service (JPRS), "American Visitors give Impressions of Anti-U.S. Struggle: 'How did the Americans Speak of Vietnam," Hanoi Lao Dong, Oct 21, 1970, 45-6. TTU.

[1008] Douglas Pike, "The Viet-Cong Strategy of Terror," U.S. Mission, Vietnam, 1970, 82, TTU; Rothrock, 175N37.

[1009] Collier and Horowitz, *Destructive Generation*, 226; Armstrong, Trumpet, 165, 188.

[1010] Clipping of Max Friedman, "North Korea feature film to premier this weekend," Nov. 7 1974.

Question: ". Identify yourself.

Answer: "…Alex Hing of the San Francisco Red Guards."

Off camera, Eileen Arthur Cormier, National League of Families, asked Hing if her organization representing the POW families could deliver the returned letters. Hing said, no, the U.S. People's Anti-imperialist group, he, would deliver the POW letters.

Robert Scheer lauded the humanitarianism of Hanoi allowing the POWs' letters. U.S. Customs checking names on letters "could be used against (the POWs) by the US government." The Government had "no concern for their wellbeing…" "The US government is a criminal government that got those pilots [to] perform the highest war crimes…"

Customs seized 374 POW letters checking for names and serial numbers. By 8:00 pm Customs was seeking to return the letters.

Hanoi and COLIFAM Threaten Loss of POW Mail. Robert Scheer said, "We are not allowed to allow the US government to play any …role whatsoever in connection with those letters…" Scheer said, "I can assure you that there will be no future delivery of letters if the US government insists on seizing them…"

COLIFAM was Hanoi's annointed channel for POW mail. Robert Scheer carried Hanoi's mailbag. He was bagman from POW hell. He thought he was a messenger from communist utopias, North Korea.

Comrades in Arms. Pham Van Dong and General Giap[1011] received Robert Scheer and the others quite well: "Our delegation …met openly with the peoples governments and were received as *comrades-in-arms.* We are fellow combatant against US imperialism." The delegation was in the international service of communist imperialism, Vietnamese, North Korean, Cuban, Soviet, or Chinese.

[1011] Photo with General Giap is at "U.S. Anti-imperialism Delegation," *Journeys Toward Peace: Internationalism and Radical Orientalism During the U.S. War in Vietnam,*
http://digitalunion.osu.edu/r2/summer09/caldwell/Pages/eldridgecleaver.html

Above: Delegation poses with North Vietnamese General Giap.

Photo: General Giap with Cleaver Anti-Imperialist
Delegation.

Ellen Brown: "We [Huey Newton and the Black
Panthers] have offered our troops to assist the Vietnamese people
in their current struggle for liberation…."

On September 18, 1970 in a "friends" letter, Cora Weiss
condemned Custom's temporary seizure of POW letters…"in
seeming disregard for the families… at the initiative of the North
Vietnamese … mail has increased. …We are not responsible for
the consequences that acts of government interference may
produce."[1012]

The messages of Sheer and Weiss to POWs and their
families was clear. We are as Hanoi's designated agents, make
the rules, hold the mail and hold the POWs. You, members of
POW families, are hostages.

Cleaver in Exile. Instead of landing in New York with
his followers, Eldridge Cleaver, in Scheer's words, 'unjustly
forced into exile" traveled on to Algiers. Algeria gave
diplomatic recognition and embassies to national liberation
fronts. Cleaver opened a U.S. Peoples Embassy. Cleaver soon
left Algiers for the better climes of Paris, returning in 1975, a
Mormon and a conservative Republican.

Cleaver later told what he learned about conducting
intelligence operations with enemies of the United States. If
someone "…goes to Qaddafi. … Qaddafi is not giving away
anything. He has some strings attached. …intelligence things,
but also military things."[1013] Similarly, "When we went to

[1012] Cora Weiss to Friends, COLIFAM, September 18, 1970.
[1013] An Interview with Eldridge Cleaver, Eldridge Cleaver was interviewed at his
Berkeley apartment by REASON editors Bill Kauffman and Lynn Scarlett, February
1986.

Hanoi…They would ask us to say things in international forums, things that they couldn't say…"

***

Weather Underground Free LSD guru Timothy Leary

On September 12, 1970 the Weather Underground Organization helped LSD guru Timothy Leary, imprisoned for drug dealing, escape from the California state prison at San Luis Obispo. Leary's Brotherhood of Eternal Love, an LSD and marijuana smuggling operation, through Michael Boyd Randall (aka Michael Thomas Garrity) paid the Weathermen either $25,000 or $50,000 for the breakout..[1014]

Leary Cash for Dynamite. "Kelly," likely Bernardine Dohrn, told Leary the cash was to buy dynamite.[1015] Timothy Leary observed, "Dope dealers raise twenty-five thousand dollars to finance the breakout. And the bread goes to the maniac guerrillas."

Timothy Leary (William John McNeill) and Rosemary Leary (Sylvia Edith McGaffin) fled[1016] to sanctuary in Algeria.

In October, Stew Albert, Jennifer Dohrn, Bernardine's sister, and Brian Flanagan flew to Algeria via Canada to meet Leary and Cleaver.[1017] Jennifer said, "(Cleaver) had the Chinese, Koreans and the North Vietnamese looking for us. … Kim II Sung and he sent a wire to Cairo saying that they should find us…we were their comrades."[1018]

[1014] Timothy Leary, *Confessions of a Hope Fiend,* 35; *Hashish Smuggling and Passport Fraud: the Brotherhood of Eternal Love,* Hearing before the Subcommittee to Investigate the Administration of the Internal Security Act and Other Internal Security Laws of the Committee on the Judiciary, United States Senate Ninety-third Congress First Session 1973, U.S. Government Printing Office 23-638 Washington: 1973, 29-31. http://www.ebooksread.com/authors-eng/united-states-congress-senate-committee-on-the/hashish-smuggling-and-passport-fraud--the-brotherhood-of-eternal-love--hea-tin/1-hashish-smuggling-and-passport-fraud--the-brotherhood-of-eternal-love--hea-tin.shtml

[1015] *Hashish Smuggling and Passport Fraud: the Brotherhood of Eternal Love*, Hearing before the Subcommittee to Investigate the Administration of the Internal Security Act and Other Internal Security Laws of the Committee on the Judiciary, United States Senate Ninety-third Congress First Session 1973, U.S. Government Printing Office 23-638 Washington: 1973, 31, 37. http://www.ebooksread.com/authors-eng/united-states-congress-senate-committee-on-the/hashish-smuggling-and-passport-fraud--the-brotherhood-of-eternal-love--hea-tin/1-hashish-smuggling-and-passport-fraud--the-brotherhood-of-eternal-love--hea-tin.shtmla

[1016] FBI, FOIA, Weather Underground. The primary source is Acting SAC Chicago to Director, memo, "Foreign Influence-Weather Underground Organization," August 20, 1976, 306.

[1017] FBI, FOIA, Weather Underground. The primary source is Acting SAC Chicago to Director, memo, "Foreign Influence-Weather Underground Organization," August 20, 1976, 232, 289.

Destroying "US Imperialism." After boasting about the Leary liberation, on September 15, 1970 Bernardine Dohrn issued the fourth communiqué from the weather underground, saying, "With the NLF and the North Vietnamese…we know that peace is only possible with the destruction of U.S. imperialism."[1019]

Police were alerted.

NYPD Raids Bronx Bomb Factories. After having three sites under court ordered surveillance since July on November 3, 1970 police raided three Weatherman bomb factories at 284 St Ann's Avenue, 605 West 111th Street, and 2427 Webster Avenue in the Bronx, New York finding explosives and maps for 50 buildings in New York and Chicago.

Of six arrested for conspiracy to commit arson, make bombs and commit murder police, four were Weather, Donald Cavellini, 27, Jefferson Bernard, 19, Beth Rosenthal Katz, 27, and Timothy Doyle, 28.[1020]

On November 11, 1970, Jennifer Dohrn played a tape recording to the press of Leary from Algeria.[1021]

FBI Director Hoover said, "The Black Panthers are supported by terrorist organizations." Hoover meant the Weather Underground bombers, Hayden's International Liberation School/Red Family (terrorist wannabes), and Quadafi financed terrorist operations.

In contrast, the CIA "found no indication of any relationship between the Fedayeen and the Black Panthers."[1022] Wrong question. Wrong answer. Wrong analysis. Again.

***

[1018]"Getting High With Jennifer," *Good Times,* January 8, 1971 cited in *Hashish Smuggling and Passport Fraud: the Brotherhood of Eternal Love,* Hearing before the Subcommittee to Investigate the Administration of the Internal Security Act and Other Internal Security Laws of the Committee on the Judiciary, United States Senate Ninety-third Congress First Session 1973, U.S. Government Printing Office 23-638 Washington: 1973, 80-83. http://www.ebooksread.com/authors-eng/united-states-congress-senate-committee-on-the/hashish-smuggling-and-passport-fraud--the-brotherhood-of-eternal-love--hea-tin/1-hashish-smuggling-and-passport-fraud--the-brotherhood-of-eternal-love--hea-tin.shtmla

[1019] Copy in Acting SAC Chicago to Director, memo, "Foreign Influence-Weather Underground Organization," August 20, 1976, 161.

[1020] Martin Gansberg, "6 Are Seized Here As Bomb Plotters," *New York Times,* November 3, 1970, 1, 29.

[1021] FBI, FOIA, Weather Underground. The primary source is Acting SAC Chicago to Director, memo, "Foreign Influence-Weather Underground Organization," August 20, 1976, 312.

[1022] CIA, FOIA, Family Jewels, 283.

Hanoi soon had a star, a Navy lieutenant, perhaps recruited in Paris, to take a leadership role in VVAW, a tiny but reliably pro Hanoi group of veterans, all angry, but few combat veterans of Vietnam.

Operation RAW (Rapid American Withdrawal). Back from a Paris meeting with communists in June, John Kerry joined VVAW, sponsored by Jane Fonda, Mark Lane, Donald Sutherland, Sen. George McGovern, Sen. Edmund Muskie, Rep. John Conyers, etc.[1023]

On September 7, 1970, Kerry took leadership of VVAW Operation RAW (Rapid American Withdrawal). During the Labor Day weekend of September 4-7, 1970, 150 Vietnam veterans marched 86 miles to Valley Forge State Park. The march concluded with a rally of 1,500 and speeches by John Kerry, Joe Kennedy, Rev. James Bevel, Mark Lane, Jane Fonda, Donald Sutherland, Rep. Allard Lowenstein, Mike Lerner, and Army First Lt. Louis Font.

Jane Fonda "on the bed of a pick-up truck," condemned the Nixon administration, "a beehive for cold blooded killers." John Kerry followed suit,
[I]t is not patriotism to ask Americans to die for a mistake ...it is not patriotic to allow a president to talk about not being the first president to lose a war and using us as pawns in that game.

Phony Photo Obscures Kerry-Fonda Alliance. In 2001, Rich Taylor (aka "Registered"), a conservative graphic parody artist, photo shopped Kerry standing next to Jane Fonda at a podium on June 13, 1971. Fonda was there with Kerry in spirit. She was photographed at the RAW rally with Kerry on September7, 1970, helped fund Kerry, VVAW and Winter Soldier. They worked on "Winter Soldier."[1024]

No phony photo was necessary to show the association of John Kerry and Jane Fonda.

Kerry gloated in 2004 over exposure of the phony Fonda-Kerry photo showing Kerry having a close association with Jane Fonda, he was downplaying. The prank, removed from FreeRepublic Web site within three hours, gave Kerry a club to strike his Swift Boat veteran critics.[1025] The Taylor fabrication distracted from the truth.

[1023] VVAW, "Operation RAW," a flyer at FBI, FOIA, VVAW.

[1024] "Doctored Kerry Photo...," *San Francisco Chronicle*, Feb 20, 2004.

[1025] Scott Swett and Tim Ziegler, *To Set the Record Straight: How the Swift Boat Veterans, POWs and the New Media Defeated John Kerry*, New American Media

Soon a genuine photo was discovered showing John Kerry at the Valley Forge rally of RAW on September 7th with Fonda. Kerry appears above Jane Fonda sitting three rows behind her. Fonda admitted, "We were at a rally for veterans at the same time. I spoke, Donald Sutherland spoke, and John Kerry spoke. "I don't even think we shook hands." Kerry's staff said they were "only acquaintances."[1026]

VVAW, Kerry and Fonda. Fonda and Kerry raised funds and worked on VVAW activities together. Moreover, a VVAW resolution of August 31, 1970 listed Jane Fonda on the Steering Committee of VVAW's Winter Soldier Investigation.[1027] As a member of the VVAW's Executive Committee, Kerry would have known about the tours of Fonda and Al Hubbard starting VVAW chapters and fundraising.

Americans and the communists were frequently coming together to discuss the strategy and tactics of peace on Hanoi's terms.

***

Americans and Vietnamese Coordinate Fall Actions and Themes, 1970
Vietnamese comrades...create a United Front in the fight
against American aggression

Robert Greenblatt joined a broad coalition of antiwar and social justice organizations at a Strategy Action Conference in Milwaukee September 11-13, 1970. Delegates represented the United Church of Christ, AFSC, FOR, WILPF, WRL, SANE, CALC, NSA, and WSP.[1028]

In May,[1029] the New Mobe had transformed itself into the National Coalition against War Racism Oppression and eventually into the Peoples Coalition for Peace and Justice (PCPJ).

The Communist Party of Washington State says the CPUSA "played an important role in the struggle against the war in Vietnam." In Washington local members Taimi Halonen, Thorun Robel and Marc Brodine chaired the People's Coalition

Publishing, 2008, 67-68.
[1026] http://www.snopes.com/photos/politics/kerry.asp
[1027] FBI, New York to Director, NY 100-160644, October 1, 1970.
[1028] William Poole, "The Anti-Defense Lobby Part 2: The Peace Movement, Heritage Foundation, #11.
[1029] Frank J. Rafalko, *MH/CHAOS: The CIA's Campaign Against the Radical Left and the Black Panthers*, Annapolis: Naval Institute Press, 2011, 142.

for Peace and Justice (PCPJ) in Seattle,[1030] The PCPJ represented the CPUSA endorsed multiple issue-united front strategy bringing in the alienated single issue Trotskyites.

***

All Communists wanted unity and coordination. The Soviet Embassy in Hanoi wrote,

Our Vietnamese comrades led an active effort to create a United Front in the fight against American aggression… guided by…the material and moral aid of the Socialist countries, particularly the Soviet Union and China.[1031]

Diplomatic offensive is…designed to coordinate…American antiwar movement." On September 17, 1970 the Binh Tan Province Standing Committee of the People's Revolutionary Party issued a directive, COSVN Directive 27, reporting policy to influence U.S. Congressional elections and public opinion on the war.

…Higher headquarters [COSVN Directive 27] has decided to conduct a new diplomatic offensive…coinciding with …the senatorial [sic] elections in November 1970. …Our delegation at the Paris Conference will make a declaration…coordinated with the struggle of the American people to …rally those people who want peace, independence, and neutrality. … We are to coordinate armed, political, and military proselyting activities with the new diplomatic offensive at the Paris Conference.

The cadre is also told to "listen to…broadcasting stations to clearly understand the content of propaganda themes."[1032]

8-Point Plan. In Paris Mme. Binh proposed an 8-point plan on September 17, 1970 whose first point was "…negotiations would begin at once on the release of all prisoners…when the date for total withdrawal of allied troops is set."[1033] Set the date was a recurring theme.

[1030] CPUSA, Washington District, "Communist Party of Washington State, brief history," 3/12/2002 at www.cpusa.org/article/article print/379/

[1031] CIA, FOIA, "Political Report of the Embassy of the USSR in the Democratic Republic of Vietnam For the Year 1970," [TFR 136-22A, [handwritten "22"] Top Secret, Copy No. 3 "12" Mar 71, Issue No. 114 [Stamp "TsK KPSS, 10987, 16 Mar 71 180-A/ Subject to Return to the General Section TsK KPSS"] DRV, city of Hanoi, March 1971, 6. [Handwritten "124, 125, 126"].

[1032] Directive No. 6 CT/Bt, Executive Committee of Binh Tan Party division, PRP of Vietnam, Sept 17, 1970 in U.S Mission to South Vietnam, Viet-Nam Documents and Research Notes, Document No. 101, Part IV, Saigon, January 1972, pp. 36-39.

[1033] Cora Weiss to Dear…, COLIFAM, February 24, 1971, 1.

In late September Madame Binh, Xuan Thuy, Wilfred Burchette and *Le Monde's* Jacques Decornoy met Rennie Davis, Richard A. Falk and Robert Greenblatt in Paris. Davis, Falk and Greenblatt wrote, "The Thieu regime is in its deepest trouble…and …may be on the verge of collapse. Nixon's support of Thieu doomed any settlement.[1034]

Dong to Chou: "influence the anti-war public opinion in the U.S." In Beijing on September 19, 1970 Premier Pham Van Dong told Chinese Premier Chou en lai to counter Nixon's Vietnamization plan, Hanoi needed to
Step up the diplomatic struggle…We have to influence the anti-war public opinion in the U.S. that includes… political, business, academic and clerical circles…

Hanoi's diplomatic demands were not new, "We want further to corner Nixon by influencing public opinion in the U.S. …"[1035]

100,000 Chinese Unremarkable? Chairman Mao told Dong Henry Kissinger was a "stinking scholar" who knew nothing about diplomacy. Mao wondered "Why have the Americans not made a fuss about...more than 100,000 Chinese troops [wearing Chinese uniforms] help you building railroads, roads and airports although they knew about it? Dong replied, "Of course they are afraid."[1036]

***

Fonda Helps Vietnamese Acquire Canadian Visas. According to "reliable" source of the Royal Canadian Mounted Police, RCMP, on September 23, 1970 Jane Fonda telephoned Tommy Douglas, long an alleged Communist and leader of the New Democratic Party, NDP. Tommy Douglas, father of Shirley Douglas Sutherland was an actor and Fonda's FTA comrade Donald Sutherland's father in law. Fonda asked Douglas to "start work on getting visas into Canada for the Vietnamese who were scheduled to participate in a citizen's inquiry in Quebec.[1037] At

---

[1034] Rennie Davis, Richard A. Falk and Robert Greenblatt, "The Way to End the War: the Statement of Ngo Cong Duc," *The New York Review of Books*, Volume 15, Number 8, November 5, 1970.

[1035] 77 Conversations cited in Larry Berman, *No Peace, No Honor*, 78-9, 302.

[1036] Westad, Odd Arne, et al, (eds.) *77 Conversations between Chinese and Foreign Leaders on the Wars in Indochina, 1964-1977,* Cold War International History Project, Working Paper no. 22, Washington, D.C. 1998, 177 cited in Jung Chang and Jon Halliday, *Mao: The Unknown Story*, 578 and in Berman *No Peace...*79.

[1037] Jim Bronskill, "Files on Tommy Douglas detail antiwar chat with Fonda," *Canadian Press*, Feb. 20, 2011 cites an Oct. 1, 1970 RCMP memo.

the time there were a number of regional inquiries conducted in Canada on U.S. war crimes, in effect coordinating with the upcoming Winter Soldier war crimes testimony and confessions in Detroit—just across the border from Windsor Canada.

***

Americans Attend Communist Conferences

WPC Conference, New Delhi, October 16-18, 1970. The Presidential Committee of WPC held a conference in New Delhi, India. The The Communist Party of the Soviet Union gave free tickets to the Soviet Peace Committee and WPC. The WPC appreciated "the growing strength of the (U.S. antiwar) movement...will continue to support the initiatives taken by the U.S. movement."[1038] Three American delegates in New Delhi flew to Moscow afterwards on Soviet-subsidized Aeroflot.

Moscow: Inquiry on U.S. War Crimes, October 22-25, 1970. The three Americans were delegates to an International Commission on Inquiry on U.S. War Crimes. Alexander Berkov, the Soviet representative, at WPC "played a dominant role in the preparation for the Commission."[1039] David Dellinger met privately with the Vietnamese communist concerned about a weakened antiwar movement. They urged demonstrations earlier than May 1971.[1040]

Abbie Hoffman in Paris. Abbie Hoffman and his wife Anita were in Paris at October 25-30, 1970 on an Appeals Court approved travel for the convicted rioter in Chicago.[1041] Their contact at 16 *Boulevard Rasrail*, Jean Jacque Lebel, was a French artist, socialist and a member of anarchist groups, *Noir et Rouge* and *Informations et Correspondances Ouvrières*. Redacted FBI files do not reveal if the Hoffmans met Hanoi representatives in Paris. Mrs. Hoffman, along with Mrs. Jerry Rubin, Judy Gumbo and Genie Plamondon, had met the Vietnamese

---

[1038] World Peace Council President Committee Meeting, Conference Letter, February 23, 1970, Helsinki cited in Frank J. Rafalko, *MH/CHAOS: The CIA's Campaign Against the Radical Left and the Black Panthers*, Annapolis: Naval Institute Press, 2011,138, 141.

[1039] Frank J. Rafalko, *MH/CHAOS: The CIA's Campaign Against the Radical Left and the Black Panthers*, Annapolis: Naval Institute Press, 2011, 141.

[1040] Frank J. Rafalko, *MH/CHAOS: The CIA's Campaign Against the Radical Left and the Black Panthers*, Annapolis: Naval Institute Press, 2011, 156.

[1041] FBI, FOIA, Abbot Howard Hoffman, SECRET, URGENT, Teletype, Director FBI to Director CIA, 10/1/70, 10/12/ 70; [redacted] New York office, FBI, memo (FD 204), Abbot Howard Hoffman, 10/30/70; Chicago to Director, Teletype, Abbot Howard Hoffman, 10/2/70, 2.

communists in Stockholm and Hanoi in May and the Hoffmans would meet the Vietnamese communists again in Paris in March 1971.

***

American Public Opinion: Not in Hanoi's Favor

Hanoi's efforts to effect public opinion were working, but in the opposite direction. In late September 1970, Nixon's approval rating was 64%. Some 47% thought Nixon was not acting strongly enough against student disorders and 71% that college administrators were too lenient.[1042]

"Dove" Senators Lose. In the November elections of 1970 voters threw four incumbent "doves" in the U.S. Senate out of office: Al Gore, Sr., D-Tennessee; Ralph Yarborough, D-Texas; Joseph Tydings, D-Maryland and Charles Goodell, R-New York.

So far, President Richard Nixon had defeated the best efforts of the mass antiwar movement. The movement did not reflect the public opinion it had hoped to affect.

***

New strategies and tactics were needed. Among them was exploitation of dissent inside the military.

"Indoctrinate...enemy soldier's dependents [to] call their [relatives]...to defect." On November 13, 1970, Directive No. 11/CT of the South Viet-Nam Liberation Army detailed its guidance on proselyting enemy troops.

Target soldiers and their families:

> We should indoctrinate...enemy soldier's dependents [and then to] call their husbands, sons, and brothers to defect and come home.

Focus on propaganda themes from Paris:

> The Paris Conference will be used as our propaganda themes...The bellicose and obdurate U.S...clique...sows bereavement among...the dependents of their own soldiers... We support those who turn their guns against the Americans and their cruel commanders.... Listen to the radio. Take notes of broadcasts...[1043]

[1042] H.R. Haldeman, *The Haldeman Diaries: Inside the Nixon White House*, New York: Berkley Books, 1994, 235.

[1043] Directive No. 11/CT of the South Viet-Nam Liberation Army, November 13, 1970 in U.S Mission to South Vietnam, Viet-Nam Documents and Research Notes, Document No. 101, Part IV, Saigon, January 1972,pp 40-42.

Viet Cong and Black Panthers. On November 14, 1970 the deputy military commander of the People's Liberation Armed forces, Mrs. Nguyen Thi Dinh, replied to a letter from the Defense Minister of the Black Panthers, Huey Newton, who had earlier offered, "to send volunteers to fight shoulder to shoulder…against (our common enemy) the U.S. imperialist aggressors…." VC Commander Dinh said, "When necessary, we will call for your volunteers…. We are firmly confident that …our ever closer coordinated struggle will surely stop the bloody hands of the U.S. imperialists."

Concluding, "best greetings for 'unity, militancy, and victory…" [1044] Four days later on November 18, 1970, the San Francisco office of the FBI entered the residence of Huey P. Newton to place a microphone to intercept conversations.[1045] Perhaps the FBI's interest was not in the widely advertised Black Panther's breakfast programs.

Dinh's "ever closer coordinated struggle" was occurring on all fronts and under all weather conditions.

***

From Cuba with Love

"From Santa Barbara to Boston…" WUO Fall Offensive 1970. On September 3, 1970, the CIA Director was informed the Weather Underground, WUO, had targeted the CIA.[1046] Projects MERRIMAC and RESISTANCE were gathering news clips and reading FBI files on such threats. The CIA also was working with Capitol area police agencies to provide security for its personnel and facilities in the Washington area. On October 5, 1970, the Weathermen bombed the police statue in Haymarket Square in Chicago for the second time.

On October 6, 1970, Bernardine Dohrn's sister, Jennifer Dohrn, played a Bernardine tape recording saying it was the beginning of a WUO fall offensive. Bernardine

---

[1044] "Black Panther Party Offers Volunteers to RSVN,NFLSV," Hanoi VNA International News Service in English 0546 GMT 20 Oct 1970 TTU and "PLAF Deputy Commander Replies to Black Panther Troop Offer," Liberation Press Agency (Clandestine) in English to East Europe and the Far East, 1610 GMT 14 Nov. 1970 TTU archive cited in James Rothrock, *Divided We Fall*, 2006, pp. 142-43N17.
[1045] December 21, 1976; FBI, San Francisco to Director, "Request of Attorney General for Information Concerning Surreptitious Entries, Nitel 8:15 PM October 16, 1975.
[1046] CIA, FOIA, Family Jewels, 282.

promised the fall offensive would "spread from Santa Barbara to Boston, back to Kent and Kansas."[1047]

On October 8, 1970 in Santa Barbara, as predicted, a National Guard facility was bombed by, as predicted, one of the "families or tribes" calling itself the "Perfect Park Home Grown Garden Society."[1048] On October 10, 1970 on Long Island, New York, the WUO bombed the Queens Courthouse "in solidarity with the current New York prison revolts" at Attica. That day the Women's Brigade of the WUO took credit, and "Proud Eagle tribe" on October 14 bombed "war research" at the Center for International Affairs at Harvard College, Boston.

It was as promised, "From Santa Barbara to Boston."[1049]

On the Tony East Side: Cuban Mission at United Nations

Georgie Anne Geyer and Keyes Beech report by October 1970 "approximately 4,000 Americans have visited Cuba …over the last decade."[1050] A "carefully watched" building, an "elegant five-story gray stone mansion at 6 E. 67th Street on the tony east side of New York is the Cuban mission to the UN." It is "the major Cuban source of influence, ideology and dollars for American radicals…dispensed under the huge picture of Che Guevara."[1051] Moreover, "Radical leaders admit privately they see the Cuban mission 'very often' …but please don't print that, they're not supposed to do that, you know."

A Cuban Intelligence officer was a control operative for Mark Rudd suggesting propaganda slogans for demonstrations.[1052] Geyer and Beech saw "hardcore

---

[1047] Bernardine's tape is cited in FBI, FOIA, Weather Underground. The primary source is Acting SAC Chicago to Director, memo, "Foreign Influence-Weather Underground Organization," August 20, 1976, 178-9.

[1048] FBI, FOIA, Weather Underground. The primary source is Acting SAC Chicago to Director, memo, "Foreign Influence-Weather Underground Organization," August 20, 1976, 180.

[1049] FBI, FOIA, Weather Underground. The primary source is Acting SAC Chicago to Director, memo, "Foreign Influence-Weather Underground Organization," August 20, 1976, 189.

[1050] Georgie Anne Geyer and Keyes Beech, "Cuba: School for US Radicals," Chicago Sun Times, October 1970.

[1051] Georgie Anne Geyer and Keyes Beech, "Cuba: School for US Radicals," *Chicago Sun Times*, October 1970 cited in FBI, FOIA, Weather Underground. The primary source is Acting SAC Chicago to Director, memo, "Foreign Influence-Weather Underground Organization," August 20, 1976, 42.

[1052] Frank J. Rafalko, *MH/CHAOS: The CIA's Campaign Against the Radical Left and*

indoctrination and even collaboration…. "American radicals have been copying… Latin urban guerrilla techniques of sniping, assassination, political kidnapping and even bank robbery."[1053]

The Weathermen followed the French Marxist Regis De Bray who said, like Mao, "…the political and the military are not separable, but form one organic whole, consisting of the people's army."[1054]

***

Fonda's Excellent Canadian Adventure

Canadian Coordination? In October 1970, Jane Fonda traveled to Canada to give an anti-war speech at Ontario's Fanshaw College. Fonda may have coordinated with the Vietnamese there. The Vietnamese were participating in the upcoming Fonda funded Winter Soldier program. Five Vietnamese planned to appear by closed circuit television from Canada.[1055] Immediately afterwards Americans and Vietnamese met to debrief in Windsor.

Vitamins and Political Prisoners. Returning from Canada in early November 1970, U.S. Customs in Cleveland stopped Jane Fonda. A cop declared, "Here is another Commie." Jane Fonda demanded, "Let me by. Let me go to the bathroom." An officer refused to move. "Get the f--- out of here, you pig." Then, "I pushed him out of the way." Police say she tried to kick the police officer in the groin.[1056]
My arrest was unusual….I wasn't beaten …because I am white, because I am a movie actress, because I have lawyers. Some of the best people in America are in prison today for their beliefs. … The two Berrigans, Angela Davis, Bobby Seale, the Soledad Brothers ... Why do you smile?[1057]

the Black Panthers, Annapolis: Naval Institute Press, 2011, 158.

[1053] Georgie Anne Geyer and Keyes Beech, "Cuba: School for US Radicals," *Chicago Sun Times*, October 1970 cited in FBI, FOIA, Weather Underground. The primary source is Acting SAC Chicago to Director, memo, "Foreign Influence-Weather Underground Organization," August 20, 1976, 42.

[1054] FBI, FOIA, Weather Underground. The primary source is Acting SAC Chicago to Director, memo, "Foreign Influence-Weather Underground Organization," August 20, 1976, 48.

[1055] VVAW, newsletter, program section, fragment, n.d. [pre-WSI], 13.

[1056] Andersen, 237; "Cause Celeb", *Time,* November 16, 1970; Fallaci, February 1971, 147.

[1056] Andersen, p. 235; "Cause Celeb", *Time* November 16, 1970; Fallaci, February, 1971, 147.

[1057]Fallaci, (February, 1971 147.

In a *Playboy* interview, Fonda claimed the police took her address book in Cleveland. Interesting reading if ever recovered.

According to *Time,* Henry Fonda called Jane, "my alleged daughter…every time there's a parade or peace rally…it will make the war last that much longer…it doesn't escape the attention of Ho Chi Minh."[1058] Jane responded to her father,

He…sincerely thinks that I am manipulated by someone. He believes that there is an organization behind me. …There is no point in telling him that I am doing this on my own, that nobody ever influenced me politically. [Roger Vadim, Elizabeth Vailland?]

Fonda's New Kind of Soldier: "Blow grass and Stargaze."

Beginning on November 3, 1970 Fonda toured fifty-four college campuses and raised funds to support the GI Office, VVAW, and the VVAW Winter Soldiers Investigation of American War Crimes.

At one November stop, Jane described her favorite G.I.s:

> They're a new kind of soldier. …When they're sent out on patrol …just…a little ways. They lie down on a little knoll and blow grass and stargaze. … they're not even performing the basic functions of soldiers.[1059]

She also asked, "When the time comes for these guys to make a decision ... will they kill people in Vietnam?"[1060]

Jane's sentiments were identical to the Viet Cong's *Binh Van*, action against the military, as described by Douglas Pike:

> A military patrol leader could lead his patrol noisily down a well-traveled path and after an hour return ... The effect was…mediocrity ... when excellence was vital.[1061]

Both Jane Fonda and the NLF's Viet Cong sought exactly the same slothful sabotage, malingering, slowdowns,

---

[1058] J. Borough, *The Fabulous Fonda's,* 269.
[1059] Lee Winfrey, "Jane Fonda - an LP Record with a Socialist Sermon", *Detroit Free Press* (November 22, 1970).
[1060] *Fabulous Fondas,* 275-6, 280; *Time,* January 3, 1972.
[1061] Pike, *Viet Cong,* 258.

inefficiency and mediocrity in the performance of U.S. and South Vietnamese troops.

***

COLIFAM, Hanoi Dribbles Out MIA News, POW Letters.

MIAs. On November 13, 1970 Cora Weiss, Dave Dellinger and Rennie Davis met the press at the Diplomat Hotel in New York City.[1062]
They brought little news on MIAs (most lost in South Vietnam). Only four MIAs were revealed as live POWs.[1063] Six others had died in captivity and ten had never been Hanoi's POWs.[1064] Hanoi provided a list of 335 POWs. Sidney Peck from Stockholm conference brought 571 letters.

Bad Santa. COLIFAM handed out a copy of POW Cdr. Robert James Schweitzer's Christmas message to his son Erik.[1065] DRV revealed its "humanitarian policy" to allow 5 kilograms Christmas packages per POW.

A Few Grateful. Families receiving their first letter in months or years were thrilled. John H. Fellowes, not listed as a POW for fifty months and feared dead wrote a note to his family. Mrs. Fellowes said, "It's wonderful. It's wonderful. I can't express myself," She thanked everyone including COLIFAM.[1066] Mrs. Allen Colby Brady was the "luckiest person in the world" receiving her only letter from her husband since his capture in January 1967, three years and eleven months ago. Mrs. Brady thanked, not COLIFAM, but the National League of Families[1067] whose members had badgered the North Vietnamese in Paris, Stockholm, Vientiane.

[1062] FBI, New York to Director, "COLIFAM IS-Misc Registration Act; 00-New York," TELETYPE 830PM URGENT November 12, 1970.

[1063] John H. Fellowes, Ben Markbury Pollard, George Everett Day, James J. Connell listed in COLIFAM News Release, "Four Added to List of Confirmed POW's, Families Receive 571 Letters, November 13, 1970; FBI, Director to White House Situation Room, ATT: Dr. Henry A. Kissinger, COLIFAM, November 14, 1970.

[1064] Cora Weiss to Dear Families, no letterhead, n.d.; FBI, Domestic Intelligence Division, Informative Note, November 14. 1970; Vietnam Committee for Solidarity With the American People, *Viet My,* to Dear Mrs. Cora Weiss, November 20, 1970.

[1065] Voice of Vietnam, English, November 2, 1970, text in FBI, New York to Director, "COLIFAM IS-Misc; Registration Act; 00-New York," TELETYPE 830PM URGENT November 12, 1970.

[1066] Tom Laughlin, "Postman's 'Love letter' read 50 times," Ledger-Star (Norfolk), November 14, 1970.

[1067] Ron Golobin, "I'm the luckiest person in world,' says wife," Ledger-Star, November 14, 1970.

Mary Crow, wife of Lt. Col. Frederick A. Crow, was happy to receive a father's letter to his son Patrick on his seventh birthday. Promised in April, it was delayed (dated two months before its delivery), and it made no mention of a stream of letters and packages from his family to Crow. A coincidence? Mrs. Crow had worked on "Operation Action" delivering 100,000 signatures to Paris urging Hanoi to provide information on all POWs.[1068] Had Mrs. Crow's actions delayed her mail?

**

Lawyers' Committee in Hanoi. From about November 9-23, 1970 three lawyers, Peter Weiss (husband of Cora), William Standard and identified CPUSA member Morton Stavis, representing the CPUSA influenced Lawyers' Committee on American Policy Toward Vietnam, traveled to Hanoi to carry POW mail.

Threats: No Mail, No Release Except on Hanoi's Terms. In the lead up, Mrs. Peter Weiss, Cora Rubin Weiss, had written a letter to the families of official 335 POWs list. Weiss told the wives we still "have no way of guaranteeing that prisoners will get each letter...some have been returned." Cora Weiss said the problem was the "irregular flights" and U.S. postal channels were "risky and unpredictable."

No Release. There will be no release of any husband or son,"...until there [is]...some movement in Paris...to the proposals... [of] Mme. Binh on Sept. 17." Otherwise, "there will be no further move vis-à-vis POWs." To be perfectly clear, nothing would happen on POWs

Until the two conditions are met—setting a fixed date for total withdrawal...and agreeing to withdraw support from the Thieu Ky Khiem regime. ...Upon fixing that date and agreeing to withdraw support, prisoners from both DRV [and] PRG...will be released."

Cora Weiss later said she had verified these conditions for a POW release with Premier Pham Van Dong and editor Hoang Tung.[1069]

No torture. Cora Weiss enclosed news articles saying prisoners were not being tortured anywhere but in South Vietnam.[1070] The President simply had to comply.

[1068] Norman M. Covert, "Letter From POW Brightens Birthday," Daily Press (Newport News), November 14, 1970.

[1069] Cora Weiss to Dear…, COLIFAM, February 24, 1971, 1.

[1070] Mrs. Cora Weiss to Dear families, COLIFAM, October 30, 1970; FBI, SAC, New

Provocative Packages. On November 22, the lawyers returned to New York from Hanoi with 326 letters from 297 pilots. Morton Stavis, Center for Constitutional Rights, CCR, ominously reported, "The authorities told me that they receive many 'provocative' packages and letters" containing metal objects, small clothes "(...based on the erroneous [sic] assumption that the men have lost a lot of weight)" and letters "don't stick to the rules regarding content." Stavis said, "They told me that many letters coming as a result of provocative and unfriendly campaigns in the U.S. are clogging the postal channels."

Cora Weiss concluded with the reminder to see the POWs ever again required setting the date for American withdrawal [and betraying an ally, South Vietnam].[1071]

***

Fonda: Communism—Pray on Your Knees, November-December 1970
Fonda: La Pasionaria, not yet Mother Bloor.
Meanwhile, *Newsweek* was writing about Jane Fonda, "The sexy ... actress is a modern La Pasionaria, if not quite yet a Mother Bloor." *Newsweek* was not referring to icons of domestic female achievement, Paris Hilton, Betty Crocker, Julia Childs, or Martha Stewart. La Pasionaria and Mother Bloor were notorious Communist cadre.[1072] Besides being a CPUSA organizer, Mother Bloor's son, Harold Ware, headed a Soviet espionage network in the US government.[1073]

"Pray on your knees...we someday become Communist." Jane Fonda relished her new starring role as La Pasionaria or Mother Bloor, perhaps without benefit of a party card or paying its dues. Her favorite line was: "If you understood what Communism was ... you would pray on your knees that we someday become Communist." Bob Mulholland, Tom Hayden's and the California Democrat Party's top political gun, denied Fonda's historic uttering. "That's a fabrication, Jane never said that," Bob Mulholland told the author.[1074] The record is clear. She said precisely such words.

York to Director, "COLIFAM IS-MISC Registration Act," AIRTEL November 11, 1970.
[1071] Mrs. Cora Weiss, Dear Friends, COLIFAM November 23, 1970.
[1072] *Herald of Freedom*, (October 5, 1979).
[1073] Klehr, *Heyday of Communism*, p. 143.
[1074] Morton Downey show, "Jane Fonda on Trial," 1988; Bob Mulholland to Canfield and David Demshki in an elevator at the California Capitol annex in 1988.

On November 21, 1970, before 2,000 students (and other witnesses) and reporter Lee Winfrey at Michigan State University, Jane Fonda said:

> "I would think that if you understood what Communism was, you would hope, you would pray on your knees, that we would someday become Communist."

Jane continued:

> "I think that the majority ... are scared of the word Socialism. It's a good message (Socialism) and the more people give it, the better."[1075]

On December 11, 1970, Jane Fonda repeated her winning lines at Duke University:

> I am a socialist; therefore I think we should strive toward a socialist society, all the way to communism. ...If you understood what communism was, you would hope and pray on your knees that we would someday become communist...[1076]....Whether the transition is peaceful depends on the way our present governmental leaders react....We must commit our lives to this transition. We can't bow to intimidation because we've come too far.[1077]

Such words did not make Jane Fonda a member of the CPUSA, but it did ingratiate her to such folks.

***

Rescuing POWs: The Son Tay Raid-

Early on November 28, 1970, a 101 man joint Air Force-Army commando force helicoptered into a compound guarded by towers at Son Tay a mere 23 miles west of Hanoi. A

[1075] Lee Winfrey, "Jane Fonda - an LP Record with a Socialist Sermon", *Detroit Free Press* November 22, 1970.
[1076] Karen Elliott, Dallas *Morning News,* Dec. 11, 1970; Other sources: Andersen, 236; *National Vietnam Veterans Review,* (September/October, 826; J. Borough, *The Fabulous Fondas,* (1973), 272; *Time,* (November 16, 1970);
[1077] Jane Fonda, *Dallas Morning News*, (December 11, 1970). See also: Poole, Heritage report # 13, 13.

Viet Cong defector said there were POWs there. Earlier aerial photos confirmed their presence showing coded arrangements of rocks and laundry in patterns indicating 55 POWs wanting a rescue.[1078] Yet the camp had camp emptied on July 14 in anticipation of the annual Red River flood in August. Indeed a year later in 1971 in August and September floods did destroy many flood control and water works and at least one surface to air missile site. Two days before the raid a Hanoi source of the DIA revealed Son Tay was empty,[1079] but the raid went ahead in the hopes the source was wrong.

Leak or Poor Intelligence? Though the planning of the operation was a secret even to the President,[1080] there was wild and false speculation of a security breach.[1081] For one example, *Edward J. Emering,* says,

The Gold Star Order was ...presented to PAVN General Tran Ba Thanh, who served as an ARVN officer on the South Vietnamese Prime Minister's staff ... provided invaluable intelligence to Hanoi. It is believed that he alone was responsible for the failed Son Tay prison raid, which attempted to rescue captive U.S. military personnel.[1082]

Was the Son Tay raid an intelligence failure? Sec Defense Melvin Laird said, the intelligence was good "except for our not having a camera that would see through the rooftop of buildings."[1083]

Americans Thrilled. The families and POWs were thrilled. Thousands of telegrams flooded the White House praising the attempted rescue. An Opinion Research Corporation survey of POW and MIA family members found that eighty-one percent approved of the rescue attempt and 84 percent would approve of another attempt.[1084]

[1078] Dale Van Atta, *With Honor: Melvin Laird in War, Peace and Politics*, Madison: University of Wisconsin, 2008, 211-212.
[1079] Lt. Gen. Ronald L. Burgess, "The Defense Intelligence Agency: National Intelligence and Military Intelligence are Indivisible," *The Intelligencer*, Volume 18, Number 3, Summer/Fall 2011, 12.
[1080] Dale Van Atta, *With Honor: Melvin Laird in War, Peace and Politics*, Madison: University of Wisconsin, 2008, 211-15.
[1081] Schemmer, Benjamin F. *The Raid*, Harper & Row, Publishers, 1976 206-210; Gargus, John, *The Son Tay Raid: American POWs in Vietnam Were Not Forgotten*, Texas A&M Press.2007, 249-251.
[1082] *Edward J. Emering,* "The Gold Star Order and *Orders, Decorations and Badges of the Socialist Republic of Vietnam"* http://www.vwam.com/vets/nvameds/goldstar.html
[1083] Dale Van Atta, *With Honor: Melvin Laird in War, Peace and Politics*, Madison: University of Wisconsin, 2008, 215.
[1084] "Son Tay Raid, " EHistory Archive,

Hanoi and Friends Outraged. Cora Strikes Again.
Cora Weiss wrote the families that the POWs might never get out
if Nixon pulled such stunts. Weiss drafted a petition to be sent to
the POWs

…the only way to get you home is by ending the war—not by
commando raids. …Our President has cynically exploited the
deep concern of the American people… My New Year's
Resolution is to let no day pass without pressing our government
to set a date of June 30, 1971…"[1085]

**Seymour Hersh Condemns Intelligence. Who Knew
Less?** Cora Weiss sent a news clip of Seymour Hersh, New York
Timesman and My Lai muckraker, trashing the Defense
Intelligence Agency, DIA, for a bad reading of aerial photos (not
seeing through roof tops?)

Many Times men, Homer Bigart, David Halberstam,
Harrison Salisbury, had their own trouble interpreting things on
the ground before their very eyes. The Times men relied on
gossip at the bar of the Continental Hotel or briefings by Hanoi's
spy reporter Pham Xuan An at the Givral coffee shop. Hanoi or
its agents, such as Pham Xuan An, often provided the reporters
both photos and text. Seymour Hersh received a Pulitzer Prize
for his reporting on Vietnam. He had never set foot there.[1086]

**Cora's Cornucopias Cookie Jar: $170.81 Funds
Worldwide Travel.** By December 10, 1970 Cora Weiss would
distribute internally a one page financial statement showing a
COLIFAM balance of $170.81 of the $5,323.40 raised in 1970.
COLIFAM's world travelers were not being paid out of Cora's
cookie jar. Round trip, Hanoi, cost $1,500.

Who Paid For Worldwide Travel? CALC's Rev.
Fernandez said prominent people. Al Hubbard, VVAW, said the
(the Soviet subsidized) CPUSA paid the travel bills. Many flights
were booked through the CPUSA owned Anniversary Tours
allowing the CPUSA to subsidize some flights. Some Soviet and
Romanian secret police defectors later said the World Peace
Council and the Stockholm Conference had paid these bills.
Others said Soviet front monies were laundered through the
wholly Soviet controlled Russian Orthodox Church to the World
Council of Churches and to assorted peace conferences. Taking

---

http://ehistory.osu.edu/vietnam/essays/sontay/0012.cfm
[1085] Petition n.d. see also: CALC, American Report, *Review of Religion and American
Power*, December 4, 1970.
[1086] Peter Braestrup, Big Story, 521.

money from their pews some tax and IRS exempted mainline churches such as the United Methodists, United Church of Christ, United Presbyterian Church and the Episcopal Peace Fellowship either gave money to peace groups or laundered millions of dollars through the tax exempt National Council of Churches, World Council of Churches and its American affiliate[1087] and the Youth Project.[1088] Ruth Gage-Colby directed all tax-deductible ad revenues for a dinner in her honor be given to antiwar activities.[1089]

Few believed WSP's Cora Weiss was a Girl Scout selling cookies to pay for her worldwide COLIFAM operations. She had her father's Rubin Foundation fortune and associated fronts could fund their causes outside of the modest public COLIFAM balance of $170.81.

Evidence: "Insufficient to support a solicitation"
There was lots of smoke, lots of clues, but no fire, no arson attributable to COLIFAM? In December the Assistant Attorney General, Internal Security Division, informed the FBI that the "available admissible evidence ...is insufficient to support a solicitation of registration under the Foreign Agents Registration Act or a criminal prosecution under the Logan Act against COLIFAM. All offices are to dispense with further interviews of relatives of servicemen detained in North Vietnam."[1090]

The Justice Department lawyers had said, "Quit. Give it up." Hanoi's agent COLIFAM won. POWs, MIAs and their families lost.

***

[1087] David Jessup, "Preliminary Inquiry Regarding Financial Contributions to Outside Political Groups, by Boards and Agencies of the United Methodist Church 1977-79," (paper) April 7, 1980; David Emerson Gumaer, "Apostasy: The National Council of Churches at nccwatch/articles/apostasy.htm?200815; ucc.org/aboutus/short-course/the_united_Church_of_Christ.html; Rael Jean Isaac, "Do You Know Where your Church Offerings Go?," *Reader's Digest*, January 1983, 120-125; Robert L. Wilson, *Biases and Blind Spots: Methodism and foreign Policy Since World War II*, at cmpage.org/biases/; Max Friedman, Council for Inter-American Security, study in lieu of testimony to Chairman of House Ways and Means Committee, Lobbying and Political Activities of Tax-Exempt Organizations, Hearings, subcommittee on Oversight, March 12-13, 1987, 398.
[1088] "Methodist Church Funding examined," *Information Digest*, May 16, 1980, 161.
[1089] Ruth Gage-Colby Testimonial Committee, letter for January 20, 1972 dinner.
[1090] Director to New York, COLIFAM IS—Misc, AIRTEL, December 24, 1970; Chicago to Director, memo, COLIFAM IS—Misc, Sac, December 16, 1970; New York to Director, COLIFAM IS—Misc, AIRTEL December 29, 1970;

The Hanoi, the enemy, continued to smell American fear and defeat and see victory in its future.

Mass action in coordination": Stockholm Conference on Indochina- Nov. 28-30, 1970

November 28-30, 1970, a delegation of antiwar Americans attended a World Conference on Vietnam, Laos, and Cambodia staged by the Soviet controlled Stockholm Conference on Vietnam. Alexander Berkov, Soviet representative of WPC was highly influential in preparations for the conference, including "drawing up a list of invitees."[1091] In May 23-24, 1970, the Stockholm Conference had invited New Mobe to become a member. In June, the Stockholm Conference had declared it "stands with the people of Indo-China" and "their legitimate representatives," DRV, PRG, the Lao Patriotic Front and the Royal Cambodian Government of National Unity."

Many of the thirty-five American delegates to World Conference on Vietnam, Cambodia and Laos November 28-30, 1970 received Soviet-subsidized Aeroflot transportation.[1092]

Among the Soviet, Berkov vetted American invitees and attendees of the Stockholm Conference in late November 1970, were representatives of New Mobe, CPUSA, WSP, American Deserters Committee, WILPF, Lawyers Committee on American Policy Toward Vietnam, CALC, and Chicago Peace Council.[1093]

Hanoi Thanks Antiwar Movement. A spokesman of the NFL expressed gratitude for the "worldwide mass movement, fighting against American aggression in Indochina. By November, Minh Giam of the office of North Vietnamese Premier Pham Van Dong urged, Support the anti-war movement ...and establish a broad program of mass action in coordination with the activities of this movement in the spring of 1971."[1094]

[1091] Frank J. Rafalko, *MH/CHAOS: The CIA's Campaign Against the Radical Left and the Black Panthers*, Annapolis: Naval Institute Press, 2011, 141.

[1092] Frank J. Rafalko, *MH/CHAOS: The CIA's Campaign Against the Radical Left and the Black Panthers*, Annapolis: Naval Institute Press, 2011, 138, 141.

[1093] David Dellinger, Rep. Ron Dellums (D-CA), William Douthard, Sidney Peck, Mrs. Jerrie M. Meadows, and Willie Jenkins of either New Mobe or its predecessor NCAWWR; Mrs. Janey Hayes of WSP; Mrs. Pauline Rosen of CPUSA[1093] and WSP; Bruce Beyer, Gerry Condon, Mike Powers, John Woods of American Deserters Committee; Estelle Cypher and Eleanor Fowler of WILPF;; And Stan Faulkner of Lawyers Committee on American Policy Toward Vietnam; Carlton Goodlett and Gil Green of CPUSA; Rev. Thomas Hayes of CALC; Ron Young of FOR, Silvia Kushner of Chicago Peace Council.

Nguyen Van Hieu said, "to the American representatives here" that "… Nixon…is obliged to consider…American opinion….We are particularly pleased at the increasingly close cooperation between the American antiwar movement and urban South Vietnamese…"

Conference Sets Themes and Campaign Schedule. On December 20, 1970 the Stockholm conference sent letter number 5 planning 1971 to "follow the main theme and slogan we propose" and a proposed campaign schedule:

> April 3-4-…actions in the United States against the American aggression in Indochina, on the occasion of the anniversary of the assassination of Martin Luther King. …May 1-16—the US movement will mobilize massive nationwide action to end the war against Indochina…

Further,

…We call upon all countries where war resisters, such as American GIs reside, to create…sanctuary or asylum." …We call special attention to…Americans facing the penalty...Angela Davis, Erika Huggins, and Bobby Seale and John Sweeney who faces the death penalty on the charge of desertion from the field of battle. [1095]

***

Hanoi had issued its orders to the People's Coalition for Peace and Justice, PCPJ, to hold demonstrations in May.[1096]

Pattern of Coordination, Collaboration. A House Committee noticed, "The program of action for 1971 adopted… was in many respects identical to that of the American antiwar movement, demonstrating again the coordination that exists between American antiwar activists and the international Communist 'peace' movement." And "From New Mobe through NCAWRR down to (People's Coalition for Peace and Justice) PCPJ, this pattern has never varied…American antiwar movement and North Vietnamese victory were mutually supportive.

[1094] William T. Poole, The Anti-Defense Lobby Part 2: "The Peace Movement, Continued", *Institutional Analysis #11,* September 19, 1979; John Schmitz, 207-215. http://www.heritage.org/Research/GovernmentReform/IA11.cfm
[1095] Schmitz, 209-214.
[1096] Max P. Friedman, "More Proof Reds Behind 'Peace, *Manchester Union Leader,* May 8, 1971. Friedman had infiltrated the antiwar movement.

Angela Davis. On December 22, 1970 the Hanoi controlled South Vietnam Liberation Women's Union condemned the U.S. for "detaining Angela Davis, an active peace-fighter." Police held Davis for allegedly smuggling a gun into the Marin County jail. The gun was used to murder Judge Haley. Angela Davis, an active CPUSA leader, was as progressives were apt to say "working for peace."[1097]

Sidney Peck. On November 30, 1970 Radio Hanoi[1098] played a Sydney Peck, a co-chairman of New Mobe:

> Question: …would you…tell our listeners something about the (anti-war) movement that really concerns you?

> Peck: …Nixon was compelled to initiate…withdrawal [and to] say that the silent majority was with him. But the truth…is that the antiwar movement reflects a great majority of opinion…

> Question: …what do you think of Madame Binh's proposal (on September 17)…?

> Peck:"… [The] first important thing is to *set a time, to fix a date* when those (military) forces (of the U.S.) will be withdrawn."[1099] [Precisely the Communist line "set a date."]

***

National Citizens Commission of Inquiry on U.S. War Crimes in Vietnam

Vets Allege War Crimes. Ralph Schoenman of Bertrand Russell's Hanoi-scripted war crimes tribunals formed the National Citizens Commission of Inquiry on U.S. War Crimes in Vietnam in November 1969 in New York. Its major activists in 1970-71 were Michael Uhl, Tod Ensign and Jeremy Rifkin closely tied to self-described socialist Rep. Ron Dellums of California, Oakland and Berkeley.[1100]

December 1-3, 1970 vets took public testimony on atrocities in Washington, DC. Some 35 veterans claimed to

---

[1097] "NLF Women's Union Condemns Treatment of Angela Davis," Liberation Press Agency, 1613 GMT, Dec. 23, 1970, TTU archive cited in Rothrock, 149N23.
[1098] Hanoi in English to American Servicemen in S. Vietnam 1300 GMT 30 Nov 1970. Interview with Prof. Sidney Peck on GIs antiwar movement in the U.S.
[1099] "Peck Describes Antiwar Movement in the United States," Hanoi in English to American Servicemen in South Vietnam, 1300 GMT, Nov 18, 1970, 10-12, TTU.
[1100] Michael Uhl, "That's Vietnam, Jake," *The Nation* July 9, 2001
http://www.thenation.com/article/thats-vietnam-jake?page=0,2

have committed or have witnessed war crimes.[1101] Robert
Bowie Johnson moderated and Noam Chomsky and Jeremy
Rifkin commented afterwards.

**Ron Dellums Promotes Congressional Investigation
of War Crimes**. Rep. Ronald V. Dellums (D-Ca) placed the
vets crimes testimony in the *Congressional Record* on March
1, 1971. Dellums announced a joint resolution of Dellums and
others[1102] to conduct a congressional war crimes investigation.
The "terrible realities of war atrocities [are] ...an integral
component of our illegal, insane and immoral adventurism in
Southeast Asia."[1103] Later Dellums chaired an unofficial, ad
hoc committee hearing from April 26-29, 1971.[1104]

***

For the VC things were not going as well on their
home front as they were in the USA.

South Vietnam Taking back Hamlets. Back in
Vietnam, Nguyen Van Thanh, a defector and former VC
commander, spoke to Jeffrey Race. Thanh said VC cadres in
Long An province were finding traveling and recruitment
difficult and their military units weakened. Thanh explained
what the Viet Cong faced:

> One... [it was] a partial reconstitution of the
> government's village apparatus. A second had
> been the psychological impact of the
> government's land- reform proposals, widely
> propagandized...A third... the considerable
> expansion of the Popular Force and People's
> Self-Defense Force organizations."[1105]

[1101] Daniel Alfiero, Richard Altenberger, Daniel K. Amigone, Robert Asman, Kenneth
J. Campbell, Bob Connelly, T. Griffiths Ellison, Donald Engel, Tod Ensign, Louis Paul
Font, Gail Graham, Chuck Hamilton, Steven Hassett, Robert Bowie Johnson, Jr.,
Norman Kiger, Robert J. Lifton, Gordon S. Livingston, Peter Norman Martinsen,
Robert J. Master, Michael Paul McCusker, Ed Melton, Elliott Lee Meyrowitz, Greg
Motoka, Edward Murphy, Kenneth Steve Noetzel, Barton Osborn, Sam Rankin, Larry
Rottman, Chaim Shatan, Gary Thamer, Greg Turgeon, and Phillip Wingenbach.
[1102] Diggs, Charles Rangel, Bella Abzug, Collins, Roncallo, Mitchell, Rosenthal,
Augustus Hawkins, Ryan, Scheuer, Edwards of California, Eckhardt, Conyers,
Kastenmeier, Mikva, Seiberling, Burton, Koch, Helstoski, Dow and Badillo.
[1103] National Veterans Inquiry on U.S. War Crimes in Vietnam, Washington D.C.,
Congressional Record, March 1, 1971, 4238.
[1104] *The Dellums Committee Hearings on War Crimes in Vietnam: An Inquiry into
Command Responsibility in Southeast Asia.* Edited and with an introduction by the
Citizens Commission of Inquiry. New York: Vantage, 1972.
[1105] Jeffrey Race, *War Comes to Long An: Revolutionary Conflict in a Vietnamese*

233

The Saigon had neutralized the residual Viet Cong forces in the over two years since the Viet Cong suicide missions in Tet 1968. The VC shadow government cadre was a ghost of its former self.

Land to Tiller. The lives of most Vietnamese was been "eternally impoverished tenant farmer families" according to Bill Laurie.[1106] In early 1968, Thieu began distributing government owned land to peasants. In February 1969, Thieu froze private repossessions of land and froze increases in rent for one year. In 1969 even these early promises to farmers were bearing fruit. Finally, in March 1970 Thieu instituted the Land to the Tiller program. The farmer received the land he worked and the landowner was paid fair compensation in government bonds. The land reform won popular support.

Hanoi Fights Land to Tiller. By August 11, 1970 Hanoi appealed "smash the U.S. Vietnamization scheme and especially to defeat its pacification program." To "maintain a political base...stay close to the people and the land."[1107] In the north, the solution was to murder by quota of evil capitalist landowners.

By February Xuan Thuy, Hanoi negotiator in Paris, was pleading for its American comrades in NPAC and PCPJ to unite in light of a "serious situation, the success of Vietnamization and pacification and the impact of allied military operations in Cambodia and Laos. [1108]

The Communists had no place left to hide except in broad daylight on the Second Front.

***

All was not lost for the Communist forces. Things would get better, much better for the North Vietnamese on the

Province (Berkeley: University of California Press, 1972), 270 cited in Mark Moyar, "VILLAGER ATTITUDES DURING THE FINAL DECADE OF THE VIETNAM WAR, 1996 Vietnam Symposium, "After the Cold War: Reassessing Vietnam,"18-20 April 1996,
http://www.vietnam.ttu.edu/vietnamcenter/events/1996_Symposium/96papers/mo yar.htm
[1106] Bill Laurie to Canfield and others, May 26, 2009.
[1107] Hanoi Broadcast Editorial: A Directive for Intensified 'People's War' in South Vietnam, Hanoi Domestic Service in Vietnamese, 1430 GMT, 11 August 1970 and "Push Forward the People's War in Villages and Hamlets," *Quan Doi Nhan Dan*, August 11, 1970, Pike Collection, TTU, Virtual Archive Item Number 2121709004.
[1108] Max P. Friedman, "More Proof Reds Behind 'Peace," *Manchester Union Leader*, May 8, 1971. Friedman had infiltrated the antiwar movement.

Second Front in the United States in 1971. The year 1970 would close with early evidence of that good news for the enemy.

People's Peace Treaty

After three days in December 1970 in Moscow, Saigon, and Paris twelve members of the (American) National Student Association, NSA, and others (Mark Rasenick, Doug Hostetter, Keith Parker) spent two weeks in Hanoi, signed "joint declarations of peace" and the People's Peace Treaty.

Along with Hanoi's student group, North Vietnam Student Union, the NSA claimed to represent South Vietnamese organizations, National Student Union, and Liberation Student Union.

In Hanoi, Pham Van Dong, told NSA president and PCPJ leader David Ifshin and others, the treaty was important.[1109] Some in the American delegation made broadcasts over Radio Hanoi. According to a copy in his FBI FOIA files, Ifshin said, The U.S. government does not go to South Vietnam to fight for democracy...but they go there... to murder the people of Vietnam...to make South Vietnam into one large military base. ...We call on GIs to strengthen the antiwar movement...to demand an end to all U.S. involvement in Vietnam."

POW John McCain remembers hearing the Ifshin broadcast repeatedly piped into his cell.[1110]

People's Peace Treaty: "Set the Date." "Drafted by the North Vietnamese," [1111] the People's Peace Treaty, echoing the Madame Binh formula of September 17, 1970, demanded America "*set the date*" for immediate withdrawal, overthrow the Thieu-Ky-Khiem government in Saigon and accept the neutralization of Cambodia and Laos.

The North Vietnamese promised to form a coalition government and to guarantee the safety and freedom of South Vietnamese who had "collaborated" with the U.S. and Saigon.

For these terms of abject surrender built on promises very likely to be broken, Hanoi would release its American

---

[1109] *Organizational Trends*, Vol. 1, No. 3, July 1984.
[1110] Mark Libbon, "McCain friendship with SU's radical student leader," October 6, 2008 at
blog.Syracuse.com/politicalnotewook/2008/10/mccains_friendship_withsus_ra.html;
Time, May 13, 1996 .
[1111] *Guardian*, February 13, 1971; House Committee on Internal Security, *Annual Report* 1971.

hostages, the POWs. Moreover, Hanoi's armed forces would remain inside South Vietnam.

"Popularizing Hanoi's...terms ...disguised." The terms of the People's Peace treaty favored entirely the Communist side of the conflict and became "a propaganda devise by the NSA (National Student Association) and the PCPJ (People's Coalition for Peace and Justice) in popularizing Hanoi's negotiating terms ...disguised by the People's Peace Treaty."[1112]

Hanoi's blueprint in hand, the American friends of the Viet Cong acted accordingly. In Washington the FOR joined an interfaith effort to "set the date" for US withdrawal and surrender.[1113] Within weeks, January 8-10, 1971, the New University Conference and the Chicago Movement Meeting adopted the People's Peace Treaty.[1114] The People's Peace Treaty was quite the rage for everyone "working for peace" on Communist terms.

"Student Leaders: Communist Agents. Indeed, the South Vietnamese signers of the People's Peace Treaty were Viet Cong agents. Student Huynh Tan Mam was a secret member of the Viet Cong and a cheerleader of the North Vietnamese conquest. And Doan Van Toai said, "For four years I wrote secret reports providing intelligence [to] ... the National Liberation Front."[1115]

As the NSA delegation was leaving Hanoi, on December 19, 1970, an Hanoi Circular promoted the youth emulation movement in South Vietnam. The Circular declared to achieve "the liberation of the South" and "reunification of the country" depended upon the "peace-and-justice-loving youths of the world, and especially...progressive American youths and students...."[1116]

During January 1971 Doan Van Toai, a Viet Cong agent, would speak at Berkeley and Stanford universities as

---

[1112] House Committee on Internal Security, *Annual Report* 1971.
[1113] Records of the Fellowship of Reconciliation, USA,FOR-USA), DG 013, Section 2, Series G, G-7, in Box 18, Swarthmore College Library at Swarthmore.edu/library/peace.
[1114] Wintersoldier.com ... page=peoples
[1115] Doan Van Toai, "A Lament for Vietnam," *New York Times Magazine*, March 29, 1981, 1-2 of 13; Doan Van Toai, in Collier and Horowitz, *Second Thoughts...*, 70.
[1116] Circular Calls for Youth Emulation Movement in SVN, Hanoi in Vietnamese to South Vietnam 0330 GMT 19 Dec. 1970, Pike Collection, Virtual Archive, TTU, Item Number 2311602038.

vice president of the Saigon Student Union denouncing the Thieu regime.[1117]

American Authors of Communist People's Treaty. After Tom Hayden's letter of introduction, Robert Greenblatt helped the North Vietnamese write the People's Peace Treaty.[1118] Douglas Hostetter, a Vietnamese-speaking Mennonite of Vietnam Christian Service and the United Methodists, also traveled to Saigon and Hanoi to work on the treaty[1119] and met Pham Van Dong.[1120] Greenblatt, Hostetter and others returned home to seek its adoption among American groups.

The charade of phony groups and not a few dupes would distribute petitions and hold signing ceremonies for months thereafter.

***

COLIFAM's Christmas 1970 Crew

As the National Student Association group was departing, December 18-26, 1970 at the invitation of the South Vietnam People's Committee in Solidarity with the American People (*Viet My*) [1121] COLIFAM sent another delegation to Hanoi.

In the COLIFAM delegation were Anne M. Bennett of WSP, Ron Young of FOR and his wife Trudi Young of WSP, and Sister Mary Luke Tobin of Catholic Peace Fellowship.[1122] The secretary of the South Vietnam People's Committee in Solidarity with the American People (*Viet My*), Tran Trong Quat, met the group. Quat said that U.S. bombing and rescue attempts made seeing the POWs difficult.

"It Did Not Look Like a Prison." At dusk on Christmas day, four named Vietnamese, Mr. Quat, Prof. Tri, Mr. Lu, Prof. Due, escorted the American visitors to a POW

[1117] Doan Van Toai, "A Lament for Vietnam," *New York Times Magazine*, March 29, 1981, 10 0f 13.

[1118] Icord, March 13, 1972, H-172. Members of A People's Peace Treaty organization in Versailles in 1972 were Dianne Apsey, Mae C. Bremer, Frank H. Joyce, Nancy Woodside.

[1119] Luke S. Martin, *A Vietnam presence; Mennonites in Vietnam During the American War*, Morgantown: Masthof Press, 2016, 387.

[1120] Doug Hostetter, Records, 1967-2001, Boxes 5,39 of 62, Mennonite Church USA Historical Committee and Archives at mcusa-archives.org/personal_collections /HostetterDoug.html.

[1121] FBI, New York to Director, COLIFAM IS-Misc, TELETYPE 11 25 PM NITEL December 11, 1970.

[1122] FBI, New York to Director, COLIFAM IS-Misc, TELETYPE 535 PM NITEL December 22, 1970.

camp. They arrived on a dark, but mesmerizing scene of oddly "familiar surroundings…college or seminary quadrangle. It did not look like a prison. The prisons…in South Vietnam were fortified, cold, harsh looking places (as are prisons in the USA)." The POWs called this Potemkin setting the Plantation.

The Vietnamese convinced the peace delegation they treated U.S. "pirates" and "war criminals" better than their own people. Such credulity could only be found in the twilight zone of those seeking world peace and utopian societies and willfully blind to contradictory facts and common sense.

The antiwar group entered a large room, sat at a large table and were served tea. "We were not subjected to a search. We were trusted." Was it the camaraderie of innocents or of comrades?

Finally, they met "five tall men—Americans," Bill Mayhew, Mark Gartley, Edison Miller, Paul Gordon Brown, and Robert Schweitzer.
"They all said 'we are in good health and are treated well.' …They moved quickly, they moved normally. …They had good food, meat almost every day along with vegetables, fruit, French bread, cookies and sometimes warm milk with sugar."

And "Many times the men said to us, 'End the war. We want to go home.' And 'we know we cannot go home until the war ends.'"[1123]

After a U.S. Customs check in Seattle of POW letters looking for new names of POWs,[1124] the group arrived in New York on December 27, 1970 with 649 letters and Christmas cards claiming the POWs were in excellent health and spirits.[1125] All concerned had accomplished their mission with letter, perfect performances.

***

Influencing U.S. Public Opinion:
Soviet Report, U.S. Intelligence Evaluations on 1970
The Soviet Embassy in Hanoi wrote in its year-end report for 1970:

[1123] "Committee Delegation Speaks to American Pilots at Christmas," American Report: Review of Religion and American Power, January 15, 1971 found in FBI FOIA, C, COLIFAM.
[1124] FBI, New York to Director, COLIFAM IS-Misc, TELETYPE, 1230 PM URGENT, July 27, 1970; FBI, Director to White House Situation Room, ATTN: Dr. Henry Kissinger, COLIFAM, December 27, 1970.
[1125] Cora Weiss, Dear Families, December 28, 1970.

The DRV-RyuV leadership is endeavoring to win the sympathy of world public opinion. ...It has expanded its activities...developing contacts with ... organizations advocating an end to the Vietnam War. The Vietnamese have attached great significance to this influence, in their favor, on US public opinion and to the assistance in consolidating forces opposed to Nixon's policy in Indochina.[1126]

Soviets: Progressive Forums; "For this our Vietnamese comrades need our help". The Soviet Embassy report offered political advise as well as military and economic aid, "Our Vietnamese comrades...should use progressive international ... forums for...advancing their program. ....our Vietnamese comrades need our help." The USSR organized, funded and directed many progressive groups and seduced others with subsidized conferences, communications and travel.

The Soviet embassy recognized things had gone badly on the battlefield in South Vietnam. A protracted struggle was expected. The Vietnamese had to look to "a longer struggle by combining military, political, and diplomatic means via mobilization of all forms and resources ..." There was evidence the Vietnamese knew what to do. "Visits to the DRV by various youth, women, and other delegations happened to increase in 1970."[1127]

The Soviet empire had delivered 1.2 million tons of cargo in 270 shiploads in 1970 to the DRV, provided hundreds of KGB and GRU officers and technicians, trained thousands of Vietnamese and maintained antiaircraft batteries.[1128] A dozen "Socialist" regimes gave 374 million rubles in military

---

[1126] CIA, FOIA, "Political Report of the Embassy of the USSR in the Democratic Republic of Vietnam For the Year 1970," [TFR 136-22A, [handwritten "22"] Top Secret, Copy No. 3 "12" Mar 71, Issue No. 114 [Stamp "TsK KPSS, 10987, 16 Mar 71 180-A/ Subject to Return to the General Section TsK KPSS"] DRV, city of Hanoi, March 1971, [TFR 136-37][handwritten "127"].

[1127] CIA, FOIA, "Political Report of the Embassy of the USSR in the Democratic Republic of Vietnam For the Year 1970," [TFR 136-22A, [handwritten "22"] Top Secret, Copy No. 3 "12" Mar 71, Issue No. 114 [Stamp "TsK KPSS, 10987, 16 Mar 71 180-A/ Subject to Return to the General Section TsK KPSS"] DRV, city of Hanoi, March 1971, [TFR 136-40] handwritten "129", "161"].

[1128] Stanislav Lunev, *Through the Eyes of the Enemy*, Washington: Regnery Publishing, 1998, 170.

aid and committed another 513 million rubles in military aid for 1971.[1129]

Only Soviet funds, weapons and propaganda assistance kept Vietnamese communists in a war against a super power, the USA.

***

[1129] CIA, FOIA, "Political Report of the Embassy of the USSR in the Democratic Republic of Vietnam For the Year 1970," [TFR 136-22A, [handwritten "22"] Top Secret, Copy No. 3 "12" Mar 71, Issue No. 114 [Stamp "TsK KPSS, 10987, 16 Mar 71 180-A/ Subject to Return to the General Section TsK KPSS"] DRV, city of Hanoi, March 1971, [TFR 136-42][handwritten "108","165"].

Part IV. 1971 Summary.

During 1971 treason was on the march as the leaders of the peace movement enthusiastically gave aid and comfort to the enemy in war sometimes with millions of witnesses, sometimes secretly.

Jane Fonda. Actress Jane Fonda, age 32, came of age continuing to "work for peace" disseminating communist war crimes propaganda in national and Pacific tours, fundraising for the peace movement, and staging a Winter Soldier show trial of American war crimes in coordination with Vietnamese communists in Canada.

Senator George McGovern. A Senator and antiwar candidate for President, George McGovern, (D-South Dakota), begged Vietnamese communists to give him a complete list of American POWS in exchange for a bill to set a date for unilateral withdrawal.

John Kerry. A U.S. Navy Lieutenant, often wearing U.S. Army fatigues, John Kerry, burst on the scene leading a tiny organization called Vietnam Veterans against the War, VVAW, tossing away war medals, wowing a Senate hearing, meeting Vietnamese communists in Paris, and putting on display POW wives as trophy supporters of a Viet Cong peace plan. John Kerry denies attending meetings where a VVAW leader, Scott Camil, advocated murdering U.S. Senators.

Daniel Ellsberg. A former civilian employee of the Department of Defense and Rand corporation, Daniel Ellsberg stole and distributed classified documents, the Pentagon Papers, to antiwar reporter Neil Sheehan, and the Soviet-friendly Institute for Policy Studies. McNamara civilians collected the papers, only some from the Pentagon.

Pentagon Papers. The New York Times, Neil Sheehan, cherry picked a few documents out of 43 volumes showing the war was a lie from beginning to end and obscuring evidence to the contrary. An unprepared Department of Justice, with one day's notice, lacking access to secret documents and to specific threats to national security, failed to persuade the US Supreme Court that an absolute freedom of press trumped national security. Justices detailed the evidence and arguments that might have swayed them to rule in favor of national security. In effect, the Court and the press decriminalized espionage and treason during war into the present day "leaks."

The Clueless, CIA. CIA Intelligence Estimates opined that the antiwar movement was nothing to worry about. In fact, the peace movement gathered up timely intelligence on US military actions. Leaders of the movement repeatedly met the enemy in Paris, Budapest, Moscow, Winsor, Vancouver, Toronto, Stockholm, Oslo, Helsinki, Beijing, and Saigon. They helped Hanoi write the Peoples Peace Treaty. They organized a massive "spring offensive" in Washington in April and May.

POWs as Pawns. Like John Kerry, Walter Cronkite and COLIFAM exploited POWs. COLIFAM abused and recruited POW families, and controlled POW mail. They followed communist playbooks on the treatment and use of POWs. The communists and their American comrades worked mightily to encourage desertion and malingering of GIs and to recruit GIs and deserters to the movement.

The Media. The media gave lavish coverage to Hanoi's American agents of influence in the antiwar movement claiming American war crimes,a and ignoring communist atrocities, The Vietynamese communists burned hundreds of civilians alive at Duc Duc and turned heavy artillery on fleeing refugees in Cambodia. CBS blamed U.S. bombing and Cambodian cowardice.for NVA and Khmer Rouge slaughter in of innocents in Cambodia

The Enemy. On Radio Hanoi, in multiple meetings, and in directives and circulars, Vietnamese Communists praised, advised, coordinated and instructed antiwar activists to unity antiwar groups. They also instructed antiwar leaders to follow the Hanoi propaganda lines. Promote Hanoi/Viet Cong peace plans, "set the date" for U.S. unilateral withdrawal and POW releases.

VVAW Proposals: Killing Senators and American Values. The year ended with VVAW's Scott Camil offering a plan to assassinate pro-war US Senators. No member of VVAW, including John Kerry, bothered to inform law enforcement of this high crime. VVAW attacked symbols of patriotism, Betsy Ross, Statue of Liberty and Christianity.

***

Chapter 9. Hanoi Tutors American Spokesmen.
Unify, Set the Date for Withdrawal and POW Releases.

Opening 1971: CIA Estimates of Foreign Influence.
On January 5, 1971 a CIA a memo declared foreign involvement in the antiwar movement was nothing much. "Definition and Assessment of Existing Internal Security Threat," said the main (foreign) assistance [was]...exhortation and encouragement... through international conferences..." There was "no evidence" of foreign "control [of] of U.S. Left movements." There was no capability of "supporting terrorist or sabotage" [Cubans and Weathermen?] or [widespread] "fomenting...subversion in the United States Armed Forces...or in colleges, and universities and mass media."

The CIA report was reassuring when judged by its own artificial criteria. No control. In short, the groups were not capable of mounting a fully successful revolution inside America. The CIA concluded "Foreign funding, training, propaganda does not play a major role in the U.S. New Left, but at present the U.S. New Left is basically self-sufficient and moves on its own impetus."[1130] 1971 would prove otherwise.

The issue of "control" was irrelevant if, using many hundreds of volunteers, foreigners influenced American politicians. The CIA saying antiwar groups were self-sufficient was breathtaking. Most of the organizations had treasuries with next to zero balances, most activists had no visible means of support and yet they traveled across the nation and the planet. Cuba was training thousands of Venceremos activists. The Soviets and the Vietnamese hosted conferences with hundreds of people. Trips to foreign capitals lasted weeks at a time often with free airline tickets, lodging, food, entertainment.

While FBI reports found foreign funding, training and indoctrination, except for Cuba, the CIA found little and reported less.

[1130] CIA, Report, "Definition and Assessment of Existing Internal Security Threat," January 5, 1971 cited in Church Commission, 700.

The powerful influence of Hanoi would be proven in the opening days of 1971 with a propaganda show using America Vietnam vets, real and counterfeit.

****

Winter Soldiers—January 1971
Winter Soldier Investigation of American War

Crimes. Fully committed to Communist scripts, recited in public, Jane Fonda and comrades mouthed every line and verse of the propaganda of Hanoi and international communism. Despite rabid Hanoi assistance, the Bertrand Russell war crimes tribunal of 1966-67 never quite caught on in the USA. The idea for an American-conducted war crimes inquiry very likely began with either Mark Lane and/or a group of Americans from over 70 organizations in a meeting of February 7-8, 1970 in Vancouver initiated by Carlton Goodlett and Irving Sarnoff of the New Mobe and the KGB-financed World Peace Council. Neil Sheehan's initial coverage in the *New York Times* gave credence to the need for a War Crimes Tribunal against the United States.[1131] Also Bill Moyers of *Newsday*.[1132]

Jane Fonda Funded Tales of American War Crimes. Jane Fonda produced a propaganda spectacular. Fonda sponsored, raised funds and helped select witnesses for a televised war crimes tribunal against the United States, the Winter Soldier. Fonda's United States Servicemen Fund (USSF) helped fund the Winter Soldier program. During the fall, touring 54 college campuses, Jane Fonda raised $10,000 for the VVAW Winter Soldier Program.[1133] Overall, somewhere between $50,000 and $75,000 was raised and spent.[1134]

[1131] Jules Witcover, "Veterans Ask Inquiry Into Alleged Atrocities," *Los Angeles Times*, December 4, 1970; Neil Sheehan, "Taylor Says by Nuremberg Rules Westmoreland May Be Guilty," *The New York Times*, January 9, 1971; Neil Sheehan, "Five Officers Say They Seek Formal War Crimes Inquiries," *The New York Times*, January 13, 1971; Neil Sheehan, "Should We Have War Crimes Trials?" *The New York Times Book Review*," March 28, 1971.

[1132] "For a War Crimes Inquiry," Editorial, *Newsday* [Long Island and New York City], Bill Moyers as Publisher March 22, 1971.

[1133] *Saturday Review*, (September 10, 1970); *New Republic*, (March 13, 1973); *Time*, (November 16, 1970); *Detroit Free Press*, (November 22, 1970); *Fabulous Fondas*, 266, 271; Frook, 52. Other notable contributors were Emil Mazy, Richard Austin, Mark Lane, Dick Gregory, Phil Ochs, Graham Nash, David Crosby, Alison Montgomery, Barbara Dane, Donald Sutherland, and USSF. Gerald Nicosia, *Home to War: A History of the Vietnam Veterans' Movement, Crown, 2001*.

[1134] Other notable contributors were Emil Mazy, Richard Austin, Mark Lane, Dick Gregory, Phil Ochs, Graham Nash, David Crosby, Alison Montgomery, Barbara Dane, Donald Sutherland, and USSF. Gerald Nicosia, *Home to War: A History of the Vietnam Veterans' Movement, Crown, 2001*.

The "Winter Soldier Investigation" was conducted out of a Howard Johnson Motel in Detroit between December 31, 1970 and February 2, 1971. Months before the event VVAW members Mike Oliver, Jeremy Rifkin, Bill Crandell, Al Hubbard, Scott Moore, "Jane Fonda and associates," e.g. Mark Lane, screened and selected over 100 vets to testify.[1135]

Mark Lane: KGB's Ghost Writer. Jane Fonda's tutor, Mark Lane, had written a book *Conversations with Americans* detailing American atrocities in Vietnam. According to Vasili Mitrokhin, a KGB archivist, KGB agent Genrikh Borovik helped Mark Lane "research."[1136]
Neil Sheehan of the *New York Times,* in a rare instance of objectivity, reported many of Mark Lane's "eye witnesses" had either never served in Vietnam or were not where atrocities they "witnessed" occurred.[1137]

Winter Soldiers Coordinate with VC in Canada. With Mark Lane's encouragement, Jane Fonda and VVAW, coordinated their "Winter Soldier" planning with Hanoi representatives in Canada. Winter Soldier recorded T.V. testimony from Cambodians and Vietnamese in Windsor, Ontario, Canada across the Ambassador Bridge in Detroit.[1138]

Who Were the VVAW? The VVAW, in late 1970 was a very small group of no more than 1,000 and at its peak never exceeded 7,000 members out of the 9,000,000 Vietnam era vets, or less than one half of one percent of the 2.6 million Americans who served in Vietnam.[1139] VVAW's minuscule membership was surprisingly low since anyone, veteran or civilian, could be a member. VVAW members were certainly not among the 91% of Vietnam Vets who were "glad [to have] served in Vietnam."[1140]

What Did the VVAW do Against the War? VVAW's leaders were a unique breed with a radical portfolio of militant actions favoring the enemy in war. Over its history VVAW's top

[1135] Gerald Nicosia, *Home to War: A History of the Vietnam Veterans' Movement, Crown, 2001.*
[1136] Christopher Andrew and Vasili Mitrokhin, *The Sword and the Shield: The Mitrokhin Archive and the Secret History of the KGB*, Basic Books, 1999.
[1137] Guenter Lewy, *Commentary*, (February, 1976), 42; See also, B.G. Burkett, *Stolen Valor.*
[1138] *Time*, November 16, 1970.
[1139] Stephen Morris, "John Kerry's Other Vietnam War: Why would we trust this man to be our president? *National Review,* October 31, 2004.
[1140] *Parade*, November 11, 1980.

leaders and spokesmen[1141] participated in the disruption of the 1968 Democratic Convention and the 1972 Republican Convention. VVAW barricaded the Statue of Liberty and flew the American Flag upside down. VVAW hoped the Vietnam War "precipitated a social revolution ... fast ... very fast." VVAW camped on the Capitol mall in Washington (despite a U.S. Supreme Court injunction), wearing fatigues, and coolie hats, tossed war medals over a barricade protecting the Capitol, saying, "here's my merit badge for murder." VVAW disclosed military intelligence on deployments of U.S. military forces and attempted espionage on secret U.S. weapons.

VVAW: Fellow Travelers. VVAW members joined both the orthodox Maoist (Stalinist) Venceremos organization (also Revolutionary Union-Revolutionary Communist Party) and the Symbionese Liberation Army, the kidnappers of Pattie Hearst. To meet communists, VVAW leaders traveled to Cambodia, Soviet Union, China, France, Sweden, Cuba, Canada, Poland and Vietnam. One member, Scott Camil, hatched a plot to murder U.S. Senators and no one informed authorities. VVAW organized illegal tours to North Vietnam during the war and admitted Hanoi "called the shots" on acceptable antiwar activities. VVAW members worked in the Carter White House and for Senator John Kerry. After the war, a VVAW contingent traveled to North Vietnam to lay a wreath at the tomb of Ho Chi Minh. There Ho's embalmed corpse lays for reverential public showings in a massive mausoleum set in a large plaza. Long lines pass the tomb's guards up red carpeted marble stairs. Moscow embalmers Valery Bykov and Yuri Denisov-Nikolsky annually nurse the VVAW-revered corpse of Ho Chi Minh.[1142]

Winter Soldiers: VVAW Confessed to Horrendous War Crimes. Over five weeks, some 150 American alleged servicemen appeared to testify to war crimes they "committed or witnessed." Gerald Nicosia described Scott Camil, heroically as "formerly a gung-ho Marine, now looking Christ-like with long hair and beard chiseled Semitic features." VAW's Scott Camil testified to:

> burning of villages with civilians in them,
> the cutting off of ears,

[1141] Some of the most active VVAW leaders were: John Kerry, Peter Bourne, Robert Muller, Al Hubbard, Hayden Fisher, Joe Remiro, William Harris, John Kniffin, Scott Camil, Ron Kovic.

[1142] AFP, "Vietnam honours Russian embalmers of Ho Chi Minh," May 29, 2009.

cutting off of heads,
torturing of prisoners,
calling in of artillery on villages for games,
corpsmen killing wounded prisoners,
napalm dropped on villages,
women being raped,
women and children being massacred,
CS gas used on people,
animals slaughtered,
Chieu Hoi [surrender]passes rejected and the
people holding them shot,
bodies shoved out of helicopters,
tear-gassing people for fun and
running civilian vehicles off the road.[1143]

Michael Noetzel said Green Berets used snakes and electroshock and 12 Viet Cong soldiers were thrown from helicopters to their death in 1963.[1144] The helicopter tosses got wide media coverage.[1145] Joe Bangert claimed to have gone on secret CIA missions, seen deformed children, bloody bodies strung up on wire and children murdered for flipping fingers at GIs on Route 1. Others testified to torturing prisoners; cutting off body parts for trophies; throwing Viet Cong suspects out of helicopters[1146]; mutilating and gang raping women, etc.

As a moderator of the Americal Division Panel at the Winter Soldier Investigation, Chicano Barry Romo testified that the racist military dehumanized the enemy and made it easy and normal to kill civilians.[1147]

Jane Fonda told Italian journalist Oriana Fallaci: "...[G]enerals ...exchange[d] transistor radios for the cut genitals or the cut ears of the Viet Cong, Fonda said, "There is a camp in Maryland, it's called Fort Holabird, where they're trained to torture the prisoners." [Editor: they are trained to

---

[1143] Camil's testimony at winter soldier Web site is at http://www.wintersoldier.com:80/staticpages/index.php?page=20040315221225656
[1144] FBI, fragment, n.d. [post-WSI report], 3.
[1145] "Red POWs Pushed Off Copter, Witness Says," *Los Angeles Times*, December 3, 1970; GI's threw 2 Viets to death, agent says." *The Detroit News,* December 3, 1970.
[1146] "Red POWs Pushed Off Copter, Witness Says," *Los Angeles Times*, December 3, 1970; "GI's threw 2 Viets to death, agent says." *The Detroit News,* December 3, 1970.
[1147] Vietnam Vets, "John Kerry and VVAW (Vietnam Veterans Against the War)", *Bella Ciao,* Sunday August 29, 2004 - 22:36, http://bellaciao.org/en/spip.php?article3093

resist torture, not to conduct it.] Asked about the treatment of Viet Cong prisoners, former POW of the Viet Cong George Smith testified, "We just beat them and put them in barbed wire cages that were about three or four feet high."[1148] Torture allegations was widely covered.[1149]

Fonda, Kerry's and Mark Lane's "Winter Soldiers" asserted barbarities were not simply the depravity of individual soldiers. They were policy[1150] training and generals actively promoted war crimes.

Congress Outraged. Thousands learned of the Winter Soldier testimony through radio and underground press coverage, books, newspapers, and magazine articles.[1151] Senator Mark Hatfield put the "Winter Soldier" transcripts into the Congressional Record.[1152] The Winter Soldier Investigation was filmed.[1153]

An outraged anti-war Senator, Mark Hatfield, demanded that the Commandant of the Marine Corp conduct an investigation of such American barbarities in Vietnam.

Marine Corps Investigation: Witnesses Not in Detroit, Not in Vietnam. The Marine Commandant did. Yet under instructions from VVAW, most of its "Winter Soldier" witnesses, even with immunity from prosecution for their own claimed misdeeds, refused to be interviewed by investigators.

[1148]**http://lists.village.virginia.edu/sixties/HTML_docs/Resources/Primary/Winter_Soldier/WS_23_POW.html**

[1149] Jerry Oppenheimer, "We could hear them screaming," *The Washington Daily News*, December 3, 1970; "A Tale of Torture and Murder," *The Daily Freeman* (Kingston, N.Y.), December 3, 1970; "Yanks tortured Red prisoners, two GIs testify," *Chicago Daily News*, December 3, 1970; Jules Witcover, "New Vietnam Atrocity Charges Little Noticed; War Veterans Make Allegations of Bizarre Tortures, Crucifixion of Enemy Soldiers," *Los Angeles Times*, December 8, 1970; Lucien K. Truscott IV, "'We can't sleep man,' Veterans Inquiry into War Crimes," *The Village Voice*, December 10, 1970; "Ex-GI Says He Saw Americans Commit Executions, Atrocities." *The Florida Times-Union*, December 3, 1970; Powell Lindsay, "Viet Veterans Tell of GI Atrocities,". *The Pittsburgh Press*, December 2, 1970.

[1150] "Torture was policy, Viet war vets say." *The Cleveland Press*. December 3, 1970; "War Veterans at Inquiry Feel 'Atrocities' Are Result of Policy." *The New York Times*, December 4, 1970. Lee Dye, "4 Officers Challenge To Brass on Policies in South Vietnam," *Los Angeles Times,* January 21, 1971. "Ex-GI Says He Saw Americans Commit Executions, Atrocities." *The Florida Times-Union*, December 3, 1970.

[1151] See: Vietnam Veterans Against the War, the *Winter Soldier Investigation: An Inquiry into American War Crimes*, Boston: Beacon Press, (1972). See also: John Kerry, *The New Soldier*.

[1152] April 6, 1971.

[1153] http://lists.village.virginia.edu/sixties/HTML_docs/Resources/Primary/Winter_Soldier/WS_entry.html

248

Still others listed as giving testimony had not been in Detroit. Some told grisly stories, used the names of other Vietnam vets.[1154]

One "witness" had been coached on his answers, but lacked details sufficient to validate his own "Winter Soldier" testimony. VVAW member Steve Pitkin filed a legal affidavit saying John Kerry and others had coerced him into testifying to atrocities.[1155]

VVAW member Joe Bangert claimed he went on secret CIA missions served in a Light Observation Squadron whose major duties were hard labor giving logistical support to fighting units. Bangert might be able to testify to hearsay, but not what he saw.[1156]

U.S. Army Investigation: No One to Prosecute. The Criminal Investigation Division of the U.S. Army identified 43 alleged witnesses whose stories, if true, qualified as war crimes of which 25 refused to cooperate, 13 provided information insufficient to prove a crime, five could not be located. After initial investigation none warranted criminal prosecution.

CID reported 11 individual WSI witnesses changing their horrific stories once faced with an Army investigation. Those retracting their prior testimony were Douglas Craig, Larry Craig, Donald Donner, John Lytle, Robert McConnachie, Ronald Palosari, Donald Pugsley, Kenneth Ruth, James Henry, David Stark, and George Smith.

George Smith's story of Army beatings and barbed wire cages, he modified. The South Vietnamese tortured not Americans.[1157]

Many disproven mythological incidents persist.

Tossed From Helicopter: Media Stunts. A detailed follow up CID investigation found only one documented, staged, instance of a corpse, not a living person, being thrown out of a helicopter and the U.S. government disciplined the sick perpetrators. This mirage hangs today in a war crimes museum.

[1154] Guenter Lewy, *America in Vietnam*, 1978, 317; FBI, memo to E.S. Miller, subject: VVAW, internal Security. Nov. 24, 1971 TTU archive; Mackubin Thomas Owens, "Vetting the Vet Record," *National Review Online*, Jan. 27, 2004, 1,6. cited in Rothrock, 124-125N78.

[1155] Steve Sherman at Vietnam Myths Conference, Session 3 at wwwviet-myths.net/session03t.htm.

[1156] Steve Sherman, Vietnam Myths conference at wwwviet-myths.net/session03t.htm.

[1157] Scott Swett, "Newly Discovered Army Reports Discredit 'Winter Soldier' Claims," *FrontPageMagazine.com* February 25, 2008.

Ears. The televised October 9, 1967 edition of the "CBS Evening News" a soldier cutting an ear off the body of a dead enemy was staged on the dare of reporters with Don Webster and John Smith providing the knife. The soldier was convicted of violating the Rules of Land Warfare and the Uniform Code of Military Justice. Smith and Webster were uncharged and CBS refused to correct its broadcast.[1158]

Burning villages. A TV correspondent provided his own Zippo lighter to burn down an abandoned village used for Marine training.[1159]

Not a Policy. That some servicemen or combat units committed war crimes in Vietnam is undeniable, despicable and almost always investigated. The "Winter Soldier" charges such barbarities were U.S. policy and routinely unprosecuted are false, but useful propaganda.

Not a Story. The military did not fully release investigations and did not distribute their conclusions that WSI claims were mostly false.

Scott Swett observes, "US military leaders during the Vietnam era failed to understand that home-front psychological warfare operations pose at least as great a threat to the military's ability to successfully complete its mission as enemy operations in the field."[1160]

***

Fonda, Winter Soldiers Debriefing with Vietnamese "Students" in Canada

Immediately after WSI hearings in early February 1971, Jane Fonda and other WSI participants and a group of North Vietnamese students met at a United Auto Workers (UAW) union hall in nearby Windsor, Canada. Gerald Nicosia writes "several carloads of veterans drove across the border to Windsor, Canada, to meet with a delegation of Vietnamese

---

[1158] Guenther Lewy, *Commentary*, (February, 1978), 42-43; Robert Elegant, "How to Lose a War: The Press and Vietnam," *Encounter*, (London), vol. LVII, August 1981, 73-9- at Wellesley.edu/Polisci/wj/Vietnam/readings/elegant.htm; William V. Kennedy, *THE MILITARY and The MEDIA: Why the Press Cannot Be Trusted to Cover a War*, Westport: Praeger, 1993 excerpts at http://www .viet-myths.net/Kennedy.htm

[1159] Robert Elegant, "How to Lose a War: The Press and Vietnam," *Encounter*, (London), Vol. LVII, August 1981, 73-9 at Wellesley.edu/Polisci/wj/Vietnam/readings/elegant.htm.

[1160] Scott Swett, "Newly Discovered Army Reports Discredit 'Winter Soldier 'Claims," *FrontPageMagazine.com* February 25, 2008.

students in exile, who had been denied visas by the Canadian [?] government to come to Detroit for the hearings."[1161]

By a happy coincidence, also on February 2-3, also in Windsor, also with Vietnamese, Chicago Seven attorneys, William Kunstler and Leonard Weinglass, attended a religious "service of liberation." The FBI was told the meetings would "not involve formal discussions…"[1162] Very likely this was a debriefing with Vietnamese of the Winter Soldier proceedings. VVAW and Fonda had planned a reception[1163] with Vietnamese at the end. Weathermen got some Cuban cash.[1164]

POW Mother Wants to Meet Vietnamese in Winsor. A likely participant was Virginia R. Warner, mother of POW Jim Warner, who signed a VVAW letter on February 1, 1971. She said, "Since I would like to meet the Vietnamese people, I really hope they will come to Windsor." She said the U.S. was exploiting POWs. "End the war so prisoners can come home …I'm not proud…my son helped to bomb Vietnam and I don't want any more Vietnamese people killed… I'm sure Jim is being treated just fine because his letters are just great."

According to Scott Swett of Winter Soldier.com, POW Jim Warner accused John Kerry of exploiting his mother's fears to extort his mother into writing the letter.[1165] Whatever her motives, Mrs. Warner appeared on March 16 with John Kerry joined by mothers Judy Keyes and Patricia Simon who also had sons in the war[1166] and Mrs. Warner appeared in still other VVAW events later.

Meanwhile, her son, Capt. James Warner, was tortured to make Hanoi propaganda tapes, ate "grease" sandwiches, and provided the only regular medical treatment some of his camp mates received.[1167]   Among those not invited to the

---

[1161] Gerald Nicosia, *Home to War: A History of the Vietnam Veterans' Movement*, Crown, 2001.

[1162] FBI, FOIA, Abbie Hoffman, Teletype, Director to Legat Ottawa, Abbott Howard Hoffman, Security Matter—Anarchist, January 28, 1971, 1-2.

[1163] FBI, New York to Director, NY 100-160644, October 1, 1970.

[1164] Max Friedman, "Behind Terrorism in the U.S.: Castro's Cuba," *Washington Intelligence Report*, Washington: the U.S. Anti-Communist Congress, Inc. Volume III, Number 10, November 1970, 4.

[1165] News Release, Feb. 1, 1971, Winter Soldier Investigation, 967 Emerson Street, Detroit, Michigan 48215, Telephone (313) 822-7700 at wintersoldier.com …page=Warner.

[1166] Washington Post, March 17, 1971; FBI, SAC WFO to Director, VVAW IS-Miscellaneous, AIRTEL, April 15, 1971, 2.

Windsor reception for the Vietnamese Communists was a white-haired lady who on the afternoon of the last day of the WSI, stood up marched toward the podium waving the American flag saying that everyone on the stage was a "communist." She said, "My son is in Vietnam. You should speak with him if you want the truth."[1168]

***

Talking Peace, Organizing Revolution

Rep. Ron Dellums (D-California [Berkeley]) upon taking office in January 1971 "in his office in the House...mounted an exhibit of atrocities committed by the United States in Vietnam."[1169]

Terror. An article, "Suppressed Issue: Guerrilla War in the USA," in *Scanlon's* magazine in January, revealed a dramatic increase in acts of sabotage and terrorism in the United States from 16 occurrences in 1965 to 546 in 1970.[1170]

Best Offer: US Surrender. On January 7, 1971 in Paris, Madame Binh turned down Nixon's offer of October 7, 1970 for an internationally supervised ceasefire in place, an Indochina peace conference including all parties in South Vietnam and a timetable for withdrawal once there was an overall settlement.[1171] Instead, Binh insisted upon total and unconditional withdrawal by June 30, 1972 and a coalition government not including President Thieu or Vice President Ky.[1172]

***

The People's Coalition for Peace and Justice (PCPJ)

Sidney Peck. On January 8-10, 1971, the National Coalition Against War, Racism, and Repression, NCAWRR,

---

[1167] Stuart I. Rochester and Frederick Kiley, *Honor Bound, American Prisoners of War in Southeast Asia 1961-1973,* Annapolis: Naval Institute Press, 1999, 381, 433, 444.

[1168] FBI, Detroit, LHM, Re: Winter Soldier investigation WSI, February 4, 1971, 1.

[1169] Former Congressman Ron Dellums Organizing for Peace Forces Us to Challenge All Forms of Injustice," *Democracy Now,* Monday May 25, 2015.

[1170] FBI, FOIA, Weather Underground. The primary source is Acting SAC Chicago to Director, memo, "Foreign Influence-Weather Underground Organization," August 20, 1976, 51.

[1171] Public Papers of the Presidents of the United States: Richard Nixon, 1970 (1971), 825-828 cited in Willard J. Webb, *History of the Joint Chiefs of Staff, The JCS and the War in Vietnam,* 1971-1973. 570, 584.

[1172] (C) Msg, US Fel France 291 to State, 7 Jan. JCS in 29585 cited in Willard J. Webb, *History of the Joint Chiefs of Staff, The JCS and the War in Vietnam, 1971-1973,* 584.

met in Chicago. It favored melding multiple issues, Vietnam and social justice.

Sidney Peck, among its most prominent leaders, was a former CPUSA member, a Marxist sociologist, an activist in the Soviet-controlled World Peace Council and soon a leader of NAWWR's renamed successor, the People's Coalition for Peace and Justice, PCPJ.[1173] Peck had the authority to sign checks of New Mobe and PCPJ.

People's Peace Treaty and Protests. The NCAWRR approved the Hanoi written "Joint Treaty of Peace Between the People of the United States, South Vietnam, and North Vietnam," AKA the "People's Peace Treaty." It scheduled demonstrations for April 2-4, 1971 commemorating the death of Martin Luther King and a May 1971 "a multi-issue action" demonstration in Washington, D.C.

Mayday Planning. Members of PCPJ and Mayday Collective attended a February 1971 Student and Youth Conference on a People's Peace in Ann Arbor, endorsing the People's Peace Treaty and May actions. Working with Arthur Waskow of the Institute for Policy Studies, Rennie Davis of the Collective sought "to create an atmosphere of struggle in May 1971 that leads to an international crisis."

In February, Student Mobe had a National Conference on Vietnam at Catholic University. Major leaders were SWP/YSA and CPUSA. The University took photos Max Friedman forwarded to DC Police intelligence. Those photographed at this public meeting were Debby Busten, Maceo Dixon, Jerry Gordon, Helen Gurewitz, Don Gurewitz, Julius Hobson, Tina Hobson, and John Studer.[1174]

Viet Cong Endorses PCPJ. The PCPJ's multiple issues included "Set a date now for complete withdrawal of US military ...[and] set a date for guaranteed annual income for a family of four."[1175] Madame Binh, expressed her appreciation for "this initiative of the American anti-war movement" and wished "the best successes to your spring activities and plans for mass demonstrations in May."[1176]

[1173] FBI, Information Digest special Report.
[1174] Courtesy Max Friedman.
[1175] CIA, Special Information Report, Feb. 17, 1971, TTU archives, 2 cited in Rothrock, 115N63.
[1176] William T. Poole, The Anti-Defense Lobby Part 2: "The Peace Movement, Continued", *Institutional Analysis #11,* September 19, 1979.http://www.heritage.org/Research/GovernmentReform/IA11.cfm

VVAW "We would shoot them [US Senators] all."

During February 1971 after the WSI in Detroit and debriefings in Winsor, Canada, VVAW leaders met in New York at 156 Fifth Ave. sharing offices with PCPJ. VVAW leaders, including John Kerry, Scott Camil, Mike McCusker (Oregon) and others, discussed plans for upcoming Dewey Canyon III protests in April in Washington.

Scott Camil. In an oral history interview Scott Camil remembers, "I put a plan on the floor which caused a ton of disruption. ...We would go into the [Congressional] offices...schedule the most hard-core hawk[s] for last—and we would shoot them all."[1177] Camil told Tom Lipscomb he tried to persuade John Kerry to support his plot.[1178] A Nicosia article in the *Los Angeles Times* reported, Camil "proposed 'taking out' the prominent senators and congressmen who consistently voted in favor of the war."[1179]

Camil reports John Kerry "totally flipped out."[1180] The plan was rejected as merely "impractical."[1181] Still Scott Camil was elevated to a VVAW regional director and the members of VVAW, who had discussed an assassination plot, including John Kerry, did not report these talks to the police and no one

[1177] Scott Swett and Tim Ziegler, *To Set the Record Straight: How the Swift Boat Veterans, POWs and the New Media Defeated John Kerry*, New American Media Publishing, 2008 60n63 cites Scott Camil, interview by Stuart Landers (discovered by Ron Kolb), October 20, 1992, transcript, University of Florida, Oral History Archive.
[1178] Scott Swett and Tim Ziegler, *To Set the Record Straight: How the Swift Boat Veterans, POWs and the New Media Defeated John Kerry*, New American Media Publishing, 2008 61n64 cites Swett Interview with Thomas Lipscomb December 2006.
[1179] Scott Swett and Tim Ziegler, *To Set the Record Straight: How the Swift Boat Veterans, POWs and the New Media Defeated John Kerry*, New American Media Publishing, 2008 61n65 cites Gerald Nicosia "Veteran in Conflict: Sen. John Kerry's Struggle for Leadership of a Vietnam Veteran's Antiwar Group in 1971 Ended with His Resignation at a Stormy Meeting in Kansas City, Where Militants Advocated Violence Against the U.S. Government," *Los Angeles Times*, May 23, 2004, Los Angeles Times magazine, LAT magazine Desk, Pat I, 10.
[1180] Scott Swett and Tim Ziegler, *To Set the Record Straight: How the Swift Boat Veterans, POWs and the New Media Defeated John Kerry*, New American Media Publishing, 2008 60n63 cites Scott Camil, interview by Stuart Landers (discovered by Ron Kolb), October 20, 1992, transcript, University of Florida, Oral History Archive.
[1181] Scott Swett and Tim Ziegler, *To Set the Record Straight: How the Swift Boat Veterans, POWs and the New Media Defeated John Kerry*, New American Media Publishing, 2008 61n65 cites Gerald Nicosia "Veteran in Conflict: Sen. John Kerry's Struggle for Leadership of a Vietnam Veteran's Antiwar Group in 1971 Ended with His Resignation at a Stormy Meeting in Kansas City, Where Militants Advocated Violence Against the U.S. Government," *Los Angeles Times*, May 23, 2004, Los Angeles Times magazine, LAT magazine Desk, Pat I, 10.

resigned from VVAW to object to planning assassinations of
U.S. Senators.[1182]

PCPC Disputes With NPAC

On February 5, 1971 PCPJ sent a memo explaining its
spring action campaign and differences with NPAC. PCPJ
followed Hanoi's lead on propaganda themes and set the date
for unilateral US withdrawal and promote the People's Peace
Treaty.

PCPJ sought unity with NPAC on common dates, but
NPAC had plunged ahead scheduling events on April 24, 1971
and insisting on making Vietnam the single issue and using
peaceful, legal tactics. Militant PCPJ wanted "sustained
nonviolent direct action and civil disobedience."[1183] On the
26th, David Dellinger, advised "using force without violence"
such as tax resistance, sit-ins, and general strikes.[1184]

Hanoi Demands Unity of PCPJ and NPAC

As the wheels of the antiwar movement might have
seemed to be moving off in many wild and uncertain
directions, on February 27, 1971, Hanoi's Ambassador and Paris
negotiator, Xuan Thuy, called for unity within the American antiwar movement and gave specific guidance on propaganda
themes:
..I call upon the progressive American people and all anti-war
organizations in the United States to unite closely, to associate
all forces and strata of the population ... making a wide and
strong movement…to demand an end to [the] war[s] of
aggression in South Vietnam, Laos and Cambodia, to demand
the withdrawal of all American troops from Indochina, and let
the Indochina's people settle their own internal affairs."[1185]

**NPAC/PCPJ, New Found Unity of Purpose and
Schedule.** Responding to Xuan Thuy's prodding on March 2,
1971 the feuding NPAC and PCPJ hastily announced their

[1182] Scott Swett and Tim Ziegler, *To Set the Record Straight: How the Swift Boat
Veterans, POWs and the New Media Defeated John Kerry,* New American Media
Publishing, 2008 61n67 cites Richard Stacewicz, *Winter Soldier: An Oral History of
the Vietnam Veterans Against the War,* New York: Twayne Publishers, 1997, 76.
[1183] PCPJ, memo, to Area Contacts and Potential Contacts, Spring Action Campaign,
February 5, 1971.
[1184] "Dellinger Calls for Peaceful Non-Violent Force in Spring," The *Eagle,* February
26, 1971, 4.
[1185] *Guardian,* March 20, 1971; Cong. Record April 6, 1971; Max P. Friedman, "More
Proof Reds Behind 'Peace, *Manchester Union Leader*, May 8, 1971. Friedman had
infiltrated the antiwar movement.

newfound unity of purpose, co-sponsorship of events not in May, but on April 24, 1971. Echoing her Hanoi masters, on March 6, 1971 NLF's Madame Binh said she "hoped...the Vietnamese and American people...could coordinate their actions...to ending the war and reaching a correct political solution..."[1186] Unity and correct themes became the common public declarations of the leadership of the antiwar movement, Mobe, New Mobe, Spring Mobe and PCPJ. The "Hanoi Lobby" was what undercover agent Max Phillip Friedman called travelers to Hanoi and Paris.

***

Laos: No Sanctuary, No Secrets—Lam Son 719

The Sanctuary. Since soft on communism Averill Harriman and President Kennedy had brokered the "neutralization" of Laos, they created a *de facto* sanctuary for North Vietnamese forces, Hanoi's own "secret" war. The Hanoi occupied Laos at will, constructing roads and barracks and filling supply depots with modern Soviet and Chinese mortars, rockets, and 130 MM artillery all along the Ho Chi Minh Trail. They did so, no longer with their mythical bicycles and legendary coolies, but with thousands of heavy Russian Molotova trucks.[1187]

Laos was "King's X," off limits to allied military attacks upon the Hanoi troops and supplies. During the battles in Laos, Saigon Vietnamese directed US bombing upon concentrations of enemy troops, tanks, artillery and caches of war material wherever they were found.

U.S. Plans. U.S. military plans to occupy and hold strategic parts of the Ho Chi Minh trail with 50,000-60,000 troops were never implemented. In early 1971, President Nixon approved a smaller, 16,000 troops, temporary operation[1188] highly dependent upon secrecy.

Marvin Kalb, Leaks Warn Enemy. On February 2, 1971, Marvin Kalb led the CBS news with a story about an impending South Vietnamese military raid into Laos—a sanctuary, the Ho Chi Minh trail. "The initial objective is said to be the clearing of Highway 9 running east to west...then the

---

[1186] "PRG Paris Delegates confer with U.S. Peace Group," Paris VNA to Hanoi VNA, 0740 GMT, March 8, 1971, 23, TTU cited in Rothrock 171-2N29.

[1187] Bill Laurie, *Godzilla at Khe Sanh: Viet Nam's Enduring Hallucinatory Illusions*, unpublished manuscript to author August 26, 2009.

[1188] Bill Laurie to Mike Benge and others, April 1, 2009.

South Vietnamese are suppose to continue ...towards Sepone (Tchepone)..."

Briefing the press before the invasion, General Abrams embargoed news on the Laos operation as an absolute "imperative for safety and security ...and success... According to Maj. Gen. Nguyen Duy Hinh, "The press seemed to be able to pick up leads ...into news dispatches ...gave every detail ...as of the end of January..."[1189]

Alerting the enemy a week before the operation, Kalb and/or CBS violated General Abram's trust[1190] Hanoi concentrated its usual defenses against an amphibian invasion and/or an air assault above the DMZ. The Kalb and other leaks allowed Hanoi to move all available forces, except one division, into Laos.[1191]

Curiously, super spy Pham Xuan An received a Battle Exploitation Medal, First Class, for delivering the battle plans of South Vietnam for Lam Son 719,[1192] perhaps cheating Marvin Kalb out of his news scoop, Pulitzer, or his own post war Ho Chi Minh medal.

Also forewarned on February 8, 1971, the PCPJ protested Nixon's policy in Laos. Communist Rep. Bella Abzug said an antiwar coalition was forming in Congress to force withdrawal.[1193] Sec. Defense Mel Laird warned of building opposition in Congress.

On the same day as the Washington protest of PCPJ, after leaks on all fronts and several delays in LAMSON 719, Saigon's finally moved into Hanoi's sanctuary in Laos. On February 11 and 18, Madame Binh and Xuan Thuy denounced the raid as an allied extension of the war.

[1189] Maj. Gen. Nguyen Duy Hinh, *LAM SON 719,* Indochina Monographs, U.S. Army Center Of Military History, n. d. 151.
http://www.vlink.com/nlvnch/lamson719/lamson7.html.
[1190] (TS-GP 1) Msg, COMUSMACV 0775 to CJCS and CINPAC, 2400802z Jan 71; (TS-GP 1) Msg, JCS to CINPAC and COMUSMACV 300526z Jan 71; (TS-GP 1) Msg, COMUSMACV 9122 to CINPAC and CJCS 300829z Jan 71.
[1191] Lewis Sorley, *A Better War: The Unexamined Victories and Final Tragedy of America's Last Years in Vietnam*, New York: Harcourt, 1999, 242.
[1192] Thomas A. Bass, *The Spy Who Loved Us: the Vietnam War and Pham Xuan An's Dangerous Game*, New York: Public Affairs, 2009, 6, 217, 278n; Kyle Horst at Texas Tech Vietnam conference in March 2008. TTU video.
[1193] Memo, M.A. Jones to Mr. Bishop, "House Resolution 410; To Authorize the House Committee on Judiciary to Investigate the FBI," May 11, 1971 in FBI, FOIA, Bella Abzug file, USA Survival, http://www.usasurvival.org/ck01.20.11.html

Answering who was invading whom, Laotian Prime Minister Souvanna Phouma said,
Certainly the primary responsibility rests with the Democratic Republic of Vietnam, which scornful of international law… began and continues to violate the neutrality and territorial integrity of the Kingdom of Laos.[1194]

Viet Cong Mobilizes Antiwar Movement. Madame Binh urgently cabled Huey Newton of the Black Panther Party— and many others,
ALERT YOU/ LAOS INVASION WITH TENS OF THOUSANDS U.S. SAIGON, THAI TROOPS/ ACTION INTENSE, US AIR FORCE/URGENTLY CALL ON YOU TO MOBILIZE PEACE FORCE, YOUR COUNTRY CHECK DANGEROUS VENTURE INDOCHINA." [1195]

Huey Newton had previously pledged troops to fight alongside the Viet Cong. Nancy Kurshan, wife of Jerry Rubin remembers, "When the U.S. attacked Laos, we organized a protest demonstration at Kent State." Kurshan spray painted US OUT of Laos. She was allowed to leave town without prosecution.[1196]
Weather Retaliates Bombing U.S. Capitol. To protest the invasion of Laos in early morning of Feb. 28, 1971, the Weather bombed a ground-floor bathroom of the U.S. Capitol. On March 1, 1971, President Nixon called FBI Director Hoover for a report on the explosion at the Capitol, "it sounds like the Weatherman group." On Feb. 28, 1971 the WUO issued communiqué #8 "…We attacked the Capitol because it is…the worldwide symbol to the US domination of the planet. …. It was a "criminal invasion of Laos...US B-52s are dropping the equivalent of Hiroshima every two days…" In disbelief, "…the

[1194] Recording, WIEU, 13 February 1971, ASC, quoting Souvanna's statement cited in Lewis Sorley, *A Better War: The Unexamined Victories and Final Tragedy of America's Last Years in Vietnam*, New York: Harcourt, 1999, 245.
[1195] Telegram at SNCC Papers, Reel 53, Howard University cited in Yohuru Williams, "American exported Black nationalism: The Student Coordinating Committee, the Black Panther Party, and the Worldwide Freedom Struggle, 1967-1972-SNCC," *Negro History Bulletin*, July-Sept 1997; As quoted in Todd L. Newmark, "Theoretical Framework," Vietnam, December 1997, 69 cited in Lewis Sorley, *A Better War: The Unexamined Victories and Final Tragedy of America's Last Years in Vietnam*, New York: Harcourt, 1999, 245-6.
[1196] Nancy Kurshan, "From Tiger Cages to Control Units," *Counterpunch*, November 1-3, 2013.

US claims to be responding to the presence of the North Vietnamese in Laos, to be attacking the Ho Chi Minh trail." Not so. It was really "a direct attack on the people of Laos. …Sixty percent of the Laotian people have been made homeless…."

Parroting the precise lines of the revered dead, Ho Chi Minh, the Weather communiqué claimed America had a war policy of 'kill all, burn all, destroy all."[1197] The Weatherman was never brought up on charges of plagiarism let alone perjury, treason or terrorism.

San Francisco Bomb Factory. In April 1971, the FBI discovered a quickly abandoned WUO bomb factory on Pine Street in San Francisco. Rented for one year in April 1970, Mark Rudd says, "The hurried Weathermen had left behind a lot of important stuff." This included C-4 explosives, concealed shivs in ballpoint pens and voice-activated bomb switches…timed to go off when a victim spoke."[1198]

Among WUO fingerprints found at the bomb factory, including those of Mark Rudd, were Karen Ashley, Bill Ayers, Kathy Boudin, Peter Wales Clapp, John Willard Davis, David Joseph Gilbert, Naomi Esther Jaffe, Michael Thomas Justesen, Howard Machtinger, Julia Nichamin, Jeffrey David Powell, Sheldon Rosenbaum, Michael Louis Spiegel, Lawrence Michael Weiss, Kathlyn Platt Wilkerson. Among those identified using aliases, according to the FBI, were Mark Joseph Real and Clayton Van Lydegraf.[1199]

Actually Van Lydegraf, not an alias, was in his sixties, a life-long Communist purged from the CPUSA and the Maoist People's Labor Party.[1200] The raid gave up WUO aliases, cars and apartments.[1201]

Lam Son 719 Goes Badly for Weeks. Meanwhile, Lam Son 719 went very badly for weeks. Besides the fierce

---

[1197] Copy in FBI, FOIA, Weather Underground. The primary source is Acting SAC Chicago to Director, memo, "Foreign Influence-Weather Underground Organization," August 20, 1976,165-7.

[1198] Peter Jamison, "Time Bomb: Weather Underground leaders claimed their bombings were devised to avoid bloodshed. But FBI agents suspect the radical '70s group killed a S.F. cop in the name of revolution," *SF Weekly*, September 16, 2009.

[1199] FBI, FOIA, Weather Underground. The primary source is Acting SAC Chicago to Director, memo, "Foreign Influence-Weather Underground Organization," August 20, 1976, 196, 201, 384.

[1200] Ron Jacobs, The Way the Wind Blew, Xv.

[1201] Mark Rudd, *Underground: My Life With the SDS and the Weathermen*, New York: Harper Collins, 2009, 239.

and forewarned North Vietnamese defenders, every other thing went wrong. Initial operations were severely hampered by: a dirt track Route 9 with ruts and weather cuts in the road 20 feet deep; key southern commanders and staff killed in helicopter accidents; a timid commander Lt. Gen. Hoang Xuan Lam halting the advance; President Thieu's interference; slow helicopter maintenance; poor communications between units; and defective coordination of infantry, tanks, helicopters, Navy and Air Force aircraft.

Amidst the initial disorder was extraordinary gallantry. Tran Ngoc Hue led a hard fighting 2nd Battalion of the 2nd Regiment of the 1st ARVN out of six enemy encirclements, 26 survived. Tran Ngoc Hue spent 13 years in a North Vietnamese prison.[1202]

Saigon Airlift and Breakout. Beginning on March 3, six Saigon battalions were airlifted out of the stalled offensive into positions close to Tchepone. Survivors of the ARVN 1st Infantry Division and B-52s obliterated massive caches of armaments. U. S. airpower and firefights of ARVN troops inflicted massive casualties on enemy forces losing 16 of its 33 battalions and half of its tanks and artillery.

US intelligence estimated 13,000 of the enemy killed, So. Vietnamese Gen. Nguyen Duy Hinh said 19,360 and the enemy's own tally was 16,224. The operation's preemptive attack stopped a spring offensive and NVA combat operations 1971.[1203] A Polish member of the International Control Commission said the North Vietnamese 'could not hide....'' Its heavy casualties. The French Mission in Hanoi said,
Lam Son 719 had a devastating effect upon the morale of the NVA. ... [This included] "...increased defections....[This] caused the morale of all but the NVA officer corps to disintegrate."

Further,
during the operation the NVA lost the equivalent of 16 of the 33 maneuver battalions ... that's a complete loss of those battalions...at least 75 of some 110 enemy tanks were... destroyed...[1204]

[1202] Andrew Weist, "Vietnam's Forgotton Army," in Joachim Le Tinh Thong, (ed.), *The Missing Pieces in the Vietnam War Puzzle*, the Vietnamese-American Nationalist in Diaspora, Wesminster, April 28, 2010, 153.
[1203] Lewis Sorley, *A Better War: The Unexamined Victories and Final Tragedy of America's Last Years in Vietnam*, New York: Harcourt, 1999, 246-266.

Al Haig and Defense Secretary James Schlesinger thought Lam Son was a big loss. Why was that? Perhaps we know.

ARVN Redux: "Cowards." Despite very heavy enemy casualties in Laos and major destruction of Hanoi's stockpiled war materials and despite ARVN casualties being a fraction of NVA losses, Saigon's early withdrawal with initial heavy casualties was another opportunity to do a rewrite on Neil Sheehan's well-worn Ap Bac template, the cowardice of the ARVN.

A reporter concocted a story of a "rout" of hundreds of healthy South Vietnamese troops swarming helicopters wearing phony bandages to escape fighting. This false story was repeatedly republished. What the reporter believed was cowardice was prudence, ARVN troops covering their cuts with first aid bandages in an infectious jungle. For maximum effect the reporter added to the story a picture, in his mind only, of troops swarming helicopters.

Robert Elegant: "Media sought…the victory of the enemy.' A veteran *LA Times* reporter in Asia, Robert Elegant, investigated the helicopter-swarming story. It never happened.[1205] Elegant, once honored by the Overseas Press Club, would soon be denied publication at his old haunts and be eventually exiled.[1206] The *Times* hired Robert Scheer.

Media Declares Saigon Defeat. No one believed official Saigon casualties of 6,000 ARVN, 19,000 PAVN.[1207] Elegant said, "Never before Vietnam had the collective policy of the media sought…the victory of the enemies of the correspondents' own side."[1208] Ambassador Ellsworth Bunker said the press had a "vested interest in failure."[1209]

[1204] Lewis Sorley, *A Better War: The Unexamined Victories and Final Tragedy of America's Last Years in Vietnam*, New York: Harcourt, 1999, 261-3.

[1205] Robert Elegant, "How to Lose a War: The Press and Vietnam," *Encounter*, (London), vol. LVII, August 1981, 73-9- at Wellesley.edu/Polisci/wj/Vietnam/readings/elegant.htm

[1206] Robert Elegant, "How to Lose a War: The Press and Vietnam," *Encounter*, (London), vol. LVII, August 1981, 73-9n11.at Wellesley.edu/Polisci/wj/Vietnam/readings/elegant.htm

[1207] Maj. Gen. Nguyen Duy Hinh, *LAM SON 719*, Indochina Monographs, U.S. Army Center Of Military History, n. d. 151 http://www.vlink.com/nlvnch/lamson719/lamson7.html.

[1208] Bill Laurie, "Vietnam, the Media and Lies," at http://veteransforacademic freedom.org/2010/01.

[1209] Lewis Sorley, *A Better War: The Unexamined Victories and Final Tragedy of*

Communists Brief antiwar activists. In Vancouver in April 1971 Lao communists told antiwar activists three fourths or 15, 400 of allied troops in Lam Son 719 were killed, wounded or captured, including 200 Americans. In Khe Sanh during this period the communists said the US suffered 4,800 casualties, 100 pilots, 444 tanks and 486 planes including 306 helicopters.[1210]

On April 7, 1971 Nixon announced Saigon's battlefield successes in Laos allowed an American withdrawal of 100,000 troops by November. Casualties were down and the Hanoi had not launched their anticipated spring 1971 offensive despite a buildup of military supplies[1211] now destroyed in Lam Son 719.[1212]

America's Last Years in Vietnam, New York: Harcourt, 1999, 266.
[1210] Kathleen Gough Aberle, "An Indochina Conference in Vancouver," *Bulletin of Concerned Asian Scholars*, Vol. 3, Number 4, (Summer-Fall) 1971.
[1211] Haldeman, *Diaries*… 346.
[1212] General Abrams in Bernard C. Nalty, ed., *Vietnam War: the History of America's Conflict in Southeast Asia, Smithmark Publishers, 1996,* 253 cited in Van Atta, 349.

Chapter 10: The Manipulators: Media, Cora Weiss, Fonda, Hollywood and the People's Peace.

Nixon "Set the Date"

Dismissing demands from Hanoi and US agents, Nixon refused to set a date for total US withdrawal without the enemy's ending the war as well. The next day Madame Binh condemned the President's failure to set a date. Xuan Thuy insisted the date set be June 30, 1971.

With Hanoi's exploitation of American sensitivity, POW welfare and POW releases increasingly became topics for negotiations.

***

Kate Webb, UPI Reporter Captured, Charmed by Vietnamese Troops in Cambodia

On April 7, 1971, Hanoi's troops operating inside Cambodia, captured Australian Kate Webb an intrepid hard drinking, smoking UPI reporter, and five other Asian reporters while driving between Phnom Penh and the deep-water port on the Gulf of Thailand at Sihanoukville.

Reported dead in an obituary in the *New York Times*, she survived 23 days of forced marches, interrogations, and malaria.

Under interrogation, Webb proved her progressive *bona fides* listing references of "especially progressive" journalists. Her *curriculum vita* proved her an internationalist seeing the war as an anti-colonial struggle with "Communism a convenient rationale." Webb was unconvinced Tet was a U.S. military victory. To Webb COSVN, Hanoi's headquarters, controlling the Viet Cong was imaginary.[1213]

In *War Torn*, reviewers say Webb discovers "a humanistic side of the Viet Cong." She tells "a fascinating account of humanity, humor and compassion that is both moving and captivating." Her so human captors gave Webb parachute silk for menstruation. They watched her in her underwear. Soldiers lit her cigarettes. She feared being killed by rescuers[1214] or US bombs, not her captors. Force marched "muddy, leech-ridden and exhausted, but otherwise unharmed."

[1213]Joyce Hoffman, *On Their own: Women Journalists and the American Experience in Vietnam*, Philadelphia: Da Capo Press, 2008, 195-196, 197, 199, 215-6, 222, 227.
[1214] Kate Webb, *On the Other Side: 23 Days with the Viet Cong*, Quadrangle Books,

Though soldiers bound her arms with wire, vine and tape and confiscated notebooks, cameras and watches and forced marched her barefoot on hot asphalt, bamboo splinters and stones, she sympathized with the enemy. "The Viet Cong are human beings. They are soldiers and not much different from soldiers on this side. They ... have sore feet." Comparing scarred feet, there was little difference between soldier and prisoner.

Webb was uncertain why she was released.

After the spring of 1971, captured journalists faced almost certain death. Only three of over two dozen were released. Twenty-five journalists were dead, missing and presumed dead.[1215]

Journalists had many ways to collaborate with the enemy—writing nice stories about Communists, like Katy Webb, and bad stories about U.S. troops, like Kalb and Cronkite.

***

Aiding the Enemy—Kalb, Cronkite, COLIFAM

Cronkite. Following the leaks of the Laos invasion plan by Marvin Kalb, Pham Xuan An and/or an unknown member of Congress, on February 15, 1971, CBS's Walter Cronkite gave Hanoi other useful intelligence. Cronkite revealed that former prisoner of war Lieutenant David Matheny was now training pilots. The Vietnamese said they would release no more POWs. David Dellinger said Hanoi was unhappy with a former POW training pilots.

The baritonic Walter Cronkite intoned authoritatively the Geneva Accords prohibited a repatriated prisoner from returning to active military service. Actually, the Geneva accords prohibited return to combat, which Matheny had not done.[1216] Former POWs Maj. Joe Victor Carpenter and Maj. Fred Neale Thompson also returned to military service at stateside bases. Of course, former POWs George Smith and John Sweeney had joined the other side.

1972.

[1215] Joyce Hoffman, *On Their own: Women Journalists and the American Experience in Vietnam*, Philadelphia: Da Capo Press, 2008, 223.
[1216] Vanderbilt Television News Archive, http://openweb.tvnews.vanderbilt.edu/1971-2/1971-02-15-CBS-6.html

COLIFAM: **Cora to POW Families: Set the Date.** As the "Winter Soldier" fest was concluding, on February 24, 1971 Cora Weiss told POW families again setting the date for U.S. withdrawal would insure release of POW releases. Premier Pham Van Dong had told her so in an interview. Weiss said she could do nothing about prisoners in Laos or South Vietnam since "neither are under the ...control of Hanoi." COSVN, NLF, PRG, Pathet Lao?

Cora Weiss: U.S. Actions Stop POW Mail.
"Escalated war has curtailed travel (and mail) a bit,"[1217] she told POW families. She blamed a reduction in POW mail on "heavy bombing raids over Laos ...The absence of regular travel means the absence of regular mail."[1218]

Some families, side stepping Cora, used USPS or the Red Cross and received the same or a greater number of letters from POWs. During COLIFAM's existence, the Red Cross delivered more mail to Hanoi than COLIFAM, but the actual POW receipt of letters is unknown.

Meanwhile invigorated by the Winter Soldier claims of War Crimes, Jane Fonda becomes still more revolutionary, or dare we say Communist?

***

Fonda, a Revolutionary Woman February 1971.
"I would pick up a gun." In the February issue of *McCall's*, Italian reporter Oriana Fallaci interviewed Fonda. Her answers ranged from the silly to deadly.
And please, Oriana, should I die tomorrow, please tell them...that I was serious. I am sure I am ready to risk my life ... should the need to fight arise... And I would pick up a gun, no matter how scared I was.[1219]

Executions of Hated Americans?
Fonda Spares Agnew From Execution. Post Winter Soldier, the CIA opened the foreign mail of citizens in the Detroit area suspected in an alleged plot to assassinate CIA director Richard Helms and Vice President Spiro Agnew. The CIA also kept watch on a foreign national, a Latin American, "Miss King.[1220]

[1217] Cora Weiss to Dear..., COLIFAM, February 24, 1971, 1-2.
[1218] Cora Weiss to Dear families, COLIFAM, March 15, 1971.
[1219] Fallaci, February 1971, 123, 141.
[1220] CIA, FOIA, Family Jewels, 26. See also: Karen DeYoung and Walter Pincus, "CIA will air decades of its dirty laundry: Documents include details of spying, assassination

In February Jane Fonda reassured her enemy, conservative Vice President, Spiro Agnew, come the revolution his life would be safe in her hands.

I feel pity for him… He grew up in a society that is predicated on hate and war. ... If an international court of law ever tried him as a war criminal, I would not like to see him executed. He might be salvageable. It's the American myth that must be destroyed, not its victims."[1221]

Fonda, a Black Panther financier, Jane did not join the audience cheering a Black Panther for saying, "We will kill Nixon."[1222]

Hate America, Forbidding Speech. Like Fonda and VC directives, Richard Barnet of the pro-Hanoi Institute for Policy Studies wrote, "There is much to hate about America and nothing so much as American militarism from which so many other evils flow." All Americans in Vietnam committed war crimes and ought to be forbidden to "preach or advocate" the use of military force against any [Soviet backed] "national liberation movement."[1223]

It was an Orwellian factoid that so much hate proclaimed itself peace and love and that those with long careers of hate were celebrated for their humanity. Che, Mao, Castro.

Jane Fonda Goes Stalinist
Wilfred Burchett Birthday Party. In April 1971, Fonda joined a long list[1224] of hard-core leftists, public and identified Communists and joiners of front organizations and causes sponsoring the Wilfred Burchett Sixtieth Birthday. The

---

attempts," June 23, 2007.

[1221] Fallaci, February 1971, 152.

[1222] William Good "CUPPP: Active Fund-Raiser for Black Panthers,"

[1223] *Information Digest*, Vol. XIII, #6, March 21, 1980, 88, 94 cites a Barnet essay in *Washington Plans an Aggressive War and his 1972 book, The Roots of War.*

[1224] Ad, "The Wilfred Burchett 60th Birthday Committee," *Guardian* February 27, 1971, 9. Among the other sponsors were many publicly acknowledged or identified Communist Party members, antiwar activists and travelers to Hanoi. Norma Becker, Barbara Bick, Allan Brick, Noam Chomsky, Mary Clarke, Carl Davidson, Rennie Davis, Dave Dellinger, Richard Fernandez, Jim Forest, Carlton Goodlett, Robert Greenblatt, Gus Hall, Terrance Hallinan, Dorothy Healy, Al Hubbard, David Ifshin, William Kunstler, Sylvia Kushner, Corliss Lamont, Mark Lane, Howard Levy, Brad Lyttle, KGB funded soviet agent and publisher Carl Marzani, Stewart Meacham, William Moyers, ,Grace Paley, Sidney Peck, Orville Schell, Pete Seeger, Stanley Sheinbaum, Jack D. Spiegel, Benjamin Spock, I.F, Stone, Paul Sweezy, Amy Swerdlow, Ethel Taylor, Cora Weiss, Dagmar Wilson, Dr. Quinton Young, Trudi Young, Howard Zinn.

reporter worked for the Soviet secret police, the KGB. The celebration was nearly two years after Soviet defector Yuri Krotkov said he was Burchett's KGB control. [1225]

By the spring of 1971, having aligned herself with Stalinists, Angela Davis, Wilfred Burchett and the CPUSA, Jane Fonda denouncing other radicals as "Trotskyite."[1226] As for mere liberals she said: "I'm not a do-gooder. I'm a revolutionary, a revolutionary woman."[1227]

While shooting "Steelyard Blues" in Berkeley, Jane said it was "a film which says stealing is not theft, property is theft."[1228] Fonda expropriated, stole, $100,000 out of the salaries of cast and crew of "Steelyard Blues" and donated it to the peace movement.[1229]

Many claimed opposing the imperial USA gave them the high moral ground to kill war criminals in high office.

***

Paris--Citizens Conference on
Ending the War in Indochina, Paris.

On March 3-10, 1971 American Friends Service Committee (Stewart Meacham), Clergy and Laymen Concerned (Richard Fernandez) and the Fellowship of Reconciliation (Allan Brick) sponsored 170 Americans for a weeklong Citizens Conference on Ending the War in Indochina at the Hotel Garnier and the Modern Palace Hotel in Paris.[1230] Rev. Richard McCollum and Mrs. Jane Whitney represented the Syracuse Peace Council.[1231] Elaine Schmitt Urbain, CALC founder and supporter of Daniel Berrigan, came from Westchester.[1232] Bud Ogle, student leader at University of Virginia, represented Charlottesville chapter of CALC.[1233] Rev.

[1225] William T. Poole, "Campaign For Economic Democracy: Part I, The New Left in Politics," Institutional Analysis, No. 13, The Heritage Foundation, Washington, D.C., September 1980,

[1226] Bo Burlingham, "Politics under the Palms, *Esquire*, February, 1977, 118.

[1227] Philip Abbott Luce, (Orange County, Ca.) *Register*, (1979), G8; Jeffery Klein, *Mother Jones*, February/March, 1980, 42.

[1228] Frock, 52.

[1229] Emphases mine, Fallaci, 148.

[1230] FBI, Memo, "Travel of U.S. Citizens to Paris, France, sponsored by Clergy and Laymen Concerned About Vietnam, American Friends Service Committee, and Fellowship of Reconciliation, March 3-10, 1971," March 23, 1971 File No. 100-11392 at FBI, FOIA, A, AFSC.

[1231] "Paris for Peace," Peace Newsletter, Syracuse Peace Council, February 1971 SPC 657, 1.

[1232] "The Rupert Schmitt Family," at www.bmcproject.org/Biographies/aaTDownload/SCVHMITTurbainElaineBIO/Schmit

Bruce Pierce came from Michigan with nine others. Harriet Price, a member of AFSC came from Hancock County, Maine.[1234]

Graduate student in history and Presbyterian minister Arthur "Bud" Ogle condemned the American people for being "Good Germans' …(despite) destruction …equal to the ravages of Hitler."[1235] Allan Brick met Dai Dong, the Vietnamese name of a French Communist and an indoctrinator of French POWs, Georges Boudarel, who former French POWs accused of crimes.Prof. Shawn McHale of George Washington University said Boudarel/Dong was "part and parcel" of "horrendous" implementation of *dich van*, proselytizing French POWs. Dai Dong/Georges Boudarel was not prosecuted.[1236] He regretted his treatment of POWs advising others to read Solzhenitsyn's *Gulag Archipelago* before visiting Vietnam.[1237]

The clerically sponsored Americans met with representatives of the Hanoi, PRG, NLF, the National United Front of Cambodia, the Laotian Student Union and "various South Vietnamese groups opposed to the war (…Buddhists, Catholics, students, and…dissident members of the…National Assembly)." Among the Vietnamese were Xuan Thuy, negotiator and Madame Nguyen Thi Binh (neither sat down), Thich Nhat Hanh, Pere Thi, Le Trang, Venerable Chau.

Only 12 out of the 170 attended a short symbolic meeting with U.S. Ambassador, David K. E. Bruce, U.S. negotiator in Paris.[1238]

In contrast the Hanoi approved group spent a full seven days with the enemy wanting to "set the date" for U.S. withdrawal and promising a coalition government without Thieu or Ky. "Our theme …was what is essential for peace? …[T]he answers were an American ceasefire and

---

[1233] *The Cavalier Daily*, February 25 and March 19, 1971.

[1234] Guide to Harriet Price Papers," Folger Library, Special Collection, University of Maine.

[1235] *The Cavalier Daily*, February 25 and March 19, 1971 from Ellen Cousins.

[1236] "Dai Dong meeting in Paris," Fellowship of Reconciliation-USA, DG 013, Section II, Series C, Executive Secretaries/Directors, Swarthmore Peace Collection. At the time a Georges Boudarel taught Vietnamese History in Paris. Former French POWs remembered him as Dai Dong, an indoctrinator who allowed prisoners to starve to death. In 1991 some sought to charge him with crimes against Humanity. See: Alan Riding, "Paris Journal; Vietnam Echo Stuns France: Case of Treachery?" THE NEW YORK TIMES, March 20, 1991.

[1237] McHale to Vietnam Studies group, 6 January 2004 at www.lib.washington.edu/SouthEastAsia/vsg/elist_2004/georges%20 boudarel.html

[1238] "Bring the GIs Home Message from Paris," *Courier-Post* (Camden), undated (mid-March 1971) in FBI, FOIA, "A", AFSC.

withdrawal..."[1239] About 150 out the 170 Americans signed a telegram to President Nixon asking him to set a date for U.S. withdrawal and to stop all support of Saigon.[1240] Surrender Now.

"Indochina Specialists." The attending journalists, all "Indochina Specialists," were Wilfred Burchett, Serge Thion, Jacques Decornoy, Madeleine Riffaud and Jean Lacourture.[1241] The "Indochina Specialist" group were accomplished conduits for Hanoi's propaganda. **Jean Lacouture** was a biographer of Ho Chi Minh and an expert on Cambodia. **Madeleine Riffaud**, the French Communist Party's reporter,[1242] calling herself Sister Tam, lived among the Viet Cong[1243] during the war and was a highly decorated hero of the North Vietnamese government.[1244] **Serge Thion,** a French sociologist and a sympathetic student of the brutal Cambodian Revolution, would become a Cambodian holocaust denier.[1245] *Le Monde's* **Jacques Decornoy** lived among the Pathet Lao communist guerrillas, reported U.S. bombing of "innocents" in Laos, but wrote nothing about why the US bombed Laos. Hanoi's troops and supplies destined for Saigon.

Safe Passage in Journalist Kill Zones, Laos and Cambodia. Jacques Decornoy traveled to the battlefields of Laos[1246] where other reporters were executed. Precisely during the months of April and May 1971 the guerrillas of Khieu Samphan in Cambodian clubed to death seventeen journalists.[1247]

[1239] "Bring the GIs Home Message from Paris," *Courier-Post* (Camden), undated (mid-March 1971) in FBI, FOIA, "A", AFSC.

[1240] "Returning Pair See No Progress in Visit to Paris Peace Talks", News clip Bethlehem, Pennsylvania, undated (mid-March 1971) in FBI, FOIA, "A", AFSC.

[1241] "Bring the GIs Home Message from Paris," *Courier-Post* (Camden), undated (mid-March 1971) in FBI, FOIA, "A", AFSC.

[1242] Ly Van Sau (Trans. Hoang Quan), "New battlefield" in Paris (Part 1)," *Vietmaz*, JANUARY 25, 2013 http://www.vietmaz.com/2013/01/new-battlefield-in-paris-part-1/

[1243] Madeleine Riffaud, *Dans les maquis, 'Viet Cong,"* Paris: Julliard, 1965.

[1244] "Veteran French journalist presented with Viet Nam's Friendship Order, " Ministry of Foreign Affairs, Government of Vietnam. August 24, 2012.
http://www.vietnamembassy-mexico.org/vnemb.vn/tin_hddn/ns050826155858

[1245] Serge Thion, "Letter to the Signatories,' *Phnom Penh Post*, october2-November 2, 1995, 89. abbc.net/totus/CGCF/file23thion.html.

[1246] Jacques Decornoy, "Life in the Pathet Lao Liberated Zone," in Nina Adams and Alfred McCoy (eds.), *Laos: War and Revolution*, New York: Evanston and London: Harper Colophon books, 1970, 411-423; Noam Chomsky cites Decornoy in July [3, 7-8], 1968 issues of *Le Monde* in Chomsky's letter, "Cambodia," in June 4, 1970 issue of the New York Review of Books. At nybooks.com/articles/10923.

[1247] Jean Lacouture, "The Revolution that Destroyed Itself," *Encounter*, May 1979 in Robert Elegant, "How to Lose a War: The Press and Vietnam," *Encounter*, (London), vol. LVII, August 1981, 73-9- at

None of the approved "Indochina Specialists," Decornoy, Thion, Riffaud, Lacouture, met such fates in the same neighborhoods.

Civilian Kill Zones, Cambodia. During May, according to Reuters, the Viet Cong cut throats, disemboweled and buried 200 villagers on Route 3 between Phnom Penh and the port of Kampot for refusing to dig ditches big enough across a road to slow Cambodian .[1248] In September, outside of Phnom Penn, the Communists executed another 300 for joining in an anti-Viet Cong rally.[1249]

Singalong Among Fraternal Comrades. The conference ended in passionate moments of among fraternal comrades. **Songfest.** At a Hanoi reception folk singer Judy Collins sang a French song, a Vietnamese girl sang a love song, llides Christopher sang the black national anthem and all joined in singing "We Shall Overcome." The happy event closed with singing the Vietnamese national anthem.[1250] Rev. William T. Gramley said, "I wish Americans could hear such songs. ...." Overall, "there was laughter, tears, and friendly embraces." Dancing with the Devil.

Upon his return to Bethlehem, Pennsylvania the Rev. William T. Gramley declared POWs were being treated humanely [1251] and spoke of love and friendship. "[O]ur desire to love others and to be loved by them…grassroots friendship."[1252] Mrs. Allides Christopher wanted to "bring about a cessation of this war so that our brothers can stay here in (the) fight against oppression in America."[1253]

Jane Fonda, Mark Lane, and VVAW member Michael Hunter met Madame Binh privately in Paris. Also Gabriel Kolko.

Kolko: "Deeply Rewarding Meetings." Hanoi vetted others had great access. Professor Gabriel Kolko remembers, "I had continuous, intensive, and deeply rewarding meetings

Wellesley.edu/Polisci/wj/Vietnam/readings/elegant.htm
[1248] "Murder of 200 by Reds Reported in Cambodia," Washington Star, May 30, 1971
[1249] "Cambodia Says Reds Executed 300 Villagers," Washington Star, Oct. 15, 1971.
[1250] William Gramley, "North Vietnamese Reception High Point of Paris Trip," *Globe-Times*, N.D. (mid-March 1971) in FBI, FOIA, A, AFSC.
[1251] "Returning Pair See No Progress in Visit to Paris Peace Talks, News clip Bethlehem, Pennsylvania, undated (mid-March 1971) in FBI, FOIA, "A", AFSC.
[1252] William Gramley, "North Vietnamese Reception High Point of Paris Trip," Globe-Times, N.D. (mid-March 1971)
[1253] "Bring the GIs Home Message from Paris," *Courier-Post* (Camden), undated (mid-March 1971) in FBI, FOIA, "A", AFSC.

('frequent discussions') with National Liberation Front and North Vietnamese personnel working in Europe."[1254] Jay Veith reports a translated cable "...circa late 1974 [saying] they were being supplied by Gabriel Kolko with congressional testimony."[1255] Espionage if classified secret.

Abbie Hoffman Late to Paris. Abbie Hoffman, a convicted Chicago conspirator and his wife Anita Susan Kushner met David Dellinger JFK Airport, perhaps for a briefing or to deliver a message to the Vietnamese before flying on American Airlines 114 to Paris on March 18. The Hoffmans had arrived too late for the official Paris conference with the Vietnamese. It had taken an Appeals Court approval to travel out of country under the pretext of Abbie Hoffman meeting his French publishers, M. Mario Machueck and Robert Laffont.[1256] The Hoffmans met privately with the Vietnamese, Anita for the third time since meetings in Stockholm and Hanoi. Madam Binh had tea with the Hoffmans, refused to be recorded, but gave Abbie Hoffman a ring made from the metal of an American plane shot down over Vietnam. Speaking of his meetings in Paris, at University of Oklahoma on April 28, 1971 Hoffman urged support for the People's Peace treaty, Mayday Tribe demonstrations in Washington, U.S. troop rebellions and sending recorded tapes to Radio Hanoi --like those of John Lennon and Yoko Ono.

Hoffman said, "The only dope worth shooting was Richard Nixon."[1257]

WPAX. On March 1, 1971 Hoffman wrote Mathew Rinaldi of the U.S. Servicemen Fund, about his plans for radio WPAX to beam radio to U.S. troops in Southeast Asia. "Jane Fonda will personally be bringing the first week's show to

---

[1254] Gabriel Kolko, *Vietnam; Anatomy of a Peace*, London: Routledge, 1997, 15.
[1255] Jay Veith to author, July 12, 2011; Incoming cable from Vo Van Sung (Paris) to Nguyen Co Thach (Hanoi) 25 December 1974, Volume 187, Archives Office, Foreign Ministry in *Major Events: The Diplomatic Struggle and International Activities During the Resistance War Against the Americans to Save the Nation, 1954-1975*, For internal Distribution only, Ministry of Foreign Affairs, Hanoi, 1987, 436.
[1256] FBI, FOIA, Abbot Howard Hoffman, Director FBI to Legat Paris, 3/19/71.
[1257] FBI, FOIA, Abbot Howard Hoffman, [redacted] Washington memo and transcript of Hoffman speech at University of Oklahoma, April 9, 1971, 10; FBI, FOIA, Abbot Howard Hoffman, Teletype, Oklahoma City to Director FBI, David Tyre Dellinger, AKA, ET Al (Travel of defendants), 4-29-71, 2; AP, STILLWATER, "Hoffman Says Antiwar Drive at Critical Point," April [29 or 30], 1971; FBI, FOIA, Abbot Howard Hoffman, Chicago, LHM, Transcript of Abbie and Anita on "Howard Miller's Chicago" TV show, May 19, 1971; FBI, FOIA, Abbot Howard Hoffman, Report of [redacted] New York, 6/22/71.

North Vietnam on March 15."[1258] The VVAW later sold eight cassette tapes and a bound transcript of conversations with the Vietnamese for $45.[1259]

***

Fonda Fulminates: London, Fort Bragg

In London, after private meetings in Paris, believing the crudest Hanoi propaganda, Jane Fonda described America atrocities "applying electrodes to genitals, mass rape, slicing off body parts, scalping, skinning alive..."[1260] In Fayetteville near Fort Bragg, North Carolina March 13-14, Fonda led show funding USSF, a financing sponsor of Winter Soldier headlining Dick Gregory, Peter Boyle, Elliot Gould, Barbara Dane, Donald Sutherland and Swamp Dogg.[1261]

On March 17, 1971, according to an FBI source, "The North Vietnamese in Moscow bought a plane ticket for Fonda to travel to and from the United States to Moscow and Hanoi ...though the trip was discontinued as all visas to North Vietnam were later cancelled."[1262]

***

Fonda's Hollywood comrades. Entertainment Industry for Peace and Justice

In planning for Hollywood celebrations of May Day 1971 Jane Fonda, Shirley and Donald Sutherland formed the Entertainment Industry for Peace and Justice, EIPJ,[1263] in March 1971.

Other EIPJ activists were Barbara Bain, Dick Benjamin, Peter Boyle, Gower Champion, Tyne Daly, Gordon Davidson, Cass Elliott, Ruthie Gorton, Lou Gosset, Dick Gregory, Burt Lancaster, Dalton Trumbo, Don Johnson, Martin Landau, Sue Lyon, France Nguyen, Phil Ochs, Suni Paz, Paula Prentice, Bert Schneider, George Takei, Marlo Thomas, Tuesday Weld, Rev. Cecil Williams, Jon Voight.

[1258] Exhibit 2, U.S. House, Internal Security Committee, *Investigation of Attempts to Subvert the United Sates Armed Services,* cited in *The Pink Sheet,* October 29, 1973, 3.
[1259] *National VVAW News,* n.d. 1971.
[1260] Christopher Andersen, *Citizen Jane,* London: Virgin Books, 1990, 241. Also Scott Swett and Tim Ziegler, *To Set the Record Straight: How Swift Boat Veterans, POWs and the New Media Defeated John Kerry,* New American Media 2008, 8.; "Timeline," *Wintersoldier.com* May 21, 2005, 10 at www.wintersoldier.com cited in Rothrock p. 126N83.
[1261] Flyer reproduced at www.quakerhouse.og/QH%20Exhibit/panel5.htm.
[1262] Jack Anderson, column, May 11, 1972 cited in *The Pink Sheet,* October 29, 1973, 3.
[1263] Contemporary flyer announcing event in possession of author.

Sponsors of a mid-April fundraiser for EIPJ at the home of director Richard Quine were Karen Black, James Earl Jones, Jack Nicholson, Richie Havens, Michelle Phillips, Tom Smothers, Elliott Gould, Jon Voight, as well as Fonda and Donald Sutherland. Attendees were Burt Lancaster, Mama Cass Elliot, Ryan O'Neal, Quincy Jones.

Donald Sutherland introduced film excerpts of "Winter Soldier," premiered at Cannes and at the Whitney Museum in New York, focusing on VVAW claim war crimes were American policy. Lancaster read a statement from Daniel Berrigan and introduced Fonda who described EIPJ as part of a broad coalition for peace and justice. Fonda said the talents and resources of EIPJ would help the movement with TV commercials, a telethon, fundraisers, shows, speakers, pamphlets, documentaries etc. Fonda claimed 1,100 members of EIPJ.[1264]

Fonda's EIPJ printed up flyers for an event on May 23, 1970 at the Hollywood Bowl, (rescheduled from May 2), called "Acting in Concert to End Genocide and Repression." Fonda, the Sutherlands and others spent too much of their time in self-criticism and consciousness-raising. Lacking adequate planning, the May EIPJ event seemed to be moving toward a certain disaster.

Fonda and her flaky friends were saved by the timely intervention of the liberal Democrats they hated. The Los Angeles City Council threatened to deny their event the use of the Hollywood Bowl. Saved by the gavel, the event faded away. At one EIPJ meeting in June, Jane said, "What is needed is victory for the Viet Cong."[1265]

Years later Jon Voight said, he "was surrounded by people were heavily programed Marxists…very, very deep."[1266] There was "Marxist propaganda underlying the so-called peace movement." He said, "I didn't even realize it at the time…the communists were behind organizing all of these rallies and things."[1267]

Pathetically Passionate at Pierce College. On March 31, 1971, speaking at Pierce College in Woodland Hills

---

[1264] Kathy Orloff, "From Movies to Music: Show Biz Attacks the War," Chicago Sun-Times Service, April 21, 1971.

[1265] Copy of EIPJ flyer in possession of author. See: Bo Burlingham, *Esquire,* 1977.

[1266] Glenn Beck show, Fox News, June 11, 2009.

[1267] Jon Voight, op ed. *Washington Times,* July 28, 2008, http://www.washingtontimes.com/news/2008/jul/28/voight/

California, Fonda believed the worst about her country, "exterminating an entire population" in Vietnam and "violating every single...war crime." U.S. POWs were "treated more humanely" than Korean and Japanese POWs in past wars. She compared the brig at Camp Pendleton with the "tiger cages" in Vietnam. She said the American imperialism in Vietnam was the same as the American occupation of California and Texas, "a history of racism and genocide." American society needed to be restructured to remove "racism and sexism and poverty." She said "everyone in jail is a political prisoner." She claimed soldiers were in mutiny in Vietnam, deserting and fragging their officers. "I ...met...soldiers who have said they killed more officers than they have Vietnamese people." She closed urging her student audience to read KGB agent Wilfred Burchett's book *Vietnam Will Win.*[1268]

***

Fonda's Pacific Tour of Military Bases, March-April 1971.

F--- the Army. In late March 1971 Jane began a month-long F--- the Army, FTA, tour of the Pacific making 21 appearances before 64,000 servicemen at bases in Hawaii, the Philippines and Okinawa. Mixing readings, songs and skits FTA was "political vaudeville"[1269] with deadly dialogue. The military's basic training sought was "to strip away...the human being, ...to follow orders, [such as] ...peel skin off live Vietnamese women..."[1270] according to Jane Fonda. FTA women sang "Tired of Bastards F---king Over Me" doing a farcical can-can and claiming women WACs had to "service the servicemen." Playing the race card, an FTA film actor said, "the only place a black man should fight is where he's being oppressed, and I'm not being oppressed in Vietnam... I'd go to jail first."[1271] FTA's readings from Communist Dalton Trumbo's "Johnnie Get Your Gun" said no war was worth fighting. Donald Sutherland did mock play-by-play descriptions of the battlefield as a sports event.

[1268] Jane Fonda, Speech at Pierce College, March 31, 1971 taped for replay on KPFK radio.
[1269] Burlingham, *Esquire*, February 1977, 118; *Time* January 3, 1972.
[1270] *Ramparts*, May 1972, 32.
[1271] *Ramparts*, May 1972, 32.

Jane said, "We must oppose …those blue-eyed, murderers - Nixon, Laird and …ethnocentric American white male chauvinists."[1272]

Vivian Gornick of the *Village Voice* wrote, "As the month progressed…the FTA was surrounded, wherever it went, by agents of the CID, the OSI, the CIA, the local police, the various national investigating agencies of the countries it visited." It was a "miracle of frightened attention…from the U.S. military . . . Men were confined to base, 'riot conditions' were declared, GIs were photographed." Fonda joked about soldiers "fragging," murdering their officers. An obscenities spewing Fonda was "seemingly enjoying herself." And "Fonda maintained that even her disapproving father was moved to tears when he saw the film…the Pentagon couldn't stop!" On July 14, the FTA stopped.[1273]

The FTA had faced considerable. Saigon denied FTA venues and visas. One American General said, the FTA show was "detrimental to discipline and morale."[1274] Sometimes a third of the GIs walked out.

Most of South Vietnam's hamlets preferred Fonda's demons, "blue-eyed, murderers - Nixon, Laird and …ethnocentric American white male chauvinists," over the VC alternatives.

***

Duc Duc: A Story Seldom Told—March 1971

On March 31, 1971, Walter Cronkite intoned that Saigon was "claiming," implying something was surely questionable, the VC had attacked Duc Duc, South Vietnam, killing 200 civilians. Three days later on April 2nd CBS film showed villagers digging through rubble, reported 107 dead and 135 medically evacuated. CBS film had villagers saying Saigon had not protected them, but not saying from whom they needed protection. The Viet Cong killed women and children. **Many… died of suffocation as the flames sucked oxygen…."** The *Stars and Stripes* staff reporter on the mass murder scene in Duc Duc, Spec 4 Dan Evans, gave a less nuanced report of more than 300 killed and 2,000 homeless as

---

[1272] *Time*, January 3, 1972, 71.
[1273] J. Hoberman, "G.I. Jane A Hollywood Daughter's Radical Past Winds up on the Cutting Room Floor," *The Village Voice,* May 2 - 8, 2001 at http://www.villagevoice.com/news/0118,hoberman,24337,1.html
[1274] *New Republic*, March 13, 1971.

a result of a "Monday night systematic smashing and burning" at 2:30 am.[1275] Another AP and *Stars and Stripes* story attributed 200 deaths to the Viet Cong "blasting houses and setting fires...Huge areas were leveled by raging fires, and many... died of suffocation as the flames sucked oxygen...." As the Viet Cong retreated its "killing and burning" destroyed 1,500 homes.

Duc Duc v. My Lai. Major Franklin Trapnell, an eyewitness to Duc Duc, heard news of the conviction of William Calley for the massacre at My Lai simultaneously with the horrors of Duc Duc. Trapnell noted more innocent civilians were massacred at Duc Duc than at My Lai and for no reason whatsoever. Jack Cunningham's research of the Vanderbilt Television archives revealed Duc Duc in six stories and My Lai in 602 stories.[1276] My Lai casualties were less, but the TV coverage was 100 times greater than Duc Duc. It reminded Uwe Siemon-Netto of an American TV crew disinterested in filming a mass grave at Hue, we are "not here to spread anti-Communist propaganda."[1277]

For every William Calley at My Lai there were scores more like Lance Corporal William R. Prom, Hospital Corpsman Second Class David Robert Ray and Combat Engineer Jimmy Wayne Phipps. All gave their lives in a series of battles defending the people of Duc Duc (Phu Da) and other hamlets in the An Hoa valley. These under reported soldiers were recipients of the Congressional Medal of Honor for their selfless service. They symbolized the honor of most Vietnam veterans. William Calley represented very few in the US military.

Vinh Binh. As the residents of Duc Duc were being burned alive, communist mortars and sappers were killing 28 more civilians, including 16 children, five women. in Vinh Binh province. Still another 15 were killed and 22 wounded when terrorists threw grenades into a private gathering. In 34 separate contemporary incidents 67 civilians were killed, 87 civilians wounded and 30 kidnapped.[1278] Such Viet Cong terrorism was commonplace, therefore not news.

[1275] Spec 4 Dan Evans, "2,000 Left Homeless by NVA Terror Attack," *Stars and Stripe,* April 1, 1970 copy at http://home.earthlink.net/~duc_duc_massacre/.
[1276] http://home.earthlink.net/~duc_duc_massacre/
[1277] Uwe Siemon-Netto, *DUC: A Reporter's Love for a Wounded People, Amazon,* 2013, 232.

John Kerry on My Lai. On April 1, 1971, Lt. John Kerry, USN (reserve), back from Vietnam after three months service with three Purple Hearts, a Bronze Star, and Silver Star, spoke to a VVAW crowd on Wall Street. Kerry said convicting William Calley for My Lai massacre was "scapegoating one man" when "the real guilty party is the United States of America."[1279] Kerry, like Hanoi, mentioned neither the current massacre at Duc Duc nor the selflessness of Americans dying protecting rather than butchering peasants. "The real guilty party" was the communist policy of terror. Lenin in *Novaia Zhizn,* 14 July 1918, "Terror is an absolute necessity during times of revolution."

Hanoi's bald faced line was "if the American people only knew …, Americans would demand an end to atrocities and the war."[1280]

Hanoi was operating in Vancouver.

***

Vietnamese Meet to Unify Divided American Women, Vancouver and Toronto April 1971.

April 1-6, 1971, six Indochinese women met 600-1,000 Americans women in Canada for two conferences, the Conference of Indochinese and North American Women, CINAW in Vancouver and an April 9-11 a "sister" conference, the Indochinese Women's Conferences, IWC, held in Toronto.

Muriel Duckworth of Voice of Women, WILPF, and WSP organized the CINAW conference.[1281] In Vancouver student groups[1282] loaned rooms free of charge and "helped to finance the conference."

Indochinese Communists were Vo Thi The, Women's Union of the Democratic Republic of Vietnam, a professor of

---

[1278] "NVA Burn Viet Town: NVA Terrorists Turn Town Into 'Ashtray,'" AP and Stars and Stripes, April 1, 1971 copy at http://home.earthlink.net/ ~duc_duc_massacre/

[1279] Michael T. Kaufman, "U.S. Veterans of Vietnam War Rally on Wall Street for Peace," *NY Times*, April 2, 1971.

[1280] "Impressions from the Conference of Indochinese and North American Women, April 1971, Sponsored by Voice of Women, WILPF, WSP," *Memo*, 2:1 (Fall; 1971), 16.

[1281] Muriel Duckworth, "Impressions from the Conference of Indochinese and North American Women April 1971, Sponsored by Voice of Women, WILPF, WSP," *MEMO*, 2, No.1, Fall 1971, 16.

[1282] University of British Columbia, Student Union Student Unions of Simon Fraser University and Vancouver City College.

Vietnamese literature and history; Nguyen Thi Xiem, Institute for the Protection of Mothers and Newborn Babies, a medical researcher and obstetrician. Representing the Women's Union of South Vietnam were Phan Minh Hien, a teacher, and Dinh Thi Huong, housewife. From Laos were two members of the Executive Committee of the Lao Women's Union, teachers Khampheng Boupha and Khemphet Pholsena. Three interpreters were Nguyen Tri, a professor of French at the University of Hanoi, Trinh Van Anh, South Vietnam, and Souban Srithirath from Laos.

American War Crimes. Nguyen Thi Xiem, representing the Institute for the Protection of Mothers and New Born Babies, claimed "women's uteruses, bowels and urinary tracts were perforated by pellet bombs causing miscarriages." She declared the superiority of Hanoi's health care. Hanoi medicine was preventing small pox, polio and other diseases still found in South Vietnam. Dinh Thi Huong claimed 800 "tiger" caged prisoners died at Con Son in 1971.

The 600 conference women were so wildly divided by race, sexuality and nationality they split the first the six days into three separate conferences: April 1-2 for the (Canadian) Voice of Women, VOW, WILPF, and WSP. About 300 Third World delegates (Black, Chicano, Asian, Native American and Canadians) met April 3-4; Women's Liberation groups met April 5-6.

The identified "old (WSP) friends" of the Vietnamese from meetings in 1965 and 1968 in Jakarta and Paris were Shirley Lens, Mary Clarke, Cora Weiss, Beula Sanders, and Amy Swerdlow of WSP and others. The "new friends" were "many strains of feminism: maternal, equal rights, socialist, radical lesbian, third world, and women of color globally oriented, anti-war, or anti-imperialist perspectives among feminists…"[1283] Carol Anne Douglas and Fran Moira were among this women's liberation group.[1284] They were active in Off Our Backs. The lesbians in the Women's Liberation group held flags "OUT NOW" for both men and the war.

Revolutionary Women. The Indochinese women disagreed, "We are suppressed not by men but by the system.

[1283] Karin Aguilar-San Juan review of Judy Tzu-Chun Wu, *"Radicals on the Road" In the Vietnam War Era, diacritics, Jun 9, 2014,* http://diacritics.org/?p=23511
[1284] Carol Anne Douglas and Fran Moira, *The Guardian,* New York, April 17, xxx, 5, Critical Asian Studies .org/bcas/back_issueshtml?page=1

[W]e … relate men in our struggles. … together we can be successful." Vietnamese women were "working anti-aircraft machinery while still being mothers… for the sake of themselves, their families and their nation." Women made real sacrifices. Vo Thi The said, "My husband is in the Army, so we rarely see each other." Pran Hinh Hien was separated from her husband and children for most of ten years. The Viet Cong "limit the number of children a woman may have and encourage women to marry later."

In a Vancouver workshop the Indochinese said, WHO IS THE MAIN ENEMY?...Our common enemy is the united States… Our two struggles cannot be replaced…together we can be successful.[1285]

The Third World groups identified were Los Siete de la Raza, Soledad Defense Committee, Angela Davis Defense Committee, Los Angeles Asian Involvement, San Francisco Red Guards, Native Canadian, and Chinese Youth Defense Committees

There was much hugging, laughing and weeping, but behind it all was hard core WSP organizational politics, hardline Hanoi orders.

Hanoi Instructions: Unify. The Indochinese, seeking American unity, sought to "strengthen our solidarity." Hanoi's Ambassador and Paris negotiator, Xuan Thuy called for unity. (*We repeat*):

[1285] Gough, 17.

I call upon the progressive American people
and all anti-war organizations in the United
States to unite closely, to associate all forces
and strata of the population irrespective of
their skin color, religion, and political trend,
thus making a wide and strong movement....

In Vancouver this message of unity was repeatedly
conveyed. "The main question is unity for the common goal -
END THE WAR." Despite the disunity there was "a
widespread longing for unity and for clarification of goals."
The DRV, Laotians, and the South Vietnamese delegations
gave similar "independent" messages of unity. They all wanted
a Stalinist united front to win. Hanoi, "In general our policy is
to unite everyone ...with the revolution voluntarily at
any...stage..."

Racism, poverty and unemployment would remain
after war, "Yet the war has greatly increased these conflicts; At
present the American people have the capacity to mobilize
broad unity in order to stop the war."

The communist knew the underside of the antiwar
movement.
We have followed antiwar activities...We have taken note of
the demonstrations, petitions, and many other actions. They all
help...The most important thing is to mobilize larger forces...
If we are larger and more united, we can achieve greater
success. We need unity. ...As Ho Chi Minh said, 'Unity, unity,
larger unity; success, success, bigger success.' The greater the
difficulties, the broader must be the force in order to defeat the
enemy. The more we consolidate, the more we weaken and
divide the enemy.[1286]

Unity on Common Objectives. When asked "What do
you need from us," the communists answered with tactical
instructions:

demand that Nixon set a date before the end of
1971 for complete withdrawal of all troops,
material and bombing from Indochina. ...a
large mobilization on April 24 will be very
valuable and all groups should cooperate
provided their demand is total withdrawal.[1287]

[1286] Kathleen Gough Aberle, "An Indochina Conference in Vancouver," *Bulletin of
Concerned Asian Scholars*, vol. 3, Number 4 (Summer-Fall) 1971.

U.S. POWs could be released once the U.S. "set a date" for the withdrawal of all troops and military material and cessation of bombing.Workshops discussed the state of anti-war movement being followed closely.

Toronto. In Toronto, the Indochinese talked to G.I. wives, veterans, deserters, and draft resisters. The Vietnamese Women's Union invited WSP's Amy Swerdlow, Irma Zigas (WSP and WRL) and Willie Barrow of Operation Push to visit Hanoi in September 1971.[1288]

Besides aiding in the cover up of Viet Cong terrorism, on the home front some took up the cause of carrying Hanoi's terms for ending war not peace, but a communist military victory.

Promoting the People's Peace Treaty, 1971

From April 11-17, 1971 AFSC joined by WILPF, lobbied members of the House and Senate urging them to support the "People's Peace Treaty."[1289] PCPJ and Jane Fonda also sponsored the "peoples" treaty which National Students' Association leader David Ifshin and 15 others signed in Hanoi in early December 1971.[1290]

Ghost Writers. The widely acclaimed South Vietnamese students in the People's Peace Treaty were fakes. Doug Hosteller, a Mennonite serving with Vietnam Christian Service, met the "president" of the nonexistent South Vietnamese Student Association, Student Huynh Tan Mam, who was a secret spy of the VC and a cheerleader of Hanoi's conquest in 1975.

Broken Promises. The Nine Point People's Peace Treaty called for immediate and total U.S. withdrawal, removal of Thieu-Ky government of South Vietnam, followed by POW releases and a ceasefire. The "Treaty" promised (and subsequently violated): a ceasefire; safety to South Viet officials; democratic elections in the South (not North); and independence of Laos and Cambodia. The House Committee on Internal Security said, "This so-called treaty, ... fully

---

[1287] Gough, 18-19.

[1288] Amy Swerdlow, *Women Strike for Peace: Traditional Motherhood and Radical Politics in the 1960s* University of Chicago Press, 230-231; *Baltimore Afro American*, June 24, 186, 6.

[1289] Boston to Director, 5:49 am 4/10/71 NITEL 4/10/71, page two, at FBI, FOIA, A, AFSC.

[1290] CIA, FOIA, "Travel of U.S. student leaders to North Vietnam to negotiate a separate peace treaty," December 14, 1970, Cable, reference: 1988-001490

supports the communist position on Vietnam." No promises kept. No ceasefire, no safety, no elections and no sovereignty. The Communists sought a totaletarian victory.

June 25-27, 1971 the People's Coalition for Peace and Justice, PCPJ, held a conference at St. Michaels' Church in Milwaukee, Wisconsin. Among the major agenda items were ratification of the People's Peace Treaty, promoting the slogan, "Set the date," and support of Huynh Tan Mam, a student, and a Viet Cong agent, to whom drafting the People's Peace Treaty was attributed.[1291] With Hanoi's guidance, Robert Greenblatt and Doug Hostetter were the likely authors of the script of the People's Peace Treaty. PCPJ set October 13th for nationwide protests and November 6th for a militant march in DC.

Meanwhile April protests moved rapidly forward…

[1291] FBI, Indianapolis to Director, People's Coalition for Peace and Justice, National Conference, Milwaukee, Wisconsin, AIRTEL, July 9, 1971.

Chapter 11. The Spring Offensive.
Friends of the Spring Offensive—April 1971
Moral and Material Support. Having continuing contact with Madame Binh and Xuan Thuy, the PCPJ and affiliated organizations like VVAW were getting advice for their April-May demonstrations.

A Viet Cong Circular 06/71 said so. "The antiwar movement in the US…has been guided and supported by our delegation at the Paris peace talks." Circular 06/71 correctly identified the PCPJ and NPAC leading demonstrations. The Circular also described future protests.[1292]

The spring actions included VVAW's Dewey Canyon III rally, PCPJ demonstrations and the May Day Tribe's planned Mayday riot.

Money No object for VVAW Protests. Those needing funding were getting it. VVAW members, whose New York office phone had recently been disconnected for failure to pay, were told at VVAW meetings "money was no object…all …money …obtained from New York." Senators Hatfield and McGovern paid VVAW for the Dewey Canyon III project. Robert Kennedy speechwriter Adam Walinsky raised $50,000 from Democratic Party financiers Edgar Bronfman, Abraham Feinberg, and Philip Levin.[1293] John Kerry said VVAW spent $94,000 for an ad in the Sunday *New York Times* of April 11, 1971.[1294] VVAW bought airline tickets (San Francisco, Portland) and paid for food, housing, rental cars, and bus fares.[1295] VVAW New York rented six buses. Four left empty.[1296] Many others made their own way bumming rides, hitch hiking[1297] and using crash pads of acquaintances.

[1292] Current Affairs Committee, Ba Ria Sub-Region Party Committee, Viet Cong Circular 06/71, 23 July 1971, captured 21 August 1971.CDEC # 08-1395-71.
[1293] 8/25/1972 FBI Information Digest Special Report on VVAW, http://www.wintersoldier.com/staticpages/index.php?page=InfoDigestGuide
[1294] FBI, WFO to Director, VVAW. Internal Security-Miscellaneous, TELETYPE 853PM Urgent April 13, 1971, 1-3; FBI Informative Note, April 13, 1971.
[1295] Ads in Albuquerque Tribune, Albuquerque Journal, New Mexican Lobo contact George Smith, VVAW office at UNM cited in FBI, Albuquerque to Director, VVAW-IS-Misc, TELETYPE 6:58PM URGENT April 16, 1971.
[1296] FBI, New York to Director, Demonstrations Sponsored by VVAW, at Washington DC, Four eighteen dash twenty-three seventy-one IS dash Miscellaneous, VIDEM, TELETYPE, 4:05 PM URGENT April 18, 1971, 1.
[1297] During the sixties the author as both sailor and student hitchhiked throughout California, across the nation and through Europe. Slept in cars, roadsides and youth

East Bloc Provides Propaganda. General Ion Michai Pacepa, the defected Romanian spy chief before the Iron Curtain fell says,

I produced the very same [Kerry like] vitriol…almost word for word and planted it in leftist movements.

…KGB chairman Yuri Andropov managed our anti-Vietnam War operation. He often bragged about having…poisoned domestic debate in the U.S. … 'Our most significant success."[1298]

Pacepa said atrocity stories intended to outrage and recruit:

> aid or to conduct operations to help Americans dodge the draft or defect, to demonize its army…to conduct protests, demonstrations, and boycotts…[1299]

Communist Cash. Pacepa says the Stockholm Conference received $50 million a year from the World Peace Council and an additional $15 million annually from the International Department of the CP-USSR to conduct operations in Europe. " I would print up these materials in hundreds of thousands of copies. …along with counterfeit pictures." [1300]

Col. Stanislav Lunev, a defector from Soviet military intelligence, GRU, wrote, the "GRU and KGB helped to fund just about every antiwar movement organization in America and abroad." Lunev says incredibly "the GRU and KGB had a larger budget for antiwar propaganda in the United States than it did for economic and military support of the Vietnamese."[1301] Politics was the winning strategy.

If true, and the magnitude of his claim is extraordinary, then much of the disorder of the era may be attributed in some considerable measure to a secret foreign propaganda apparatus nurtured by Soviet agents and financed by the billion-dollar budgets of the Soviet General Staff of the GRU, Soviet military intelligence.

Lunev claimed that the GRU alone budgeted more than $1 billion for propaganda and peace movements against

---

hostels and abused the hospitality of strangers. 'Twas a different time.

[1298] Ion Mihai Pacepa, "Kerry's Soviet Rhetoric," National Review, April 22, 2004.
[1299] Pacepa quoted in MacKubin T. Owens, "They Charge War Crimes…" *National Review*, May 3, 2004.
[1300] Ion Mihai Pacepa, "Kerry's Soviet Rhetoric," *National Review*, April 22, 2004.
[1301] Stanislav Lunev, *Through the Eyes of the Enemy*, Washington: Regnery Publishing, 1998, 78.

Vietnam War. "It was a hugely successful campaign and well worth the cost. The antiwar sentiment created an incredible momentum that greatly weakened the U.S. military."[1302] It is worth repeating, Lunev claimed, "the GRU and the KGB helped to fund just about every antiwar movement and organization in America and abroad." According to Lunev the GRU spent twice as much on the antiwar movement, through fronts and third parties, than on military and economic support.[1303] These Soviet funds, (except for FBI agent SOLO carrying cash for the CPUSA), were difficult to trace. The KGB funneled funds through Cuban, Czech, Bulgarian, Hungarian, Romanian, and Polish secret services.[1304] How were peace groups funded? "Funding was provided via undercover operatives or front companies. These would fund another group that in turn would fund student organizations," according to Stanislav Lunev.[1305]

In addition, Oleg Danilovich Kalugin, former head of KGB operations in the United States says,
Soviet intelligence was really unparalleled. ... The KGB programs -- which would run all sorts of *congresses*, peace congresses, youth congresses, *festivals*, *women's movements*, *trade union* movements... all sorts of *forgeries* and faked material -- [were] targeted at politicians, the academic community, at the public at large. It was really a worldwide campaign, often not only sponsored and funded, but also conducted and manipulated by the KGB. And this was again part and parcel of this campaign to weaken [the] military, economic and psychological climate in the West."*[1306]*

[1302] Stanislav Lunev, *Through the Eyes of the Enemy: The Autobiography of Stanislav Lunev* , Regnery Publishing 1998 cited in Wikipedia, J.R. Nyquist, "A balanced perspective," WorldNetDaily.com, October 9, 2000 at http://www.worldnetdaily .com/news/ article.asp?ARTICLE ID=19869

[1303] Stanislav Lunev, *Through the Eyes of the Enemy*, Washington: Regnery Publishing, 1998, 170.

[1304] Frank J. Rafalko, *MH/CHAOS: The CIA's Campaign Against the Radical Left and the Black Panthers*, Annapolis: Naval Institute Press, 2011, 134 cites Lora Soroka, *Fond 89: Communist Party of Soviet Union on Trial*, Stanford: Hoover Institute, 2001, 301; Theodore Shackley and Richard A. Findlay, *Spymaster:My Life in the CIA*, Dulles, VA: Patomac Books, 2005, 48; Lunev, 78.

[1305] Lunev, 78.

[1306] CNN, The Cold War experience: Espionage, "Inside the KGB: An interview with retired KGB Maj. Gen. Oleg Kalugin
http://www.cnn.com/SPECIALS/cold.war/experience/spies/interviews/kalugin/;"Active Measures," Answers.com at http://www. answers. com/topic/active-measures
http://www.answers.com/topic/#wp- note-Lunev

Post War Soviet Financing. By 1980 and 1982 the CIA estimated that Soviets spent $3-4 million a year on propaganda and disinformation of which $600,000 or so was spent on "peace offensives" with money funneled through the World Peace Council and Communist parties. FBI agent Ed O'Malley told the House Permanent Select Committee on intelligence in 1982 that KGB "devote serious attention to the antiwar movement in the United States."[1307] Well documented is Soviet organization and financing of involvement in the peace movement in Europe to the tune of hundreds of millions of dollars[1308] against intermediate range missiles, the neutron bomb, and for the nuclear freeze.[1309]

In a meeting between former Senator John Tunney with KGB agents on March 5, 1980, Tunney said Senator Edward Kennedy blamed bad relations and the dangers of war upon the U.S. Government, President Jimmy Carter. Not the peaceful Soviets. Kennedy was impressed with General Secretary Leonid Brezhnev's commitment to peaceful détente. "The atmosphere of tension and hostility towards the whole Soviet people was being fueled by Carter."[1310] The Soviets may have invested earlier in Kennedy's go between, John Tunney. Representative John V. Tunney of California contacted the Bureau on August 9, 1966, and reported that he had been visited by an unnamed Soviet official in Washington, D. C., on August 9, 1966. According to Representative Tunney, he and the Soviet official discussed the war in Vietnam in general terms ... Representative Tunney stated he had put the Soviet in his place throughout the entire conversation and had not agreed with anything the Soviet had stated. Representative Tunney ...felt the Soviet probably would not contact him again but he

---

[1307] "The KGB: Eyes of the Kremlin," *Time*, Feb. 14, 1983; Elizabeth Pond, "The West wakes up to the dangers of disinformation," *Christian Science Monitor*, February 28, 1985.
[1308] *Soviet Active Measures*, Hearings before the House Permanent Select Committee on Intelligence, July 13-14, 1982, 7.
[1309] Sergei Tretyakov cited in Pete Earley, *Comrade J: Untold Secrets of Russia's Master Spy in America After the End of the Cold War*, Penguin Books, 2007, 167-177; Dennis Kux, "Soviet Active Measures and Disinformation," *Parameters*, Vol XV, No. 4, 21, 22,23; Jeffrey G. Barlow, *Moscow and the Peace Offensive*, Heritage Foundation, Backgrounder No. 184, May 14, 1982; Opposition to the Bomb: The fear and occasional political intrigue behind the ban the bomb movement, CNN http://www.cnn.com/SPECIALS/cold.war/experience/the.bomb/opposition/
[1310] Unspecified Mitrokhin Papers cited in Kevin Mooney, "Ted Kennedy's KGB Correspondence, " *American Spectator,* 6.22.10.

desired to make this first meeting a matter of record in FBI files."[1311]

By 1980 the former congressman and now U.S. Senator, John V. Tunney, was apparently very trusted in Moscow.

According to KGB chief Viktor Chebrikov's memo to Gen. Secretary Yuri Andropov on May 14, 1983, Senator Ted Kennedy sought to help the Soviet media reach the American media, Walter Cronkite and Barbara Walters, in opposition to President Reagan's foreign policy and in support Soviet peaceful intentions.[1312] In particular, Reagan was supporting Pershing II, MX missiles and Strategic Defense Initiative, SDI. Sen. Kennedy actively promoted a U.S. nuclear freeze movement,[1313] which in Europe, if perhaps not the USA, was Soviet funded and controlled.

It is likely the KGB made similar investments in the American peace movement during the Vietnam War as Lunev claims, perhaps too fulsomely.

The recruitment of John Kerry and funding of VVAW, would have high payoffs for communist propagandists and their financiers. Out of base locations, VVAW kept track of movements of US forces. A few members sought to gather technological secrets, including nuclear ones, and pass them on to the Soviets.

***

VVAW Stages Mock Operation Dewey Canyon III

On April 18, 1971, about 1,000 protesters dressed as Vietnam vets camped out in Washington, D.C. They called it Operation Dewey Canyon III, "a limited incursion into the country of Congress."

The disheveled horde, longhaired and unshaven, wore tattered and dirty Army fatigues and brought with them wine, beer, marijuana, and young runaway girls.[1314] They carried Viet

---

[1311] W. A. Branigan to C.D. Brennan Subject: Contacts…Russia, August 16, 1966 in Federal Bureau of Investigation (FBI) File, 105-HQ-229897, *Contacts between representatives of the Soviet Union and members or staff personnel of the United States Congress, 1964 – 1972*, Released 16-February-2011, Posted 10-June-2013, Section II, 353.

[1312] Tim Sebastian, "Teddy, the KGB, and the top secret file," *The Sunday Times,* Feb. 2, 1992; Paul Kegor, *The Crusader: Ronald Reagan and the Fall of Communism,* 2006; Jamie Glazov, "Ted Kennedy and the KGB," *Frontpage,* May 15, 2008; Kevin Mooney, "Ted Kennedy's KGB Correspondence, " *American Spectator,* 6.22.10.

[1313] Seymour Hersh, *The Shadow President*, 60-63.

[1314] Lance Gay, "Bivouac With Wine, Pt, Music and Girls," *Washington Evening Star,*

Cong flags and pro-communist signs and banners. Armed with toy rifles, they mocked "search and destroy" missions and pretended to massacre civilians.

Kerry Claims Massacres. That day April 18, 1971, VVAW spokesman, John Kerry told NBC's Meet the Press, "I committed the same kinds of atrocities as thousands of other soldiers...in that I took part in shootings in free-fire zones... conducted harass-and-interdiction fire...used .50-caliber machine guns, ...in the burning of villages."[1315]

Terrible things are done in war including use of arms to kill people and to destroy things. James Rothrock asks, "Could it be Navy Officer training [as distinct from infantry training] failed to teach Kerry that interdiction fire, search and destroy, bombing and killing the enemy are fundamentals of war?"[1316]

Who Killed Civilians? The antiwar movement almost universally described "heavy firepower in the populated rural areas as the most immoral of all allied actions during the war," because of higher civilian casualties, property damage and refugees.

Yet most of the responsibility for the destruction caused by allied firepower and any related indictments of immorality belong to the communists ... [who]... chose to launch military attacks from hamlets and take refuge in them when allies attacked, thereby drawing fire on the hamlets. Many chose to dress in civilian clothes...On many occasions they chose to draw fire on hamlets ...firing at the allies and the fleeing..."[1317]

Just like Al Quaida, Hamas, Hezbullah and ISIL today use human shields. Under the rules of war, the communist use of civilian shields made the villages legitimate targets during firefights. Human wave attacks immorally killed their own troops.

The communists gave no assistance to injured, starving, and displaced civilians for whom they were largely

---

April 20, 1971; FBI, LHM, [REDACTED], Demonstration Sponsored by VVAW Washington, DC April 18 through April 23, 1971, 4.

[1315] NBC interview of John Kerry cited in Brian Williams, NBC News, Mar 16, 2004. See also: John E. O'Neill and Jerome R. Corsi, *Unfit for Command*, Regnery, 2004, 153; Newsmax 2/16/ 04.

[1316] James Rothrock, *Divided We Fall*, Authorhouse, 2005, 123.

[1317] Mark Moyar, *Phoenix and the Birds of Prey; The CIA's Secret Campaign to Destroy the Viet Cong*, Annapolis: Naval Institute Press, 1997, 289.

responsible. It was the communists, drawing fire amongst civilians, brought death and destruction to hamlets and did little afterwards to mitigate the horrific consequences of their own actions far outside of the norms of international law, moral values and common decency.[1318]

***

Greetings and Accolades: Arlington, Madame Binh, Today Show, *Daily World*

Assaulting Arlington Cemetery. On the 19th of April VVAW converged upon the gates of Arlington Cemetery intending to place two wreaths at the Tomb of the Unknown. They were not welcomed. Finding the gate locked and guarded, some smashed their plastic M-16s against the gate. One vet cried. His father was buried in Arlington.[1319]

Viet Cong Greetings and Guidance. On April 20th, Madame Nguyen Thi Binh sent greetings to "American Friends," the united front, "Friends of various circles and political and religious tendencies. ..." The Viet Cong leader gave instructions. "We demand that Mr. Nixon put forth a reasonable deadline [set the date] for a total U.S. troop withdrawal..." Binh hoped "the antiwar movement...will further *coordinate* so it will be effective...."[1320]

Cora: Set the Date. April 20, 1971, Barbara Walters and Hugh Downs gave Cora Weiss a long, ten-minute, interview on the "Today Show." Weiss described COLIFAM's personalized mail service and said repeatedly setting the date for US withdrawal, freed POWs.[1321]

Communists Congratulate unity. On the 21st, from Hanoi, the South Vietnam People's Committee in Solidarity with the American People (*Viet My*) committee praised unity. your April 24th demonstrations, May 5th moratorium and other spring activities...The Vietnamese people...highly appreciate the broad coalition of different American antiwar groups....[1322]

[1318] Mark Moyar, *Phoenix and the Birds of Prey; The CIA's Secret Campaign to Destroy the Viet Cong*, Annapolis: Naval Institute Press, 1997, 288-91.

[1319] FBI, LHM, [REDACTED], Demonstration Sponsored by VVAW Washington, DC April 18 through April 23, 1971, 3-4.

[1320] Madame Binh Sends Letter to Antiwar Americans," Paris VNA to VNA Hanoi, 1331 GMT, April 20, 1971 in FBIS, "Principal Reports From Communist Radio Sources, I. Madame Binh Sends Letter to Antiwar Americans..." (Paris VNA), 22 April 1971 also cited in Rothrock, 132-33N6.

[1321] FBI, Norfolk LHM, COLIFAM, April 28, 1971; FBI, SAC New York to Director AIRTEL, April 20, 1971; FBI , SAC, New York to Director, memo, COLIFAM IS-Misc., April 27, 1971; FBI, New York, LHM, COLIFAM, June 10, 1971.

Kerry Protests Supreme Court. On April 22, 1971 John Kerry was in a front-page photo in *Daily World* handing former Attorney General Ramsey Clark a sheet of paper. Police arrest 127 veterans for "obstructing the administration of justice" on the steps of the Supreme Court. As VVAW's counsel, Ramsey Clark protested an order from Chief Justice Warren Burger to vacate their "liberated" campsite on the Capitol Mall.[1323] VVAW stayed in place defying the Supreme Court order. John Kerry walked a few blocks to the U. S. Senate.

***

Kerry Wows Senate Foreign Relations Committee "Reminiscent of Genghis Khan."

At a hearing of the Senate Foreign Relations Committee on April 22, 1971, covered by television cameras, Naval Officer John Kerry dressed in U.S. Army combat fatigues wore his Silver Star, Bronze Star and three Purple Heart ribbons. Echoing the words of VVAW mantra on American atrocities Kerry said,

[U.S. servicemen] had personally raped, cut off ears, cut off heads, taped wires from portable telephones to human genitals and turned up the power, cut off limbs, blown up bodies, randomly shot at civilians, razed villages in fashion reminiscent of Genghis Khan, shot cattle and dogs for fun, poisoned food stocks and generally ravaged the countryside of South Vietnam.[1324]

Singing From the Same Hymnbook. Kerry's words were indistinguishable from those of Scott Camil in the Winter Soldier Investigation and more important those of Ho Chi Minh and his disposable cannon fodder, the Viet Cong.

On April 8, 1966, Ho Chi Minh said that American tactics followed a "burn all, kill all, and destroy all" of using "napalm bombs, poison gas, and toxic chemicals to massacre our compatriots and ravage our villages." The NLF wrote:

> You …probably hear about the U.S.-Diem
> troops indulging in cannibalism, disemboweling

[1322] "Vietnam Organizations Laud American Antiwar Campaign," Hanoi VNA International News Service, 1621 GMT, April 21, 1971, FBIS, TTU Archive cited in Rothrock, 140-41N15.

[1323] "Nixon and High court Defied. Vets hold Peace Line; Jail and threats Fail," *Daily World*, April 22, 1971 at wintersoldier.com… /CDW0423_1.jpg

[1324] Complete Testimony of Lt. John Kerry to Senate Foreign Relations Committee, *Congressional Record* April 22, 1971, 179-210.

a man, and *eating his liver* ... Young men eat
...liver ... during ...party or fishing trip.[1325]
The USSR was the mentor of Ho and the VC.

Soviet Disinformation: America. Chemical and Biological Warfare. Though USSR used chemical and biological weapons in Vietnam, using the forum of the UN, claimed the US was the leading user of chemical weapons [1326] and biological weapons. The US interrogated communist prisoners to uncover any possible unauthorized and illegal use of vectors for bubonic plague and malaria.[1327] At the urging of the Vietnamese, the Soviets circulated disinformation about American use of chemical weapons in Vietnam.[1328] As a paid KGB agent Australian Wilfred Burchett claimed the US use in Vietnam, as he had in Korea, of chemical warfare. The Soviets forged documents of a Gordon Goldstein of the U.S. Office of Naval Research "confessing" to U.S. biological warfare in Thailand and Vietnam.[1329]

And before the Senate, Kerry continued, [Americans] are more guilty [sic] than any other body of violations of those Geneva Conventions in the use of free-fire zones, harassment interdiction fire, search-and-destroy missions, the bombings, the torture of prisoners - all accepted policy by many units in South Vietnam.

Kerry said these were not rogue operations, but "crimes committed on a day-to-day basis with the full awareness of officers at all levels of command."

Last man to die in Vietnam? Kerry asked, "We are asking Americans to think about that because how do you ask a man to be the last man to die in Vietnam?"[1330] Hanoi Hannah

---

[1325]Che Van Vien, "Sparkling Fires in the South," in Douglas Pike, *Viet Cong...*, 438.
[1326] Huber, Mark, "THE UNITED NATIONS LIBRARY: PUTTING Soviet Disinformation INTO CIRCULATION," *Backgrounder #487*
Heritage Foundation, February 18, 1986, 7-8
http://www.heritage.org/Research/RussiaandEurasia/upload/87526_1.pdf
[1327] Garnett "Bill" Bell with George J. Veith, *Leave No Man Behind: Bill Bell and the Search for American POW/MIAs from the Vietnam War*, Madison: Goblin Fern Press, 2004, 39.
[1328] CIA, FOIA, "Political Report of the Embassy of the USSR in the Democratic Republic of Vietnam For the Year 1970," [TFR 136-22A, [handwritten "22"] Top Secret, Copy No. 3 "12" Mar 71, Issue No. 114 [Stamp "TsK KPSS, 10987, 16 Mar 71 180-A/ Subject to Return to the General Section TsK KPSS"] DRV, City of Hanoi, March 1971, [TFR 136-47][handwritten "211-212"].
[1329] Soviet archives cited in Fedora, "Goodfellow's Bedfellows: Who's in Bed with the Washington Post," Original Freeper research July 4, 2006 at freerepublic.com/focus/f-news/1660323/posts

and Trinh Huu Tuan repeated the refrain "…the last man to die in Vietnam," on Radio Hanoi, in propaganda pamphlets,[1331] and POW interrogations. [1332]

Swett and Ziegler say, "Kerry and the Vietnamese Communists were singing from the same hymnbook."[1333]

On different page of the hymnal, Kerry told Senator Fulbright Binh's Eight Points was the preferred peace plan …until he was instructed in July to shuffle a few points. "If the United States were to set a date for withdrawal prisoners of war would be returned."

From Paris, Madame Binh expressed her "profound, warm feelings" to VVAW for its adding "significance" to the anti-war protests.[1334]   Kerry and Cora Weiss had all taken up the Communist theme, "set the date."

***

VVAW Throws Away American War Medals

On April 23, 1971, John Kerry led members of VVAW in a protest tossing American war medals and ribbons over a fence in front of the U.S. Capitol "We came here to undertake one last mission, to search out and destroy the last vestige of this barbaric war," Kerry said. Among those tossing their medals are Rep. Ron Dellums, (D-California),[1335] and Barry Romo.[1336]

Stolen Medals… and Valor. Paul Withers of Boston came to the microphone claiming to be a former Green Beret. He said he had received nine purple hearts and a long list of other medals, including the Distinguished Service Cross.[1337]

[1330] Edward Epstein, *San Francisco Chronicle*, Oct 17, 2004; Notra Trulock, *Accuracy in Media*, Jan 27, 2004. O'Neill and Corsi, *Unfit for Command*, 99-106.

[1331] Swett and Ziegler 19n94 cite Viet Cong leaflet Duc-Pho National Front for Liberation to "US officers and men," archives of John Boyle, historian, 19th Engineer Battalion (Combat, Army).

[1332] Swett and Ziegler cite 19n93 cite Richard Tomkins, "Ex-POWs slam Kerry's war protest activities UPI, August 3, 2004.

[1333] Scott Swett and Tim Ziegler, *To Set the Record Straight: How Swift Boat Veterans, POWs and the New Media Defeated John Kerry*, New American Media 2008, 19n90-94 cite Hanoi Hannah, Vietnam Veterans Radio Network's Vrn Catalogue of Radio Hanoi Tapes; Trinh Huu Tuan to PBS, American Experience: Vietnam Online, Viewer Mail, June 1997;Don North, "Voices from the Past: The Search for Hanoi Hannah, *Vietnam Generation Journal & Newsletter* 3, no. 3 (November 1991); Richard Tomkins, "Ex-POWs slam Kerry's war-protest activities," UPI, Aug. 3, 2004.

[1334] Swett and Ziegler 16n72-3 cite ABC Evening News, April 22, 1971 and "Vietnamese patriots praise anti-war vets," *Daily World*, April 23, 1971.

[1335] Tim Wheeler and Gene Tournour, "Vets Dump Medals, Nixon Ducks March," *Daily World*, April 23, 1971 at Wintersoldier.com … CDW0424_1.jpg

[1336] *Vietnam HD*, History Channel, November 2011.

The name Withers does not appear in an alphabetical list of the 1,055 recipients of the Distinguished Service Cross.[1338] Similarly, a Purple Heart website cites Medal of Honor recipient Robert Howard receiving 9 Purple Hearts.[1339] Again, the Purple Heart not mention Withers as a recipient of nine. While the "absence of a name should NOT be construed to definitively negate a veteran's claim to this award," the VVAW members made numerous false claims or exaggerations at Winter Soldiers "hearing."

Valor, Stolen. B.G. Burkett and Glenna Whitley in *Stolen Valor* document 1,700 persons fabricating war stories. Lying about service in Vietnam gained veterans benefits for those who had not earned them, made political points and answered the embarrassing question, "What did you do during the Vietnam War?" **Stolen Benefits.** By 2000 service in Vietnam had become honorable. The Veteran's Administration gave more than 600 veterans benefits for having been a POW in the Vietnam war though only 400 POWs were known to be alive.[1340] Later others would claim exposure to Agent Orange and to PTSD to acquire VA benefits.

Medals/Valor, Borrowed and Purchased. Scott Swett reports some VVAW members were carrying medals for others not at the rally. VVAW member Steve Pitkin remembered someone with long hair holding a bag filled with military ribbons and medals and offering them to VVAW members. Pitkin said that most of the medals were from the Korean War, not Vietnam. Pitkin said VVAW cleaned out the local Army-Navy stores. Disgusted, Pitkin grabbed a handful of medals and threw them into a mob of reporters and marched off.[1341]

VVAW Answered. Five weeks later on June 1, 1971, Vietnam Veterans, Bruce Kesler and John O'Neil announced the formation of Vietnam Veterans for a Just Peace at the

---

[1337] Tim Wheeler and Gene Tournour, "Vets Dump Medals, Nixon Ducks March," *Daily World*, April 23, 1971 at Wintersoldier.com … CDW0424_1.jpg
[1338] http://www.homeofheroes.com/valor/0_DSC/4_rvn/dsc_rvn_list.html
[1339] http://www.homeofheroes.com/medals/purple_heart/purple_heart.html
[1340] Doug Sterner, Restoring Valor; fakewarriors.org; Mike Benge to author and others January 19, 2014; The 600 included 23 POWS of Gulf War in 1991.
[1341] Pitkins recollections are at
http://www.wintersoldier.com/staticpages/index.php?page=YesterdaysLies1.
Armond Noble, publisher of Military magazine, says that phony vets often have chests filled with medals worn in inappropriate patterns.

National Press Club demanding, "Don't Call us War Criminals." They challenged Kerry to a debate and asked the media to stop giving "prominence… to (an) embittered little group of 1,000 out of 2 ½ million" Vietnam veterans." In contrast over 500,000 Vietnam Veterans had joined the VFW. In three years, O'Neil said, "I never saw one war crime committed by Allied Forces." Yet the Viet Cong committed kidnappings and assassinations, daily.[1342] The VVAW now claims it was "more interested in putting their ideas through the media than in building a big organization."

John Kerry's New Soldier. After the spring offensive in Washington, Kerry compiled his testimony and speeches into a book *The New Soldier,* a book that disappeared from circulation during the 2004 Presidential election, but has since reappeared.

Its cover showed six disheveled soldiers holding the American flag upside down, mocking the famous photo from Iwo Jima. Inside, Kerry wrote, "We were sent to Vietnam to kill Communism. But we found instead that we were killing women and children." And "We created a nation of refugees, bomb craters, amputees, orphans, and prostitutes, and…in the words of …Tacitus: 'where they made a desert they called peace.'"[1343]

James Webb, Marine recipient of the Navy Cross, author of *Fields of Fire*, and Reagan Secretary of the Navy, a U.S. Senator, and Democrat candidate for President in 2016, said in an NPR editorial:

> For most veterans it was not that Kerry was against the war, but that he used his military credentials to denigrate the service of a whole generation of veterans. …
> (The VVAW) stories of atrocious conduct, repeated in lurid detail by Kerry before the Congress, represented not the typical experience of the American soldier, but its ugly extreme. That the articulate, urbane Kerry

---

[1342] "Don't Call Us War Criminals." Bruce Kesler and John O'Neil, statements before National Press Club, June 1, 1971; *Evening Star*, June 1, 1971; *New York Times*, June 2, 1971; *Washington Post*, June 2, 1971; *Chicago Tribune*, June 2, 1971. Evening Star, June 1, 1971.
[1343] John Kerry, *The New Soldier*, New York: Collier Books, 1971; Marc Morano, "Kerry Denials at Odds With 1971 Book He Authored," *CNSNews.com* Feb 20, 2004.

would validate such allegations helped to make life hell for many Vietnam veterans, for a very long time.[1344]

While John Kerry and Cora Weiss successfully sowed disunity among Americans, the Vietnamese communists had demanded and gotten a united front among antiwar factions.

***

Answering Hanoi Call
Antiwar Groups Reunite in Spring Actions

Strange Bedfellows. On April 24, 1971, less than two months since Xuan Thuy and Madame Binh gave their March 6th instructions, the Trotskyite NPAC joined the Stalinist influenced PCPJ. Soon, the PJPJ, NPAC, SMC, May Day Collective, and the Vietnam Veterans Against the War shared addresses, 1029 Vermont NW in Washington, D.C. The united front organized the "Spring Offensive."

On the 24th, Ho Thu, chairman of the South Vietnam People's Committee in Solidarity with the American People (*Viet My*) cabled both the NPAC, and the competing Justice, PCPJ, of which Kerry's VVAW was a part. Ho Thu "acclaim[ed] the *broad* spring offensive…initiated by…progressive organizations…" and said [We] highly value your…struggle for *unity*."[1345]

The PCPJ provided housing, nonviolent training, legal aid and medical aid. Two weeks of activities included April 24-April 30 of rallies and lobbying Congress, Selective Service, IRS, HEW and Justice Department.

May 1-5 were days of civil disobedience and stop the government on May 5.[1346] Ron Young, Fellowship for Reconciliation, told the *Washington Post* that PCPJ had raised $15,000 for bail from telephone and street solicitations and from Methodists and Quakers.[1347]

Rally at Capitol Mall, April 24, 1971

[1344] Mackubin Thomas Owens, "Kerry operated on the Radical Fringe of the Vietnam Anti-War Movement," *Weekly Standard*, September 2004.

[1345] Emphases added. "Ho Thu Acclaims U.S. Antiwar Demonstrations," Liberation Radio (Clandestine), 1000 GMT, April 27, 1971, TTU archive cited in Rothrock pp. 138-139N12

[1346] PCPJ, flyer, "Join the Peoples Lobby; Come to Washington, April 24 To Stay, two days to two weeks," April 1971.

[1347] Paul Valentine, "Protesters Raise $15,00 For Demonstrators' Bonds," *Washington Post*, May 5, 1971.

Reflecting the skills of experienced hard left organizers, the struggle on the second front was impressive. On April 24, some 250,000 demonstrated on Capitol Mall thereafter another 200,000.

Communist Influentials, Local, International. John Kerry, a Naval Officer, out of uniform, wearing U.S. Army fatigues, addressed the rally. Other speakers on April 24, included Abe Feinglass (CPUSA), Coretta King, Ralph Abernathy, and Rep. Bella Abzug (NY). Feinglass, Abzug, and Abernathy were members of the CPUSA and Soviet fronts, including the World Peace Council, WPC, the International Association of Democratic Lawyers, IADL and the World Federation of Trade Unions, WFTU. Also Jack O'Dell, [1348] an aide to the late Dr. Martin Luther King Jr., and to Rev. Jesse Jackson. O'Dell was a CPUSA leader, in contact with Soviet intelligence and active in Mobe.

Abe Feinglass, standing at Kerry's side with a clipboard, controlling the program,[1349] was vice-president of the KGB/CPSU (Communist Party of the Soviet Union) controlled and financed WPC.[1350] In the rape of Anne Bailey, a VVAW member in Moscow, the U.S. Peace Council and CPUSA protected the Moscow police. Anne Bailey was treated like she expected any rape victim in the USA. "She was asked if she enjoyed it." WPC/CPUSA covered up and gave no apologies.[1351]

FBI testified before the House Internal Security Committee to KGB manipulation of the demonstrations, e.g.

1348 Identified as a member of the CPUSA in hearings roughly entitled "Communist Party Operations or Organization in the South), HCUA, 1956. Also identified as CPUSA National Committee member, report, 1961, HCUA. Also headed the CPUSA front, "*Freedomways*" magazine - See New Mobe study, 1970 and Hoover, FBI testimonies 1970, 71. Max Friedman to author, February 25, 2008.

1349 As seen on MSNBC's "John Kerry: Bringing the War Home,"

1350 Max Phillip Friedman, "JOHN KERRY: AMBITION AND OPPORTUNISM," winter Soldier Web site.

http:/http://www.wintersoldier.com/staticpages/index.php?page=KGBKerry See also: Senate Internal Security Subcommittee (SISS), a hearing held in Executive Session, "Extent of Subversion in Campus Disorders: Testimony of Max Phillip Friedman", Part 2, Oct. 15, 1969.

1351 National Coordinators of VVAW/WSO, Winter Soldier Organization, National Office to The Officers of the National Alliance Against Racist and Political Oppression, January 14, 1975 in FBI FOIA, VVAW, Section 75, FBI, Report of SA [REDACTED], Chicago, "Vietnam Veterans Against the War /winter Soldier Organization (VVAW/WSO, October 29, 1975, 55-56.

The National Council of American-Soviet Friendship and the US PC were KGB fronts.[1352]

Town Criers. Protesters, attired in burlap and faux blood, walked the halls of Congress crying for peace. On the Capitol steps John Conyers (D-MI), Bella Abzug (D-NY) and Ogden Reid (R-NY) spoke to the crying.[1353]

Hanoi. April 26th, Dang Thai Mai, vice chairman of the South Vietnam People's Committee in Solidarity with the American People (*Viet My*) welcomed the "1971 spring offensive" and "*consolidating* the solidarity of the Vietnamese people with the American people....and "warmly hail the antiwar movement...which is surging up forcefully. Welcome the...working people, youth... intellectuals, mothers and women, religious believers... statesmen, and servicemen." He said, "The struggle...constitutes a great encouragement to the fight of the Vietnamese people...."[1354]

Boston. Mai also welcomed "two American scientists in Hanoi, Arthur Galston of Yale and Ethan Singer [or Singner] of Boston University" Upon his return professor Galston said, "American science played an outstandingly important role in the destruction of Vietnam. . American science has a responsibility to play a role in the reconstruction of that country."[1355]

Late April and May. Between April 27 and May 6, 1971 another 175-185,000 people gathered in Washington.

In the April 27, 1971 issue of the *Daily World*, "Notes on the Washington Rally," John Kerry quotes Communist playwright and winner of the Stalin Peace Prize, Bertolt Brecht. "Your Army has one defect—your soldier can think. ...We have taken one last mission to, to search out and destroy the last vestige of this barbaric war..." On the platform: Peter, Paul and Mary and Rev. Ralph Abernathy. In the crowd were American Servicemen's Union and the Communist fronts, Veterans of the Abraham Lincoln Brigade and Veterans for Peace.[1356]

[1352]"Soviet Active Measures," hearings, House Permanent Select Committee on Intelligence, July 13-14, 1982.

[1353] Richard Halloran, "Sack-Clad Protesters in Capital Plead for Peace," *New York Times*, April 26, 1971.

[1354] "Americans Attend Hanoi Solidarity Meeting," Hanoi VNA International News Service, 1633 GMT, Apr. 26, 1971, 8-10. TTU archive cited in Rothrock, 144-5N18.

[1355] Cora Weiss, "AID FROM THE US TO VIETNAM, A Brief and Incomplete Review," September 1975, projections attachment, Texas Tech, Vietnam Center.

The May Day took a more militant posture than the April protests, but the government was ready. On May 2, the police cancelled a permit for 30,000 protestors.

Stop the War or Stop the Government: May Days 1971. The May Day leaders in PCPJ vowed to "stop the war or stop the government," blocking traffic intersections and buildings. They planned mass actions, "sustained" civil disobedience, disrupting traffic and occupying buildings. The "dynamics" were intended to provoke police attacks, violence, and mass arrests bringing down the judiciary.[1357]

While 100,000 alone rallied in San Francisco, the big event was in the Belly of the Beast in Washington, D.C.

Mass Arrests. During six hours of May 3, some 7,000 were arrested for fighting the police and blocking intersections. Abbie Hoffman and two others were arrested for constructing a barrier with cinder blocks, bricks and a 16 foot long 2 x 8s at Wisconsin. R. Daniel Ellsberg remembers, "…We went with our affinity group (including Noam Chomsky, Cindy Fredericks, Marilyn Young, Mark Ptashne, Zelda Gamson, Fred Branfman and Mitch Goodman), to the Mayday actions blocking traffic in Washington."[1358] Also Howard Zinn.

Tear gas stopped a march on the Pentagon.

On the 4th, another 2,000 were arrested outside the Justice Department. On the 5th protestors forced the closure of the U.S. Capitol and another 1,000 were arrested and hauled off the Capitol Steps as Bella Abzug and three other members of Congress hailed the protest. Edith Green, D-Ore, an opponent of the war told Abzug, she supported peaceful protests, "But I will not go on record in support of bands of crazies…The right ..to persuade is one thing. The right to coerce is another."[1359]

The 7,000 arrests on one day are the most in U.S. history, including the Civil War. There were 14,517 arrests in the May melees.

As the organizers had intended, the mass arrests had not allowed procedures complying with every particular of the

[1356] "Notes on the Washington Rally," The *Daily World,* April 27, 1971, 11 at wintersoldier.com… CDW0427_3.jpg
[1357] Richard Starnes, "Troubled spring dawning," *Washington Daily News*, March 11, 1971; William Basham, "Second Anti-war Group to Camp Out near Mall," *Washington Star*, April 23, 1971.
[1358] Daniel Ellsberg, "A Memory of Howard Zinn," *Anti-war Blog*, January 27, 2010, http://antiwar.com/blog/2010/01/27/a-memory-of-howard-zinn/
[1359] UPI, teletype, May 6, 1971.

law. Many arrest forms were not filled out. Judge Harold Green ordered immediate releases without trial. Some of those improperly arrested later received $10,000 as compensation. Paid to stop the government. What the KGB and GRU couldn't finance of the anti-imperialist movement, U.S. taxpayers could.

Hanoi's Unending Gratitude. In Paris on May 10, 1971, Nguyen Minh Vy, a deputy minister of the DRV, said the demonstrations were "a great success. …It is hard to find the words to express our feelings."[1360] As late as April 20, 2016, Madame Binh thanked a New York reunion of the May 1971 assault on the U. S. government. "The Vietnamese people have great appreciation for the peace and antiwar movements in the United States and view those movements' contribution as important in shortening the war.[1361]

Solidarity Forever, 2016. Attending the May 2-3, 2016 reunion of May Day 1971 in Washington were Judy Gumbo Albert (aka Judith Clavir), Leslie Bacon, Noreen Banks, Eddie Becker, Tim Butz, Carole Cullum, Rennie Davis, Michael Drobenare, Daniel Ellsberg, Mark Looney, Jack Mallory, Barbara Nerenberg, Sheila O'Donnell, Walter Teague, Skip Williamson.[1362]

***

**Vietnamese Issue Instructions,
Directive No. 31, Paris, Budapest**

Enemy's Intimate Knowledge of U.S. Antiwar Movement--Viet Cong Directive 31. During the "spring offensive" on April 28, 1971 the Viet Cong, oft described as uniformed peasants isolated from world affairs, issued Directive No. 31 OT/TV[1363] ordering VCI cadre to "step up …the anti-Vietnam War movement of the Americans."

[1360] Pauline Rosen of the Communist Party and Women Strike for Peace quotes *World Magazine*, June 26, 1971.
[1361] Richard Pollock, "War Activists Helped Their Victory," *Daily Caller*, May 29, 2016.
[1362] See: Facebook posts.
https://www.facebook.com/45thanniversary/posts/582978775196259
https://www.facebook.com /45thanniversary/posts/590330131127790
[1363] Directive No. 31 OT/TV, April 28, 1971 captured in the field by the 23rd infantry Division forwarded to Commander, United States Military Assistance Command, Vietnam (COMUSMACV)and to Combined Documents Exploitation Center, CDEC, at the United States Military Assistance Command, Saigon, Vietnam. Directive 31 is CDEC Doc Log No. 05-1660-71 and item number 2150901041 on line at the Vietnam Archive at Texas Tech. Also cited in small part in Thomas Lipscomb, "Hanoi Approved of Role Played by Anti-War Vets, *New York Sun*, October 26, 2004 at nysun.com/article/7356A. The Combined Documentation Exploitation Center (CDEC)

Directive No. 31 very precisely identified the activities of every major antiwar organizations from March through May 1971 including: the "nationwide alliance for peace" [i.e. National Peace Action Coalition, NPAC], the Alliance of Americans for Just Peace [i.e. Peoples Coalition for Peace and Justice, PCPC], the "US war veterans who have fought in Vietnam" [i.e. Vietnam Veterans Against the War, VVAW,] and "the families of those US soldiers who were KIA or captured" [i.e. COLIFAM].

The Directive No. 31 also noted 'a law court to denounce the crimes of the US" [i.e. Winter Soldier Investigation], the "return of medals" [VVAW medal toss] and the demonstrations on April 24. The Directive proved Hanoi's puppet, NLF, had a very detailed playlist of the anti-war movement inside the USA.

Directive 31 listed future events as if they had already occurred. It covered the planned May 1 signing of the "People's Peace Treaty," between "student" groups. Directive 31 dated April 28th informed, "On 5 May, all universities in the US were shut down to celebrate the first anniversary of opposing Nixon's invasion of Cambodia. On 16 May, the whole country unanimously backed the antiwar demonstrations staged by US servicemen."

The Directive described antiwar activities of American soldiers on specific battlefields—Laos, Khe Sanh, on Route 9. The "fighting spirit [of (U.S. troops)] is lowered while dissension between officers and NCOs and between the 'white' and 'black soldiers is deepened."

Targeting South Vietnamese public opinion and American soldiers fighting in South Vietnam, Directive 31 instructed Viet Cong cadre, "taking advantage of this occasion," in part, to
do the following: …keep track of the information on the American's struggle campaign…to emphasize the upsurge of the American's struggle campaign… was due to the successive defeats suffered by U.S. troops…especially on Route 9 in lower Laos. …

Use media.

---

was created in October 1966 under the MACV Assistant Chief of Staff for Intelligence (J-2), with the mission of receiving and exploiting captured enemy documents as a source of military intelligence for assessments and planning.

Spread rumors…use newspapers…and radio stations to spread the struggle movement …back the struggle movement of the American people…

Pass the word

Make the [South Vietnamese] people fully understand that the American people stand up against the warmongers for the sake of peace in Vietnam…

Directive 31 sought to

motivate US servicemen [in South Vietnam] to provide full support to the spring struggle of the American people…start rumors and exaggerate our victories…encourage US servicemen to participate in the antiwar movement…

There were approved propaganda themes to be used among the troops:

> [D]esseminat[e] leaflets...and the following slogans among US troops in base areas: participate in the spring struggle campaign…stage demonstrations… to return home…do not execute combat orders… demand your immediate return… Motivate US soldiers to support the struggle of US veterans, students, and people of all classes…by refusing to conduct sweep operations, provide reinforcements …and demanding to return home to meet their parents, wives, and children…motivate students to conduct propaganda activities among US soldiers.

Meanwhile Hanoi and the Viet Cong met antiwar leaders in Paris and Budapest to thank the antiwar movement, instruct them on the proper propaganda themes and to plan future actions.

***

Chapter 12. Hanoi Guidances and Pentagon Papers Set the Date

Communist Guidance in Paris and Budapest

Paris-Binh and Sarnoff –May 1971. During the week of May 10, 1971, American activists met Vietnamese Communists in Paris to debrief the spring offensive and to plan future actions. Sidney and Louise Peck, Robert Greenblatt, Carol Kitchen and Jack Davis met Nguyen Minh Vy, Xuan Oanh, and Madame Binh.[1364] A circular No. 6 of July 23, 1971 to VC in South Vietnam describes the "guidance" given to Americans meeting them in Paris in May 1971.[1365]

Nguyen Minh Vy, Deputy Minister to Hanoi's Paris delegation said, "We felt that he "Spring Offensive of the American antiwar movement was a large success. …It is hard to find the words to express our feelings." In contrast, Nguyen Minh Vy is dissatisfied with the Mayday slogan, "Stop the war or we will stop the government," implying the Vietnamese were losing, victory was inevitable.

Madame Binh said, the People's Peace Treaty was good for organizing, but too complex for mass agitation. She wanted groups to popularize, "Set the Date" for U.S. withdrawal. Rep. John G. Schmitz (R-California) called "set the date" unilateral U.S. withdrawal and surrender.[1366] Communist "guidance" was marching orders.

Budapest-World Peace Council. Hanoi was happy with the USA spring offensive and said so at a meeting of a Soviet front, the World Peace Council, in Budapest, Hungary on May 12-16. The "warmest reception" the 30-member American delegation received, "was from the Vietnamese delegates, who affirmed that the Spring Offensive had given a new thrust to the world forces opposed to U.S. imperialism and its naked aggression in Indochina."[1367] Several PCPJ-affiliated groups attended.[1368]

[1364] John Schmitz, "Set the Date," *Congressional Record* E6812, July 1, 1971.
[1365] Circular 06/71, Current Affairs Committee , Ba Ria Sub-Region [VC Region 7]Party Committee, 23 July 1971, captured 21 August, 1971, CDEC Log number 08-1395,71; summarized in Bulletin Number 45, 456 on 27 August 1971, CDEC Document Log Number 08-1395-71.
[1366] John Schmitz, "Set the Date," *Congressional Record* E6812, July 1, 1971.
[1367] Pauline Rosen of the Communist Party and Women Strike for Peace quotes *World Magazine*, June 26, 1971.
[1368] Gannon, *A Biographical Dictionary of the Left*, [1969-1973] Belmont (Mass.):

Madame Binh said, "I wish to thank here particularly our American friends."[1369] Similarly, Romesh Chandra, Sec. General of the WPC "praised the 25 United States delegates." Chandra complimented the united front Hanoi had demanded in March. He praised "this linking of the anti-war movement with the key problems facing the people of the USA at home" and applauded "the vast development and growing unity of the U.S. peace movement."[1370] Ruth Gage-Colby who attended the Budapest conference was later credited with "helping to fashion unity of all major peace groups"[1371] as instructed by Hanoi in February.

Now unified, a single simple message was instructed and accepted.

***

Viet Cong and Americans agree: "Set the Date"

The CIA reports: "Antiwar leaders met with Mme. Nguyen Thi Binh...[S]he...both criticized and praised antiwar activists for their May efforts. Additionally, she indicated several desirable changes in American antiwar tactics that have since been adopted by American organizations." And like Binh, Chandra urged "massive demonstrations... with the central slogan 'Set the '71 date'...on the American antiwar movement..."[1372]

Back in the U.S. John Rankin Davis, brother of Rennie Davis, passed on the North Vietnamese suggestions, instructions, to PCPJ and to the May Day tribe: "Set the date by December 1971...[L]obby Congress... Support.... Sen. George McGovern and Rep. Bella Abzug."[1373]

Both NPAC and PCPJ, besides uniting in common antiwar actions, would also adopted "Set the Date" for US withdrawal and quit claiming to "stop the government."[1374] The

---

Western Islands, Vol. III, 572.

[1369] *Daily World*, June 16, 1971.

[1370] June 16, 1971, Daily World cited in William T. Poole, The Anti-Defense Lobby Part 2: "The Peace Movement, Continued", *Institutional Analysis #11*, September 19, 1979.**http://www.heritage.org/Research/GovernmentReform/IA11.cfm**

[1371] Dear friend of peace letter, Ruth Gage-Colby Testimonial Committee, scheduled January 20, 1972 at Biltmore in New York. Copy in possession of author from Max Friedman.

[1372] CIA, *Situation Information Report*, June 9. 1971, TTU Archives cited in Rothrock, 118N68.

[1373] CIA, *Situation Information Report*, June 9. 1971,p. 3 TTU Archives cited in Rothrock, p.118N69.

[1374] CIA, *Situation Information Report*, July 23, 1971,p. 1 TTU Archives cited in

Vietnamese finally understood ordinary Americans did not like disorder. Pauline Rosen, CPUSA and WSP, told *World Magazine*, "... the Vietnamese delegates...affirmed that the Spring Offensive had given a new thrust to the world forces opposed to U.S. imperialism and its naked aggression in Indochina."[1375]

Congress On Board? On May 17, 1971 Radio Hanoi reported the impact of the antiwar movement on Congress. "...Deepening Internal Division in U.S. Political Circles," was demonstrated by "the recent fierce spring offensive" revealing "broad segments of the American population participate in the Vietnam antiwar movement on an unprecedented scale." The impact was clear in "the weariness and antiwar mood in the U.S. Congress." Identical to Hanoi's instructions in Paris and in Budapest, some bills in Congress demanded, "Nixon set a date for the total withdrawal..."[1376] And on May 17 Senator George McGovern called in VVAW's Scott Camil to testify that in Vietnam his unit tortured, killed, raped and mutilated the Vietnamese. McGovern read it all into the *Congressional Record* saying, it was "exactly what the Nazi force did...during World War II."[1377] A claim that Senator Richard Durbin would make and retract about the war in Iraq.

Hanoi's Comrades in Congress Follow Party Line. On June 12, 1971, Hanoi's Vietnam News Agency, VNA, reported on the vote of June 11, 1971 in the Senate on the McGovern-Hatfield amendment proposing to defund the war after December. The VNA quoted Senator Mark Hatfield appealing to the "conscience of America" and Senator Ted Kennedy charging Nixon of having "grossly mislead" the American people about an expanding war.[1378]

Rothrock, p.119-120N70.

[1375] June 26, 1971, *World Magazine* cited in William T. Poole, The Anti-Defense Lobby Part 2: "The Peace Movement, Continued", *Institutional Analysis #11*, September 19, 1979.http://www.heritage.org/Research/GovernmentReform/IA11.cfm

[1376] "The U.S. War of Aggression in Vietnam and the Deepening Internal Division in U.S. Political Circles," Hanoi Domestic Service in Vietnamese 1430 GMT 17 May, 1971,1-2, TTU Archive cited in Rothrock, *Divided...* 293-5n77.

[1377] E4465-5/17/71 cited in FBI *Information Digest Special Report on VVAW*, Aug. 25, 1972 at www.wintersoldier.com.

[1378] "Congressional, Other Opposition against Indochina War Reported," *Hanoi Vietnam News Agency*, International Service, FBIS, 1552 GMT, June 12, 1971, TTU Archive cited in Rothrock, *Divided... 291-2n74*.

June 25-27, 1971 the PCPJ, held a conference at St. Michaels' Church in Milwaukee, Wisconsin. Among the major agenda items were ratification of the People's Peace Treaty, promoting the slogan, "Set the Date," and supporting Huynh Tan Mam, a student and a Viet Cong agent, to whom drafting the People's Peace Treaty was attributed.[1379] PCPJ set October 13th for nationwide protests and November 6th for a militant march in Washington.

As the year 1971 progressed it became harder to claim that the antiwar activists and North Vietnamese propagandists were not locked at the hips and using the same lips. As they had since Harrison Salisbury's reports from Hanoi in 1965-66, the communists and antiwar activists adopted identical numbers as well as words.

***

Political Prisoners by the Numbers: North and South
On May 17th, 1971 Madame Ngo Ba Thanh, a law student in Spain, France and at Columbia University, now chairman of Women's Actions for the Right to Live, sent a letter to the Foreign Relations Committee of the U.S. Senate. Claiming to represent a noncommunist Third Force[1380] Madame Binh wrote, "the U.S. war of aggression 'has resulted in 200,000 political prisoners, drinking, opium smoking, prostitution….'"[1381] Media and antiwar reports promptly parroted the newly approved number of 200,000 political prisoners.

In testimony before Congress, Father Chan Tin (Stephano Nguyen Tin) representing the Committee to Reform the Prison System in South Vietnam claimed widespread torture, described the "tiger cages" and said the true number of political prisoners was 202,000.[1382] The Thieu regime jailed Father Chan Tin, as did the Communists after 1975.

And that was how a bogus number became the official public record.[1383] In September 1973 Rep. Bella Abzug met

---

[1379] FBI, Indianapolis to Director, People's Coalition for Peace and Justice, National Conference, Milwaukee, Wisconsin, AIRTEL, July 9, 1971.
[1380] Bergman *Women of Vietnam…*, 104-105.
[1381] "Saigon Women Appeal to U.S. Committee for End of War," Liberation Press Agency, 1512 GMT, May 17, 1971, TTU archive cited in Rothrock pp. 149-150N24.
[1382] **Tôn Thât Manh Tuong**, "Chân Tin: A Non-Violent Struggle for Human Rights in Viet Nam," *Nobody Gets Off the Bus: The Viet Nam Generation Big Book*, Volume 5, Number 1-4, March 1994.
http://www3.iath.virginia.edu/sixties/HTML_docs/Texts/Scholarly/Tuong_Chan_Tin_bio.html
[1383] D.E, Bordenkircher, S.A. Bordenkircher, *Tiger Cage: Untold Story*, Abby

Madame Ngo Ba Thanh and Chan Tin and other "third force" leaders Ho Ngoc Nhouan and Huy Tan Nam and others in Saigon to discuss Thieu's 200,000 political prisoners. These "third force" leaders, claimed persecution for their political views rather than their role as secret agents of the Viet Cong.[1384] They were not believed inside Saigon. On October 15, 1973 a mob in a Saigon trashed Madame Ngo Ba Thanh's car. For her phony support of a "third force" in Saigon, she would be rewarded after liberation.

How Many "Political" Prisoners? According to South Vietnamese Premier Nguyen Cao Ky, "We held no more in detention or internment than any other country fighting for survival." The imprisoned engaged in assassinations, espionage, and terrorism were not civilian noncombatants,[1385] not political activists. They were combatants, legitimate prisoners of war.

Moreover, 200,000 was just false. At war, Ky claimed a total 47,000 prisoners of war either captured on the battlefield or terrorists lawfully convicted as combatants.[1386] Don Bordenkircher and staff came up with 45,000 by the end of 1968 and 43,717 by December 1972. A US Embassy study revealed civilian "political" prisoners had actually declined from 38,000 to 35,000 since 1970. Indeed by May 1, 1973, after the Paris Accords, the Thieu government had released 27,000 healthy North Vietnamese POWs.[1387] Both 27,00 and 47,000 were far less than 200,000.

"Political Prisoners" Refuse Return to Hanoi. Hanoi's political prisoners was feigned. In May 1971, Saigon offered to release 570 sick and disabled NVA prisoners. On May 29, 1971, the International Red Cross, IRC, found only 13 of 570, two % wanted to return home. Ninety-eight percent favored Saigon's prison life. In WW II and Korea expatriates from Communist regimes also did not wish to be returned to their homelands. In 1971, Hanoi turned back the loyal 2% returning home by sea.[1388] On October 31, Saigon released

Publishing, 1998, 77, 197.
[1384] Bella Abzug, "Documents on South Vietnam's Prisoners, *Congressional Record*, Vol 119, No. 133.
[1385] Mark Moyar, *Phoenix and the Birds of Prey; The CIA's Secret Campaign to Destroy the Viet Cong*, Annapolis: Naval Institute Press, 1997, 210.
[1386] Nguyen Cao Ky, How We Lost…, 177
[1387] George J. Veith, *Black April: The Fall of South Vietnam, 1973-75*, New York: Encounter Books, 2012, 28.

3,000 prisoners pledging loyalty to it. Over the course of the war 100,000 switched sides, deserting the Viet Cong and pledging loyalty to Saigon.

Hanoi used all POWs as pawns, its own and Americans.

The media and the peace movement aided Hanoi exploitation.

***

POWS Pawns of Media, Hanoi, Peace Movement

Anthony Lewis, Hanoi: Keep U.S. POWs...Until Surrender. On May 22, 1971 Anthony Lewis published an article on interviewing Xuan Thuy. Cora Weiss of COLIFAM shared a copy with POW families. Before POW releases, Thuy said, "What I need is a precise date for withdrawal of all forces." Then POWs go home.

Commenting on the Lewis's sycophantic flack job for Xuan Thuy, a witless columnist, Tom Wicker, whined that if Nixon kept troops in Vietnam then the troops and the POWs would be there forever.[1389] Making the POWs hostage to a settlement on Hanoi's terms had become a winning tactic for American supporters of Hanoi.

Cora Weiss Teases Families. On June 8, 1971 Cora Weiss wrote POW families saying bombing had reduced mail service. Since March, no mail had reached Hanoi. Weiss reminded the families, setting the date for withdrawal would "trigger immediate arrangements for release of prisoners."

She suggested families pressure the Senate to set a date.

Peggy Duff. No Torture. Weiss enclosed from the *New York Times* a letter from Peggy Duff of the International Confederation for Disarmament and Peace. Peggy Duff had accompanied David McReynolds of the War Resisters League, WRL, to Saigon in 1966 to talk to dissident Buddhists. The serially credulous Peggy Duff was a British democrat socialist, an occasional critic of Stalinist show trials and opposed Soviet tanks crushing the Hungarian Revolution in 1956. Yet Duff believed the communist line, no torture of US POWs.

[1388] (S-NOFORN-GP 1) COMUSMACV COMMAND HISTORY, 1971, X-3. NY Times, 4 JUN 71, 1. (C) Msg, US Del France 9980 to State, 10 June 71, JCS in 62334.
[1389] Tom Wicker, "Illogical in Vietnam," *New York Times*, May 25, 1971.

Cora Weiss enclosed a Mother's Day column from a mother whose son had died in Vietnam. The column included a large cartoon, of rolling hills to the horizon covered with thousands of gravestones, and captioned "For Mother's Day".[1390] Sweet, Cora.

POW Releases: Hanoi's Surrender. On June 24, 1971, Le Duc Tho arrived in Paris claiming to carry a new proposal, removal of all US forces by December 31, the release of all POWs and, of course, the removal of the Thieu and Ky government opposing Hanoi. With Weiss, Lewis, Wicker and others running interference it seemed a very good game plan for Hanoi.

***

Joint Chiefs Want More Targets; Laird Opposes

Bombing NVA troops and supply caches in Laos in Lam Son 719 effectively devastated the enemy with up to 70% casualties and destroyed stockpiles of food and weapons intended for an NVA invasion during 1971. With US ground forces rapidly withdrawing, the Joint Chief's wanted freer use of airpower to aid Saigon. In particular Chairman Moorer wanted to hit SAM sites and MIG bases. The antiwar movement and Congress worried Sec. Defense Laird. Further Laird argued such actions would violate the "deal" made by LBJ with Hanoi to halt bombing [if the NVA did not build up DMZ forces.] Over Moorer's objections Laird refused to give target authority to field commanders to decide targets.[1391]

June 1971- Pentagon Papers

If the court does not temper its doctrinaire logic with
a little practical wisdom, it will convert the
constitutional
Bill of Rights into a suicide pact.
Justice Robert H. Jackson, *Terminiello v. Chicago*

Neither Pentagon Nor History: the Pentagon Papers, Political Origins and Intent. The June 13, 1971 issue of the *New York Times* published very selected parts—9 ½ percent of 7,000 pages--of the Robert McNamara commissioned

---

[1390] Cora Weiss to Dear Friends, COLIFAM, June 8, 1971.
[1391] Dale Van Atta, *With Honor: Melvin Laird in War, Peace and Politics*, Madison: University of Wisconsin, 2008,383-386.

study of the Vietnam War, forever thereafter known as the Pentagon Papers.

Largely without consulting the White House, State Department or CIA, Robert McNamara, Secretary of Defense in 1967 asked a small group of six part time public employees to answer 100 questions about the war. Only a dozen were historical questions.[1392] This six-month project grew to a large task force of 36 analysts, largely civilian employees at the Pentagon, to write a history of the Vietnam War to discover what had gone wrong in the Pentagon. McNamara's successor, Clark Clifford, seeing nothing but catastrophe ahead in Vietnam,[1393] finished the report.

The "what had gone wrong" pessimism of McNamara and Clifford and its mostly civilian supervisors and writers, e.g. Clark Clifford, John McNaughton, Morton Halperin, Leslie Gelb, Mel Gurtov, Paul Warnke, is found scattered the final report.

The papers selectively covered America's Cold War assistance to the colonial French against the communists, but neglected the earliest U.S. preference, e.g. Edward Lansdale, that the French free their colonies in Indochina after the Japanese defeat. After the Hanoi communists attempted to force the unification of the three distinct parts of Vietnam,[1394] all U.S. presidents favored stopping the communist conquest, a worldwide threat during the Cold War.

Military Role Minimized. Most of the Pentagon Papers, internal memorandum of the bureaucrats, never actually reached senior policy officials for their concurrence or approval. One of the few career military officers involved in the research, Col. William R. Simons had little access to material from the Joint Chiefs of Staff and none from the President's National Security Council. Col. Simons had no access to critical National Security Agency intercepts of the North Vietnamese communications during the Gulf of Tonkin.[1395] The massive number of documents allowed the war's critics and the media opportunistically to pick

---

[1392] Mai Elliott, *RAND in Southeast Asia: A History of the Vietnam War Era*, Santa Monica: RAND corporation, 2010, 416-17.

[1393] LBJ, *Vantage Point*, 148.

[1394] John M. Del Vecchio, *For the Sake of All living Things*, New York: Bantam 1991,474.

[1395] Mai Elliott, *RAND in Southeast Asia: A History of the Vietnam War Era*, Santa Monica: RAND corporation, 2010, 418-19 cites Prados and Porter, *Inside the Pentagon Papers*, 2004, 19.

and choose those documents that carried their antiwar agendas forward.[1396]

Lacking Military Perspectives. Pentagon Papers were largely not papers produced in the Pentagon. Neither a majority of the documents, their signers, nor the task force staff originated in the Pentagon or from military sources or military authors.

Of the military resources, most came from the Office of the Secretary of Defense, International Security Affairs, McNamara's civilian whiz kids, a decidedly non-military lot. The civilians did not explain their own past failures in military strategy. Their analytical civilian brethren, the CIA, also came out quite well. The CIA provided only positive documents about the CIA.[1397]

Whiz Kids Blame Others for their Mistakes. It was quite a trick to be able to blame Presidents Kennedy and Johnson for the bad advice the civilian analysts, inexperienced in both the politics and military arts, had themselves given the Commanders in Chief and the nation's military commanders.

The whiz kid's no-win doctrines, limited war, war without strategy, signals without bombs, war without force, were presumptively pessimistic about military success. Victory was not in the rules of the game cards the wonder boys had invented. Victory was not an option. Peace now, victory never. The Communist enemy was defeated in battle after battle, but was never finished off.

In today's world, one sees the same in over fascination with computer modeling based on sparse or nonexistent data. Absent a wealth of facts, assumptions fabricate "facts" out of thin air.

The enemy was able to return repeatedly to fight another day at times, places and tactics of its own choosing. There might be light at the end of the tunnel, but the tunnel simply had no end, no exit. There was no military strategy other than avoidance of defeat. The end was an ignoble peace cloaked in a thin mask of honor soon shredded.

[1396] Michael Lind, *Vietnam: The Necessary War,* New York: Simon& Schuster 1999, 192-193;Karnow, *Vietnam: A History*, 414, 648; Nixon, *No More Vietnams, 138-139* cited in Rothrock, *Divided... 250n35.*
[1397] Mai Elliott, *RAND in Southeast Asia: A History of the Vietnam War Era*, Santa Monica: RAND corporation, 2010, n35421.

Who Were the Liars and Fools? By 1968, pessimism ruled and the McNamara-Clifford report showed it.

Those who had been optimists, mostly the warriors, the military officers, were surely liars and fools, the whiz kid analysts felt. As Walter Cronkite would say, "And that's the way it is," in most histories of the Vietnam War the optimists were surely the liars. War, always messy and horrific, is best left to the warriors.

The Vietnamese Communists, waging the psychological war between optimistic and pessimistic feelings, won the political war of wills, disarmed the enemy and finished him off the old fashion way with superior firepower.

The Pentagon Papers, selected and analyzed by the whiz kids, represented the loser's manifesto blaming others for their own failures. Robert Elegant has accused some journalists of doing the same, making partial apologies for not reporting communist terror, but redoubling efforts to blame others, Presidents and Generals.

The deed done all that remained was distribution.

***

Daniel Ellsberg's Copy Machine Team. The Rand Corporation was an analytical contributor to the Pentagon Papers. Daniel Ellsberg worked at the Rand Corporation near Venice in Santa Monica where copies of the 47 volume work were stored. **Ellsberg a Slacker.** At the Rand Corporation, Ellsberg was a flawed human being and employee. Dan Ellsberg worked little, wrote little and produced next to nothing.[1398] Ellsberg was not trusted. He later lied about his contribution to the Pentagon study and about his privileged access to the whole study. He later admitted he had mental problems as his RAND colleagues observed.[1399]

In the early fall of 1969 Ellsberg made his own personal copy of the Pentagon papers before giving a copy to his employer, the Rand Corporation. Ellsberg with the assistance of Vu Van Thai, a former South Vietnamese Ambassador to the U.S. under a Rand Corporation contract,[1400] began passing still

---

[1398]Mai Elliott, *RAND in Southeast Asia: A History of the Vietnam War Era*, Santa Monica: RAND corporation, 2010, 423-4.

[1399] Mai Elliott, *RAND in Southeast Asia: A History of the Vietnam War Era*, Santa Monica: RAND corporation, 2010, 424, 427,429, 430, 433, 485.

[1400] Vu Van Thai Contract #70663 with RAND, October 1 1969 at ACLU-So Cal, Box 270.

other copies to the Soviet-friendly Institute for Policy Studies and perhaps others. Some claim, others not,[1401] that Ellsberg, through Vu Van Thai, also sent photocopies to Hanoi and to the Soviet Embassy in Washington.[1402]

Assisting photocopying the many volumes was a young advertiser, antiwar volunteer and future billionaire, Lynda Rae Harris Sinay [later Reznick], and pro-Communist Anthony Russo, and experienced Vietnamese politician Vu Van Thai.

Who Was Vu Van Thai? Vu Van Thai, a French trained engineer, married a French girl, advised Ho Chi Minh and the united front Viet Minh. In a Communist Party purge, Vu Van Thai's father was murdered. Vu came South in 1954 as an economist for Ngo Dinh Diem, called Diem a "dictator," was exiled to the UN in 1960, worked under a USAID contract for Togo, wrote Marxist economic analyses of the developing world,[1403] became Ambassador to the United States under Nguyen Cao Ky in January 1966. Vu thought the Ky regime was "sincere about its program of social revolution."[1404] It got off to a slow start.[1405]

Vu Van Thai also had been a protégé of "Albert" Pham Ngoc Thao was suspected of being Hanoi's top secret agent inside the Saigon government. Viet Cong expert and scholar Douglas Pike said Pham Ngoc Thao, "Although he was never uncovered as a Viet Cong spy,…[but he was] …promoted posthumously to the rank of Colonel in People's Army of Viet Nam …"[1406] His family later confirmed his status as an Hanoi spy.[1407]

Hilarie Du Berrier, a French-American journalist and others believed that not only Pham Ngoc Thao, but also his

---

[1401] "I doubt that Dan was sending copies to Hanoi and the USSR via Vu Van Thai. Dan's interest was in getting copies before Members of Congress," Frank Scotton to Roger Canfield CC Sherman Stephen Dec 31, 2015.

[1402] "The Soviet Union has a complete copy of the forty-seven volumes," George Carver to Director, 9 July 1971, in CIA, FOIA, Family Jewels, 287; Covert *Cadre*, 48N4; Hilaire Du Berrier in both *The New American*, April 27, 1987, 43 and his *H du B Reports*, June 1989, 6.

[1403] Vu Van Thai, "Technology in Focus—Emerging Nations," JSTOR, Technology and Culture: Vol. 3, no. 4, *Proceedings of the Encyclopedia Britannica*, 602.

[1404] "A Taste for Tulips," *Time,* Friday April 29, 1966.

[1405] Frank Scotton says, "If Nguyen Cao Ky had a program for social revolution, it is a mystery to me. I was in Viet Nam during the Ky administration. He did appoint Nguyen Duc Thang (one of the famously honest generals) as Minister of Revolutionary Development. But Thang barely understood what Tran Ngoc Chau had in mind, and nothing really began cooking for rural recovery and development until Chau brought Nguyen Be to the training center in Vung Tau. Frank Scotton to Roger Canfield CC Sherman Stephen Dec 31, 2015.

[1406] Pike, Chapter 1, *War in Shadows*, Boston: Boston Publishing Co., 1988, 6.

[1407] https://www.theguardian.com/g2/story/0,,214575,00.html

protégé Vu Van Thai, was a Hanoi agent. Vu's helping steal and distribute the Pentagon Papers benefited propaganda the war was illegal, immoral and unwinnable.

Passing Around Copies of the Pentagon Papers. Daniel Ellsberg, misremembers he decided to release the Pentagon Papers in the fall of 1970 after a Yale-Harvard football game (on November 21).[1408] Yet months earlier in September 1970, the pro-Soviet Institute for Policy Studies, holding the papers since 1969, conducted a conference, "U. S. Strategy in Asia," based on the stolen and still un-released, Pentagon Papers. On September 1, 1970, John Bross asked the Director of the CIA to lift Ellsberg's security clearance.[1409] Ellsberg's decision to go public, made in the fall of 1970 was, of course, a full year after Ellsberg had secretly copied the Pentagon Papers and began passing private copies around. It was March 1971 before Neil Sheehan, an unsympathetic reporter on the war in Saigon, of the *New York Times* began receiving parts of the Pentagon Papers from Ellsberg.[1410] The *New York Times* published parts of the papers another nine months later in June 13, 1971.

President Nixon Reacts to the Pentagon Papers June 13, 1971. Happy with his daughter Tricia's wedding the previous day and the declining number of American deaths in Vietnam, President Nixon's initial responses after the publication were tentative and thoughtful. While liberals at the *Times* angered him, e.g. Neil Sheehan who Nixon called a "bastard" on the Vietnam War, Nixon was more concerned about the nation's security than he was about his enemies.

If Treason by Whom? On tape recordings, Nixon told Kissinger, "it's unconscionable on the part of the people that leaked it."[1411] It was treason. "This is treasonable action on the part of the bastards that put it out."[1412] Nixon tells Haldeman, "it's an aid to the enemy…" just like Alger Hiss had done, "this [release] turns it over to the enemy."[1413]

[1408] Wm. F. Buckley, "Ellsberg in the Dock," *National Review*, August 18, 1972, 918.
[1409] "3 September 1970," CIA, FOIA, Family Jewels, 282.
[1410] Powell, *Covert Cadre,* 48 cites Harrison Salisbury, *Without Fear or Favor.*
[1411] Nixon to Kissinger 6 13 71 15:09 pm, Nixon Presidential Materials Project, Selected Conversations from the period 1971/06/13-16 concerning the Pentagon Papers, National Security Archives, George Washington University.
[1412] Nixon to Kissinger 6 13 71 15:09, Nixon Presidential Materials Project, Selected Conversations from the period 1971/06/13-16 concerning the Pentagon Papers, National Security Archives, George Washington University.
[1413] Nixon to Kissinger 6 13 71 15:09, and Nixon to Haldeman 6 14 71 3:09 pm. Nixon Presidential Materials Project, Selected Conversations from the period 1971/06/13-16

Others shared Nixon's views.

Former President Lyndon Johnson termed the leak "close to treason." General Hyman and General Lemnitzer, Chairman of the Joint Chiefs of Staff early in the war and later Supreme Commander of NATO, denounced it as "a traitorous act." Most of Ellsberg's own colleagues thought him a traitor including his mentor Albert Wohlstetter and Gus Shubert who said most Rand employees thought Ellsberg was a "loathsome traitor."[1414] Rand had an economic interests in separating itself from the leak of its government contract.[1415]

When pressed about a decision to prosecute the *New York Times*, Nixon told John Ehrlichman, "Hell, I wouldn't prosecute the *Times*. My view is to prosecute the goddamn pricks that gave it to them."[1416] After all, the *Times* was an enemy that couldn't be expected to do anything else. Nixon had also leaked documents to the press during his own tough fight against a recipient of the Soviet Order of the Red Star, Alger Hiss and Hiss's many high-placed friends.[1417]

On the first day, Alexander Haig and Henry Kissinger persuaded Nixon that the leak of the Pentagon Papers was monumental despite being embarrassing only to the Kennedy and Johnson administrations. Alexander Haig told Nixon that the publication was "a devastating security breach...of the greatest magnitude"[1418] And Kissinger said, "I'm absolutely certain that this violates all sorts of security laws... ...this is everything the Defense Department [unclear—'possessed]"[1419]

Trust in Government. On the first day, Nixon also began to see the current significance of the history. The impact was "… massive against the war."[1420] Kissinger said, "it just

---

concerning the Pentagon Papers, National Security Archives, George Washington University.

[1414] Wells *Wildman: The Life and Times of Daniel Ellsberg*, New York: Palgrave, 2001, 418, 453 cited in Mai Elliott, *RAND in Southeast Asia: A History of the Vietnam War Era*, Santa Monica: RAND corporation, 2010, 468, 470.

[1415] Frank Scotton to Roger Canfield CC Sherman Stephen Dec 31, 2015.

[1416] Nixon to Ehrlichman 6 14 71 7:13pm, Nixon Presidential Materials Project, Selected Conversations from the period 1971/06/13-16 concerning the Pentagon Papers, National Security Archives, George Washington University.

[1417] Sam Tanenhaus, *Whittaker Chambers, A Biography*, New York Random House, 1997; Nixon, July 1, 1971 cited in Kutler, *Abuse of Power*, 9. Transcripts on website of University of Virginia, Miller Center of Public Affairs, Presidential Recordings Program.

[1418] Haig to Nixon 6 13 12:18.

[1419] Kissinger to Nixon 6 13 71 15:09.

[1420] Nixon to Kissinger 6 13 71 15:09.

shows a further weakening of resolve."[1421] And "It hurts us with Hanoi, because it shows how far our demoralization has gone." Nixon responds, "Good God." [1422]

H.R. Haldeman immediately saw the long-term implications of the Pentagon papers as a lack of trust in government:

> Don't hurt us politically so much—they hurt others—but what they really hurt—and this is what the intellectuals—and [what] the motivation of the *Times* must be [,] is that it hurts the government…Rumsfeld was making this point this morning—but out of the gobblegook, comes a very clear thing…you can't trust the government; you can't believe what they say: you can't rely on their judgment… It shows that people do things the president wants to do even though it's wrong, and the president can be wrong.[1423]

In the early days through Walt Rostow, former President Johnson, said publishing the Pentagon Papers was "an attack upon the whole integrity of government…."[1424]

Leaker Suspects. Nixon wanted to find and prosecute the source of the leak, saying first he'd "fire the top guy"[1425] responsible at the Pentagon[1426] Nixon told Kissinger, "cleaning house… people have got to be put to the torch for this sort of thing—this is terrible."[1427] Nixon and Kissinger were unable to trust the "bureaucracy."

Talk of possible leakers turned immediately to names like Clark Clifford, Morton Halperin, Leslie Gelb and finally Dan Ellsberg. There was the former Defense Secretary, Clark Clifford and the "peaceniks over there" in the Pentagon.[1428] Clifford had finished the McNamara study and had become so actively antiwar that he had angered former President Johnson. With Halderman, Nixon discussed Sam (sic, Leslie) Gelb now at the Brookings Institute and Morton Halperin who had

---

[1421] Kissinger to Nixon, 6 13 15:09

[1422] Nixon to Kissinger 6 13 71 15:09.

[1423] Haldeman to Nixon, 6 14 71 3:09 pm

[1424] Kissinger to Nixon and Mitchell 6 14 71 7:19 pm.

[1425] Nixon to Haig 6 13 1971 12:18pm

[1426] Nixon to William Rogers 6 13 71 13:28pm

[1427] Nixon to Kissinger 6 13 71 15:09

[1428] Haig to Nixon 6 13 71 12:18.

possession of many of the Pentagon's most closely held secret files. And Tony Lake. The suspects were antiwar and recently or currently on the federal payroll at the highest levels.[1429]

Charles Huston warned a year before Brookings had extensive Pentagon files and recommended retrieval, but that had not been done.

In these early June days of 1971 Nixon was certain he had the culprit in his sights. Nixon instructed Haldeman to "get out the story on Gelb" and to "smoke out" the Brookings Institute where Gelb and Halperin worked--using Nixon's friends in the press and Congress.[1430]

In a three-way conversation between Nixon, Mitchell and Kissinger, it was learned that Walt Rostow believed among those with access to copies of the Pentagon Papers was "a gentleman by the name of Ellsberg, who is a left-winger that's now with the Rand Corporation."[1431] The CIA was tasked to perform the deed of removing documents from Rand. Under Halperin, a former aide to Kissinger, Brookings had far more classified documents than Rand.

The Nation's Security and the Pentagon Papers. The CIA assessed the damage from disclosure of the Pentagon Papers. Whatever Defense Secretary Laird thought, both the President and the CIA opposed publishing the whole or sanitized parts of the Papers.[1432]

The publication of the Pentagon Papers would harm national security. Nixon told an interagency group he wanted to revoke all clearances and to retrieve all classified documents from Harvard, Brookings, Rand, Cal Tech and the Regents of the University of California.[1433] The Department of Defense dispatched a security squad to Rand's headquarters in Santa Monica and John Ehrlichman of the White House hired a former CIA employee, Howard Hunt, as a security consultant.[1434]

Neither the U.S. Supreme Court, nor thieving journalists, nor history believed Richard Nixon. Nixon and top agency officials feared loss of: coded messages, war contingency plans, informants/agents, and foreign cooperation.[1435]

[1429] Ray Wannall, *The Real J. Edgar Hoover: For the Record,* Paducah: Turner Publishing Company, 2000,116.

[1430] Nixon to Haldeman 6 14 71 3:09 pm

[1431] Mitchell to Nixon and Kissinger, 6 14 1971 7:19pm.

[1432] "8 July 1971," CIA, FOIA, Family Jewels, 286.

[1433] "2 July 1971," CIA, FOIA, Family Jewels, 285, 286.

[1434] "8 July 1971," CIA, FOIA, Family Jewels, 286.

It was absurd to believe no vital secrets were contained in seven thousands pages of classified materials.

Secrets Still Important. These issues are relevant into the 21st Century where Army Private Bradley Manning and IT specialist Edward Snowden stole and distributed thousands of secret documents. Mark Bowden writes too many critics of government secrecy, are "at war with the concept of secrecy itself…" Governments keep secrets for legitimate reasons as well as reasons that are dubious, abusive, nefarious, in short wrong. Good secrets protect surprise in war and in criminal investigations, preserve candid discussions and negotiations, protect the identities, indeed the lives, of spies and the effectiveness of technical and other methods of acquiring information.[1436]

The Real Secrets of the Pentagon Papers. David Rudenstine, author of *The Day the Presses Stopped*, who reviewed the historical documents of the Pentagon Papers cases, concluded that the Pentagon Papers contained real secrets and Nixon and Kissinger honestly believed national security was at stake.[1437] Henry Kissinger said secret third party negotiations jeopardized countries not wanting publicity.

Other losses might be incalculable. The verbatim, classified documents would enable the Soviets to break the codes of all other classified messages for the many days over the decades covered by the Pentagon Papers. The NSA said allowing enemy intelligence services to compare the plain English text of coded U.S. communications with the intercepted cipher text permitted the breaking of U.S. secret codes (As the U.S. had done in the VENONA project).

Once decoded these would reveal hidden secret sources and methods including the names of agents and locations/targets of wiretap, microphone and other technical capabilities. The Pentagon Papers had revealed at least one big secret. NSA was able to intercept Soviet communications inside the Soviet Union, including voices inside the limousines of Soviet leaders.[1438]

[1435] Nixon, No More, 139.
[1436] Mark Bowden, "What Snowden and Manning Don't Understand About Secrecy," *The Atlantic*, August 23, 2013.
[1437] David Rudenstine, *The Day the Presses Stopped*, 8-9.
[1438] National Security Agency, http://history.sandiego.edu/gen/20th/nsa.html

Prosecution? Attorney General Mitchell and John Erlichman pressed Nixon immediately to prosecute the New York *Times*. Facing a deadline and against his own instincts, President Nixon gave the go ahead for the Justice Department to try to warn off the New York *Times* and failing to prosecute the T*imes*.

In the event a poorly prepared case lost.

The Bungled Case Against the New York *Times*. As for losing the cases in court David Rudenstine says the lawyers in the Justice Department did not believe the courts would ever allow the press to publish stolen, classified material. Further, the Justice Department made a poor case because of lack of sufficient time and limited access to secrets. An attorney later told the CIA Director "Justice {Department) did not cite the appropriate provisions of the Code and has presented the case poorly."[1439] The government did not initially cite any specific material would threaten national security; nor did the judge ask the government to do so[1440] (Viewing of specific materials in *camera* would later become the routine practice subsequently under the Foreign Intelligence Surveillance Act, FISA).

The Justice Department briefs ultimately provided a largely generic, not a specific, list of secret disclosures. Disclosure would cause direct and immediate damage to the national security of the United States in several ways. Disclosure would be harmful by revealing secret diplomacy, candid comments about other nations, names and missions of CIA agents. Also activities of the National Security Agency, military contingency plans, U.S. estimates of Soviet intentions in Vietnam. Enemies would learn U.S. judgments on Soviet capacity to deliver particular weapons to North Vietnam, U.S. considerations of a nuclear option if there was a Chinese attack on Thailand and a U.S. Ambassador's assessments of Soviet responses to a range of U.S. military options in Vietnam. There was information about a possible South Vietnamese military action in Laos. The U.S. perspectives on U.S. POWs in negotiations.[1441]

[1439] "23 August 1971," CIA, FOIA, Family Jewels, 290.

[1440] David Rudenstine, *The Day the Presses Stopped*, 105-107.

[1441] This description is based upon the characterization of the Griswold brief at George Washington University Web site, which dismisses each and every such damage in their entirety. The lawyers simply assert, argue, and insist that there cannot be any military consequences whatsoever. "The Brief for the United States (Secret Portion)," in "The Pentagon Papers: Secrets, Lies, and Audiotapes, (The Nixon Tapes and the Supreme

This list did not persuade judges whose favored part of the Constitution, the First Amendment, trumped the war powers of the President and excised national security out of the national polity. It was an astonishing decision weakening the powers of the President in war. The courts said the government had a "heavy burden" of justifying prior restraint of free speech. The government had not made the case.

Publish First. Consequences Later. Had the government made a strong evidentiary case of "a grave and immediate danger to the security of the United States," it might have prevailed. The generic dangers presented were not enough under the near absolutist court doctrine of no "prior restraint" of free speech.

Using far, far fewer secret Soviet messages than in the Pentagon Papers, covering some eighteen months in the 1940s and only partially decoding them, the U. S. VENONA project discovered a Soviet spy network of at least 300 agents inside the USA. Known years before the Vietnam War, the FBI and NSA held these important secrets until 1996. Like VENONA had proven, the clear text of Pentagon Papers would allow decoding of crypted American documents.

Indeed, the issue of actual damages was in fact moot. The real damage had already been done when Ellsberg *et al* delivered 18 copies of the forty-seven volumes of the Pentagon Papers to the press and CBS's Walter Cronkite interviewed Ellsberg from a secret location.[1442] And an FBI double agent reported that someone sent the whole to the Soviet Embassy,[1443] or to one of Hanoi's agent close by.

The Court Cases on the Pentagon Papers. Inadequate evidence of dangers to national security were presented to justify denying publication. Would publication pose grave and imminent danger to national security? On appeal, Attorney General John Mitchell asked the Solicitor General Erwin Griswold to argue the case only hours before the case was to be heard. Griswold had never seen the

---

court Tape), The Secret Briefs and the Secret Evidence," National Security Archives 1-11, at gwu.edu/-nsarchiv/NSAEBB/NSAEBB48/secretbrief.html.
[1442] June 23, 1971 according to Rudenstine, note 11.
http://books.google.com/books?id=JR4LIbHYaLYC&pg=RA1-PA72&lpg=RA1-PA72&dq=william+rehnquist+pentagon+leaks&source=web&ots=iR1VypuaL2&sig=V67B4UquMeUQkmf5tEbJp_lQ_dY#PRA2-PA11,M1
[1443] Ray Wannall, *The Real J. Edgar Hoover: For the Record,* Paducah: Turner Publishing Company, 2000, 128.

Pentagon Papers.[1444] All the material was classified. Secretary Laird told Griswold there were only "six or seven paragraphs in the whole thing that were dangerous." Pentagon staff had previously developed a "voluminous list" of items too sensitive to publish. This was whittled down to 33 items. Undercutting his own now piddling case, Griswold said it was "much too broad."[1445] Laird and Griswold sabotaged the case.

There were two final court cases, in New York and Washington, D.C. concerning United States activities in Vietnam.[1446]

The Pentagon Papers Before the U.S. Supreme Court. Incredulously, the Supreme Court ruled in the final Pentagon Papers case the government's allegations of grave danger to the national security provided an insufficient foundation for enjoining publication by the *Washington Post* and the *New York Times* of classified documents. In the ten cases involving the Pentagon Papers, seven of nine justices, except Justices Black and Douglas, had "appeared willing to accept prior restraints on the basis of danger to the national security in some circumstances." But there was no agreement on a standard to do so and the government's case of generic, unspecified, dangers to national security did not persuade the seven judges open to the concept.

Justice Brennan said, a "generalized claim of threat to national security from publication of cryptographic information would constitute an adequate basis for establishing a prior restraint" and "…where properly classified government information is involved, a prior review requirement may be permissible."[1447] Justice Stewart with Justice White concurring wrote, "I am confident that the Executive is correct…But I cannot say that disclosure… will surely result in direct, immediate and irreparable damage to our Nation or its people."[1448]

[1444] David Rudenstine, *The Day the Presses Stopped*,243.

[1445] Sanford J. Ungar, The Papers and the Papers, E..P. Dutton, 1972, 31; Dale Van Atta, *With Honor: Melvin Laird in War, Peace and Politics*, Madison: University of Wisconsin, 2008, 374.

[1446] New York Times Co. v. United States, supra.

[1447] United States v. Marchetti, supra; See: "THE GOVERNMENT'S CLASSIFICATION OF PRIVATE IDEAS,"HEARINGS BEFORE A SUBCOMMITTEE OF THE COMMITTEE ON GOVERNMENT OPERATIONS HOUSE OF REPRESENTATIVES, NINETY-SIXTH CONGRESS, SECOND SESSION, FEBRUARY 28; MARCH 20; AUGUST 21, 1980, Printed for the use of the Committee on Government Operations, U.S. Government Printing Office, Washington, 1981, 260-298.

Justice White, with Stewart concurring, did not deny "substantial damage to public interest. Indeed, I am confident that their disclosure will have that result…because the material poses substantial dangers to national interests… a substantial part of the threatened damage has already occurred." Allowing publication White continued, "does not mean that…publicat[ion]… will be immune from criminal action… I would have no difficulty in sustaining convictions…" Justice Marshall: "At least one of the many statutes in this area [control of sensitive information] seems relevant to these cases."

Chief Justice Burger, a dissenter, No District Judge knew all the facts. No Court of Appeals Judge knew all the facts. No member of this Court knows all the facts …because these cases have been conducted in unseemly haste… it is hardly believable… that a newspaper… would fail to… report [theft] forthwith to responsible public officers. This duty rests on taxi drivers, Justices, and the New York *Times*. … [W]e literally do not know what we are acting on …the result is a parody of the judicial system… I am in general agreement [to]… penal sanctions… relating to the national defense.'

Justice Harlan, dissenting, with Burger and Blackmun joining, `… the Court has been almost irresponsibly feverish in dealing with these cases."

Justice Blackmun, dissenting, said he was in "substantial accord' … about criminal prosecution. … I hope that damage has not already been done. If, however, damage has been done and if, with the Court's action today, these newspapers proceed to publish the critical documents and there results … `the death of soldiers, the destruction of alliances, the greatly increased difficulty of negotiation with our enemies, the inability of our diplomats to negotiate,' to which list I might add the factors of prolongation of the war and of further delay in the freeing of United States prisoners, then the Nation's people will know where the responsibility for these sad consequences rests."

[1448] New York Times Co. v. United States 403 U.S. 713(1971) cited in Senator Strom THURMOND, "STATEMENT ON THE NOMINATION OF DR. MORTON HALPERIN, Senate - July 15, 1994, S9106-9113, http://www.fas.org/irp/congress/1994_cr/s940715-halperin.htm

In summary, a series of court injunctions failed to stop the piecemeal publication of these classified documents in the *New York Times* on June 13, 1971, and soon thereafter in the *Washington Post*, the *Boston Globe*, the *St. Louis Dispatch* and ultimately Bantam Books.

Daniel Ellsberg and Anthony Russo had stolen the Pentagon Papers, which was thought at the time to be a crime.

***

Pursuing Daniel Ellsberg and the Press

Investigating Reporters and Leakers. By July 1971, the White House was calling Director Hoover for updates on investigations of the individual New York Times reporters who had acquired the papers.[1449]

Ellsberg psychology? David Young of the White House asked CIA Director Helms to do an "indirect personality assessments of Daniel Ellsberg" from news clips and State and Justice files. Dr. Malloy worked with Howard Hunt and Gordon Liddy in producing two psychological profiles on Ellsberg completed on 12 August and 9 November 1971. The first CIA study praised Ellsberg as "brilliant, success-oriented" man who believed in "a higher order of patriotism... (who had) a special mission" on the Vietnam War.[1450] This CIA work on Ellsberg was judged "insufficient."[1451] Meanwhile, on September 3, 1971 Howard Hunt sent his private agents to break into the offices of Ellsberg's psychiatrist, Dr. Lewis Fielding, in Beverly Hills, but also found a 'dry hole'.

Interviews of Ellsberg's colleagues at Rand would have been more productive.

Ellsberg Indicted. On June 28, 1971, a Federal Grand Jury recommended an indictment of Daniel Ellsberg for unauthorized possession, access, and control of Top Secret documents, "United States-Vietnam Relations, 1945-1967," relating to national defense and that he converted these

---

[1449] Hoover to Tolson, memo, 8:54 AM, July 6, 1971.

[1450] Mai Elliott, *RAND in Southeast Asia: A History of the Vietnam War Era*, Santa Monica: RAND corporation, 2010, 476 cites *Los Angeles Times*, "CIA Ellsberg Study Reported as Laudatory," August 4, 1973.

[1451] CIA, FOIA, Family Jewels, 441-442. In 1973-1974, the author and colleague, Andy Crosby, consulted with a CIA psychometrician, David Smith, seeking advice on psychological tests that might be useful for police officer selection. This was a nationwide study of best practices in state and local law enforcement agencies (IACP-IPMA project funded by the Police Foundation). At that time the CIA had not found anything valid or reliable for screening its agents and warned us that our own research would reveal the same. It did.

documents to his own use. On December 20, 1971, Daniel Ellsberg and Anthony Russo were indicted for conspiracy, espionage, theft and misuse of secret documents in Los Angeles, Ca. Lynda Sinay and Vu Van Thai, copiers and distributors of the Pentagon Papers were unindicted co-conspirators.

The press had reinforcements.

Largely operating in the open, antiwar activists were assisting Hanoi on many fronts and venues.

****

Chapter 13: Directives and Pleadings.
Peace Advocates Meet the Enemy
Stockholm, Moscow, Oslo, Paris-
June 1971

Stockholm. On June 5, 1971, Larry Levin, Tom Hayden and others attended the Soviet, CP-USSR and KGB, funded Stockholm Conference on Vietnam.[1452]

In Chicago on June 15, 1971, John Kerry told newsmen he was planning a three-week trip to South Vietnam to see "what is really happening there," focusing on drugs, morals and refugees. As Madame Binh instructed others in Budapest, John Kerry, joined the pro-Hanoi chorus requesting Congress to "set the date" for the total and complete withdrawal of all US troops and supplies from Vietnam.[1453]

A VVAW delegation toured Moscow, Oslo and Paris. On June 22, 1971, Larry Rottman, VVAW New Mexico-Arizona, John Onda,[1454] VVAW, Pittsburgh and one other VVAW member, either John Randolph "Randy" Floyd or Ken Campbell, flew out of New York[1455] to **Moscow** via London.[1456] They had discussions with North Vietnamese, NLF, and Soviets.[1457] They picked up Russian literature.

June 20-26, 1971, the VVAW delegation visited Bertrand Russell's the International Commission for Inquiry into U.S. War Crimes in Indochina in **Oslo,** Norway[1458] Among the participants were Russell, Hanoi friendly reporters Wilfred Burchett, Roger Pic, Chesneaux, Riffaud, American Gabriel Kolko and Jean Paul Sartre.[1459] VVAW picked up literature.

[1452] Photo on Levin Website; On the conference see Papers of British Communist Party official, Jack Askins, Anti-Vietnam War Movement, Ref. Code MSS.189/V/1/12/6 cited at http://dscalm.warwick.ac.uk/DServe/dserve.exe?dsqIni= Dserve.ini&dsq App=Archive&dsqCmd=NaviTree.tcl&dsqDb=Catalog&dsqItem=ASV/1/12&dsq Field=RefNo, archives@warwick .ac.uk <archives@warwick.ac.uk. Open archive upon 1970 conference upon request http://mrc-catalogue.warwick.ac.uk/records/ASV/1/12/6

[1453] Ted Pearson, "John Kerry plans tour of South Vietnam in July," *Daily World*, June 16, 1971 at wintersoldier.com ... CDW0616_1.jpg

[1454] "Soviet Youth Secure and Confident," *Daily World*, August 28, 1971 cited in FBI, Pittsburgh Memo, VVAW, November 26, 1971.

[1455] Frank J. Rafalko, *MH/CHAOS: The CIA's Campaign Against the Radical Left and the Black Panthers*, Annapolis: Naval Institute Press, 2011, 138.

[1456] FBI, Director to Albany, Memo, VVAW IS-New Left, August 3, 1971.

[1457] FBI cites *Albuquerque Journal*, July 29, 1971.

[1458] VVAW, *First Casualty*, August 1971 cited in FBI, New York, "VVAW, Inc", Bureau file 100-448092, October 12m, 1971.

They also later met the North Vietnamese in **Paris**.[1460] The Vietnamese told Larry Rottman they were "interested in a fast settlement of the war, but the (US) is fearful of losing face."

On July 14, 1971 Larry Rottman, John Randolph "Randy" Floyd, and Ken Campbell VVAW members returned to New York on Aeroflot Number 311 back from their tour of Finland, Moscow, England, France and Norway. One of the three carried Russian literature and a report on the International Commission for Inquiry into United States War Crimes in Indochina held in Oslo, Norway on June 20-26. 1971.[1461]

At a July 20 staff meeting of VVAW, it was decided that no American flag would fly "over any VVAW office anywhere."[1462] In the fall the VVAW would be selling eight cassettes and a bound transcript of conversations between the U.S. and Vietnamese delegations for $45.

Private Meetings in Paris. In late June, Cora Weiss, Richard Falk, David Dellinger and Ethel Taylor spent "several days in extensive talks" with Madame Binh and Xuan Thuy. "Setting the date" would "trigger … release of the prisoners." …every day of delay…is another day of continued separation." Madame Binh said once the date was set the VC prisoners could also receive mail.[1463] Richard Falk wrote Nixon used the prisoners as a smokescreen to continue the war. Getting the POWs out required ending US air forces, naval power and Saigon aid. Surrendering without getting the POWs seemed reasonable to Falk[1464] later infamously saying the victims of 9 11 got what they deserved.

***

Viet Cong's Seven Point Peace Plan

On July 1, 1971 Madame Binh announced a new Seven-Point plan in Paris and the Liberation Press Agency and the *New York Times* printed it:

1. Set a date for unconditional US withdrawal;
2. Remove government of Nguyen Van Thieu;

[1459] http://rmc.library.cornell.edu/EAD/htmldocs/RMM04285.html#d0e379
[1460] FBI, Director to Albany, Secret, VVAW-IS New Left, August 3, 1971.
[1461] FBI, New York, Memo, VVAW, Inc, Nov 4, 1971, BUFILE (100-448092)and NYFILE (100-160644), 3.
[1462] VVAW, Staff Meeting Minutes, July 20, 1971, 1 at ice.hc.net.
[1463] David Dellinger and Cora Weiss to Dear families, COLIFAM, July 8, 1971.
[1464] Richard Falk, "Mr. Nixon and the Prisoner Smoke screen,: *New York Times*, June 29, 1971.

3. Allow North Vietnamese armed forces to remain in south;

4. Reunify North and South;

5. Neutralize South Vietnam;

6. Pay reparations to North Viet Nam;

7. Accept Hanoi promises as guarantees of Treaty provisions.

It was a seven-ingredient recipe for U.S. surrender, betrayal of its ally, and mobilization of the antiwar movement.[1465]

China, July 1971. Meeting in China in July the PRG, Hanoi's political front in the south told members of the Committee of Concerned Asian Scholars to "unity, unify, unify" around the PRG's Seven Point Peace Proposal.[1466]

***

Another Set of Orders.

COSVN Circular 05/T71. The Central Office of South Vietnam, COSVN, a military organ of the North Vietnamese issued Circular 05/T71, directing VC cadre to use the "Seven Point" peace plan to proselytize soldiers and to mobilize antiwar activities:

> aimed at expanding the political front…into foreign counties including the U.S…to motivate soldiers …and political factions to coordinate with the people's struggle to oppose the Americans and… demand the withdrawal of American troops…[1467]

Kerry Following the Viet Cong Playbook:

John Kerry- "Set the Date." At a press conference in Washington on July 22, 1971, John Kerry, called for Nixon to accept the NLF's 7- point peace proposal.[1468] In particular, set the date for unconditional US withdrawal so that the POWs could come home.

Kerry Uses POW Wives. Per Hanoi instructions to all antiwar groups, at his side Kerry gathered some POW wives,

---

[1465] Robert K. Brigham and Le Phuong Anh (Trans.) The Liberation Press Agency, July 1, 1971, at wintersoldier.com … page=7pointplan.

[1466] Gough, 28-29.

[1467] U.S. State Department, U.S. Mission in Vietnam, Viet-Nam Documents and Research Notes, The PRG's 'Diplomatic Offensive,' Document No. 101 Part IV, January 1972, 8-

[1468] The New York Times, "Anti-War Veteran Accused of Exploiting P.O.W. Issue," July 23, 1971; Daily World, July 24, 1971. Both articles had a photo with members of POW families.

parents and sisters. UPI photographed Kerry with Mr. and Mrs. Richard Sigler of Lakewood, Colorado, parents of Gary Richard Sigler. Also Francis Ford of Wahala, Florida, likely a relative of David Edward Ford. The communist *Daily World* printed the photo and a story on Radio Hanoi applauding Kerry.[1469] A *New York Times* photo showed Kerry with Sheila Cronin and Delia Alvarez.[1470] Captured in 1976, Mike Cronin was tortured, wrote unbelievable confessions, and taught the tap code to other POWs.[1471] Delia's brother, Everett Alvarez, was the longest held POW in the north[1472], suffered greatly there and was unhappy with Delia's antiwar activities.[1473]

In September 1974, the communists were still enjoying the distress they caused Alvarez. In an article in *Vietnam Courier* gleefully described his mother, Chole, and sisters Delia's antiwar activities and Alvarez's unfaithful wife, Tangee.[1474] POW Gary Richard Sigler later told of being subjected to the "rope trick" and repeated beatings.[1475] Michael Cronin later was active in a group of former POWs to oppose Kerry's election to the presidency in 2004.

Most Wives Refuse. Most POW families refused to be stage props for John Kerry and the Viet Cong. On July 22, 1971, the *New York Times* reported some POW family members refused a place on the platform with John Kerry. From the audience one family member shouted, "That's a lie." Another asked, "What office are you running for." One accused Kerry of "constantly using our own suffering and grief" to advance his political ambitions. The *Washington Star* reported four women relatives of POWs, under VFW escort, accusing Kerry of using the POWs for his own personal political

---

[1469] Captioned photo at wintersoldier.com ...Daily_World_1.jpg. Swett and Zigler cite Summary of Radio Hanoi's *Voice of Vietnam, July 26, 1971* from the Vietnam Veterans Radio Network VVRN Catalogue of Radio Hanoi Tapes; *Daily World*, July 24, 1971, 3.

[1470] "Anti-war Veteran Accused of Exploiting P.O.W. Issue, in wintersoldier.com ... Kerry7Points.

[1471] Mike Cronin's very informative oral history is at http://www.thinkport.org/pdfs/vietnam_war_stories/8Invasion/Mike-Cronin-Interview-Transcript.pdf

[1472] At nine years, March 1964 to March 1973, Floyd James Thompson, was longest held POW in south and north.

[1473] Craig Howes, *Voices of the Vietnam POWs*, New York: Oxford University Press, 1993,155n164.

[1474] "Comment," *Vietnam Courier*, Monthly, Sept. 1974.

[1475] http://www.scopesys.com/cgi-bin/bio2.cgi?bio=S027

327

purposes. The women called those POW relatives supporting Kerry, "stupid."

Mrs. Floyd Harold Kushner, said the ladies protesting Kerry had bad manners.[1476] She was unaware her husband had barely survived the really bad VC manners of captivity, starvation, disease.[1477]

Following communist protocols could be demanding, but on July 22, 1971 per the instructions of the Viet Cong's Circular 33 and Cora Weiss, John Kerry had used the POWs and their families as hostages and propaganda props.

How to Exploit POW families: The Playbook.
Exploiting POW family members came right out of the Viet Cong playbook for VC cadre. Kerry's actions coincided with Viet Cong circulars and Madame Binh.

The long-standing Vietnamese policy of exploiting POW families was clear:

> The *Binh van* cadre were interested in personal information from POWs …to gain the support of the individual POW, his family and friends, and the American public. …*Binh van* element attempted to spread dissention and anti-war sentiment throughout the United States."[1478]

The personnel effects of American soldiers were intimate, personal and powerful. "Anti-Vietnam war movement was spreading in the United States, and there exists a requirement to furnish this (Anti-Vietnam war) movement with personnel belongings of US servicemen."[1479] Another said, "…Corpses …should be secretly buried after removing all personnel effects." Another 1970 document ordered …capturing American personnel effects…for forwarding to Hanoi."[1480]

According to Bell and Veith, it was a long-standing Viet Cong directive that personal:
Documents were needed…to develop propaganda broadcasts oriented toward POW/MIA family members… in November

---

[1476] Mary McGrory, "POW Drive in Confusion," *The Evening Star*, July 23, 1971.
[1477] Craig Howes, *Voices of the Vietnam POWs*, New York: Oxford University Press, 1993,214n64.
[1478] Garnett "Bill" Bell and George J. Veith, "POWs and Politics: How Much does Hanoi Really Know," Center for the Study of the Vietnam Conflict Symposium, "After the Cold War: Reassessing Vietnam," Texas Tech University, 19 April 1996.
[1479] Bell and Veith
[1480] Standing Committee of the southern arm of the Politburo, cited in Bell and Veith.

1967...Hanoi announced the death of USMC Lance Corporal James O. Pyle. ... Pyle was alive... but...letters containing the address of his parents in America was captured..."[1481]

Retired Captain James H. Warner says in "Stolen Honor:"

> ...The interrogator showed me a transcript of testimony that my mother had given at something called the Winter Soldier hearings. ...He said that John Kerry had helped organize the...hearings because he was so motivated because he had been an American officer, served in the U.S. Navy. The interrogator ...starts pounding on the table see, 'Here, this naval officer, he admits that you are a criminal, and you deserve punishment'...

POW and Col. Leo K. Thorsness says:

> Without question, we were held captives longer, because of the antiwar people; from the Kerrys to Fonda and Hayden...They encouraged the enemy to hang on. ...they were experts at the PR.[1482]

Retired Air Force Brig. Gen. Robinson Risner, seven years, four months as a POW-said:

> ...We had more than one person come to Vietnam, who the Vietnamese told me [were helping them win] the war in the streets of America. ...I didn't think it was right for an American... (to) bolster the Vietnamese morale.

Circular 06/71. On July 23, 1971, Duong and Bo of the Ba Ria Sub-Region Party Committee issued Circular 06/71 describing coordination, guidance and support the VC Paris office was giving the US antiwar movement. "The antiwar movement in the US is a spontaneous movement which has been guided and supported by our delegation at the Paris peace talks." Circular 06/71 mentioned the "Seven Point" plan and setting a timetable for US withdrawal, but concentrated on identifying major organizations friendly to the Viet Cong

---

[1481] Bell and Veith
[1482] http://www.frontpagemag.com/Articles/ReadArticle.asp?ID=15108

namely PCPC, NPAC, and specifying antiwar events on the 1971 calendar.[1483]

VC battlefield units down to the lowest units were well informed, perhaps propagandized, about the actions and political importance of their American friends in larger struggle combining military and political struggles.

Directive No. 19/CT/TV On August 5, Party officials ordered indoctrination of VC cadre on the Seven Point peace proposal. They were instructed to avoid illusions of peace and to intensify "the struggle against the forthcoming enemy congressional and presidential elections." The cadre were warned not to allow Nixon's trip to Red China to distract them. Stick to approved propaganda themes, e.g., "Nixon must immediately proclaim the final date of US troop withdrawal."

According to Directive No. 19, the antiwar movement was playing a critical role: "The Americans have considered the war waged by the US government in SVN unjust and inhuman" and are forcing Nixon to end it immediately. The Directive gave the VC cadre in South Vietnam the US protest calendar:

> The anti-war movement of the US people...struggling for peace and justice will take the date of 6 November...the autumn struggle phase. Many large-scale demonstrations are to be conducted on 6 August (to commemorate ...a nuclear bomb...dropped by US imperialists on Hiroshima...) Also on 13 Oct, all the people in the US will cease activities and oppose the war.

PCPJ Gets Back in Step. As if it were instructed by Directive No. 19/CT/TV to the Viet Cong, the PCPJ instantly switched its priority from the People's Peace Treaty to the Seven Points, "the most important political initiative of the Vietnamese liberation fighters."[1484]

***

[1483] Circular 06/71, Current Affairs Committee , Ba Ria Sub-Region [VC Region 7]Party Committee, 23 July 1971, captured 21 August, 1971, CDEC Log number 08-1395,71; summarized in Bulletin Number 45, 456 on 27 August 1971, CDEC Document Log Number 08-1395-71.

[1484] "Coalition rejects 'fraudulent' invitation Urges 'peoples' movement," *Daily World*, December 4, 1971, 4.

To San Francisco from Vancouver with Love.
On September 4, 1971 some 1,500 women marched from Fisherman's Wharf in San Francisco under a six-foot poster of Madame Binh emblazoned, "Sisters Fight for Life, Support PRG 7-point peace proposal…to the Presidio headquarters of the 6th U.S. Army. Le Anh Tu said women know "true revolutionary struggle is born out of love (for our sisters) and hatred (for the oppressor)."[1485]

Poster from The Good Times Collective for a woman's anti-war march on the Presidio, 1971.

American peace activists had easily skipped a single step from September 1970's Eight Points to July 1971's Seven Points without missing a beat in their long perfectly cadenced march with their Hanoi comrades. By 1973 Le Anh Tu would author following the latest changes in the Hanoi/IPC line after U.S withdrawal.[1486] At Temple University's Vietnam Center Le

---

1485 September Women's Action Committee, "Women's Presidio March 1971, *San Francisco Good Times,* September 17, 1971,
http://foundsf.org/index.php?title=Womens_Presidio_March_1971&printable=yes
1486 Le, Anh Tu, *Dollars to Saigon, or, An elephant and his Thieu,* Philadelphia, PA: National Action/Research on the Military Industrial Complex, 1973; Le Anh Tu, Eric Prokosch, and Truong Dinh Hung, eds. and translators, *After the Signing of the Paris Agreements: Documents on South Vietnam's Political Prisoners.* Cambridge, MA: NARMIC (National Action/Research on the Military Industrial Complex, a project of the American Friends Service Committee) and the Vietnam Resource Center, July 1973.

Anh Tu Packard is today a frequent economic consultant to Hanoi.[1487]

The sellout of South Vietnam had the strangest bedfellows.

***

Blind Ambition: George McGovern
Collaboration in Paris

George McGovern's Secret Talks with the Enemy, September 11-12, 1971. For six hours over two days, September 11-12, 1971, Senator and presidential candidate George McGovern, D-South Dakota, met secretly with Xuan Thuy and Dinh Ba Thi, deputy of Madame Binh of the PRG, in a Verrieres commune outside of Paris. Among the McGovern party were Frank Mankiewicz, Pierre Salinger and others.

McGovern sought a list of American POWs for which he in return, as a U.S. Senator, along with Sen. Hatfield, would offer legislation to set a date for US withdrawal. "Supply me with a list of these (POW) prisoners…would strengthen me politically …" He expanded, "It would strengthen those of us in the peace movement in the United States if in the near future we could release a full list of prisoners that you are holding." Thi replied, "Our people have special sentiments toward the Senator, as well as other American friends who are fighting for an end to the war."

On the next day, McGovern met Xuan Thuy who thanked McGovern for his resolution in the Senate setting a date for withdrawal.

McGovern again proposed linking U.S. troop withdrawal to POW releases. Thuy said, "Mr. Nixon is unwilling to act in the way proposed by you." Thuy lied.

Kissinger Betrayal? On August 16, Henry Kissinger had secretly offered Thuy a withdrawal of U.S. forces for the release of the POWs saying he didn't care if Thieu survived. Tho told Kissinger Thieu could be removed by a coup or an assassination.

[1487] http://www.temple.edu/vietnamese_center/Lectures/; Packard, Le Anh Tu [Lê Anh Tú Packard]. "Asian American Economic Engagement: Vietnam Case Study." In *Across the Pacific: Asian Americans and Globalization.* Editor Evelyn Hu-DeHart. Philadelphia: Temple University Press, 1999; Packard, Le Anh Tu [Lê Anh Tú Packard], and Stephan S. Thurman. "A Model Design for Vietnam As an Open Economy in Transition." *ASEAN Economic Bulletin* 13, no. 2 (1996): 241-264.

Xuan Thuy did offer to help McGovern's election in any way possible, including not helping Nixon in negotiations.[1488]

CUT Funds for POWS? In a letter to Thuy, McGovern offered still more to get the POWs (and political credit). McGovern asked Xuan Thuy if a Congressional cut off of funds would lead to the release of POWs. If not, would they make a partial release of POWs?[1489]

Le Duc Tho told Henry Kissinger, "I don't know why I'm negotiating with you. I have spent six hours with Senator McGovern. Your anti-war movement will force you to give me what I want."[1490]

POWs for Sale? McGovern's partner Senator Mark Hatfield offered POW Mike Benge's sister ransom, maybe $20,000 to $40,000, for Benge's release. His sister refused, "saying (her brother Mike Benge) would be infuriated if ..(he)... knew what ..(Hatfield) was proposing." Indeed, "she recorded the conversation and then took it to an attorney (former Marine) to see if Hatfield could be brought up on charges." [1491]

According to Benge, "there was an effort to ransom out some POWs by the anti-war crowd. ... Several families were approached by them saying POWs could be bought out for a sum of money." Still, "the only outright buyout of a POW that I know of happened in Laos...." In email to Mike Benge, Rosemary Conway, a CIA operative in Laos after January 1974, says CIA Director Bill Colby "paid the $ 1.2 million U.S. $ for my release."[1492]

While sensing technology was making great strides detecting NVA infiltrations down the Ho Chi Minh Trail,[1493] Hanoi was retaining its superiority in the technology of politics. Hanoi's instructions to the antiwar movement continually improved.

Hanoi rejected the entreaties of both Kissinger and McGovern to end to the war on any grounds except complete victory.

[1488] McGovern Papers, Mudd Library, Princeton University, cited by Larry Berman, *No Peace, No Honor*, 83-91,93-95, 302.
[1489] Larry Berman, *No Peace, No Honor*, 100.
[1490] Larry Berman, *No Peace, No Honor*, 101.
[1491] Mike Benge email to author, May 14, 2009 1:43 PM.
[1492] Mike Benge email to author, May 15, 2009 4:45 PM.
[1493] Lewis Sorley, *A Better War: The Unexamined Victories and Final Tragedy of America's Last Years in Vietnam*, New York: Harcourt, 1999,278.

Circular No. 33:
Viet Cong Intelligence and Guides to Anti-war
Movement

On July 16, 1971, Viet Cong Circular No. 33/VP/TD entitled "On Antiwar Movements in the US" detailed Vietnamese communists knowledge and assistance to groups within the U.S. antiwar movement:

> The anti-war movements in the US...have been widely developed ...At the beginning, only a small number of people... but now they have rallied a large number of people including members of the Senate and House.... The spontaneous antiwar movements in the US have received assistance and guidance from the friendly [Viet Cong/North Vietnam] delegations at the Paris Peace Talks....The PCPJ [People's Committee [sic] for Peace and Justice]...maintains relations with us...

Circular 33 said the

> "PCPJ...has made progress...with the following strategic alternation: 1.strengthen internal unity, contact other associations [and] social classes...and take part in ((U.S. Congressional elections)) and plant progressive people in the Senate and House of Representatives....2. Step up motivation of US soldiers..."

A section titled "PREPARATION FOR THE FALL (1971) ANTIWAR MOVEMENT" said the Pentagon Papers "enabled antiwar organizations...to motivate the [American] people."

The Circular revealed the value of using Madame Binh's 7-Point Peace Plan to stimulate concerns POWs and recruit families:

> The seven-point peace proposal ...not only solved problems concerning the release of US prisoners but also motivated the people of all walks of life and even relatives of US pilots detained in NVN to participate in the antiwar movement.[1494]

334

Circular 33 says, Nixon and Thieu are "very embarrassed because the seven-point peace proposal is supported by the people's (political struggle) movement and the antiwar movements in the US:"

> All local areas, units, and branches must widely disseminate the seven-point peace proposal, step up the people's (political struggle movements both in cities and rural areas, taking advantage of disturbances and dissensions in the enemy's forthcoming (RVN) Congressional and Presidential elections. They must coordinate more successfully with the antiwar movements in the US so as to isolate the Nixon-Thieu clique."

The Circular urged disrupting South Vietnamese elections.

Circular 33 expresses pleasure with the progress made in the increase of GI antiwar efforts of 1971 over 1970. In meetings with movement people in 1970, Hanoi had pressed hard on organizing among GIs.

Circular 33 shows full awareness of the PCPJ and NPAC split over the united front strategy, and chastises the Mayday Tribe for generating public discount over "impeding …traffic." Instead of encircling the White House and the Pentagon, the demonstrations blocked road intersections thus impeding…traffic. This caused their people to discontent and gave President new reasons to suppress demonstrations.

Indeed, Metropolitan Police arrested nearly 10,000 and squelched the May Day Tribe in May.

In Paris in September Hanoi was still telling antiwar leaders to "stop bickering and unite" to conduct more demonstrations.[1495]

[1494] "On Antiwar Movements in the US," Circular No. 33/VP/TD, CDEC doc log no: 12-1370-71,Hoai Huong District Party Committee, VC Binh Tuy-province, VC Region, 16 July 1971. The circular is item number 2150901039b at the Vietnam Archive at Texas Tech. Links to a copy of full text of document are also at: Thomas Lipscomb, "Hanoi Approved of Role Played by Anti-War Vets," *New York Sun*, October 26, 20045 at nysun.com/article/7356A and Art Moore, *WorldNetDaily*, October 28, 2004 and Freepnet/Kerry/staticpages/index.php?page=vccircular
[1495] Frank J. Rafalko, *MH/CHAOS: The CIA's Campaign Against the Radical Left and the Black Panthers*, Annapolis: Naval Institute Press, 2011, 156.

Yet the July Circular indicates the PCPJ and NPAC are patching things up with common events in the near future commemorating Hiroshima on August 6, 1971 and demonstrations on October 13th and November 6, 1971, precisely the PCPJ schedule adopted in Milwaukee weeks before. A September 1, 1971 PCPJ "Dear Friend" letter, "Call for Action to End the War in Indochina" describes "unity negotiations, …meetings [of] ..labor leaders and representatives of NPAC and Peoples Coalition have been taking place since June."[1496] The Circular, PCPJ and NPAC are in close coordination.

The antiwar movements in the US are trying to find means to cooperate... They are also trying …to support the seven-point peace proposal (of the PRG) and oppose the distorted interpretation made by the White House, the Pentagon and CIA." [1497]

Instructions to Cadre and Americans Clear. On July 23, 1971, Circular 06/71 sent to VC cadre in VC Region 7 repeated most of Circular 33. Movement responses to the needs of Hanoi were also prompt. On September 21, 1971, the US launched air strikes against air defense targets in North Vietnam. In Sweden, the American Deserters Committee, ADC, close by the Stockholm Conference on Vietnam, immediately picketed the U.S. Trade Center in Stockholm in opposition to renewed U.S. bombing of North Vietnam.[1498]

Greetings and Salutations. The Vietnamese were grateful. On October 10th, 1971 Ho Thu, chairman of the South Vietnam People's Committee in Solidarity with the American People (*Viet My*) sent a letter to the committee. We

> "highly appreciate the last spring offensive of *various strata*… including war vets and active servicemen… [spring and fall] actions…demanding that the Nixon administration seriously respond to the *7-point peace* initiative…."[1499]

[1496] "Dear Friend," in a "Call to Action to End the War in Indochina," September 1, 1971.
Rothrock 116-118 quotes the Circular in detail.
[1497] Cited in THOMAS LIPSCOMB, Hanoi Approved of Role Played By Anti-War Vets, *New York Sun*, April 14, 2006.
[1498] FBI, Legat Copenhagen (100-49) to Director (100-454113), "American Deserters Committee-Sweden, October 12, 1971.
[1499] "Our Wishes for Your Victory in the 1971 Fall offensive, Letter From Mr. Ho Thu

Thanks for following our instructions!

The movement was following instructions on GIs, 7-point peace plan and set the date.

Deserter Greetings. A letter from the American Deserters Committee to the NL F reported on Radio Hanoi on December 20, 1971 announced. "We [deserters] warmly greet …the (NLF) and salute the courage of the Vietnamese people. …The U.S. must set the date…Full victory will most certainly be yours."[1500] The deserters' goal, communist victory.

Latin Support. On November 2, 1971 in Valparaiso, Chile a Soviet front, World Federation of Democratic Youth, passed a resolution endorsing the Seven-Point Peace Plan, to "set the date" for full withdrawal from Indochina and to build the Nguyen Van Troi Hospital in Hanoi. American members of WFDY, the communist Young Workers Liberation League, attending were Jarvis Tyner, Naomi Chesman, Victoria Stevens, Jeff Schwartz and Roslinda Basso of La Raza Unida.[1501]

VVAW Pride. The VVAW was also following Hanoi's orders. In October Saigon soldiers circulated VVAW petitions to US troops urging withdrawal and release of POWs.[1502] The October 18, 1971 issue of a VVAW flier bragged, "We have sent delegations to the World Peace Council conferences in Budapest and Stockholm, the Seventeenth World Conference Against Atomic and Hydrogen Bombs in Hiroshima and to Hanoi and Paris to meet with our Indochina brothers and sisters."[1503]

Message to VVAW: Get in Line. As in the May Day assault, after Hanoi counseling, VVAW changed their plans for future actions. On December 13, an FBI memo and night teletype reported,

> according to a source the North Vietnamese delegation in Paris is unhappy with plans by the VVAW to stage five separate protest demonstrations …because they wanted one

---

to American People," *Vietnam Courier* October 10, 1971, 1-2, TTU archives cited in Rothrock, 145N19.

[1500] Message, American Deserters Committee, Moscow, Vietnam News Agency, VNA in Vietnamese and English to VNA Hanoi 1743 GMT 20 Dec 71, TTU archive cited in Rothrock, *Divided...*

[1501] "World youth step up anti-imperialism drive," Daily World, November 3, 1971.

[1502] COMMUSMACV, Subj: Vietnam Veterans Against the War in Vietnam, 1300, 14 Oct71.Copy from Jay Veith.

[1503] Copy of "VVAW History, page 3," October 18, 1971, section 6, 10.

massive demonstration in Washington, D.C. on Christmas Day.[1504]

VVAW SNAFUs. The Hanoi cancelled a planned trip of VVAW to Hanoi in December.[1505] On December 17th, Scott Camil cancelled the Christmas Day Peace Action in Atlanta, in favor of "a massive demonstration on January 15, 1971 in Washington D.C."[1506] According to a [redacted] FBI source, the Arkansas Chapter of VVAW decided to send Christmas cards to Governor Bumpers and to the Arkansas delegation in Congress, showing children with war toys wanting to "grow up to defend peace and freedom" and inside, four GIs holding the decapitated heads of two civilians.[1507]

Some did a better job than VVAW of following Hanoi's leadership.

***

Cora Weiss's Extortion of POW Families. Cora Weiss's rough manners were revealed again in a letter to families of POWs in August. Because of bombing in Laos and North Vietnam, "deliveries of mail have decreased." Threats like the Son Tay raid "may also be a factor contributing to the dwindling mail." What needed to be done was clear. "The solution to the problem is for the president to set the date…but it is up to each of us to pressure the president…" Cora Weiss provided the talking points from the Lao Patriotic Front, an AP clip entitled, "POW List Pledged if US Sets Deadline," a graveyard cartoon captioned, "Mother's Day," and an op ed from Madame Binh of August 9, 1971 published in the *New York Times*.

The Binh op ed got strategic. Set a date and the POWs will be released the same day. Binh understands "American people's…desire to see their children" and promises, "American soldiers can be repatriated." Besides a date, she also wants the Thieu regime gone.[1508] Binh, titular of the VC, does

---

[1504] FBI, Domestic Intelligence Division, Informative Note, December 13, 1971.

[1505] FBI, [Redacted] to Bureau; ATTN: Domestic Intelligence Division, 7:51 pm NITEL, December 13, 1971, 2.

[1506] FBI, [redacted "Northwest" office], to Director, 7:30 pm NITEL, December 12, 1971.

[1507] FBI, [Redacted] to Bureau; ATTN: Domestic Intelligence Division, 7:51 pm NITEL, December 13, 1971,5.

[1508] Nguyen Thi Binh, "Mrs. Binh: Our Plan for Peace," New York Times, August 9, 1971.

not mention U.S. POWs in South Vietnam under VC or POW mail, all under her fictional NLF jurisdiction.

A few POWS cooperated with the enemy.

POWs Protest War. On October 13, 1971 at a VVAW rally at the University of Florida, Gainesville, VVAW leader Scott Camil played a tape of POWs, one of Capt. Kishner [Floyd Kushner] condemning American atrocities and expressing a desire to go home to his family. In another tape POW John A. Young is heard saying he supports the North Vietnamese and condemns the United States.[1509] Kushner, a medical doctor, not a military man, was a long time captive of a VC unit where many POWs died of disease, starvation, beatings and executions. After arriving in Hanoi POW senior officers persuaded Kushner to make no more statements. In contrast, Young, an enlisted man chaffing under arbitrary military authority, was a proud voluntary member of the Hanoi Peace Committee. Young was "grief stricken over the death of Ho Chi Minh" in September 1969 and betrayed his POW cellmate Sgt. Harvey Brande.[1510]

The antiwar pretense of caring for the POWs proceeded.

Mail Dribbled Out. On October 28, 1971 WSP's Amy Swerdlow and two others returned from Hanoi to Los Angeles with only 33 pieces of mail from hundreds of prisoners. They held a press conference and read some names, Alvarez, Miller, Martin, Schultz, Stirm, Ferr, McSwain, and Stafford.[1511] On November 4, 1971 in Paris Ambassador Porter asked why the North was reducing the amount of mail POWs could send home.[1512] During most of 1971, only 50 families of POWs out of 300 had received letters.[1513]

Fernandez. Hanoi, caught playing with the mail, on December 21, 1971 CALC's Rev. Richard Fernandez, a COLIFAM courier returned from Paris to JFK airport with 1,001 letters from 229 POWs, including 18 from POWs in the South. David Dellinger and Cora Weiss forwarded the mail

---

[1509] FBI, Jacksonville, LHM, "Anti-War Speak Out Rally by Student Mobilization and VVAW," Gainesville, Florida, October 28, 1971, 2,5.
[1510] Craig Howes, *Voices of the Vietnam POWs: Witnesses to Their Fight*, New York: Oxford University Press, 1993, 100-104.
[1511] FBI John Edgar Hoover, to [redacted]COLIFAM, November 1, 1971.
[1512] (C)msg. US Del France 18673 to State, 4 Nov 71, JCS in 38131.
[1513] FBI, Norfolk, LHM, COLIFAM, December 20, 1971; Scott Swett 57n44 cites FBI, VVAW files, HQ 100-448092, Section 05, 230.

with their own messages. There was bombing 25 miles from Hanoi and Nixon should set the date as Congress had recently voted.[1514]

COLIFAM was Hanoi's agent holding the POWs, their families and their letters hostage.

***

The Guns of August 1971:
VVAW joins PCPJ-WRL in Hanoi,
Kerry in Paris.

Kerry in Paris. In August 1971, John Kerry made his second known trip to meet the Vietnamese communists in Paris to discuss a POW release.[1515] The August 26, 1971 issue of the *Denver Post*, covering the National Student Association Congress at Ft. Collins, Colorado, reports John Kerry, 28, being a national leader of VVAW. Kerry tells the *Post,* he had just returned from Paris where he had talked to the peace delegations, including the North Vietnamese. Hanoi said, "Everything is on the table," but only if the U.S. set a definite date for withdrawal. Only then, could the POWs be released and negotiations begin. Kerry said Nixon was "absolutely immoral."[1516]

Also speaking at the NSA meeting, perhaps reading John Kerry's words in the *Denver Post,* were George McGovern, Rep. Pete McCloskey, Benjamin Spock, and Daniel Ellsberg.

By 2004 John Kerry would falsely claim he thought meeting with North Vietnamese "would be disastrous to the credibility of the [VVAW] organization…"[1517] Yet in 1970 and 1971 he did meet with Hanoi officials and planned a third meeting. The *Denver Post* clipping and two redacted FBI files confirm his trip to Paris to meet the enemy as an VVAW officer as do Kerry biographer, Douglas Brinkley and VVAW historian Gerald Nicosia.[1518] Kerry thought he was swifter than the truth.

VVAW Joins PCPJ-WRL in Paris/Hanoi

[1514] David Dellinger and Cora Weiss, Dear friends, COLIFAM, December 21, 1971; FBI, New York, LHM, COLIFAM, January 20, 1972.

[1515] Gerald Nicosia, "Veteran in conflict," LA Times, May 23, 2004.

[1516] August 26, 1971 issue of the *Denver Post* cited in FBI, Denver Memo, VVAW-IS-New Left, September 3, 1971, 15-16 at FBI, FOIA, VVAW, Section 5, 231.

[1517] John M. Glionna, *LA Times,* Mar. 23, 2004.

[1518] "Kerry Visited Vietnam Peace Talks," Fox News cites Gerald Nicosia and Doug Brinkley.

VVAW's Joe Urgo, in Paris. August 13-21, the PCPJ and the WRL sponsored VVAW staffer Joe Urgo's trip to Paris with [redacted] members of the WRL and WSP.[1519] Like Kerry, Joe Urgo and the enemy talked about "international action of active duty personnel to demonstrate against the war."[1520]

Hanoi. Exchanging Tapes. In Hanoi, with WRL's David McReynolds, Joe Urgo offered the communists VVAW tapes for broadcast over Radio Hanoi urging U.S. soldiers to stop fighting.[1521] Urgo took 36 letters for PCPJ to POWs and returned with 34 letters for families.[1522] Hanoi denied Urgo's request to see POWs.[1523]

Hanoi instead gave Urgo four tapes of POWs held by the PRG, the VC. [1524] One POW voice recommended the NLF's Seven Points plan and opposed the killing women and children. Another POW praised the patriotism of PCPJ and VVAW. Yet read carefully, two POWs spoke in code.[1525] One was disturbed by "stories" of atrocities and "reports" of the VVAW medal tosses. One accused the U.S. of "waging the most vicious and ignoble war of all times."

Urgo toured training camps and factories of the NVA.[1526] WRL's David McReynolds visited a hospital where he was shown US antipersonnel bombs with [nonlethal] plastic pellets that could not be X-rayed [1527]or removed from the bodies of wounded innocents.

Pham Van Dong. Meeting the PCPJ, VVAW and NPAC delegation, Pham Van Dong "highly praised the antiwar activities… especially in the 1971 spring offensive" where the VVAW had choreographed the "Dewey Canyon," medal toss.

[1519] FBI Surveillance November 19, 1971 cited in O'Neill and Corsi 133.

[1520] FBI, [Redacted]to Director, 8:50 NITEL, Nov 16, 1971

[1521] FBI, [Redacted Office] Memo, "VVAW Regional Coordinators and National Steering Committee Meeting Weekend November 12-15, 1971 Kansas City, Missouri," November 24, 1971,7.

[1522] VVAW, John A. Lindquist, Regional Coordinator for Wisconsin, VVAW Newsletter, November 29, 1971 cited in FBI, Memo, VVAW Milwaukee Division, Milwaukee, December 2, 1971, 3.

[1523] Liberation News Service, LNS, Packet 378, September 25, 1971 cited in FBI, NY to Director, AIRTEL, Nov 29, 1971, 5.

[1524] FBI, VVAW, Member[s] of subject organization, n.d., 6.

[1525] Swett and Zigler cite transcripts of recorded messages from US servicemen captured in South Vietnam, August 1971, FBI VVAW, HQ 100-448092, section 11, 174-181.

[1526] FBI, Memo, VVAW Steering Committee Meeting Kansas City, Missouri, November 12, 13, 14, 1971

[1527] David McReynolds, "Looking Back at St. Paul," *The Lunatic Gazette*, 16 September, 2008.

Radio Hanoi said, "The American guests …welcomed the Seven Point peace initiative…and promised to push on [with] their coordinated antiwar actions."[1528]

The trip "had an enormous impact…convincing me that I was on the side of the Vietnamese now," Joe Urgo said.[1529] Urgo debriefed his talks in Hanoi at the VVAW National Steering Committee meeting in Kansas City, MO on November 12-15, 1971. John Lindquist, VVAW Wisconsin wrote in a newsletter,

We also discovered two POWs who …listed as MIA and informed their families they were alive…We have taped-recorded letters written by three [four?] POW brothers… The brothers even have an organization of POWs Against the War…[1530] [POW Peace Committee]

***

Kerry's July "Resignation" from VVAW Never Happened

Though histories report John Kerry resigning from VVAW in July 1971 and his denying[1531] being an active spokesman for VVAW, the contemporary press and FBI informants show Kerry remaining a VVAW spokesmen and member of its executive committee until late November 1971. And he continued his VVAW associations thereafter. John Kerry met the Vietnamese communists in Paris in August 1971, a month after his alleged resignation from VVAW.

VVAW Speaking Tour. After John Kerry's July "resignation" and forgotten second trip to Paris in August, during 1971, Kerry spoke for VVAW at least four public events at the University of Nevada, Las Vegas, Georgetown University, University of Pittsburgh, and University of Oklahoma.[1532] On September 27, Kerry spoke at Georgetown University about electoral politics. Some thought, "Kerry is an

---

[1528] "Pham Van Dong Receives Two Antiwar Delegations," Hanoi International News Service, 1557 GMT, August 26, 1971, TTU Archive cited in Rothrock, *Divided…171n35*

[1529] Wells interview with Urgo, Wells *The War Within*, 526.

[1530] VVAW, John A. Lindquist, Regional Coordinator for Wisconsin, *VVAW Newsletter*, November 29, 1971 cited in FBI, Memo, VVAW Milwaukee Division, Milwaukee, December 2, 1971, 3.

[1531] John M. Glionna, "FBI Shadowed Kerry During Activist Era," *LA Times* Mar. 22, 2004.

[1532] FBI Memo, [redacted office], "VVAW Regional Coordinators and National Steering Committee Meeting Weekend November 12-15, 1971 Kansas City, Missouri," November 24, 1971, 2.

opportunist with personal political aspirations," weakening VVAW.[1533] On September 30, Kerry spoke at the University of Nevada criticizing Nixon's secret plan for peace and saying there was no honor in Vietnam. Associated Students gave Kerry $1,200.[1534] That day the House rejected withdrawal within six months, but favored a "date certain" with release of POWs.[1535] "Set the date." On October 13 in Norman, Oklahoma, a paper of the People's Workshop, *The Well*, identified John Kerry as a national spokesman for VVAW.

Kerry, VVAW Spokesman, Oklahoma City-- November 5-7, 1971. Kerry was invited to speak by the Oklahoma VVAW on November 2nd,[1536] according to the FBI and the *Oklahoma Daily* of November 3, 1971.[1537] Kerry was the main speaker at the November 5-7, VVAW Steering Committee in Norman Oklahoma.[1538]

Kerry urged VVAW to vote for anti-war candidates. Kerry declared VVAW members against "any type of violence." Yet Kerry told the *Sunday Oklahoman*, if the "government doesn't change, ... those who are talking about seizing it will have every right to go after it."[1539]

Kerry Plans Trip Three to Paris. Al Hubbard and Kerry planned to meet the communists in Paris November 15-20, 1971.[1540] The FBI the CPUSA might be paying because Hubbard attended PCPJ meetings with CPUSA members, Gil Green and Jarvis Tyner.[1541] Indeed, Hubbard claimed the Communist Party promised to pay expenses. Intent clear, there is no evidence Kerry made the third trip.

[1533] FBI, Washington Memo, VVAW, Inc, 100-448092-483

[1534] FBI, Las Vegas, Memo[s], "VVAW, John Kerry Speech, University of Nevada, Las Vegas, September 30, 1971," September 30 and October 4, 1971 cite *Yell*, (UNLV), Oct 6, 1971 and *Las Vegas State Journal*, Sept 30, 1971;

[1535] NY Times, 28 Sept 71, 3; 1 Oct 71,9; 20 Oct 71, 1; 11 Nov 71, 1.

[1536] Kerry is on national executive committee. FBI, Bufile (100-448092)NYFILE (100-160644)Memo, New York, VVAW, Inc, Nov 4, 1971

[1537] FBI Oklahoma City to Director, 7:45 pm NITEL November 4, 1971.

[1538] FBI, Oklahoma City to Director, Regional VVAW Convention sponsored by Oklahoma VVAW, University of Oklahoma November 5,6,7 IS-New Left" Teletype, November 8, 1971

[1539] Bryce Patterson, "Veterans Against War Chief..." *Sunday Oklahoman*, Nov 7, 1971.

[1540] FBI, [Redacted] to Bureau, ATTN: Domestic Intelligence Division, 5:40 pm URGENT TELETYPE, Nov 10, 1971, 2; FBI, New York to Director, URGENT TELETYPE, Nov. 12, 1971.

[1541] FBI, New York to Director, VVAW, Inc... November 11, 1971, 1,2; FBI, New York to Director, "VVAW IS-New Left, URGENT TELETYPE, November 12, 1971, 2.

What Kerry told the *Oklahoman,* the Weathermen confirmed some antiwar activists, within Weather and VVAW, justified violence.

***

Chapter 14. Bombs, Assassinations, Massacres, and Killing Christmas.

Weatherman Bombings

On August 28, 1971 in San Francisco at the Ferry building and in Sacramento, the Weather Underground Organization bombed offices of the California Department of Corrections "in retaliation for the assassination of George Jackson." Hit on the same day was the San Mateo office of the Department of Rehabilitation.[1542] The bombed target, Department of Rehabilitation, did not abuse prisoners, political or otherwise. It provided services to the physically disabled. OOPS.

In September 17, 1971 in Albany, New York the Weather Underground Organization bombed the offices of the Department of Corrections "in retaliation for the brutal assault against the Attica Prison uprising,"[1543] which had killed 29 inmates.

On October 15, 1971, the "Proud Eagle Tribe" of the Weather Underground Organization bombed the office of William Bundy. Bundy had been President Johnson's Assistant Secretary of State and was since at the Herman Center for International Affairs at MIT.[1544]

FBI Microphones Weather Supporters. In a measured response on December 16, 1971 the FBI installed, Attorney General approval, a microphone in the New York residence of a "suggested participant in Weather Underground support apparatus," followed on January 18, 1972, a microphone in a car in Chicago and another in a New York residence March 23, 1973.[1545]

Others, hands clean of gunpowder residue, held more dignified proceedings about the evils of America in Vietnam.

[1542] Cathy Wilkerson, *Flying Close to the Sun*, New York: Seven Stories Press, 2007, 369; FBI, FOIA, Weather Underground. The primary source is Acting SAC Chicago to Director, memo, "Foreign Influence-Weather Underground Organization," August 20, 1976, 182.

[1543] FBI, FOIA, Weather Underground. The primary source is Acting SAC Chicago to Director, memo, "Foreign Influence-Weather Underground Organization," August 20, 1976, 182.

[1544] FBI, FOIA, Weather Underground. The primary source is Acting SAC Chicago to Director, memo, "Foreign Influence-Weather Underground Organization," August 20, 1976, 183.

[1545] FBI Top Secret, "Re: Surreptitious Entries," HQ files 100-457986,100-459597, 100-454261, NY files 100-165434, 100-171161, Chicago file 100-49663 60, 61, 17.

***

Grand Jury Investigation of America-
Project Air War

On October 22-25, 1971 the PCPJ with whom the Vietnamese "maintain relations" (Circular No. 33) sponsored a "Grand Jury Investigation" of America at Washington's First Congregational Church. Tom Hayden, David Dellinger, Rennie Davis, John Froines, Staughton Lynd, Richard Falk and Iqbal Ahmad spoke. Other sponsors were Barbara Bick, Tim Butz, Rev. Ben Lewis, and Margery Tabankin.[1546]

Project Air War. Fred Branfman was back from Laos, the Ho Chi Minh trail, and beginning Project Air War which was, Branfman testified, killing more civilians than soldiers. Branfman's tale of Laos became, "Using official figures, my group, Project Air War, calculated that the Nixon administration killed, wounded or made homeless more than 6 million civilians between Jan. 20, 1969, and the fall of 1972."[1547]

One of Branfman's sources was a communist Pathet Lao soldier Ngeun who Branfman met again in 1993. Ngeun said, "I had to eat grass to survive. Fred, I had to eat grass." Branfman said, "I was naïve and wrong in my belief that if the North Vietnamese and the Pathet Lao won it would usher in a better world. Communism is obviously no better than capitalism. But I certainly have no regrets that I tried to stop the bombing."[1548] No better. Ngeun ate no grass under capitalism.

Guilty as charged the "Peoples'Grand Jury" of PCPJ indicted not only the Vietnam War, but also the "social and economic basis of American Society." On the 25th, Xuan Thuy spoke to a People's Armistice Day at Sylvan Theater.[1549]

***

Fall Protests Peter Out—October 1971

[1546] DC PCPJ letter of September 13, 1971 to Sisters and Brothers signed by Al Spencer and Sue Orrin. Max Friedman met Tabankin working on the Moratorium in Friedman to Canfield and others December 2009.

[1547] http://dir.salon.com/story/opinion/feature/2004/04/13/peacesoldier/index.html

[1548] Fred Branfman, "What would it be like to hide in a cave day after day for five years?" Christian G. Appy, *Patriots: The Vietnam War Remembered From All Sides*, New York: Penguin Books, 2003, 219.

[1549] Hand printed and drawn PCPJ leaflet of September 1971 listing upcoming events in October 1971 from Max Friedman; *Washington Post*, October 23, 24, and 25, 1971; Zaroulis, *Who Spoke Up*, 371; Tom Wells, *The War Within: America's Battle over Vietnam*, NY: Henry Holt, 1994,528.

The long planned PCPJ rallies of October 13, 1971 sputtered away with a few hundred appearing in most cities and several thousand in New York. The war was winding down: U.S. troops were withdrawing, draft calls were down, cash was short and the old leftist divisions reappeared.[1550] Nonetheless, on October 18, 1971, Hanoi reported all was well. There were protests at city halls across the U.S. "condemning the Vietnam war as immoral," and supporting the Seven Point peace plan. Hanoi named its American supporters, Ron Dellums, Bella Abzug and Mayor Lindsay of New York.[1551]

November Rallies, a Little Better. On November 6, 1971 PCPJ regional rallies did a little better than the October events mobilizing 40,000 in San Francisco, 30,000 in N.Y, 15,000 in Denver and 10,000 in Boston.[1552]

Unity in Atlanta. Among the unity sponsors of a regional rally in Atlanta on November 6, 1971 were Atlanta Peace Action Coalition and PCPJ. Individual sponsors included U.S. Senators Birch Bayh, Vance Hartke, John Tunney; black leaders Rev. Ralph Abernathy, Rev. Jesse Jackson, Coretta Scott King, Rev. Fred Shuttleworth, and labor leaders Abe Feinglass, Leon Davis, Harold Gibbons, Victor Reuther. Also Daniel Ellsberg and actors Ossie Davis and Ruby Dee.[1553]

Mass antiwar demonstrations had peaked with the Moratorium and Nixon's "Silent Majority" speech in late 1969.

The Viet Cong cadre in America might be small in numbers, it was relentless, influential and hateful. Some were murderous.

***

VVAW Releasing POWs and Murdering US Senators.

Releasing POWs? November 12-14, 1971, VVAW leaders met in Kansas City at the University of Missouri. Mike Oliver read a telegram from Al Hubbard in Paris[1554] reporting a possible POW release to VVAW. five delegates there.[1555]

[1550] Tom Wells, *The War Within*, 526-29.
[1551] "Commentary Applauds U.S. Antiwar Fall Offensive: The American People Warn the Nixon Administration," Hanoi Domestic service in Vietnamese 1430 18 Oct 71, cited in Rothrock, *Divided... 292-3n75*
[1552] Zaroulis, *Who Spoke Up*, 371.
[1553] Flyer, United Nov. 6 Action Committee, Atlanta, circa October 1971.
[1554] FBI, Director to President 11:50 am Teletype, Nov. 16, 1971.
[1555] FBI,[Redacted] to Director, 7:55 urgent TELETYPE, Nov. 15, 1971, 3.

Arriving late, Hubbard described his trip to Paris where Vietnamese suggested VVAW might travel to Hanoi near Christmas and receive a group of released POWs.[1556] Over several weeks, Hubbard talked to Xuan Thuy[1557] and representatives of the PRG and NLF.

Communist Financing? To avoid the taint of Communist money, a "neutral" woman, (tied to an unnamed northeastern paper company)[1558] paid for Hubbard's travel expenses to Paris. Yet in Kansas City Hubbard said the CPUSA USA sponsored and financed his trip.[1559] Yet FBI claimed an inability to verify CPUSA financing.[1560]

VVAW Killing Senators? In Kansas City the delegates expressed a strong desire for action and initiative voting to contact 2,000 GIs in Vietnam to organize refusals to take up arms.

"**Special Proposal.** One item on the Kansas City agenda was "…VIII. Future Actions…D. SPECIAL Proposal."[1561] A concerned J. Edgar Hoover, cryptically wrote to selected offices, "… information developed by informants, if accurate, indicate drastically increased militant posture of VVAW of considerable concern to internal security interests of U.S."[1562] [Redacted] wrote to E.S. Miller of "emergence of definite militant and possible violence-prone posture of VVAW."[1563]

At a closed 2:30 Agenda meeting 60 attended.[1564] The 4:30 pm general meeting discussed civil disobedience at Christmas, burning Christmas trees and offering sanctuaries for deserters.

[1556] FBI, [Redacted] to Director, 9:55 pm urgent TELETYPE, Nov 18, 1971, 2; FBI, [Redacted] to Director, TELETYPE 806PM URGENT November 19, 1971, 2-5.
[1557] FBI surveillance reports November 11, 14 and 19, 1971 cited in O'Neill and Corsi.
[1558] FBI, [Redacted] to Director, TELETYPE 806PM URGENT November 19, 1971. Possibly the Great Northern Paper Company?
[1559] FBI, [redacted] to E.S. Miller, November 24, 1971, 1; FBI, [Redacted Office] Memo, "VVAW Regional Coordinators and National Steering Committee Meeting Weekend November 12-15, 1971 Kansas City, Missouri," November 24, 1971,6.
[1560] FBI, New York to Director, ATTN Domestic Intelligence Division, 12:55 am TELETYPE, Nov. 13, 1971; FBI, SAC, New York (100-160644)to Director (100-448092, VVAW, INC, IS-New Left, AIRTEL, November 29, 1971, 3.
[1561] FBI, [Redacted Office] Memo, "VVAW Regional Coordinators and National Steering Committee Meeting Weekend November 12-15, 1971 Kansas City, Missouri," November 24, 1971,4.
[1562] FBI, Director to New York, Jacksonville and two [redacted], VVAW, IS-New Left, Teletype, Nov 18, 1971.
[1563] FBI, memo, [Redacted] to E.S. Miller, November 24, 1971
[1564] Second Venceremos Brigade, Cong. Record, Nov. 8, 1972, E9080-9098, on page 8147 of hearings, Denver, Colorado. Max Friedman to author, February 25, 2008.

Camil's Plan to Assassinate U.S. Senators. At a party after 11:00 pm on Friday the 12th, Scott Camil held forth to eight witnesses, three delegates from Arkansas [Roger DeVito[1565]], the regional coordinator for Missouri and Kansas [John Upton], a delegate from Montana [Carl Larson], and three from St. Louis [Rich Bangert].

Camil had a secret firearms training program and out of which he yearned to form "Phoenix" [assassination]like "readiness groups." It was Camil's rendition of Che Guevara's revolutionary cells, the Weathers affinity groups, "foco" collectives, and Tom Hayden's revolutionary Red Family collective.

Did Camil's "Phoenix" groups have military objectives? "Yes ...political elimination" of the "governmental chain of command." This required men be assigned to each assassination. Terry DuBose, Texas, remembers, "there was actually some discussion of assassinating... Senators during ...Christmas... They were people...with hot head rhetoric. ...They had a list of Senators (Jesse)Helms, John Tower...They approached me about John Tower...he was from Texas."[1566]

Historian of VVAW, Gerald Nicosia, writes, Camil "proposed the assassination of the ...conservative members of Congress... (He) called together eight to ten Marines to organize... [and] attempted "to parcel out the hit jobs." John Upton, VVAW Kansas-Western Missouri, says, "A lot of people were convinced *this was the way to do it.*"[1567]

Some number of the eight eyewitnesses, say Camil's ideas were "favorably received" and "quietly disseminated ...at the party."[1568]

A closed meeting was called. It met for an hour at secure location, a Mennonite Hall.[1569] Scott Camil wanted a

---

[1565] All names in brackets in this section are from the roster of VVAW regional coordinators in *The 1st Casualty*, VVAW, Vol. I, No. 3, 1971. http://www.vvaw.org/veteran/article/?id=1026

[1566] Richard Staciewicz, *Winter Soldier: An Oral History of the Vietnam Veterans Against the War,* 1997, 295. Emphasis in original.

[1567] Scott Swett, 47-48n1 cites Gerald Nicosia, *Home to War*, 220-2; Nicosia also cited in Thomas Lipscomb, "How Kerry Quit Veterans Group Amid Dark Plot," *New York Sun*, Mar 12, 2004, 1; Scott Stanley, *Insight*, Mar 23, 2004.

[1568] FBI, Kansas City, Memo, VVAW Steering Committee Meeting Kansas City, Missouri, November 12, 13, 14, 1971. 2, 3; See: testimony of informant William Lemmer in "The Gainesville Eight," *Time*, August 20, 1973.

[1569] On changes in locations see: Gerald Nicosia, *Home to War*, 221-2.

discussion of his "readiness squads." Another proposal was to kidnap a Senator to pressure an ending to the War. This was rejected.

A [redacted] agenda item was not discussed in the plenary meeting. The [redacted] item was held over to the next Steering Committee in February.[1570] In fact, the Agenda committee had vote voted not to allow Camil to bring the assassination proposal up on the floor of the general session in Kansas City.[1571]

John Kerry Debates Assassination Plan. John Kerry was not at the Friday night party, he arrived the next day on Saturday morning.[1572] Once there Kerry participated in debates in closed meetings about the Camil assassination plan. As a national officer, Kerry was present in the agenda meeting. The FBI says, "some of the delegates present were: [redacted[1573]] Kansas City... Mike Oliver; John Kerry; Scott Camil..."[1574] Randy Barnes and Terry Dubose, VVAW coordinator for Texas, both corroborate Kerry's presence in the agenda meeting. Randy Barnes, an advocate of Kerry for President, says Kerry voted against Camil's assassination proposal.[1575]

Unlike the FBI informants, John Kerry never reported this criminal conspiracy.

Kerry Covers up Assassination Plot. Despite fighting and losing a two-day political dispute, with many witnesses John Kerry would later deny he even attended the Kansas City meeting.[1576] The *Los Angeles Times* confirms Kerry attended the meeting, FBI surveillance, and Kerry's flawed memory, but the *Times* studiously fails entirely to mention the biggest news story in Kansas City and perhaps the nation in those days in November, 1971, Scott Camil's assassination plot.[1577]

[1570] FBI, Director to President 11:50 am Teletype, Nov. 16, 1971, 4; FBI, [Redacted] to Director, 7:55 urgent TELETYPE, Nov. 15, 1971,4.

[1571] FBI, [Redacted] to Director, TELETYPE 806PM URGENT November 19, 1971, 7-8.

[1572] FBI, Kansas City, Memo, VVAW Steering Committee Meeting Kansas City, Missouri, November 12, 13, 14, 1971. 8 pages

[1573] Likely Rich Bangert, representing Eastern Missouri-Illinois, *The 1st Casualty*, VVAW, Vol. I, No. 3, 1971. http://www.vvaw.org/veteran/article/?id=1026

[1574] FBI, Kansas City, Memo, VVAW Steering Committee Meeting Kansas City, Missouri, November 12, 13, 14, 1971; Steve Gilbert, "Kerry, Kansa City, and the FBI Files," American Thinker, September 7, 2004.

[1575] Thomas Lipscomb, "How Kerry Quit Veterans Group Amid Dark Plot," New York Sun, Mar 12, 2004, 1; Scott Stanley, Insight, Mar 23, 2004.

[1576] John M. Glionna, *LA Times* Mar. 23, 2004.

[1577] John M. Glionna, *LA Times* Mar. 23, 2004.

Douglas Brinkley, author of *Tour of Duty*, a laudatory account of John Kerry, says Kerry "clearly knew about the assassination plot...and never went to authorities."[1578] Except for the FBI informants, likely Bill Lemmer and Dwight Crews, no other VVAW member reported the conspiracy. In 2004 John Kerry would first deny he was in Kansas City let alone participated in any talk of assassinations. Kerry put pressure on eyewitnesses to refresh their memories. Kerry finally retracted his denials as the files of VVAW and the FBI proved his participation.[1579] John Kerry could not remember this "historical footnote...of his work to end the difficult and decisive war."[1580] Mere footnote.

VVAW Coup. On Saturday, the 13th, after discovering and challenging Hubbard's phony claim of military service in Vietnam and failing to remove Hubbard from the leadership,[1581] John Kerry, Mike Oliver and Skip Roberts resigned from the executive committee. Hubbard, Joe Urgo, Jon Birch (Pa.-Del.) and Larry Rottman would become the new VVAW leadership.

When did Kerry Leave VVAW? Kerry's claims in 2004 he left VVAW in July 1971 notwithstanding, on November 13, 1971 Kerry told his VVAW comrades he would remain an active spokesman.[1582] Kerry did speak for VVAW into mid-1972. On November 16, 1971 President Nixon received an FBI "Priority" message. Hoover said John Kerry remained tied to VVAW.[1583]

Camil's Preparations for Revolution. The assassin cheerleader, Scott Camil chaired the end of the conference. Camil declared all future meetings ought to be closed to all but national and regional leaders. "We're [not] a conservative

---

[1578] John Fund, "Kerry's Other War Record: His antiwar activities deserve more scrutiny from the press," *Opinion Journal*, March 29, 2004.

[1579] Scott Swett and Tim Ziegler, *To Set the Record Straight: How the Swift Boat Veterans, POWs and the New Media Defeated John Kerry*, New American Media Publishing, 2008, 48-51.

[1580] Josh Gerstein, "Kerry Retreats From His Denial On Vietnam Meet," *New York Sun*, March 19, 2004.

[1581] FBI, Memo, "VVAW Regional Coordinators and National Steering Committee Meeting Weekend November 12-15, 1971 Kansas City, Missouri," November 24, 1971, 7; FBI, [Redacted Office] Memo, "VVAW Regional Coordinators and National Steering Committee Meeting Weekend November 12-15, 1971 Kansas City, Missouri," November 24, 1971,5.

[1582] FBI, Director to President, 11:00 am Teletype, Nov 16, 1971.

[1583] FBI, Director to President, Telegraph, 11:50am November 16, 1971.

organization." The VVAW leadership was far more militant than its membership.[1584]

According to FBI Jacksonville's "source one," back home in Gainesville, Camil said, "Look out. There is going to be violence. I do not mind being a martyr." The informant claimed VVAW had shotguns, pistols, and knives stored in the attic of Camil's house and the VVAW was shooting in the countryside.[1585] "Paranoid" Camil suspected VVAW's Florida chapters were infiltrated.[1586]

As to the new militancy of VVAW, particularly the Senator assassination plot, the FBI sent an urgent teletype its offices in Jacksonville, Little Rock, New Orleans, and New York to investigate fully [redacted] a "matter of extreme importance to highest U.S. government officials" including a [redacted] proposal that VVAW had decided not to discuss in the Kansas City meeting.

In a letter shortly after Kansas City, Camil complained, "I presented my idea. ... It was defeated and instead we end up having five different actions planned for Christmas."[1587] Camil now urged using the release of POWs to stir up the American people.[1588]

Vietnamese Communists "CALL THE SHOTS"

The new VVAW leadership, Al Hubbard, Joe Urgo, Jon Birch and Larry Rottman replied to Camil:

The VVAW had already voted down the POW issue precisely because Hanoi had rejected "any attempt to force or pressure the North Vietnamese into any POW releases."
All members of the VVAW who have been in contact with the PRG/DRV people know the POW issue is not, to them, 'the single most explosive issue of the war.' It is their wish that we

---

[1584] FBI, [Redacted] to Director, TELETYPE 806PM URGENT November 19, 1971, 11-12.

[1585] FBI, Jacksonville LHM "VVAW Gainesville, Florida," November 24, 1971, 1-2.

[1586] FBI, Jacksonville to Director LHM, "VVAW Gainesville IS-New Left, Scott Camil IS-New Left, AIRTEL Nov 24, 1971, 2.

[1587] Scott Swett and Tim Ziegler, *To Set the Record Straight: How the Swift Boat Veterans, POWs and the New Media Defeated John Kerry*, New American Media Publishing, 2008 62n68 cites Scott Camil, "Open letter to all Vets," *Wisconsin Historical Society Archives, Vietnam Veterans Against the War Records*, Florida Chapters correspondence, Box 2, Folders 12-15, 290.

[1588] Scott Swett and Tim Ziegler, *To Set the Record Straight: How the Swift Boat Veterans, POWs and the New Media Defeated John Kerry*, New American Media Publishing, 2008 cites Scott Camil, "Open letter to all Vets," Wisconsin Historical Society Archives, *Vietnam Veterans Against the War Records*, Florida Chapters correspondence, Box 2, Folders 12-15, 290.

do not hassle them about it. They are the ones under the falling bombs and in front of ARVN /American/CIA/mercenary bullets, and, for the <u>horror they continue to endure.</u> THEY CALL THE SHOTS.[1589]

The Camil faction of VVAW needed to leave propaganda and terror to the pros, their communist instructors "calling the shots."

***

The 1971 Battles for Baray Cambodia

December 1, 1971 tragically culminated a three month anticommunist Cambodian operation, Chenla II, to regain territories occupied by tens of thousands of Hanoi troops and its allied Khmer communists. Cambodian forces moved along Highway 6 into territories north and east of Cambodia's capital of Phnom Penn. On August 26th the Cambodians recovered Vietnamese occupied Baray and on September 1, regained Kompong Thmar too.

Pon, a witness in Baray, reported Khmer Rouge troops "threw [Chinese] grenades into the houses of those who had sheltered the Vietnamese... In some cases they killed entire families." In Baray Cambodian President Lon Nol's forces found 62 tombs and mass graves, containing 180 corpses.[1590]

Far worse was yet to come.

On October 5, the Cambodians engaged the Communists in hand-to-hand combat in Phnom Santuk and declared victory on October 25. Too soon. Cambodian battalions of about 20,000 and refugees of 40,000-50,000 fled not only from NVA artillery and rockets, but also from the murderous Communist Khmer Khrom.

Soon imprecisely known as the Khmer Rouge, the Khmer Khrom torched and forcefully evacuated 400 hamlets[1591] and "thousands and thousands" of peasants. The infirm, elderly

---

[1589] Scott Swett and Tim Ziegler, *To Set the Record Straight: How the Swift Boat Veterans, POWs and the New Media Defeated John Kerry*, New American Media Publishing, 2008 5n19 cites Letter from Jon Birch, Larry Rottman, Joe Urgo, and Al Hubbard to Scott Camil Wisconsin Historical Society Archives, *Vietnam Veterans Against the War Records*, Florida Chapters correspondence, Box 2, Folders 12-15, 286-287. All emphases in the original.

[1590] Ke Pauk: One of Pol Pot's leading military commanders, was responsible for the murders of many thousands of Cambodians, but escaped justice. Ben Kiernan, *Guardian*, Thursday February 21, 2002 http://www.guardian.co.uk/Archive/Article/0,4273, 4360122 ,00.html

[1591] John M. Del Vecchio, *For the Sake of All living Things*, New York: Bantam 1991, 472-3.

and tiny children straggled out along 70 kilometers of Highway 6 stretching from north to south through Kompong Thmar, Puk Yuk, Tang Krasang, Baray, Rumlong, Tang Kouk, Pa Kham, and Skoun toward the south.[1592]

On the night of October 26, the NVA assaulted Cambodian troops thinly strung out along Route 6 and encircled a battalion. On October 27th, a Cambodians counterattack suffered great casualties.[1593]

For days on end, the NVA used obliterating shelling, 130 mm guns, 122 mm rockets, 120 mm mortars, upon helplessly trapped residents, 9,000 in Pa Kham, 8,000 in Tang Kouk, 12,000 in Rumlong[1594] and perhaps another 8,000 refugees running toward Rumlong. John Del Vecchio writes, "The concentration of artillery on tiny Rumlong was greater than that on mighty Stalingrad in 1941-42" and massacred no less than 8,000 civilians.[1595]

After a three-month liberation, on December 1, 1971, North Vietnamese and Khmer Rouge forces drove Cambodians out of Kompong Thmar and nearby Baray. NVA artillery turned the Baray area into rubble and killed as many as 20,000 civilians.[1596]

Neither the slaughtered civilians nor the Cambodians soldiers counted much to the press. The media did not tell the story of the flesh, bone and blood of the massacres at Kompong Thom, Baray, Tang Kouk. Instead the story was the raw materials of the abandoned tanks, trucks and guns of the fleeing [cowardly] Cambodians.[1597]

The CBS Evening News with Roger Mudd of December 1, 1971 gave twenty seconds to North Vietnam's

---

[1592] John M. Del Vecchio, *For the Sake of All living Things*, New York: Bantam 1991, 418, 436

[1593] "In for the Duration," *Time* Monday, Dec. 20, 1971
http://www.time.com/time/magazine/article/0,9171,878972,00.html?promoid=googlep

[1594] John M. Del Vecchio, *For the Sake of All living Things*, New York: Bantam 1991, 440, 442.

[1595] John M. Del Vecchio, *For the Sake of All living Things*, New York: Bantam 1991, 435, 473.

[1596] John M. Del Vecchio, "Cambodia, Laos and Viet Nam? The Importance of Story Individual and Cultural Effects of Skewing the Realities of American Involvement in Southeast Asia for Social, Political and/or Economic Ends," 1996 Vietnam Symposium "After the Cold War: Reassessing Vietnam," 18-20 April 1996.

[1597] John M. Del Vecchio, *For the Sake of All living Things*, New York: Bantam 1991, 455, 458.

butchery in Baray and Kompong Thmar in Cambodia. Cambodian defeat was news.

A day after the Baray slaughter ABC's Harry Reasoner gave 30 seconds, CBS's Walter Cronkite, 30 seconds and NBC's John Chancellor, 10 seconds, to Cambodian troops fleeing Baray. On December 3, ABC's Harry Reasoner gave another 20 seconds to Cambodians fleeing the North Vietnamese.[1598] Cowards not innocents.

The media spin was the anticommunists, whether Americans, South Vietnamese or Cambodian, were running away. Communists were winning, they were the heroes no matter how many thousands of anonymous innocent women and children the Communists butchered.

Senator Kennedy, GAO, NBC, and CBS Attribute Atrocities to US Bombing. As for who the media held responsible for killing civilians, on December 5, NBC's Garrick Utley gave 50 seconds to a General Accounting Office, GAO, study attributing rising civilian casualties and refugees in Cambodia almost entirely to U.S. bombing. GAO said little about indiscriminate North Vietnamese artillery turned on fleeing civilians.

There was a simple apparent explanation for GAO indifference to human suffering. Senator Edward Kennedy had requested the GAO, an arm of Congress deferential to elected members of the majority party, to study the subject.[1599] Senator Ted Kennedy paid for the GAO report and the media happily broadcast it free.

As the outgunned neophyte Cambodians troops retreated, the U.S. bombed the NVA and Khmer Khrom forces pressing on the capitol of Phnom-Penh. 25,000 South Vietnamese troops fought in the rubber plantations of eastern Cambodia. The Cambodians made a last ditch desperate defense of Phnom-Penh.[1600]

Cambodian Cowards. On December 7 NBC's Garrick Utley reported communists rocketing Phnom Penh. Cameras focused on Cambodian women defending it all…implicitly

---

[1598] Vanderbilt Television News Archive, http://openweb.tvnews.vanderbilt.edu/1971-12/
[1599] Vanderbilt Television News Archive, http://openweb.tvnews.vanderbilt.edu/1971-12/
[1600] "In for the Duration," *Time* Monday, Dec. 20, 1971. http://www.time.com/time/magazine/article/0,9171,878972,00.html?promoid=googlep

because the cowardly men had fled. Utley made no mention of the NVA artillery butchering civilians in Baray just days before.

None Dare Call it Victory. In the event the South Vietnamese troops, relieving pressure on the Cambodian capital, rescued Phnom Penh a city now flooded with refugees. Disaster faded away as the Communists were driven back. A December 9th story of ABC's Howard K. Smith covers South Vietnamese, using U.S. helicopter gunships, overrunning a Communist base camp in Cambodia. A Denis Cameron story followed on the village survivors of Kompong Thom.

NBC's John Chancellor gave only 10 seconds to the Cambodian's finally successful defense of Phnom Penh and the South Vietnamese winning its battle on the border. Losing to the Communists was news. Defeating Communist was not news fit to print or broadcast.

On December 17 CBS's Walter Cronkite and NBC's John Chancellor reported the deterioration of Cambodian defenses along [a hundred kilometer] Highway (sic) 6 and martial law in Phnom Penh. On December 20 Cronkite said the news on Indochina war was not good. Communists surrounded Cambodian troops near Phnom Penh.

CBS's Bob Schieffer featured Professor Raphael Littauer pontificated American aerial bombing of the Ho Chi Minh trail created the refugees. History would record maps showing B-52 bombings where the refugees had been[1601] without noting that American bombing had targeted three advancing NVA divisions and that the U.S. bombing came after the civilians had fled to safety.

To this day, short of John DelVecchio's account in *For the Sake of All living Things*, there is deafening silence about North Vietnamese's indiscriminate shelling of innocent civilians in Cambodia, a wealth of recurring stories missed or downplayed. It was the same silence that met North Vietnam's many main force battles using heavy artillery against civilians in 1964, 1968, 1972 and 1975.

Project Air War. Fred Branfman's Project Air War, protecting the sacrosanct and pristine life of gentle Lao villagers along the Ho Chi Minh Trail, was now on the evening

---

[1601] John M. Del Vecchio, *For the Sake of All living Things*, New York: Bantam 1991, 472.

news. On December 21 ABC's Denis Cameron gave nearly 2 minutes to North Vietnam's move on Kompong Thom, 80% destroyed and many wounded civilians.

The pictures of devastation were followed immediately by pictures of the US 7th Air Force. This implied falsely that the U.S. airpower had destroyed Kompong Thom and its people. On Dec 23 NBC's Garrick Utley reported U. S. air power in the Cambodia with no mention of NVA artillery. The TV news time remaining that day was given over to delays in release of a U.S. Army report on My Lai massacre,[1602] an old story about hundreds of civilian casualties blackening out news coverage of the contemporary communist slaughter of tens of thousands of civilians in Cambodia.

***

Hanoi Invasion in 1972 to Spur "Antiwar Dissidence."

In December 1971 in Hanoi the 20th Plenum of the Politburo approved main force invasion of South Vietnam with Soviet tanks and artillery. A COSVN Resolution, Gen. Giap, and Minister of Justice of the Viet Cong Provisionary government, PRG, Truong Nhu Tang all indicated a major objective of the offensive was political struggle, "spurring antiwar dissidence in the United States."[1603]

Public Supports Nixon. After all of the propaganda barrages from Hanoi and New York, remarkably, 50-55 percent of the American people still supported President Nixon's Vietnam policy in late 1971.[1604] Only 15% thought Vietnam was the biggest problem facing the nation.[1605]

Perhaps it was the Christmas season. Christmas 1971 offered bountiful opportunities for the antiwar movement and the Vietnamese.

[1602] Vanderbilt Television News Archive, http://openweb.tvnews.vanderbilt.edu/1971-12/
[1603] Lt. Gen. Ngo Quang Truong, The Easter Offensive of 1972, Indochina Monograms, Washington DC: U.S. Army Center of Military History, 1980, 157; Tang Vietcong Memoir, 210; cited in Phillip B. Davidson, *Vietnam At War: the History: 1946-1975*, New York: Oxford University Press, 1991, 676.
[1604] John M. Del Vecchio, *For the Sake of All living Things*, New York: Bantam 1991,

[1605] Gallup cited in Louis Sorley, *A Better War...*, 282.

***

The Christmas Spirit: CBS and VVAW

In Kansas City the VVAW had discussed civil disobedience at Christmas and burning Christmas trees. On Hubbard's trip to Paris the North Vietnamese suggested VVAW might be traveling to Hanoi near Christmas and accept a release of POWs to a VVAW delegation.[1606]

Terry DuBose, VVAW Texas, who Scott Camil had asked to assassinate Sen. John Tower (R-Texas) remembers, "There was actually some discussion of assassinating some Senators during the Christmas holidays."[1607]

POWs Home by Christmas? On November 10, 1971 Barbara Webster, aide to Cora Weiss reported, "The North Vietnamese in Paris called the Committee in Liaison on Sunday the 7th, to ask us to send a representative to discuss a prisoner issue with them. ...I spent Tuesday with two members of Vietnam Committee of Solidarity with the American People and Mr. Nguyen Minh Vy..."

The POW news? Eleven pound Christmas packages and cards were allowed. The POW families could enjoy Christmas at home with husband, son, or father, if President Nixon had allowed it.

The Vietnamese reiterated with me...they have no communications with any American representative except the Committee of Liaison. There is only one channel for Nixon and that is already in existence. All he needs to do is announce the date...at least some of you would share Christmas with your husband, son, or father..."[1608]

Fernandez Bearing Gifts. On December 21, 1971, Rev. Richard Fernandez, a COLIFAM courier, returned from Paris bearing gifts, 1,001 letters from 229 POWs, including 18 from POWs held by the VC in the South. (All other VC POWs were dead, released or escaped.) David Dellinger and Cora Weiss forwarded mail to families with the message of bombing 25 miles from Hanoi and Nixon ought to set the date for withdrawal as had Congress.[1609]

[1606] FBI, [Redacted] to Director, 9:55 pm urgent TELETYPE, Nov 18, 1971, 2; FBI, [Redacted] to Director, TELETYPE 806PM URGENT November 19, 1971, 2-5.
[1607] Richard Staciewicz, *Winter Soldier: An Oral History of the Vietnam Veterans Against the War,* 1997, 295.
[1608] Barbara Webster to Dear friends, November 10, 1971.

Desecrating God, Country, Liberty, Christmas: Commentators and Communists. Christmas Eve 1971 arrived with ABC's Howard K. Smith showing military troops at Christ's birthplace in [Muslim Arab] Bethlehem and American planes bombing Laos, Cambodia and North Vietnam. Bethlehem needed protection from Muslim Arabs dominating it. America was bombing the safe havens in Indochina from whence communists were killing Americans.

Not to be outdone, CBS Walter Cronkite and Bob Schieffer aired a long five-minute story on the victims of the air war using Communist film. Cronkite repeated Hanoi's claims of alleged civilian casualties and one million refugees. Bob Schieffer showed Communist film of wounded civilians, alleged dead victims of U. S. air strikes, air raid rubble…refugees. Millions were homeless. Schieffer didn't know when the bombing would end.[1610]

The utter futility of self-defense in war made surrender the nobler option, especially during Christmas. The advice atheists and agnostics give to Christians.

By the end of 1971, the Communists had made some 24,756 terrorist attacks upon civilians in South Vietnam since 1965[1611] but these were morally less than the occasional accidental killing of civilians by US bombing errors.

Assaulting Lady Liberty. On Sunday December 26, 1971 some 15 longhaired, bearded VVAW members wearing fatigues, Fidel Castro look-alikes, and a radio disk jockey boarded the last 4:00 pm tourist ferry from Manhattan to Liberty Island.

Among the group were Joe Bangert, Michael Parker, Don Bristow-Carrico, Vin MacLellan, Eugene Halpern, Robert Barracca, Jr., Tim MacCormick and nine others.[1612] The VVAW cadre hid until tourists left, occupied the Statue of Liberty, barricaded themselves inside and from Lady Liberty's torch hung the American flag upside down. For twenty hours, park service police stood by as a judge deliberated. Peter Weiss

---

[1609] David Dellinger and Cora Weiss, Dear friends, COLIFAM, December 22, 1971; FBI, New York, LHM, COLIFAM, January 20, 1972.
[1610] Vanderbilt Television News Archive, http://openweb.tvnews.vanderbilt.edu/1971-12/
[1611] Swett and Zigler cite R.J. Rummel, *Death by Government,* New Brunswich, New Jersey: Transaction Publishers, 2000, 241, 243,258,282.
[1612] Robert D. MacFadden, "War Foes Seize Statue of Liberty," *New York Times,* December 27, 1971.

(Cora's husband), Center for Constitutional Rights, defended the VVAW.

The judge ruled VVAW might stay if they do not obstruct the tourists. With clenched fists the VVAW marched out, leaving $5 for food and carrying out "a beautiful thought…Live in peace."[1613]

To Liberty's assaulters, John Lennon and Yoko Ono sent Christmas greetings. Pete Seeger donated $200, Rep. Bella Abzug, D-NY, telephoned support and a Viet Cong negotiator in Paris, Le Mai, sent a "congratulatory message."[1614]

Other VVAW Targets. Police authorities halted a VVAW occupation of Betsy Ross House, Philadelphia, in 45 minutes and military authorities at Travis AFB, between San Francisco and Sacramento, California took 12 hours to rid themselves of VVAW cadre.

Reassembling in Washington on December 28, 1971, a VVAW troop marched from the Peace monument to the Capitol spilling blood from plastic sacks upon sidewalks surrounding the White House. While blocking the top steps of the Lincoln Memorial, 187 were arrested.

On December 30, 1971 about 309 VVAW members from Philadelphia tried to contact the Soviet delegation at the UN in New York City, but UN officials turned Al Hubbard and the others away.[1615]

***

[1613] Vin McLellan, "Protesting Vietnam Vets Seize Statue of Liberty," *Washington Post*, December 27, 1971, A-12; William Federici and Paul Meskil, "Liberty-holder's Lawyers Ordered to Explain the Court," *New York Daily News*, December 28, 1971, 3; "Retreat From the Statue," *New York Daily News*, December 29, 1971, 49; "Trespassers on Liberty," *El Paso Herald Post*, December 29, 1971, 2-B; "Viet vets leave Liberty with a thought," UPI, *Washington Daily News*, December 29, 1971, 7; FBI, Informative Note, December 27, 1971.
[1614] Josh Gerstein, "How Kerry's Group Plotted Against Statue of Liberty," *New York Sun*, April 14, 2004.
[1615] FBI, New York, Memo, December 30, 1971.

Part V. January-June 1972 Summary

January-June 1972, were days of horrible war and hopes for peace punctuated by a Hanoi invasion, protests, bombings, and treason. President Nixon orders bombing of the previously off limits Port of Haiphong, the supply center for Soviet war material. Despite a sophisticated propaganda assault upon America's "Air War," it and South Vietnamese ARVN gallantry halt Hanoi's massive Easter Offensive.

From Washington to Paris to Hanoi, hundreds of peace activists gather and find comfort with the enemy in Versailles, Milly-la-Foret, Paris, Hanoi, Stockholm, giving Hanoi explicit advice on actions and propaganda themes. The Beatles' John Lennon funds Rennie Davis efforts to disrupt the Republican convention in San Diego. Convention moved to a Miami moat like location, they fail, but Hayden recruits Ron Kovic and other veterans to interrupt Nixon's acceptance speech. Hayden and Fonda form the Indochina Peace Campaign (IPC). COLIFAM continues to exploit POWs and families.

VVAW leaders meet Soviet bloc secret services, gather detailed military intelligence on troop movements and try to acquire information on weapons systems. The terrorist Weather Underground of Ayers and Dohrn, continue domestic bombing. Jane Fonda prepared for a trip to Hanoi.

In early January 1972, President Nixon approved the withdrawal of another 70,000 troops. At 150,000 America was well on its way out of Vietnam. Nixon had reduced troop levels by 400,000 from their peak of 550,000. On the ground Saigon was largely on its own against Hanoi's massing again for a grand offensive to end it all. America's diminishing presence retained the capacity to wage an air war in support of its ally.

***

Chapter 15. Easter Political Offensive: Condemn USA

Air War Threatens Hanoi Invasion

Since U.S. ground troops were fading away, Hanoi and its antiwar comrades focused their propaganda on the horrors of American air power in Vietnam, Laos and Cambodia. This focus on the US air war coincided with the planning of a major NVA spring offensive. Hanoi in December 1971 approved a massive main force invasion of South Vietnam in early 1972 one of whose objectives was stirring up antiwar activists in the USA. The likely U.S. response was being called "escalation" before the fact and it would come "especially in the air." The horrific Saigon ground forces having to counter the NVA, also got more attention.

Political Will. In early January, anticipating an NVA offensive, but confident of southern defenses, General Abrams said the battlefield was not a problem. "You go to the weakest thing in the whole setup…the will of the American government." If the enemy attacked and held a key city for a week, "the press…will say Vietnamization has failed. … [T]he most important front of all—the American political scene."[1616]

Getting tortured and starved POWs home was a human link in American will and Hanoi knew it.

Morality of the Air War. Fred Branfman's claims to the contrary, during the Vietnam War the moral restraints of two Presidents and the active assistance of some of the Hanoi's friends in U.S. effectively limited the bombing—the air war. On the side of morality:

- American mines were set for deep draft freighters to avoid sinking civilian craft;
- vehicles 200 yards off the Ho Chi Minh Trail went free;
- many targets, such as populated areas, heavy industry, canals, dikes, dams, were flat off-limits.[1617]

[1616] Lewis Sorley, *A Better War: The Unexamined Victories and Final Tragedy of America's Last Years in Vietnam*, New York: Harcourt, 1999, 352.
[1617] The North switched to shallow vessels to avoid mines. A U.S. bombing retaliation upon the construction was surgically accurate. Bombing hit on the southwest edge of

- There was a no fly zone near the Chinese border. A rogue aircrew bombed an off limits Chinese Cultural Center and "the ammo stored there cooked off for a week."[1618]

POWs Freed If Air War Ended. Hanoi and its surrogates linked the release of POWs directly to American acceptance of their every demand. Kissinger says to Nixon, "The other side (is) using...the prisoners brutally. What I've always said to the wives...I don't believe your husbands want you to have America surrender." Nixon replied, "They're still, basically, patriots."[1619]

On January 17, 1972, Richard Falk on COLIFAM letterhead wrote to POW families,

The resumption of the large scale air war ...in 1971 should be ...of grave concern for all...who seek to end the Vietnam War and secure the release of American POWs...We urge...the end of combat operations by a date certain prior to June 1, 1972... [There is] no other way to secure prisoner release. We hope you will join us ...to build public support for this position.[1620]

The peace movement propaganda apparatus required financing.

Taxpayer Financing of Antiwar Movement. On January 20, 1972 a testimonial dinner was held for Ruth Gage-Colby in New York. Tax-deductible funds would "help finance" antiwar activities. Gage-Colby's contributions to peace included travels to meet the enemy in Budapest and Hanoi and helping unify "all major peace groups."[1621]

Haiphong missing 27 foreign vessels. See: "U.S. Jets Strike Haiphong Shipyard," San Francisco *Examiner* and *Chronicle*, August 6, 1972, 13. See: Perloff, 122 who cites the twenty-six pages in the 1985 Congressional Record required summarizing the "Rules of Engagement" during the Vietnam War. See also: Eschmann, 74-5, 80.

[1618] Mark Berent, "Rules of Engagement," in Santoli, *To Bear Any Burden*, 143.

[1619] Richard M. Nixon, Henry A. Kissinger, White House Telephone, Conversation No. 17-125, January 1, 1972, 10:57 am -11:19 am, transcript, 6.

[1620] Richard Falk to Dear friends, COLIFAM, January 17, 1972.

[1621] Dear friend of peace letter, Ruth Gage-Colby Testimonial Committee, scheduled January 20, 1972 at Biltmore in New York. Copy in possession of author from Max Friedman. Among the familiar leftist patrons of the dinner were members of the Senate, Sen. Frank Church, Sen. Vance Hartke, Sen. Walter Mondale, Sen. John Tunney. Members of the House included Rep. Bella Abzug, Rep. Herman Badillo, Rep. Seymour Halpern, Rep. Patsy Mink, Rep. Charles Rangel, Rep. William Fitts Ryan, Rep. Benjamin Rosenthal. Former members of Congress were Robert Abrams, Frank P. Graham, Ernest Gruening, Allard Lowenstein, Wayne Morse, and Jeanette Rankin. Old reliables included Roger Baldwin, Mr. & Mrs. Leonard Boudin, Katherine

POW Families Lobbied to Support Hanoi. In late January, Pacific News Service reporter and *Rampart's* Asian Editor,[1622] Banning Garrett returned from Hanoi with 541 letters from POWs. Cora Weiss told families she was refusing any letters sent to MIA, or previously believed to be alive at capture. [1623]

Weiss enclosed a James "Scotty" Reston column declaring Hanoi victories in Cambodia and Laos, hence, urging Nixon to stop prolonging a losing war.[1624] Cora's clipping file lacked a February 2, 1972 story of the North executing 20 villagers for refusing to obey.[1625]

Robert Miller, ABC, asked Cora Weiss whether her delivery of a large batch of POW mail was a Viet Cong ploy to distract from Nixon's disclosure of secret peace talks. Weiss replied the letters were written months before the secret talks.[1626] The late delivery showed Hanoi delaying POWs letters for impact with COLIFAM complicity. .

VC Peace Plan. On February 2, 1972 Madame Binh released clarifications on the PRG's (NVA's) 7-Point proposal making clear the POWs were hostages whose ransom was setting a date for US, resignation of Thieu government. Also …stop …pacification policy, disband concentration camps," free political prisoners, and "guarantee… democratic liberties."[1627]

Unstated. Pacification had to be stopped. It was working.

Removing Thieu, Easy. After a seven-hour talk with Xuan Thuy in Paris on February 5, 1972 Richard J. Barnet and Peter Weiss of the IPS told POW families Hanoi's lie-- Kissinger never brought up the POWS. Removing Thieu could be easy. Unstated A coup and assassination had removed

---

Camp, Noam Chomsky, Age Feinglass, Jerry Gordon, Corliss Lamont, Robert Jay Lifton, Rev. Paul Moore, Victor Reuther, Stanley Sheinbaum, Gloria Steinem, I F Stone, Amy Swerdlow and George Wald. Writer and entertainer patrons were Ossie Davis, Ruby Dee, Joseph Heller, Murray Kempton, Pete Seeger, and Dalton Trumbo.

[1622] Banning Garrett, "The Strange Economics of the Vietnam War," *RAMPARTS*, Vol. 10, No. 5. November 1971.

[1623] Cora Weiss to Dear friends, COLIFAM, January 31, 1972.

[1624] James Reston, "Nixon Report: Shrewd Politics, But no Peace," New York *Times*, January 26, 1972.

[1625] AFP, "Monk Says North Executed Villagers," Washington *Post*, February 2, 1972.

[1626] FBI, New York to Director, COLIFAM IS- New Left, NITEL 123AM, February 1, 1972; FBI, New York, LHM, COLIFAM, February 10, 1972.

[1627] Found in part in COLIFAM to Families of captured servicemen in North Vietnam, March 17, 1972.

Diem. Le Duc Tho told Kissinger, "You can replace (Thieu) in many ways...You can swap him...Ways are not lacking."[1628]

Freedom. Barnet and Weiss suggested that freeing Saigon's political prisoners, stopping censorship and allowing political meetings might lead to a breakthrough in negotiations.[1629] It was Hanoi, not Saigon, which had political prisoners, censorship and no protests.

***

Air Defenses Preparations for Major Offensive in 1972

Hanoi, not Washington, was preparing for a massive escalation, its Easter offensive 1972, as they had in 1965 and 1968 and would again in 1975. Hanoi's divisions were well equipped with Soviet air defenses as well as trucks, tanks and artillery.

Anti-aircraft Expertise. During February and March 1972 four high-level Soviet delegations visited Hanoi, including: the commander-in-chief of armed forces of the USSR, Marshal Pavel Batitsky, accompanied by commander of the anti-aircraft missile forces, Lt. General of Artillery F. M. Bolddarenko; and head of anti-aircraft radar forces, Lt. Gen. M.T. Beregavoi. NVA participants were Tran Quy Hai and Tran Sam.[1630] Clearly, Hanoi and Moscow viewed the American air war as a major threat to its planned Easter offensive. UPI reported an increase in supplies of anti-aircraft weapons during 1972.[1631]

***Times* Stuck on Stupid.** The New York *Times* reported, "...Although Marshal Pavel Batitsky, commander of the Soviet Air Defense Forces, had visited Hanoi ... North Vietnamese leaders did not inform him of the imminent launch date of their Easter Offensive."[1632] Assuming the timing of Soviet high military visits was merely a happy coincidence,

---

[1628] Loi and Vu, Negotiations in Larry Berman, *No Peace, No Honor*, 106

[1629] Richard J. Barnet and Peter Weiss, "Memo to: Families of Prisoners of War, Re: Recent activity around the negotiations in Paris," News Releases, February 7, 1972.

[1630] "Soviet Chief of Staff Kulikov Holds Talks in Hanoi," FBIS Trends, 31 December 1974, 11.

[1631] VNA, 27 March 1972; K.C. Thaler, UPI, London, 23 February 1972 both cited in J.C.K., "Hanoi's Growing Soviet Ties," Radio Free Europe Research, March 27, 1972 online at Open Society Archive, 67-4-164. Batitsky was a go- to guy, the designated assassin of secret police chief Lavrenty Beria in 1953 according to Lt. Gen. Vadim Volkovitsky in June 2010.

[1632] Stephen J. Morris, "The War We Could Have Won," NY *Times*, May 1, 2005. http://www.nytimes.com/2005/05/01/opinion/01morris.html?pagewanted=print&positi on=s

complaining about Hanoi's precise calendar was petty quibbling. In 1971, the Soviets provided a million tons of the necessary equipment, antiaircraft, tanks and heavy artillery for a major invasion. .

***

Aiding and Abetting the Enemy.

When Barbara Walters interviewed Chief of Staff, H.R. Haldeman, on NBC's *Today* show, Haldeman said U.S. Senators and the anti-war movement were "consciously aiding and abetting the enemy of the United States." They favored "putting a Communist government in South Vietnam." On February 9, Nixon said his opponents had a right to propose to "overthrow [of] the government of South Vietnam or ...satisfy the enemy." Yet they must also take "responsibility for the enemy failing to negotiate...until after the election."[1633]

CBS: US Bombing Hospitals. On the CBS Evening News for Wednesday, Feb 16, 1972, Roger Mudd led with a Banning Garrett, Pacific News Service reporter and *Rampart's* Asian Editor, story and film of a December bombing of the Tranh Hoa hospital in North Vietnam. Ruins and victims were shown and antipersonnel bombs claimed. Pentagon replied US did not bomb hospitals, but suggested another explanation, the crash landing of a shot-down jet.[1634] **Banning- CIA running Drug Traffic?** Banning Garrett of pro-Hanoi *Ramparts* magazine wrote astonishing things—like the CIA was in charge of the opium trade in Asia.[1635] Beijing and Hanoi Vietnamese, not the CIA, peddled drugs to American troops in Vietnam.[1636] Joseph Westermeyer and William M. Leary conducted years of research having little impact on tall tales about the CIA, such as the movie *Air America*.

Westermeyer writes,

American-owned airlines never knowingly transported opium in or out Laos, nor did their pilots ever profit from its transport. Yet every plane in Laos undoubtedly carried opium at some time, unknown to the pilot and his superiors—just as had

[1633] Larry Berman, *No Peace, No Honor*, 119
[1634] CBS Evening News for Wednesday, Feb 16, 1972, Abstract and Metadata, Vanderbilt University, 1972-2007.
[1635] *Frank Browning and* Banning Garrett, "The CIA and the New Opium War," *Ramparts*, May 1971;
[1636] Phillip B. Davidson, *Vietnam At War: the History: 1946-1975*, New York: Oxford University Press, 1991.

virtually every pedicab, every Mekong River sampan, and every missionary jeep between China and the Gulf of Siam.[1637]

Similarly, Ron Chepesiuk traced the heroin trade to Leslie "Ike" Atkinson and William "Jack" Jackson operating out of Jack's American Star Bar in Bangkok. Heroin was never smuggled out in the coffins of dead US troops.[1638]

Based on history, some astonishing things were predictable.

Doug Pike Predicts Night of the Long Knives. On February 17, 1972 a subcommittee of the Senate Committee on the Judiciary released the testimony of Doug Pike predicting the results of a communist conquest:

> If the Communists win decisively...what is the prospect? First all foreigners would be cleared out....especially the hundreds of foreign newsmen.
>
> A curtain of ignorance would descend. Then would begin a night of the long knives. The Communist would create a silence. The world would call it peace."[1639]

The Pike's report fell in the dark woods. No one was there.

George Wald in Hanoi. In late February 1972 Nobel Prize winner George Wald arrived in Hanoi after 5-weeks in China. Wald interviewed POW David Wesley Hoffman and four other POWs, claimed the U.S. targeted civilians and hospitals for bombing, used inhumane napalm and fragmentation bombs and OWs were in good condition, well fed and cared for.[1640] On Radio Hanoi Wald said the POWs

---

[1637] Joseph Westermeyer, *Poppies, Pipes and People: Opium and its Use in Laos,* Berkeley: University of California Press, 1982, 51 cited in William McLeary, "Supporting the 'Secret War': CIA Air Operations in Laos, 1955-1974," cia.gov/libray/center-for-the-study-of-intelligence/Kent-csi/docs/v43i3a07p.htm. See also Richard Botkin, *Ride the Thunder: A Vietnam War Story of Honor and Triumph,* New York: WND Books, 2009, 208 cites Curtis Peebles, *Twilight Warriors: Covert Air Operations against the USSR,* Annapolis: Naval Institute Press, 254-5; The CIA's role is claimed in Christopher Robbins, *Air America: The Story of the CIA's Secret Airlines,* New York: G.P. Putnam's Sons, 1979, 138.

[1638] Ron Chepesiuk, *Sergeant Smack: The Legendary Lives and Times of Ike Atkinson, Kingpin and His Band of Brothers,* Rock Hill and Thunder Bay: Strategic Media, 2010 review by Bertil Lintner, Asia Times Online.

[1639] Douglas Pike, *The Viet-Cong Strategy of Terror,* United States Mission, Viet-Nam, 1970, 42; also cited in U.S. Congress, Senate, Committee on Judiciary, *The Human Cost of Communism in Vietnam,* Washington, U.S. Government Printing Office, February 17, 1972, 2-3.

were "violently against the war and want our country to get out as quickly as possible."[1641] Wald had parroted the Hanoi line on every point every time.[1642] George Wald claimed Hoffman's description of being hung on a hook by a broken arm was not physiologically possible. The arm would have come apart.[1643] Perhaps Wald was unfamiliar with research conducted by "Fidel" in the Zoo POW camp. **Wald Invigorated.** On February 24, 1972, George Wald returned from China and North Vietnam where he talked to POWs and carried back 86 POW letters.[1644] Wald joined the presidential campaign of Senator George McGovern and was arrested for occupying the US Capitol.

Bombing SAM Sites. From November 1971 through March 1972 President Nixon ordered 20 air strikes against SAM sites posing a danger to US aircraft. **No Good Deed Unpunished.** General John D. Lavelle was publicly accused of conducting unauthorized strikes and cashiered on the very day Hanoi began its 1972 spring offensive. Nixon said, "It was proper to relieve and retire him," though privately Nixon said, "I just don't want him to be made a goat, goddamnit," and "It's just a hell of a damn. And it's a bad rap for him, Henry." Kissinger said, "I think this will go away." In two months the SAM sites would be back on the authorized target list,[1645]but Lavelle's reputation was destroyed.

VVAW, Hanoi and East Bloc

During January and February 1972, the Stockholm Conference, the World Peace Council, Soviet Peace Council and the Japanese Gensuiko sponsored and funded VVAW's Al Hubbard's long tour of Paris, Budapest, Moscow, Hanoi, and Japan.[1646]

Pete Seeger. By mid-February Hubbard was in Hanoi. He met New York Timesman Seymour Hersh and folk singer

---

[1640] Clinton, *The Loyal...*237-242.

[1641] Frank J. Rafalko, *MH/CHAOS: The CIA's Campaign Against the Radical Left and the Black Panthers*, Annapolis: Naval Institute Press, 2011, 150.

[1642] Papers of George Wald, boxes 4, 19, 27, 103 at oasis.lib.Harvard.edu/oasis/deliver.

[1643] Clinton, *The Loyal...*239.

[1644] FBI, New York to Director, Teletype, February 25, 1972; FBI, New York, memo [Redacted] title, March 17, 1972.

[1645] Richard Sisk, "Nixon Transcripts: Air Force General John Lavelle wrongly took the fall for secret bombing of North Vietnam," *Daily News*, August 6, 2010; Editorial, New York Times, August 7, 2010.

[1646] FBI, Houston, Memo, "VVAW National Steering Committee Meeting, Houston, Texas, April 7-11, 1972" May 11, 1972, file No. 100-448092-14501, 11, 12, 37, 39, 52.

Pete Seeger. Seeger made a radio broadcast telling servicemen to lay down their arms and come home. As Seeger described it, "I start with the song, 'Turn, Turn, Turn,'...Then I say, 'yes this is Pete Seeger...some of my friends will say, 'What the hell are you doing up there? Perhaps the question is 'What are any of us doing in this part of the world?'[1647]

Hubbard met with Pham Van Dong and Le Duc To talk about "what could be done to end imperialist aggression." They extended an open invitation to any VVAW member. In Hanoi, Hubbard also met people from Sweden, Algeria, Finland, Australia, and Denmark.

Hubbard met with several POWs calling themselves "Captured U.S. Servicemen Against the War." Hubbard filmed POWs David Wesley Hoffman, Larry Stolz, and Dale Koons and recorded James Dickinson Cutter saying the POWs had adequate medical care and lived in "pleasant surroundings under decent conditions."

Tortured POW. Later Lt. Commander Hoffman told the House Committee on Internal Security,
I was personally tortured...to meet a delegation in February 1972. ...It is completely obvious... We were not at liberty to say what we wanted. It was a completely programmed thing. And if you made the wrong response, you stood a very definite chance of some severe consequences.[1648]

Hubbard toured Quang Binh, near the DMZ, and other provinces to evaluate the air war and to establish a relationship with the NLF.

Docs Didn't Get Memo. Doctors told Hubbard they were unaware of fiberglass pellets or chemical warfare in North Vietnam.[1649]

VVAW Plans Hanoi Tour. A Houston meeting of VVAW on the April 11, selected its nominees for a proposed trip to Hanoi. The most notable were George Smith, Indiana-Ohio, a former POW and IPC activist and Scott Camil, Florida advocate of the assassination of pro-war U.S. Senators.[1650] The

---

[1647] Pete Seeger, "Strummin' Banjo in North Vietnam," *Saturday Review*, May 13, 1972, 32 cited in House... "Compilation of Broadcasts...," 7691.
[1648] House, Hearings on Restraints on Travel to Hostile Areas: Hearings before the Committee on Internal Security, 93rd Cong., 1st sess., 1973, 3-4 cited in Rothrock *Divided...* 186n10
[1649] FBI, Houston, Memo, "VVAW National Steering Committee Meeting, Houston, Texas, April 7-11, 1972" May 11, 1972, file no. 100-448092-14501, 11-13.

FBI transmitted the list to the President and to diplomatic and military agencies.[1651] Local FBI offices were instructed to find "possible weaknesses including pending prosecution, etc which can be exploited to bar individuals' travel..."[1652]

On May 9, 1972 John Smith of the Connecticut VVAW, wrote to the North Vietnamese Embassy, Paris offering a medical assistance team for Hanoi.[1653] Plans proceeded to send a seven-person VVAW team to Paris to meet with North Vietnamese. It would cost $30,000, but VVAW was hopeful that Jane Fonda and Soviet Union (half) would cover a major portion.[1654]

***

CP World Assembly for Peace Versailles, France
February 11-13, 1972
"A horde of Communist-controlled agitators."

Soviet controlled fronts, World Peace Council, WPC, and the Stockholm Conference on Vietnam joined by 48 French Communist Party and associated organizations sponsored a World Assembly for Peace in Versailles, France from February 11-13, 1972.

Along for the party gathering were American Communists John Gilman, Elizabeth Moos, Sidney Peck, Evelynne Perry, Pauline Rosen, Irving and Ruth Sarnoff, Abe Weisburd, Bernard Weller, Michael Zagarell and Trotskyites Deborah Bustin, Fred Halstead, and Daniel Rosenshine. Asian communists attending: Hoang Quoc Viet, Hanoi, Vietnam; Quang Ming, NLF; Thiounn Prasith, Cambodia; Gen. Singkapo Sikhoi, Laos. Red China and 70 other countries were represented as well as all major American antiwar leaders and groups.[1655]

[1650] FBI, Houston to Director, Teletype, URGENT April 12, 1972 list names. Other top candidates were Marty O. Jordan, an Indian from Arkansas; John Musgrave, Kansas; Barry Romo, California; David Evans Ross, Colorado; and Bill Marshall, Michigan, a black. Alternates selected were Peter Mahoney, Louisiana; Richard Bangert, Missouri; Mike Dedrick, Seattle; Chuck Geisler, Michigan; Gale Graham, New York; and Jon Birch, Philadelphia. For reasons unknown three names were redacted under FOIA-George Smith, David Ross and Marty Jordan on Jan 1, 1994; FBI, Acting Director to SACs (List Albany St. Louis), VVAW-IS-Revolutionary Activities, URGENT TELETYPE May 2, 1972, 7.
[1651] FBI, Domestic Intelligence Division, Informative Note, April 12, 1972.
[1652] FBI, fragment CV 100-31431, 3.
[1653] FBI, New Haven memo, VVAW, may 31, 1972.
[1654] FBI, St. Louis to Acting Director, VVAW-IS-RA, 7;56 PM NITEL, May 12, 1972; FBI fragment May 24,1972, file 100-448092, 2481-9
[1655] Icord (Mo.), Congressional Record-House March 13, 1972, H-1972-1973 lists

Also comfortable in Communist venues were members of the WILPF,[1656] AFSC,[1657] WSP,[1658] the National Welfare Rights Organization, CALC, [1659] NPAC,[1660] PCPJ,[1661]; the American Deserters Committee, the VVAW and assorted professors.[1662]

Among the other notable Americans were: Rennie Davis, planning disruption of the Republican Convention (still scheduled for San Diego) in August,[1663] the keynote speaker Sidney Peck; actress Jane Fonda; Al Hubbard, [Richard[1664]] Joe Bangert, Edward Damato of VVAW, NY-PR[1665] and Robert Greenblatt of People's Peace Treaty.[1666]

Also Fred Branfman of Project Air War; Delia Alvarez, sister of POW Everett Alvarez; Ron Ridenour, veteran-student who blew the whistle on My Lai; Margery Tabankin of National Student Association, the U.S. front for Hanoi's People's Peace Treaty; Howard Zinn.

Soviet boss Leonid Brezhnev, Pham Van Dong, and Pathet Lao Prince Souphanouvong sent messages.

Americans and their affiliations. FBI, Philadelphia, Memo, Feb 14, 1972 file no. 100-448092-2664; FBI, New York to Director, Teletype, Feb. 18, 1972 file no. 100-448092-2728; FBI, Denver, Memo, "VVAW National Steering Committee Meeting, Denver, Colo, February 18-21, 1972 Internal Security-new Left," March 17, 1972, 29, 31. Also American Deserters Committee (Sweden).

[1656] Jean E. DeLord, Miriam Edera, Anne Florant, Cathern Flory, Libby Frank, Margaret Hayes, Joyce McLean, Beatrice Milwe, Maggie Olesen, Irma Prior, Helen Rees, Pat Samuel, Jean Thurman. Icord, H-172-3.

[1657] Bronson P. Clark, Eleanor Clark, Wallace Collett, Bob Eaton, Virginia Hill. Icord, H-172-3.

[1658] Madeline Duckles, William Goodfellow, Blanch Haber, Elizabeth A. Lichtenberg, Elizabeth Moos, Pauline Rosen, Frieda Schiffman. Icord, H-172-3.

[1659] Ed Deberry, Mary Glendinning, Maria Holt, Josephine Irwin, Robert S. Lecky, Max Surjadinvasta. Icord, H-172-3.

[1660] Lucille Banta, Peter S. Bergman, Ruth Gage Colby, Stephanie Coontz, Bonnie Garvin, Jerry Gordon, Fred Halstead, Elsie M. Monjar, Evelyn Perry, Daniel Rosenshine, Irving Sarnoff, Ruth Sarnoff, Jean Tibbils. Icord, H-172-3.

[1661] Barbara Dane, Ned Dobner, John Froines, Mary Lee Barbara Gilbertson, John Gilman, James Lafferty, Joseph Miller, Marece Neagu, Sidney Peck, Daphne Pounos-Clinton, Vivian Raineai, George Vickers, Lee Webb. Icord, H-172-3

[1662] Leonard P. Adams, Odell Lee, William Goodfellow, David Marr, Gabriel Kolko, Howard Zinn. Icord, H-172-3

[1663] Also Pam Cole and George Katsiaficas, Icord, H-1972-3.

[1664] FBI reports cover "Richard" Bangert a VVAW member in top ranks of its leadership in the middle west.

[1665] FBI, New York to Director, Teletype, Feb 18, 1972; also Everett Brown Carson, Robert Dunne, Lori Reidman in Ichord, H-1972-73.

[1666] Also Dianne Apsey, Mae C. Bremer; Frank H. Joyce and Nancy Woodside, Ichord H-1973.

Photo: Peace Conference, Versailles, France February 1972
Roger Canfield, March 2008, Museum Hanoi Hilton

The Critics. Career U.S. diplomat William J. Porter, Ambassador to the Paris Peace Talks, claimed that a "horde of Communist-controlled agitators"[1667] attended the Versailles confab. VVAW's Al Hubbard said, "true." A Pentagon briefer told the press, "Totally predictable speakers…produced a totally predictable resolution condemning U.S…and supporting the PRG's seven points." [laughter]. Speeches "were of monumental dreariness."[1668] In retrospect, the Pentagon's levity summarily dismissed the actual significance of the antiwar movement's impact on the outcome of the war. Rep. Richard Ichord of Missouri said, "We are not by any stretch of the imagination, dealing with 'doves' for peace but 'hawks' on the other side."[1669]

The American media took the event seriously.

The Cheerleaders. The *New York Times* headlined, "800 Rally Near Paris Say U.S. Sabotaged Talks" and the Assembly made the NBC evening news with John Chancellor. The Assembly unanimously endorsed the Viet Cong's, PRG's, 7-point peace plan "almost word for word," reported the Jonathan Randal of the *Washington Post*[1670] and summarily rejecting a Nixon 8-Point plan.

[1667] "Peace Group Backs Plan of Viet Cong," *Washington Star*, February 14, 1972; "Paris Antiwar Assembly Blasts United States, Backs Hanoi," *Washington Post*, Feb. 14, 1972.

[1668] Lewis Sorley, *Vietnam Chronicles*, Texas Tech University Press, 788.

[1669] Ichord, March 13, 1972, H-172.

[1670] *Washington Star*, February 14, 1972.

Coordinated Worldwide Actions. The Viet Cong platform summarily adopted, the issues were tactical. The PCPJ and NCPAC settled their Stalinist v. Trotskyite differences. They formed, again, as they had at the request of Xuan Thuy in 1971, a "united and broad based left" in a "joint struggle...on the Indochina question"[1671] The Assembly adopted a call for coordinated worldwide actions to "efficiently help" demonstrations. It called for "support of...progressive and antiwar forces in the United States," the united front.

VVAW's Al Hubbard reported his private discussions with the Vietnamese, focusing upon specific tactics in the antiwar movement and upcoming antiwar actions.

Scheduling. The plenary session of the Assembly in Versailles then adopted a specific six week antiwar program, virtual instructions, for the U.S. antiwar movement for April and May: April 1 defense of Harrisburg defendants Berrigan et al, Angela Davis; April 15, Tax Resistance Day; and in early May, actions inside military bases.[1672] Protests encouraged "draft evasions, desertions, resistance, demonstrations which now effect even soldiers."[1673]

John Lennon. An Assembly document spoke approvingly of demonstrations at the Republican Convention in San Diego in August [and later in Miami] caused considerable concern at the White House. The FBI aggressively investigated the VVAW. The FBI developed an interest in John Lennon who helped finance the efforts of Rennie Davis, Jerry Rubin and Abbie Hoffman to disrupt the Republican Convention in 1972 as they had the Democratic Convention in 1968.

At the plenary of the Assembly Hubbard showed photos of bombed hospitals and "mass casualties of children and adults." Hubbard claimed South Vietnam had 100,000 political prisoners and 10 million refugees.

**Delegates Committed to Communist Victory:
Flags, Shirts and Songs.**

[1671] Max Friedman marginal notes in Icord (Mo.), Congressional Record-house March 13, 1972, H-1972-1973 lists Americans and their affiliations, 1973, 1976 the objectives; *Daily World* Feb. 19, 1972 carried Sidney Peck's address to the Assembly.
[1672] FBI, Denver, Memo, "VVAW National Steering Committee Meeting, Denver, Colo, February 18-21, 1972, Internal Security-new Left," March 17, 1972, 31-33.
[1673] [Unsigned, likely John Dougherty and or Bernard Wells], Intelligence Evaluation Group Committee and Staff, "Foreign Support for Activities Planned to Disrupt or Harass the Republican National Convention," 21 March, 1972, CIA, FOIA, Family Jewels,553-4.

At the end, six blocks of demonstrators marched in a cold rain carrying Viet Cong and North Vietnamese flags, chanting "Nixon-Fascist, Murderer." VVAW member Joe Bangert says, "We had a great banquet with the diplomatic delegations of both the DRVN and the PRGSVN and later some music began- [PCPJ's] Barbara (Dane) sang the 'Song of the Coats' …" Bangert sang, "We Will Liberate the South" (Giai Phong Mien Nam) the national anthem of the NLF in Vietnamese and the Ballad of Uncle Ho. "It was a show stopper…"[1674]

After the Assembly in Versailles, Jane Fonda met separately with Viet Cong and North Vietnamese officials in Paris acquiring Vietnamese slides of "Viet Cong" heroics and U. S. bombing—likely the same slides received from the North Vietnamese by VVAW's Al Hubbard and doubtless many others.

The Assembly in Versailles coincided with the World Peace Congress and the World Federation of Democratic Youth, which Joe Urgo of VVAW and other Americans attended.

Withholding POW Mail At Versailles three wives of POWs entered the Assembly asking the Vietnamese to reveal the fate of their husbands. The women were promptly ushered out.[1675] Back from Versailles, one person returned with 40 letters from POWs.[1676] On February 20, 1972 Tran Trong Quat of the South Vietnam People's Committee in Solidarity with the American People (*Viet My*) reinforced rules for POW mail. He complained of mail containing "strange addresses," names not on Hanoi's official list of U.S. pilots. The Air War was hurting POW mail. On March 20, 1972 New York Times man, Seymour Hersh, returned from Hanoi to hand off Hanoi's POW mail to Daniel Berrigan announcing he was joining COLIFAM.[1677] Berrigan, escort to three POWS, was surely on Hanoi's approved list since it had selected all of COLIFAM's members.

Hanoi's Fronts for Peace.

[1674] http://www.pegseeger.com/html/ewancheers.html
[1675] *Congressional Record-House* March 13, 1972, H-1971.
[1676] FBI, New York to Director, COLIFAM- IS-New Left, TELETYPE 215 AM February 17, 1972; FBI, New York, LHM COLIFAM, February 23, 1972.
[1677] *Daily World*, March 21, 1972; FBI, SAC New York to Director, COLIFAM IS-New Left AIRTEL, March 21, 1972;

VVAW. In March 1972 VVAW's Al Hubbard met vice Premier Nguyen Duy Trinh in Hanoi. "For his part the DRV vice-premier highly praised the activities of the VVAW and other antiwar organizations in the United States."[1678] **Women.** Similarly, on March 8, 1972, International Woman's Day, NLF figurehead Madame Nguyen Thi Binh sent a message to women in the U.S.: '…The South Vietnamese women have been encouraged by the news of their American sisters' actions. …All my sincere wishes for your success in this spring drive!"[1679] **Organized Labor.** George Meany AFL-CIO supported the Vietnam War, but David Livingston, district 65, Distributive Workers Union, Harold Gibbons, VP of Teamsters Union, and Clifford Caldwell, VP of Amalgamated Meat Cutters tried to form an antiwar labor group. They spent eight days in Hanoi where they were shown bombed hospitals and schools (and a workers' rest home) and met POWs Capt. Edwin A. Hawley and Cdr. and collaborator Walter "Gene" Wilber.

They met with Hanoi's negotiator Le Duc Tho for two hours. Le Duc Tho's message to Henry Kissinger: Hanoi would accept a three-part government in South Vietnam. Le kept repeating Hanoi did "not visualize a Communist government…in South Vietnam."[1680]

All Hanoi wanted was peace and friendship with the US. *Au contraire,* Hanoi was making final preparations to launch a major main force invasion of South Vietnam at the very moment Le Duc Tho was talking to his few friends in the American labor movement. At press conference, David Livingston, a labor leader back from Hanoi, said the Vietnamese would fight for generations.

In Paris, Nguyen Minh Vy asked about Harold Gibbons. Gibbons was a Teamster vice president active in Labor for Peace who the White House wanted fired by the Teamsters who endorsed Nixon's policies.

[1678] "Nguyen Duy Trinh Receives U.S. Antiwar Veteran," Hanoi VNA International Service in English at 1501 GMT 27 March 1972 cited in Rothrock, *Divided… 166-67n20*

[1679] Bergman, *Women of Vietnam…,* 160-3.

[1680] Rick Nagin, "Unionists report on Vietnam trip," *Daily World*, April 4, 1972; Jacoby Sims, "Livingston to spur labor fight on war," *Daily World*, April 13, 1972, 3.

In Cambodia, Communist forces rocketed the city of Phnom Penh killing 102 and wounding 200 mostly women and children.[1681] ***

NVA Hits South at Easter, Protesters Outraged...over U.S. Air Strikes March 30, 1972 to April 26, 1972

Intelligence. During late 1971 and early 1972, the Defense Intelligence Agency, DIA, noticing NVA buildups, predicted an invasion across the DMZ. The CIA dismissed the idea of an attack—it would directly violate the Geneva Peace Treaty Hanoi had signed. Similarly, Mel Laird had limited bombing targets in the North expecting Hanoi to honor its prior deal with LBJ not to build up forces across the DMZ.

Hanoi's Massive Invasion. With American troops drastically reduced inside South Vietnam, on Good Friday, March 30, 1972, the North launched a conventional main force attack on the South across the DMZ. The 14 regular NVA divisions were well equipped with tanks--600 T-54, T-55, and PT-76 – artillery-- 130 mm, 152 mm and 160 mm--and SA-2 anti-aircraft missiles. As well as strengthening Hanoi's air defenses, the Soviet's had trained 25,000 elite troops in the Soviet Union for the attack.[1682] The NVA force was about the size of the German Army's assault in the Battle of the Ardennes in WWII, which in three days took the lives of nearly 20,000 Americans in the largest battle of WWII for the USA.

In early 1972, after months of Hanoi and friends whining about US escalation of the "Air War," bombing Hanoi's sanctuaries in Vietnam, Cambodia and Laos, the peaceniks said nothing about the Northern invasion of the only democracy in Indochina, South Vietnam.

Named "Nguyen Hue Offensive" after the Vietnamese defeat of the Chinese in 1789, North Vietnam sought a final victory and, at minimum, to prevent the re-election of President Nixon. Outcome uncertain. In Gen. Vo Nguyen Giap's prior major offensive at Tet in 1968, he suffered 100,000 casualties.[1683]
***

[1681] "Enemy Massacres Civilians in Assault on Phnom Penh," Washington *Post*, March 22, 1972.

[1682] Uwe Siemon-Netto, *DUC: A Reporter's Love for a Wounded People, Amazon*, 2013, 233.

[1683] Walter J. Boyne, "The Easter Halt," *Air Force Magazine* online, September 1998 Vol. 81, No. 9. http://www.afa.org/magazine/Sept1998/0998easter.asp

Antiwar Actions a Part of Invasion Plan. As planned in the December COSVN Resolution approving the invasion, *dich van* actions among the enemy, the antiwar movement, were an integral part. The North needed, asked for and received help from its comrades in arms in the rear of the common enemy, Hanoi's Second Front in America.

On April 3, 1972 Madame Binh telephoned a PCPJ demonstration in Harrisburg. Pennsylvania. "Let us unite... end U.S. commitment in Vietnam.... Let us demand ... Nixon...respond to *PRGRSV's correct proposals...*"[1684]

Protests Against US Air War. On April 4, 1972, the fifth day of the northern invasion--a representative of Hanoi in the Paris phoned the 'movement' in the US telling them to expect to take action in response to expected escalations of bombing.[1685] An FBI telegraph predicted, "demonstrations, to counter expected escalation of bombing by American Air Forces in South Vietnam [of] ...North Vietnamese forces in Quang Tri Province..."

Indeed, in early April President Nixon decided, as Hanoi had anticipated, to double deployments of U.S. air and naval power in Indochina to help defeat the invasion against the wishes of the Secretaries of Defense and State, Melvin Laird and William Rogers.[1686]

Westmoreland Unwelcomed at Yale. On April 4, some 250 people gathered up by VVAW and New Mobe chanted and carried Viet Cong flags to protest the Army Chief of Staff Westmoreland. A crowd pushed and shoved police and shouted Gen. Westmoreland down when he tried to speak outside Mory's with his student sponsors.[1687] Driven out of town, he skipped his planned speech at Yale. No arrests were made.[1688]

Paris Meetings of PCPJ, March, April 1972. On March 28-31, 1972 Bob Levering representing PCPJ, held discussions with DRV and PRG about sending a series of

[1684] Madame Binh Telephones Harrisburg Peace Rally," Liberation Radio (Clandestine)1900 GMT, April 3, 1973, cited in Rothrock, 133N7.
[1685] FBI, New York to Director(100-448092), VVAW, Telegraph, 1040 pm urgent, April 4, 1972; FBI, Domestic Intelligence Division, Informative Note, April 4, 1972
[1686] Phillip B. Davidson, *Vietnam At War: the History: 1946-1975*, New York: Oxford University Press, 1991, 701-2.
[1687] General William C. Westmoreland, *A Soldier Reports*, New York: Dell, 1976, 481-482.
[1688] FBI, New Haven to Director (ATTN: DID), 1:40 am NITEL, April 5, 1972, 1-2.

American delegations to Paris. Levering spent six hours with Nguyen Minh Vy, Nguyen Mai, and Csi Phan of the DRV on the 28th and the next day three hours with Mme. Pham Than Van and Dinh Ba Thi of PRG.

Since Nixon had cut off negotiations, PCPJ's Levering wanted "lines of communication (for) Vietnamese delegations…with the American people." Dinh Ba Thi welcomed support in condemning Nixon's "sabotage" of peace talks. "Credible" people "willing to work when they returned home was good." Next week?

Thi stressed three messages. 1. Vietnam was still an "American war," increasingly ferocious and oppressive with B-52 strikes, 200,000 political prisoners and "tiger cages." 2. Thieu must go. 3. Nixon wanted to subjugate the Vietnamese people.

Thi suggested "People's Peace Talks." By "credible" delegations. Thi requested Rep. Ron Dellums and other Congressmen. Thi recommended delegations meet with Tran Dinh Lan and Huynh Trung Dong of the Union of Vietnamese Residents in France. The Union was a Hanoi front for recruiting agents.

On the 29th Vy of DRV agreed with communicating with delegations, but they were not official peace talks. Nguyen Minh Vy insisted the Vietnamese were serious about negotiations but Nixon had rejected Vietnamese offers. Sabotaging peace talks permitted the US to escalate the war. The antiwar delegates were needed to join with DRV and PRG in condemning Nixon for sabotaging peace talks.[1689]

Within a week the planned PCPJ delegation arrived in Paris.

April 6-8, 1972 Cora Weiss and Bob Levering sponsored a delegation visiting representatives of Hanoi, PRG, Cambodian communists in Paris. The "peace and justice" group included Marcus Raskin, founder of Institute for Policy Studies, Sister Mary –Luc (sic, Luke) Tobin, Stoney Cookes and Maria Jolas. At *Choisay–le-Roi* they met for five hours with Nguyen Minh Vy. At 2 *Place de Barcelone*, 16 e they meet with representatives of GRUNC, Cambodians for two hours. At *Verrieres-le-Buisson*, they met Madame Binh At 8

[1689] Bob Levering, "Report On Paris Trip for Peoples Coalition for Peace and Justice," PCPJ March 28-31, 1972.

Villa Montsouris, 14e they met S. George and M. Dong of UVF, Union of Vietnamese in France, a front for Hanoi intelligence and twelve other representatives of Union of Vietnamese in France front groups for Catholics, Buddhists, military, students in Paris.[1690]

Marcus Raskin dictated an 87 minute report to Tom Ross at the Chicago *Sun Times,* which "made several hundred mid-west and Western papers. ...radio news [sic] and a short AP dispatch."[1691]

Also on April 4, 1972, the *Boston Globe* reported the VVAW poster boy, John Kerry, running for Congress. The FBI ceased all investigations of John Kerry henceforth.

"Media visibility...benefit our friends." "[Rep. Bella] Abzug, [Rep. Patsy Takemoto] Mink and [WSP's Amy] Swerdlow left last night (April 20, 1972) for Paris." Rep. Mink said, "We're going to Paris because we think that's where the action should be, not Vietnam." Pressed to reveal who arranged their trip, PCPC, Mink-Abzug-Swerdlow refused their opportunity to credit "the peace movement let alone PCPJ" which miffed Cora Weiss. Abzug and Mink were already known Communist sympathizers who may not have wished to advertise those allegations.[1692] Abzug, Mink and Swerdlow were scheduled to meet "PRG, DRV and other Vietnamese groups." They planned a taped interview with WBAI "for beeping to NPAC rally."[1693]

"Mark Raskin called Max Palevsky for the next trip" to Paris, April 28 cancelled. Those asked to go were Mary Clark and David Hunter. Raskin planned a Moratorium Day for May 4, 1972 featuring actress Shirley Maclaine, South African Bishop Crowther (in Los Angeles) and Orville Schell,[1694] founder of leftist Pacific News Service and China scholar-advocate of Maoist socialism. Cora Weiss contacted the

---

[1690] Memo of Maria Jolas in Cora Weiss files at Swarthmore (retrieved by Jay Veith), Maria Jolas, "For your Information April 6,7, 8 1972; Cora Weiss, "Memo to: PCPJ Task Force on Paris delegations from a weary Weiss," COLIFAM letterhead, April 21, 1972.

[1691] Cora Weiss, "Memo to: PCPJ Task Force on Paris delegations from a weary Weiss," COLIFAM letterhead, April 21, 1972.

[1692] "FBI's Cold War files question Mink's loyalty," *Honolulu Advertiser*, Dec. 18, 2005.

[1693] Cora Weiss, "Memo to: PCPJ Task Force on Paris delegations from a weary Weiss," COLIFAM letterhead, April 21, 1972.

[1694] http://www.discoverthenetworks.org/individualProfile.asp?indid=2239

Vietnamese "waiting for a response" about Schell's plan to go to South Vietnam after his Paris meetings.

Weiss closed her COLIFAM letter about PCPJ visitors to Paris stressing "candidates for future meetings…the quality must be tops for media visibility…to continue to benefit our friends and our cause."[1695] Quality was a criterion discussed in March now being faithfully followed by COLIFAM/PCPJ.

***

B-52s Hit North Vietnam,
Response to Hanoi's Easter Offensive

Bombing Targets? Meanwhile on April 6, Nixon authorized carrier aircraft to bomb North Vietnam, 60 miles north of DMZ. On April 10, B-52s hit Vinh, a transshipment point 150 miles into North Vietnam this time against the wishes of General Abrams and Ambassador Bunker who wanted all firepower placed on the NVA invasion forces in the South. On April 15, for the first time in the war the President authorized the bombing of targets chosen by the Joint Chiefs of Staff and U.S. commanders in both Hanoi and Haiphong.[1696]

VVAW Protest Bombing. At a VVAW meeting on April 11, nothing had been said, at least in public, among antiwar activists about the major North Vietnamese main force offensive into South Vietnam, a week old. Yet on April 16th, VVAW headquarters telephoned all regional coordinators requesting their immediate appearance in Washington to demonstrate against U.S. bombing of Hanoi and Haiphong on the steps of the Capitol the next day.[1697] Thereafter, a few members of VVAW conducted a series of poorly planned protests at the Washington Monument, the Capitol, Arlington Cemetery and the Pentagon through April 22nd. Aides of Senators William Fulbright, Charles Percy, William Proxmire and Vance Hartke helped the protestors.

Washington Demonstrations. The *Daily World* reported White House demonstrations. Speakers were Abraham Heschel (CALC), Gerhardt Elston (National Council of Churches), Sen. Mike Gravel, David Dellinger, Noam

---

[1695] Cora Weiss, "Memo to: PCPJ Task Force on Paris delegations from a weary Weiss," COLIFAM letterhead, April 21, 1972.
[1696] Phillip B. Davidson, *Vietnam At War: the History: 1946-1975*, New York: Oxford University Press, 1991,703-4.
[1697] FBI, [redacted] to Director (Att: Domestic Intelligence Div.), Teletype, April 16, 1972.

Chomsky, George Wald and Episcopal Bishop Paul Moore. Joseph Crown of the Lawyers on American Policy Toward Vietnam reported on plans to impeach President Nixon.[1698]

***

Antiwar Movement Warned Hanoi of Air Strikes

Whatever the ineffectiveness of the VVAW and other protests, FBI reports stated VVAW alerts to the antiwar movement on April 16th, gave the enemy early warnings of the bombing of Hanoi and Haiphong and likely cost American lives.[1699]

Methodists Defend Hanoi. In the midst of the northern invasion with Hanoi's murderous artillery trained on tens of thousands of fleeing civilians, in Atlanta a majority of delegates to the General conference of the United Methodist Church called American involvement in Vietnam "a crime against humanity," but refused either to declare North Vietnam's part of the war "cruel and inhuman"[1700] or to condemn Hanoi's treatment of POWs.

A hundred 100 delegates out of 900 opposed criminalizing the USA and South Korean Methodists walked out. US forces saved South Korean Christians. Hanoi's invaders were responsible for the war.[1701]

Public Favors Bombing. Despite the antiwar outrage or maybe because of it, on April 25, 1972 Gallup reported that the Americans people did not want to stop bombing. They favored stepped up bombing by a margin of 47%-41%.[1702]

Hanoi's political struggle inside the USA, *dich van,* was working rather precisely as scheduled among the peace activists, less so among the American people, and not at all upon President Nixon who bombed away against the objections of his secretaries of defense and state, Laird and Rogers.

[1698] "Peace Forces Rally in Capital Saturday," *Daily World,* Vol. IV, No. 181, April 12, 1972.

[1699] FBI Informative Note, October 25, 1973; Fidel Castro, "Fidel Sends Greetings to World, Peace Forces," FBIS, Havana in Spanish, October 29, 1973; "World Congress of Peace Forces: Peace to You Our Planet Earth," x 221269 21:56:11-22:06:08 1973 USSR; Russia; Cambodia; Northern Ireland; South Africa: Rhodesia: COLIFAM SD 25-31 October73 at Footage Farm at footagefarm.cm.co.uk.

[1700] Lewis Sorley, *A Better War: The Unexamined Victories and Final Tragedy of America's Last Years in Vietnam,* New York: Harcourt, 1999,339.

[1701] Robert Wilson, *Biases and Blind Spots: Methodism and Foreign Policy Since World War II,* Chapter 4, The Reemergence of Radicalism, 6.

[1702] Gallup, April 25, 1972

Soviet Ships Bombed—No Response. Five B-52s bombing Haiphong hit four Soviet ships, but the Soviets did nothing. Indeed, waiting for Kissinger to arrive in Moscow four days later, in Moscow the Soviets took down posters on the Sheremetyevo Airport road showing Americans slaughtering Vietnamese.[1703] And so the fear of Soviet intervention, beyond the existing billions of dollars and thousands of technicians, that had paralyzed Lyndon Johnson was unwarranted. The Joint Chiefs had been right all along.

Hanoi Mobilizes POW Families and Congress. Less than a month after Hanoi's invasion of South Vietnam, on April 25, 1972, the Committee of Liaison wrote to all families of POWs; "Since April 1, Pres. Nixon has...reordered massive bombing...(hitting)...[the port of] Haiphong and...in and around Hanoi. This incredible rain of death...creates imminent...risk to prisoners." The Pentagon claims POWs are safe, but "the Pentagon claim should be seriously challenged by prisoner families."[1704]

On April 26th Madame Binh sent a letter to the Congress, "[T]he Congress has the power to decide.... What do I want? ...The American government should withdraw all its forces *within a predetermined period.*"[1705] On April 27, 1972 Radio Hanoi quoted George McGovern saying Nixon was simultaneously ordering troop withdrawals and increasing bombing were "a piece of political trickery." They were "calculated deception to save the President's face and General Thieu's job." The bombing "is a cruel hoax that dooms our prisoners, kills innocent civilians, invites further soldiers and picks the pockets of every American citizen and taxpayer," told listeners of Radio Hanoi.[1706] Hanoi could not have said it any better than George McGovern could.

***

[1703] UPI, "GIs: Moscow Heroes?" *Baltimore News American*, 10 May 1972, 11.

[1704] COLIFAM Memo to: All families of POW's, Re" mail, April 25, 1972.

[1705] "Nguyen Thi Binh Sends Letter to U.S. Congress," Paris VNA, 0540 GMT, April 26, 1972, FBIS, TTU archive cited in Rothrock, 150N25.

[1706] U.S. Information Service, "Talking Points: Some Thoughts on the Current Vietnam Debates," USIS Saigon, April 1972, at TTU, McGovern quoted on Hanoi Radio International Service in English, April 27, 1972 cited in Rothrock, *Divided... 290-91n72.*

Chapter 16. Easter Invasion:
US Helps South Win;
Peaceniks Give Hanoi Military Intelligence

Hanoi Artillery Targets Fleeing Civilians
Kill anyone and Everyone. During the April 1972 battles North Vietnamese communists deliberately rained 130-mm guns and 122-mm rockets upon tens of thousands of civilian refugees fleeing roads running south from major battles in Quang Tri and in An Loc. Tens of thousands of civilians were strung out miles along the escape roads. Women carrying babies in baskets,[1707] were slaughtered on the escape routes along Highways 1, Bernard Fall's "Street Without Joy," and along Highway 13 known as "Horror Road." These killings were far from "selective." To "kill anyone and everyone who stood in their way" were the murderous acts of an evil regime.

Yet Jane Fonda said it was a continuation of the Vietnamese thousand-year struggle for "freedom and independence,"[1708] in her later broadcast over Radio Hanoi describing the fighting around Quang Tri

The Silence of the Pacifists. There was abject silence about this senseless slaughter of civilians among the self-anointed humanitarians and self-righteous pacifists within the peace movement. From their perspective, all the barbarism of war came from one side, the American air war campaign.

Agreeing with Douglas Pike's predictions, Robert Thompson, British counterinsurgency expert, citing massacres at Hue, Cai Be, Dak Son and defectors (Col. Tran Van Dac and Col. Le Xuan Chuyen), said this slaughter of civilians proved if Hanoi won the war a blood bath would surely follow as the inevitable human cost of communism.[1709]

On April 26, 1972 General Abrams noted that U.S. airpower had been effective in halting progress in the invasion, but "ten times the air power could not have done the job if the

---

[1707] Photos of An Loc, Highway 13 refugees, Phil Clarke, Readers Digest, from Max Friedman, July 2, 2009.
[1708] Testimony of Edward Hunter, "Analysis of Jane Fonda Activities in North Vietnam," House, Committee on Internal Security, Hearings Regarding H.R. 16742: Restraints on Travel to Hostile Areas, 92nd Cong., 2nd Sess., September 19, 1972, 7589.
[1709] Robert Thompson, "Communist Atrocities," *New York Times*, June 15, 1972.

Armed Forces of South Vietnam had not stood and fought."[1710]
And fought they did.

***

ARVN Performs Well at Quang Tri
and An Loc,
But Goes Unnoticed

The media wasted not a single honorable mentions on the South Vietnamese Airborne and Marines. Day after day they came face to face with the North Vietnamese and drove them out of Quang Tri and Binh Dinh. They successfully defended An Loc and Kontum.[1711]

An Loc. South Vietnamese President Thieu decided to hold An Loc at all costs. The President radioed top ARVN officers in An Loc ordering them to defended An Loc to the death. At An Loc 6,800 ARVN regulars and militiamen including elements of Gen. Le Minh Dao's single 18th Infantry Division, the 52d Regiment and the 48th Regiment joined the 5th ARVN division, commanded by Le Van Hung.

U.S. Air Power helps. With massive U.S. air support ARVN virtually destroyed three of four divisions of North Vietnamese. The 6,800 man elements of the South Vietnamese 18th and 5th Divisions held out for nearly two months against 30,000 NVA troops with 100 tanks and heavy artillery.[1712]

The 5th Division's Le Van Hung formed tank-destroying teams to ambushing NVA. American advisers directed air strikes against the NVA as close as twenty meters to friendly troops. Even with massive American air support, the North Vietnamese got within 300 meters of the ARVN 5th Division command post. ARVN counter-attacks stabilized the front and exhaustively held back multiple PAVN attacks including human waves and continuous heavy artillery shelling.[1713]

[1710] An Abrams cable quoted in Melvin Laird, "Personal Assessment of the Situation in RVN as of 26 April, 1972," memo for President, 4/26/72 cited in Dale Van Atta, *With Honor: Melvin Laird in War, Peace and Politics*, Madison: University of Wisconsin, 2008, 405.

[1711] Oriana Fallaci, (Trans. John Shepley)"Nguyen Van Thieu," *Interview With History*, Boston: Houghton Mifflin, 1977, 61.

[1712] Lam Quang Thi, *Hell in An Loc;* Lewis Sorley, *A Better War: The Unexamined Victories and Final Tragedy of America's Last Years in Vietnam*, New York: Harcourt, 1999, 378.

[1713] Lam Quang Thi, *Hell in An Loc, the 1972 Easter Invasion and the Battle that Saved South Viet Nam*, http://en.wikipedia.org/wiki/Battle_of_An_L%E1%BB%99c; "5th Division,"; http://www.globalsecurity.org/military/world/vietnam/rvn-arvn-

Quang Tri. ARVN Airborne and Marines retook Quang Tri, street by street, house by house using grenades and small arms. A captured North Vietnamese soldier of the 66th North Vietnamese regiment told Uwe Siemon-Netto, "Three-fourths of the men in my battalion died and I was wounded in the head."[1714]

Walter Cronkite described the NVA as having voluntarily "faded away" from Quang Tri rather than being soundly defeated.

The defeat was well earned by a few good men, Vietnamese and American.

Corporal Huynh Van Luom and Captain John Ripley. History ought to recall[1715] RVN Marine Corporal Huynh Van Luom who calmly and single handedly knocked out the lead NVA T-54 Soviet tank with a short-range, hand-held M-72 LAAW rocket stopping an NVA tank column on the Dong Ha Bridge. The bridge was strategically located at the intersection of the Cu Viet River, north-south Route 1, and east-west Route 9 to Laos. The NVA's objective was Hue on the coast splitting off northern South Vietnam..

Marine's Corporal Huynh Van Luom actions bought enough time, four hours, for U.S. Marine Captain John Ripley to climb up and down and across the razor wire protected superstructure of the Dong Ha bridge. His hands and arms shredded and bloodied, Ripley attached explosives, blowing up the Dong Ha bridge and stopping the communist march to the South China [East] Sea.[1716] Another Vietnamese Marine, Sergeant Phuoc knocked out a second tank. An American Marine, Maj. Jim Smock, took down a railroad bridge nearby. Recommended for the Medal of Honor, John Ripley received the Navy Cross[1717] and a legendary role in the history of the U.S. Marine Corps.

At the engagements surrounding Dong Ha the Vietnamese Marines, *Tuy Quan Luc Chien*, TQLC, led by Lt.

5-div.htm
[1714]Uwe Siemon-Netto, *DUC: A Reporter's Love for a Wounded People, Amazon*, 2013, 239.
[1715] Richard Botkin's *Ride the Thunder*, WND Press and him and Koster's film Ride the Thunder, 2016.
[1716] Bill Laurie to author July 8, 2009 cites Richard Botkin, *Ride the Thunder* and G.H. Turley, *Easter Offensive, Vietnam 1972*, Presidio, 1985. Bill Laurie, "Vietnam, the Media and Lies," at http://veteransforacademic freedom.org/2010/01.
[1717] Richard Botkin to author, September 2, 2012.

Col. Le Ba Binh, were a small elite force of 700 holding out against NVA forces of nearly twenty thousand NVAs. At a critical point Lt. Col. Binh broadcasted a message.
It is rumored that Dong Ha Bridge has fallen. There are Vietnamese Marines in Dong Ha. My orders are to hold the enemy in Dong Ha. We will fight in Dong Ha. We will die in Dong Ha. We will not leave. As long as one Marine draws a breath of life, Dong Ha will belong to us.

During most of the fight Binh and Ripley were denied fire support from jets and B-52s in a decision to rescue downed pilot Lt. Col. Iceal Hambleton, Bat-21. At Dong Ha, Le Ba Binh would receive his ninth wound in combat in his 10-year career in the Vietnamese Marines followed by 11 years in a reeducation camp after the war.

Col. Gerry Turley, opposed by American officers in Saigon not at the scene and sabotaged by phony communist messages of disaster, ordered the bridge destroyed. The heroics of Luom, Ripley and Binh accomplished the mission. Turley made skillful use of limited-range naval gunfire to help hold back the NVA advance. In two weeks the highly mobile NVA had advanced less than twenty miles.

"South Vietnamese Troops, not Americans" About the entire Easter Offensive, Stuart Herrington said, "It had been South Vietnamese troops, not Americans, who had faced Hanoi's thirteen divisions and enabled the defense of their land."[1718] ARVN had suffered 8,000 killed, the NVA 40,000.[1719] Binh's 700 Marines were barely 200 when ordered to withdraw from Dong Ha. Overall the Vietnamese Marines suffered 1,400 killed in action compared to 10,200 NVA killed. Most of the NVA dead and captured were young boys or old men.[1720]

The NVA defeat during the Easter Offensive at the hands of South Vietnamese troops and American air power brought Hanoi back to diplomatic negotiations.[1721]

[1718] Stuart Herrington, *Silence was a Weapon: The Vietnam War in the Villages* (Novato, CA: Presidio Press, 1982), 188.

[1719] Lewis Sorley, *A Better War: The Unexamined Victories and Final Tragedy of America's Last Years in Vietnam*, New York: Harcourt, 1999, 339.

[1720] Richard Botkin, *Ride the Thunder: A Vietnam War Story of Honor and Triumph*, New York: WND Books, 2009, 481, 483 cites Darrel D. Whitcomb, *The Rescue of BAT-21*, New York:Dell, 1999, 25-27..

[1721] Pierre Asselin, A Bitter Peace: Washington, Hanoi, and the Making of the Paris Agreement, Chapel Hill Press, 2002, xii-xiii cited in Steven Wagner, review, H-diplo, January 2004.

***

Whatever its massive setbacks on the battlefield, Hanoi clearly thought it was winning the war in the sidewalk cafes of Paris and in the streets of New York and Washington. On the diplomatic front in secret talks on May 2, 1972 Kissinger met Le Duc Tho who hailed opposition to the bombing of Hanoi and Haiphong on the streets of America and in the U.S. Senate. Le Duc Tho arrogantly insisted on South Vietnamese President Thieu's resignation "No delay. Tomorrow is best."[1722]

***

Nixon Takes Aim: Haiphong, Soviet Ships. and Congress

Haiphong in One Minute. On May 8, 1972 President Nixon approved unprecedented bombing, Operation Linebacker, including the mining of Haiphong. In only one minute, on May 9 after eight and half years of denied requests from the Joint Chiefs of Staff and field commanders, aircraft from the *U.S.S. Coral Sea* mined the harbor of Haiphong abruptly halting the movement of any ship in or out of Haiphong.[1723] During early June Alexander Haig assured Soviet Ambassador Dobrynin there would be "no air activity over Hanoi or Haiphong" during a N. V. Podgorny visit to North Vietnam.[1724]

Despite the Haiphong supply line cut and heavy ground casualties, Hanoi bragged of new victories, and a milestone, the 3,500th American aircraft shot down over North Vietnam, four times the actual tally of 944.[1725] Yet "all the Russian ambassadors...were telling everyone that the military advance of the North Vietnamese is a complete failure."[1726]

Public Supports President. Nixon's speech to the nation on May 8th, despite strong opposition in Congress and in the press, received from 59 to 76 percent public approval depending on the poll.[1727] Opinion Research Corp poll showed

---

[1722] Loi and Vu, *Negotiations*, cited Larry Berman, *No Peace, No Honor*, 128-29.

[1723] Sorley interview of Adm. Thomas Moorer, 26 September 1994 cited in Lewis Sorley, *A Better War: The Unexamined Victories and Final Tragedy of America's Last Years in Vietnam*, New York: Harcourt, 1999, 327.

[1724] Haig to Kissinger, Washington, June 12, 1972 Foreign Relations, 1969-1976, June –August 1972, 7.

[1725] Lewis Sorley, *A Better War: The Unexamined Victories and Final Tragedy of America's Last Years in Vietnam*, New York: Harcourt, 1999, 328.

[1726] Anatol Dobrynin to Kissinger, Foreign Relations, 1969-1976, June–August 1972, June 24, 1972 cites Joseph Alsop, "Moscow's View of Hanoi," *Washington Post*, June 14, 1972, a-27.

[1727] Jeffrey Kimball, *Nixon's Vietnam War* (Lawrence, Kansas: University Press of

74% supporting the mining and 25% opposed. An ABC Liberman Poll found 59% support and 42% wanting greater military action. In a separate question only 20% sought immediate withdrawal.[1728] By May 13, a Louis Harris poll had Americans favoring the mining of the port of Haiphong by well over 2-1, 59-24%.[1729] Seven years into the war, perhaps the American public had not given up on a victory. Indeed studies of public opinion during the Korean and Vietnam war and in Somalia show "a majority of the American people will accept combat deaths—*so long as the mission has the potential to be successful.* The public can distinguish between suffering defeat and suffering casualties."[1730]

Douglas Pike thought that Giap had overestimated the value of the antiwar movement.[1731]

On short notice only 600 showed up to protest in Washington.

Some antiwar activities went beyond protests favoring the enemy's positions to blatant acts of treason: intelligence, espionage and sabotage.

***

The Peace Movement Engaged in Intelligence, Espionage and Sabotage

While the Soviets provided satellite intelligence to North Vietnam[1732] and the Chinese and Cubans provided interrogators of American POWs, the antiwar movement and the Vietnamese fifth column, on the Second Front also helped gather militarily significant intelligence.

GI Coffee Houses Track Build Ups. USSF, Fonda, VVAW and others used the GI Coffeehouses to provide the anti-war movement, and Hanoi, with an overt, intelligence network hiding in plain sight. "Anti-war veterans and civilians

---

Kansas, 1998), 316.

[1728] ABC News, "American Lives, American Honor," May 11, 1972.

[1729] Tom Wells, *the War Within*, 545.

[1730] Robert F. Turner, "How Political Warfare Caused America to Snatch Defeat from the Jaws of Victory in Vietnam," in John Norton Moore and Turner (Eds.) *The Real Lessons of the Vietnam War: Reflections Twenty-Five Years After the Fall of Saigon*, Durham: Carolina Academic Press, 2002, 227 cite Peter D. Fever and Christopher Gelpi, "How Many Deaths are acceptable/ A Surprising Answer," *Washington Post*, Outlook, Nov. 7, 1999, B3.

[1731] Douglas Pike *Marxism*, 277 cited in Phillip B. Davidson, *Vietnam At War: the History: 1946-1975*, New York: Oxford University Press, 1991, 708.

[1732] Epstein, *Deception...*, 97.

in the G.I. Coffeehouse movement ... hit upon the tactic of telephoning contacts at military bases to learn what [military] build-ups and alerts, if any, were occurring."[1733]

Troop and Ship Movements. In February Al Hubbard had awed his Versailles comrades with details of American troop and ship movements. According to the *Daily World*, VVAW released "a 24-page document with information revealing air force, navy, and troop maneuvers...gathered from active-duty GI's throughout the country and Vietnam." VVAW's Detroit leader, Bill Marshall complained the FBI thought VVAW was made up of "spies, infiltrators, and saboteurs."[1734]

Air War. At a party at a VVAW Colorado conference, Tim Butz,[1735] a regional traveler[1736] and national leader was overheard saying that VVAW was "attempting to obtain intelligence...[on] the air war in Vietnam...to plan strategy and anti-war action in the United States..."[1737] Tim Butz would go on to serve as an editor[1738] of *Counterspy*. This publication revealed the identities of CIA agents, some thereafter assassinated.

Nuclear Secrets? In Japan at the end of February VVAW's Al Hubbard claimed during his military service he had transported nuclear weapons to Japan where horrific memories of Hiroshima and Nagasaki were ever present. Hubbard's sponsor in Japan, *Gensuiko*, organized annual commemoratives of the bombing of Hiroshima and Nagasaki and favored U.S. withdrawal from Vietnam, Korea and Okinawa.[1739]

[1733] Zaroulis, *Who spoke...*

[1734] "Vietnam Veterans Against the War," *Information Digest*, August 25, 1972, 10 cites *Daily World* article ND.

1735 VVAW, Organizing Committee for the Fifth Estate (OC-5), later Counterspy magazine (Phil Agee). Also with a group called PEPIC, predecessor to OC-5. Max Friedman to author, February 25, 2008.

[1736] James A. Michener, *Kent State: What Happened and Why*, New York: Random House, 1971, 98.

[1737] FBI, Denver, Memo, "VVAW National Steering Committee Meeting, Denver, Colo, February 18-21, 1972,Internal Security-new Left," March 17, 1972, 8.

[1738] Angus Mackenzie, "CIA Censors Books Bush Perfects the Cover-up, excerpted from, *Secrets The CIA's War at Home*, University of California Press, 1997. http://www.thirdworldtraveler.com/CIA/CensorsBooks_SecretsCIA.html

[1739] FBI, FOIA, Weather Underground. The primary source is Acting SAC Chicago to Director, memo, "Foreign Influence-Weather Underground Organization," August 20, 1976, 147.

The Information Office of U.S. Forces in Japan hit Hubbard back distributing a copy of a June 1971 *Air Force Magazine*. Al Hubbard, who had proclaimed he was a combat-decorated pilot and officer, was merely a staff supply sergeant with no Vietnam service, medaled or otherwise.[1740]

Military Project. In early April, Bart Savage, VVAW Chicago, told a VVAW meeting in Houston, Texas that his chapter "maintains close liaison with the Chicago area Military Project which…has military contact with bases all over the world," according to an FBI informant.[1741]

NARMIC. Al Hubbard said a New York organization, The Day After, TDA, prepared to act in the event of a US offensive.[1742] VVAW would act within days. VVAW worked closely with an umbrella group, the Ad Hoc Military Build-up Committee. AHMBC was a spin off to National Action/Research on the Military/Industrial Complex, NARMIC.

In September 1969, in Philadelphia the American Friends Service Committee, AFSC, the Soviet- and Cuban-linked Institute for Policy Studies, IPS, the pro-Castro North American Congress On Latin America, NACLA, had organized NARMIC.[1743] At least as late as November 1973, checks would be made out to AFSC/NARMIC[1744] serving as a front for NARMIC's pro-Communist co-sponsors.

Worldwide Intelligence network. AHMBC, a coalition of groups, VVAW's Chicago Area Military Project, VVAW's GI Movement and Student Mobe's antiwar GI Press Service, maintained active-duty contacts and gathered intelligence from military bases worldwide. VVAW Regional Coordinator Mike Roche set up AHMBC to gather information on military activity and to disseminate it to antiwar media.

[1740] "Hubbard Lied About His Military Career, *Mainichi Daily News*, Mar. 4, 1972; "US Forces Hit Back at Ex-Sergeant," *Japan Times*, Mar. 4, 1972 at FBI, FOIA, V, VVAW.

[1741] FBI, Houston, Memo, "VVAW National Steering Committee Meeting, Houston, Texas, April 7-11, 1972" May 11, 1972, 28.

[1742] FBI, Houston, Memo, "VVAW National Steering Committee Meeting, Houston, Texas, April 7-11, 1972" May 11, 1972, 34.

[1743] FBI *Information Digest Special Report on VVAW*, Aug. 25, 1972 cited in Fedora post to FreeRepublic.comhttp:/http://www.wintersoldier.com/staticpages/index.php?page=Info DigestonVVAW

[1744] A contemporary newspaper ad; See also, NARMIC, a project of AFSC, Catholic Peace Fellowship Records, University of Notre Dame Archives, CCPF 5/01 Folder.

***
Up to Date Intelligence on Military Deployments.

The April 7-11 meeting of VVAW in Houston, Texas revealed specific intelligence widely known before April 15th.[1745] On April 8th or 9th news of a national mobilization of US armed forces from bases across the nation interrupted the VVAW session.

In summary, the VVAW network reported six ships, 181 aircraft, 11,000 personnel had been dispatched and that within 48-72 hours another 160 planes, five ships, and 5,500 personnel would be deployed to South Vietnam. Already gone to places unknown were 21 ships, 173 planes, 8,500 personnel. Going to unknown locations in another few days were five ships, 115 planes, 1,300 personnel.[1746]

VVAW information was specific: reporting the *USS Midway* leaving for Vietnam early, the USS Kearney steaming on station off Vietnam and the *USS Constellation* remaining on station instead of returning. Bases on alert were Lowery AFB, Co., Ft. Bragg NCO School; Loring AFB (nuclear), Maine, Hanscomb Field, Mass., 3rd Marines, Okinawa; Ft Sill, OK.

On the West Coast all F-104s had disappeared. At Travis AFB, CA all cargo planes were pulled out and 1,000 persons were on alert. Westover AFB, a SAC headquarters, had alerted 21 B-52 crews and 310 personnel.

At Camp Pendleton, California the 7th Marines were put on full alert.[1747]

At Bertrand AFB "all large planes gone and all Phantoms [F-4s] have been painted jungle green."

There were many sources for this intelligence including: John Roach, "Intelligence Center" in Cambridge, Massachusetts, John Trovaso (Boston), Mike Wade (Tulsa), Chicago Military Project, and "members on active duty across the nation."[1748] The FBI added the GI movement and the GI press as sources.[1749]

[1745] FBI, Houston, Memo, "VVAW National Steering Committee Meeting, Houston, Texas, April 7-11, 1972" May 11, 1972, file no. 100-448092-14501
[1746] FBI, Acting Director to SACs (List Albany St. Louis), VVAW-IS-Revolutionary Activities, URGENT TELETYPE May 2, 1972, 3-4.
[1747] FBI, Houston, Memo, "VVAW National Steering Committee Meeting, Houston, Texas, April 7-11, 1972" May 11, 1972, file no. 100-448092-14501, 15,18-9,
[1748] FBI, Acting Director to SACs, URGENT TELETYPE, May 2, 1972; FBI, Houston, Memo, "VVAW National Steering Committee Meeting, Houston, Texas, April 7-11, 1972" May 11, 1972, file no. 100-448092-14501, 15,18-9.

Concerning the FBI. On 12 April an FBI memo from a top deputy, E.S. Miller, said, "it became obvious to informants [in Houston] VVAW has developed extremely comprehensive intelligence concerning active duty military installations..."[1750]

An article, entitled "Military Buildup," in the April issue 1972 of *SOS News* detailed deployments or alerts to mobilizing forces for Vietnam, 37 ships, 650 planes, and 33,000 personnel. The "Ad Hoc [Military Buildup] Committee [made up] of GI groups and VVAW" had "gathered this intelligence." The *SOS News* article reported demonstrations, rallies and vigils at many military bases.[1751]

On April 27, 1972, an informant delivered to the Baltimore office of the FBI, a copy of a six-page military intelligence report taken from the VVAW office in Cambridge, Massachusetts[1752] run by Mike Roach, VVAW. On June 20, 1972 Rep. Solomon inserted into the record Exhibit No. 59, "Overall Summary, Ad Hoc Military Build Up Committee" report of April 15.[1753] This twelve-page report, collected in two weeks from 38 named local sources and released before deployments were completed, was intended to stop an American defense of South Vietnam two weeks after North Vietnam's massive Easter invasion begun on March 30, 1972.

Beating the Pentagon. Disclosures of the VVAW and Ad Hoc committee were made three to four weeks before the official Pentagon report on redeployed American forces was released.[1754] Lt. Col. James Rothrock (USAF-Ret.) calls these disclosures unlawful, unpatriotic and traitorous.[1755]

Hanoi's Military Intel Agents were identified in the report. [1756]

[1749] FBI, Acting Director to SACs (List Albany St. Louis, VVAW-IS-Revolutionary Activities, URGENT TELETYPE May 2, 1972

[1750] FBI, [redacted] to E.S. Miller, memorandum, RE: Vietnam Veterans Against the War, VVAW, 100-448092, April 12, 1972.

[1751] "Military Buildup," *SOS News*, April 1972 at Sir No Sir Library—Reading Room, sirnosir.com/archives.

[1752] FBI, Baltimore Memo, December 13, 1972.

[1753] Exhibit No. 59, "Overall Summary, Ad Hoc Military Build Up Committee" report of April 15, House, Investigation of Attempts to Subvert, Part 3, 7338-7345 cited in Rothrock Divided 236-41 and entire exhibit text is Appendix N, 438-450.

[1754] House, Investigation of Attempts to Subvert, Part 3,734-45, 7375,7479, 7480,7486,7488.

[1755] Rothrock, *Divided...* 241.

[1756] The 38 named sources of the Ad Hoc Military Build Up Committee report of April 15, 1971 were: Steve Dilts, Gene Parker and Jim Walkly of Liberated Barrack, a GI

Nixon War Build Up. VVAW and Ad Hoc committee intelligence on U.S. deployments was very good. In early April Nixon had radically increased forces: by 20 May doubling the Air Force fighter and bomber jets and B-52s; tripling Navy carriers and their aircraft squadrons from two to six aircraft carriers; bringing six cruisers and 44 destroyers off the coast; and quadrupling aircraft sorties from 4,000 to 17,000 from March to April.

This was the air war that Hanoi had feared and failed to restrain with the help of the antiwar movement. Off shore naval artillery helped allied forces at Quang Tri and Hue. B-52s, fighters and gunships helped to defend Kontum and An Loc. C-130's and helicopters supplied and medevac'd South Vietnamese. Bombing and mining in the North greatly crippled Soviet and Chinese supply lines.[1757]

***

Antiwar Movement Responds to U.S. Defense of South Vietnam.

Zaroulis writes, "The Anti-war Movement had had (two days) advance notice of the bombing of Hanoi-Haiphong" on April 15, 1972.[1758] Actually the warning was close to a week.

Austin Report. On April 17, 1972 the VVAW, the Gay Liberation Movement and Trotskyite groups gathered in

---

coffee house in Honolulu; Ruth of Pacific Counseling Services, Tokyo; Kent Hudson, Center for Servicemen's Rights, San Diego; Mike Buckley, VVAW, Cambridge; "Dale," Angeles City, Philippines; Katherine Robert and Nancy Hause, covering Travis AFB, Fairfield, CA; Alan Miller, Pacific Counseling Services, covering Hamilton AFB, Novato, CA; Robert Ratford, Shelter Half Coffee House covering March AFB (an error in the original, Shelter Half was outside Ft. Lewis, Tacoma, Washington); Terry Christian, Los Angeles SOS covering Norton AFB, Redlands, CA; Tim McAfee covering Mather AFB, Sacramento; Stan Richardson, The Covered Wagon, Mt. Home AFB, Mt. Home, Idaho; Tom Spaulding, The Covered Wagon, Shaw AFB, Sumter, So. Carolina; Buddy Tiger, Johnson AFB, Goldboro, NC; Fred Breukblman, Dover AFB, Dover, Del.; Lisa Schiller, McGuire AFB, Wrightstown, New Jersey; Chuck Harrison, Plattsburg AFB, Potsdam, NY; Fred Miller, Westover Action Project, Westover AFB, Chicapee, Mass; Tom, Frank Neisser, LISP, Hanscom Field, Bedford, Mass.; Jim Page, Loring AFB, Caribou, Me; David Jones, Norfolk, VA; George Stein and Mike Roche, Ad Hoc Military Buildup Committee, Cambridge, Mass; Tom, PCS, Oakland; Lenny Spiegle, PCS, California; Mike Oliver, San Francisco, VVAW; Bill Marshall, VVAW, Detroit; Matt Renauldt, USAF. Exhibit No. 59, "Overall Summary, Ad Hoc Military Build Up Committee" report of April 15, House, Investigation of Attempts to Subvert, Part 3, 7338-7345 cited in Rothrock Divided 236-41 and entire exhibit text is Appendix N, 438-450.

[1757] Phillip B. Davidson, *Vietnam At War: the History: 1946-1975*, New York: Oxford University Press, 1991, 702, 705.

[1758] Zaroulis, *Who Spoke Up...*, 380.

Austin, Texas to declare the bombing of North Vietnam was "bombing hell out of civilians." A [redacted] VVAW member read six pages detailing movements of American troops and material from the U.S. to Vietnam. The San Antonio FBI wrote, "the communiqué listed by name and size more than thirty U.S. Navy ships and personnel complements as well as Marine, Army, and Air Force units giving their origin and destination in many cases."[1759]

The VVAW Intelligence Center closed taking a last shot, a conspiratorial claim, that Nixon had commissioned a Rand Corporation study on what would be the "popular reaction" to suspending the 1972 presidential election.[1760] If true, it would have been silly.

Public Supports President and Bombing. Only days after the Democrat Convention nominated McGovern, a Harris poll showed the public favored Nixon's Vietnam policy over McGovern's by a margin of 55-33. Moreover, however outraged the peace movement, no less than 59% of the American people supported the bombing of Hanoi and Haiphong,[1761] which all the VVAW observed military redeployments had made possible.

McGovern said, "Begging is better than bombing. I would go to Hanoi and beg if I thought that would release the boys one day earlier."[1762]

FBI and Military Downplay VVAW Intelligence Gathering. During WWII such intelligence gathering activities of a few Japanese on the West Coast led to the internment of thousands of Japanese, some citizens some not. FBI Director then called internment a "capitulation to public hysteria."[1763]

Vietnam was entirely different. After consulting with local military authorities, FBI Sacramento reported there were errors in the intelligence, the information was available to the public and "carefully prepared to deliberately not violate statutes."[1764] Similarly, San Diego FBI reported intelligence

---

[1759] FBI, San Antonio to Director, TELETYPE, 10:30pm URGENT April 18, 1972, 1-2.
[1760] FBI, Acting Director to SACs (List Albany St. Louis), VVAW-IS-Revolutionary Activities, URGENT TELETYPE May 2, 1972, 4.
[1761] Harris Poll cited by Zaroulis, *Who Spoke Up...,* 389.
[1762] "Begging Is Better Than Bombing," Washington Post, June 24, 1972.
[1763] Ray Wannall, *The Real J. Edgar Hoover: For the Record,* Paducah: Turner Publishing Company, 2000, 69
[1764] FBI, Sacramento to Director, TELETYPE, 7:30 pm urgent April 22, 1972, 1-2;

was non-specific, unconfirmed or reported after the fact, unclassified.[1765] The information had not come from official, classified, documents, but from AHMBC and VVAW human contacts worldwide. A Domestic Intelligence Division, Informative Note, reported that an AHMBC telephone was disconnected,[1766] but "intensive investigation [was] continuing to develop any information warranting prosecutive and espionage violations..."[1767]

The FBI was a law enforcement agency. The FBI would have trouble distinguishing war from illegal activity, crime, and sometimes counterintelligence from criminal prosecution, up to and after September 11, 2001.

These CYA reports from bureaucrats missed several points. Often the best intelligence is acquired from open, public sources and the VVAW and others had actively and publicly proclaimed their intent to aid the enemy in war. They were willing partners in Hanoi's political struggle, *dich van,* inside the United States and Hanoi had asked them directly for military intelligence.

Meanwhile during 1972 some would cheerfully go further down the path to treason.

***

Espionage: Vietnamese Seek Intelligence on New U.S. Weapons

Hanoi asked the antiwar movement to engage in espionage.

July 20-27, 1972 the Anti-War Union, a Rennie Davis spin-off of PCPJ,[1768] and a Weather Underground affiliate sponsored a "movement" group, Colin Stuart Neiburger, Marsha Rhoda Steinberg, Carole Cullum, visit to Paris to meet with the North Vietnamese:

> The Vietnamese...stated they would be interested in having any information...concerning development of new weapons by the US.... Such information would

---

Legat, Manila, Philippines also responded on May 15, 1972.

[1765] FBI, San Diego to Director, 10:11 pm NITEL April 24, 1972.

[1766] FBI,[Redacted]to E.S. Miller, VVAW-IS-Revolutionary Activities, April 28, 1972.

[1767] FBI, Domestic Intelligence Division, Informative Note, April 26, 1972.

[1768] FBI, Washington Field to Acting Director, VVAW-IS, TELETYPE, June 27, 1972.

be especially helpful…before such weapons were used on the battlefield."[1769]

The Vietnamese also passed out the latest of their own antiwar literature[1770] to their newly recruited espionage agents.

Project Corona Harvest. By October, VVAW member Steven Hawkins had returned from Copenhagen, Denmark at a conference where he testified on "Corona Harvest," the testing of new gases and anti-personnel weapons he said. Project Corona Harvest was a secret Air Force study evaluating the effectiveness of air power in Southeast Asia since 1954. Hawkins had been in Vietnam in February and learned about the automated air war and electronic battlefield. Hawkins said the Soviet Union had paid his airfare to Copenhagen.[1771]

The Vietnamese would discover, first hand, new weapons, smart bombs, in December 1972.

***

FBI Pursuit of Weather Underground

Meanwhile, the FBI had been trying to capture the Weather Underground fugitives. The FBI's Ed Miller claimed and Director Clarence Kelly denied FBI Director had knowledge of some 14-18 surreptitious entries in 1972-1973.[1772] The record suggests that Squad 47, Division 4 of the New York Office conducted the surreptitious entries.[1773] The squad focused on members of the fugitive Weather Underground.

FBI Targets Hard Core. These included above ground contacts of Weather leaders: Mark Rudd (February 15, 1972)[1774], Bernardine Rae Dohrn (Jennifer Dohrn and Judith Alice Clark) on March 7, 23, April 4, June 5, 12, 1972, December 11 and 20th 1972 at two addresses, Howard Machtinger (Leonard Machtinger) April 16, 1973,[1775] "Van Lydegraf,"[1776] and Judith

---

[1769] FBI, FOIA, Weather Underground, p. 28 or 361 C

[1770] FBI, FOIA, Weather Underground. The primary source is Acting SAC Chicago to Director, memo, "Foreign Influence-Weather Underground Organization," August 20, 1976, 343, 361.

[1771] FBI, New York, NY 100-160644, October 26, 1972.

[1772] Director to Attorney General, Surreptitious Entries, May 19, 1976. Director Kelly Memorandum for Mr. Jenkins, July 12, 1976.

[1773] Memorandum to Mr. J. B. Adams, Re: Civil Rights Division, Criminal Investigation, Surreptitious Entries, … PURPOSE… New York Office in 1972 and 1973, May 11, 1976.

[1774] FBI, FOIA, SAC Philadelphia to Director (Attention: Automatic Data Processing Unit, Subject: [Redacted] SM-New Left, oo: Philadelphia, March 2, 1972.

[1775] FBI, FOIA, ADIC, New York to Director NITEL, Surreptitious Entries, April 5,

Flatley.[1777] Other targets included the VVAW (November 1972), Black Panther Party (November 1970)[1778] and redacted other targets.[1779]

FBI supervisors believed the activities of the Weathermen and the Black Panthers made them international rather than domestic targets. By a vote of four to zero, a Justice Department, Review Committee for Executive Order 11652, on April 4, 1976 concluded both investigating Weatherman was in the interest of national security and the FBI's domestic sources and methods, including informants and surreptitious entries, in the investigation needed to be protected.

The review committee characterized the investigation of Weathermen as a matter of "national security based on… [both] advocating the overthrow of the Government and its overt use of violence seeking this end. This ruling provides that sources and methods of intelligence, including informants and surreptitious entries utilized in the Weatherman investigation, are correctly classifiable in the interest of national security."[1780]

Subsequent investigations and prosecutions ended with the conviction of FBI officials E.S. Miller and Mark Felt and President Ronald Reagan's later pardon of both.

***

1976; Legal Counsel to Director, Memorandum, "Surreptitious Entry Investigation, December 9, 1976.

[1776] FBI, FOIA, Portland to Director, July 19, 1977.

[1777] Nicholas M. Horock, "Linked to FBI Memo: Newark Field Office Said to Have Been Told to 'Do Anything' in Weatherman Search," *New York Times*, October 6, 1977.

[1778] Keys acquired on November 28, 1971. See: Memorandum SA [redacted] #14 to SAC, New York, "Vietnam Veterans Against the War, Inc IS-New Left (NY 100-160644)" Personal Folder, Sub C, JUNE, December 13, 1971; [redacted] to J.G. Deegan, Memorandum, "Request by Department of Justice to Interview SA [redacted] Regarding His Knowledge of Surreptitious Entries," December 21, 1976; FBI, San Francisco to Director, "Request of Attorney General for Information Concerning Surreptitious Entries, Nitel 8:15 PM October 16, 1975.

[1779] H.N. Bassett to Mr. Callahan, Top Secret Memorandum, JUNE, "Surreptitious Entries," May 11, 1976.

[1780] [redacted] to Mr. Ash, Memorandum, "Surreptitious Entries, Classification Matter, September 3, 1976. *Emphasis* in Memorandum, FBI, FOIA.

Chapter 17. Political Organizations, Conventions, Propaganda.

Hanoi Changes Political Tactics. Complying with Hanoi's new, less confrontational, tactics, the VVAW flirted with electoral politics and Hayden and Fonda shifted to lobbying Congress.

These changes in tactics reflected a changed political arena. Reduced protest numbers in the fall of 1971 and tepid protests to stop tNixon's bombing of Haiphong and Hanoi during the Easter offensive in 1972, showed that Nixon had taken the wind out of the sails of mass anti-war politics.

Nixon had withdrawn 400,000 out of 550,000 troops and announced no more draft calls, a matter of particular interest to the privileged college youth who made up the "don't draft me" cadre.

Nixon was also cavorting with Mao and making new nuclear weapons deals with the Soviets.

Yuri Andropov, KGB Chief, said not to worry: "We'll win the Vietnam war…in the streets of America."[1781]

McGovern and VVAW. In Los Angeles on May 25, 1972 at a regular local meeting of the VVAW, an FBI informant said an unidentified representative of McGovern for President spoke to the group promising a leased station wagon for the use of VVAW "barnstorming" of college campuses from Los Angeles from May 30-June 2, 1972. VVAW travelers would have helped McGovern to get out his vote in the California Democratic primary election in June. On May 31, the FBI informed the acting Attorney General, FBI director L. Patrick Gray and H.R. Haldeman in the White House about the alleged McGovern campaign's offer to VVAW.[1782] A Gallup poll of August 30, 1972 would show Nixon leading McGovern 64% to 30%.[1783] The RNC's best strategy would have been to lease a fleet of vans for VVAW, driving Democrat anti-McGovern voters to the polls to vote for Nixon.

[1781] Shevchenko, 288, 284.
[1782] FBI, [Redacted] to E.S. Miller, VVAW-Internal Security-Revolutionary Activity, May 31, 1972; FBI, Acting Director to Acting Attorney General, VVAW-Internal Security-Revolutionary Activity, May 31, 1972; L. Patrick Gray, III to Hon. H.R. Haldeman, May 31,1972.

North Vietnamese Interest in Republican and Democrat Conventions. In February 1972 the CIA informed the secret multiagency Intelligence Evaluation Group Committee and Staff[1784], (IES), and John Dean in the White House the Assembly in Versailles had discussed, but had not formally adopted a specific resolution to disrupt the upcoming Republican Convention in San Diego (August 21-24) and the Democrat Convention (July10-13).

Without benefit of a memorandum of understanding, Rennie Davis, Jane Fonda, Ron Kovic, Scott Camil and others had plans to disrupt the Republican Convention and Hanoi and others were interested. With Chicago 1968 a vivid memory Republicans were alert.

John Lennon Funds and Hanoi Endorses: Rennie Davis's Plan to Disrupt Republican Convention

The IES report, "Foreign Support for Activities Planned to Disrupt or Harass the Republican National Convention," noted an unidentified representative of Rennie Davis assigned to the Republican Convention in San Diego met with the Viet Cong (PRG) in Paris.

Rennie Davis led the San Diego Convention Coalition, SDCC, to disrupt the 1972 Republican Convention. The SDCC planned to conduct demonstrations and to play videos and live telephone calls from VC delegation in Paris and from Communist China.[1785] On January 27th the North Vietnamese sent a solidarity letter to SDCC expressing "great delight" in SDCC's formation and extended "best wishes of militant solidarity and friendship."[1786] Rennie Davis had long time fraternal relations with Hanoi in Bratislava, Hanoi and Paris.

[1784] Staff. John Dougherty, Bernard Wells reporting to Robert Mardian and William Olson at Justice. Richard Ober, CIA reporting to James Angleton and another. Contributors were DOJ, FBI, DOD, Secret Service, NSA, CIA and occasionally Treasury and State). Source: CIA, FOIA, Family Jewels, 548, 584.

[1785] [Unsigned, likely John Dougherty and or Bernard Wells], Intelligence Evaluation Group Committee and Staff, "Foreign Support for Activities Planned to Disrupt or Harass the Republican National Convention," 23 Feb. 1972, CIA, FOIA, Family Jewels,551-2; See also Ichord *Congressional Record—House*, March 13, 1972, H-1975-76.

[1786] [Unsigned, likely John Dougherty and or Bernard Wells], Intelligence Evaluation Group Committee and Staff, "Foreign Support for Activities Planned to Disrupt or Harass the Republican National Convention," 24 April 1972, CIA, FOIA, Family Jewels,555-6.

Beatle's icon John Lennon[1787] donated $75,000 to Rennie Davis's Election Year Strategy Information Committee, EYSIC. EYSIC was founded in John Lennon's basement. Yoko Ono's Project Yes, covered Davis's trip to Versailles February 11-13, 1972.[1788] Following PCPJ's lead, the Soviet allied, Stockholm Conference, International Confederation of Disarmament and Peace, ICDP, finally included the Republican conventions on its "Spring Offensive," protest calendar in its publication, *Vietnam International*.[1789] A memo to CIA Director Colby reported Rennie Davis was the only American "we reported on to the IEC" –White House and Justice.[1790]

In mid-May an unidentified visitor to the Vietnamese communists in Paris dropped by the offices of both PCPJ and NPAC in New York to report on "plans for action" at the party conventions.[1791]

PCPJ soon announced members of the Stockholm conference would be participating in demonstrations at the Republican Convention.

The GOP changed the convention to Miami where a narrow peninsula provided moat-like security.

Rennie Davis's Antiwar Union, AU, switched planning to Miami. The AU sent a delegation to Paris to meet with officials of the North Vietnamese and the Viet Cong.

Demonstrations Against Bombing. PCPJ promised Republican Party National Coalition would conduct "dramatic demonstrations" against bombing. there would be a "People's Campaign Against Bombing," conducted at military bases and the sites of defense industries. The Stockholm conference would speak on American bombing of dikes in North Vietnam.

VC Endorsement? Rennie Davis's AU asked the Vietnamese who Americans should support in the 1972 Presidential election? The Vietnamese wanted to know the

---

[1787] FBI Director to H.R. Haldeman, April 25, 1972;

[1788] Fedora at FreeRepublic.com citing John Lennon's FBI file.

[1789] [Unsigned, likely John Dougherty and or Bernard Wells], Intelligence Evaluation Group Committee and Staff, "Foreign Support for Activities Planned to Disrupt or Harass the Republican National Convention," 23 May 1972, CIA, FOIA, Family Jewels,555-7.

[1790] [initials redacted] memorandum for: Mr. Colby 14 May 1973, CIA, FOIA, Family Jewels,546.

[1791] [Unsigned, likely John Dougherty and or Bernard Wells], Intelligence Evaluation Group Committee and Staff, "Foreign Support for Activities Planned to Disrupt or Harass the Republican National Convention," 14 June 1972, CIA, FOIA, Family Jewels,559.

political mood in the United States. AU delegates promised the Vietnamese that the AU would "educate the American people about… (not) voting for Nixon, and the need to end the war and defeat Nixon."[1792] Still another AU group, led by Rennie Davis, was scheduled to meet the Vietnamese on August 1.[1793]

Hence, three meetings with the Vietnamese on the subject of the Republican Convention in Miami proved peace activist solidarity with Hanoi's aims. Yet the CIA neither caught nor understood such solidarity between "domestic" groups and foreign powers.

***

Meanwhile: Rocks and Bombs

Portland Protest. In Portland, Oregon on May 11, 1972, at a Student Mobe and VVAW sponsored march some 150 protestors broke away from the 500 person crowd, on a rampage throwing bricks, rocks and concrete, breaking windows at offices of timber company Georgia Pacific, Armed Forces Recruiting Main Station and two banks, spraying paint on building, chanting antiwar slogans and screaming obscenities. At the Georgia Pacific building several citizens and a security guard, using mace, halted fifty rioters surging toward the flagpole to tear down the American flag. The FBI had confiscated bricks delivered earlier in the day to no effect.

The Portland Police gave the vandals a motorcycle escort and arrested no one.[1794]

Weather Underground Bombs the Pentagon. On May 19, 1972, the Weather Underground Organization bombed the Pentagon in retaliation for U.S. bombing of Hanoi in response to Hanoi's massive Easter offensive. "Today we attacked the Pentagon." Weather Underground Communiqué #12 declared an Hanoi victory. "In the last six weeks the massive offensive organized by the Vietnamese people has

---

[1792] [Unsigned, likely John Dougherty and/ or Bernard Wells], Intelligence Evaluation Group Committee and Staff, "Foreign Support for Activities Planned to Disrupt or Harass the Republican National Convention," 26 July 1972, CIA, FOIA, Family Jewels,561-2.

[1793] [Unsigned, likely John Dougherty and or Bernard Wells], Intelligence Evaluation Group Committee and Staff, "Foreign Support for Activities Planned to Disrupt or Harass the Republican National Convention," 2 August 1972, CIA, FOIA, Family Jewels,563.

[1794] Acting Attorney General to Acting Director, "Antiwar Demonstration Sponsored and Student Mobilization, Portland, Oregon, May 11, 1972. Internal Security-Revolutionary Activities, May 25, 1972; Domestic Intelligence Division, Informative Note, May 24, 1972.

shattered the Nixon strategy of 'Vietnamization' (and) pacification."

The WUO deplored the "lie of aggression from the North…US air and naval shellings are…against the Vietnamese while U.S. mines and war ships are used to blockade the harbors of the Democratic Republic of Vietnam." Some "3,000,000 Vietnamese have died in the fighting." The solution was Madame Binh's peace proposal.[1795]

Thus spake the WUO and Hanoi through Bill Ayers, Bernadette Dohrn and others. In fact, the 1972 Easter offensive had failed leaving the NVA with nearly 100,000 casualties, mostly on the battlefields of South Vietnam. The ARVN forces had successfully defended all but one (Quang Tri) of 44 provincial capitals.

Weather Underground Organization had not missed a single issue of current concern to the enemy.

Keeping in touch with the North Vietnamese was the best way to stay on top of current events and propaganda themes.

***

PCPJ, VVAW in Hanoi, *Milly-la-Foret*

PCPJ-Hanoi May 1972. On May 25, 1972 an American PCPJ delegation arrived in Hanoi: Robert Lecky, CALC; Rev. Paul Mayer; Marge Tabankin, National Student Association; William Zimmerman, Medical Aid for Indochina (an unindicted co-conspirator in a planned kidnapping of Henry Kissinger by the Harrisburg 8[1796]). In Hanoi the PCPJ delegation met Nguyen Duy Trinh, toured bombed rubble and interviewed and filmed eight American POWs: Capt. James D. Cutter, Capt. Lynn E. Geunther, Capt. Edwin E. Hawley, Lt. Col. Edison Miller, Capt. Kenneth S. Fraser, Cmdr. David Hoffman, Cmdr. Walter E. Wilbur; Lt. Norris A. Charles.

[1795] Weather Underground #12 copy in FBI, FOIA, Weather Underground. The primary source is Acting SAC Chicago to Director, memo, "Foreign Influence-Weather Underground Organization," August 20, 1976, 170-74, 183.

[1796] On January 12, 1971, Dr. Eqbal Ahmad, Father Philip Berrigan, Sister Elizabeth McAlister, Father Neil McLaughlin, Anthony Scoblick (a married priest), and Father Joseph Wenderoth were indicted on federal charges of conspiring to kidnap Henry Kissinger among other charges. Mary Cain Scobliick and John Theodore Glick was added later. Cited co-conspirators Father Daniel Berrigan, Sister Beverly Bell, Marjorie Shuman, Paul Mayer (a married priest), Sister Jagues Egan, Thomas Davidson and William Davidon. See: Syracuse Peace Council, *Peace Newsletter*, SPC 657, February 1971, 7; "How to Grab the Brain Child," *Time*, May 10, 1971.

The POWs expressed extensive interest in the antiwar movement, in the campaigns of Nixon's opponents, George Wallace and George McGovern, in the progress of Congress in ending the war. POW Hoffman asked Americans to unite against the war. POW Cutter said, "We receive better food than the Vietnamese." POW Charles said, "Vote."[1797] The eight POWs signed a statement to 'People of the United States and the Congress...'" saying the bombing was killing "many innocent people" and no bombing would ever get the Vietnamese "to come begging for peace."[1798] The only solution was Binh's seven-point proposal.

Certainly, Charles, Miller and Wilbur were progressives. Cutter had made prior statements of good care. Later Lt. Commander Hoffman told the House Committee on Internal Security:

> I was personally tortured...to meet a delegation in February [and May?]1972. ...It is completely obvious... We were not at liberty to say what we wanted. It was a completely programmed thing. And if you made the wrong response, you stood a very definite chance of some severe consequences."[1799]

Plagues of Old Testament. Rev. Paul Mayer, New York Theological Seminary, said he didn't know if all POWs held the views of the POWs PCPJ had visited. Back home, joined by Jane Fonda, Cambodian Sokhom Hing, and Holly Near in Redbank, New Jersey Rev. Mayer compared the devastation in Vietnam to the plagues of the Old Testament.[1800]

Cora Weiss reported a "terrifying week in North Vietnam where through village after village of rubble they watched children being carried from schools on stretchers, endured 17 air raid alerts, saw planes shot down..."[1801] Similarly, the *Daily World* reported on spot inspections of

[1797] Terry Ryan, "8 POWs Eager for News," *The Evening Star* (Washington), June 10, 1972.

[1798] May 1972- Text of letter from Eight US Pilots Detained in North Vietnam found in Ellen Ray to Dear families, COLIFAM, May 24,1972. Dated day before made public in Vietnam suggests COLIFAM wrote it or North Vietnamese telegraphed a copy.

[1799] House, Hearings on Restraints on Travel to Hostile Areas: Hearings before the Committee on Internal Security, 93rd Cong., 1st sess., 1973, 3-4 cited in Rothrock *Divided...* 186n10

[1800] "U.S. Policy Criticized at Rally," unidentified clipping circa September 24, 1972.

[1801] Cora Weiss to Dear families, COLIFAM, May 30, 1972.

civilian targets.[1802]The group returned with 306 letters from POWs.

VVAW Meets Enemy Vets at *Milly-la-Foret…*France. On June 25, 1972, sixteen VVAW members, flew out of JFK on Air France Flight 022[1803] into Orly International Airport in Paris on June 26, 1972. A VVAW check for $1,440 from a recently near empty VVAW account paid the airfares. The FBI wondered where the money came from. Manufacturers Hanover, was uncooperative, but the FBI noted the Paris reservations suggested foreign funding.[1804]

For three days the VVAW delegation met with military war veterans and "war victims" from France, China,[1805] North Vietnam, Pathet Lao, Cambodian Liberation, and the NLF at the International Center for the Denunciation of War Crimes at Milly-la-Foret, France.[1806] They met North Vietnamese and NLF civilian experts on war crimes.

By October 1972 by some accounts the Vietnamese would be desperately rushing negotiations complaining of American delays, probably fully aware of the impending crushing defeat of McGovern.

Vietnamese worried about dikes. The Vietnamese worried about Americans bombing dikes and making rain. The Vietnamese gave VVAW photos of bomb damage, including, allegedly, dikes,[1807] for distribution in USA. [Redacted] received a war trophy, a cup made of shrapnel from bombs dropped over North Vietnam.[1808] The Vietnamese asked the VVAW to move its national office out of New York.[1809] Maybe Hanoi knew the FBI had VVAW's bank account and office covered.

VVAW Assassins and Communists. The VVAW voted 15-1 to "completely support the fight against capitalism."

[1802] "4 Back from DRV tell of murder in the air," Daily World, May 31, 1972; FBI, New York, LHM, "Peoples Coalition for Peace and Justice, June 5, 1972.

[1803] FBI, New York to Director, file NY 100-160644, June 25, 1972.

[1804] FBI, Acting Director to Sac New York, VVAW, NITEL June 26, 1972; FBI Director to Sec State and Director, CIA, June 25, 1972; New York to Acting Director, TELETYPE, VVAW-IS-Revolutionary activities, June 26, 1972.

[1805] FBI, Los Angeles memo, VVAW, file 100-448092-1676, July 20, 1972, 2.

[1806] FBI, Memo, Member of subject organization, VVAW, N.d. 4

[1807] FBI, Los Angeles to Acting Director, NITEL 9:24 PM July 7, 1972. Donald Ullrich promised dike photos, but not available at his press conference in Los Angeles.

[1808] FBI, memo, "VVAW National Steering Committee Meeting, July 21-24, 1972, Milwaukee, Wisconsin, N.D. 16.

[1809] FBI, Los Angeles memo, VVAW, file 100-448092-1676, July 20, 1972, 3.

Tom [redacted] offered to "come to Hanoi and execute all 1,500 POWs."[1810] Tom [Redacted] said, "I will do everything …even at the expense of my life to annihilate that dog Nixon, Laird, and any other who stand in the way." Thomas Zangrilli, Ron Kovic's best friend,[1811] shocked the VVAW majority,[1812] some of whom considered Scott Camil's plot to kill pro-war Senators.

A CIA profoundly stupid report said the "meeting was arranged…bring former enemies together to seek a common understanding about what can be done to end the war."[1813]

Blood donations. In Cuba on July 5, 1972, five members of VVAW in the Venceremos Brigade, Jean-Pierre Wendell, Leland Lubinsky, Fred Werner, Alan Morris, and Albert Morgan, proudly donated blood to the communists.[1814] By November 1972 VVAW New York would demand the reunification of Korea and democratic reforms in South Korea. VVAW was affiliated with the North Korean front American-Korean Friendship and Information Center.[1815] Also Pyongyang's friends were AFSC, the *Guardian* and the Workers World Party.[1816]

The VVAW bought the whole international communist agenda while the media was giving shocking aid to Hanoi atrocity propaganda.

***

[1810] FBI, Los Angeles memo, VVAW, file 100-448092-1676, July 20, 1972. Thomas Zagarelli must be distinguished from CPUSA member Michael Zagarell.
[1811] Gerald Nicosia, *Home to War*, 235-36.
[1812] FBI, Los Angeles memo, VVAW, file 100-448092-1676, July 20, 1972, 3.
[1813] Central Intelligence Agency, *Special Report, Vietnam Veterans Against the War*," July 7, 1972, TTU Archives cited in *Rothrock Divided…* 166n19.
[1814] "Vietnam Veterans Against the War," *Information Digest*, August 25, 1972, 10.
[1815] VVAW national newsletter, national covering VVAW chapter news, (n.d.)
[1816] "North Korean Terrorism," *Information Digest*, Vol. XVII, # 12, June 22, 1984, 186.

Photos: Napalmed girl horrifies whole world, War Remnants Museum, Roger Canfield. Saigon March 2008.

***

Reporting on War: Napalmed Girl.

Phan Thi Kim Phuc. On June 8, 1972 the Viet Cong attacked and occupied Trang Bang. Civilians and ARVN soldiers fled from the Cao Dai Temple to safer ARVN positions down the road. As the South Vietnamese retaliated bombing the now Viet Cong occupied village a South Vietnamese pilot of an A1-E Skyraider dropped a napalm canister upon the fleeing villagers. AP photographer Nick Ut caught the scene of fleeing civilians and within his lenses was a 9 year old girl, Phan Thi Kim Phuc, her clothes burned off screaming and running naked down the road. It was an accident. Either the canister fell short of its target[1817] or the pilot mistook the fleeing group as Viet Cong.

It was one of the most memorable photos of the war displaying the inhumanity of American firepower, the air war. In truth it was South Vietnamese action and an accident at that. No American was involved at any level. It was an entirely South Vietnamese operation of the Vietnam Air Force.[1818] Nick Ut won a Pulitzer and the World Press Photo of 1972. Phan Thi Kim Phuc and her family were evacuated by air to a Saigon hospital where she underwent 14 months of care and before returning to her village.

ARVN Beats Communist Offensive —Summer 1972. By the summer the North Vietnam's Easter Offensive of 1972 had failed on the battlefield. The South Vietnamese ground forces had fought well in their own defense and driven back the massive Communist, 14 divisions, forces. North Vietnamese rifle companies found they were no match for South Viet Nam's military forces.[1819] All ARVN units did well,

---

[1817] Stuart A. Herrington, *Stalking the Viet Cong: Inside Project Phoenix*, New York: Ballantine, 1982, 208.
[1818] Statement of Lt. Gen. (Ret) James F. Hollingsworth at vhfcn.org.
[1819] Karnow, Stanley. *Vietnam: A History.* The Viking Press; New York. 1983,658-9.

the elite 1st ARVN Division, Hac Bao, the ARVN Rangers, including local Regional and Popular Forces.

Truong Nhu Tang's *A Viet Cong Memoir* says:

> ...American arms were again scoring victories, just as they had during Tet, [and] in Cambodia...As the summer (of 1972) wore on, our losses had become prodigious, ...territorial advances could not be sustained . ..

Tang added, [D]espite this, [it]...was...a decisive triumph.[1820]

Hanoi Battlefield Losses. NVA General Tran Van Tra wrote about Nguyen Hue offensive and the ARVN's counter offensive, "Our troops were exhausted and their units in disarray... We had not been able to make up our losses... and coping with the enemy was very difficult." [1821]

Eastern bloc observers, the Polish and Hungarian representatives on the ICCS, reported "not one NVA division was as good as the (South Vietnamese) Air Force, Marine or Airborne divisions and not one VC unit, of those still functioning as such (after Tet), were as good as regular ARVN units."

Doug Pike said, the 'RVNAF out-fought" the VC/NVA.[1822]

Indeed, NVA's legendary General Vo Nguyen Giap, victor of Dien Bien Phu and architect of the North's strategy in the South, was relieved of his command in 1972 for incompetence[1823] and demoted from Vice-Chairman.[1824] Giap's forces had lost half a million men—including nearly 100,000 deserters.[1825]

[1820] Truong Nhu Tang with David Chanoff, and Doan Van Toai. *Vietcong Memoir: An Inside Account of The Vietnam War and Its Aftermath.* Harcourt Brace Jovanovich, Publishers; San Diego. 1985, 203. See also: Dinh in Gettleman (ed.), 1985, 209-10.
[1821] John M. Del Vecchio, "Cambodia, Laos and Viet Nam? The Importance of Story Individual and Cultural Effects of Skewing the Realities of American Involvement in Southeast Asia for Social, Political and/or Economic Ends," 1996 Vietnam Symposium "After the Cold War: Reassessing Vietnam," 18-20 April 1996, Texas Tech University
[1822] Bill Laurie to Mike Benge and others, April 1, 2009.
[1823] John M. Del Vecchio, "Cambodia, Laos and Viet Nam? The Importance of Story Individual and Cultural Effects of Skewing the Realities of American Involvement in Southeast Asia for Social, Political and/or Economic Ends," 1996 Vietnam Symposium "After the Cold War: Reassessing Vietnam," 18-20 April 1996 cites Betson, Bill (Captain, USA; Instructor, USMA). "The Battle of Ban Me Thuot--1975." A lecture delivered at The Westside YMCA, New York, New York. (c) 1985.
[1824] http://www.vietnam.ttu.edu/star/images/408/4080407002b.pdf
[1825] Nguyen Cao Ky, How We Lost..., 162.

***

Political Prisoners and VC Combatants.

By July 1972, in response to the Easter offensive, South Vietnam's President Thieu arrested 15,000 Viet Cong suspects and political opponents, releasing most months after the failure of the North Vietnamese offensive. There was no increase of prison population during this period of a major North Vietnamese offensive.[1826]

Rep. Ogden Reid (D-NY) claimed nearly all of those arrested were "unarmed, noncombatant civilians." They were all political prisoners.

Combatants and POWs Are Not Political Prisoners.

Historian Mark Moyar compares these civilian Viet Cong to the military leaders of the Confederacy in the American Civil War. Abraham Lincoln imprisoned 38,000 confederate sympathizers and spies. The US Supreme Court approved of the detention of 70,000 Japanese men during World War II. The Geneva Accords of 1949 allowed arrest and humane and legal treatment of subversive civilians. The Internal Security Act of 1950 allows the President "to…detain [with] reasonable grounds to believe that such a person will probably …engage in…acts of espionage or sabotage."

Most of the VC cadres were not ordinary civilians. They were genuine combatants, comrades in arms of the North Vietnamese and of not a few Americans collaborators.

In contrast Hanoi simply executed suspects. naoi

Communist Policy: Take no Prisoners, Assassinations-Binh Dinh.

Meanwhile, Hanoi, occupying the northern province of Binh Dinh from April through July, massacred 250-500 hamlet and village chiefs, deputies, pacification, police and militiamen. Two French priests were crucified, the innocent family of an interpreter was executed and 600 males were marched off to a "re-education center."[1827] It was another bloodbath warning, but the New York *Times*, citing unnamed "other American officials," wrote that Hanoi would seek reconciliation if they won the war.[1828] The *Times*

[1826] Mark Moyar, *Phoenix and the Birds of Prey; The CIA's Secret Campaign to Destroy the Viet Cong*, Annapolis: Naval Institute Press, 1997, 208n18 cites Moyar's interview of Robert Komer, Phoenix creator and leader.

[1827] Malcolm W. Browne, "Saigon Replaces Highlands Commander," *New York Times*, 11 May 1972.

[1828] Joseph B. Treaster, "Saigon Officials Executed," *Star and News*, 4 August 1972, P-5.

had found it easier to believe Hanoi lies than facts written in human blood. It was not alone.

North Vietnamese Win on the Second Front— Again. Truong Nhu Tang, Minister of Justice for the Viet Cong, gives perspective:

> American leaders...focused on the military dimension.... the spring (1972) offensive was...a battlefield exercise.... [W]e were pursuing a mix of political and military objectives. ... [W]e could hope to take and hold territory.... Far more important, though, were the political goals... to get the United States out of Vietnam ...isolating the Thieu regime [and] weaken[ing] still further Nixon and Kissinger's ability to make war, by bringing domestic opposition to their policies to a head . . . .[T]he U.S. Congress...prohibited funds for American operations in Cambodia and Laos... These were the signs that told us the [spring 1972] offensive was a success.... [W]e received them with as much satisfaction as we received news of any military victory.[1829]

Hanoi's Propaganda Offensive. After battlefield losses in the spring and summer of 1972, Hanoi launched a propaganda barrage in America among the anti-war movement and the western media.[1830]

During June 1972, the Hanoi controlled Viet Cong issued a "Plan Concerning the Motivation of the People in the Immediate Future," implementing Resolution Binh Gia 5. This agit prop directive detailed ten specific propaganda themes in part: "conduct propaganda on the support we obtain from the progressive American people and the world movement."[1831]

Truong Nhu Tang, says,

> The idea that...American intervention was immoral was gaining widespread credence in the United States, according to our intelligence

---

[1829] Tang, *A Viet Cong Memoir* 209-10.

[1830] Truong Nhu Tang, *A Viet Cong Memoir*, 203.

[1831] Agit Prop Directive- June 1972, "Plan Concerning the Motivation of the People in the Immediate Future," CDEC Doc Log No. 09-1113-72, Pike Collection, Item number 2311618014.

analysts, not only among the militant antiwar groups, but also in the population generally.[1832]

Photo: Many Thanks to the People of the World for Your Support Hanoi Propaganda Poster Showing American Protest, 1972, Nguyen Trinh Than

Saigon's 200,000 Political Prisoners. One theme: South Vietnam had 200,000 political prisoners.[1833] At an International Pax Christi meeting in Strasbourg, France Tom Cornell of the Catholic Peace Fellowship joined the Fellowship for Reconciliation in pleading for relief for Thieu's political prisoners and Vatican assistance.[1834]

Some POW Families Support Hanoi Policies. On June 1, 1972 representatives of POW-MIA Families for Immediate Release spoke before the House Committee on Foreign Affairs claiming to represent 500 POW-MIA families, accepting Madame Binh's Seven Points, and seeking a Congressional resolution to set a definite date for U.S. withdrawal and the release of POWs. Sheila Cronin, Mrs. Shirley Culbertson and Mrs. Gerald Gartley testified.[1835]

[1832] Tang, *A Viet Cong Memoir,* 209-10.

[1833] This and similar themes constituted the North's propaganda war against the South until Northern arms could once again be used to win the war. See: Hung, *Palace File,* 166-167N17-18.

[1834] Thomas C. Cornell, "Catholic Peace Fellowship Ten years Old," *The National Catholic Reporter*, April 25, 1975;

[1835] House Committee on Foreign Affairs, Hearing June 1, 1972, 127-143.

Ring Around Congress. On June 22, 1972 WSP organized women and children, holding hands, to circle the Congress in "Ring Around the Congress," demanding "an immediate cutting off of the funds which perpetuate …slaughter…." Among the most notable sponsors were 25 of the usual activists, singers, actors.[1836]

Also there was a scant group of wives and relatives of POWs: Sheila Cronin, sister of a POW and the director, POW-MIA Families for Immediate Release; Jane Dudley, POW mother; Minnie Lou Gartley, POW mother; and Virginia Warner, POW mother.[1837]

Occupy Entrance to Chambers of the U.S. Senate. On June 27, 1972 hundreds of "prominent professionals and artists" called Redress gathered near the chambers of the U.S. Senate. Brig. Gen. Hugh Hester (ret.) said, the U.S. was "doing the same thing that Hitler did. …We're killing thousands and thousands of people." Senators Edward Kennedy, Mike Gravel and Jacob Javits spoke.

As the group laid down on floor mimicking death, George Plimpton said, "We place these deaths at the door of our representatives." Some 115 were arrested among them was: Hanoi's secret agent Nguyen Thi Ngoc Thoa; National Student Association president Marge Tabankin; author Grace Paley; actor Jon Voight; actress Candice Bergen; WSP's Cora Weiss: and Dr. Benjamin Spock.[1838]

***

Hanoi's Campaign to Protect Dikes from Bombing. Another propaganda theme was the claim that the U.S was intentionally bombing dikes protecting hundreds of thousands of Vietnamese from floods during the May-October rainy season. On June 25, 1972 in Milly-la-Foret, France VVAW members had heard that Hanoi worried about Americans bombing dikes and making rain. The Vietnamese gave VVAW

[1836] Rep. Bella Abzug, Joan Baez, Norma Becker, Mary Clarke, Ruth Gage Colby, Judy Collins, Ruby Day, Jane Fonda, Betty Friedan, La Donna Harris, Dolores Huerta, Coretta Scott King, Sylvia Kushner, Shirley MacClain, Jeanie Plamondon, Jeanette Rankin, Ginette Sagan, Gloria Steinem, Barbara Streisand, Margery Tabankin, Ethel Taylor, Marlo Thomas, Sister Mary Luke Tobin, Cora Weiss, and Trudi Young. In part from sponsors list of Ringaround Congress, June 22, 1972.
[1837] Women Strike for Peace, "Ringaround the Congress," June 22, 1972.
[1838] Betty Medsger, "115 Arrested Lying on Floor In Protest at Senate Door," *Washington Post*, June 28, 1972.

photos of bomb damage, including, allegedly, dikes,[1839] for distribution in the United States.

It was an absurd claim easily refuted by fundamental facts on the ground.

Historic Vulnerability to Floods. Over the millennia the Red River laid down silt creating a river delta of 9,800 square kilometers no more than three meters above sea level. Seventy percent of the agriculture and 80 percent of the industry of modern North Vietnam is in this flood-vulnerable Red River Delta where 19 million live.

Over nearly 2,000 years the Vietnamese built an extensive 3,500 kilometers system of levees. In 1971 a 14-meter flood overtopped 6-8 meter levees, inundated 250,000 hectares, displaced 2.7 million people and drowned 100,000. In 1978 floods wiped out a third of Vietnam's food supply.[1840]

Photo: Roads and buildings at flood risk on both sides of levees. Roger Canfield, Hanoi, March 2008.

During the Vietnam War erosion, sedimentation, leakage and deforestation had already weakened the dike system, which could accurately be described as ancient, old and deteriorating. Indeed dikes had failed in every two or three annual floods, e.g. 1968, 1969 and 1971.[1841]

[1839] FBI, Los Angeles to Acting Director, NITEL 9:24 PM July 7, 1972. Donald Ullrich promised dike photos, but not available at his press conference in Los Angeles.
[1840] Bill and Peggy Herod, "The Sino-Vietnamese Conflict and U.S. Policy," FRIENDSHIPMENT, late 1979.
[1841] "The Dikes: Battered by floods or Bombs?" *Time*, July 31, 1972; Giang Chau, *Vietnam Investment Review*, Sept 24, 2007; Dr. To Trung Nghia, Flood Management in the Red-Thai Binh River Basin-Viet Nam, Asian Development Bank, a power point presentation, circa 2005; Meng, Viet Nam Country Report 1999, at www.adrc.or.jp/countryreport/VNM/VN99/Vietnam99.htm; "Flood prevention a top priority," Viet Nam News, August 8, 2006, at

America's leaders considered but because of the human costs ultimately rejected quickly ending the war by bombing dikes. Such facts did not prevent the Communists from claiming American bombing. Nor did such facts prevent Jane Fonda and others from enthusiastically parroting the Communist line unfiltered.

Meanwhile what started as a drip, Watergate, finally inundated President Nixon and the South Vietnamese.

***

June 17, 1972- Watergate Burglary

U. S. Government's ineffective responses to the Pentagon Papers caper, in part, led the rogue White House "plumbers unit" to illegally break into Daniel Ellsberg's psychiatrist's office in September 1971, conduct wiretaps and ultimately to burglarize the Democrat Headquarters at the Watergate Hotel on June 17, 1972. The cover up brought down the President and limited presidential war powers.

***

Hayden's Exile to Venice. After the riots at the Democratic Convention in Chicago in August 1968, Tom Hayden moved to Berkeley in 1969 to form his own radical revolutionary commune, the Red Family, and a combat training group the International Liberation School. After a while the Red Family collective threw him out and Tom moved to Venice, California where he found an American vet beneficial to him and Hanoi. .

Ron Kovic. In 1970 purged from his own Red Family Hayden met Ron Kovic, an embittered paraplegic casualty of Vietnam. Hayden may have provided Kovic some instructions for success in the political game. A frequent guest on Robert K. Dornan's talk show, the eloquent Kovic told Dornan that Hayden and Fonda had stolen his Vietnam story for their upcoming movie "Coming Home."

Kovic at GOP Convention Miami. Remembering the tears in Kovic's eyes, Dornan and/or Rep. Pete McCloskey got Ron Kovic a pass into the Republican National Convention in Miami in 1972.[1842] There, Ron Kovic and Bob Muller of the Fonda funded VVAW, and a third vet, sitting in wheelchairs, suddenly held up a sign reading, "Stop the War" as Nixon

---

http://english.vietnamnet.vn/2006/08/601256/.
[1842] Dornan to Canfield and others in a conversation at a 1990 California Republican convention.

appeared to make his acceptance speech. Kovic and the others began shouting, "Stop the War, Stop the Bombing." A partisan Republican crowd drowned them out chanting, "Four More Years, Four More Years" for Richard Nixon. Kovic continued screaming as Secret Servicemen carried him out of the auditorium.[1843]

Kovic's book, *Born on the Fourth of July*, anti-war activities, and his associations with Hayden-Fonda eventually led to both Jane Fonda's movie *"Coming Home"* in 1978 and Oliver Stone's *"Born on the 4th of July"* in 1988. Stone's error laden film showed Kovic being attacked and thrown from his wheel chair by Republicans, which he was not. Actor Tom Cruise, played Kovic in Stone's film, and in life, as a student of politics in the Hayden-Fonda household in the late 80's.

Kovic Icon of Myth of Victimization of Vietnam Vet. Kovic's story did much to establish the mythology of the Vietnam Veteran as a demoralized, run down drunken, drugged out victim of an evil war.

Vets Proud. The truth is that 90% of those who saw heavy combat are proud to have served their country.[1844] They were satisfied with their service in the war. Some 72% agreed, "The trouble in Vietnam was that our troops were asked to fight in a war which our political leaders would not let them win."[1845]

Vietnam vets came home to families, schools and jobs to normal lives and became productive citizens.

Vets Prosperous. B.G. Burkett plumbed the depths of obscure government databases to discover Vietnam veterans had lower unemployment rates (4.3% v. 6%) than their age peers, higher per capita incomes and education levels than other vets. Some 71% took advantage of the GI Bill to improve their educations and vocational skills. Very few Vietnam veterans were imprisoned, though many prisoners claimed that they were Vietnam Vets to improve their macho status behind bars.

Drug Use Myth. Similarly, Burkett discovered that the homeless or the criminally convicted mental cases invariably were not the Vietnam vets they often claimed they were.

[1843] Zaroulis, *Who Spoke Up...*, 391-2.
[1844] Vietnam War Statistics http://www.mrfa.org/vnstats.htm
[1845] Swett and Zigler cite Michael Lee Lanning, *Vietnam at the Movies*, New York: Fawcett Columbine, 155.

During the period of U.S. withdrawal there was a serious drug problem but otherwise, a National Institute for Drug Abuse study found "the effects of military service on drug use was invisible, and the effect of service in Vietnam little more than a ripple in a stream."[1846]

In 2009, Jeremy Kuzmarov, published the *Myth of the Addicted Army*, which demolished the myth of "drug addicted American soldier—disheveled, glassy-eyed, his uniform adorned with slogans of antiwar dissent." Alcohol was the drug of choice with marijuana limited to rear areas and heroin rare anywhere. Both the antiwar movement and Nixon exploited the drug issue.[1847]

In early January 2008, the *New York Times* ran stories of 121 "War Torn" veterans of Iraq returning home to become murderers. In fact, the Iraq veterans, like Vietnam veterans, were actually five times less likely to engage in murder than civilians of the same age.[1848]

Kovic would be pushed forward several times to run for public office, but be abandoned by his "friends."

Of course, Jane Fonda would be by far Tom Hayden's best catch for Hanoi's trophy case.

***

[1846] John A. O'Donnell, et al., *Young Men and Drugs—A Nationwide Survey* cited in Gen. William C. Westmoreland, *A Soldier Reports*, New York: Dell, 1976, 489.
[1847] William O. Walker, review of *Myth of the Addicted Army: Vietnam and the Modern War on Drugs*, university of Massachusetts Press, 2009.
[1848] DEBORAH SONTAG and LIZETTE ALVAREZ, "WAR TORN, PART I, Across America, Deadly Echoes of Foreign Battles," New York *Times*, January 13, 2008; "The homicide rate for 18-34 year old civilians who have never served in the military is actually five times higher than it is for those who are now, or who have recently been in, the Armed Forces." Oliver North, "Smear Campaign," Military.com, January 17, 2008. http://www.military.com/opinion/0,15202,160277,00.html?wh=wh

Part VI. Summary
Hanoi Jane's Busy Schedule.

Over the course of two weeks (July 8-22, 1972) Jane Fonda visited Hanoi's war museum and the Bach Mai Hospital, saw damaged dikes, sat at a North Vietnamese anti-aircraft gun battery, interviewed American POWs and collaborators, wrote two articles, held a press conference, and prerecorded and broadcast (July 14-August 22) some nineteen known and transcribed radio messages[1849] to American GI's, South Vietnamese, and the world press.

Preparatory Meetings in Paris, June and July 1972. Before Jane Fonda filled the international broadcast airways, Tom Hayden, David Dellinger and Rennie Davis spent June 6-10, 1972 with the North Vietnamese in Paris. Hayden got Jane Fonda her clearance to visit North Vietnam and a plethora of "insider" information. Hayden tied down the details. After Tom Hayden's intervention, the Vietnam Committee of Solidarity with the American People, formed at least in part in his honor in October 1967 in Hanoi, formally invited Jane Fonda.[1850] In a handwritten note under her own photo, Jane Fonda wrote, "To Vietnamese youth, with love, *solidarity*, and respect for your courage and valor. Hoa Binh - Jane Fonda"[1851] .

On Fonda's travel back to the USA, she dressed for success, scripted for each audience in Moscow, Paris, New York and Hollywood.

Congress talks treason and the Justice Department did nothing. ***

[1849] Thanks to Scott Swett and Mike Benge Jane Fonda's many broadcasts over Hanoi Radio in 1972 from the Foreign Broadcast Information Service, FBIS, are available at http://ww.winter soldier.com/index.php?topic=FondaHanoi
[1850] *Vietnam Youth,* (Hanoi), Aug. 1972.
[1851] Fonda photo and autographed note in Doug Pike's Indochina Archives at U. C. Berkeley, now presumably at Texas Tech.

Chapter 18. Hanoi Jane. July-September 1972

Fonda Meets Secret Agent, Ho Nam. In Paris to pick up her visa Jane Fonda met with Ho Nam (real name Hoang Gia Huy), a secret agent of Department A13 of Foreign Intelligence Directorate of the Ministry of Public Security. Ho Nam's job was to "direct covert propaganda operations," and to recruit Americans as agents, friends and contacts. Ho Nam and another consular officer taught Fonda a North Vietnamese army fighting song. Fonda said, "I want to sing it as a gift to your soldiers."[1852] Ho Nam and Tom Hayden helped script Fonda's flurry of broadcasts and articles over eight days.

Hanoi's POW operation, COLIFAM, gave Fonda POW letters and described "serious destruction to homes, hospitals, and dikes..."[1853]

July 8, 1972- Hanoi Jane Arrives in Hanoi. "I come to Vietnam, not as a personality but as a comrade,"[1854] said Jane Fonda as she stepped off her Soviet Communist subsidized Aeroflot,[1855] plane from Moscow[1856] on July 8, 1972, a Sunday afternoon in Hanoi.[1857] Jane Fonda said, she "had come ...to recognize the hypocrisy and criminality" of the U.S. Government. To Vietnamese she said, "Your struggle, courage, and culture has forced us to recognize certain truths about our own country and what will be necessary to change it." Jane Seymour Plemiannikov, traveling under the proper surname of her estranged French husband (Roger Plemiannikov Vadim), had come to Vietnam as a "comrade." Thang Loi, a North Vietnamese, writing in *South Vietnam in Struggle* said Fonda was not just an "actress of the fast set." She was "a

---

[1852] Interview of Ho Nam in *Thanh Nien*, official newspaper of Vietnamese Communist Party's Ho Chi Minh Youth Group, 2005; Ho Nam, "The Late Minister Tran Quoc Hoan and His Relationship with an Intelligence Warrior;" 2004 cited by Merle L. Pribbenow, "Jane Fonda and Her Friendly Vietnamese Intelligence officer," *Washington Decoded*, 10 August 2011.
[1853] COLIFAM to Dear families, July 5, 1972.
[1854] Loi, *South Vietnam in Struggle*, (September 1972); "In Brief," *Militant*, (August 4, 1972).
[1855] Frank J. Rafalko, *MH/CHAOS: The CIA's Campaign Against the Radical Left and the Black Panthers*, Annapolis: Naval Institute Press, 2011, 138.
[1856] *San Francisco Chronicle*, July 23, 1972.
[1857] Fonda on Donahue Show in September, 1972.

declared enemy of Nixon and [a] stern critic of the corrupt Thieu gang of hirelings."

As the official NLF's *South Vietnam in Struggle* reported: "She went to freshly bombed sites, met with the press, interviewed bombing victims, talked to captured American pilots." She exposed "U.S. crimes" and launched "an appeal to U.S. troops and flyers over the Voice of Vietnam and Liberation Radio." She also praised "the South Vietnamese... students, intellectuals, and artists."[1858] Her schedule, her messages and her audiences evidenced good planning.[1859]

***

Fonda-War Crimes Museum

July 9, 1972. On her first full day, July 9, 1972-- Fonda visited the War Crimes Museum. She also began recording no less than 19 separate broadcasts on a wide range of topics.[1860] She had seen enough in less than one day to claim, "it is we who burn villages and massacred civilian people and raped the Vietnamese women. ...We must stop these barbarous acts. ..."[1861] The Vietnamese recorded her comments on the very next day (July 10th). Yet the museum broadcast was delayed 7 days and replaced by comments on more important developments on the battlefield.

Speaking to US Servicemen on aircraft carriers she said:

> Yesterday, [July 9] I went through the War Museum... a display...of antipersonnel weapons, ...the guava bomb, the pineapple bomb, and the spider bomb, shells that contain napalm and phosphorus and thermite.

Jane continued:

> [S]ome men in the United States ... think...much about new ways of killing people. I don't know what your officers tell you ... what...you are loading, those of you who load the bombs..."

[1858] *South Vietnam in Struggle,* (September, 1972).

[1859] Kiernan, 282; *New Youth*, (Hanoi), (August, 1972); Boroughs, *Fabulous Fondas,* 280-1; *San Francisco Chronicle,* (July 23, 1972; House Internal Security Committee, *Travel...,* (1972), 7605; Thang Loi, *South Vietnam in Struggle,* (September, 1972).

[1860] The FBIS transcripts of 19 broadcasts can be found in their entirety at > http://www.wintersoldier.com/index.php? topic=FondaHanoi

[1861] FBIS transcript, B121534 Hanoi in English to Southeast Asia 1000 GMT 10 Jul 72 B at http://www.wintersoldier.com/ index.php?topic=FondaHanoi

Now, Jane Seymour, a Vassar flunk out, lectured the troops on international law:

> …These weapons are illegal. They are outlawed …by two Hague conventions. And the use of these bombs…makes one a war criminal. The men who are ordering you to use these weapons are war criminals… and in the past, in Germany and in Japan, men …guilty of these kinds of crimes were…executed..."

POW and Capt. Gerald Coffee, "listened in disbelief ... lonely, hungry, ... and I shook my head slowly."[1862]

Since U.S. officers were "war criminals," giving criminal orders, the men hearing Jane ought to consider "executing" their officers. Jane did "not condone the killing of American Officers," but she frequently did "support the soldiers who ... think for themselves"[1863] and make their own "decisions". While Fonda was personally opposed to fragging, but it was OK if the troops had themselves decided to murder their officers.

Jane's radio messages fit the *Binh Van* program of "action against the military" to reduce troop morale. The themes were identical: the inevitability of an enemy victory; oppression by officers; and the low prestige of military service. By raising doubts about leadership, Fonda contributed, as did drugs, to a five-fold increase in the rate of fragging in the last stages of the war.[1864]

War Crimes-Napalm, Plastic Pellets, Chemical Gases.
Jane's next broadcast turned to the horrors of napalm.

> Deformed hands, necks twisted out of shape, women…working with their hands ... lovely and alive and graceful ... twisted out of shape, not dead, not spared the pain and the misery of living…."

Napalm was used against concentrations of troops and in Viet Cong tunnels. Napalm did terrible things to military forces. As for the deliberate napalming of women and children,

---

[1862] Coffee, *Beyond Survival*, cited in *Readers Digest*, December 1989.
[1863] Lofton, *Washington Times*, (July 31, 1985).
[1864] On the "fragging" rate see: General Bruce Palmer, Jr., *The 25-Year War; America's Military Role in Vietnam*, New York: Simon Schuster, 1985, 155 and Lewy, *Americans in Vietnam*.

the vast majority of burn injuries to civilians were from exploding gasoline lanterns and cooking fires. Some civilian napalm victims could be credited to the Viet Cong's use of Chinese and Russian flamethrowers as well as lighting cook stoves with gasoline.

Jane turns to other military technologies—plastic pellets.

> The victims...with thousands of holes in their body... The steel pellets have been perfected, they're now plastic, rough-edged plastic. Why? Because plastic doesn't show up on X-rays, which means that these people spend the rest of their lives with their bodies filled with plastic pellets... it causes excruciating agony."

Hanoi doctors told VVAW's Al Hubbard they had never seen plastic pellets.

Imagine U.S. experts scheming to trick Vietnamese X-ray machines. Cluster bombs were designed to disable electronics SAM, radar, and artillery sites defending legitimate military targets[1865] and to minimize damage to dikes.

Jane becomes a chemist.

> ...Women came to help victims of the chemical bombs, and the chemical toxic gases were so strong that even...long after the bomb had exploded ...they got sick. And...months later they...pass out, have headaches, ...are losing their memory...giving birth to deformed babies.

Fonda mentions "poison gasses" again in a radio broadcast on August 1, 1972--A "Fonda ... Message to Mme. Binh in Cuba." Fonda tells Madame Binh,

> We witnessed Nixon's crimes of using B-52's to massively bomb civilian targets using antipersonnel weapons, poison gasses [sic] and new toxic chemicals and barbarous bombings with napalm, phosphorous and incendiary bombs.[1866]

[1865] Eschmann, 43-44, 58, 182, 189, 202; CNN, July 2, 1998; Canfield, Roger "The roots of the Tailwind hoax," worldnetdaily, Sept 18, 1998.

[1866] Fonda's letter to Binh is quoted extensively at MME Binh RECEIVES LETTERS FROM MALIAN MINISTER, JANE FONDA, Liberation Press Agency [Clandestine] in English to East Europe and the Far East 1540 GMT 22 August 72 B, IV. 23 Aug. 72

There is no evidence that the U. S. used chemical weapons outlawed since 1925. Agent Orange, a defoliant, used in wilderness areas where no more than 3% of the Vietnamese population lived and preceded by warnings to the population were completely discontinued over a year before Fonda arrived in Hanoi. Agent Orange was discontinued because it might cause birth defects. Tear gas was used to avoid killing civilians.

When Ho Chi Minh, Bertrand Russell and Jane Fonda claimed American use of "poison gas" in the Vietnam War the story had no credibility, no legs and no footnote in most histories. Ho Chi Minh first made these allegations.[1867] Russell's War Crimes Tribunal and Jane Fonda dutifully repeated them.

And CNN's discredited and withdrawn "Tailwind" report in 1998. Official documents of the PAVN in Laos, where a U.S. "Tailwind" operation was accused of using lethal chemical weapons, detailing all weapons used, make no mention of U.S. use of chemical weapons.[1868] Claims of the use of nerve gas in the Vietnam War were very rare indeed. They were almost as rare as the claim that American soldiers gutted and ate the livers of fallen Vietnamese. The media did not bother checking that one out.[1869] If they had they would have discovered a Cambodian practice.

***

Hospitals, "Flashing Gun Barrels"
War of Extermination
July 10-12, 1972

Bach Mai Hospital. Jane visited the much-publicized Bach Mai Hospital. That day she recorded her message on Bach Mai for delayed broadcast on the 17th.[1870]

L 8, South Vietnam.

[1867] A collection of some 16 quotes from Ho Chi Minh claiming intentional use of chemicals to kill Vietnamese is at Ho Song Huong, "When Did President Ho Chi Minh Denounce the US use of Toxic Chemicals to Destroy Living Environment in Vietnam," International Scientific Conference: "Victims of Agent Orange/Dioxin in Vietnam— The Expectations," Research Centre for Gender, Family, and Environment in Development (CGFED), Hanoi, 16-17 March 2006.

[1868] Robert J. Destatte, "Search of People's Army of Vietnam Publications For Information About Possible Use of Chemical Munitions," Pentagon, Southeast Asia Division, 15 July 1998.

[1869] Roger B. Canfield, "The Roots of the Tailwind Hoax," September 18, 1998, *WorldNetDaily.com*

[1870] "Appeal on Bombing," *Washington Post*, July 18, 1972.

To the men of the Seventh Fleet: I visited a hospital today, the Bach Mai hospital. I saw a huge bomb crater in the center of the hospital...dropped there on purpose. With the kind of bombs... particularly you pilots know, that accidents...don't happen. This was no accident. It destroyed wards filled with patients. It destroyed hospital equipment. It killed some doctors. It is a terrible thing...."

Bach Mai was near legitimate targets of war: 1,000 meter from a jet airstrip at the Bach Mai Military Airfield and 20 yards from POL fuel storage facility.[1871] Moreover, the Bach Mai area was also the command and control center for North Vietnam's air defense system of SAM missiles, aircraft and artillery. One pilot described a "hospital" near a rail yard target:

> "... it must have been a hospital for sick flack gunners....a run on the railhead, it was a mass of sputtering, flashing gun barrels."[1872]

Any bombs landing on the Bach Mai Hospital was indeed accidental. POW Mike Benge was forced to see a film of Jane Fonda at Bach Mai hospital showing "courageous" and "patriotic doctors and nurse racing up stairways to shoot American "air pirates." An anti-aircraft missile in front of the hospital made it a legitimate target.[1873]

Jane continues, "Why? Why do you do this? Why do you follow orders telling you to destroy a hospital or bomb the schools?" There is no evidence any such order was ever given to destroy hospitals or schools. In fact, hospitals and schools were marked on military maps, precisely to avoid hitting them. The airfield was a legitimate target of war effectively protected by unending protests of bomb damage to the Bach Mai Hospital.

[1871] John Morocco, Rain of Fire, Boston: Boston Publishing Co., 1985, 157.
[1872] Lewy, *Commentary*.
[1873] Mike Benge to author and others, January 31, 2014.

Photo: DOD, Bach Mai Airport, December 21, 1972.

Telford Taylor, an expert on international law and a critic of the Vietnam war said the rules of engagement, the orders, American Commanders gave in Vietnam were "virtually impeccable."[1874] Just like Vietnam, in Lebanon and Iraq since, the terrorists hide in hospitals and schools to wage war amongst helpless civilians and blame Americans or allies for the deaths of the innocents. Perverse tactics create horrors in war. Firing on those targets in self-defense are not war criminals.

***

"War of Extermination" -- July 11-12th. The official NLF newspaper, *South Vietnam in Struggle,* reported Jane Fonda in tears embracing comrade Minh whose body was covered with scars. "Comrade Minh was a survivor of Saigon medieval torture," said Jane. "The fiends! The Gestapo of our time.".... She denounced (President Nixon) as a Hitler of our time, his war as a war of extermination."[1875]

[1874] Lewy, *Commentary*, February 1978, 41.
[1875] *South Vietnam in Struggle*, September 1972.

423

Photo: Hitler with Nixon Mask **Propaganda Poster ca. 1970.**

Charges of genocide were outrageous lies. During the 10-year war, the population of North and South Vietnam increased at a rate double the "baby booming" United States.[1876] Civilian deaths as a proportion of all deaths in Vietnam were half that of the Korean War. Vietnam was far from the terror bombing of World War II when in one night's firebombing 42,000 civilians died at Hamburg, 30,000 at Dresden, and 84,000 at Tokyo. It was the North Vietnamese, not Americans, who ruthlessly sacrificed 1.4 million lives of their own people to win the war and to maintain communist party power. This loss of troops and civilians was proportionately equivalent over 30 million American lives.

It was North Vietnam's war ally, the Khmer Rouge, which was preparing in 1972[1877] for a "war of extermination" of about two million of its fellow Cambodian citizens. Hanoi would attempt to exterminate the "counter revolutionary" Hmong in Laos and Montagnard in central Vietnam. Today, the communists are the "Gestapo" in Asia.

***

Saving the Dikes

July 12th-13th. Jane visited the villages of Nam Hung and Hong Phong in the Nam Sach District some 60 miles east of Hanoi where dikes had allegedly been bombed the previous day. As *Vietnamese Youth* later put it [August 1972] "Jane Fonda particularly denounced the [de]liberate bombing of the dike system and the hydraulic works." ["Yesterday"] Jane recorded a speech attacking U.S. bombing of dikes broadcast the very next day on the 14th. This pushed Jane's recordings on the War Museum and Bach Mai to later dates. Lower priority.

Jane said, "Yesterday morning [SIC 12th] I went to the district of Nam Sach to see the damage…done to the dikes…" Fonda zeroed in on moral significance of a massive assault on the dikes:

[1876] Lewy, *Commentary*, February 1978, 48.
[1877] In 1972 the Khmer Krahom began harsh measures to communize areas of Cambodia under its control in parts of Kampot Province along the southern border of South Vietnam. See: Quinn Report, American Consul Can Tho [Ken Quinn], A-008, State Department, P740017-0522-0573, *The Khmer Krahom Program to Create a Communist Society in Southern Cambodia*, file designation Airgram, February 20, 1974, 2-3.

> ...What has been going on with the hands of
> those...pulling the lever and dropping the
> bombs on the fields and on the dikes? ... These
> are peasants. They grow rice and they rear
> pigs.... Without these dikes 15 million
> people's lives would be endangered by
> drowning and by starvation. But today,
> ...American Phantom Jets are bombing
> strategic points in the dike network."

The charges were false. Of 94 strategic points, dams
and locks, two were bombed.[1878] The dam and spillway at the
Lang Chi hydroelectric power plant was not breached, but its
generators were successfully bombed.[1879] By June 1972 over
70 per cent of N. Vietnam's power capacity was disabled,
hence the high priority of Jane Fonda's agitation over dams and
dikes.

> All of you in the cockpits of your planes, on
> the aircraft carriers, ...loading the bombs...
> repairing the planes, ...working on the Seventh
> Fleet, Are these people your enemies? What
> will you say to your children...why you fought
> the war? . I beg you to consider... In the area
> where I went... there are no military targets,
> there is no important highway, there is no
> communication network.[1880]

Power plants yes.

And...*Life* magazine photographed a bombed dike atop
which three anti-aircraft guns were firing at a U.S. plane.[1881]

In *South Vietnam in Struggle*, Fonda said, "Nixon was
aware ...the 'military targets' and ...he wanted to get at the
very source of life of the Vietnamese."[1882] Of course
Presidents Nixon, Johnson and Ford all knew the dikes were
"the very source of life." According to Frank Snepp, Henry
Kissinger was told that bombing the dikes would kill 2 million
people. Nixon and Kissinger said no. "The U.S.
government...could not rationalize killing two million people.

[1878] Lewy, *Commentary*, 44.
[1879] Eschmann, 55-56.
[1880] UPI, Tokyo, "Jane Fonda's Plea from Hanoi," *San Francisco Chronicle*, Saturday,
(July 15, 1972). UPI's transcript was taken from a Vietnam News Agency news release
of the "Voice of Vietnam Radio."
[1881] *Life,* (August 4, 1972).
[1882] *South Vietnam in Struggle,* (September, 1972).

...The North Vietnamese [never] reached that level of morality," said Snepp.[1883]

All American decision makers rejected bombing dikes. The Joint Chiefs of Staff made "dams, dikes, and locks ... restricted targets ... to minimize ... damage to civilians."[1884]

W. Hays Parks, writes about the bombing of dikes:

> [T]he North Vietnamese commenced a major propaganda campaign in June 1972 alleging intentional attack of the dikes...[They conducted a]...major disinformation effort (on)...the alleged bombing of the earthwork dikes of the Red River Valley...to rally international public opinion...[1885]

The top news story that summer was the dikes and Xuan Thuy began a major part of Vietnamese propaganda campaign weeks before in Paris. George H.W. Bush, Ambassador to UN, said it was a "carefully planned campaign ...to give worldwide circulation to this falsehood." Thus dikes had moved to the top of Fonda's broadcast schedule ahead of her broadcasts from the War Museum and Bach Mai.

After the broadcast, Sec. of Defense Melvin Laird denied dams and dikes were targets, but parts of the dikes might be hit if they were near anti-aircraft sites, main roads, bridges or missile sites.[1886] Later Guenter Lewy wrote,

> Reconnaissance photos showed bomb craters on several dikes ... all in close proximity to targets of high military value; no major dike was breached or functionally damaged, and the [1972] high-water season passed without significant flooding."[1887]

The Vietnamese intentionally killed and injured innocent civilians. Hanoi neglected to repair dikes after major floods on the Red River drowned 100,000 in 1971.

[1883] Mark Moyar, *Phoenix and the Birds of Prey; The CIA's Secret Campaign to Destroy the Viet Cong*, Annapolis: Naval Institute Press, 1997, 360-61n33 cites his interview of Frank Snepp.

[1884] Eschmann, 22 N 38 cites: *Corona Haven*: USAF Air Operations Against North Vietnam, 1 July 1971- 30 June, 1972, HQ PACAF, 8 June, 1973, *Top Secret*, declassified 31 December, 1981, 98-100;

[1885] W. Hays Parks, "Rolling Thunder and the Law of War," 210-212.

[1886] *San Francisco Chronicle*, (July 18, 1972).

[1887] Guenter Lewy, *Commentary*, (February, 1978), p. 47; Hayden, *Nation*, Mar. 22, 2004.

Since Presidents Johnson and Nixon had forbidden bombing the dikes, the North Vietnamese intentionally turned the dikes into military assets. The dikes were used as "part of the road network...used to transport military equipment and personnel (into)... South Vietnam." In 2008 the author observed dikes still used as roads and inhabited flood plains. W. Hays Parks writes, the North Vietnamese placed "AAA gun positions, ground-controlled intercept (GCI) radar, and surface-to-air missile (SAM) sites atop or adjacent to dikes."

In February 1973, Bill Bell, before accompanying POWs home observed "Surface to Air Missile pads deployed on the top of dikes" and "houses of local residents were actually anti-aircraft firing positions." Blue plastic sheeting camouflaged the guns, according to Bell.[1888] They also stored petroleum supplies near or on "top of dikes as a shield against attack." Parks says, "All were legitimate targets."[1889]

Dikes Debate. While Jane Seymour Plemiannanikov had rested on the 26th and 27th, the ruling circles of "the common enemy - U.S. Imperialism" had not. On the 26th the State Department of the "common enemy" admitted that there was "incidental and inadvertent" damage to some dikes due to bombing of targets nearby. On the 27th the "criminal and traitor" Nixon said that there had never been a past/or present policy to bomb dikes and there never would be. They were not military targets. Even the military were not recommending the bombing of dikes, he said.

With such a policy "we could take them out ... in a week," a view "widely shared by the pilots" of the 366th Tactical Fighter Wing stationed at Taklia, Thailand. Maj. Stephen Levine said, "If we deliberately set out to bomb the dikes there wouldn't be any left."[1890]

Nixon continued, the issue of the dikes was "a major propaganda campaign ... the North Vietnamese are very skillful at propaganda." Indeed, Xuan Thuy made one of the first mentions of the dikes in June in Paris to Tom Hayden. June was precisely when Hanoi's blizzard of propaganda on the

---

[1888] Garnett "Bill" Bell with George J. Veith, *Leave No Man Behind: Bill Bell and the Search for American POW/MIAs from the Vietnam War*, Madison: Goblin Fern Press, 2004, 47.

[1889] W. Hays Parks, "Rolling Thunder and the Law of War,"

[1890] AP, Taklia, Thailand, "Fonda Dike Story a Lie, Pilots Say," *Stars and Stripes*, (August 31, 1972).

dikes began. In Nixon's press conference, he said the Vietnamese invited people to see bomb damaged dikes, intentionally left unrepaired before the fall rain and floods.

Left Rallies to Save Dikes. On the Second Front, on August 2, antiwar groups, AFSC, VVAW and WSP, came out in support of the North Vietnamese on the dikes issue carrying signs Stop Bombing the Dikes. Since Nixon Bombings Equal to Four Hundred Hiroshimas. They pass out leaflets, "Is Nixon deliberately causing floods in Vietnam" and McGovern for President literature in front of the Nixon campaign headquarters in Philadelphia. Bob Fields, VVAW, spoke saying that a German general had been convicted of a war crime for the flooding of Holland and likewise Nixon ought to be convicted of a war crime.[1891]

San Francisco Chronicle editor, Bill McCullam, soon wrote,

> all haters of America ... seemingly willing to act as Communist agents, began echoing the enemy claim ... It is astonishing how effectively a lie can be spread when the communist transmission belt works overtime.[1892]

McCullam mentioned Fonda's tour and film of the dikes as an example of just such agents and transmission belts. Nixon told the press the dikes issue was a Vietnamese effort to divert attention from their atrocities in the current offensive.[1893]

In the August 7, 1972 issue of *Time*, Joseph Kraft, touring North Vietnam, called the damage to the dikes incidental, but useful propaganda for Hanoi. Kraft said, if the U.S. Air Force were "truly going after the dikes, it would do so in a methodical, not a harum-scarum way."[1894]

Nixon later wrote that the war could have been won by bombing the dikes but he had rejected it, a tactic used in Korea and in WW II. As Bill McCullum said, the North Vietnamese had "defended its dike system ... using propaganda alone." It was "a master piece of successful duplicity." Indeed it was.

[1891] Philadelphia to Acting Director, 8/2/72 NITEL, files 100-54354, 100-11392 page one and two at FBI, FOIA.

[1892] *San Francisco Chronicle,* August 6, 1972.

[1893] See: "President Nixon's News Conference of July 27, [1972]," *Department of State Bulletin,* August 21, 1972; Bill McCullum, "A Memo on Dikes," *San Francisco Chronicle,* August 6, 1972.

[1894] "The Battle of the Dikes," *Time* Magazine, Aug. 07, 1972; Joseph Kraft. "Letter from Hanoi," *The New Yorker*, August 1972.

Unclassified transcripts later revealed that Nixon had seriously considered bombing the dikes. He was told it would kill several hundred thousand people. He ordered increased bombing of previously out of bounds military targets, not including dikes, in Hanoi and Haiphong, ultimately bringing the Vietnamese to the peace table in Paris.[1895] No transcript has been uncovered that Nixon actually bombed the dikes, though Tom Hayden deceitfully uses Nixon's discussion of the issue as actual proof that he did bomb dikes.

***

Jane and the Sony Repairman -- July 13th-16th. After Jane's recording on the 13th of her message on the dikes for broadcast on the 14th, she claimed later to have "traveled hundreds of miles through bombed regions." Yet except for a Hanoi photo on the 16th, claiming a July 14th visit to a Hanoi hospital, Fonda's itinerary seems blank from July 13th-16th.[1896]

When, Where and Who. It is far more likely that Jane Fonda did not spent most of the next three days, from July 13th - 16th, traveling. She was in Hanoi recording many of her remaining eighteen (19) subsequent broadcasts. She had is no other large bloc of time on her tight schedule inside Vietnam to record so many messages. Perhaps she made recordings in Paris. Maybe Fonda had spent something like two months in the Metropole Hotel in Hanoi, which its official historian, Andreas Augustin, now claims.[1897] Others have suggested KGB agent and propagandist since the Korean War, Wilfred Burchett, helped Fonda with her radio scripts.[1898]

Fonda would later claim, "Every morning a man would come to the hotel with a Sony tape recorder. I would sit down in a room alone with him and talk extemporaneously" about what she had seen the previous day.[1899] Yet Fonda's use of the military details of North's Easter Offensive (Nguyen Hue), her knowledge Hanoi's common propaganda themes and her

---

[1895] Transcripts of Nixon talking to Kissinger on March 22,1972 and June 22, 1972.

[1896] The photo is UPI-Bittman, NCP/RTD 17448, July 16, 1972 cited in *National Vietnam Veteran's Review*, Vol. 4, No. 8, 11.

[1897] Andreas Augustin, *Metropole Hotel*, The Most Famous Hotels in the World, 1986-2008 www.famoushotels.org/booms/536/making

[1898] Trahair, *Encyclopedia of Cold War Espionage, Spies and Secret Operations*, 37-38; Manne, *Left Right Left*,53, b56 all cited in Paul Kengor, *Dupes: How America's Adversaries Have Manipulated Progressives for a Century*, Wilmington: ISI Books, 2010, 327.

[1899] Fonda interview, *Playboy*, April 1974, 78.

targeting of specific audiences do not suggest that Fonda did her recording either alone or extemporaneously as she claimed.

The quality of her performances suggests at least some assistance from a scriptwriter as well as a specialist in Sony tape recorders. Indeed, three experts on psychological warfare testified before Congress about Fonda's broadcasts.

Edward Hunter, a former propaganda specialist for the OSS and the CIA who invented the word "brainwashing" to describe Communist treatment of U.S. POWs in Korea, said that Fonda's broadcasts bore on the marks of professional propaganda. Her broadcasts

fit neatly into the up-to-the-minute Communist Party line and were tactically adapted to the most recent ...fighting (Quang Tri, dikes) and 'peace' sectors. ...Their wording was highly professional in structure and aims.... Her arguments (were) adopted to different audiences. Her operations were those of a team member in the enemy's 'psywar organization.

From Hanoi's perspective, Fonda's broadcasts were intended to reduce American troop morale; to use a credible spokesman with whom other Americans could identify. They obscured the differences between friend and foe. Fonda broadcast the messages of the enemy "precisely" and repetitively. Following Marxist propaganda generally, as described in George Orwell's 1984, she used reverse logic to turn the "aggrieved party [into] "the culprit." The North Vietnamese invasion of South Vietnam became an American invasion; the Communist invasion "was the same as the American Revolution"; President Nixon was the traitor not Fonda; only Americans used the horrible weapons of war and committed war crimes, not the Viet Cong; Americans were inside South Vietnam, not the North Vietnamese army; and the enemy was military officers and the U.S. government.

In short Jane coordinated her broadcasts with the needs of the Communists. Further, Hanoi orchestrated the timing and content of her messages.[1900]

James Rothrock described one message as "a highly subliminal appeal to servicemen to disobey orders, etc., evidently prepared by professional propagandists."[1901]

[1900] Testimony of Edward Hunter, "Analysis of Jane Fonda Activities in North Vietnam," House, Committee on Internal Security, Hearings Regarding H.R. 16742: Restraints on Travel to Hostile Areas, 92nd Cong., 2nd Sess., September 19, 1972, 7582-89.

***

Most Infamous Photo of the Vietnam War

On July 17th the wire services carried photos
(AP/worldwide Photo, Warsaw, July 15, 1972), haunting Fonda
for the rest of her life. There was a smiling Jane, head tilted
girlishly and deferentially toward grinning North Vietnamese
soldiers. Fonda wore the uniform of a Vietnamese regular, war
helmet, Ao-Dai pantaloons, and shirt. She sat in the shooters
chair of an anti-aircraft gun.

A film[1902] showed a coy Jane Fonda dancing gleefully
and patting North Vietnamese soldiers upon their backs. Jane
Plemiannikov posed as if she were herself shooting the anti-
aircraft gun against, as the Vietnamese put it, "The American
Imperialist Air Raiders."

And she sang.

South Vietnam in Struggle carried the following account:

> She visited an AAC site of the capitol. She
> was greatly surprised and impressed by the fact
> that the gunners while always combat prepared
> had time to tend their lush vegetable plots, pig
> sties [sic] and poultry coops. They also
> composed and performed songs. They sang in
> chorus a song in her honor: 'We, Gunners,
> Defend Ba Dinh Square' of their own
> composition. She voiced great admiration for
> their courage, optimism and love for peace.
> She praised their sense of purpose as
> combatants and their taste for music as young
> men.
> She obliged them with 'Rise Up and March
> On' in Vietnamese, a song she had learned
> from Saigon Youth and students who sing in
> anti-U.S.-Thieu demonstrations.
> 'I apologize for my Vietnamese accent,' she
> said. 'After the war I hope I can come back to
> learn Vietnamese. May you shoot down many
> more U.S. planes? Vietnam will win!' she
> exclaimed when taking leave. Her American

[1901] James Rothrock, *Divided…* 158.

[1902] AP/worldwide Photo, Warsaw, July 15, 1972; *San Francisco Chronicle,* July 29,
1972; Also: "The New Left," (Act 1 film footage).

431

voice spoke out our Vietnamese wish and conviction.

A Bolshevik once said, "We simply give the order to sing to anyone who knows how to sing the songs we need."[1903] Of course, in Paris secret agent Ho Nam and another consular officer taught Fonda the army fighting song, not Saigon youth. In Paris Fonda told Ho Nam "I want to sing it as a gift to your soldiers."[1904]

Jane sang and sang and sang….

***

"Women and the mothers…weeping" Day Ten

This is Jane Fonda speaking from Hanoi, and I'm speaking…to the U.S. servicemen…on the aircraft carriers in the Gulf of Tonkin, in the 7th Fleet in the Anglico Corps [Air & Naval Gunfire Liaison Company]…. You are very far away…and so it's…hard for you to, to understand in…human terms…. Never in my life have I been in a country…so loving…. You see people holding hands, …hugging… working….

There's an expression…to describe Vietnamese women: 'Feet in the dust and hands in the mud.' And you see of these beautiful Vietnamese women … their hands in the mud planting the rice…. The women and the mothers in the United State are weeping for the…death and destruction …caused to the mothers of Vietnam. This war is the most terrible crime…ever…created against humanity. How can…the people of the United States have caused this…terrible suffering…? …what do you think? That the Vietnamese people are going to row across the Pacific in canoes?

[1903] V. Pereverzev cited in *Utopia in Power…*,270N139.

[1904] Interview of Ho Nam in *Thanh Nien*, official newspaper of Vietnamese Communist Party's Ho Chi Minh Youth Group, 2005; Ho Nam, "The Late Minister Tran Quoc Hoan and His Relationship with an Intelligence Warrior;" 2004 cited by Merle L. Pribbenow, "Jane Fonda and Her Friendly Vietnamese Intelligence Officer," *Washington Decoded*, 10 August 2011.

Three years later millions of boat people, fleeing prison and death, used anything floatable, driftwood, baskets. Few found canoes.

***

Nam Dinh--"Criminal...Lies" July 17th Fonda visited Nam Dinh, a "textile" center suffering damage to "non-military" targets. The Vietnam News Agency printed Fonda's comments in *Nhan Dan* the very same day. Comments prepared without yet visiting the place?
As the elections...near Richard Nixon is using...criminal
...lies...to fool American...opinion...that he is trying to end the war... .He [is] killing more people...than...before,
...and...bombing the dikes...endangering crops and animals.
I "will expose the lies...."[1905]
The best lie was Nam Dinh being a "cotton and silk textile town...nothing of military significance." Anti-aircraft gun batteries and surface-to-air-missiles defended Nam Dinh, a major river and rail center having a railroad yard, a supply depot, an oil storage area, and a power plant. Harrison Salisbury lost the Pulitzer Prize copying NVA propaganda pamphlets on Nam Dinh not attributing his information to its source.[1906]

***

"Siren Song...Rotten and Wrong"
POWs Meet Fonda, July 18th. On Day Eleven, Jane Fonda interviewed "a picked few,"[1907] seven, American POWs. Most of the POWs were not enthusiastic. Fonda's voice was being heard night and day on camps' loudspeakers. Ranking officer Col. George Day said, "How terrible it is to hear that siren song...so rotten and wrong."[1908]
The Vietnamese tortured some POWs into meeting Jane Fonda. POW Michael Benge, an advisor to the Civil Operations and Rural Development Support, CORDS, pacification program, told his jailors he was going to tell Jane about POW treatment.
> "Because of this I spent three days on a rocky floor on my knees with outstretched arms with

---

[1905] *Nhan Dan* cites: Statement Attributed to Jane Fonda, Hanoi, VNA, International Service in English, 0719, GMT, 17 July, 72 B.
[1906] Lewy, *Commentary,* p. 45; Karnow, *Vietnam,*
[1907] Jim Stockdale in Tom Carhart, *National Vietnam Veterans Review,* (November, 1982).
[1908] Andersen, 255.

a piece of steel placed on my hands, and
beaten with a bamboo cane every time my
arms dipped."

Benge lost a part of his left foot.[1909] The Vietnamese
flogged George Day with a fan belt. His buttocks like
"hamburger," he still refused.[1910] Navy Lt. Commander David
Hoffman, under pain relented:

...In a body cast from the waist up with my
arm out in front of me. I was placed on a table
and then on a chair...on top of the table. And
there was a hook on the ceiling...probably 20
feet or so. The rope was strung around my
arm...Then... the table was kicked out from
under me. I dropped the length of this
rope...inches off the floor. They would...drop
me again, until eventually I came very close to
passing out.[1911]

John McCain. Fonda biographer Christopher
Andersen writes POW, later US Senator, John McCain, USN,
refused a photo with Jane and had two arms broken.[1912]
Columnist George Will says McCain's refusal got him beaten
and starved for four summer months in an unventilated cubicle.[1913]
Realizing his propaganda value as the son of the Commander
of the Pacific Fleet, McCain refused to talk to any delegation.
Later to avoid more beatings he agreed to see delegations, but
not to say what was expected.[1914]

Tortured, "Eventually, I gave them my ship's name and
squadron number, and... my target...power plant." He gave
"the names of the Green Bay Packers' offensive line...as
members of my squadron." As for future targets McCain listed
old targets.[1915] Ultimately, John McCain would sign
confessions of war crimes he had not committed. "I was beaten
every two to three hours by different guards . . " In an

[1909] Mike Benge letter to Disney Co., Cosmopolitan Magazine and CBS and published
in *US Veterans Dispatch*, copy to author December 28, 2008 6:54 PM; also Andersen,
255-256.
[1910] Andersen, 255.
[1911] John Lofton, *Washington Times*, July 31, 1985. See also: Andersen, 256; Pfc.
Edward Warren, *POW*, 1972.
[1912] Andersen, 10.
[1913] George Will, *Los Angeles Times* (April 20, 1979); *Trenton Times,* April 17, 1979.
[1914] Lieut. Commander John S. McCain III, U.S. Navy, "How the POW's Fought
Back," *US News & World Report*, May 14, 1973.
[1915] John McCain, *Faith of My Fathers*, 194.

interrogation room McCain signed a confession. "It was in their language, and spoke about black crimes, and other generalities."

He said, "Every man has his breaking point. I had reached mine." [1916] Bud Day his POW commanding officer forgave McCain and he tried harder.[1917]

The Viet Cong's Military Proselytizing cadre's guidebook said:

> Special treatment was to be granted to U.S. PW's having special social standing, such as those who were the sons or relatives of American celebrities or high ranking officials in the U.S. Government. Intense propaganda and motivation should be imposed on these PW's."[1918]

McCain was surreptitiously filmed: "A journalist working on postwar film projects in Hanoi…was provided motion picture footage of U.S. POW… 20 minutes…showing a well-known American POW, now serving as an elected official, in the courtyard.[1919]

Nixon writes, "One POW had his arm and leg broken because he refused to meet with Miss Fonda."[1920] Another POW seeking to avoid meeting Jane Fonda "took his small stool and beat on his face with it until it was red with blood."[1921]

Jane later said it was laughable that POWs "were forced into seeing us."[1922] Many times thereafter, Jane would say, "POWs are lying if they state that torture is policy of the North Vietnamese."

NOTE: There is no truth to the story that POWs passed messages to Jane Fonda, gave them to their guards, and POWs were beaten as a result.

The POWs named-- Jerry Driscoll, Larry Carrigan, and A.J. Myers--deny this particular story.[1923] The rest is appears

[1916] " John McCain: Torture Worked on Me," *NewsMax.com*, Nov. 29, 2005
[1917] McCain interview on Sean Hannity's America, May 25, 2008.
[1918] Bell and Veith
[1919] Bell and Veith.
[1920] Richard Nixon, *RN*, Vol. II, 402.
[1921] Chris Noel, *A Matter of Survival,* 149.
[1922] *Pasadena Star News*, April 1, 1973.
[1923] Peter Brush, "Hating Jane: the American Military and Jane Fonda," at www.library.vanderbilt.edu/central/brush/jane-Fonda-Vietnam; Mike Benge, "Jane Fonda hoax is a dishonor to American veterans.," *Vietnamese American Review*, September 17, 2009.

to have sustained scrutiny. In short, they were beaten plenty of times for other reasons.

POW Collaborators: Edison Miller and Walter Wilber. A few POWs decided to meet Fonda voluntarily. They were Edison Miller and Walter Eugene "Ed" Wilber, who as members of a POW Peace Committee had received special treatment "...eggs, bread, bananas, and fruit, that the rest of (the POWS) did not get."[1924] They had an open window, an exercise area, books, an aquarium and a bed.[1925] They left their prison camp in civilian clothes to go sightseeing.[1926] The other POWs called them Ducks for the servile way they followed their guards around.

Without torture, Edison Miller made a Mother's Day 1970 broadcast:

> Mothers have been suffering loss and injury of sons in time of war since time began ... This war is different ... Their sons are killing fellow human beings...for an unjust cause, ...The tragedy of Vietnam is America's shame and blight on the world's conscience.[1927]

McCain said, Miller and another POW had "...said there was no reason...to obey the Code of Conduct ...it didn't apply ... in an illegal war..."[1928] Wilber and fellow peace committee member, John Young, believed that the Code of Conduct's reference to American principles gave them a blank check to do as they pleased. The first amendment trumped the code's references to God and country.[1929]

McCain continued, Miller's Mother's Day tape, "played to us time and time again...it certainly hurt morale." From his cell McCain had heard Miller make other tapes "...condemning... the United States..." Miller praised Socialist systems as "superior."[1930]

[1924] *Los Angeles Times*, (August 6, 1979).
[1925] *Herald Examiner*, (July 30, 1979).
[1926] Hubbell, *POW*, p. 595.
[1927] John Kendall, "Edison Miller: From Marine Pilot to Censured POW to Supervisor," *LA Times*, (August 6, 1979), part II, 1.
[1928] Kendall, *Los Angeles Times,* (August 6, 1979; *Herald Examiner,* (July 30, 1979).
[1929] Los Angeles Times, "News in Brief: The Nation 5:25:2, 1973; New York Times, "Ex-POW to Run in Dakota,"11:4:23, 1973; Washington Post, "Ex-POWs Plan Political Work," 4:8:6, 1973 cited in Craig Howes, Voices of the Vietnam POWs, New York: Oxford University Press, 1993, 29n68.
[1930] Kendall, *Los Angeles Times*, August 6, 1979; *Herald Examiner*, July 30, 1979.

POW Peace Committee. Edison Miller and Walter "Ed" Wilber's Peace Committee also included Alfonso Riate, Private Fred Elbert, Robert Chenoweth, John Young, Private Jim Daly,[1931] Michael Branch, Sgt. Abel Larry Kavanaugh, King David Rayford, Jr., and perhaps others. Elbert and Daly had suffered brutal torture and treatment by the Viet Cong in the South, the others had suffered less and some had voluntarily joined the other side.

The North Vietnamese gave the POW "peace committee" militarily useful tasks digging foxholes and designing anti-aircraft drills. After Nixon's May 8th bombing, the Peace Committee signed a letter saying that they must stop the bombing including "do anything ... even if it means joining the Vietnamese Army."[1932] Outraged, other POWs considered liquidating the collaborators.[1933]

Fonda's POW Show Goes On. Readied seven POWs arrived fully scripted.[1934] Over Radio Hanoi, Fonda said the POWs

> all assured me that they have been well cared for. ... listen to the radio, receive letters. ...[are] in good health.[1935] I was looking carefully in their eyes and they were not glazed,

she said.[1936]

> They all told me 'call (our friends and families)...to work in the peace movement."[1937] "Tell them to work for McGovern"[1938] "If Nixon is elected we will be here forever."[1939]

1931 James A Daly, *A hero's welcome: The conscience of Sergeant James Daly versus the United States Army,* Bobbs-Merrill, 1975; Rereleased *Black Prisoner of War: A Conscientious Objector's Vietnam Memoir,2000.*
1932 Hubbell, 582.
1933 Hubbell, *POW*, 295-6.
1934 Steven Denney, 14-15; Andersen, 256.
1935 Radio Hanoi, August 15, 1972; *San Francisco Chronicle*, July 26, 1972.
1936 AP, *San Francisco Chronicle*, July 26, 1972 and August 1, 1972.
1937 This message could have come out of a Viet Cong instruction on *Binh Van* which said: "People and troops ... should _unite_ to oppose U.S. aggression." cited in Pike, *Viet Cong,* 264.
1938 *San Francisco Chronicle*, (July 26, 1972); *Daily World*, July 28, 1972, 9.See also: Buckley, "Secretary Jane," 919; Guidry, 103; AP, *San Francisco Chronicle*, August 1, 1972.
1939 Fonda on Donahue Show, September 1972.

Yet Hoffman says, "If Miss Fonda feels for a minute that any of the people…were able to speak freely.... I reject everything I said...."[1940] Fonda said,

> …The (captured) pilots will be not released before the end of the war… The pilots will be released when Nixon understands that he has lost and not before.[1941]

After Fonda left, the POWs listened to Fonda tapes.[1942] As George Will tells it, "The North Vietnamese piped into the cells recordings [of] (Jane Fonda's voice) ... in which she …told the world how well the prisoners were being treated.[1943] Captain John F. Nasmyth, USAF, said, "It had a demoralizing effect to hear tapes of Jane Fonda…[1944] Stockdale said, "In the eyes of most of us, she was killing Americans by lengthening the war."[1945] Col. Bud Day said,

> She caused the deaths of unknown numbers of Americans by buoying up the enemy's spirits and keeping them in the fight.[1946]

***

Quang Tri "Liberation"

Fonda's Tale of Quang Tri. Fonda's fourth message broadcast on August 7 had been an astonishing tale about the "Quang Tri Liberation" to the Vietnamese people in Vietnamese. The Americans had put the people of Quang Tri into concentration camps and raped their women and now the people had risen up in support of their NLF liberators.[1947] In fact, the South Vietnamese finally liberated Quang Tri after a two-month occupation by the Northern troops.

The Truth about Quang Tri. The North had turned its guns on thousands of fleeing civilians joined, not with the Viet Cong, but with retreating Saigon troops. "When refugees fled…the Communists strafed them on the roads."[1948] In fact,

---

[1940] Andersen, 256.
[1941] From the "Third World" magazine, *Afrique Asie*, cited in the *Japan Times* of August 10, 1972.
[1942] Hubbell, *POW*, (1976), 585.
[1943] George F. Will, *Los Angeles Times*, April 20, 1979; *Trenton Times*, April 17, 1979.
[1944] *Pasadena Star News*, April 1, 1973.
[1945] Feder, "History ...", February 29, 1988.
[1946] Andersen, 255.
[1947] Hanoi Radio attributes talk on Quang Tri to Jane Fonda, B091811 Hanoi in English to American Servicemen involved in the Indochina War 1300 GMT 7 Aug 72 B at wintersoldier.com.
[1948] Nguyen Cao Ky, How We Lost… 153.

"corpses littered a four mile stretch" of highway.[1949] Local reports of the Thanh Nien Phung Su Xa Hoi, counted "5,500 dead bodies including women, children, babies."

Thousands of refugees took a terrorizing trek "50 miles from Quang Tri to Hue under bombs, bullets, rain and cold with their babies, children, cows and pigs…"[1950] And "Skinny buffalos and cows" intermingled with humans "lips blue with cold and hunger." A woman held her baby and cried, "All my family are dead. No one could escape. My father, my mother, my children."[1951]

Phan Nhat Nam's eye- witness account:

> I was on kilometer 9 from Quang Tri (on Highway1) in the area of Mai Dang Hamlet, Hai Lam Village. …I could not speak, weep, or cry out at the scene before me. ...My arms fell useless. …I knew nothing, absolutely nothing of my own body…Nine kilometers of…death in each grain of sand, death in every leaf, death scattered in each strip of flesh, in each bundle of vertebrae, or bone, death in scattered heads and in bent, blackened hands. …[O]n each meter an average of two shattered skeletons. …One could not distinguish this arm, that leg, that skull…The army engineers steamrolled the long road…bundles of bones crushed together with clothes…the human 'trash' moving fast, as a black, slimy grease shone on the tar—the 'tar' of human flesh. …What kind of person could fire…artillery from high points…onto…masses of fleeing people? …Northern soldier…who do you liberate when you kill like that…. What kind of hatred do you have for a disheveled woman carrying her child amidst a flow of shattered people? [1952]

[1949] *San Francisco Chronicle*, August 11, July 18, July 21, 1972.
[1950] Cao Ngoc Phuong, "Dear Friends" letter, Thanh Nien Phung Su Xa Hoi, undated 1972;
[1951] Phai Doan Phat Giao Viet Nam, the Vietnamese Buddhist Peace Delegation to Paris, *Newsletter*, April 21, 1972 cites *Dong Noi Daily*, 11/4/72 [April 11] and 10/4/72 [April 10] at FBI, FOIA.
[1952] Phan Nhat Nam, *Mua He Do Lua*, cited in James Banerian and the Vietnamese Community Action Committee, *Losers Are Pirates: A Close Look at the PBS Series*

Stanley Karnow, likely sitting in Hong Kong, blamed the slaughter upon American air power,[1953] an exclusive story. That was Fred Branfman's "Air War," Hanoi's propaganda.

In Binh Dinh province, in three months the communists executed 300-500, imprisoned 6,000, and confiscated 1/3 to 1/2 of the rice crop.[1954] Mark Moyar reports a former VC cadre from Binh Dinh province commenting on Allied shelling, strafing, and bombing, "I thought that the attacks were mostly caused by the presence of Front forces in the hamlets, but [sometimes] …they weren't justified." This could be blamed on poor intelligence or careless GVN or American leaders. "With regard to all the attacks resulting from VC activities, they blamed the Front, sometimes openly."[1955]

Saigon itself had come under indiscriminate rocket fire.[1956]

By late July 1972, Nixon reported 860,000 refugees, 45,000 casualties (15,000 dead). Such was the "liberation" (during the Easter Offensive) of Quang Tri, Hue, An Loc, Binh Dinh province and other areas benefiting from the humanitarian policies of the North.

Yet by October 758,000 had been resettled in refugee camps.[1957]

After Fonda's "Quang Tri Liberation" message, she broadcast to "the U.S. men who ... have been sent here to fight."[1958] Her fifth message.

On the 20th the "Voice of Vietnam" broadcast her recorded press interview with Jean Thoraval during prime time 8:00 PM in England, Europe, Africa and the Middle East. Her sixth.

"Vietnam: A Television History," Phoenix: Tieng Me Publications, 1984, 231-3.
[1953] Stanley Karnow, Vietnam, 641 cited in James Banerian and the Vietnamese Community Action Committee, Losers Are Pirates: A Close Look at the PBS Series "Vietnam: A Television History," Phoenix: Tieng Me Publications, 1984, 197.
[1954] San Francisco Chronicle, August 4, 1972
[1955] 5. Rand Vietnam Interviews, Series AG, No. 573, 3, cited in Mark Moyar, "VILLAGER ATTITUDES DURING THE FINAL DECADE OF THE VIETNAM WAR, 1996 Vietnam Symposium, "After the Cold War: Reassessing Vietnam,"18-20 April 1996,
http://www.vietnam.ttu.edu/vietnamcenter/events/1996 Symposium/96papers/moyar.htm
[1956] Ky, How We lost…, 153.
[1957] "Land Reform and Refugee Resettlement – Aid Successes in South Viet-Nam," U.S. Department of State, July 1974.
[1958] 7/20/72, 1,300 GMT.

'What are You Doing?'

July 21-22. Days Fourteen and Fifteen, Fonda's seventh broadcast to "U.S. pilots." She said,

> Nixon is continuing to risk your lives ... How does it feel to be…pawns? ... Tonight when you are alone, ask… 'What are you doing?' Accept no ready answers fed to you by rote from basic training…. But as men, as human beings, can you justify what you are doing? …The people beneath your bombs have done us no harm.[1959]

Five hours later, the Viet Cong's clandestine Liberation Press Agency carried Fonda's eighth broadcast to "The South Vietnamese People" in English.[1960] We do not know the reactions of the South Vietnamese. Bill Laurie who spent many years in South Vietnam says:

> There's an old Vietnamese slang term, *Coc Vang* ... [meaning] ... literally a golden toad, figuratively, a stupid, wealthy effete idiot ... I know fully well what South Vietnamese people think of ... [Hayden/Fonda] ... utter fools and gullible snots.[1961]

Liars. On day fifteen, July 22nd, Fonda met Vice Premier Nguyen Duy Trinh assuring him of "triumph" over America.[1962] Radio Hanoi broadcast her ninth to "U.S. Flyers and Airmen. She said, "All of you, in your heart of hearts, know the lies--cheating on body counts[1963],

> [S]hould you allow these same liars to decide for you who the enemy is? ... If they told you the truth, you wouldn't fight, you wouldn't kill."[1964]

Combatant. Comrade. *South Vietnam in Struggle* reported,

[1959] 7/21/72, 1,000 GMT; Andersen, 254.

[1960] 7/21/72, 1513 GMT.

[1961] Bill Laurie to Author, (1 January, 1989). Doug Pike expressed similar and independent use of the term useful idiot to the author on January 6, 1989.

[1962] UPI-Bittman archive, NXP/RTK, 1745505, July 22, 1972 Hanoi, shown in *National Vietnam Veterans Review*, Vol. 4, No. 8, p. 10.

[1963] With Hanoi admitting a loss of 1.1 million souls after the war, it might be useful to think of the cheating on body count as a matter of margins of errors or very good guesses.

[1964] Andersen, 255.

On her parting with the land she [Fonda] described as a great school of life, she declared that her Vietnamese friends had instilled in her strength, courage and confidence, the love of man and life full of pervading optimism."[1965]

And...

All through her visit to Vietnam Jane behaved like a real *combatant* ... Thank you, Jane. Thank you for your courage. Thank you for inspiring comradeship.[1966]

Perhaps as her recorded voice reached "U.S. Flyers and Airmen," she flew off for a 30-minute stopover in Vientiane, Laos.[1967] She had more important places to b, Moscow for two to three days.

***

Fonda's Choreographed Return: Moscow, Paris and New York

Moscow Layover. "For two days no one heard anything about her," said *South Vietnam in Struggle.* [She was in Moscow.] This is not literally true. Fonda's words were still being heard in recorded radio messages. Her 10th broadcast was her "Letter to Southern Youth" in Vietnamese on the 23rd.[1968] Recorded in *Vietnam Youth* she said:

The U.S. must withdraw all its troops from South Vietnam and set a terminal date for this withdrawal and cease its support for the Thieu Regime, a regime hated by every South Vietnamese.[1969]

On her "Letter to Southern Youth" she wrote a note on her photo: "To Vietnamese Youth with love, solidarity, and respect for your courage and valor. Hoa Binh, Jane Fonda"[1970] She was encouraging the 16-17 year olds conscripts into the Northern controlled Viet Cong.

On the 24th, while she was in Moscow, the UN's Secretary General joined the chorus asking the US to stop bombing dikes and Radio Hanoi broadcast her eleventh

---

[1965] *South Vietnam in Struggle,* September 1972.
[1966] *South Vietnam in Struggle,* emphasis added, September 1972.
[1967] AP, Vientiane, Laos, "Jane Fonda on Way Home," *San Francisco Examiner-Chronicle,* July 23, 1972.
[1968] 0300 GMT, 7/23/72.
[1969] *Vietnam Youth,* August 1972.
[1970] See: "Jane Fonda: I Accuse..." *Vietnam Youth,* August 19, 1972.

message to "U.S. Pilots and Airmen." This same message was repeated as her twelfth broadcast on July the 25th near the time [1300 GMT] Jane Fonda "made her appearance" in Paris at Orly Airport.

Paris Reception-- Peasant Suit of Black Pajamas. Arriving in Paris Jane Fonda wore a South Vietnamese peasant suit of black pajamas, red tunic, and a peasant's conical palm hat. Her Vietnamese military uniform, worn in Hanoi, now packed away,[1971] Fonda wore a Viet Cong peasant's disguise. She was in the act of becoming Viet Cong, a new role, new audience.[1972]

Indeed.

At Orly Airport the press asked about "criticism against her ... for allegedly calling to disobey orders." Yes she said, "There is a very serious traitor in our midst and I think it is Richard Nixon." Trying to stop the war didn't make Jane, a traitor. It was "someone," like Nixon, "who was committing the most heinous crimes.... ever committed." She said, "Men like [Nixon and Agnew] are war criminals... but Jane insisted, "I would not like to see him [Agnew] executed."

Why did she speak on Radio Hanoi? "I will speak wherever... I can appeal" to the "humanness of the American people."[1973] In Vietnam she had "expressed...shame of being an American....[1974] She went there to reach particular Americans. "It was the only way I could reach the pilots."[1975] Not the humane Americans, the "war criminals."

She said, "There were some (pilots) who said 'I just can't do it anymore' ... so I at least hoped, if a pilot had access to new information... as a human being he would eventually say 'I can't bomb anymore."[1976] A very sympathetic Hal Jacobs said of Jane's broadcasts, "Everyone in the anti-war movement knew it to have been [an] attempt to influence U.S. pilots to stop participating in a criminal war."[1977]

[1971] Thang Loi, *South Vietnam in Struggle*, September 1972. The [bracketed] description is from AP, Paris, *San Francisco Chronicle*, July 26, 1972.

[1972] Thang Loi, *South Vietnam in Struggle*, September 1972.

[1973] Fonda's remarks in Paris are from: AP, Paris, "Jane Fonda Calls Nixon a Traitor," *San Francisco Chronicle*, July 26, 1972, 12; See also: *Militant*, August 4, 1972; Buckley, "Secretary Jane."

[1974] *South Vietnam in Struggle*, September 1972.

[1975] Fonda on Donahue show, September 1972.

[1976] *Playboy*, April 1974, 78.

[1977] Jacobs, *Tikkun*, June 1989, 109.

Thang Loi wrote:

> So Jane Fonda, an 'actress of the fast set' has become an outstanding anti-war militant, having accepted the challenge of the Fascist of our time, enemy number one of peace. The dogs can keep barking, but Jane and her anti-war caravan will go on.

The Vietnamese were pleased having given her the now familiar ring made from the debris of an American aircraft shot down.[1978] At Fonda's request from Bangkok, Vietnam's official spy recruiter, Ho Nam, met Fonda at Orly airport.[1979]

A few Americans feigned amusement. William F. Buckley said, Jane had been "secretly studying every international law" and Agnew would be sentenced to "a lifetime [sic] study of the thoughts of Jane Fonda."[1980] Whatever Jane's intellect, she was deadly serious.

Talk with Saigon Students, July 26, 1972—"a common enemy - us imperialism." The day after her Paris press conference, Radio Hanoi broadcast in English her thirteenth message, "Talk with Saigon Students" on July 26, 1972.[1981]

> This is Jane Fonda in Hanoi. I am very honored to be a guest in your country, and I loudly condemn the crimes. ...against your country. A growing number of people in the United States not only demand an end to the war, an end of the bombing, a withdrawal... but we identify with the struggle of your people. We have understood that we have a common enemy - us imperialism. We have understood that we have a common struggle and that your victory will be the victory of the American people.. . Your struggle and your

---

[1978] Andersen, 257.

[1979] Interview of Ho Nam in *Thanh Nien*, official newspaper of Vietnamese Communist Party's Ho Chi Minh Youth Group, 2005; Ho Nam, "The Late Minister Tran Quoc Hoan and His Relationship with an Intelligence Warrior;" 2004 cited by Merle L. Pribbenow, "Jane Fonda and Her Friendly Vietnamese Intelligence officer," *Washington Decoded*, 10 August 2011.
[1980]

[1981] "Jane Fonda discusses Vietnam War with Saigon students," B261715 Hanoi in English to American Servicemen involved in the Indochina War, 1300 GMT 26 Jul 72 B, Radio Hanoi.

courage... has inspired all of us in the deepest part of our hearts.
We follow very closely... the brave people who are speaking out for peace and independence, who are being put away into prisons in the - - in the tiger cages."
In our country people are very unhappy. People have no reason for living. They are very alienated from their work, from each other, and from history and culture. We know what U.S. Imperialism has done to our country ... So we know what lies in store for any Third World Country that could have the misfortune of falling into the hands of a country such as the United States and becoming a colony ...We hope very soon that, working together, we can remove the American cancer from your country... [1982]

Doan Van Toai, a student protest leader, believed Fonda. The Communists had a strategy - a people's war for the hearts and minds of the American people. "The secret strategy made the American people ... the chief target."

The Communists appealed to decent values: "A hatred of colonialism, an abhorrence of violence, a belief in social welfare and liberal democracy." South Vietnam failed such standards.[1983] "For four years I wrote secret reports providing intelligence [to] ... the National Liberation Front,"[1984] said Doan Van Toai.

New York Makeover ; Now a Patriot. Arriving in New York on the 28th, Fonda escaped from demonstrators carrying signs. One said, "Hanoi Rose."[1985] Meanwhile, her

---

[1982] Pieces of the text of Jane Fonda's message of July 26th are found in a number of secondary sources. The author apologizes for any inaccuracies in the sequencing of Fonda's phrases or sentences. See: William T. Poole, "Campaign for Economic Democracy..." Heritage Foundation, Institutional Analysis, #13, September, 1980, 12; Chris Noel, *Matter of Survival*, 148; Feder, "History...", February 29, 1988; "Fonda's Anemic Apology", *Human Events*, (July 21, 1988); Bruce Herschensohn, *Police Gazette*, (October, 1987), 7.

[1983] Doan Van Toai, "Vietnam: How We Deceived Ourselves," *Commentary*, (March, 1986), 43: Chanoff, David and Doan Van Toai, *Portrait of the Enemy*. Random house; New York. 1986.

[1984] Doan Van Toai, in Collier and Horowitz, *Second Thoughts...* 70.

[1985] Andersen, p. 258.

fourteenth broadcast on Radio Hanoi addressed "U.S. Servicemen" in Vietnam.[1986] Cora Weiss told the POW families she had brought back 241 letters and Fonda had

> observed damage to civilian targets, dams and dikes…. If the present unrestricted bombing isn't stopped the damage to dikes and dams will cause unprecedented catastrophe to the people of Vietnam.[1987]

The next day at the Drake Hotel Jane Fonda again answered questions about treason. In New York she was saying, "I would no more tell the soldiers to defect and go over and fight with the Vietnamese. It is absurd they are needed at home." Wrong question. She had called for disobedience, desertions, and mutiny. And, no one asked her why she felt soldiers were needed at home. Her answer at least in Vietnam had been to fight at home against "a common enemy - U.S. Imperialism."

She was, she continued, just a garden-variety anti-war protestor -- her third role-played in a week. "Anyone that is speaking out against the war is carrying on a propaganda - a propaganda for peace, a propaganda against death, a propaganda for life." Again no one held her to her two-day old identity with the struggle of the Saigon students for victory against United States Imperialism. No one remembered her just discarded military and now peasant costumes.

She asked the critical question. "What is a traitor?" Not answering it, she said, "I cried every day I was in Vietnam. I cried for America." Why cry for America? She said, "the bombs are falling on Vietnam but, it is an American tragedy." She said, "I believe that the people in this country who are speaking against the war are patriots." (Not traitors)

In New York she was now a patriot. In Hanoi she had starred as an internationalist - a comrade. Jane Fonda changed flags as she did military uniforms and stage costumes. "She felt the pilots would stop bombing if she could 'tell them what they are doing." According to A.P. "She said her comments were intended to direct the pilots' attention to what she described as death and destruction on the ground." She intended the pilots to stop the bombing they were being ordered to do. Disobedience? Desertion?

[1986] 7/28/72, 2000 GMT.
[1987] Cora Weiss to Dear friends, COLIFAM July 28, 1972.

Jane admitted that the transcripts of her broadcast of July 17th were accurate and typical of her other broadcasts.[1988] On the 17th she had said, "Why do you follow orders? ... The men who are ordering you to use these weapons are war criminals ... and in the past ... were tried and executed." Some American servicemen may have remembered from their own military training that following orders was defense for neither Nazi nor any other war criminal. American servicemen were war criminals—just as the Vietnamese communists said they were.

Last Shots at Troops. On July 29th, her voice droned on in her fifteenth broadcast, "Message to Saigon Soldiers." She told the South Vietnamese troops that they were but "cannon fodder for U.S. imperialism ... " serving "racist aggression ... [in] ... a white man's war."

Desertion was a solution.

> We read with interest about the growing number of you who understanding the truth and joining with your fellow countrymen to fight... .For example... the 56th Regiment of the Third Division of the Saigon Army ...is taken into the ranks of the National Liberation Front, including officers, who may retain their rank.[1989]

On the 30th there was her sixteenth to "American GI's."[1990]

***

Hollywood- Dikes, hydrologist, engineer

Flying back home to Hollywood, at a Los Angeles Airport news conference on the 30th of July, Fonda was defending her statements on dikes. On the 28th, the State Department had said the U.S. had hit only 12 locations along 2,800 miles of dikes. Minor damage. Fonda now admitted the bombing was merely near the dikes. Still, she said, it was "systematic and on purpose."[1991] "It's not only the dikes that are being bombed but all the things that have to do with irrigation and flood control."[1992] By "all the things that have to do with irrigation and flood and control," Jane likely meant dams, canals and locks. Two of 94 such "things" had been hit.

[1988] AP, New York, *San Francisco Chronicle*, (July 27, 1972, p. 13.
[1989] 7/29/72, 1000 GMT. See also: Andersen, 259.
[1990] 7/30/72, 2000 GMT.
[1991] AP, Los Angeles, *San Francisco Chronicle*, (July 31, 1972).
[1992] VNA, International Service in English, 1503 GMT (1 August '72B.

Continuing her learned discourse on seismology, hydrology, and civil engineering, she said, "The bombs falling on the side of the dikes are dangerous because they cause earthquakes and weaken the dikes at the base causing fissures in the dike walls." Moreover, Jane said, tricky Nixon had directed bombing near the sides of dikes to avoid charges of bombing dikes! How clever! How evil! According to AP Jane had herself seen "28 bomb craters along [side] a crucial dike."

Pilots accused of bombing dikes were not very fond of Fonda. AP reported, "they write rude things about her on bombs they drop on the North Vietnamese." As for deliberately bombing dikes, Col. George W. Rutter, Commander of 366th Tactical Fighter Wing said, "I think it's a four-letter function in Anglo-Saxon." Jane Fonda was "no pin-up girl among American pilots."[1993]

***

On July 31, 1972, Jane Fonda, back from Hanoi, had announced she was giving up her acting career to join Tom Hayden's Indochina Peace Campaign (IPC).[1994] In September and October, Tom and Jane toured ninety cities for IPC in the states of Michigan, Ohio, Illinois, Pennsylvania, New Jersey, New York and California. Hanoi's own People's Peace Treaty sponsored such events.[1995]

Fonda's Hollywood Homecoming

In Hollywood, July 31, 1972, Jane announced a double feature the premier of "F-ck The Army," FTA,[1996] and giving up her acting career to join (Tom Hayden's) Indochina Peace Campaign.[1997] American-International Pictures pulled "FTA" from theatres in a week,[1998] but the Vietnam News Agency had Fonda saying, "Genocide is more important than anyone's career."

Rep. Robert H. Steele, R-Conn, wanted an Oscar for Jane for "the rottenest, most miserable performance by any ...

[1993] AP, 8/31/71.

[1994] *San Francisco Chronicle*, August 1, 1972. Indeed after the releases of "Doll House" and "Steelhouse Blues," she would not make another American film until 1977's "Fun With Dick and Jane."

[1995] Jane Fonda in Michigan spurs peace drive," *Daily World*, September 15, 1972, 9.

[1996] Kiki Levathes, "F.T.A. To Open: Fonda Political Film," *Washington Post*, July 2, 1972.

[1997] *San Francisco Chronicle*, (August 1, 1972); Alan Myerson quoted in Bo Burlingham, *Esquire*, (February, 1974), 118.

[1998] Dennis Lim, "Jane Fonda's antiwar years with the FTA," *Los Angeles Times*, February 22, 2009.

American in ...history..."[1999] The Hollywood Women's Press Club gave Jane Fonda the "sour apple" award for worst image of Hollywood. Jane said, "They don't give the Academy Award to...me ... I'm a renegade actress.... " She had many Oscar nominations and had been awarded an Oscar that very spring.

There still was Jane's career on Radio Hanoi. Her seventeenth, on August 1, Viet Cong Liberation Radio, was a "Fonda ... Message to Mme. Binh in Cuba."[2000]

> We...send a warm kiss to you, to the heroic sons of the Vietnamese people, and to the Vietnamese children... conducting the most valiant fight in history... . Nixon... [is] ...causing death and destruction perhaps as serious as the bombing of Hiroshima....We witnessed Nixon's crimes...using anti-personnel weapons, poison gasses and new toxic chemicals and barbarous...napalm, phosphorous and incendiary bombs. ... We saw...Nixon's...scheme of destroying dikes ... at the flood season. Never has history witnessed...such a barbarous plan which seriously threatens...15 million...."[2001]

In *Phu Nu Vietnam*, "The Struggle of the Vietnamese People Has Awakened the American People's Conscience, " Jane wrote/signed:

> ...American women are... struggling to liberate themselves. ... This struggle ... is ... an anti-imperialist struggle.... Struggling very heroically, women ... can hold weapons ...[2002] We have contemplated... Vietnamese women...in the rice fields, wearing rifles on their shoulders, ... handling anti-aircraft guns, fighting on the battlefield.... You...smile, you sing ... you love.... These virtues have disappeared ...in Capitalist countries. I am very lucky to come here ... After my return ... I

[1999] Guidry, 105.
[2000] 8/1/71, 1400 GMT.
[2001] "Jane Fonda Sends Message to Mme. Binh in Cuba," Liberation Radio [Clandestine] in Vietnamese to South Vietnam, 1400, GMT, 1 August, 1972.
[2002] Dinh was the Military Commander of the Viet Cong's People's Liberation Army.

will report all these things [recorded]. ...
[Y]our victory is the victory of all people. The
Vietnamese women's victory is the victory of
women the world over.[2003]

Such a communist "victory" cost American lives, both
those following "criminal" orders and those following Jane's
advice to soldier slothfully.

***

Congress Talks the Talk: Treason

While Jane was still in Hanoi, Rep. Fletcher Thompson thought
charges of treason ought to be brought against Jane Fonda.
"Giving aid and comfort to the enemy" was, he (and the U.S.
Constitution) said "treason."[2004] On day twelve in Hanoi, Jean
Thoraval, an *Agence France Presse* reporter known for anti-
American stories, interviewed Jane. What about Rep.
Thompson's accusations of treason? The Vietnamese account is:

> In [a] ... remark occasioned by the question of a
> journalist [Jean Thoraval] who revealed that
> American bellicose elements have threatened to
> put her to trial for treatise [sic] Jane Fonda said,
> 'I want to publicly accuse Nixon here of
> betraying everything the American people have
> at heart, betraying their long tradition of freedom
> and democracy. The tragedy, I feel is not for the
> Vietnamese people who will soon discover their
> freedom and democracy, but for the American
> people because for the Americans it will take a
> long, long time to wipe out their crimes
> committed by Nixon in their name."[2005]

It was Nixon, not Fonda, who was betraying America.

To bolster his charges of treason, Rep. Thompson
placed the full text of Fonda's broadcast of the 17th into the
Cong. Record. Thompson said,

> obviously she is attempting to get them [the
> pilots] to disobey orders ... Jane knows that
> there are no orders to bomb hospitals ... [H]er

[2003] Jane Fonda, "The Struggle of the Vietnamese People Has Awakened the American
People's Conscience," *Phu Nu Vietnam* (in Vietnamese), No. 297, (1 August, 1972),
16-17S.
[2004] *San Francisco Chronicle*, July 19, 1972.
[2005] *Vietnam Youth*, (August, 1972).

statements ... [are] designed to cause American troops to disobey the orders of their country."

It was the Viet Cong, not Americans, who were under standing orders to "assassinat[e] 30,000 school teachers, policemen, and civil officials ...." It was they, said Rep. Fletcher Thompson, who "bombed school buses, cafes, indiscriminately ... [and] ... executed (4,000) at Hue [in 1968] and buried them in a common grave by bulldozer."

Moreover, "that (Fonda) condemned her country and not the enemy 'puts the lie' to her concerns for humanity," said Rep. Thompson.[2006]

Soon Fonda would tell TV host Phil Donohue the Viet Cong assassinated only about a dozen people a week, but that was OK, they were "enemies of the people."[2007]

Besides the topic of treason, Fonda said she had "traveled hundreds of miles throughout the bombed regions" and been forced into a roadside shelter the day before--probably while returning from "the textile center" Nam Dinh to interview American POWs. Fonda condemned the criminality of the U.S., praised the courage of the North Vietnamese, and was "more convinced than ever of the victory of the Vietnamese people." The North's official Vietnam News Agency said Fonda "particularly denounced the deliberate bombing of dike systems and hydraulic works."[2008]

***

Hanoi Happy with Jane.
Antiwar Movement... Gave Us Confidence... in the Face of Battlefield Reverses. PAVN Sr. Col. Bui Tin would take the unconditional surrender of South Vietnam on April 30, 1975. Once retired Col. Bui Tin told the *Wall Street Journal* how persons like Jane Fonda aided Hanoi.[2009]

> It was essential to our strategy. Every day our leadership would listen to world news over the radio at 9 a.m. to follow the growth of the American antiwar movement. Visits to Hanoi by people like Jane Fonda and...ministers gave us confidence that we should hold on in the face of battlefield reverses. We were elated

[2006] *Congressional Record*, (July 20, 1972), 24764-24765.
[2007] Fonda on Donohue show, September 1972, author's videotape.
[2008] *San Francisco Chronicle*, (July 21, 1972).
[2009] Arnaud de Borchgrave, Monday, April 19, 2004, Newsmax.

when Jane Fonda, wearing a red Vietnamese dress, said at a press conference that she was ashamed of American actions in the war and that she would struggle along with us.[2010]

The anti-war movement, which led to the collapse of political will in Washington, was "essential to our strategy." America lost the war, said Bui Tin, "because of its democracy. Through dissent and protest, it lost the ability to mobilize a will to win."

Back home many still said Fonda gave aid and comfort to the enemy--treason. *South Vietnam in Struggle* said, "Her activities infuriated the U.S. ruling circles into wanting her to be prosecuted for 'treason' for 'intelligence with Communists."[2011] North Vietnam reported:

> The U.S. reactionary circles are launching a campaign of harassment ... to intimidate… progressives … The brave acts of Miss Fonda …have caused the Nixon clique to be greatly confused and isolated from U.S. and world's peoples."

It was "their old plots of intimidation, terrorism, and oppression..."[2012]

The "intimidation, terrorism and oppression" Fonda faced was laughable. Intelligence agencies kept a close watch on Fonda, but officials hid under their desks cowering. Sec. of State Henry Kissinger wanted to talk with her, but she refused.[2013] William Olson, Chief of the Internal Security Division of the Department of Justice claimed no investigation and "Treason is not involved in the technical sense."[2014]

On August 10th, the House Committee on Internal Security lacked a vote to subpoena Fonda to testify. The Committee voted 8-1 asking the Justice Department to do a report or something.

All but declaring victory Fonda said, "I welcomed the Committee…studying…my broadcasts…. [T]here there is no basis for… charges…."[2015] On August 14, U.S. Attorney General

---

[2010] Stephen Young, "How North Vietnam Won the War," *Wall Street Journal,* 3 August 1995.

[2011] Loi, *South Vietnam in Struggle,* September, 1972.

[2012] Hanoi Domestic Service in Vietnamese, 1115 GMT, 7 Aug. 72.

[2013] Andersen, 257.

[2014] UPI, August 10, 1972; Andersen, 260.

[2015] AP, Washington, *San Francisco Chronicle,* (August 11, 1972).

Kleindienst told the committee: "...[S]he...denies [sic] most statements [sic], there doesn't seem to be any indication of treason.... [T]reason has to depend on a declaration of war." Fonda had denied nothing. The Foreign Broadcast Information Service (FBIS) had recorded her every broadcast.

In pertinent part, Jane Fonda had not denied asking, "Why do you follow orders? ... [T]he men are ordering you ... are war criminals ... and in the past were tried and executed." Apparently, having read nothing, heard nothing they were saying nothing.

Officials claimed Jane Fonda had not asked U.S. troops either to lay down their arms or to pick them up against their officers. By following law more appropriate for the arrest of a common prostitute, it is true that "Barbarella" had not spoken the precise script to qualify her for an overnight stay in a Washington hotel to testify before a Congressional Committee or to speak to a government lawyer.

Then, of course, there was the matter of no formal declaration of war. It would be 2002 before Henry Mark Holzer and Elizabeth Holzer published the lawyerly case for Jane's treason in *Aid and Comfort*.

As for American troops, they didn't need any "stinking lawyers." By 2002 books were being written claiming to say Jane Fonda had not said what thousands had heard with their own ears, taped or read in the original unexpurgated text.

Troops Talk Back. Men who saw their comrades die in Vietnam never appreciated the value of fine legal reasoning under gunfire. Jane Fonda was a traitor—forevermore. Tom Beasley, a platoon leader for the First Calvary Division said, "...When a guy in my platoon got killed by gunfire ... I didn't need an Act of Congress to tell me who the enemy was."[2016] Army Special Forces officer, Peter Laurence,[2017] "While my friends were being killed (Fonda)...helped the people who were killing them. "[2018] John Dramesi, a six year POW said, "...I just can't believe that reasonable people wouldn't see her actions in Hanoi as treasonous."[2019] John Dramesi's POW

[2016] Chris Noel, 153.
[2017] Peter Laurence provided the author with a wealth of news clips on Fonda.
[2018] Peter Laurence, *San Jose Mercury*, (October 11, 1984).
[2019] Chris Noel, 154. A Vietnam Green Beret, Lawrence provided the author with a box of Fonda clips.

roommate, Ed Atterbury, had been beaten to death after their escape and capture.[2020]

No Guts. No Prosecution. Jim Parker, rifleman with the 101st Airborne Division said, "...no one in ...in the Government has the guts to go after her."[2021] Henry Kissinger: "She knew precisely what she was doing -- she wanted Hanoi to win...totally immoral."[2022]

This author, who spent over twenty years in close proximity to platform patriots, politicians, believes Tim Parker had it about right - no guts from Kissinger or the others. Peter Collier, says Jane Fonda committed "no fault treason." No fault treason cost dearly in blood and treasure, but in the end American blood and treasure was more plentiful than political courage.

***

In the fall of 1972, a last stand.

The House Internal Security Committee offered a bill protecting U.S. passports, the paper, from the desecration of enemy ink upon entry and exit. The House Committee could not decide, but the VFW still resolved that Fonda be prosecuted for treason. The Justice Department dropped its treason investigation for lack of a declaration of war.[2023]

Fonda's 18th and 19th radio shows to "American Servicemen" hit the airwaves on August 15th and 22nd. On August 22, the well-scripted actress was broadcast saying she had witnessed destruction ... [of] ... schools, hospitals, pagodas, ...factories, houses and the dike system"[2024]

In late September working class neighborhood of Philadelphia jeered Fonda's comments at a rally. She claimed big business wanted the war to acquire cheap Vietnamese labor.[2025] Actually, Hanoi's liberation provided the world with cheap labor, both prostitutes and near slave labor.

On October 3, 1972 a peacetime treason statute providing a ten-year sentence and a $10,000 fine for

---

[2020] Lieut. Commander John S. McCain III, U.S. Navy, "How the POW's Fought Back," US News & World Report, May 14, 1973.
[2021] Chris Noel, *Matter of Survival*, (1987), 151.
[2022] Andersen, 257.
[2023]"I Committed No Crime," *Washington Post*, September 16, 1972.
[2024] FBIS, "Hanoi Radio attributes talk on DRV visit to Jane Fonda," B 221928 Hanoi in English to American Servicemen involved in the Indochina War, 1300GMT 22 August 72; Almost exactly same words in Fonda interview, *Playboy*, April 1974, 78.
[2025] "Hostile Reception for Jane Fonda," *Washington Post*, September 30, 1972.

unauthorized travel to Hanoi was rushed to the floor of the House of Representatives passing 230-170, some 17 votes short of a 2/3rds vote required.[2026]

Fonda's immunity from treason was widely shared among those willing to love the enemy and hate their own country in war.

1972-175 would prove treason to be profitable as Volume II will show.

***

[2026] Senate Internal Security Subcommittee, Hearings, *The Nationwide Drive Against Law Enforcement Intelligence Operations*, part 2, July 14, 1975, 174.

POSTSCRIPT: America and the Vietnam War

Representing a major battle in the Left's war against Western Civilization and its protector, the United States of America, the discovery of the truths of the Vietnam War continue into the future. In the mythology or the facts of the war the true soul of America is found or expunged from human memory. In a generation no one will be alive who experienced the war in Vietnam and at home. In another generation all that will be remembered is what is then told about a place perhaps still called AmeriKa.

Fair Oaks, California, September 2019.

Biographical Information -- Dr. Roger B. Canfield

Canfield is a founding member of Vietnam Veterans for a Factual History, After serving in the Navy (1959-1964), Canfield "fought the Vietnam War on campus and in the California

Legislature." He earned PhD degree in

Photo: Dr. Roger Canfield, Mekong Delta, Vietnam, March 2008. Credit: Courtesy of Doug Shoffner.

Government from the Claremont Graduate School. Among other teaching, he was Assistant Professor at the MPA program at the John Jay College of Criminal Justice at the CUNY. Thereafter, civilian Commander of Technical Services Division of the San Mateo Police Department; Chief of Staff, Press Secretary and Policy Consultant for California State Senators and Assemblymen; a daily political columnist, "Under the Dome," for the Sacramento *Union* and executive director of the U.S. Intelligence Council, a private public policy group. He has written on civil disorder, water , California politics and policy, environmentalism, international travel, and China as well as Vietnam. He is the author of four books on the political and intelligence operations of China in the USA, *China Doll* (with Richard Delgaudio, 2000), *Stealth Invasion* (2002), *China Traders* (2000), and *China's Trojan Horses* (2002) with 2 million copies in circulation. Films: Producer/Screenwriter *Betrayal: The True Story of Richard Nixon, Alger Hiss, and Whittaker Chambers,* in association with Kennan Johnston, producer, forthcoming; Staff Historian, *Ride The Thunder: A Vietnam War Story of Honor and Triumph*, Richard Botkin, a

457

Fred Koster Film, 2015. He spent most of 2014-16 as a communications consultant for three political campaigns for Attorney General of California and US Senate and since as a volunteer and writer. Many publications are at http://www.americong.com, VVFH.org, *Military Magazine, California Political Review and California Globe.*

Appendix I--American "Peace Activist" Meetings[2027] with Enemy During War, 1968-1972 by Date and Place.

1968

January 23, **Haiphong and Hanoi,** Quaker Action Group, AQUAG.

February 28, **Japan,** deserters.

February 1968, **Budapest,** 67 Western Hemispheric Communist parties.

November, **Stockholm,** American Deserters Committee, ADC

February, **Havana,** Tom Hayden, Carl Davidson, Todd Gitlin, Gerry Long, Susan Sutheim, Ed Jennings, Joe Horton, Paul Hugh Shinoff, and Les Coleman and 40 other Americans.

Moscow, North Korea, two SNCC leaders.

February, **Havana,** Ted Gold, Mark Rudd and twenty other SDS.

February 9, **Vientiane, Laos** Daniel Berrigan, Professor Howard Zinn.

February 17, **Hanoi,**. Berrigan, Zinn.

March, **Hanoi** Mary McCarthy, Franz Schurmann, Harry Ashmore, William Baggs and Charles Collingwood.

March, **Hanoi,** Charles Collingwood, Harry Ashmore and William Baggs.

April, **Hanoi,** Steve Halliwell.

April, **Sweden,** Ken Cloke.

April 3-6, **Paris** WSP.

Paris, American contacts.

May 3-17, **Hanoi,** Robert Greenblatt, Susan Sontag and Andrew Kopkind.

May 15, **Hanoi,** Naomi Jaffe and three other SDS members.

June 16, July, **Paris,** Greenblatt and Dellinger.

July, **Hanoi,** Richard Barnet and Marcus Raskin of IPS.

Prague and to Budapest, Greenblatt.

July 3-6, **Paris,** Hayden, Stuart Meacham, Vernon Grizzard, and Anne Weills Scheer.

July 17-August 1, **Hanoi** Hayden, Stuart Meacham, Vernon Grizzard, and Anne Weills Scheer.

July 26, **Havana,** five SDS and 300 others.

June 16, **Prague,** Robert Greenblatt and Dellinger.

July, **Grenoble** William Standard, Carey McWilliams, Richard Falk, Hans Morganthal, and Quincy Wright.

July 28-August 6, **Sofia, Bulgaria** Howard Jeffrey Melish, Leslie Cagan and some fifty to seventy-one other Americans.

August 11-14, **Kyoto, Japan,** 23 Americans.

August 25-28, **Ljubljana, Yugoslavia,** Bernadine Dohrn, Judi Bernsten, Larry Bloom, Jeff Blum, Ruth Chamberlain, Bernardine Dohrn, Bryan Flack, Ruth Glick, Martin Kinner, Ellen and Fred Lessinger, Miles Mogulescu, Paul Schollmen, Mollje Struerer, and Daniel Swinney.

August 26-27, **Mexico, Havana,** Douglas Bernhardt, Michelle Clark, Ross Danielson, Pam Enriques, Larry Erander, Nancy Figeroa, Nick Freudenberg, Daniel Friedlander, Thomas Good, George Greunthal, Fred Halper, Louise Halper, Mark Hershel, (illegible) Iglesias, Hilda Ignatin, Jim Kulk, Jim Mitchell, Holly Moore, Steve Moore, Thomas Mosher, Mary Nalcoln, Morris Older, Sue Orrin, Mark Shapiro, Helen Shiller, Russell Smith, Jeffrey Swanson, Cliff Taylor, Joseph Webb, Marilyn Webb, and Bill Yates.

Summer **Cuba,** Barbara Stone.

July–October, **Cuba,** Carol "Kali" Grosberg.

August and September, **Yugoslavia, Hungary, Germany and Sweden,** Bernadine Dohrn.

[2027] Does not include Radio Hanoi, correspondence, telephone contacts in FBIS broadcasts and NSA intercepts.

September 3, **Budapest, Hungary**, twenty-eight Americans

September 10- September 23, **Paris**, John Davis.

Prague Stockholm, John Davis.

September 12-16, **Frankfurt, West Germany**, Bernardine Dohrn and Bill Ayers.

Late September, **Paris** Howard Zinn, Jonathan Mirsky, George Kahin of Cornell, Marilyn Young and Douglas Dowd.

October 24-30, **Paris and Stockholm** Rabbi Balfour Brickner.

November 8, **Japan** Ernest P. Young,

November 28-December 1, **Montreal,** Douglas Dowd, Howard Zinn and 500 other Americans.

1969

January 1-10 **Havana,** Carl Oglesby, Bruce Goldberg, Russ Neufeld and Dan Friedlander.

May 14-16, **Stockholm** World Peace Council's Conference on Vietnam, 1969.

April **Cuba, East Berlin, Hanoi**, new left.

April **Prague** office of the SDS Bernardine Dohrn and Steve Halliwell.

May 16-18, **Stockholm,** George Carrano, Donald McDonough, Anatol Rapaport, Noam Chomsky and Gabriel Kolko, John Wilson, Sherman Adams, Amy Swerdlow, Serita Crown, Althea Alexander, Joseph Elder, Bob Eaton, Bronson Clark, Joseph Crown, Richard Falk, Stanley Swerdlow, Doris Roberson, Carlton Goodlett, John McAuliff.

June 10-17, **Phnom Penh, Hanoi**, Joseph Elder

June 5-17, **Moscow**, Irving Sarnoff, , Barbara Bick, Arnold Samuel Johnson, Charles Fitzpatrick, Barbara Ruth Bick, Rennie Davis, David Tyre Dellinger, William Douthard, Douglas Fitzgerald Dowd, Carlton Benjamin Goodlett, Terrence Tyrone Hallinan, Gersho Phineas Horowitz, Arnold Johnson, Sylvia Kushner, Stewart Meacham, Sidney Peck and Irving Sarnoff

June 21-23, **East Berlin**, Dick Gregory; Stanley Faulkner, , Valeri Mitchell, Sonia Karose, Estelle Cypher, Susan Borenstein, Karen B. Ackerman, Herbert Aptheker, Barbara Bick, Mary Clarke, Martin Hall, Jarvis Tyner, Irving Sarnoff; Mary Angie Dickerson, Eleanor Ohman, Pauline Rosen and Carlton Goodlett.

July, **Stockholm** Irving Sarnoff.

July 9-15, July, **Havana,** Carlos Antonio Aponte, Robert Jay Barano, Christopher Kit Bakke, Thomas Wilson Bell, Edward "Corky" Benedict, Kathie Boudin, Cristina Bristol, Aubrey Brown, Robert Burlingham, George Cavalletto, Peter Clapp, Luis John Cuza, Lucas Daumont, Carl Alfred Davidson, Dianne Donghi, Bernardine Dohrn, Diane Westbrook Faber, Richard Rees Fagen, Ted Gold, Kenneth Alan Hechter, Frank Petras James, Nino Jeronimo, Gregory, Nina, Saul Irwin and Valerie Landau, Sandra Hale Levinson, Gerald "Jerry" William Long, Robert Schenk Love, Beth Susan Lyons, John "Shorty" Marquez, Albert Martinez, Howard Jeff Melish, David Millstone, Robert Edward Norton, Orlando Ortiz, Diana Oughton, Rose Paul, Verna Elinor Richey Pedrin, Jesus Maria Ramirez, Jose Ramirez, Eleanor Raskin, Patricia Ellen Shea, Jane Spielman, Jeronomi Ulpiano, Joanne Washington, Robert Wetzler, Myra Ann Wood, and Mary Woznich

August 4, **Hanoi** , SDS group

October 10-17, **Paris**, Rennie Davis and David Dellinger.

October 11-12, **Stockholm**, Irving Sarnoff and Ron Young.

October 15, **Havana,** George Cavalletto.

Late November, **Havana**, Julie Nichamin, Diana Oughton, John Butney (phonetic), Bruce Goldberg, Brian Murphy, Bill Thomas, Bill Drew, Phoebe Hirsch, Jerry Long. Arlene Bergman, Allen Young, Jerry Long; John McAuliff, Al Martinent. Weathermen: : Nichamin, Pierre Joseph Barthel, Neal Birnbaum, Marianne Camp, Sonia Helen Dettman, Linda Sue Evans, Laura Ann Obert, Nicholas Britt Riddle, Sheila Marie Ryan, Jeffrey David Sokolow, Mallorie N. Tolles, Robert Greg Wilfong, and Donna Jean Willmott, Willie Brand and Wendy Yoshimira, Bert Garskof, Sandy Pollack, Leslie Cagan.

December 1969 **Hanoi**, Cora Weiss, Ethel Taylor and Madeleine Duckles.

1970

January 31, 1970 **Quebec, Montreal,** Sylvia Kushner Katherine Camp, Arnold Johnson, and Stewart Meacham Stanley Faulkner, Joseph Crown, Pauline Rosen, Rev. Richard Norford

February 7-8, **Vancouver, British Columbia**, Carlton Goodlett and Irving Sarnoff and 125 others.

March 24- June 10, **Hanoi, Stockholm, Moscow,** Nancy Kurshan Rubin, Anita Susan Kushner Hoffman, Judith Gumbo Genie Plamondon.

March 28-30, **Stockholm** Robert Greenblatt, Irving Sarnoff, William Davidon, Doug Dowd, Carlton Goodlett, Sylvia Kushner, Noam Chomsky, Richard Fernandez, Nancy Kurshan Rubin, Anita Hoffman Judith Clavir and 34 other Americans.

February 13-April 28, **Havana,** Venceremos: Second Contingent, Edith Crichton, David Ira Camp, John De Wind, Nancy Frappier, Vicki Gabriner, Joyce Greenways, Ann Hathaway, Robert Hackman, Marguarita Hope, Lenore Ruth Kalom, Jonathan Lerner, Jeffrey Melish, Jed Proujansky, Daniel Ross Slick, Marguerite "Mini" Smith, Carlie Tanner, "Daren" [Karen] B. Ackerman, David L. Berger, Carol Brightman, Angela Davis, Ellis Jay Goldberg, William Joseph Maher, Karen Beth Nussbaum, Stephen William Shriver, Shari Whitehead.

April 13, **Hano**i Noam Chomsky, Douglas Dowd and Rev. Richard Fernandez

April 12-22, **Hanoi** 1970 Institute for Policy Studies—Charlotte Bunch-Weeks, Gerald Shin, Frank Joyce and Elisabeth Sutherland-Martinez.

late May, **Paris**, John Kerry and his new wife Julia Thorne.

May 22-24, **Toronto**, Joseph H. Crown, William Standard, Richard Falk and 97 other U.S. lawyers.

May, **Prague, Czechoslovakia,** Ann Hathaway, Eleanor Ruth Kalom, Jonathan David Lerner and Carlie Tanner

June 25-July 2, **Paris**, Adam Schesch and 31 Minnesotans.

July 27, **Havana**, third Venceremos Brigade, Jon Frederic Frappier, Eda Godell Hallinan, Richard Gutman and others.

August 27, **Cuba** Robert Greenblatt,, Nancy Kurshan (Rubin), and Judy Clavir, (Judy Gumbo)

Continuous, **Cuban intelligence,** Bernardine Dohrn, Martin Kenner, Mark Rudd, Julie Nichamin, Karen Koonan, Kathy Boudin, Gerry Long, Karen Ashley, Jeff Jones and Jennifer Dohrn.

August 25-27, **Helsinki**, Dave Dellinger, Bernardine Dohrn and others.

August and early September 1970, **USSR, North Korea, North Vietnam, Algeria, and China**, Eldridge Cleaver, Robert Scheer, Regina Blumenfeld, Randy Rappaport, Alexander Hing, Janet Austin, Hideko Pat Sumi, Anne Froines Janet Kranzberg Elaine Brown, Judith Clavir Andrew Truskier.

September 18-23, **Pyongyang**, Eldridge Cleaver and Byron Booth.

Algeria Cleaver.

September 23, **Canada**, Jane Fonda, Tommy Douglas

October 22-25, **New Delhi, India, Moscow,** three Americans.

November 9-23, **Hanoi**, Peter Weiss, William Standard and Morton Stavis.

November 28-30, **Stockholm**, David Dellinger, Rep. Ron Dellums, William Douthard, Sidney Peck, Jerrie M. Meadows, Willie Jenkins, Janey Hayes, Pauline Rosen, Bruce Beyer, Gerry Condon, Mike Powers, John Woods, Estelle Cypher, Eleanor Fowler, Carlton Goodlett, Gil Green Rev. Thomas Hayes, Stan Faulkner Ron Young Silvia Kushner and 15 other Americans.

December **Moscow, Saigon, Paris, Hanoi,** 1970 Mark Rasenick, Doug Hostetter, Keith Parker, David Ifshin and eight other NSA members.

People's Peace Treaty, Robert Greenblatt, Douglas Hostetter.

December 18-26, **Hanoi,** Anne M. Bennett, Ron Young, Trudi Young, Mary Luke Tobin

1971

March 3-10, **Paris,** Gabriel Kolko Rev. William T. Gramley, Allan Brick, Mrs. Allides Christopher, Rev. Richard McCollum, Mrs. Jane Whitney, Elaine Schmitt Urbain, Bud Ogle, Rev. Bruce Pierce, Harriet Price and 160 other Americans.

Paris. Jane Fonda, Mark Lane, and Michael Hunter.

April 1-6, **Vancouver and Toronto, Canada**, 600-1,000 American women.

May 10, **Paris**, Sidney and Louise Peck, Robert Greenblatt, Carol Kitchen and Jack Davis

461

May 12-16, **Budapest, Hungary,** Ruth Gage-Colby, John Rankin Davis, Pauline Rosen and 25 other Americans including VVAW.

June 5, 1971, **Stockholm,** Larry Levin, Tom Hayden and others

June 20-26, **Moscow, Oslo and Paris.** VVAW Larry Rottman, John Onda, John Randolph "Randy" Floyd, Ken Campbell

Late June, **Paris** Cora Weiss, Richard Falk, David Dellinger and Ethel Taylor.

September 11-12, **Paris.** George McGovern, Frank Mankiewicz, Pierre Salinger

On September 21, **Stockholm** American Deserters Committee, ADC.

Late October, **Hanoi** WSP's Amy Swerdlow and two others.

December 21, **Paris,** Rev. Richard Fernandez, a COLIFAM courier.

August, **Paris,** John Kerry

Paris VVAW staff member Joe Urgo's trip to along with a [redacted] member of the War Resisters League, WRL, and [redacted] of Women's Strike for Peace, WSP.[2028]

Hanoi, David McReynold.

Paris, Al Hubbard.

1972

February 5, **Paris,** Richard J. Barnet and Peter Weiss of IPS.

late February **Hanoi, China,** George Wald.

January-March, **Paris, Budapest, Moscow, Hanoi, and Japan,** Al Hubbard.

Mid-February-March, **Hanoi,** Al Hubbard, Seymour Hersh and Pete Seeger.

February 11-13, **Versailles, France,** John Gilman, Elizabeth Moos, Sidney Peck, Evelynne Perry, Pauline Rosen, Irving and Ruth Sarnoff, Abe Weisburd, Bernard Weller, Michael Zagarell, Deborah Bustin, Fred Halstead, Daniel Rosenshine, Rennie Davis, Jane Fonda; Al Hubbard, [Richard?] Joe Bangert, Edward Damato, Robert Greenblatt, Fred Branfman, Delia Alvarez, Ron Ridenour, Margery Tabankin, Howard Zinn.

End of March, **Hanoi,** David Livingston and other labor leaders.

April 6-8, **Paris,** Cora Weiss, Bob Levering Marcus Raskin, Sister Mary –Luc (sic, Luke) Tobin, Stoney Cookes and Maria Jolas.

April 20 **Paris,** Rep. Bella Abzug, Rep. Patsy Takemoto Mink and Amy] Swerdlow.

May 19-21, **Canada,** a VVAW member.

Mid-May? **Paris,** Rennie Davis

On May 25, **Hanoi,** Robert Lecky, Rev. Paul Mayer; Marge Tabankin, William Zimmerman

Late June **Paris,** Peter Mahoney, Rich Bangert, John Bochum, Stanley Michelson, Joseph Hirsch, Gary Steger, Forest Lindley, David Baily, John Turner, "Jack" Bronaugh, Willie Sykes, Ronald Sable, Thomas Zangrilli, Sean Newton, Toby Hollander, Paul Richards, Donald Ullrich all sixteen VVAW members

July 5, **Cuba,** Jean-Pierre Wendell, Leland Lubinsky, Fred Werner, Alan Morris, and Albert Morgafive members of VVAW in Venceremos Brigade.

June 6-10, **Paris,** Tom Hayden, David Dellinger and Rennie Davis

Most of July 1972 **Hanoi, Moscow** Jane Fonda.

August 4, **Hanoi** ,Dr. George Perera and John A. Sullivan.

July 29 to August 12, **Hanoi,** General Ramsey Clark.

End of August, **Paris,** David Dellinger and Cora Weiss.

September 11, **Hanoi,** Mrs. Charles, Mrs. Gartley, Elias, Weiss, Dellinger, Coffin, Mrs. Mary Anne Hamilton and Rev. Harry Bury.

October 4-17, **Hanoi,** 1972, Drs. Gardner, Simon and Wolf and one other.

In October 1972, **Copenhagen, Denmark,** CALC, and VVAW member assisting ADC.

During October **Hanoi,** Jane Hart (nee Senator Philip Hart), Mrs. D. Goodwin, Muriel Rukeyser and Denise Levertov COLIFAM sponsored.

End of October 25, **Hanoi,** Joseph Crown, Malcolm Monroe, Lawrence Velvel and John Wells.

Late October **Paris,** Cora Weiss and Richard Barnet.

November 12, **Hanoi**, Hayden, Howard Zinn, Rev. David Hunter, Fred Branfman, Susan Miller, Carolyn Mugar, Jan Austin.

December 11, **Hanoi**, Joan Baez; the Episcopal Rev. Michael Allen of Yale Divinity; Barry Romo , Gen. Telford Taylor.

Adams, Herbert/ NA/1965.

Allen, Rev. Michael/ accompanied Telford Taylor, Joan Baez; associate dean, Yale Divinity School/1972.

Aptheker, Herbert/ historian; member, U.S. Communist Party; accompanied by Tom Hayden and Staughton Lynd/1965.

Arnett, Peter/ accompanied Cora Weiss; war reporter, author (with Michael Maclear), *The Ten Thousand Day War: Vietnam 1945-1975* (NewYork: St. Martin's Press, 1981)/1972.

Ashmore, Harry S./ journalist; author (with W. C. Baggs), *Mission to Hanoi. -A 1968 Chronicle of Double Dealing in High Places* (New York: Putnam, 1968)/1967 and 1968.

Austin, Jan/ editorial board, Ramparts; editor, War Bulletin; accompanied both Eldridge Cleaver and Tom Hayden/1970 and 1972

Baez, Joan/ accompanied Telford Taylor; singer; Amnesty International/1972.

Baggs, William C./ editor, Miami News; accompanied Harry Ashmore/ 1967 and 1968

Barnet, Richard J./ co-director, Institute for Policy Studies; author (with Ralph Stavins and Marcus G. Raskin), *Washington Plans an Aggressive War* (New York: Random House, 1971)/1969.

Barrow, Willie/ accompanied Irma Zigas; minister/1971.

Bennett, Anne/ accompanied Ronald Young and Trudi Schutz Young/1970.

Benson, Sally/ NA/NA.

Berrigan, Rev. Daniel/ priest; POW escort; author, *Night Flight to Hanoi: War Diary With 11 Poems* (New York: Macmillan, 1968)/1968.

Bevel, Diane Student Nonviolent Coordinating Committee; accompanied Grace Newman/1966.

Blumenfeld, Regina/ accompanied Eldridge Cleaver/1970.

Boardman, Betty/ Quaker activist (delivered medical supplies in ketch to Haiphong)/1967.

Branfman, Fred/ accompanied Susan Miller-Coulter, Tom Hayden, and Howard Zinn-, director, "Project Air War"/1972.

Brown, Elaine/ vice minister of information, Black Panther Party/1970.

Brown, Rev. John/ Episcopal priest; accompanied Tom Hayden and Rennie Davis/1967.

Brown, Robert/ accompanied Tom Hayden and Rennie Davis/1967.

Burrows, Vinnie/ actress; poet/NA.

Bury, Rev. Harry/ priest; International Assembly of Christians in Solidarity With the Vietnamese/1972.

Butterfield, Fox/ reporter, *New York Times*; accompanied Cyrus Eaton, his grandfather/1969.

Caldwell, Clifton/ vice president, Meat Cutters Union/1972.

Camp, Katherine/ Coordinating Committee, People's Coalition for Peace and Justice; national chairwoman, Women's International League for Peace and Freedom; Steering Committee, New Mobilization ("Mobe")/1971.

Carmichael, Stokely/ chairman, Student Nonviolent Coordinating Committee; member, International War Crimes Tribunal,1967/1967.

Champney, Horace/ crewmember of ketch Phoenix 1967.

[2029] With minor edits from: Clinton, James, *The Loyal Opposition: Americans in North Vietnam, 1965-1972,* University of Colorado, 1995. Posted by redvet Facilitator, Vietnam Veterans against the War/Anti-Imperialist
http://www.oz.net/~vvawai/ Hawaii Chapter
http://groups.google.com.vc/group/alt.gossip.celebrities/msg/428da4d0fc9af29b Does not include meetings in Paris and across the globe.

Charles, Olga/ wife of POW Lt. Norris Charles; accompanied husband back to States/1972.

Chomsky, Noam/ professor, MIT; accompanied Douglas Dowd and Richard Fernandez; principal organizer, Resist/1970.

Clark, Ramsey/ former U.S. attorney general; Amnesty International, U.S./1972.

Clarke, Mary Women Strike for Peace; Coordinating Committee, People's Coalition for Peace and Justice/1965.

Cleaver, Eldridge/ minister of information, Black Panther Party/1970.

Clement, Marilyn/ accompanied woman associated with Operation Push, Chicago/NA.

Cobb, Charles/ accompanied Julius Lester; member Student Nonviolent Coordinating Committee; member, Commission of Inquiry to North Vietnam, International War Crimes Tribunal/1967.

Coffin, Rev. William Sloane/ chaplain, Yale University; POW escort; Committee for a Sane Nuclear Policy/1972

Collingwood, Charles/ CBS News reporter/1967.

Collins, Judy/ folksinger/NA.

Cook, Terrie/ Coordinating Committee, People's Coalition for Peace and Justice/1971.

Craven, Joseph (Jay)/ Coordinating Committee, People's Coalition for Peace and Justice/1971.

Davis, Rennie/ project director, National Mobilization Committee; leader, SDS; Coordinating Committee, People's Coalition for Peace and Justice; May Day Collective; Steering Committee, National Antiwar Conference; POW escort/1967 and 1969.

Dellinger, David/ chairman, National Mobilization Committee to End the War in Vietnam; editor, *Liberation*; Coordinating Committee, People's Coalition for Peace and Justice; POW escort; member, War Crimes Tribunal, Stockholm and Copenhagen, 1967; Committee of Liaison; Fifth Avenue Vietnam Peace Parade Committee; Steering Committee,1969, National Antiwar Conference; author/1966 and 1967 and 1972.

Deming, Barbara/ editorial board, *Liberation* magazine/1966.

Douglas, John/ SDS; accompanied Rennie Davis and POWs; filmmaker, Newsreel/1969.

Dowd, Douglas/ professor, Cornell University; New Mobilization Committee to End the War in Vietnam ("Mobe"); New Universities' Conference participant; Resist; Steering Committee, National Antiwar Conference Coordinating Committee, People's Coalition for Peace and Justice/1970.

Drath, Phillip/ crewmember of ketch Phoenix/1967.

Duckles, Madeline/ accompanied Cora Weiss and Ethel Taylor; Women Strike for Peace; member, Women's International League for Peace and Freedom.

Eaton, Anne accompanied husband, Cyrus 1969/1968.

Eaton, Cyrus/ 86-year-old Cleveland industrialist/1969.

Eaton, Robert/ crewmember of ketch Phoenix/1967.

Egleson, Nicholas/ president, SDS; accompanied David Dellinger/1967.

Elder, Joseph/ American Friends Service Committee/1968.

Evans, Linda/ member, SDS/1969.

Falk, Richard/ professor, Princeton University; POW escort; Amnesty International, U.S.; author, *The Vietnam War and International Law* (Princeton NJ: Princeton University Press; vol. 1, 1967; vol.2, 1969; vol. 3, 1972; and vol. 4, 1976)/1972.

Faun, Richard/ accompanied Betty Boardman; employed by Canadian Broadcasting System/1967.

Feinberg, Abraham/ rabbi; accompanied David Dellinger/1967.

Fernandez, Richard/ minister; Clergy and Laity Concerned About Vietnam; Coordinating Committee, People's Coalition for Peace and Justice; Steering

465

Committee, National Antiwar Conference; National Coalition Against War, Racism, and Repression/1970.

FitzGerald, Frances/ author, *Fire in the Lake: The Vietnamese and the Americans in Vietnam* (Boston: Little, Brown, 1972)/NA.

Floyd, Randy/ American Deserters Committee, Sweden/1972.

Fonda, actress, Indochina Peace Campaign, July 1972. [un mentioned by James Clinton].

Forest, James/ secretary, World Peace Committee/1970.

Fruchter, Norman/ SDS; POW escort; founding member of Newsreel; co-organizer with Tom Hayden of Newark (New Jersey) Community Union Project (NCUP)/1967 and 1969.

Froines, Ann/ wife of John Froines, Chicago Seven/1970.

Fulmer, Mark/ student; accompanied David Kirby/1968.

Gartley, Minnie Lee/ mother of POW Navy Lt. Mark Gartley/1972 .

Gerassi, John/ author, *North Vietnam: A Documentary* (Indianapolis, IN: Bobbs-Merrill, 1968); member, first investigating team, International War Crimes Tribunal/1967.

Gibbons, Harold/ vice president, Teamsters Union/1972.

Gordon, Lorraine/ accompanied Mary Clarke; Women Strike for Peace/1965.

Greenblatt, Robert/ professor, Cornell University; Steering Committee, New Mobilization; New University Conference; accompanied Andrew Kopkind, Susan Sontag, and Franz Schurmann/1968.

Griffith, Patricia/ wife of Cornell University chemistry professor; administrative secretary, Nov. 5-8 "Mobe" Committee/1966.

Grizzard, Vernon/ accompanied Anne Weills, Stewart Meacham, and POWs; SDS; member, National "Mobe"/1968.

Gumbo, Judith Clavir/ accompanied Nancy Rubin and Genie Plamondon/1970.

Hall, Gus/ general secretary, U.S. Communist Party/1972.

Hamilton, Mary Anne/ International Assembly of Christians in Solidarity With the Vietnamese; accompanied Rev. Harry Bury/1972.

Hart, Jane/ wife of Sen. Philip A. Hart, Democrat, of Michigan/1972

Hart, John/ reporter, CBS News/1971.

Hayden, Tom/ founder, SDS; project director, "Mobe"; author, *The Love of Possession Is a Disease With Them* (Chicago: Holt, Rinehart and Winston, 1972) 1965 and 1967 and 1972 , 1974.

Heick, William/ accompanied Betty Boardman; employed by Canadian Broadcasting System/1967.

Herring, Frances/ accompanied Mary Clarke; professor, University of California, Berkeley/1965.

Hersh, Seymour/ investigative reporter, New York Times; University of California, Berkeley author, *My Lai 4. A Report on the Massacre and Its Aftermath* (New York: Random House, 1970)/1972.

Hunter, Rev. David/ deputy general secretary, National Council of Churches/1972.

Ifshin, David/ president, National Student Association; Coordinating Committee, People's Coalition for Peace and Justice chairman, Black Antiwar Antidraft Union; Young Workers'/ 1970.

Johnson, James A/ Liberation League; one of Fort Hood Three; accompanied Rennie Davis and POWs; SDS/1969.

Kahin, George McT./ professor of government, Cornell University/1971 and 1972.

King, Alexis/ women's liberation movement; accompanied Eldridge Cleaver/1970.

Kirby, David/ student/1968.

Kirkpatrick, Kenneth/ American Friends Service Committee/1970.

Koch, Jon Christopher/ accompanied Harold Supriano, Michael Myerson, and Richard Ward; former radio producer/1965.

Koen, Rev. Charles/ minister; national chairman, Black United Front/1971.

Kolko, Gabriel/ historian/NA [1975].

Kolko, Joyce/ economist/NA [1975].

Kopkind, Andrew/ SDS; accompanied Robert Greenblatt and Susan Sontag; editor, New Republic/1968.

Kraft, Joseph/ news correspondent/1972

Kramer, Robert/ SDS; accompanied Rennie Davis and POWs; founding member, Newsreel/1969.

Kransberg, Janet/NA/NA.

Krause, Ruth/ accompanied Mary Clarke; Women Strike for Peace/1967.

Lawson, Phillip/ Methodist minister; Executive Committee, New "Mobe"/1970.

Lecky, Robert/ accompanied Paul Mayer; editor, Clergy and Laity Concerned About Vietnam; minister/1971.

Lens, Shirley/ accompanied Mary Clarke/1965.

Lerner, Judy/ Women Strike for Peace/NA.

Lester, Julius/ member, fourth investigating team, International War Crimes Tribunal/ 1967.

Levertov, Denise/ poet; accompanied Jane Hart/1972.

Lewis, Anthony/ reporter, New York Times/1972.

Livingston, David/ president, District 65, Distributive Workers of America/ April 1972.

Lockwood, Lee/ news photographer/1967.

Lynd, Staughton/ professor, Yale University; author, accompanied Tom Hayden; editor, *Liberation*/1965.

Lynn, Conrad J./ accompanied Hugh Manes; associated with International War Crimes Tribunal; lawyer/1967.

Manes, Hugh R./ lawyer; member, Third Commission of Inquiry, International War Crimes Tribunal/1967.

Massar, Ivan/ crewmember of ketch Phoenix/1967.

Mayer, Rev. Paul/ New York Theological Seminary; People's Coalition for Peace and Justice/1972.

McCarthy, Mary/ accompanied Franz Schurmann; author, *Vietnam* (New York: Harcourt, Brace, and World, 1968)/1968

McEldowney, Carol SDS; accompanied Rev. John Brown, Tom Hayden, and Rennie Davis/1967

McReynolds, David/ director, War Resisters League; accompanied by a Vietnam veteran/1971.

Meacham, Stewart/ accompanied Anne Weills and Vernon Grizzard; POW escort; education secretary, American Friends Service Committee; co-chairman, "Mobe"; National Coalition Against War, Racism, and Repression; Coordinating Committee, People's Coalition for Peace and Justice; Steering Committee, 1969, National Antiwar Conference/1968.

Meyers, William/ member, Lawyer's Committee on American Policy Towards Vietnam; accompanied Richard Barnet/1969.

Miller-Coulter, Susan/ director, Episcopal Peace Fellowship; New "Mobe," organizer, March Against Death, September 1969/1972.

Mugar, Carolyn/ accompanied Tom Hayden and Howard Zinn; Indochina Peace Campaign/1972.

Muste, A. J./ 82-year-old pacifist; Fellowship of Reconciliation; chairman, Fifth Avenue Vietnam Peace Parade Committee/1967.

Myerson, Michael G./ international secretary, W.E.B. Du Bois Clubs; accompanied John Christopher Koch, Harold Supriano, and Richard Ward/1965.

Near, Holly/ actress; accompanied Jane Fonda/1972.

Neilands, J. B./ professor, University of California; member, Third Commission of Inquiry, International War Crimes Tribunal/1967.

Newman, Grace/ sister of Dennis Mora (one of Fort Hood Three); Fort Hood Three Defense Committee/1966.

Paley, Grace/ National Resist; Greenwich Village Peace Center; poet and author; accompanied Rennie Davis/1969.

Parker, A. (Zeus)/ college student body president/1970.

Peck, Sidney/ professor, Case-Western Reserve University; co-chairman, New Mobilization Committee; Coordinating Committee, People's Coalition for Peace and Justice; coordinator, "Mobe"; Steering Committee, National Antiwar Conference; National Coalition Against War, Racism, and Repression; Wisconsin State Committee, U.S. Communist Party (while a student)/1970.

Pfeiffer, Egbert W./ professor of zoology, University of Montana; accompanied Mark Ptashne/1970.

Plamondon, Genie/ accompanied Judith Gumbo and Nancy Rubin/1970.

Ptashne, Mark S./ professor of biochemistry, Harvard University/1970.

Rappaport, Randy/ NA/1970.

Reed, Charles/ secretary, American Friends Service Committee/1971.

Reynolds, Earle L./ captain of ketch Phoenix/1967.

Romo, Barry/ accompanied Telford Taylor and Joan Baez; former U.S. Army lieutenant; Vietnam Veterans Against the War/1972.

Rothstein, Vivian/ accompanied Rev. John Brown, Rennie Davis, and Tom Hayden; SDS /1967.

Rubin, Nancy Kurshan/ accompanied Judith Gumbo and Genie Plamondon/1970.

Rukeyser, Muriel/ poet; Greenwich Village Peace Center/1972.

Russell, Margaret/ accompanied Mary Clarke/1965.

Salisbury, Harrison/ editor, New York Times; author, *Behind the Lines: Hanoi, December 23, 1966-January 7, 1967* (New York: Harper and Row, 1967)/1966.

Scheer, Robert/ editor, Ramparts; author, *How the United States Got Involved in Vietnam* (Santa Barbara, CA: Center for the Study of Democratic Institutions, 1965)/1970.

Schmidt, Phyllis/ accompanied Mary Clarke/1965.

Schneider, Mr./ member, A Quaker Action Group/1970.

Schoenbrun, David/ reporter, CBS News; author/1967.

Schoenman, Ralph/ secretary to Bertrand Russell; author, *A Glimpse of American Crimes in Vietnam* (London: Bertrand Russell Peace Foundation, 1967)/1966

Schurmann, Franz/ professor, University of California; author (with Peter Dale Scott and Reginald Zelnik), *The Politics of Escalation in Vietnam* (Greenwich, CT: Fawcett Publications, 1968)/1968.

Seeger, Pete/ folksinger/1972.

Seeger, Toshi/ accompanied husband, Pete Seeger/1972.

Sontag, Susan/ author, *Trip to Hanoi* (New York: Farrar, Straus, and Giroux, 1969)/1968 .

Stavis, Morton/ accompanied Peter Weiss; Lawyer's Farrar, Straus, and Giroux, 1969) Committee on American Policy Towards Vietnam; Center for Constitutional Rights/1970.

Stetler, Russ/ NA/1966.

Storey, Rasheed/ chairman, Communist Party, New York/1972.

Sumi, Hideko (Pat)/ leader, Movement for a Democratic Military/1970.

Supriano, Harold E./ accompanied Jon Koch, Michael Myerson, and Richard Ward/ 1965.

Swerdlow, Amy/ accompanied Irma Zigas; Women Strike for Peace; professor, Sarah Lawrence College; author, *Women Strike for Peace* (Chicago: University of Chicago Press, 1993)/1971.

Tabankin, Margery/ accompanied Rev. Paul Mayer; president, National Student Association/May 1972.

Taylor, Ethel/ accompanied Cora Weiss and Madeline Duckles/1969.

Taylor, Telford/ U.S. Army prosecutor, Nuremberg Trials; professor of law, Columbia University; author/1972.

Tyner, Jarvis/ vice presidential candidate, U.S. Communist Party; national chairman, Young Workers Liberation League/1972.

Wald, George/ Nobel laureate; professor, Harvard University/1972.

Ward, Richard E./ accompanied Harold Supnano and Michael Myerson; freelance writer/1965.

Wefers, Mark/ student/1970.

Weills, Anne/ POW escort; member, National "Mobe"/1968.

Weiss, Cora/ Committee of Liaison; POW escort; Women Strike for Peace; co-chairperson, National Mobilization Committee; Steering Committee, National Antiwar Conference; Coordinating Committee, People's Coalition for Peace and Justice; Jeannette Rankin Brigade/1969 and 1972.

Weiss, Peter/ Lawyer's Committee on American Policy Towards Vietnam/1970.

Westover, Martha/NA/1970.

Williams, Robert/NA/1966.

Williams, Mrs. R./ accompanied husband, Robert/1966.

Wilson, Dagmar/ accompanied Mary Clarke; president, Women Strike for Peace; vice chairperson, Spring Mobilization Committee/1967.

Woodward, John/ professor/1971.

Young, Ronald/ member, Fellowship of Reconciliation; coordinator, People's Coalition for Peace and Justice; Washington Action Committee; Steering Committee, New "Mobe"; National Coalition Against War, Racism, and Repression; accompanied Anne Bennett and Trudi Schutz Young/1970.

Young, Trudi Schutz/ accompanied Ronald Young; national coordinator, Women Strike for Peace; Coordinating Committee, People's Coalition for Peace and Justice; "Mobe"; organizer, 1969 March Against Death/1970.

Zietlow, Carl/ crewmember of ketch Phoenix/1967.

Zigas, Inna/ Women Strike for Peace/1971.

Zimmerman, William/ accompanied Rev. Paul Mayer; Medical Aid for Indochina/1971.

Zinn, Howard/ professor, Boston University; POW escort; accompanied Tom Hayden and others; author, Vietnam. *The Logic of Withdrawal* (Boston: Beacon Press, 1967) /1968 and 1972 .

***

The following is a partial chronological list of terrorist acts which were a part of the Viet Cong campaign of terror against the civilian population of South Vietnam from 1968-1969.

January 20, 1968: An armed propaganda team enters Tam Quan, Binh Dinh province, gathers 100 people for a propaganda session; one prominent village elder objects and is shot to death.

January 30, 1968: On the night of the new moon marking the new lunar year during a negotiated truce, a Vietnamese communist force of approximately 12,000 invaded Hue quickly turned it into one of the saddest cities on Earth. The communists stayed for 26 days, during which time they executed nearly 6,000 Hue civilians who the National Liberation Front Central Committee had blacklisted as enemies of Communism. After being forced to withdraw from Hue, South Vietnamese officials found the bodies of over 3,000 men and women buried in a river bed with their hands tied behind them. Many had been buried alive.

April 6, 1968: A band of communists enters That Vinh Dong, Tay Ninh province; they sell several thousand piasters worth of "war bonds" and then depart, taking with them a school teacher, the hamlet chief's two daughters and nephew and six other males age 15 or 16.

May 5 - June 22, 1968: Some 417 rockets are fired indiscriminately into Saigon, chiefly in the densely-populated Fourth District. The rockets are 107mm Chinese-made and 122mm Soviet-made. Result: 115 dead, 528 hospitalized.

May 29, 1968: A band of communists stops all traffic on Route 155 in Vinh Binh province; 50 civilians are kidnaped, including a Protestant minister; 2 buses and 28 three-wheeled taxis are burned.

June 28, 1968: A major attack is made against the refugee center and fishing village of Son Tra, south of Da Nang. In all, 88 persons are killed and 103 are wounded by mortar and machine gun fire, grenades and explosive charges. Some 450 homes are destroyed leaving 3,000 of the 5,000 persons there homeless. Later, villagers gathering bamboo to rebuild the center are fired on from ambush.

July 28, 1968: Four gun-wielding terrorists, two of them women, detonate a 60-pound plastique charge in city room of Cholon Daily News, most prominent of city's seven Chinese-language newspapers, after ordering workers out of building; the four escape before police arrive.

September 1, 1968: Doctors at the American Division's 27th Surgical Hospital report two Montagnard women have been brought in for treatment for advanced anemia. It is determined that the North Vietnamese had been systematically draining them of blood for treating their own wounded.

September 12, 1968: A communist report (captured in Binh Duong province) from the Chau Thanh district Security Section to the provincial party Central Committee says that seven prisoners in the district's custody were shot prior to an expected enemy sweep operation: "we killed them to make possible our safe escape," the report says.

September 26, 1968: A grenade is thrown into the crowded Saigon central market, killing one person and wounding 11.

December 11, 1968: A band of terrorists appears at the home of the provincial People's Self-Defense Force chief in Tri Ton, Chau Doc province; they bind his arms with rope and lead him 50 yards from his home where they fire a burst from a submachine gun into his body.

[2030] Ted Sampley and Xuan Nhi, Vietnamese American Youth, "Vietnamese Communist Party's Crimes Against Humanity, a petition to Mrs. Mary Robinson, UN High Commissioner for Human Rights and to all Human Rights Organizations, 2002.

January 6, 1969: The Vietnamese Minister of Education, Dr. Le Minh Tri, is killed when two terrorists on a motorcycle hurl a hand grenade through the window of the car in which he is riding.

February 7, 1969: A satchel charge is exploded in the Can Tho market place, killing one and wounding three.

February 16, 1969: Communists invade and occupy Phuoc My village, Quang Tin province, for several days. Later, survivors describe a series of brutal acts: a 78-year old villager shot for refusing to cut down a tree for a fortification; a 73-year old man killed when he could not or would not leave his home, pleading that infirmities prevented him from walking; an 11-year old boy stabbed; several families grenaded in their homes.

January 19, 1969: A bicycle bomb explodes in a shop in Kien Hoa province (Truc Giang), killing six civilians and wounding 16.

February 24, 1969: Terrorists enter the Catholic Church in Quang Ngai province, assassinate the priest and an altar boy.

February 26, 1969: A bicycle bomb explodes in a shop in Kien Hoa province, killing a child and wounding three other persons.

March 4, 1969: Rector of Saigon University, Professor Tran Anh, is shot by motorcycle-riding terrorists; previously he had been notified that he was on the "death list" of something called the "Suicide Regiment of the Saigon Youth Guard."

March 5, 1969: An attempt is made to assassinate Prime Minister Tran Van Huong by hurling a satchel charge against the automobile in which he is riding. The attempt fails and most of the terrorists are captured.

March 6, 1969: An explosive charge explodes next to a wall at Quang Ngai city hospital, killing a maternity patient and destroying two ambulances.

March 9, 1969: Terrorists enter Xom Lang, Go Cong province, take Mrs. Phan Thi Tri from her home to a nearby rice field where they behead her, explaining that her husband had defected from the communists.

March 9, 1969: A band of communists attack Loc An, Loc My and Loc Hung villages in Quang Nam province, killing two adults and kidnaping ten teenage boys.

March 13, 1969: Kon Sitiu and Kon Bobanh, two Montagnard villages in Kontum province, are raided by terrorists; 15 persons killed; 23 kidnaped, two of whom are later executed; three long-houses, a church and a school burned. A hamlet chief is beaten to death. Survivors say the communists' explanation is: "We are teaching you not to cooperate with the government."

March 21, 1969: A Kontum province refugee center is attacked for the second time by a PAVN battalion using mortars and B-40 rockets. Seventeen civilians are killed and 36 wounded, many of them women and children. A third of the center is destroyed.

April 4, 1969: A pagoda in Quang Nam province is dynamited, killing four persons, wounding 14.

April 9, 1969: Terrorists attack the Phu Binh refugee center, Quang Ngai province and fire 70 houses, leaving 200 homeless. Four persons are kidnaped.

April 11, 1969: A satchel charge explodes in the Dinh Thanh temple, Long Thanh village, Phong Dinh province, wounding four children.

April 15, 1969: An armed propaganda team invades An Ky refugee center, Quang Ngai province, and attempts to force out the people living there; nine are killed and ten others wounded.

April 16, 1969: The Hoa Dai refugee center in Binh Dinh province is invaded by an armed propaganda team. The refugees are urged to return to their former (communist dominated) village, but refuse; the communists burn 146 houses.

April 19, 1969: Hieu Duc district refugee center, Quang Nam province, is invaded and ten persons kidnaped.

April 23, 1969: Son Tinh district refugee center, Quang Ngai province, is invaded; two women are shot and 10 persons kidnaped.

May 6, 1969: Le Van Gio, 37, is kidnaped and later shot for refusing to pay "taxes" to a communist agent who entered his village of Vinh Phu, An Giang province.

May 8, 1969: Communist sappers detonate a charge outside the Postal-Telephone Building in Saigon's Kennedy Square, killing four civilians and wounding 19.

May 10, 1969: Sappers explode a charge of plastique in Duong Hong, Quang Nam province, killing eight civilians and wounding four.

May 12, 1969: A communist sapper squad attacks Phu My, Binh Dinh province, with satchel charges, rockets and grenades; 10 civilians are killed, 19 wounded; 87 homes are destroyed.

May 14, 1969: Five communist 122mm rockets land in the residential area of Da Nang, killing five civilians and wounding 18.

June 18, 1969: Three children are wounded when they step on a communist mine while playing near their home in Quan Long (Ca Mau) city, An Xuyen province.

June 19, 1969: In Phu My, Thua Thien province, communists assassinate a 54-year old man and his 70-year old mother.

June 24, 1969: A 122mm communist rocket strikes the Thanh Tam hospital in Ho Nai, Bien Hoa province, killing one patient.

June 30, 1969: Communist mortar shells destroy the Phuoc Long pagoda in Chanh Hiep, Binh Duong province; one Buddhist monk is killed and ten persons wounded.

June 30, 1969: Three members of the People's Self-Defense Force are kidnaped from Phu My, Bien Hoa province.

July 2, 1969: Two communist assassins enter a hamlet office in Thai Phu, Tay Ninh province, shoot and wound the hamlet chief and his deputy.

July 17, 1969: A grenade is thrown into Cho Con market, Da Nang, wounding 13 civilians, most of them women.

April 22, 1960: A communist unit attacks the Chieu Hoi center in Vinh Binh province killing five persons, including two women and a youth, and wounding 11 civilians.

July 18, 1979: Police report two incidents of B-40 rockets being fired into trucks on the highway, one in Quang Duc province in which three civilians were wounded and one in Darlac province which killed the driver.

July 19, 1969: Communist seize and shoot Luong Van Thanh, a People's Self-Defense Force member, Tan Hoi Dong, Dinh Tuong province.

July 30, 1969: Communists rocket the refugee center of Hung My, Binh Duong, wounding 76 persons.

August 5, 1969: Two grenades are thrown into the elementary school in Vinh Chau, Quang Nam province, where a school board meeting is taking place. Five persons re killed and 21 are wounded.

August 7, 1969: Communist sappers set off some 30 separate plastique charges in the U.S. Sixth Evacuation Hospital compound, Cam Ranh Bay, killing two and wounding 57 patients.

August 13, 1969: Officials in Saigon report a total of 17 communist terror attacks on refugee centers in Quang Nam and Thua Thien provinces, leaving 23 persons dead, 75 injured and a large number of homes destroyed or damaged.

August 26, 1969: A nine-month-old baby in his mother's arms is shot in the head by terrorists outside Hoa Phat, Quang Nam province; also found dead are three children between ages six and ten, an elderly man, a middle-aged man and a middle-aged woman, a total of seven, all shot at least once in the back of the head.

September 6, 1969: Communists rocket and mortar the training center of the National Police Field Force in Dalat, Killing five trainees and wounding 26.

September 9, 1969: South Vietnamese officials report that nearly 5,000 South Vietnamese civilians have been killed by communist terror during 1969.

September 20, 1969: Communists attack Tu Van refugee center in Quang Ngai province, killing 8 persons and wounding two, all families of local People's Self-Defense Force members. In nearby Binh Son, eight members of a police official's family are killed.

September 24, 1969: A bus hits a mine on Highway 1, north of Duc Tho, Quang Ngai province; 12 passengers are killed.

October 13, 1969: A grenade is thrown in the Vi Thanh City Chieu Hoi center, killing three civilians and wounding 46; about half those wounded are dependents.

October 13, 1969: Communists kidnap a Catholic priest and a lay assistant from the church at Phu Hoi, Bien Hoa province.

October 27, 1969: Communists booby trap the body of a People's Self-Defense Force member whom they have killed. When relatives come to retrieve the body the subsequent explosion kills four of them.